**NATIONAL
GEOGRAPHIC**

COMPLETE
NATIONAL PARKS
OF EUROPE

*In memory of our dear friend
and colleague Ford Cochran*

NATIONAL
GEOGRAPHIC

COMPLETE
NATIONAL PARKS
OF EUROPE

460 PARKS, INCLUDING FLORA & FAUNA, HISTORIC
SITES, SCENIC HIKING TRAILS, AND MORE

JUSTIN KAVANAGH

NATIONAL GEOGRAPHIC
WASHINGTON, D.C.

CONTENTS

Introduction **7**

WESTERN EUROPE **8**

United Kingdom **12**
Ireland **34**
France **48**
Belgium **60**
Netherlands **64**
Germany **88**
Switzerland **108**
Austria **114**

NORTHERN EUROPE **124**

Iceland **128**
Greenland **136**
Denmark **140**
Norway **148**
Sweden **190**
Finland **216**

SOUTHERN EUROPE **254**

Portugal **258**
Spain **262**
Italy **282**
Malta **316**
Greece **320**

EASTERN EUROPE **336**

Czechia **340**
Poland **346**
Lithuania **362**
Latvia **368**
Estonia **372**
Belarus **378**
Slovakia **382**
Hungary **390**
Slovenia **400**
Croatia **404**
Bosnia & Herzegovina **414**
Serbia **418**
Montenegro **422**
Kosovo **428**
Albania **432**
North Macedonia **446**
Bulgaria **450**
Romania **456**
Moldova **468**
Ukraine **472**
Turkey **490**
Georgia **496**
Russia **502**

CREDITS

Acknowledgments **526**
About the Author **526**
Illustrations Credits **527**
Index **530**

*Opposite: The territorial Ural owl casts a cold eye
on Oulanka National Park, Finland.
Previous pages: Kirkjufell (Church Mountain), in Snæfellsjökull
National Park, often called "Iceland in miniature"*

INTRODUCTION

When the United States introduced the first national park—Yellowstone—in 1872, it became a worldwide beacon for environmental conservation. Scottish-American naturalist and "father of the national parks" John Muir recognized how much we needed the green spaces that mankind was busy devastating to fuel the industrial revolution: "Thousands of tired, nerve-shaken, over-civilized people are beginning to find out that going to the mountains is going home; that wildness is a necessity." Sweden saw the light and protected nine wildernesses in 1909, and the rest of Europe soon followed. Now, the continent boasts more than 460 national parks of its own, all of which you can find within these pages.

More than a century later, our wilderness spots are more vital than ever, both for us and for the animals that make their homes in Europe's green spaces: Capercaillie, polar bears, Dalmatian pelicans, golden eagles, European bison, Mediterranean monk seals, and Apollo butterflies are just some of the creatures whose habitats the parks protect. Europe's parks also preserve human heritage at sites such as Agia Paraskevi Monastery in Greece's Víkos-Aóös National Park, Hadrian's Wall in England's Northumberland National Park, and at the expeditionary remnants of Norway's Svalbard parks and the Russian Arctic National Park. All are places where humankind sought enlightenment and spiritual renewal in the serenity of nature. Now, with our efforts in preserving these wild places, we can find our own comfort and reprieve within these sacred parks.

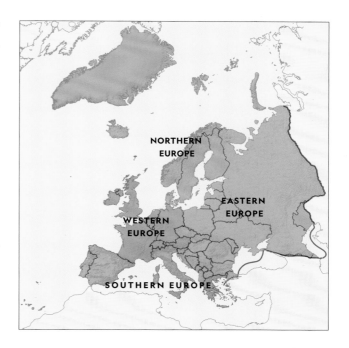

HOW TO USE THIS BOOK

This book divides Europe into four sections: Western, Northern, Southern, and Eastern. Within each chapter, countries appear in geographic order as we make our way eastward from the British Isles to Europe's borders with Asia. Greenland and Iceland, although geographically west of Ireland and Britain, appear in Northern Europe, in acknowledgment of their Scandinavian forebears. The map above is color-coded by chapter. Each chapter includes a regional map highlighting basic topography, and country maps that outline the locations of each park.

Happy trails stretch across Europe: horse riders and hikers on the North York Moors

WESTERN EUROPE

Scotland

Edinburgh ⊛

Northern
Ireland
Belfast ⊛

IRISH SEA

IRELAND ⊛ Dublin

The Pennines

UNITED
KINGDOM

NORTH

SEA

Wales

England

Amsterdam

The Hague ⊛

NETHERLANDS

Cardiff ⊛

London ⊛

Brussels ⊛

BELGIUM

GERMANY

CELTIC

SEA

ENGLISH CHANNEL

LUXEMBOURG

ATLANTIC

OCEAN

Channel Islands
(U.K.)

Paris ⊛

LIECHTENSTEIN

BAY

OF

BISCAY

FRANCE

Bern ⊛

SWITZERLAND

P

MASSIF

CENTRAL

L

A

MONACO

PYRENEES

MEDITERRANEAN

SEA

WESTERN EUROPE

From the lowlands of Belgium and Holland to the soaring Alpine spine of Austria and Switzerland, western Europe is a region of geographic and cultural contrasts. Its national parks reflect this diversity: Germany's Black Forest is a haven for day hikers, while the French Pyrénées attract adventure seekers from afar. The fringes of the continent—Ireland, Scotland, and Wales—are home to stunning rugged wildernesses, such as Connemara or Loch Lomond and the Trossachs. These extremities of Europe largely remain sparsely inhabited, wind-blasted, and rain-soaked reservoirs of ancient Celtic cultures.

BALTIC SEA

Berlin

Vienna

AUSTRIA

N

0 100 kilometers
0 100 miles

Above: Western Europe towers with great mountain ranges; Écrins National Park, France
Previous pages: Sgwd Ddwli waterfall, in Britain's Brecon Beacons National Park, Wales

UNITED KINGDOM

Great Britain stands alone in western Europe, as an island cleaved geographically and geologically apart from the mainland, and as a nation with a rich mix of four indigenous cultures. To ramble its national parks is to go from a gentle stroll through the New Forest in southern England to a strenuous hike along the Roman ruin of Hadrian's Wall in Northumberland in the north; you can scale 3,560-foot (1,085-m) Mount Snowdon in Wales before contemplating the higher heights of Scotland's Loch Lomond and The Trossachs National Park. Britain's wildernesses have long inspired a literary tradition that exalts nature's wonders: The Romantic poets colonized the Lake District, just as the Brontë sisters wrought gothic fiction from the stark highlands of the Yorkshire Dales.

Opposite: An inviting lane in Wharfedale, Yorkshire Dales

BRECON BEACONS

Sandstone hills roll down to the celebrated Valleys of South Wales.

The lyrically named Brecon Beacons mountain range in southern Wales sweeps down toward the Valleys, recalled by a local singing legend as "The Green, Green Grass of Home." The sandstone peaks of Pen y Fan (2,907 feet/886 m) and Corn Du (2,864 feet/873 m) face north over sheer cliffs, and horseback riding and hiking paths offer spectacular routes across the Beacons. Likewise, the four sandstone ridges of the Black Mountains to the northeast are connected by level, horizontal spines with fine valley views.

The old quarries of Llangattock ridge in the Black Mountains

The national park is geographically and geologically divided into four parts. The Beacons consist of ancient red sandstone, soft rock carved out by relentless rain-swollen Welsh rivers. The Black Mountain region is defined by elevated moors and glacial lakes. To the south, water has sculpted outcrops of carboniferous limestone into a karst landscape of waterfalls, caves, and sinkholes. To get a vivid sense of the underground karst geology of the region, visit the Dan yr Ogof, an 11-mile (17-km) cave system located at the National Showcaves Centre. Lower down, the valleys unfold as a maze of green fields and hedgerows.

WELCOMING HABITATS

This mix of landscapes ensures a diversity of natural habitats, and the park teems with birdlife: You'll spot kestrels, reed warblers, ravens, peregrine falcons, and ring ouzels. In the west of the park, the Red Kite Feeding Station offers a chance to study and photograph this rare bird of prey up close. In springtime, you might spy a creature akin to a tiny dinosaur in a park pond. This is the great crested newt, a protected species, whose dull brown color is countered by its orange underbelly. The marsh fritillary is now sadly in decline, but this bright butterfly sports impressive orange- and black-checkered wings and is found in marshy grasslands, particularly around Penderyn. The Brecon Beacons also has its share of badgers, Welsh mountain ponies, and Welsh mountain sheep. Fforest Fawr (Great Forest) UNESCO Global Geopark, in the western half of the park, incorporates an International Dark Sky Reserve.

STONE WITNESSES

The park is filled with landmarks of Welsh and Celtic history. Prehistoric chieftains were buried here, and huge heavy boulders were hewn to form the stone circles of pagan rituals. The red sandstone and local limestone facilitated the building of Neolithic tombs, Iron Age hill forts such as 4,000-year-old Y Garn Goch, early Christian churches, and Norman castles such as Carreg Cennen. The industrial revolution altered the landscape, pocking its beauty with quarries and mines, and stitching canal and railway lines across South Wales to transport limestone, coal, and iron to the valleys and beyond.

The Gospel Pass takes in rugged moorland with fine views. The park's best known hike is the 10.5-mile (17-km) Beacons Horseshoe, which stretches across ridges joining three peaks, including Pen y Fan. A day's hiking is well rewarded with a pint and a pie at the Skirrid Mountain Inn in Llanvihangel Crucorney, the oldest pub in Wales.

AT A GLANCE

Sandstone peaks ▪ Rolling Welsh valleys ▪ 519 square miles (1,344 sq km) ▪ Norman castles ▪ Skirrid Mountain Inn ▪ beacons-npa.gov.uk

BROADS

East Anglia's waterways and marshlands host a wealth of rare wildlife.

The Broads National Park in the east of England is one of Britain's best kept geographical and geological secrets. Under wide skies and open horizons, the park's marshy flatlands and waterways offer a surprising contrast to the rest of the mountainous island of Britain. These fenlands sit atop Norfolk's chalk beds, and the alkaline waters that course through the Broads form a labyrinth of gorgeous wetlands and semisubmerged forests, alive with all sorts of rich flora, aquatic wildlife, and several rare wading birds. In mid- to late summer, the marshes become a riot of maroon, as purple sea lavender bursts into bloom.

CALL OF THE WILD

The Broads often echo to the booming mating call of the bittern, or the butterbump as locals call this large brown-plumaged bird. The powerful sound carries far over the still waters and is heard up to one and a half miles (2 km) away. Unlike other birds of the heron family, this rare breed flies with its distinctive brown- and white-striped neck retracted. The unmistakable call of the cuckoo is another pleasant sound of summer, although their numbers are declining sharply. The Norfolk coast is also host to an increasingly rare, dark-bellied variety of the vocal Brent goose. One success story is the marsh harrier, which has come back from the verge of extinction to populate these parts aplenty, finding rich pickings in the wetlands.

Another endangered inhabitant of the Broads is the water vole, whose decline has been caused partly by the predatory and invasive American mink. On the endangered list, too, is the European eel, once a staple catch of fishermen in North Norfolk. These amazing sea creatures spawn in the Sargasso Sea before crossing the Atlantic Ocean. Another slithery creature to watch out for here is the adder, Britain's only venomous snake, which makes its pit in the heathland and dunes near Horsey. Britain's largest butterfly, the swallowtail, can now only be found in the Broads; Hickling Broad is one of its favored fluttering grounds. Horsey is home to a colony of grey (Atlantic) seals; in winter locals wrap up and watch seal pups waddle their way to the water.

THE HUMAN FOOTPRINT

Human activity has shaped the Broads for centuries, and a series of canals trace the cargo routes that transported goods and agricultural produce before the railways came to Victorian Britain. The small port of Staithes once thrummed with boats unloading flour, coal, and timber, while its moorings now host only pleasure craft. Windmills were once used to drain these wetlands, and several still stand as testament to a time when local landlubbers learned to harvest the North Sea winds. The man-made maze of dikes and ditches weaves East Anglia's agricultural narrative of grazing and arable farming. At the heart of the park is the charming city of Norwich, England's first UNESCO City of Literature and its only city within a national park.

A boat's mast on the River Thurne frames Thurne Windmill.

AT A GLANCE

Biodiverse waterways and fenlands ▪ 117 square miles (303 sq km) ▪ Seven rivers, 63 broads (lakes) ▪ Norwich, UNESCO City of Literature ▪ visitthebroads.co.uk

CAIRNGORMS

Granite mountains and glacier lakes sparkle in Britain's largest national park.

Twilight on the heather at Mar Lodge Estate in Aberdeenshire: the time to go roamin' in the gloaming

They call it "the gloaming" here in the Highlands—that ethereal shade between daylight and nightfall. This is the bewitching hour when the Scottish twilight can play tricks on your eyes as you roam the rugged plateaus of Cairngorms, Britain's largest national park. Here, at the Celtic edge of Europe, you might well imagine that the granite rock over there winked at you, or that a purple patch of heather just waved mysteriously in the day's darkening shade. It's easy to see how folktales of faeries gained credence in these parts.

HIGHLAND SPECTACLE

Cairngorms National Park encapsulates 1,748 square miles (4,528 sq km) of highland spectacle that often glistens as light reflects on the glassy granite rocks scattered across this elevated wilderness. The Highlands themselves are a 3,000-foot-high (914-m) plateau, a staging ground for hikers and climbers to take on five of Britain's six highest peaks. Ben Macdui soars highest at 4,295 feet (1,309 m). Adventurous souls who scale these heights are rewarded with unforgettable views of ice age landscapes, with deep valleys showing the paths carved out by ancient glaciers as they plowed through granite bedrock. Dotted on the mountains' northern side are corries, mountain lakes that mirror Cairngorms' fast-changing skies. Hills are still bearded with

the Scots pine remnants of ancient Caledonian forests. The names roll off native tongues: Abernethy, Glen Tanar, and Rothiemurchus are woods that have stood for 300 years or more.

The high plateau has a subarctic climate that fosters rare alpine flora and hosts bird species, including the ptarmigan, a species of grouse that changes its feather colors seasonally to adapt to the grays and browns of this Scottish wilderness, or the whiter northern climes of the Arctic.

The ptarmigan's main foe is the soaring golden eagle, whose fearsome wingspan can stretch to six feet (2 m). These eagles are dexterous enough to hunt down the weaving mountain hare that zigzags across the slopes. Ospreys nest hereabouts in spring, and Loch Garten Nature Reserve is a good place to observe them in their natural habitat.

LOWER VALLEYS

The lower valleys have long been used for sheep farming, forestry, and deer hunting, a pastime British royalty have enjoyed since Victorian times. Autumn is the best time to watch herds of 50 or more red deer, Britain's largest wild mammal, as they roam the park. In the October rut (mating season), you can witness fearsome clashes as males with massive antlers vie for dominance.

The post–ice age Caledonian pine forest in the foothills offers the gentler spectacle of red squirrels and pine martens gathering sustenance for winter hibernations. The western capercaillie is a species of wood grouse that roosts among pines, and you may even spot a Scottish wildcat, an endangered species sporting a short bushy tail with black stripes. To guarantee a sighting, visit Newtonmore's Highland Wildlife Park.

ROYAL PATRONAGE

Human activity has spanned the centuries long before Cairngorms became a national park in 2003. This followed the construction of a funicular railway in 2001 that brings visitors almost to the top of Cairn Gorm. The ski areas at Aviemore, Glenshee, and the Lecht have been popular since the 1960s, but the patronage of British royalty first put Cairngorms on the map. For a taste of the country life of the British royal family, visit Balmoral Castle and the

A large capercaillie fans his tail and gurgles seductively in a courtship display called lekking.

stone cottage where Queen Victoria wrote in her diary of the peace that she and Prince Albert found in the Highlands. A visit to Tomintoul is worthwhile for the hairpin drive up to this little village. Then head north to Glenlivet distillery, where samples of single malt will steel the soul for a walk in any weather.

HIKING & BIKING

The best time for walking is in August, when the heather spreads a purple blanket over much of the park's moorland. Loch an Eilein has an easy loop around the loch, affording a view of the island castle ruin. You can opt for easy climbs such as Cairn Gorm and Mount Keen or steeper challenges such as Cairn Toul or Ben Avon. The summit of Meall a'Bhuachaille, some 2,657 feet (810 m) above Glenmore,

offers more spectacular views, while Lairig Ghru is a tough 20-mile (31-km) hike along mountain passes aglint with huge granite boulders.

Cairngorms is also a bikers' delight. Glenmore Campsite on the shores of Loch Morlich is a good starting point for several walks and mountain bike trails, and also has canoe, dinghy, and windsurf rentals available in summer on the lake. Cairn Gorm Mountain is Britain's largest winter sports center with miles of fine pistes for skiers and snowboarders. You can also try dogsledding at the Cairngorm Sleddog Centre. When you've tired of roaming, and before the gloaming descends, why not take the railway toward the peak of Cairn Gorm, and enjoy the bird's-eye view from the Ptarmigan Restaurant, the highest in Britain.

AT A GLANCE

Classic Scottish Highlands ▪ 1,748 square miles (4,527 sq km) ▪ Britain's largest national park ▪ Caledonian pine forests ▪ Golden eagles ▪ visitcairngorms.com

DARTMOOR

Granite tors, brooding moorlands, and a sense of haunted history

Here in Britain's southwestern corner, tall granite tors (exposed rocky hilltops) point upward from lonesome moorlands and heathery cleaves (valleys) toward skies that darken stormily and suddenly. When the winds blast and the rain stings, the only shelter is ancient woodland that seems to echo with the souls of ancient Britons. This is the home of Dartmoor National Park.

The rugged granite that shapes the Dartmoor uplands dates from the Carboniferous period, pushed up as outcrops of the vast volcanic rock that underlies these moors. Further tectonic activity over millennia pushed the tors toward the surface while centuries of erosion exposed the higher rock, which now stands as great stone columns, dramatic markers of geological history.

Foggintor Quarry granite was used to build Nelson's Column and London Bridge.

STORIED STONES

Human history is also narrated in the granite, which has been used to house the living and the dead for millennia. Prehistoric menhirs (standing stones), stone circles such as the Grey Wethers, *kistvaens* (box-like stone tombs), enduring clapper bridges, and primitive settlements have long been carved from the subterranean stone and all are scattered atop the moors. The world's longest row of standing stones (1.9 miles/3.1 km) is at Upper Erne.

The moorlands provide rich habitats for the park's wildlife. The bee fly—a fly without a sting—and the real bee pollinate the purple flowers of devil's-bit scabious, while the long-beaked snipe wades in marshes for snails and water insects. The hardy Dartmoor pony can sometimes be seen sheltering from storms leeward of the tors. This small, squat breed has served humankind since Neolithic times, notably as beasts of burden in the medieval tin mines.

A HAUNTED LANDSCAPE

The heart of Dartmoor is aswirl with dark myths and legends. These moorlands are said to be a place of pixies, haunted by a headless horseman and a huge black dog. A pack of satanic hounds supposedly stalks Wistman's Wood, one of Britain's last prehistoric oak forests.

During the Great Thunderstorm of 1638, the village of Widecombe-in-the-Moor was allegedly visited by the devil, and anyone who has walked these parts at night would acknowledge this wind-blasted moorland as a place Satan might favor. Dartmoor has inspired artists and writers, such as Sir Arthur Conan Doyle, whose *Hound of the Baskervilles* howled to bloodcurdling effect. Harry Potter was a recent fictional visitor. In the realm of the all too real, the Dartmoor Prison Museum in Princetown documents the local penitentiary's grim history. In Tavistock, a brighter past beckons at Buckland Abbey, an Elizabethan country house. The national park's main visitors center in Princetown has exhibits about Dartmoor's history, culture, and wildlife, as well as changing displays of local art. The centers in Postbridge and Haytor offer maps and guidebooks, including information on the West Devon Way, a fine 37-mile (59.5-km) hike.

AT A GLANCE

Brooding moorlands ▪ 368 square miles (954 sq km) ▪ Dark folklore and literary legacy ▪ Granite tors ▪ West Devon Way ▪ dartmoor.gov.uk

EXMOOR

Open moorland and valleys with walking trails provide a hiker's heaven.

Stretching for 34 miles (55 km) along the southern shores of the Bristol Channel, Exmoor National Park is a short drive from its sister park to the south at Dartmoor. The mood in Exmoor is lighter and airier, and the park incorporates the fine walking realms of Brendon Hills, the East Lyn Valley, and the Vale of Porlock. Exmoor's open, elevated moorland spans West Somerset and North Devon, and its combes (wooded valleys) provide welcome contrast within the hilly landscape. The moor itself takes its name from the River Exe.

ROCKS & PASTURES

The geological foundations of these hills are sedimentary rocks dating from the Devonian and early Carboniferous periods with Triassic- and Jurassic-age rocks on lower slopes. The sandstone cliffs along the park's coast are a hiker's delight, punctuated dramatically with ravines and waterfalls. Those who venture inland early in the morning might chance upon the park's most famous residents, its 5,000-odd red deer, but their russet coats can be hard to pick out amid the red and brown hues of bracken and heather. The alpha exemplar of the species, a red stag known as the Emperor of Exmoor, was Britain's largest known wild land animal until it was killed in 2010.

The park also hosts managed herds of sturdy Exmoor ponies, which help to keep the growth of rough pasturelands in check. In summer months, these pastures become aflutter with many varieties of butterfly, and their names evoke the full swath of nature's palette: the clouded yellow, the green hairstreak, the holly blue, the orange tip, the brown argus, the grayling, the meadow brown, the green-veined white, and the marbled white. Watch too for otters in the park's marshy pools and buzzards circling overhead.

BEASTS, BATTLES & POETS

Like Dartmoor, the remote wilds of Exmoor have given rise to many legends, among them a cryptozoological feline creature that many a shaken hiker has reported. Known locally as the Beast of Exmoor, this phantom animal might stalk the moors for wild horses or sheep. Back in the material world, Exmoor Horn sheep have long supplied the local mills with wool renowned globally for its rugged, hard-wearing, yet soft consistency.

Exmoor's rich history dates all the way back to the late Mesolithic era (8000 to 4000 B.C.), from which several flint implements called microliths have recently been unearthed. Burial sites and standing stones are evidence of mankind's presence during the Neolithic (4000 to 2000 B.C.) and Bronze Age (2000 to 700 B.C.). Later, the Romans left several forts in the area, mainly on the south of the park. The region's most impressive medieval structure is the Norman-built Dunster Castle. Situated forbiddingly atop a tor, it is now a welcoming country house.

The pick of Exmoor's many fine hiking trails is the Coleridge Way, a 51-mile (82-km) trek, much of it paved, which follows the footsteps of poet Samuel Taylor Coleridge from his cottage at Nether Stowey in the Quantocks all the way to Lynmouth.

This Exmoor trail leads to the Tarr Steps, a clapper bridge over the River Barle.

AT A GLANCE

Moorlands and valleys ■ 267.5 square miles (693 sq km) ■ Coastal walks along the Bristol Channel ■ The Beast of Exmoor legend ■ The Coleridge Way trail ■ exmoor-nationalpark.gov.uk

LAKE DISTRICT
An enchanted idyll long eulogized in literature

The Lake District was a bucolic balm for 19th-century city dwellers in England's industrial north.

There are few more iconic British landscapes than the lakes, forests, and fells (high, barren terrains) found within Lake District National Park. For many Anglophiles, this is the England of their imagination. For many English nature lovers, this is England.

The word "fell" comes from the Old Norse word *fjall,* and it offers a fine geographical example of the multilingual makeup of the English language. The sheer beauty of the Lake District would inspire many English wordsmiths to craft their art in homage to the wonders of the natural world as manifested in the county of Cumbria. Among these, William Wordsworth was the most influential, and his poetry still inspires many a visit to the Lake

District (see sidebar). Founded in 1951, the 912-square-mile (2,362-sq-km) national park has consistently been one of Britain's most popular ever since. The towns of Windermere, Bowness, Grasmere, and Keswick are all charming starting points for forays into the multifaceted wilderness. There are several excellent walks from the stations of the Ravenglass and Eskdale Railway, whose miniature steam and diesel locomotives draw tiny carriages up from Ravenglass on the coast to the foothills at Dalegarth.

GEOLOGIC WONDERS

The glacial lakes of Wast Water and Windermere are the central attractions of the park, the deepest and longest bodies of water in England. Much of the national park takes the

form of a highland massif. This was caused by a granite batholith—a large swath of rock that has crystallized below the Earth's surface—being pushed upward. Exposed plutons that are visible in the Lake District include the Ennerdale, Skiddaw, Carrock Fell, Eskdale, and Shap granite outcrops. Scafell Pike, the highest mountain in England at 3,210 feet (979 m), looms large among these igneous peaks. Climbing the Pike takes about six hours from Borrowdale, and the view at the rocky peak is rich reward for the effort. A gentler hike is the Cumbria Way linking Ulverston with Carlisle, with plenty of cozy country pubs along the way for thirsty travelers.

Keep an eye to the sky for ospreys,

red kites, and peregrine falcons, which all enjoy a wide choice of land and lake fauna to prey upon. Golden eagles are being reintroduced to the region. The lakes are stocked with three rare and endangered fish species: the vendace, the schelly, and the arctic char. In the forests, Britain's indigenous red squirrel evokes fond memories of Beatrix Potter's Squirrel Nutkin.

The natural English settings of Ms. Potter's stories continue a long tradition of the Lake District as a wellspring of literary inspiration. The area's association with the Romantic poets of the 19th century and with Victorian writers such as John Ruskin helped convince UNESCO to deem the park a World Heritage site.

VARIED ADVENTURES

For those who prefer to venture into nature far from the madding

Poetic wellspring: Wordsworth's Dove Cottage in Grasmere

crowd, the wide-open coastline of the southern Lakeland around Morecambe Bay offers 117 square miles (303 sq km) of tidal sands. Guided tours take you across the sand and through rivers in an unusual expedition. The nature reserves on Whalney Island bring you into the realm of seals, orchids, hen harriers, and natterjack toads. The Cumbrian coast railroad snakes and loops on skeletal viaduct legs across the three estuaries of the Rivers Kent, Leven, and Duddon, on a 100-mile (161 km) coastal adventure from Carnforth to Carlisle. Carlisle's sandstone castle is foreboding, and its Norman cathedral has fine medieval stained glass, wood carving, and sandstone sculpture.

Wherever you roam in the Lake District, you'll find hundreds of miles of trails, and the visitors center at Windermere (in a former country house called Brockhole) provides information on walks to suit all fitness levels and ambulatory ambitions. But be prepared for sudden mists and rain on the fells with wet gear and a good map. And remember that after the rain comes the rainbow.

The Lake Poets

Every English schoolchild knows the poem "I Wandered Lonely as a Cloud," and many have visited the lakeshores of Ullswater where William Wordsworth composed "Daffodils." Wordsworth and his sister Dorothy were born in what is now Wordsworth House in Cockermouth. The poet spent six decades living in the Lake District, as a schoolboy at Hawkshead and later in Grasmere (1799–1813), and at Rydal Mount (1813–1850). Today, visitors flock to Dove Cottage in Windermere, where much of his poetry was written. Wordsworth and his wife are buried in the churchyard of Grasmere. Although Wordsworth, Samuel Taylor Coleridge, and Robert Southey, England's poet laureate, would become known as the Lake Poets, other literary greats who spent time in the District include Percy Bysshe Shelley, Sir Walter Scott, Nathaniel Hawthorne, John Keats, and Alfred, Lord Tennyson.

AT A GLANCE

Iconic Lake District landscape ▪ 912 square miles (2,362 sq km) ▪ Windermere town and lake ▪ Literary legacy ▪ lakedistrict.gov.uk

LOCH LOMOND & THE TROSSACHS

Scotland's first national park brings the Lowlands and Highlands within reach.

Scotland's most celebrated national park centers around the "bonny, bonny banks" of Loch Lomond, Britain's largest inland stretch of water by surface area. The park measures 720 square miles (1,865 sq km) and incorporates several impressive mountains and the Trossachs (from the Gaelic *Na Trosaichean* meaning "rough terrain"), straddling the divide between the Scottish Lowland and the Highlands. This gorgeous northern wilderness covers a broad variety of geography that includes 21 *munros* (Scottish mountains), two forest parks, 22 lochs, and more than 50 designated nature conservation sites that host a rich range of wildlife. There are also two national nature reserves within the park: Loch Lomond National Nature Reserve and the Great Trossachs Forest National Nature Reserve. This region was the realm of the infamous Scottish outlaw Robert Roy MacGregor (1671–1734), subject of the 1995 movie *Rob Roy*.

WATCHING WILDLIFE

The park's present inhabitants include ospreys, which nest around the bountiful lochs; pine martens, which can be seen at the feeding station at David Marshall Lodge; and red squirrels, which are losing ground to invasive grey squirrels. Otters and water voles are also common sights along waterways and lakes. However, don't blame the local whiskey if you spot a bunch of Australian wallabies on an island on Loch Lomond—they were introduced by a local landowner. Dragonflies and damselflies dance around the lakeshores, and the plenteous salmon and trout in the park's rivers and lakes make this one of Europe's most popular destinations for fishing. Loch Lomond is known for its perch and pike, while there are few better rainbow trout fisheries than the Lake of Menteith.

Loch Lomond first gained popularity as a travel destination when Sir Walter Scott was moved by local legend to write the romantic poem *The Lady of the Lake*. Travelers today can admire the scenery aboard cruises of Loch Lomond that start out from Tarbet, Argyll and Bute, and Balloch. On Loch Katrine, the historic steamship *Sir Walter Scott* takes visitors into the wilderness, while an extensive water taxi service connects most lochside communities.

The visit of Queen Victoria led 19th-century Britons to frequent these Scottish waters. You can find echoes of this time at Luss, a scenic conservation village on the shores of Loch Lomond with its historic village houses, sandy shoreline, and cobbled streets. In 2002, the area of Loch Lomond and the Trossachs was designated as Scotland's first national park.

TRAILS & TREKS

To really escape into nature, the park offers several superb long-distance trails including the West Highland Way, Rob Roy Way, and the Three Lochs Way. These trails wind past several country parks and estates worth visiting, such as Balloch Castle and Mugdock Country Parks. You'll also come across many old railway lines, lochside paths like the Clyde Sea Lochs Trail, and forest treks. Higher trails that offer wonderfully scenic vantage points can be found in Queen Elizabeth Forest Park in the southeast part of Loch Lomond and The Trossachs National Park; in the west side of the park, Argyll Forest Park has fine woodlands to explore; the park abounds with native birch and oak forests. The highest peak around here is Ben Lomond, and a climb up its 3,248 feet (990 m) reveals spectacular views all around, not least the sight of Ben Nevis some 40 miles (65 km) in the distance.

The visitors center at the southern end of Loch Lomond Shores in Balloch offers information on all trails and park activities, and is the most accessible gateway to the park. It also has an aquarium, shops, and restaurants nearby.

Scottish skies darken over Ben Lomond, Loch Ard, and the Trossachs near historic Aberfoyle.

AT A GLANCE

Classic Scottish wilderness ▪ 720 square miles (1,865 sq km) ▪ West Highland Way, Rob Roy Way, and Three Lochs Way trail ▪ S.S. *Sir Walter Scott* steamship ▪ lochlomond-trossachs.org

NEW FOREST

A royal forest with protected grazing commons and a wealth of wildlife

These woodlands were long the hunting grounds of English royalty.

The New Forest National Park embodies much of English history. Proclaimed a royal forest by William the Conqueror in the 11th century, the New Forest was used as a source of wood for Britain's Royal Navy as the British Empire expanded in the 18th century. In the park today, you might come across one of its 10 *verderers,* unpaid officers who enforce the rights of common pasture that have been passed down from medieval times, when the New Forest was mentioned in the Domesday Book.

HEALTHY HABITATS

The park spans southwest Hampshire and southeast Wiltshire, and stretches across 218.5 square miles (566 sq km) of open pastureland, heathland, and woodlands in southeast England. The superficial deposits above the sedimentary Hampshire Basin provide a variety of habitats for rare species of flora and fauna. The New Forest cicada is now feared extinct, but many species still thrive in the area's deciduous woodland, valley bogs, and dry and wet heaths. Rare plants grow in the wet heaths, including marsh gentian, marsh club moss, and wild gladiolus. Take a closer look among the flora and you'll find rare insects such as the southern damselfly and the mole cricket.

The chirping of crickets is superseded by birdsong of heathland birds, including the Dartford warbler and the woodlark, and the plaintive cry of the Eurasian curlew. The European nightjar, the European stonechat, the common redstart, and the tree pipit all add to the lovely cacophony of the heathlands and forests. The common snipe arrives in winter and breeds in the bogs. The woodlands trill with the sound of wood warblers, stock doves, European honey buzzard, and northern goshawk.

The undoubted star of the animals is the New Forest pony, known for its sturdiness, strength, and sure-footedness. Horses have been bred here since before the last ice age; remains dating back to 500,000 B.C. have been found in the general area of the New Forest, and DNA has revealed a shared ancestry with Celtic-type Asturcón and Pottok ponies.

Apart from the rich agricultural value of its pasturelands, the New Forest also hosts all three British native snake species. The adder thrives on open heath and grassland. The grass snake stalks the damper climes of the valley mires. The rare smooth snake slithers along sandy hillsides through heather and gorse.

TRAILS TO EXPLORE

The New Forest Centre in Lyndhurst, which also hosts the New Forest Museum, offers information on the park's many trails. Shorter loops include the 1.9-mile (3-km) Radnor Trail starting from Bolderwood, while the 7.3-mile (11.6-km) Brook to Minstead Trail passes by the Rufus Stone, witness to the mysterious death of King William II. For a modern-day take on the region, try the 5-mile (8-km) Burley Food Trail and enjoy a taste of New Forest Cider.

AT A GLANCE

England's ancient royal forest ▪ Diverse birdlife ▪ 218.5 square miles (566 sq km) ▪ The Snakecatcher pub ▪ A choice of nature trails ▪ newforestnpa.gov.uk

NORTHUMBERLAND

Varied habitats and rich heritage at the Roman Empire's northernmost border

Northumberland, England's wildest and most remote national park, spans centuries of history at an extremity of ancient civilization. Rolling along the border between England and Scotland, the Cheviot Hills are a hikers' paradise. They slope down into moorland to where Kielder Forest now blankets the landscape. Here too lies the biggest man-made lake in northern Europe, covering some 250 square miles (647 sq km), part of the nearby Kielder Water and Forest Park. The main attraction of Northumberland National Park is found in its southernmost area, where the central section of Hadrian's Wall evokes the Roman occupation of Britain. Beyond this point, the wild Celtic tribes of Scotland and Hibernia (Winterland—now Ireland) were never conquered by the Romans.

ROCKS TELL THE STORY

The Romans found no shortage of raw materials while constructing their wall to keep out the northern ancient Britons, including the Picts. Northumberland's geology is vast and varied, and the region is rich in Silurian, carboniferous, igneous, and metamorphic rock, as well as more recent quaternary deposits. Hadrian's Wall (also known as Picts' Wall) in its central section follows a hard, resistant igneous rock escarpment, known as the Whin Sill.

Humans have inhabited these parts for more than 10,000 years, and the park has many fascinating archaeological sites, from prehistoric monuments to Pele Towers, built as a defense against Border reivers, fearsome raiders along the Anglo-Scottish border. A visit to the Sill National Landscape Discovery Centre, located by Hadrian's Wall, is a good way to orient yourself.

STARRY SKIES & HISTORIC TRAILS

Thanks to Northumberland's remoteness and sparsity of densely populated towns and cities, the nights around here offer brilliantly starry skies, unpolluted by light. Much of the region has been designated Northumberland International Dark Sky Park, the largest such protected area in Europe. The wonders of the heavens can be enjoyed in the observatory with superb telescopes in Kielder Forest Park, which runs astronomical events year-round.

In daytime, some of the best trails on which to enjoy the park include the well-beaten Pennine Way, the six-mile (10-km) Shepherds Cairn Walk, which leads to a poignant memorial site, and the three-mile (5 km) Kirknewton Hillfort Trail, which lets you explore a 2,000-year-old Iron Age hill fort high in the Cheviots. Or plot a section of Hadrian's Wall to hike along, and go marching in the footsteps of ancient Romans. Bird-watchers should watch for the colorful, shimmering wing feathers of the northern lapwing, with its distinctive long black "quiff." You'll do well to spot well-camouflaged red or black grouse as they tiptoe through the heather. Wild goats and roe deer roam these hills too, and look underfoot for waxtops—colorful, waxy-topped fungi.

Hikers follow Hadrian's Wall, England's Roman-era border with Scotland.

NORTH YORK MOORS

Brooding moorland, cozy fishing villages, and spectacular coastal cliffs

The North York Moors meet the sea at coastal towns such as Staithes.

North York Moors National Park stretches across harshly beautiful moorland and secluded hills, before ending abruptly in the spectacular cliffs of England's northeastern coast. In contrast to the bucolic beauty of the Yorkshire Dales to the west, this wilderness is dramatically moody.

The park is bounded to the east by the impressive cliffs of the North Sea coast and to the north and west by the steep scarp slopes of the Cleveland Hills and the Hambleton Hills above the Vale of Mawbray. The Tabular Hills and the Vale of Pickering bound the North York Moors to the south.

Most of the park's landscape consists of a moorland plateau, interspersed with deep dales or valleys where agriculture and woodland adds variety to the bleak Highlands. The largest dale is Eskdale, carved out by the River Esk, which winds eastward to the North Sea at Whitby. The geology of the North York Moors gives a fascinating insight into sea levels and marine life over many millennia. The Jurassic-period rocks that predominate in the region were mostly deposited in subtropical seas 205 to 142 million years ago. The Yorkshire coastlines from Staithes to Filey exhibit the variety of marine

and delta-deposited rocks caused by fluctuations in sea level, varying from shales to sandstones and limestones derived from coral.

Inland on the elevated plateau, heather decorates the park with its seasonal spectacle. The moorlands offer a safe haven for several rare species of bird, such as the merlin and golden plover. Heathland plants abound so wildlife can feast on the crowberry and hide amid wiry leaves and silvery or purple flower heads of wavy hair grass. Bog plants thrive here too: Sphagnum moss abounds, and the blooms of cotton grass add white dots to yellow galaxies of flowering bog asphodel. Bracken blankets the slopes of the moors, providing habitat for the small perching whinchat bird. Juniper, dwarf cornel, bog rosemary, and cloudberry have traditionally thrived on the uplands of the North York Moors, but all are now vulnerable to the hastening caprices of climate change.

Hikers on the moors might hear the hoot of the short-eared owl and birdsong of the skylark and snipe. They should keep an eye out, too, for Britain's only poisonous snake, the adder, which feasts on the mice, voles, and lizards that also call the moorlands home.

EXPLORING THE PARK

There are many ways to experience the natural wonders and the many historic sites of the park. A ride on the North Yorkshire Moors Railway, which runs 18 miles (29 km) from Pickering north to Grosmont, affords great views of the moorlands. The line has operated as a steam railway since 1973. The station stops are also starting points for several fine walks; one trail leads from the village of Goathland and takes you to Mallyan Spout, a 70-foot (21-m) waterfall.

Just west of Goathland you can explore Wade's Causeway, a remarkable paved road that dates from the later stages of the Roman occupation.

The park has several Bronze Age burial mounds, and the Cleveland Way National Trail runs around the southern and western perimeter of the massive Roulston Scar Hillfort, believed to date back to around 400 B.C. The 109-mile-long (175-km) trail also incorporates much later industrial history, passing numerous alum quarries and works on the coast, including the Peak Alum Works, near Ravenscar. It also sweeps down the coastline, passing castles, ancient stone crosses, and fishing villages.

A day spent beachcombing in Runswick Bay is an excellent way to get a flavor of this once pirate-infested coastline.

Starting at Ravenscar, fine scenic coastal walks follow the abandoned railway track and the clifftop path to Robin Hood's Bay, a fishing village picturesquely piled on a narrow cleft, three miles (5 km) to the north. Other charming villages are Staithes and Whitby, where 13th-century abbey ruins cling precariously to the clifftops. At the top of the 199 Church Stairs stands the Norman Church of St. Mary, its interior woodwork reputedly the work of ships' carpenters. Bram Stoker set part of his novel *Dracula* (1897) in the graveyard. No visit to Whitby is complete without a salty taste of smoked kipper, the local delicacy, especially good for breakfast.

Near the market town of Helmsley, you'll find the 12th-century Rievaulx Abbey, where Cistercian monks cradled their faith in Europe's Dark Ages. At Lastingham, St. Mary's Church hosts a crypt for some of the region's early Norman settlers. And at Hutton le Hole, you can explore more recent social history at the Ryedale Folk Museum, a collection of restored local buildings. The Cawthorn Roman Camps Trail is an easygoing one-mile (1.6 km) walk to the escarpment on which sat Roman fortifications. Their remains now overlook the central moorlands of the park.

The ruins of 13th-century Whitby Abbey overlook the North Sea.

AT A GLANCE

Roman ruins ▪ 554 square miles (1,435 sq km) ▪ Iron Age hill fort ▪ The North Yorkshire Moors Railway ▪ Cleveland Way National Trail ▪ northyorkmoors.org.uk

PEAK DISTRICT

The Dark Peak and the White Peak contrast purple moorland with limestone caves.

The Peak District is split into the Dark Peak, which consists mainly of gritstone with a purple moorland covering, and the limestone region of the White Peak, hollowed out with caves and rocky gorges. The area has been inhabited from the Mesolithic era, with archaeological finds showing human activity through the Neolithic, Bronze, and Iron Ages. The Romans and Anglo-Saxons realized

national park, designated in 1951. Its proximity to Manchester, Stoke-on-Trent, Derby, and Sheffield means it is easily accessed by road and rail.

EXPLORING THE AREA

For modern-day nature lovers, 34 miles (55 km) of converted railway lines make up four distinct trails within the park. The 17-mile (27-km) High Peak, as well as the Monsal, Thornhill, and Tissington Trails

dubbed the Black Harry Trails, as many converge on the junction of Black Harry Gate, named for the 18th-century highwayman who robbed travelers on the moor.

The park's natural habitats are increasingly prized, given their surrounds are so densely populated with humankind. The hedgerows of the Peak District still rustle with foxes, and the dales are some of the safer British breeding grounds for hedgehogs. Caves house vast dormitories of bats, and kestrels, owls, and buzzards swoop to prey on the moorlands. The maroon hues of the heathers' autumnal flowering give the Dark Peak its name. Much more concentrated is the endangered Derbyshire feather moss: It is limited to a *single* riverbed in Cressbrook Dale. The exact location is a well-kept secret to deter trophy hunters.

The Victorian resort of Buxton is a good base from which to explore the Peak District, with the elegant Buxton Opera House and the Old Original Bakewell Pudding Shop, where you can taste the Bakewell tart, a district delicacy. Scarcely a mile from town is the limestone Poole's Cavern. Here, just 28 steps take you into a subterranean realm of stalactites and stalagmites two million-odd years in the making. To the northeast of Buxton you'll find the Castleton caves, each a geologist's delight.

Purple heather softens the region's gritstone and limestone outcrops.

the area's agricultural potential, and the medieval era saw the growth of mining. Richard Arkwright built cotton mills here to kick-start the industrial revolution, and the Victorians used their newfangled railways to escape into nature.

Situated at the southern end of the Pennines, in the resource-rich crucible of the industrial revolution, is the locale of Britain's first

offer hikers and cyclists a variety of routes to access sites such as Arkwright's Cromford Mills, the Monsal Tunnels (a series of lit railway tunnels), and Tissington Hall, a 17th-century Jacobean mansion house.

Apart from these four trails, the park has routes for horse riders and mountain bikers in the Longstone Edge area, accessible from Bakewell and the Monsal Trail. These are

AT A GLANCE

Poole's Cavern ▪ 555 square miles (1,437 sq km) ▪ The industrial revolution reinvented ▪ Railway line cycling ▪ The High Peak Trail ▪ peakdistrict.gov.uk

PEMBROKESHIRE COAST

Ancient ruins, oceanic wildlife, spectacular cliffs, and elevated heaths

Pembrokeshire Coast National Park is a microcosm of the seascapes and weather-sculpted coastlines of southwest Wales. Britain's smallest city, St. David's stands as a testament to Wales's patron saint at the westernmost extremity of this rugged peninsula. This is where the saint founded his great cathedral circa A.D. 550—with heavenly views of the ocean from elevated plateaus atop limestone cliffs.

The dramatic seascapes and weather-beaten wilderness of southern Wales conferred the region with an elemental and spiritual significance in Welsh history. The patron saint of Wales was born within the present-day confines of the park and in medieval times a pilgrimage to his cathedral was a mark of great devotion. St. David's Cathedral has many fine elements, including a beautiful rose window at its west end, a 14th-century rood screen in its east end, and a nave with a carved 16th-century oak roof. One choir stall here is permanently reserved for the British monarch.

EXPLORING THE AREA

Signs of almost 30,000 years of human habitation are everywhere, from Neolithic tombs to Norman castles. You can experience one such Norman stronghold firsthand by spending a night at Roch Castle Hotel, built in the 12th century.

Access to the park via St. David's

The Green Bridge of Wales sea arch, a highlight of the Pembrokeshire coast

leads onto the best area for walkers: the 11 miles (18 km) of coastline that winds along from Solva and Whitesands Bay. The four-mile (6-km) round-trip from Whitesands Bay around St. David's Head incorporates Iron Age and Stone Age relics, as well as the beach from where St. Patrick set sail in the fifth century to convert the Irish. The four-mile (6-km) walk starting in Bosherton leads around St. Govan's Head, passing the tiny Chapel of St. Govan, wedged into a crack in the cliffs. The five-mile (8 km) Cemaes Head loop incorporates much of the park's weather-carved coastal landscapes and passes cliffs filled with colonies of seabirds.

The southern limestone cliffs of the park, the oceanic shelf, the glacial floodplains, and the heaths that stretch across volcanic hills all provide a wide range of wildlife habitats. The world's largest species of dolphin, the rare Risso's dolphin, can regularly be viewed around Bardsey Island, while the Atlantic seal can be spotted on the rocky shorelines during the fall calving season. Nearby Skomer Island is known for its puffin colonies.

The Wales Coast Path traces the coastline from the Severn to the Dee, and details of many excellent walks can be downloaded from the Wales Coast Path website *(walescoast path.gov.uk)*. Offshore, the islands of Ramsey, Skokholm, and Skomer offer bird and wildlife sanctuaries accessible by boat. The cliffs and beaches of the Gower Peninsula arguably have some of the finest coastal scenery in Britain. Small wonder then that the Welsh have invented their own unique sport of traversing the coast by a combination of swimming and climbing, an activity they call "coasteering."

AT A GLANCE

Classic coastlines ▪ 243 square miles (629 sq km) ▪ Walk Cemaes Head ▪ Rare marine life ▪ Coasteering ▪ Surfing ▪ pembrokeshirecoast.wales

SNOWDONIA

Legends and adventure amid the rugged, rocky mountains of North Wales

The Great British summit of Mount Snowdon: Think of it as your trial run for Everest. Sir Edmund Hillary and his team did just that when they set up camp at Pen-Y-Gwryd Hotel in Nant Gwynant in 1953, before their historic ascent of Mount Everest later that year. King Arthur is another legend who conquered a giant hereabouts, before burying the body near the summit of Snowdon, the highest peak in Wales at 3,560 feet (1,085 m). The hardest ascent of the great peak is the ascent of the cliffs at Clogwyn Du'r (or Old Cloggy), first scaled in 1798. Thankfully, there are easier ways to the top.

REACHING THE SUMMIT

Riding the Mountain Railway to the summit has been the easiest way to conquer Mount Snowdon since the rack-and-pinion railway opened in 1896, and the views through the steam are exquisite. The ultimate Snowdon experience, of course, is climbing to the top. The gentlest and most popular hiking trail, the five-mile (8-km) Llanberis Path, cleaves closely to the Mountain Railway. The 3.5-mile (5.6-km) Watkins Path is a slightly steeper ascent, and the four-mile (6.5-km) Crib Goch Trail is thought to be the toughest of all; with a razor-sharp glacial ridge to navi-

The Mountain Railway takes riders all the way to the summit of Mount Snowdon.

gate, this route is strictly for those with a head for heights. For Iron Men and Women, the Welsh 3000s combine the summits of Snowdon with 15 other 3,000-foot-plus (914-m) peaks on an epic 30-mile (48-km) trail. Snowdonia National Park boasts a total of nine mountain ranges containing over 90 peaks and 100 lakes.

Don't be surprised to spot fossilized seashells on your way up or down any of the park's peaks: This region was once covered by ocean. Aside from hiking and climbing, mountain biking is another popular park sport, especially off-season. Going up is a strenuous workout, but coming down is a freewheeling joy.

WATCHING WILDLIFE

These mountains are home to many species of Welsh wildlife and wildflowers. In higher grounds, the Snowdon lily and other hardy arctic-alpine plants thrive in extreme conditions. Lower down, oak, alder, and wych elm forests carpet the foothills.

As wild goats ramble the slopes, peregrine falcons and rare ospreys circle the skies. The red kite, national bird of Wales, soars magnificently above the Snowdon massif, distinguishable by its uniquely forked tail feathering.

The polecat is a ferret-like creature that stalks the higher realms of the park. Polecats faced extinction in Victorian times but their more recent

protected status has helped the species achieve a comeback. To view the elusive otter, stake out any of the elevated *llyns* (lakes) in the park, such as Llyn Tegid (Bala Lake) in Penllyn, an area often referred to as the Welsh Lake District. Llyn Tegid is, allegedly, home to Teggie, the Welsh version of the Loch Ness monster.

EXPLORING THE AREA

Many of the windswept llyns are ideal for sailing and windsurfing, and kayaking in the white-water stretches of the Afon Tryweryn and Dee Rivers is also popular. For those of a gentler disposition, the Dolgellau (Mawddach) Trail takes in historic wool mills and the Corris Mine, as well as many historic listed buildings. At Llanberis, for example, the National Slate Museum offers fascinating insight into the harsh lives of North Wales's slate miners. To travel even further back in time, take a hike to the ruins of 13th-century Dolbadarn Castle, home of Welsh prince Llywelyn the Great. The rugged Snowdonia National Park is still the very heartland of this proud nation: Two out of every three of its approximately 26,000 inhabitants speak Welsh as their first language. Listen in the shops and pubs for its beautifully lyrical lilt. One other piece of advice to park visitors: Bring reliable rain gear. Crib Goch in Snowdonia is the wettest place in Britain.

AT A GLANCE

Glacial mountains ▪ Legendary landscapes ▪ 823 square miles (2,132 sq km) ▪ Snowdonia's Mountain Railway ▪ The Llanberis Path ▪ snowdonia.gov.wales

SOUTH DOWNS

Chalk cliffs, gnarled ancient yew forests, greensands, and heathlands

Stretching across some 87 miles (140 km) of Southern England, South Downs National Park is best known for the chalk hills of the South Downs. The chalk in the cliffs that now face out into the English Channel was formed in the late Cretaceous epoch, when the entire region was submerged under the sea. Later, in the Cenozoic era, this chalk was raised up as part of the Weald uplift, caused by the same continental plate movements that formed the Alps. Like the cliffs of Dover farther west, these white landmarks have stirred a sense of homecoming for returning British sailors, explorers, and empire builders across the ages.

To the north, the park's geography changes as the chalk downland gives way to the Western Weald, an area of densely forested sandstone and clay hills.

VARIED HABITAT

A variety of landscapes provide vital habitat for a wide range of flora and fauna. The streams of the Meon and the Itchen attract wild trout, grayling, and salmon with their chalk-filtered, alkaline waters, and the fly-fishing here is superb. Animals that form exoskeletons, such as snails and shrimps, likewise thrive in the calcium-rich water. The streams are also exceptional for their insect life.

Farther east, on the sheep-grazed downland of East Sussex, nature takes unexpected turns with the appearance of rare plants such as the round-headed rampion (aka the Pride of Sussex), with its intricate cluster of purplish blue flower heads, and many species of orchids.

The colorful local flora is complemented by the spectacle of delicate butterflies such as Chalkhill blues with their pale silvery blue (male) and checkered brown (female) wings. The Adonis blue has similarly brilliant hues. Look also for green woodpeckers hunting ants on the grasslands, and for red kites and buzzards hovering overhead.

The bog, pond, heath, and grassland of Shortheath Common are home to 23 species of dragonfly. This is also a nesting ground for the nightjar, after its long migration from South Africa. Nearby in Woolmer Forest, once a medieval royal hunting ground, all Britain's native reptile and amphibian species are found. Watch for adders, smooth snakes, great crested newts, and sand lizards.

In West Sussex, beech plantations, and mystical yew groves offer secluded habitats for specialist species. The Kingley Vale Trail takes you through an ancient yew forest and over lovely chalk grasslands. The area is also one of the key archaeological sites in Southern England, with 14 ancient scheduled monuments. Elsewhere in the park, you can seek out remnants of the Iron Age hill forts of Cissbury Ring, Chanctonbury Ring, Old Winchester Hill, Bignor Roman Villa, and Lewes Priory. A national trail, the 100-mile (161-km) South Downs Way, runs the entire length of the park.

The Seven Sisters chalk cliffs loom above the English Channel at Seaford.

AT A GLANCE

White chalk cliffs ▪ 628 square miles (1,627 sq km) ▪ The Seven Sisters ▪ The South Downs Way ▪ southdowns.gov.uk

YORKSHIRE DALES

Heather moorland carpeting limestone layers above labyrinths of caves

A hiker pursues the park trail along Ribblehead Viaduct.

The landscape of Yorkshire Dales National Park varies from lush pasturelands to wild upland moors to hills cut by broad valleys with rushing rivers. Here too are the region's picturesque small, neat villages, cozy little pubs, and drystone walls delineating farmers' fields.

The spectacular scenery of the Yorkshire Dales is due to the area's unique geology, which is mainly carboniferous limestone. The karst landscape is pocked by caves and potholes, making the Dales popular with subterranean adventurers.

Aboveground, each dale has its own appeal. Wharfedale runs northwest from the lower edge of the Dales. At the entrance to the park is Bolton Abbey, built in the 12th century. Its great east window still stands, flanked by tall arches. Nearby Grassington is the location of one of the park's information centers as well as the Grassington Folk Museum.

EXPLORING THE DALES

Around Nidderdale, look for the strangely shaped gritstone outcrops of Brimham Rocks on the road to Fountains Abbey. Founded by Benedictines in 1132, this abbey was soon in the hands of the Cistercians, on its way to being the richest abbey in Britain, with wool, lead, quarrying, and agricultural operations. Some of the buildings and the giant vaulted undercroft remain. In 1720, the property was bought by John Aislabie, who along with his son created Studley Royal water garden and 1,800 acres (730 ha) of landscaped grounds—grottoes, cascades, temples, lakes, deer parks, and alcoves.

Two miles (3 km) east, the Norman Cathedral of St. Peter and St. Wilfrid at Ripon has a fine 13th-century front with twin towers, and a seventh-century crypt. At nearby Masham, beer lovers should visit Theakston Brewery, established in 1827, for a tour of the "tower-style" brewery that uses gravity to good effect. Wensleydale is famous for its cheese and pastoral beauty. At Aysgarth, the river rushes spectacularly over the limestone steps in two long falls.

Swale Dale is the most rugged of the Yorkshire Dales. Richmond, at the eastern foot of the dale, boasts the largest cobbled marketplace in Britain. It also has a huge Norman castle perched on a knoll, its great curtain walls enclosing a 100-foot-high (30-m) keep.

Although the wildlife of the Dales is mostly the same as in nearby national parks, some of the flora is unusual: The alpine pennycress is a metallophyte, a plant that can tolerate or absorb heavy metals that are found in the soil around former lead mines. This plant has white or purple flowers with violet anthers and heart-shaped seedpods. The Dales also host five rare mosses, including incurved feather moss, Yorkshire feather moss, slender thread moss, and long-leaved flapwort.

Yorkshire Dales National Park is intersected by the popular Pennine Way National Trail, which includes a stretch that runs alongside a spectacular monument to Victorian engineering, the Ribblehead Viaduct.

AT A GLANCE

Limestone scenery ▪ 680 square miles (1,762 sq km) ▪ Ribblehead Viaduct ▪ Pennine Way National Trail
▪ yorkshiredales.org.uk

IRELAND

Ireland is Europe's westernmost outpost, long romanticized as a green haven warmed by the temperate Gulf Stream waters of the Atlantic. The landscapes of this oft invaded Celtic nation have inspired poets, playwrights, and holy men and women seeking heavenly solitude on Earth, a place where monastic ruins are as commonplace as those of Norman castles. Although the midland bogs that fueled 20th-century Ireland have now morphed into nature parks, dramatic topographies still rim the island: The Wicklow Mountains rise south of Dublin; the Lakes of Killarney offer a scenic prelude to the Wild Atlantic Way that stretches north to the rugged wilds of Connemara and Donegal; and the glacial limestone moonscapes of the Burren in Clare and Galway host alpine, arctic, and Mediterranean wildflowers.

Glenveagh National Park

Donegal

Northern Ireland (U.K.)

Donegal Bay

Sligo

Wild Nephin Ballycroy National Park

Newport

Connemara N.P.

IRELAND

Dublin

IRISH SEA

Galway

ATLANTIC OCEAN

Aran Islands

Burren N.P.

Wicklow Mountains National Park

Wicklow Mts.

Wicklow

Ennis

Shannon

Nore

Barrow

Limerick

Suir

Tralee

Killarney
Killarney National Park

Cork

N

0 ____ 40 kilometers
0 ____ 40 miles

CELTIC SEA

Opposite: Kerry's Lakes of Killarney mirror a golden Irish dawn.

BURREN

A surprising diversity of flora and fauna in a haunting limestone wilderness

The Burren's karst landscape hosts an astounding range of arctic, alpine, and Mediterranean wildflowers.

The Irish word *boireann* means "rocky land," and at first glance the Burren National Park in County Clare looks like a lunar landscape, devoid of any signs of life. Yet look a little closer and this bleak limestone wilderness reveals Ireland's greatest diversity of wildflowers, an extraordinary mix of arctic, alpine, and Mediterranean plants. Dig into its history, and you'll find that the Burren is a man-made landscape, a once dense woodland deforested by settlers and invaders. Along the sparse gray hills lie ancient tombs and dwellings, the ruins of churches, ring forts, and holy wells. And at the outer edges lie villages where swirling traditional Irish music still echoes down the ages.

The Burren National Park stretches its limestone pavements across 4,083 acres (1,653 ha) of northwest Clare. Its northern boundary is Galway Bay; it is bounded to the east by the Atlantic, and to the south and east by Clare's pasturelands. At the center cluster a series of dome-shaped hills with rounded tops and stepped flanks of pale gray limestone. The park has multiple entry points, including the Burren Centre in Kilfenora, which provides maps and walking guides helpful to start your explorations.

To delve deeper into the karst geology of the Burren, visit the nearby Aillwee Cave to see stalactites and stalagmites, underground rivers and waterfalls, and the region's labyrinth of caves and passages.

The Burren is a karst region, formed of rough, cracked limestone. Its striated landscape was formed beneath ancient oceans and pushed above sea level by a great geological upheaval. The surface of the limestone is split into deep, narrow channels (*grykes*) a few inches wide and several feet long, with long strips of rock (known as clints) in between these channels. When the invading general Edmund Ludlow reported to Oliver Cromwell in 1651, he noted that the Burren "had not any tree to hang a man, nor enough water to drown a man, nor enough earth to bury him." The New Model Army would improvise other ways to inflict their murderous intent on the Irish. But Ludlow also noted: "Their cattle are very fat, for the grass growing in tufts of earth of two- or three-foot square that lie between the rocks, which are of limestone, is very nourishing."

BURREN BLOSSOMS

Indeed, the Burren's nutrient-rich soil and plentiful rainwater gathers in the grykes, finding a nurturing space between rocks. The result is the extraordinarily varied range of plants that flourishes here: Some 75 percent of Ireland's native wildflowers are found in the Burren, including 24 species of orchids. These limestone crevices are sheltered from salty wind, watered by frequent rainfall, and warmed by the Gulf Stream off the Clare coast and by sunlight reflected into their depths off pale limestone. Some botanists believe that certain arctic and alpine plants found here are descendants of seeds that moved south in melting Ice Age glaciers 10,000 years ago.

Northerly plants like mountain avens flourish next to southerly plants such as yellow hoary rock-rose. Streams bring acid bog peat into hollows of alkaline limestone so that acid-loving plants such as heather and saxifrage thrive alongside lime-loving plants like spring gentian. This produces a riot of color across the gray hills and coastal shelves: June heralds the flowering of brilliant blue trumpets of spring gentians, and vivid magenta of bloody cranesbill.

The creatures that make their home on this limestone landscape are rare for Ireland: Multiple species of butterfly feast on the flora, while pine marten (small weasels), badger, and stoat (ermine) all thrive in these rocky parts.

THE HUMAN FOOTPRINT

Although there is little sign of human settlement on the Burren interior today, due to a dearth of surface water—the karst draws rivers underground—and to the ethnic cleansing implemented by Cromwell during his conquest of Ireland (1649–1653), evidence of previous inhabitants abounds. The 5,000-year-old portal dolmen of Poulnabrone evokes the pomp and ceremony prehistoric Burren dwellers observed in burying their chiefs. The stone-walled Celtic ring forts of Cahermacnaghten and Caherballykinvarga are easily reached by road; the medieval law school at Cahermacnaghten once taught students the tenets of Brehon law.

Rathborney Church, dating from A.D. 1500, was built inside a pre-Christian circular earthen rampart here, while the nearby ruins of Corcomroe Abbey and of the church at Dysert O'Dea both display fine stonework. Several fine fortified towers and houses also survive, including Newtown Castle and Leamaneh Castle. Many holy wells dot the Burren landscape: Locals have visited these sacred sites since pagan times, seeking cures for headaches, bad backs, tooth trouble, failing eyesight, and other ailments.

Poulnabrone Dolmen, a Neolithic portal tomb, held 33 human remains.

AT A GLANCE

Limestone landscapes ▪ 5.7 square miles (15 sq km) ▪ Arctic, alpine, and Mediterranean flora ▪ Pine marten and ermine ▪ Seven walking trails ▪ burrennationalpark.ie, theburrencentre.ie

CONNEMARA

An Irish dreamscape of cliffs, bogs, and wild Atlantic weather

Set on the westerly edge of Europe ("next parish Newfoundland," as the locals say), the Connemara region sweeps scenically across the western realms of County Galway. The wild rugged countryside, much of it Ireland's largest *Gaeltacht* or native Gaelic-speaking area, is framed by the magnificent Maumturk Mountains. Mist rolls inland over rugged Atlantic coastlines and shrouds lonesome loughs (lakes) that teem with salmon and trout; the lake and river fishing here is among Europe's best. Twisted treetops at 90-degree angles testify to the force of gales that blast the elevated boglands hereabouts. The area called Connemara, which has no officially mapped boundaries, is as wild and enchanting as the jigs and reels that animate life in the west of Ireland.

Pollacapall Lough reflects Kylemore Abbey and the Connemara skies.

PONIES & THE PIOUS

As an entity, Connemara National Park protects an area of 7,307 acres (2,957 hectares) within this western wonderland. It thus encompasses the Twelve Bens, a series of smaller mountains that offer a variety of hikes and climbs to suit all comers. Diamond Hill, accessible from the visitors center in Letterfrack, is the focus of the most popular loop walk (4.3 miles/7 km). Hikers might spot mountain hares, red deer, and stoats, although these short-tailed weasels are more nocturnal in their habits. Any walk along western trails will bring a sighting of the delightfully short Connemara pony grazing in green valleys. This breed was originally brought to Irish pastures by the Vikings who raided the island between the 8th and 10th centuries A.D., eventually settling along the east coast. Local legend has it that when galleons from the Spanish Armada ran aground off Galway in 1588, the breed was diluted by the arrival onshore of a stock of Andalusian horses. These Spanish horses interbred with the native stock, giving Connemara its local species of strong, hardy horse.

Nearby, Kylemore Abbey is an elegant nunnery founded in 1920 by Benedictine sisters who were fleeing war-torn Europe. A choice of several easy walking trails, a miniature cathedral, and Victorian walled gardens make for a restful and reflective visit.

THE ASHFORD ESTATE

East of Connemara National Park, the stately Ashford Castle dates back to 1228, and offers visitors regal repose on an estate that was initially a Norman stronghold and later the hunting grounds of the Guinness family. The estate's Ireland School of Falconry lets you hunt with birds of prey in the English gardens and wild woods along the banks of Lough Corrib. Various woodland walks cross the estate, including the Pigeon Hole Loop, which leads through the village of Cong out to the Pigeon Hole Cave between two lakes. This cave, accessible via a staircase, vividly demonstrates the porous subterranean karst landscape that accommodates the flow of water from the upper (Mask) to the lower (Corrib) lake.

AT A GLANCE

A classic Irish wilderness ▪ 11.4 square miles (29.5 sq km) ▪ Kylemore Abbey ▪ Connemara ponies ▪ Pigeon Hole Loop ▪ connemaranationalpark.ie

GLENVEAGH

A walker's wonderland with a castle and a dark history

Encircling the crystalline waters of Lough Beagh, on the eastern side of the Derryveagh Mountains, the hilly sweep of Glenveagh National Park covers 23,887 densely wooded acres (9,667 ha) in the northwestern county of Donegal. Mount Errigal towers over the park at 2,464 feet (751 m), adding the element of shade to dramatic light that has long attracted painters and photographers to this region.

GLEN OF THE BIRCHES

The central valley within the park is called Glenveagh (*Gleann Bheatha* in Gaelic) meaning the "glen of the birches." To the southwest are the ice-carved cliffs of the Poisoned Glen, a corruption of another Gaelic name that actually translates as "heavenly glen" (Gaelic for "heaven" is *neamh,* and for "poison" is *neimhe*). This strange juxtaposition of evil and Eden runs throughout the sad history of the locale.

Glenveagh Castle—started in 1870 and completed in 1873—is the park's focal point. This castellated mansion, with its neo-Gothic architecture of ramparts, turrets, and a round tower, was built for John George Adair of granite in the Scottish baronial style, looking onto Lough Veagh. Adair gained lasting notoriety for the infamous Derryveagh Evictions, during which 244 tenants were ousted from their land in the harsh winter of 1861.

Locals claim that the landlord considered the tenants a blight on his vision for the valley. His actions caused many homeless families to perish in freezing conditions. His wife, Cornelia, left a gentler legacy: She laid out the beautiful rhododendron gardens and introduced the red deer that are now Ireland's largest herd. A more recent resident is the golden eagle, which was reintroduced to the northwest of Ireland in 2000, having been hunted to extinction in the 19th century. Numerous other avian residents also find sustenance in the many lakes hereabouts, including Lough Veagh, which boasts natural stocks of brown trout, salmon, and arctic char. The informal gardens of the castle play host to a multitude of exotic and delicate plants brought from faraway climes including Chile, Madeira, and Tasmania. These plants are sheltered from the harsh Atlantic winds of Donegal by windbreaks of pine trees.

The grounds of the castle also feature terraces, an Italian garden, and a Belgian Walk, so named for the Belgian soldiers who constructed it while billeted at the castle during World War I. The stronghold, modeled on Scotland's Balmoral Castle, was briefly occupied by the Irish Republican Army in 1922, during the Irish Civil War. Later, Hollywood's most famous hermit, Greta Garbo, favored the pink-striped candy room when she wanted to be alone within the castle keep. The sale of Glenveagh Castle to the Irish government in 1975, by its Philadelphian owner, Henry Plumer McIlhenny, enabled the creation of the national park.

Glenveagh Castle, built of local granite, is a four-story rectangular keep.

KILLARNEY

An emerald gem set in an ancient woodland rich in history

The Long Range, a narrow channel, leads from the Meeting of the Waters to the Upper Lake.

The magnificent Macgillycuddy's Reeks Mountains provide a brooding backdrop to this most romantic wilderness, now protected under the designation of Killarney National Park. This is a wild expanse of 25,000 acres (10,117 ha), where lush, moss-carpeted woodlands sweep down to steely gray lakes that mirror the ever changing Kerry skies. These stunning and surreal landscapes were aptly praised by Victorian and Edwardian visitors as the "Mecca of every pilgrim in search of the sublime and beautiful in Nature—the mountain paradise of the west."

The blanket boglands come spectacularly alive each summer with purple heather and yellow gorse splashed across sun-brightened vistas as the ancient oak and yew woods offering shady green relief. Year-round, the Gulf Stream washes this southwest region of Ireland with its warming waters, allowing plants and animals from southern Europe to thrive here. Sika deer and native red deer roam the park, and the reintroduced white-tailed eagle now soars above Killarney's lovely lakes. Fishermen catch and release any Killarney shad, a critically endangered fish endemic to Lough Leane. This freshwater member of the herring family, known locally as the *goureen,* became trapped in the lake some 16,000 years ago.

The Lakes of Killarney are best observed from the famous Ladies' View, an overlook pointing north over the narrow Gap of Dunloe and the gorgeous Upper Lake. The Torc Cascade, beside Middle Lake, is another must-see—it cascades

AT A GLANCE

Ireland's iconic landscape ▪ 39.7 square miles (103 sq km) ▪ Lakes of Killarney ▪ Muckross House ▪ Nature trails ▪ killarneynationalpark.ie

60 feet (18 m) down a staircase of rock shaded by sycamore and mountain ash.

ANCIENT OCCUPANTS

Despite the air of otherworldly mystery enshrouded within the velvety green forests of the park, human beings have inhabited these lands for more than 4,500 years, and historic sites abound. Bronze Age copper miners were the earliest visitors, followed by St. Finnian in the seventh century. He founded a leper colony and monastery on Innisfallen Island, where generations of holy men continued to thrive for 850 years. These scholarly monks were believed to have educated the high kings of Ireland. Today, Ireland's only herd of native red deer can be spotted swimming across to the island to graze among the ancient ruins. The deer wear a deep red color in summer, and the males' large antlers are on powerful display during the fall rutting season.

Also look for the imposing Ross Castle on the banks of Lough Leane, built in the 15th century by the O'Donoghue clan. The castle's *bawn,* or walled tower, has been restored to its former glory.

MUCKROSS HOUSE

The true heart of the park is the elegant Muckross House and estate. The Tudor-style mansion has hosted many of the park's preeminent visitors, from Queen Victoria in 1861 to George Bernard Shaw. Travelers continue to visit Muckross House, now an operational hotel, and its beautifully kept gardens of rhododendron and azalea. Both the house and estate were presented to the young Irish state in 1932, thus facilitating the establishment of Ireland's first national park at Killarney.

Killarney NP Trails

As cars are banned from most of the park, Killarney's beauty is best experienced on foot:

Blue Pool Nature Trail: Starting behind Muckross Park Hotel, this gentle 1.4-mile (2.3-km) trail skirts a small lake colored deep blue-green, thanks to copper deposits in the soil.

Cloghhereen Nature Trail: This walk is accessible for those with visual impairment by means of a rope guide along a trail lined with plants identifiable by smell and touch. An audio guide is available from Muckross House visitors center.

Mossy Woods Nature Trail: This 1.2-mile (2-km) walk starts from Muckross Lake, passes through moss-covered woodland atwitter with birds, and includes spectacular mountain views. Along the way are several strawberry trees (Arbutus), a botanical misfit in northern Europe.

Muckross House boasts 65 rooms, once hosted Queen Victoria, and served as a hunting lodge for Arthur Guinness.

WICKLOW MOUNTAINS

Two nature reserves cradled within the mountainous Garden of Ireland

Wicklow Mountains National Park is a mosaic of more than 49,000 acres (19,830 ha) of blanket bogs and woodland located atop the elevated eastern county known as "the Garden of Ireland." The parklands enclose two nature reserves: The larger protects the heath of Glendalough Valley as well as the Upper Lake and its surrounding slopes. The smaller conserves valuable oak woods.

Set within vast boglands that blaze seasonally with the colors of gorse, bracken, and heather, the park's landscape is further animated by a series of small corrie lakes glimmering with reflected light. Lakes such as Lough Bray Upper and Lower were carved out by glacial ice at the head of glaciers that swept through these highlands during the last ice age, the Pleistocene epoch that ended about 11,700 years ago. Vast granite peaks, like that of Lugnaquillia (3,031 feet/924 m), are visible from the park, their hot igneous rock having solidified some 400 million years ago to form schist-capped mountains. Between these summits run deep glacial valleys, including Glenmacnass, Glenmalure, and Glendalough.

DRAMATIC ENTRANCES

Traveling south from Dublin, the

Glendalough's round tower was built more than 1,000 years ago.

dramatic spectacle of the Wicklow Mountains is first experienced along the narrow Military Road, one of Ireland's most scenic drives, which leads south to the park. This route was built in the early 1800s to move British troops quickly to the mountains, where rebel forces could easily melt into the dense, inaccessible landscape. The best point of present-day access to the national park is from the visitors center at Glendalough.

Hikers following the Wicklow Way, a 79-mile (127-km) trail that transects the park, attain a rich reward in the valley of Glendalough ("glen of the two lakes," in Gaelic). Here you'll find the ruins of a monastic city dating from the sixth century, when a monk named Coemgen (Kevin) built his church in this sheltered valley (see sidebar). The presence of a Bronze Age tomb suggests that the site may already have been considered sacred.

VARIED INHABITANTS

Wicklow Mountains National Park plays host to many of Ireland's mammal species. Large herds of deer—many a hybrid of indigenous red deer and sika deer that escaped from the nearby Powerscourt Estate—roam these hills. The deer were reintroduced in the 20th century, having previously been hunted to near extinction here by the Anglo-Irish aristocracy. Foxes, badgers, and hares continue to inhabit the uplands, and around Glendalough's Upper Lake you'll spot red squirrels, plentiful in the pine woodlands.

Birds of prey thrive here too: Peregrine falcons, merlins, kestrels, and hawks all find rich pickings in the wooded mountain terrain. Avian rarities to look for are hen harriers, whinchats, ring ouzels, dippers, and the disappearing red grouse.

Ireland's Sacred Vale

St. Kevin's monastic settlement of Glendalough, founded in the sixth century, grew quickly as the hermetic holy man attracted many more followers than he probably wanted. Following his death, thousands of theological students flocked here from across Europe, as Rome fell and Europe descended into the Dark Ages. Between A.D. 775 and 1071, the site was repeatedly attacked by Vikings but persevered until invading English soldiers finally destroyed the monastery in 1398. However, the ruins of its small church, better known as St. Kevin's Kitchen, as well as the larger Cathedral of Sts. Peter and Paul, and the magnificent 102-foot-high (31-m) round tower all still stand as testament to the saint's faith and perseverance.

AT A GLANCE

Majestic mountain scenery ▪ 85 square miles (220 sq km) ▪ Glendalough monastic site ▪ The Wicklow Way trail ▪ wicklowmountainsnationalpark.ie

Aerial view of Glendalough, Ireland's sacred vale, with St. Kevin's monastic site in the foreground and the upper and lower lakes beyond

WILD NEPHIN BALLYCROY

An Atlantic blanket bog hosts a rich tapestry of wildlife habitats.

Wild Nephin Ballycroy's isolated, mountainous setting overlooking the western seaboard of northwest Mayo makes this, Ireland's newest national park, a remote getaway for walkers and campers. Small wonder that in 1937 the travel writer Robert Lloyd Praeger reflected, "Indeed the Nephin Beg range of mountains is, I think, the very loneliest place in this country."

Walkways are a great way to experience Wild Nephin Ballycroy's more than 27,180-odd acres (11,000 ha) of Atlantic blanket bog at ground level without getting your feet wet. An elevated peak, a short walk from the visitors center, has signage of nearby mountains and landmarks.

Other habitats that host a wealth of wildlife include alpine heath on Slieve Carr, upland grasslands, lakes, and the fluvial catchments of the Owenduff and Tarsaghaun Rivers that empty into the sea northwest of Ballycroy.

Of particular interest is the Owenduff bog, one of the last intact active blanket bog systems in western Europe, enriched by up to 80 inches (2,000 mm) of rainfall a year. Many plants thrive within this wet bog habitat, painting the landscape from nature's rich palette. Many shades make up the grassy green background of black bog rush, purplemoor grass, deer-grass, lichens, and sphagnum mosses. This is liberally dotted with the brighter lights of orchids, lousewort, bog cotton, and bog asphodel, and the composition is completed with the vibrant pinks and purples of bell heather, milkwort, and butterwort.

LIFE IN THE PARK

The lakes in the area are edged with aquatic plants including water lobelia, pipewort, and bulbous rush. Among the rarer flora found in the park are the ivy-leaved bellflower, which blooms in July and August on the wet grassland along the riverbanks. Rare alpine heath plant species also find a home here: Purple saxifrage, alpine meadow rue, least willow, and stiff sedge all thrive at altitudes lower than their usual, colder, European habitats. Other plants that dominate these mountainous parklands include bell and ling heather, crowberry, and bilberry.

Among the mammals here are the fox, badger, mountain hare, otter, pygmy shrew, and several bat species, including Ireland's most common bat, the pipistrelle. Non-native red deer, introduced to the region in recent years, forage on the margins of the park. Pine marten are attracted to the conifer plantations on the edges. The Owenduff and Tarsaghaun Rivers teem with salmon and sea trout, and both rivers, as well as local lakes, host brown trout. Elusive otters feed on eels and salmon, and occasionally appear in the bog pools of the blanket bog.

The bog pools are vital habitat for much of the invertebrate life in the park. The predatory larval stages of dragonflies and damselflies feed on waterborne insects before metamorphosing into winged adult dragonflies and damselflies. These in turn prey on a smorgasbord of insects in the park.

AN EVER ACTIVE LANDSCAPE

The names of other insect species found here tell their own stories of an ever active landscape: the moorland hawker, the heathland skimmer, the common darter, and the black darter. Others tout their own beauty: the banded jewelwing, the common bluetip, and the spring redtail.

Wild Nephin Ballycroy also supports many bird species, among them dippers, common sandpipers, woodcock, meadow pipits, ravens, and whooper swans. Birds of prey that hunt here include kestrels and sparrow hawks, while rarer species such as merlin and peregrine falcon are also resident. Hen harriers are winter visitors. Highly gregarious Greenland white-fronted geese, with their orange legs and bills, visit Wild Nephin Ballycroy from October until April.

Wild Nephin Ballycroy is Ireland's first International Dark Sky Park.

AT A GLANCE

Atlantic blanket bog ▪ 45 square miles (116 sq km) ▪ Trout-filled lakes and rivers ▪ The Nephin Beg mountains ▪ ballycroynationalpark.ie

FRANCE

Multifaceted France, according to the French, soon becomes every visitor's second homeland. The national parks echo the eclectic range of this country's varied landscape; from soaring peaks of the Dauphiné Alps in Écrins National Park to the classic Mediterranean coastline of Calanques National Park, the mystic limestone caves of Cévennes National Park, and the exotic underwater trails awaiting divers in Port-Cros National Park. Nature's grandeur and the warmth of the Basque French seem the very epitome of the national motto of *"Liberté, égalité, fraternité"* in Pyrénées National Park near the Spanish border. The other mountainous parks of Vanoise and Mercantour offer their own elevated escapes.

Opposite: Fort Saint-Jean and Vieux Port of Marseille, in Calanques National Park

CALANQUES

France's newest national park sweeps along the Mediterranean coast.

Calanques by kayak: Turquoise sea, limestone coves, and blue skies

Calanques National Park, France's newest park (designated in 2012), is the only European national park that is continental, marine, and semi-urban. It extends over 200 square miles (520 sq km), of which 33 square miles (85 sq km) are on land; the rest is a protected marine area along the shores of the Golfe du Lion. The park ranges from Marseille to La Ciotat, encompassing landscapes of limestone in the *calanques* (steep-sided karstic valleys or inlets) in the west to the red conglomerate stone farther east.

The distinctive rugged white coastline stretching from the ninth arrondissement of Marseille eastward toward Cassis is the limestone Massif des Calanques. Mont Puget is the highest vantage point at 1,854 feet (565 m).

SATURATED IN COLOR

The geological contrast within the park can perhaps best be seen on a trip to Île Verte (The Green Island) not far off the coast at La Ciotat. The island's ochre coloring is from a pebble conglomerate that contrasts sharply with the white limestone coves between Cassis and Marseille. Combined with the sparkling blues of the Mediterranean (and the near-permanent blue skies of the French Riviera), the landscapes and seascapes of the park offer nature's take on the French tricolor. The trip to Île Verte also offers fresh sea breezes that carry the scent of Aleppo pine trees planted shortly after World War I.

The rocky, arid calanques have their own particular ecosystem, with soil being almost nonexistent. Only hardy plants that can anchor their roots into the fissures of the steep rock faces survive here. Yet the cliffs host hundreds of such plants, including the endemic Marseille traga-canth, a spiny, deciduous shrub that grows in dense cushions on the rocks, and Sabline de Marseille, a white flowering plant that blossoms in spring. Both are found only in these hills around France's second largest city. More common evergreen shrubs, such as sage, juniper, and myrtle, also thrive among the calanques.

The animals that call the park home include the white-chested, brown-winged Bonelli's eagle, and the bright green, thickset ocellated (or jeweled) lizard, which looks like a miniature medieval dragon. Watch out too for France's longest snake, the six-foot (2-m) Montpellier snake. Marine life offshore is equally diverse: You can spot dolphins, fin whales, and porpoises from the hills, while snorkelers can revel in an undersea wonderworld of sea-horses, sea urchins, barracuda, and mother-of-pearls—with the largest shellfish in the Mediterranean floating among the gorgonian coral.

The park's visitors center in Marseille offers advice on trails and activities. Water sports are popular, and a very basic hiking trail runs along the coast of Cap Sugiton from Calanque de Sugiton to Calanque de Morgiou. Wear strong hiking shoes for this and the park's other rocky routes, and a hat is a must in summer. Needless to say, no one should leave Marseille or its environs without sampling a glorious bowl of bouillabaisse (seafood stew) and a glass of one of the multitude of local wines.

AT A GLANCE

Mediterranean beaches ▪ 200 square miles (520 sq km) ▪ Water sports ▪ Limestone coastlines ▪ Fresh seafood ▪ Miles of hiking ▪ calanques-parcnational.fr/en

CÉVENNES

A divided religious history and magical limestone caves

Rich in history and geological interest, Cévennes National Park is part of a Cultural Landscape UNESCO World Heritage site located in the Languedoc-Roussillon region of southern France.

The Cévennes is a tapestry of mountains cut by valleys with crystal clear rivers and sweeping forests. The chestnut, what locals call the bread tree, is the mainstay of the Cévenol countryside, an area also known for its mulberry trees, planted to feed the silkworms that were bred in mills called *magnaneries*. The silkworm industry made Cévennes a wealthy region in the 19th century, as French fashion swept the world.

The absence of intensive farming and pesticides has ensured key habitats for many species. Although hikers in these hills should beware of wild boar, on the trails around the granitic massif of Mont Lozère (5,584 feet/1,702 m), you're more likely to come across grazing cattle and sheep. Golden eagles, peregrine falcons, and Montagu's harriers scour the hills for prey, and black woodpeckers, and owls thrive in the woods. The park has also successfully reintroduced red deer, beavers, wood grouse, mouflons (wild sheep), and black vultures.

The center of Cévennes National Park is the adjacent plateau between Le Bleymard and Le Pont-de-Montvert. There are many such calcareous (limestone) plateaus across the park. Above 2,600 feet (792 m) are the moors, where varieties of broom and coramon heather cover vast swaths of untended land. Farther down in the valleys, wild daffodils, martagon lilies, and lady's slipper orchids thrive amid the matgrass and hair grass.

PARK LEGACIES

The Cévennes were first brought to the wider world's attention with the publication of Robert Louis Stevenson's *Travels With a Donkey in the Cévennes* (1879), which became a classic of adventure literature. Today's travelers still follow the route Stevenson plotted, along the 165-mile (265-km) Robert Louis Stevenson Trail. The trail is also known as GR70, "GR" for *grande randonnée,* or "great hike."

The pastoral countryside is strewn with Protestant temples as well as Catholic churches, legacies of the awful Camisard wars, when the Huguenots (French Protestants) revolted against religious persecution, following the Revocation of the Edict of Nantes in 1685. This prolonged period of bloodshed (1702–1705) left an enduring impression on the tough, pious inhabitants, whose villages are enclosed by stone walls and whose hours are still counted by a tolling bell from a looming church belfry.

Perhaps the park's finest site is the Aven Armand Cave, a limestone cavern discovered in 1897. Its Great Hall, a forest of more than 400 fragile limestone speleothems, was created by dripping water over thousands of years. Some are nearly 98 feet (30 m) tall.

The Aven Armand Cave holds a forest of stalagmites.

AT A GLANCE

The Aven Armand Cave ▪ 353 square miles (913 sq km) ▪ Bucolic mountain hikes ▪ The Robert Louis Stevenson Trail ▪ cevennes-parcnational.fr/en

ÉCRINS

An Alpine mountain park of breathtaking beauty

The glacial Lake Lauzon, 1,640 feet (500 m) above the treeline, mirrors the Dauphiné Alps.

crins National Park encapsulates ice-capped, jagged rocky mountains, soaring peaks, glacier fields and valleys, Alpine pastures, and lush subalpine woodlands. The glacial grandeur of the landscape is augmented with a series of stunning cirques, gorges, and lakes. Designated a national park in 1973, this remote, soaring wilderness is located in the Dauphiné Alps near the Italian border in southeast France. Écrins is truly a nature lover's Alpine paradise.

The mountainous park also holds 150 peaks of more than 1,000 feet (305 m), with the highest peak, Les Écrins, reaching up to 13,458 feet (4,102 m), its side blanketed by Glacier Blanc. The first climbers to successfully summit this daunting alp were the English team of A. W. Moore, Horace Walker, and Edward Whymper on June 25, 1864. Thousands have since followed in their frosty footsteps, setting their sights on this icy, gneiss peak with its distinctive arrow shape pointing sharply heavenward.

The ice-capped and dark, jagged mountains stand in contrast to the bucolic lower meadows that in spring spread out beautiful carpets of Alpine wildflowers, mixing buttercup yellow with the deep blue of gentians and the bright whites of edelweiss and saxifrage. Nearby woodlands vary between spruce, Swiss pine, beech, alder, and juniper, while larch forests cover much of the park, starting at its northern edge near Briançon. These habitats host an array of European wildlife: Black grouse and willow ptarmigan roost in the woods; chamois and ibex (reintroduced to the park in 1977 and 1978) cling to rocky ledges; marmots and snow hares gambol in the meadows; and griffon vultures and pygmy owls glide on Alpine air currents. The park also incorporates several designated natural reserves within its borders including Pics du Combeynot, Vallée du Béranger, Vallée de Saint-Pierre, Vallée de la Séveraisse, Vallée du Vénéon, and Cirque du Grand Lac des Estaris.

HUMAN IMPACT

Although these conservation efforts are relatively recent, the mountains have been inhabited by humans since the Bronze Age, and shepherds and smugglers in particular have used the rugged mountains to profitable effect through the ages. The old town of Briançon, the highest city in France and now on the World Heritage List, suffered the fate of many border towns. The fortifications of its historical center—built by the Comte de Vauban to defend the region from Austrians in the 17th century—are an impressive monument to its spirit of resistance. The lovely village of Vallouise is worth visiting for its medieval church. The charming Alpine hamlet of La Grave, with La Meije rising 13,068 feet (3,983 m) in the background, is one of the most beautiful villages in France. The Maison du Parc in the picturesque village of Bourg d'Oisans has maps for hiking and also a good museum.

HIKING & BIKING

Away from these small clusters of civilization, the park offers an impressive 435 miles (700 km) of trails to take you high into nature. Hikes vary in length but, inevitably given the terrain, all involve some climbing: The 6.1-mile (9.9 km) Pigeon Loft Loop at Gioberney, at the heart of the national park, rewards with superb vistas of the Rouies glaciers. The ascent to Refuge du Pigeonnier at 7,949 feet (2,423 m) is worth the aching limbs, and you can overnight here if the light is fading. More intrepid

A golden eagle circles for prey.

Écrins' Golden Eagles

Écrins National Park is home to France's largest population of golden eagles. These fearsome predators use their keen senses to target likely prey from the rocks; they then ride the thermal Alpine currents before swooping with unerring precision. Golden eagles can reach amazing speeds (150 to 200 miles/241 to 322 km an hour) when diving after prey like hares, rabbits, and marmots in Écrins. The courtship ritual of golden eagles involves the male dropping a rock from its perch, then entering a steep dive to catch it in midair. The female does likewise with a small stick or piece of earth. Like swans, golden eagles mate with the same partner for life. At last count, 37 pairs had nested in Écrins aeries. The park also works with the conservation association Aquila to rehabilitate and return injured eagles to the wild.

adventurers will want to take on the legendary GR54 long-distance hike. This 123-mile (198-km) endurance test takes about 8 to 10 days, starting in Le Bourg-d'Oisans and delving deep into the park's glacial wilderness.

For a good, family-friendly long hike, try the Tour du Vieux Chaillol, an off-road *grande randonnée* that links the high mountain valley of Valgaudemar with the green landscapes of the Champsaur. This takes about five days to complete.

Mountain biking in the park comes with a "Tour de France" degree of difficulty. There are many options but for the authentic TDF challenge, try the 8.7-mile (14-km) climb from Bourg d'Oisans in the west of the park to the mountain resort of Alpe d'Huez. There are no less than 21 switchbacks to negotiate as you feel the burn all the way up to the summit of Alpe d'Huez. The views coming down, of course, will make the pain worthwhile, and you'll be able to say "done that" when the tour coverage rolls around next July. Snowshoeing and cross-country skiing are also thrilling activities in the clear Alpine air. Puy-Saint-Vincent and Vallouise offer excellent, marked trails, while those who like to go off-piste can hire a guide at any of the major resorts. These also offer a wide range of other adventure sports, such as mountain and ice climbing, gorge canyoneering, and *via ferrate* ("fixed-rope trails"). Just follow one rule: Go out with an expert and you'll probably come back.

AT A GLANCE

Soaring gneiss peaks ▪ Les Écrins ▪ 354 square miles (918 sq km) ▪ The legendary GR54 ▪ Golden eagles ▪ Quaint Alpine villages ▪ ecrins-parcnational.fr

MERCANTOUR

Azure blue lakes and Alpine meadows sloping down to the Mediterranean

Mercantour National Park is a diverse wilderness of towering mountains, glacial lakes, and forested hills, all of which wrap around several gorgeous valleys. The park's biodiversity and climactic variety spring from its location as the last promontory of the Alpine range, before the land rolls down to the Mediterranean Sea.

FLORA & FAUNA

The park hosts many tree varieties found elsewhere in French mountain regions including holm oak, fir, spruce, Swiss pine, and the ubiquitous larch. The Mediterranean olive tree and rhododendrons thrive on lower slopes. Mercantour is also home to more than 2,000 species of flowering plants, and in spring meadows are a riot of color: Clear white edelweiss, deep red or purple martagon lilies, blue bulbs of gentian, pink houseleeks, and pink moss campion all play their part. A preservation success story is the Alpine sea holly, a thistle-like plant with open umbels of steel-blue prickly flowers that was saved from near extinction and is now found only in a concentrated area of the national park. Also endemic to the park is the multiblossomed *Saxifraga florulenta*, a kind of floral chameleon that displays several shifting hues as it flowers.

Walkers may catch sight of one of several thousand chamois that inhabit the park, or hear the whistling of marmots. The ermine is more furtive, and the ibex and the mouflon (wild sheep) are seen only on higher grounds. Indeed, Mercantour is home to a rich array of wildlife including red deer and roe deer, wild boars, partridges, golden eagles, and buzzards. Since the early 1990s, about 50 Italian wolves have taken up residence here, and the park's various ecosystems—as well as local farmers—have had to adjust to this hungry arrival high on the food chain. The Alpha Park in Saint-Martin-Vésubie educates visitors on all things lupine.

The last Alpine specimen of the bearded vulture was killed at the start of the 20th century. Since 1962, this bird has enjoyed protected status and an international reintroduction program. The first wild hatching in the Southern Alps took place at Saint-Paul-sur-Ubaye in 2008.

TRACING FOOTSTEPS

Humans too have come and gone for millennia: Around Mont Bégo, several petroglyphs carved onto schist and granite faces are evidence of early inhabitants during the Late Neolithic and Bronze Ages. Further evidence can be seen in the heart of the park at the Vallée des Merveilles (Valley of Marvels). At the base of Mont Bégo, visitors are mesmerized by some 37,000 Bronze Age petroglyphs representing cattle, weapons, and humans.

Mercantour National Park has 370-odd miles (600 km) of marked footpaths, including the high mountain pass of Col de la Cayolle.

Col de la Bonette pass, one of Europe's highest roads at 9,193 feet (2,802 m)

AT A GLANCE

Alpine to Mediterranean topography ▪ 264 square miles (685 sq km) ▪ Vallée des Merveilles ▪ Italian wolves ▪ Col de la Cayolle Trail ▪ mercantour-parcnational.fr/en

PORT-CROS

Two Mediterranean islands lead to a lush undersea world of exotic marine life

Hidden away on the glorious Côte D'Azur, the islands of Port-Cros and Porquerolles and the deep-blue Mediterranean waters around them constitute what is probably France's least known nature preserve, Port-Cros National Park. Both islands are reached by boat from the mainland at Hières; both have fine sand beaches and carry the scent of their pine and eucalyptus forests on the sea breezes; and both have northern shores offering sheltered coves and beaches with southern coasts that are mainly rugged, rocky cliffs, blasted by sea breezes. The main difference? The island of Port-Cros is mountainous, while Porquerolles is flatter, making it a cyclist's heaven with various trails leading through pine vineyards, forests, and scrubland.

Mediterranean coralligenous reefs are biodiversity hot spots.

ABOVE & BELOW WATER

The vegetation is a mix of rough scrub, Aleppo pines, and evergreen oaks. Beneath the sea, Port-Cros National Park offers a great opportunity to appreciate the marine life of the Mediterranean up close. Sea grass meadows wave in the currents, and dolphins and whales are frequent passersby. From the beach at La Palud, you can enjoy an underwater trail for snorkelers or divers, which takes about 45 minutes. As you descend into a netherworld of silence and vivid color, you follow the trail along six stops with informational panels. The Maison du Parc in the village has snorkeling gear for rent; it also has information on all the park's trails.

Divers should beware of the black scorpionfish, which is deftly camouflaged on the seafloor: Its dorsal fin spines are poisonous. The beauty to this beast might be the large and lovely fan mussel, easily found among the sea grass. Watch also for the golden striped salema porgy and the brightly colored Mediterranean parrotfish, the clown in this undersea parade.

Port-Cros has 18.6 miles (30 km) of trails, and like on its island neighbor, there are no cars to contend with here. The Circuit de Port-Man is a four-hour hike round the secluded eastern half of the island, incorporating several historic buildings. To explore the western side, take the stiffer three-hour trail, the Sentier des Crêtes, which brings you to the top of 645-foot (197-m) Mont Vinaigre.

On Porquerolles, Fort Sainte-Agathe has an underwater archaeological exhibition. The park floods with day-trippers in the summer, but book ahead and you can spend the night on either island and enjoy the terrific cacophony of nature's nocturnal percussionists, the cicadas, as they rub their feet together in syncopated insect song.

Romans settled both these islands, and the remains of several forts dating from the 16th century onward can still be seen. This coastline and its islands were long a haven for the politically disaffected, and for various rapscallions, smugglers, and pirates who spread violence and crime throughout the region.

AT A GLANCE

Coral preserves ▪ 6.5 land/11 marine square miles (17/29 sq km) ▪ Shipwrecks ▪ Mediterranean beaches ▪ Coastal trails ▪ en.portcros-parcnational.fr

PYRÉNÉES

Nature's majesty matched by the largesse of the French and Basque

Clouds fill Cirque de Gavarnie, dubbed "Nature's Colosseum" by Victor Hugo.

This glorious wilderness of Alpine lakes, glacial valleys, and spectacular peaks running along the border between France and Spain is protected under the umbrella of Pyrénées National Park. Rugged scenery is glazed white in winter, and plateaus turn glorious green in summer, speckled with wildflowers. The French flock here year-round to hike, ski, climb, and enjoy a plethora of protected wildlife, or simply to breathe deep of the pure Pyrénées air.

In the eastern part of the park the Mont Perdu (Lost Mountain) World Heritage site straddles the border. The 118-square-mile (306-sq-km) site also straddles two national parks, encompassing the entirety of Ordesa and Monte Perdido National Park in Spain (see page 275).

The Cirque de Gavarnie is the park's most famous vista, a breathtaking amphitheater rimmed by peaks of up to 10,000 feet (3,048 m). Waterfalls cascade down the cirque, chief among them the Grande Cascade de Gavarnie; plunging 1,385 feet (442 m), it is Europe's highest.

Another classic Pyrenean landscape can be seen from the summit observatory at Pic du Midi, reached by cable car. There's also a star museum, and a restaurant offers diners breathtaking mountain views. Accommodations once reserved for staff are now open to the public. For an unforgettable experience, stay overnight to gaze at the stars, then catch the sunrise on the Pyrénées.

A separate, similarly named peak is the extinct volcano of the Pic du Midi d'Ossau, which towers above the Vallée d'Ossau. Grazing its slopes are herds of Pyrenean chamois, horned goat-antelopes with russet-brown coats and dark eye patches. Called *isards* by the French, these hardy natives were hunted to near extinction by the mid-1900s, but now thrive again above 3,300 feet (1,006 m) and have become a symbol of the park.

Other rare park mammals include the snow partridge, the marmot, and the mole-like Pyrenean desman, a tiny aquatic animal with a trunk-like nose and webbed feet. A declining number of Pyrenean brown bears also live in the park, pushed into the mountains by habitat loss on the lower ground. Efforts to reintroduce bears have been opposed by farmers. The Animal Park of the Pyrénées allows you to study ibex, wolves, giant otters, and other park fauna in a protected mountain setting.

LOOKING UP

The park is a bird-watcher's delight with bearded vultures, goshawks, peregrine falcons, and golden eagles swirling over mountain and valley, particularly the Vallée d'Ossau, where the ruins of Château de Beaucens now act as a bird sanctuary. Here you'll get a close view of the *vautour fauve* or griffon vulture with its wingspan of up to nine feet (2.7 m). Some 120 pairs of griffon vultures nest in the valley. Another refuge worth visiting is at Le Donjon des Aigles, offering a wide range of birds of prey. Watch for the rare Egyptian vulture, distinguishable by its white feathers.

The park is home to about 2,500 plant species, of which 200 are endemic. Pyrenean squill, rare lilies, and the delicate Pyrenean violet abound in the woodlands. Growing above the tree line is alpenrose, a vibrant flowering shrub of the rhododendron species that turns the hills bright pink in summertime. Above 7,900 feet (2,408 m), only poppies, lichens, and dwarf willow are tough enough to survive. As you walk through the park's floral spec-

Out & About

The Pyrénées offer year-round activities from springtime whitewater rafting to horse riding and mountain biking in summer to winter skiing and snowboarding. Hiking on the *sentiers balisés* ("marked trails") is a great way to experience the park. Trails include the relatively easy Cirque de Gavarnie with its glorious views. For bird-watchers, the Tour des Lacs d'Ayous, starting at Laruns, is a must. This six-hour loop passes Alpine lakes and the hunting grounds of many spectacular birds of prey. For serious hikers, the GR10 is one of France's most fabled routes, a *grande randonnée* stretching 560 miles (900 km) across the Pyrenees from the Atlantic to the Mediterranean. The less energetic visitor can enjoy the Petit Train d'Artouste, an unforgettable six-mile (10-km) ride from the peak of La Sagette to Lac d'Artouste, along one of the highest railways in Europe.

tacle, look for the rainbow of colors that swallowtail butterflies bring to the party, including luminous blues, pale yellows, and fluttering reds.

The lower hills of the Pyrénées are rooted with lush forests of beech, fir, and pine, while subalpine slopes have birch and mountain ash. The mountainous slopes are forested with yews and firs up to 5,905 feet (1,800 m). From that altitude to about 7,874 feet (2,400 m) stands of mugo pine predominate, along with a colorful springtime carpet of purple Pyrenean irises and rhododendrons.

THE PARTNERSHIP ZONE

Human life is less visible in the park, yet the ancient, pastoral way of mountain life endures here in a "partnership zone," where some 40,000 people live in 86 villages. The region was historically a cross-roads of cultures, with French, Basque, Andorran, and Spanish life commingling in these mountains. Here, hamlets perch between dizzying heights and farm fields and you might witness shepherds and their sheep as they move to higher pastures for summer grazing in a spectacle called the transhumance.

The village of Pau has a fine Renaissance castle (the birthplace of Henri IV), while the ski resort town of Cauterets offers a spa called Thermes de César, a nod to its Roman past. Cheesemaking is still a treasured tradition in the Pyrénées and you can sample ewes', goats', and cows' varieties at Les Fermiers Basco-Béarnais in the Vallée d'Aspe. For an authentic all-round Pyrenean experience, rent a *gîte* ("self-catering cottage") and experience mountain life firsthand for a week or two.

AT A GLANCE

Rare mountain wildlife ▪ 176 square miles (457 sq km) ▪ Year-round adventure sports ▪ Mont Perdu (Lost Mountain) World Heritage site ▪ Cirque de Gavarnie ▪ The Petit Train d'Artouste rail ride ▪ ee.france.fr/en

VANOISE

A rich array of Alpine flora and fauna tucked between three countries

The remote, seemingly timeless Alpine hamlet of Bonneval-sur-Arc

Vanoise National Park, located between the Tarentaise and Maurienne Valleys in the French Alps, was France's first national park, and its diversity of habitat and stunning scenery made it an easy choice to protect back in 1963. On the far side of the Italian border, the park continues into Gran Paradiso National Park. Together, the two parks cover more than 482 square miles (1,250 sq km) of Alpine wilderness.

Nestled in its towering mountains, the park's lakes are like jewels in the Vanoise crown. Thonon-les-Bains and Évian-les-Bains are charming spa towns on the banks of Lac Léman (Lake Geneva); passenger boats cross the lake from both towns to Switzerland. Aix-les-Bains, on the banks of Lac du Bourget, is another popular spa town, from where a boat can take you to visit the Benedictine Abbaye d'Hautecombe. Reconstructed in 19th-century neo-Gothic style, the abbey church holds the tombs of the Savoy kings. Annecy, another charming Alpine town, has an old quarter worth visiting for its château dating from the 12th century, as well as its pastel facades, canals and bridges, and lakeside cafés.

The park is a haven for hikers, as the Vanoise massif includes 107 peaks reaching more than 9,800 feet (2,987 m), as well as some 20 glaciers that feed many fast-running mountain streams. Best known of the summits are Grande Casse (12,648 ft/3,855 m) at the center of the park and its highest peak, Mont Pourri (12,398 ft/ 3,779 m), Grande Motte (11,995 ft/ 3,656 m), Sommet de Bellecôte (11,207 ft/3,416 m), and La Dent Parrachée (12,086 ft/3,684 m).

In these elevated habitats dwell a host of mammals, including Alpine marmots, wolves, Eurasian lynx, mountain hares, Eurasian badgers, ermines, and weasels. The park's emblem is the alpine ibex, known locally as the *bouquetin*. The ibex is a conservation success story for Vanoise, as populations have increased tenfold, from 200 to 2,000, since the park opened.

The Alpine chamois, like the ibex, live for most of the year above the tree line. They descend below the snow line in early spring and late autumn to avail of the grasslands uncovered by melting ice and snow.

PLANTS & WILDLIFE

The remote pasturelands of Vanoise provide ideal conditions for countless wildflower species, including crocuses, blue and yellow gentians, tulips, lilies, and orchids. Look for endemic alpine anemones, which flower in the color of fried eggs, with their rich yellow stamens surrounded by bright white petals.

The lower forested regions are mainly planted with conifers, including larches, arollas, firs, spruces, Scots pines, and mountain pines. Areas of quartzite and schist provide a rocky retreat for plants like blue-spiked rampions, cowberries, rock campions, and round-leaved restharrow.

Vanoise supports more than 100 bird species in the protected area. Birds of prey are a common sight soaring above the craggy peaks, including bearded vultures, Eurasian eagle-owls, and golden eagles. Less dramatic are the black grouse, black woodpeckers, rock ptarmigans, Alpine accentors, and Alpine choughs that nest in the park.

Watch, too, for the wallcreeper, a bird that nests on steep cliffs.

It stands out due to its extraordinary crimson wing feathers with white touches, a combination largely concealed amid its primarily gray and black plumage. Few artists could conceive of a more eye-catching flourish.

ALPINE ACTIVITIES

For us wingless bipeds though, the Alps are all about hiking, and you'll find information on trails at any of the park's visitors centers. One of the most memorable and iconic hiking trails, here or anywhere in Europe, is the Tour of the Vanoise glaciers. The park offers mountain huts for hikers, and your itinerary can be created "à la carte" over a period of four to seven days. Other hikes range from the 10.1-mile (16.4-km) climb to Col D'Aussois and Pointe de L'Observatoire, which takes you high into ibex territory, to the gentler 2.1-mile (3.4-km) lake loop of Lac Blanc de Termignon.

You don't have to be an adventure junkie to enjoy the Alps. In summer, the air is fresh and clear and the light sharp, and the high mountain passes are open. The best way to appreciate the magnificence of these mountains is by choosing a trail suitable to your physical fitness and hiking out into nature. Remember, however, that this is one of the great mountain ranges on Earth, and you need to take precautions before you set off. Even in summer, the weather can shift, and a bright, sunny afternoon can rapidly become a bewildering, foggy twilight. Make sure you have warm clothing, good hiking boots, a whistle, food, and a map. And tell someone where you are heading and when you should arrive; even the Saint Bernard dog of Alpine rescue legend won't find you if he doesn't know you're missing, and a cell phone probably won't work in the high mountain wilderness.

A male ibex, or bouquetin *in French, shows his distinctive horns.*

AT A GLANCE

Tour of the Vanoise glaciers ▪ Alpine ibex ▪ 204 square miles (528 sq km) ▪ Sparkling Alpine lakes ▪ Gran Paradiso's twin park ▪ vanoise-parcnational.fr/en

BELGIUM

The small country of Belgium is often overlooked, hemmed between larger nations with the North Sea seemingly its only natural outlet. But just as its territories were central to the great wars of the 20th century, Belgium's limited terrain is now key to the preservation of European wildlife and cultural heritage. As home of the European Council, Belgium has helped formulate many wise preservation policies: Its sharing of Grenspark De Zoom-Kalmthoutse Heide National Park (see page 84) with Holland shows a keen awareness of how nature transcends man-made borders. Belgium may have only one national park completely within its borders, but the idea behind Hoge Kempen—of reinventing industrial landscapes in the service of conservation—is a vital lesson for preservationists worldwide in the 21st century.

Opposite: Nature returns triumphant to the once industrialized region of Hoge Kempen National Park.

HOGE KEMPEN

New paths to the future of conservation amid medieval heathlands

The park's heaths and marshes nurture spectacular blooms of ling (aka heather), on which deer graze.

Hoge Kempen National Park is a truly pioneering preservation project, one situated in a once heavily industrialized—and still densely populated—part of Europe. The park is set in a rural area of eastern Belgium, a former coal-mining region in the province of Flanders. Its goals are to support ecotourism and education for future generations while conserving the memory of this past. Hoge Kempen's 22 square miles (57 sq km) consist mainly of pine forest and medieval heathlands, which give shelter to almost 80 percent of Belgium's Red List (threatened) species. Interspersed are a series of "garden cities" built around the former coal mines, which honor the region's urban-architectural heritage. This combination of ancient heathlands and the remnants of the 20th-century industry forms a unique cultural landscape.

COAL MINING PAST

In 1901, coal was discovered in the Limburg region, and its open spaces were quickly degraded as the fossil fuel industry thrived. When Limburg's seven mines shut in the 1990s, leaving 40,000 people unemployed, factories were proposed in the Hoge Kempen (Kempens Plateau), which had remained an oasis of untouched land within the industrial zone. Preservation prevailed in the ensuing conflict between conservation and development, and the national park was opened in 2006, in a rare success story of cooperation between industry, government, and environmental agencies. Hoge Kempen is already seen as a model for nature conservation worldwide, as evidenced in the success of similar recycling of industrial spaces, such as New York City's High Line.

GEOLOGICAL SHOWCASE

Unusually for the lowlands of Belgium and Holland, the park reaches well over 300 feet (91 m). The park is also strewn with rubble and boulders deposited by the Maas River during the last ice age and is now covered with sand blown inland by North Sea winds. In the east of the park, the Maas has gouged out a 200-foot-deep (61-m) valley. This, along with the boulders and the exposed gravel quarries, exhibit a cross-sectional geological exposure that the park presents as an "open-air museum." To the west of the Maas Valley the slope is steep, rising 147 feet (45 m) to form a small steppe, more than half of which lies within the park.

The sandy soil, mixed with gravel, was traditionally used as pastureland, resulting in typical western European heathland. This gives way to moorlands of peat and pooled water, and areas of pine forests originally planted to supply support beams for the coal mines. The eastern Flanders location of the Kempen means it is protected from the harsh weather extremes of the North Sea, and thus enjoys a more continental climate, one favoring tree species such as the sessile oak.

WATCHING WILDLIFE

In this mixed habitat hardy plants such as juniper, gorse, and bog asphodel thrive. In fall, common heather and bell heather color the park purple and provide a natural home for birds like curlews, woodlarks, and nightjars, the small birds once maligned as "goatsuckers" by medieval farmers. Black woodpeckers tap out their tattoos in these forests, which also host birds of prey such as buzzards, falcons, and hawks. The Hoge Kempen is also home

to myriad amphibians and reptiles, apparent by the croaking of moor frogs and natterjack toads heard across the marshes. Look for brook lampreys shimmying through brackish waters and viviparous lizards and smooth snakes basking on the rocks. Among the warmth-seeking insects and butterflies that flock to the south-facing slopes of the Kempen are the blue-winged grasshopper, the common yellow swallowtail, the silver-studded blue butterfly, and the Granville fritillary butterfly. Dragonflies, European beewolves, and ant lions also hover over the heathlands. For the many hikers, bikers, and horse riders on the park's trails, the most visible park creatures are the roe deer that graze extensively in Hoge Kempen.

The park offers a network of hiking trails stretching some 124 miles (200 km), containing 40 loop-shaped walks of varying lengths. These start at the six entrance gates. For serious walkers, the park's long-distance hike provides a 45-mile (72-km) signposted loop. A series of cycle paths link the national park with the cycle route network of the region, 100 miles (160 km) of mountain bike tracks in six loops. For horseback riders and horse-drawn vehicles, the park also has an 87-mile (140-km) network of mostly unpaved bridleways and paths that connect with the wider region. Campsites and hotel accommodations are available throughout the park, and support from the European Union ensures that a team of Rangers are always on hand to offer help to visitors.

Grenspark De Zoom-Kalmthoutse Heide NP

The heathlands of Zoom-Kalmthoutse Heide transcend the border between Belgium and the Netherlands (see page 84). This creates a small but vital area of protected natural habitat that is the essence of European union. The Flemish wilderness combines two former parks, the Kalmthoutse Heide in Belgium and De Zoom in the Netherlands, which now encompasses a total of 14.5 square miles (37.5 sq km).

The park's trails are a delight to walk or cycle, and are packed with wildlife-spotting possibilities. Moorlands, forests, and pools incorporate the preserved habitat of the smooth snake, the viviparous lizard, and the crested newt, as well as a host of birdlife. These flat heathlands, ablaze in purple heather for much of the summer, are also home to many rare butterflies. Look for luminous, lime-colored wings of the green hairstreak; the silver-studded blue, recognizable by the male's neon-blue wings with white edges; and the checkered skipper, with its brown wings with orange spots. *www2 .grensparkzk.nl/index_english .html*

Belgium's coal era reimagined ▪ 22 square miles (57 sq km) ▪ Industrial wastelands reconceived ▪ Medieval heathlands ▪ nationaalparkhogekempen.be/en

NETHERLANDS

The Netherlands is a flat low-lying country filled with cultivated fields, dikes, and windmills to drain the wetlands. The Dutch have always excelled at making the most out of their small nation's limited land resources. As a percentage of its landmass, no country has reclaimed more land from the sea, and no ethnic group has a keener sense of how to maximize the use of space. Consider the fact that the Dutch revolutionized the global game of soccer—and reached two World Cup finals—in the 1970s by applying basic trigonometry and breaking the rules of who could go where on the field of play. The Netherlanders bring a similar "outside the box" philosophy to their national parks pro-gram, creating parks within parks, reimagin-ing landscapes con-stantly, and packing a dizzying amount of recreational pos-sibilities into 20 relatively small spaces.

NORTH SEA
Schiermonnikoog National Park
East Frisian Islands
West Frisian Islands
Wadden Sea
Lauwersmeer National Park
Groningen
Duinen Van Texel National Park
De Alde Feanen National Park
Drentsche Aa National Park
Drents-Friese Wold National Park
Dwingelderveld National Park
Weerribben-Wieden National Park
IJssel
Zuid-Kennemerland N.P.
Amsterdam
Sallandse Heuvelrug N.P.
NETHERLANDS
De Hoge Veluwe N.P.
The Hague
Utrechtse Heuvelrug National Park
Veluwezoom N.P.
Rotterdam
Lek
Rhine
De Biesbosch National Park
Waal
GERMANY
Hollands Diep
De Loonse en Drunense Duinen N.P.
De Maasduinen N.P.
Oosterschelde National Park
Eindhoven
Maas
Grenspark De Zoom - Kalmthoutse Heide National Park
De Groote Peel N.P.
De Meinweg N.P.
BELGIUM
N
0   40 kilometers
0   40 miles

Opposite: A great crested grebe carries her chicks across Dutch wetlands in the Biesbosch.

ALDE FEANEN

As in much of the Netherlands, water, water, everywhere

Right-of-way: An equine park resident takes a shortcut to pasture.

De Alde Feanen National Park is a wildlife wetland of just 9.7 square miles (25 sq km) in the province of Frieslanda. In all, the park encompasses about 1,050 acres (425 ha) of surface water, spread across ditches, canals, peat ponds, and lakes, including the freshwater lake area of Princenhof. There are flooded morasses, peat bogs, reed beds, meadows, forested marshes, and grasslands to explore, and the park offers sailing routes as well as hiking and biking trails. Taking to the water, day or night, is probably the best way to see plants and wildlife up close.

WATERY HABITAT

The marshy conditions provide vital habitat for plants such as the critically endangered bog orchid. Yellow and white water lilies are among the water plants that thrive in the peat pits and ponds. Indeed, yellow and gold are predominant shades here: Plants typically found in the grasslands are the common marsh marigold, ragged-robin, greater yellow-rattle, and yellow loosestrife. The damp forests are rich in lichen, mosses, and mushrooms, as well as alder buckthorn and wild honeysuckle.

Fish species supported by the park include bream in open waters, and tench, perch, and pike in smaller bodies of water. Among the birds that feast in De Alde Feanen's fertile waterways are grebes and blue herons, along with rarer species such as purple herons with their long orange- and brown-striped neck, and bitterns, often identified by their "booming." The park is a vital breeding and wintering ground for migratory birds, attracting flocks of shovelers and barnacle geese who arrive from as far away as Novaya Zemlya in the Arctic Ocean. The

Miles of waterways ▪ 9.7 square miles (25 sq km) ▪ Bird-watching ▪ Art and history outdoors ▪ Guided water tours ▪ Sint Martinus Church, Wergea ▪ np-aldefeanen.nl/en larger ponds and flooded grasslands are stopping-off points for a variety of wild ducks with distinctive markings. In fall and early spring, the waters welcome thousands of waders, such as the black-tailed godwit, golden plover, and lapwing that forage and roost here.

Bird-watchers should head for the reed marshes, the nesting space of the bearded reedling, reed warbler, and reed bunting, all of which avail the abundance of insects. The swamp forest of Princenhof, with its black alder and grey willow stands, is home to a colony of large cormorants. Watch these long-necked birds dive deep for fish (up to 100 feet/30 m), then stretch their wings out to dry and dive again (they cannot fly with wet wings). Another park favorite is the white stork—look for the tall wooden poles erected to provide nesting grounds for this graceful avian with the adults flashing their distinctive long red legs and pointed red beak. The forests also host choruses of songbirds, including the bullfinch, spotted flycatcher, and nightingale.

HUMAN IMPACT

Humans too have long roosted and foraged here, many making a living as reed cutters and eel fishermen. The Skûtsje Museum in Earnewâld tells the story of Friesland's superbly crafted ships. Throughout the park, you'll pass several monumental windmills, such as the 18th-century De Ikkers, as well as historic churches including the Sint Martinus Church in Wergea, a unique neo-Gothic church built circa 1860, and Saint Peter's Church in Grou, which dates from the 13th century. History and conservation combine well to commemorate lives lost when an RAF Lancaster bomber was shot down in World War II: The memorial in De Zwaluwhaven takes the form of a 105-foot-long (32-m) wall, designed by landscape architect Nynke-Rixt Jukema, with 251 holes for sand martins to nest in. This is the number of fighter planes that took off from England on the fateful night of the crash in September 1942.

Several art museums within the park highlight Friesian artists; look too for the outdoor steel statue of ice skaters gliding on the open water titled "The Earnewâld 100."

Two good walks in the park celebrate local culture: The Dichterspaad, or Poet's Walk, runs from 5 to 15.5 miles (8 to 25 km), and leads past 18 panels with poems around Oudega; the Paad troch Grou Walk passes 21 historic buildings in Grou. Maps and information on all the park's walks, cycle paths, and boat rides are available from De Alde Feanen National Park Visitor Centre, and from the tourist offices in Grou and Earnewâld.

Windmills have long pumped out flooded wetlands on Dutch farmlands.

BIESBOSCH

Protecting part of one of Europe's last extensive freshwater tidal wetlands

The hardworking beaver is the symbol of the Biesbosch, Europe's largest freshwater tidal zone.

As an entity, De Biesbosch National Park is relatively new (designated in 1994), but the first key date in its story is 1421. This was the year De Biesbosch ("rush-woods") was formed, when a vast swath of drained and cultivated land became inundated with seawater in the devastating St. Elizabeth's flood. The dikes of this area, called Grote Hollandse Waard, were in poor repair due to political strife and failed. But the sudden loss of so much reclaimed, low-lying, or "polder," land was a lesson the Dutch absorbed well, one that remains valuable in our century of climate change and rising sea levels.

Today, De Biesbosch National Park constitutes about half of what is one of the last extensive areas of freshwater tidal wetlands in Europe. The park offers boaters and canoeists an inviting maze of rivers, creeks, and islands to explore.

The waterways are shaded largely by willow forests, their graceful canopy interrupted occasionally by open spaces of wet grasslands and fields of rustling reed.

TIDAL INFLUENCE

Boating through the park leads through the estuary of two great rivers, the Meuse and the Rhine, and on to their shared delta. It follows that water levels in the Biesbosch are tidal, peaking at flood tide, when the seawater holds back the water from the rivers, and falling at ebb tide, when the river water flows freely to the North Sea.

Around Biesboschcentrum Dordrecht in the north of the Biesbosch, this tidal difference is about 2.5 feet (76 cm), so in just a few hours visitors can witness the creeks change from mudflats to mangrove. The visitors center here runs worthwhile guided excursions through the park on foot, by canoe, and in electric boats.

The park has three main sections, and the northern section, closest to the North Sea, obviously has the most significant tidal influence. The Sliedrechtse Biesbosch takes its name from the town of Sliedrecht, which was flooded in 1421, and later rebuilt just outside the Biesbosch. This area is distinguished by its system of dunes. The western section is the Hollandse Biesbosch, the part of the national park best known for its extensive birdlife. The eastern section, the Zuidwaard, which is part of the wider Brabantse Biesbosch area, is composed mainly of willow forests with roots happily submerged.

RECLAIMING THE LANDSCAPE

Following extremely high river discharges in 1993 and 1995, the Dutch government decided to undo most of the land reclamation achieved in recent centuries, when much of the Biesbosch had been drained and turned back into polders. Planners reversed course and resolved to use the Biesbosch as a natural buffer to prevent major flooding in future. This decision—so typical of the Dutch mentality to read nature's tides and go with the flow rather than fight the environment—has effectively given the Biesbosch back to nature. The restoration of the area as an inland river delta has also resulted in an expansion of habitat for many animals within the national park.

An industrious beaver population in particular has benefited from these hydrological changes. About 300 of these herbivores now live in over 100 lodges in the park. It is also hoped that the Biesbosch will see a return of the almost extinct southern Dutch population of seals. The expanded wetlands have seen a rebound in great egret and little egret numbers, and the populations of bitterns and kingfishers have also grown in recent years. The spring of 2016 brought the arrival of the first Dutch-born ospreys, and a pair of white-tailed eagles have also made the park their home. Migrating ducks continue to visit in vast numbers and kingfishers and bluethroats make their nests in the park.

Among the many flora that thrive in the sedges and reed beds is the marsh marigold, a member of the buttercup family that spreads its floral sunshine around the wetlands each spring.

Biesbosch MuseumEiland blends into the park's landscape.

FLOOD PROTECTION

The Biesbosch had a rich history of human habitation (see sidebar) before its current role as a flood protection system for major Dutch cities. The government, conscious of the threat of rising sea levels, has breached some dikes originally built to protect farmland and dug additional drainage channels in the Biesbosch. Such measures will reduce peak flood flows to cities downstream; the excess water will be released from tightly constricted river and canal channels, and huge volumes will be allowed to spread across the Biesbosch delta, which will act as a temporary reservoir.

History in the Telling

Biesbosch MuseumEiland is a fine combination of visitors center and museum. Exhibits examine the role of mankind in shaping the area. Among the stories told are those of Biesbosch's farmers, reed cutters, and griend workers, the latter being men who lived in small, damp huts and made a living cutting willow wood in the marshy wilderness. You'll learn too how heroic World War II resistance fighters known as Biesbosch crossers used the wetlands to smuggle refugees to safety, capture fleeing Germans, and transport medicines to the occupied north of the Netherlands. The museum also explains the park's ever evolving and far-sighted water management policies; this a dialogue between the Dutch and their environment that has been going on since windmills first pumped water out of the Biesbosch in the 13th century.

AT A GLANCE

Freshwater tidal wetlands ▪ 35 square miles (90 sq km) ▪ Beaver conservation ▪ Biodiverse waterways ▪ Willow forests ▪ Biesbosch MuseumEiland ▪ Guided excursions ▪ np-debiesbosch.nl

DRENTS-FRIESE WOLD

Where shifting sands have changed habitats over time

This inviting patchwork of forests, heathlands, brook valley grasslands, and drift sands was first protected under Drents-Friese Wold National Park in 2000. From its previous incarnation as pastureland, the soil suffered mineral depletion, and heathlands and shifting sands took over. State-mandated planting of oak, pine, Douglas fir, and Japanese larch stands in the 19th century helped anchor some soils, and other sand areas were forested in the 20th century, to good effect.

The neighboring extensive marshy heathlands of the Doldersummerveld and Wapserveld are rooted with bell heather, the fluffy white bog cotton, and bog gentian. Stiff club moss and bog rosemary also thrive in the wet conditions. Heather and mouse-ear hawkweed, a yellow-flowering daisy, grow in drier areas. Sheep grazing, peat cutting, and mowing all help maintain these heaths.

HABITAT RESTORATION

The area of Aekingerzand has been restored in the 21st century by the Dutch Forestry Commission, with some trees and shrubs cut to allow the sands to shift once more. This means that creatures such as the sand lizard and the comma butterfly will not disappear. Mammals calling Drents-Friese Wold home include roe deer, hare, rabbit, hedgehog, squirrel, ermine, polecat, and the rare European pine marten, known for the yellow-colored "bib" on its throat. In the park's southwest corner lies the grazing realm of shaggy Highland cattle.

The park also hosts several reptiles, among them the smooth snake, the great crested newt, and the viviparous lizard, the only lizards known to give live birth. Watch out, while walking, for the adder, the only poisonous Dutch snake, recognizable by its sharp-edged zigzag markings. The other snakes found here, including the ringed snake, are harmless.

A wonderfully diverse birdlife takes advantage of the park's range of habitats. Stonechat, curlew, hobby, and wheatear all brood in the heathlands, and the forests welcome the red poll, hawfinch, nightingale, and crossbill, among others. The rare nightjar (once unfairly known as the goatsucker) is sometimes visible on the outskirts of the forests. The even rarer red-backed shrike prefers the rough terrain of bramble bushes, while in shifting sands you'll spot woodlark and tawny pipit. Multitudes of waders use the bogs and open-water fens during migration, including the black-tailed godwit, redshank, and common snipe.

To address declining butterfly population, Drents-Friese Wold is now home to Doldersummerveld, the first butterfly reserve in the Netherlands. Rare species such as the tan- and brown-colored grayling and Alcon blue butterflies are nurtured here.

HUMAN FOOTPRINTS

The park has also helped to restore the footprint of humankind in the area with recently restored Iron and Bronze Age burial mounds. Also on site are the uniquely Dutch *klokkenstoelen*, or "clock chairs," that originated in the Stellingwerven part of the park. Klokkenstoelen are wooden structures usually built in lieu of clock towers, inside which a sounding bell was hung.

Drents-Friese Wold National Park has also worked to maintain the classic *esdorp* landscape of the region present when medieval rural planners organized a village with farms centered around a square or church, surrounded by fields on the interior and heathland on the outskirts. You'll pass many of these historical remnants along the 80 miles (130 km) of walking paths that transect the park. There are also about 31 miles (50 km) of ATB routes (national cycling routes) in Drents-Friese Wold, incorporating the 15-mile (24-km) Appelscha loop and the 17-mile (27-km) Smilde-lus loop.

Sunrise on park heathland, where pines anchor the soil

AT A GLANCE

Iron and Bronze Age burial mounds ▪ 24 square miles (61 sq km) ▪ Dutch *klokkenstoelen,* or "clock chairs" ▪ Classic esdorp landscape ▪ Rare butterflies ▪ nationaalpark-drents-friese-wold.nl

DRENTSCHE AA

Far-sighted Dutch stewardship preserves the landscape of centuries past.

Drentsche Aa National Park is a landscape frozen in time. The preserve follows the path of the Drentsche Aa system of rivers through the bucolic Dutch province of Drenthe. The landscape around the river valley escaped the Dutch government's major agricultural reforms of the 20th century. As a result, the hedgerows, heathlands, and traditionally farmed fields *(essen)* remain much as they appeared in the paintings Vincent van Gogh created during his short stay in Drenthe in 1883, such as "Landscape With a Stack of Peat and Farmhouses."

The national park consists of about one-third of the wider National Stream and Esvillages Landscape of Drentsche Aa, which encompasses 16 traditional hamlets or *esvillages*. An esvillage *(esdorp* in Dutch) is a rural hamlet planned around an *es,* an elevated field collectively cultivated by villagers. Zuidlaren, Grolloo, Orvelte, and Annen are typical of the villages in the Drentsche Aa, and are notable for their Saxon farmhouses, cobblestone streets, and pretty village greens.

The park's remote woodlands offer secluded trails for walking and biking, and the wet heather field of the Doldersummerveld bursts into purple in summer. Also worth visiting is the overlapping Hondsrug UNESCO Geopark. Look for the *hunebeds,* granite prehistoric burial chambers built by the Funnelbeaker people some 5,000 years ago, and for the remnants of a prehistoric highway.

AT A GLANCE

Preserved ancient landscapes ▪ 38.6 square miles (100 sq km) ▪ Stone Age burial chambers ▪ Drentsche Aa river valley ▪ Hondsrug UNESCO Geopark ▪ dehondsrug.nl/verhalen/drentsch-aa

DUINEN VAN TEXEL

Coastal wildlife sanctuary for marine mammals and birdlife

Duinen Van Texel National Park is a landscape of woodlands, heaths, and salt marshes beside the beaches of this North Holland island. The park's fine natural history museum, Ecomare, offers ranger-led walks, a sea aquarium, and a seal and bird sanctuary.

Edging the grass-covered dunes of the island's western coast are salt fens and heaths where endemic plants such as the marsh orchid and orange-berried sea buckthorn thrive. The flooded dune valleys and

Dune grass roots the shifting sands.

shores buzz with birdlife: Ducks frequent the inland ponds, while waders find food along the shore. Birds of prey hover too, and to the south,

De Muy is known for its spoonbills. The creeks of the Slufter dune valley make for good bird-watching as they rise and fall with the ebb and flow of the North Sea tides. Common seals and white-beaked dolphins are sometimes visible along the shore.

Duinen Van Texel is an evolving landscape, as dune valleys flood and dunes shift. June brings a proliferation of purple as sea lavender spreads, and October reddens Duinen Van Texel as glasswort grows wild on the wetlands.

AT A GLANCE

Dramatic dunescapes ▪ 17 square miles (43 sq km) ▪ Ecomare *(ecomare.nl/en)* aquarium and natural history museum ▪ English-speaking guides ▪ Walking and biking trails ▪ npduinenvantexel.nl/299/en

DWINGELDERVELD

Expansive wet heathlands made accessible for hikers, cyclists, and a wealth of wildlife

Dwingelderveld National Park is the largest wet heathland in western Europe. More than 35 miles (60 km) of hiking paths and 25 miles (40 km) of cycling trails traverse its fens, bogs, meadows, sandy hills, and forests.

Some of the country's largest juniper thickets grow here; the juniper's fleshy cone (erroneously described as a "berry") has traditionally given Dutch gin its distinctive flavoring. Wooden pathways allow for hiking just above the water and the panoply of plant life.

Look for the varied wildlife, including adders, grass snakes, foxes, and the rare peat butterfly. The *rat-a-tat* of green, black, and great spotted woodpeckers will increase as you approach the park's pine forests; you might also spot raptors in the sky. The park offers night walks, a chance to experience a heathland and wooded wilderness while much of nature rests. Night sky enthusiasts should also visit the park's Planetron.

An enchanted, watery world

AT A GLANCE

Heathland wilderness ▪ 14 square miles (37 sq km) ▪ Juniper thickets ▪ The Planetron ▪ Night hiking ▪ nationaalpark-dwingelderveld.nl

GROOTE PEEL

A birders' paradise atop one of Europe's last raised boglands

De Groote Peel National Park is all about birds. Located between the provinces of Limburg and North Brabant, this nature preserve is one of the last uncultivated raised bogs, and it hosts one of the largest avian populations in western Europe. Although it is the Netherlands' smallest national park, De Groote Peel marshlands offer a serene habitat for a variety of birdlife. Among the park's many permanent residents are black-necked grebes, while others such as the common crane pass through in the late fall. Other notables are bluethroats, nightjars, stonechats, and water rails. Keep an ear tuned for the song of the yellowhammer; it may sound familiar, as it supposedly inspired the opening notes of Beethoven's Fifth Symphony.

The landscape of this park, like others in the Netherlands, represents a geographic moment in time, freeze-framed by the farsightedness of Dutch rural planners. This happened here midway through the 20th century when cutting peat from the raised bog was discontinued, and new trees planted. The park's 3,460 acres (1,400 ha) were thus preserved as a network of inaccessible peat swamps, lakes, heaths, and sand ridges hospitable to avian life. This forbidding landscape is bridged for human visitors by a series of raised trails over the swamps, from which you might see some of De Groote Peel's earthbound wildlife, such as the weasel, ermine, water vole, polecat, and boar.

AT A GLANCE

Raised bogs ▪ 5.2 square miles (13.4 sq km) ▪ Multitudes of birds ▪ Elevated walkways ▪ natuurparkenlimburg.nl/np/de-groote-peel

HOGE VELUWE

A country estate with a world-class art museum complementing nature's creativity

Imagine a maze of marshlands, frog-croaking heathlands, peaceful ancient pine and oak stands foraged by red deer, beech forests busy with black woodpeckers, and dunes of ever shifting sands. Think of all this encapsulated in a 13,590-acre (5,500-ha) preserve, add a world-famous Van Gogh museum and a sculpture garden, and you've arrived at De Hoge Veluwe National Park.

This park was the dream of Anton and Helene Kröller-Müller. In 1909, the couple began buying land for a hunting estate stocked with animals such as red deer, wild boar, and mouflons (horned Corsican sheep). They founded a museum to illustrate how art, architecture, and nature were three strands of the same creative life force. However, money troubles led to the park being given to the state in 1935.

FAUNA & FLORA

Today, De Hoge Veluwe National Park protects dozens of species, including the moor frog and the grass snake. Badgers, foxes, and pine martens also roam the estate. About 200 mouflons, introduced by Anton Kröller in 1921, keep the heather free of grasses and preserve the landscape's diversity. The males' large twisted horns are used to fearsome effect in the fall mating season.

"Café Terrace, Place du Forum, Arles" by van Gogh

Most of the park is forested, mainly with birch, beech, oak, and pine. The black woodpecker is a key link in the forest ecosystem:

The Kröller-Müller Legacy

The Kröller-Müller Museum, opened in 1938, is home to one of the world's largest Vincent van Gogh collections, including iconic works such as "Cafe Terrace at Night." Also among the collection of the Kröller-Müller couple are key works by Pablo Picasso, Odilon Redon, Georges-Pierre Seurat, Piet Mondrian, and Auguste Rodin. Outside is one of Europe's best sculpture gardens. Another museum, the Museonder, is located at the visitors center and focuses on the geology and biology of the Veluwe region. Jachthuis Sint Hubertus, Anton Kröller-Müller's magnificent hunting lodge, is the centerpiece of the park and may be viewed by guided tour. Renowned architect Berlage designed both the lodge and its grounds, a signature achievement of the Dutchman's career. Completed in 1920, the lodge stands as one of the Netherlands' finest buildings.

This shy, red-crested bird favors old deciduous forests with plenty of deadwood, from which they bore out their favored foodstuff, carpenter ants. Pine martens, tawny owls, and other forest dwellers happily inhabit these cavities.

The marshy conditions are ideal growing grounds for many mushrooms and toadstools, the most dramatic of which is the fly agaric. This poisonous fungus is almost a caricature of a children's book drawing of a magic toadstool: Its bright red or orange cap is dotted with white spots, which are the remains of its subterranean cowl or membrane and often wash off in the rain. You can follow the progress of park plant growth digitally via the innovative Snapshot Hoge Veluwe program, whereby the estate uses heat-sensitive camera traps to record changes in flora, as well as avian and animal activity.

CYCLIST'S DREAM

De Hoge Veluwe is also known for its fleet of 1,800 white bikes clustered near park entrances, which are free for visitors to use. Cyclists and hikers can enjoy some 27 miles (43 km) of pathways that cross the park. Hoge Veluwe is the only park in the Netherlands that charges an entrance fee, but its natural riches, combined with a visit to the Kröller-Müller Museum and sculpture garden, make it well worth the price.

AT A GLANCE

World-renowned art museum ▪ 21 square miles (55 sq km) ▪ Dutch country estate ▪ Guided tours of the Jachthuis Sint Hubertus lodge ▪ Sculpture gardens ▪ Cycling and hiking trails ▪ hogeveluwe.nl/en

LAUWERSMEER

Wild horses, fishing villages, and part of the sea reclaimed for migrating birdlife

Small fishing villages pepper the Wadden Sea coastline.

On May 25, 1969, the Lauwers Sea, formed by a flood in 1280, was separated from the Wadden Sea by the closing of a dike. The Lauwers Sea thus became the Lauwersmeer, a freshwater lake and the Netherlands' latest acquisition from the ocean. In 2003, Lauwersmeer National Park was established to protect the new flora and fauna attracted to this wilderness that spans the provinces of Friesland and Groningen.

The park's grasslands are now kept in check by grazing Highland cattle and the Konik horse, a Polish semiferal breed introduced into several European fen wildernesses.

Among the teeming birdlife are the rare sea eagle and the white-tailed eagle. Avian inhabitants include Montagu's harriers, bearded reedlings, and bluethroats. Among the thousands of birds that migrate here in winter are Eurasian wigeons, tundra swans, and barnacle geese. Birds such as golden orioles, pied avocets, and spoonbills migrate in fall and return in spring.

In 2020, a Seal Center is opening in Lauwersoog. A contemporary glass building will stand like a wading bird atop stilts in the sea, housing exhibitions on the Waddenzee ecosystem as well as a research center and rooftop pools for the once endemic gray seal.

In Zoutkamp, a fishing village with a rainbow of painted fishermen's houses, you can try the local delicacy of eels smoked in the quayside *rokerij* (smokehouse).

AT A GLANCE

Information Pavilion (HIP) in Lauwersoog harbor ▪ 23 square miles (60 sq km) ▪ Official Dark Sky Park ▪ Konik horses ▪ Lauwersoog Seal Center planned opening 2020 ▪ np-lauwersmeer.nl

LOONSE EN DRUNENSE DUINEN

A surprising desert with pine forests protecting a host of wildlife amid drifting sands

There is a little-known desert in the north of Europe. Locals jokingly refer to it as the Brabant Sahara, but the Dutch province of North Brabant is in fact home to a spacious expanse of sand, a geographical anomaly occupied at its heart by De Loonse en Drunense Duinen National Park. Despite their arid appearance, however, the shifting sands of the region are host to a vibrant ecosystem.

ANCIENT SAND

This is one of the widest wilderness in the Netherlands, and the largest sand drift region in western Europe. The dunes were formed some 10,000 years ago as sandy moorland in the early Neolithic age, when humans were changing from a nomadic life to taming a landscape demanded by sedentary agriculture. In the Middle Ages, after the local terrain became degraded due to overgrazing and peat extraction, the plains became a Dutch dust bowl, with several villages buried by raging sandstorms. In 2002, a national park was established to help protect habitats around these shifting sands into a new millennium. This includes the area of Plantloon, at the northern side of the park, which was once an English-style country estate, complete with farms, old avenues, deciduous tree stands, and meadows edged by hedgerows.

De Brand, an area of forestry and meadowlands on the southern side of the dunes, is another reserve added to the national park.

The sandy expanses of De Loonse en Drunense Duinen play host to many mosses and grasses, especially around the edges of the fragrant pine forests where heather gradually gives way to shifting sands. The whistling winds of the

Dunes formed some 10,000 years ago continue to drift in this national park.

open sands are interrupted by the sound of songbirds, and raptors ride winds in search of prey in the grasslands. Roe deer cleave to the woodlands, venturing out only to graze, and the shy badger keeps a low profile too.

TOURING OPTIONS

Expert guides lead walking tours to explain the wildlife and geography of the dunes for curious visitors. For

adventurers, the park offers GPS tours, bridle paths, and mountain bike trails. Like in any open desert landscape, nighttime can bring extreme temperature drops, so wrap up well if you plan to hike or bike after dusk. Maps and information about the nature reserve are available from the visitors center in Oisterwijk.

The park lies close to the Belgian border so it's no surprise that the area has many monuments to World War II. On your bike rides, watch for a monument at Distelberg, the cross in the dunes near Helvoirt, the Maria Chapel of Udenhout in De Brand, the Memorial for the Resistance near Bosch en Duin, and the Peace Memorial on Eftelingsestraat in Kaatsheuvel. An educational walking trail in the dunes also traces war remnants such as bomb craters and trenches.

AT A GLANCE

Desert landscapes ▪ 14 square miles (35 sq km) ▪ Expert guided walks ▪ World War II walking trail ▪ Plantloon's English landscape ▪ np-deloonseendrunenseduinen.nl

MAASDUINEN

Forests, heathlands, and parabolic river dunes from the last glaciation

Located in the Dutch province of Limburg, De Maasduinen National Park is a thin ridge of forests and heathlands straddling a sandy plateau between the Maas River and the German border. These fens, lakes, and shifting sands are home to a rich array of flora and fauna, but because the rivers are deficient in nutrients, fish are scarce. The park comprises the longest belt of river dunes in the Netherlands and planners have countered its shifting sands by rooting the landscape with oak, birch, pine, alder, and beech trees, as well as smaller plants like marsh gentian and bog myrtle. The sandy terrain suits a variety of reptiles including the smooth snake, the slowworm, the sand lizard, and the viviparous lizard. Graceful cranes, western marsh harriers, and river kingfishers are among the park's winged visitors, and bats such as common pipistrelles and brown long-eared bats hang out here too.

The park was established in 1996 and covers an area of approximately 11,120 acres (4,500 ha). At its heart lies the De Hamert estate with its stately houses. Just beside the park are the ruins of Bleijenbeek Castle; built in the 14th century, it was bombed by the British Royal Air Force (RAF) when Germans occupied it in 1945.

Visitors centers in Afferden, Well, and Wellerlooi offer maps and information on the park's various walking routes and its three mountain bike trails.

AT A GLANCE

River dunes ▪ 17.4 square miles (45 sq km) ▪ Reptilian wildlife ▪ Mountain bike trails ▪ natuurparkenlimburg.nl/np/de-maasduinen

---

MEINWEG

An environmental embodiment of the European Union

Set in the province of Limburg, De Meinweg National Park shares its wilderness with neighboring Germany: Covering 4,448 acres (1,800 ha) and founded in 1995, in 2002 the park became part of the Maas-Swalm-Nette Nature Park, a protected area straddling the German/Dutch border. That border has endured since 1815, the time when Napoleon Bonaparte personified European union. It is remarkable to think that these two nations can transcend such long-held borders in the name of conservation.

Unusual for the lowlands, this region is blessed with gorgeous rolling countryside, and De Meinweg itself is distinguished by its terraced landscape, a manifestation of the large deposits of sediment the Rhine and Maas Rivers left over centuries. There are three plateaus, the highest of which rises some 260 feet (79 m) above sea level. The mixture of forests, moors, heaths, lakes, ponds, and valleys plays host to an array of wildlife. This includes harmless adders, blindworm, wild boars, shy stoats, and dozens of butterfly species. Bell heather, bog asphodel, and marsh gentian blanket the grounds of the park, and hardy Galloway cattle (introduced from Scotland) graze the heaths. Guided hikes are available, and the walk around the bog pond at Rolvennen is particularly rewarding for seeing wildlife, as is the 11-mile (19-km) Wasser-Wander-Wege hike skirting rivers, streams, and lakes.

AT A GLANCE

Stepped plateaus ▪ 6.9 square miles (18 sq km) ▪ A transborder nature reserve ▪ Sedimentary watersheds ▪ River trails ▪ natuurparkenlimburg.nl/np/de-meinweg

OOSTERSCHELDE

A lesson in ocean barriers for our era of rising seas

Located in the province of Zeeland and founded in 2002, Oosterschelde is the largest national park in the Netherlands. It runs some 78 miles (125 km) along the country's shorelines, encompassing 13 ambitious Delta Works designed to protect a large swath of the country from flooding. Oosterschelde (Eastern Scheldt) is thus the latest exchange in a long historical negotiation with the invasive North Sea. In a country where more than a quarter of the landmass is below sea level, this is an eternal and existential dialogue.

After the North Sea flood of 1953, the Oosterschelde estuary was sealed off by means of a dam and barrier. The Oosterscheldekering (Eastern Scheldt storm surge barrier) is the largest of the area's ambitious Delta Works. A 2.5-mile (4-km) section has massive sluice gates that can be closed when storms threaten tidal surges. After the barrier was completed in 1986, the influx of seawater decreased and tidal extremes reduced to the point where no new sand is deposited on the sandbars. As a result, these are now slowly eroding, changing the character of the coastline.

UNDERWATER DISCOVERY

For visitors, the park is a portal to an incredible coastal and underwater realm. Several diving schools accommodate offshore explora-

Dog whelk stranded on seaweed

tion, where you'll share the oceans with seals and harbor porpoises. Divers will also witness the habitats of oysters, crabs, lobsters, clams, and shrimp that have fed Netherlanders for centuries. Watch too for the strangely striped cuttlefish that breed here in the warming waters of spring. You'll soon appreciate how many species of shellfish and flatfish dwell in the North Sea. Divers should beware, however: These waters are both tidal *and* seasonal, with temperatures ranging from a wintry 28°F (−2°C) to a summer high of about 75°F (24°C). The strong currents of the North Sea mean these waters are definitely *not* for beginners.

TIDAL DELIGHTS

Along the shoreline, vast tracts of land are open to the sea, becoming submerged at high tide, then drying out when the tide ebbs. At low tide, the sandbanks become a smorgasbord of rich pickings for thousands of birds, with oystercatchers, wigeon, stilt walkers, redshank, and gulls all scouring the mud for food. When the tide comes in, cormorants, ducks, and terns start diving for their dinner. In summer, seals come ashore to bask in the sun.

The mix of saltwater and freshwater habitats in the park creates a dynamic natural environment with a very diverse range of flora and fauna. Glasswort, sea lavender, and sea aster thrive in the saline grounds of shoreline and salt marshes. Apart from the saltwater edge along the Oosterschelde, the inner part of the park stretches into mudflats, shoals, and meadows. These are all accessible via many hiking and biking trails.

Beachcombing is popular with children, and a visit to a mussel farm or a walk across the tidal marshes and mudflats is always educational. The island of Neeltje Jans offers an engaging indoor exhibition explaining the history of the delta and the operation of the storm barrier.

Visitors should always check the tidal and weather forecasts before venturing onto the sands. The park website updates these daily.

AT A GLANCE

Saltwater and freshwater habitats ▪ Dutch sea barriers ▪ 78 miles (125 km) of shoreline ▪ 140 square miles (363 sq km) ▪ Neeltje Jans exhibition ▪ np-oosterschelde.nl

SALLANDSE HEUVELRUG

Scenic heathlands and a World War II cemetery

Sallandse Heuvelrug National Park is known for its picturesque heathlands and for its cemetery to the British Commonwealth soldiers killed in the last stages of World War II.

The Sallandse Heuvelrug, located in the Dutch province of Overijssel, is a moraine, an end point for unconsolidated glacial debris. As with much of the Netherlands, forests here were cut in the Middle Ages and topsoils eroded as crop fields took their toll. Large heathlands ensued when sands shifted across the region. The 20th century brought pine forests, planted to anchor the soil. Birds that typically make their home here include the European nightjar, identifiable by its sustained churring call, and the black grouse, known to American birders by its folk names of *blackcock* and *grayhen* for the male and female, respectively.

A park focal point is the Holten Canadian War Cemetery, which contains 1,393 military graves. The majority of those buried here died during the advance of the Canadian Second Corps from the Netherlands into northern Germany in April and May of 1945. The nearby museum of natural history, Natuurdiorama Holterberg, is also worth a visit. Another tribute to the victims of war stands at the labor camp of Twilhaar, where a memorial is dedicated to the men transported in 1942 from here to Westerbork camp. Almost all died at Auschwitz.

AT A GLANCE

Expansive heathland scenery ▪ Natuurdiorama Holterberg ▪ 13.5 square miles (35 sq km) ▪ World War II memorials and cemetery ▪ sallandseheuvelrug.nl/node/203

SCHIERMONNIKOOG

An unspoiled island hosts a national park of wide beaches and bird-filled mudflats.

Schiermonnikoog National Park in the province of Friesland covers an entire island, with the exception of a town and its surrounding polder. That town, also named Schiermonnikoog, dates back to 1720 and replaced the old settlement of Westerburen, which was swallowed by the sea.

Because of the influence of the tides and its location between the Wadden and North Seas, Schiermonnikoog's climate differs from that of the mainland. The landscape here hosts a surprising range of flora and fauna. The polders attract grassland birds in summer and geese in winter, and the mudflats suit wading birds and sandpipers such as the curlew. Wild plants including hawthorn, sea buckthorn, honeysuckle, and wild rose cover the vegetated dunes. The salt marshes nurture sea lavender, sea wormwood, and glasswort, ideal for birds hatching eggs in springtime. Tidal flats thrum with redshanks, barnacle geese, hen harriers, and European herring gulls. In woodlands, you'll hear the choking *chac-chac* of the Eurasian magpie, one of nature's most intelligent creatures, and lichens and mushrooms thrive in the dark soil of the pine forests. Birds of prey hover in search of the island's sparse surface wildlife, targeting hares and rabbits.

Maps and information on hiking and biking trails are available in the De Oude Centrale (visitors center) in the town.

AT A GLANCE

Varied island habitats ▪ 28 square miles (72.5 sq km) ▪ A unique island climate ▪ Birding trails ▪ vvvschiermonnikoog.nl

UTRECHTSE HEUVELRUG

A leafy green park surrounded by historic castles and estates

This peaceful urban park set within the province of Utrecht is a nature lover's delight, offering some 56 walking paths around its heathlands, shifting sands, forests, meadows, and floodplains. Utrechtse Heuvelrug National Park takes its name from a glacial ridge and is surrounded by several small towns, as well as castles and country estates that resonate with the echoes of European history. The well-maintained trails vary in length from 1.2 miles (2 km) to 13 miles (21 km), and several lead to the highest point of the park, the 226-foot (69-m) Amerongen Hill, which offers fine vistas of the Utrecht countryside. Trails also lead through much of the pine and deciduous forestry that was planted to counter the erosive effects of the region's shifting sands. The farther west you travel, the more the landscape changes into heathlands, fertile meadows, and areas of aeolian sand. You'll also pass crystalline Henschoterlake with its secluded sandy white beach, and other beautiful lakes.

Some woods hold old-growth trees such as beech and oak from the postglacial forestry, and the usual avian suspects of Dutch woods are seen and heard: Black woodpeckers, ravens, and bluethroats all inhabit the park. At ground level, the European badger, pine marten, fox, and several snake species all try to avoid contact

The park's trails put many peripheral sites within easy walking distance.

with the park's human day-trippers. In the marshlands near Amerongen Castle, the rare little bittern stands out as the smallest species of heron, with its distinctive black-and-fawn feathers and its green-tinged crown. The yellowy firecrest and the light brown-feathered hawfinch are other species you might spot in the woodlands of Utrechtse Heuvelrug. Bat, butterfly, and dragonfly species all thrive in the park's marshy areas.

NEARBY ATTRACTIONS

The country estates, historic castles, and museums surrounding the park attest to the timeless attraction to the area's stunning natural bounty. These are not within the park boundaries, but are worth a visit. Although nearby De Haar Castle appears medieval, it was built by the renowned Dutch architect Pierre Cuypers between 1892 and 1912 for Baron

Etienne van Zuylen van Nijevelt. The family entertained lavishly such celebrities as Brigitte Bardot, Coco Chanel, and Roger Moore in the elegant surrounds of the castle's French-style gardens, including a spectacular Rose Garden, with more than 1,200 plants of 79 different species.

Another nearby landmark open to the public, Soestdijk Palace, dates to the 17th century and was inhabited by members of the royal family until 2006. King Louis Napoleon ordered the construction of the landscape garden here, and its pond and winding brook are still to be enjoyed.

Also worth a visit is the Museum Huis Doorn, a manor house and national museum showcasing the life of former occupant German kaiser Wilhelm II. The last kaiser lived in exile here from 1920 to 1941, following the German defeat in World War I. The estate features fine English gardens.

AT A GLANCE

Glacial ridge landscapes ▪ 38.6 square miles (100 sq km) ▪ De Haar Castle ▪ Soestdijk Palace ▪ Museum Huis Doorn ▪ np-utrechtseheuvelrug.nl

VELUWEZOOM

Up close with some of the Netherlands' wildest spectacles

It's a powerful sound you won't forget in a hurry. The ever expressive Dutch call it *burlen,* but you really have to drag out those vowels to even begin to approximate the sound that a male red deer makes in mating season. The deep-throated roar that erupts from the stag as he seeks to impress his female of choice is quite something. You can hear this forceful call of nature for yourself in Veluwezoom National Park, if you visit one of the two wildlife observation posts sometime in September or October.

This is the oldest national park in the Netherlands, opening to the public in 1931. Unusually for the lowlands, its undulating terrain is markedly elevated in places, with the highest point in the park rising some 289 feet (88 m) above sea level. This apogee is the Posbank, a hill offering an unparalleled view of Arnhem and the surrounding Achterhoek region. From this high point you can fully appreciate Veluwezoom's varied geography, a hilly landscape mixed with forests, heathlands, and sand drifts. It's a scenic escape for hikers, mountain bikers, and equine enthusiasts. Cyclists who reach the peak of the Posbank will enjoy Daphné du Barry's statue of Queen Beatrix happily riding her royal bike!

Aside from the very vocal red deer of autumn, typical native fauna here are the badger, the wild boar, and the rare pine marten, all of which largely stick to their favored woodland haunts. As in other national parks in the Netherlands, authorities carefully manage the effects of the sand drifts. The park's elevated areas are grazed by Highland cattle and Icelandic horses; the latter imported into the region for their hardiness and their ability to munch

COUNTRY ESTATES

On the southern side of the nature preserve you'll find several estates with country houses and sprawling farms. Beekhuizen, Heuven, and Rhereroord are historical country houses, now open to the public, and are themselves complete with extensive parklands. Rozendaal Castle and the Gelders Geological Museum are worth visiting for their educational insights into

Call of the wild: Stags roar out their burlen *in an effort to woo females*

their way through the toughest of heathland vegetation. The ancestors of this breed were probably taken to Iceland by Viking-era Scandinavians in the seventh and eighth centuries, so in a way they are almost home. These long-lived horses certainly earn their keep in Veluwezoom and elsewhere on the heathlands of western Europe.

the region's history and geography.

The Veluwezoom Visitor Centre has information on the park's walking and cycling paths, and offers guided hikes. A word of advice: Bring rain gear, but if you do get caught out by inclement weather at the top of the Posbank, you can shelter in Paviljoen de Posbank, a forest café made from sustainable and eco-friendly materials.

AT A GLANCE

Netherlands hill scenery ▪ Red deer mating season ▪ 19 square miles (50 sq km) ▪ Beekhuizen, Heuven, and Rhereroord estates ▪ Paviljoen de Posbank ▪ en.visitarnhem.com/locations/2705842829/nationaal-park-veluwezoom

WEERRIBBEN-WIEDEN

An important Dutch cultural landscape with a rich rural history

This national park encompasses the largest bog of northwestern Europe in two main areas, De Weerribben and De Wieden. Part of the province of Overijssel, much of these boglands were used for peat production up to the middle of the 20th century; more recently, its reed beds have been harvested for the production of cane.

Other submerged plants, such as the water soldier, grow profusely in the brackish waters of Weerribben-Wieden; the colorful drosera, commonly known as the sundew, is an interesting carnivorous plant that thrives in the insect-infested bogs. The sundew lures, traps, and digests insects using the stalked mucilaginous glands that cover its pinkish orange leaf surfaces. Insects inhabiting these wetlands include the green hawker dragonfly and the large copper butterfly.

Birdlife here is plentiful too, with black terns, great cormorants, and egrets all in residence. Northern pike proliferate in the peaty brown waters, and otters have begun to appear in greater numbers in the lakes, ponds, and man-made canals of the park. As elsewhere across this small country, over the centuries the Dutch have left their mark on the landscape as they have manipulated the waters to their own purposes. This work started here in

The park has classic Dutch landscapes.

the 1300s, when turf was cut from areas known as *weren*. The peat was then left to dry on long strips of land, called *ribben*, which created these unique wetlands. Along the park's canals you'll find that most iconic of Dutch working buildings, the windmill, which throughout the Netherlands' history was used to pump water from the land. In Weerribben-Wieden, the windmills also pump water onto the land to cultivate growth of the lucrative reed.

TAKE TO THE WATER

The best way to understand the landscapes of Weerribben-Wieden is to rent an electric boat, rowboat, or canoe, and take to the water

(rentals are available to visitors in Giethoorn, on the edge of the park, and elsewhere). You can also take a boat tour that combines Giethoorn and Weerribben-Wieden: You start by viewing the thatched-roof houses, bridges, and canals that have given this peat diggers' water village its somewhat tongue-in-cheek nickname, "the Venice of the Netherlands." Then you sail straight into the unique fenlands of the park, with their canals, ditches, marsh forests, quaking bog, and reed beds. Boats are also available at Buitencentrum Weerribben in Ossenzijl, or board the electric boat tour at the Visitor Centre de Wieden in Sint Jansklooster.

Several of the walks through the watery wilderness are highly recommended: The Silent Kiersche Wijde Route and the Weerribben Walking Route both lead into the heart of the bogs over ancient pathways, past duck decoys and secluded reed beds. The 7.5-mile (12-km) Weerribben guided tour explores the challenging lives of the reed cutters and explains how reeds were cut in winter to thatch roofs of village houses, and how peat was dug up for fuel. Looking at the straight lines of the canals carved through the Weerribben is like studying mankind's hand-drawn efforts to contain this fluid landscape.

ZOOM-KALMTHOUTSE HEIDE

A transborder park that celebrates the beauty of nature

Ling (aka heather) adorns the heaths of De Zoom-Kalmthoutse and other Dutch national parks.

The cross-border park Grenspark De Zoom-Kalmthoutse Heide straddles the Belgian-Dutch border. It merges two former parks, Kalmthoutse Heide in Belgium and De Zoom in the Netherlands. The park is a remarkable combination of public and private interests shared across the neighboring countries: It is managed by a special commission in which both Flemish and Dutch organizations are represented and is shared by the state of Flanders, local municipalities, and several private owners.

The Belgium section of Zoom-Kalmthoutse Heide (see page 63), located in the north of the province of Antwerp, is more visited than its Dutch counterpart in the province of North Brabant.

The fact that the combined wilderness of the park has long been divided by an isolating border may well have contributed to the region's unspoiled natural state. Few cities are built on borders, which were often viewed as forbidden places frequented by smugglers, outlaws, and political refugees. One land use that was forbidden for centuries in Antwerp was the establishment of cemeteries for Jewish people; they were forced to bury their dead across the border in the Netherlands. The establishment of the European Union in the latter half of the 20th century has meant that Belgium and the Netherlands now share certain common laws and long-term conservation aims, and transborder cooperation and land management have become easier to implement under common European regulations.

THRIVING IN THE HEATH

The majority of the park's landscape consists of heath, an open area dense with heather, gorse, and coarse grasses. This habitat protects a wide variety of fauna such as the smooth snake, the viviparous lizard, the crested newt, and the moor frog. The park is celebrated for sheltering a vital habitat for rare butterfly species, including graylings, silver-studded blues, checkered skippers, and clouded yellows. Watch especially for the green hairstreak, a small butterfly with dull brown wings that conceal incredibly bright undersides of iridescent green. These are colorful tricks of nature caused by the phenomenon of diffraction, a kind of bending of light rays around an object.

Grenspark De Zoom-Kalmthoutse Heide National Park is edged by woodlands, a shaded realm where bird lovers can spot every kind of Dutch woodpecker. Other avian inhabitants of the park include hawks, falcons, stonechats, tree pipits, and nightjars.

Vegetation on the heathlands varies according to the environment: Heather thrives on dry heath, bell heather on wet heath, and moor grass proliferates where the soil became too enriched in previous centuries. The park's managers have now planned a central heath area combining wet and dry heath with minimal purple moor grass growth. They are establishing a more balanced heath biosphere across the border preserve by grazing animals and cutting sods to impoverish soil.

TAKING THE LONG VIEW

Dead trees have been left in place to provide food and habitat for a variety of wildlife and woodland organisms such as fungi. Plans are also in place to thin out the forests, to open up the canopy and promote regeneration and greater biodiversity. A more holistic approach will also weed out invasive species of plants—such as black American cherry and rhododendron—at

Amphibians thrive in the marshes of the Low Countries.

ground level, replacing them with more indigenous species. In parts of the park, the sand dunes are an open invitation to a plethora of insect life such as digger wasps, bees, and butterflies. They're also open to wind erosion, however, and to the human traffic of hikers, both of which degrade their presence in the park. Once again Zoom-Kalmthoutse Heide's planners strive for a balanced long-term approach, creating paths to circumvent the dunes and planting anchoring grasses.

The park offers a wide variety of walks, many of which follow in the footsteps of its numerous creatures, such as the Ant Trail or the Hare Trail. Perhaps the most rewarding path is the comprehensive 20-mile (32-km) Grenspark route. This complete loop of Zoom-Kalmthoutse Heide gives you a real sense of the diversity of landscapes within this forward-looking and expansive transborder park.

Parks Without Frontiers

Zoom-Kalmthoutse Heide is just one of many examples of cross-border cooperation to protect valuable wildernesses across Europe. The Austrian park of Thayatal (see page 122) is now a partner in conservation with neighboring Czechian Podyjí National Park (see page 343), reaching across the ideological border Winston Churchill dubbed the Iron Curtain. Likewise, Poland's Tatra National Park (see page 358) is twinned with Tatranský National Park (see page 389) across the Slovakian border, forming a UNESCO biosphere reserve. The shifting sands of the Curonian Spit are jointly protected by Lithuania and Russia (see pages 366 and 506). Of course, birds and animals have never recognized human-made borders.

AT A GLANCE

Cross-border nature preserve ▪ 14.5 square miles (37.5 sq km) ▪ The green hairstreak butterfly ▪ Grenspark route walking trail ▪ www2.grensparkzk.nl/index_english.html

ZUID-KENNEMERLAND

North Sea dunescapes cradle country estates of the Dutch Golden Age.

The region of South Kennemerland is known for its sand dunes. Here, Zuid-Kennemerland National Park opened in 1995, expanding an existing park. That earlier park was the brainchild of Dutch conservationist Jac. P. Thijsse, who first envisioned a nature preserve between Bloemendaal and the North Sea Canal as an oasis of retreat in the dangerous days of 1944. This was a time when the Netherlands was an occupied country and all of Europe was wracked by war.

The sand dunes here are backed by dune fields alive with thornbushes, elderberry, and sea holly. In places, freshwater seeps into these fields, allowing orchids to thrive amid the beach morning glory and the marsh grass of Parnassus. This marsh grass is not in fact a grass, but a ruggedly lovely white-flowering plant. About 20 species of butterflies flutter about the dunes, including the Niobe fritillary, recognizable by its orange wings speckled with black spots.

The dune soils are rich in lime, allowing a multitude of rare plants to grow here. Botanists and gardening enthusiasts will enjoy visiting Thijsse's Hof (Garden of Thijsse), in Bloemendaal, where South Kennemerland's 800-odd species of dune-hugging plants are displayed in less windswept conditions. The inland dunes are bearded with bacciferous shrubs and host entertaining chorus lines of songbirds including nightingales and woodlarks, two of nature's most celebrated vocalists, whose singing makes for joyous walks in Zuid-Kennemerland.

Country Estates

In the Golden Age of the 17th century, wealthy merchants of Amsterdam built luxurious estates and gardens along these forested inner dunes to escape the summer stink of the city. They traveled west to Haarlem by barge along canals and rivers, and Kennemerland became a hub of country refuges, each boasting its own signature style. Several still stand today:

Duin & Kruidberg: Chestnut and beech lanes beckon in summer; in winter bats colonize the ice cellars, and stinsen plants blossom in spring.

Elswout: The special architectural "follies" of this, perhaps the most naturally beautiful estate within the park, echo an age of untold wealth.

Koningshof: This stately red mansion faces onto a majestic meadow amid an estate seemingly swathed in a protective growth of giant beech and oak trees.

Grass growth on the dunes is kept in balance by groups of grazing Highland cattle, Shetland ponies, and Koniks (a Polish horse species). In 2007 the task of grass control was dramatically boosted by the release of a small group of wisents, or European bison, into the park. These have since become the rock stars of Zuid-Kennemerland, drawing crowds to a viewing platform to safely observe these large wild beasts.

Smaller fauna such as fallow deer, roe deer, squirrels, European rabbits, West European hedgehogs, and foxes also roam the range; meanwhile the Burgundy snail hides out in foliage, destined otherwise to be enjoyed as a local delicacy.

In addition to the dunes, the park encompasses several historic estates of the Dutch Golden Age (see sidebar), as well as forests and coastal beaches. An impressive and well-mapped network of biking and hiking routes lead to different dunes, lakes, and points of interest, including several war monuments.

The Visitors Centre De Kennemerduinen, on Zeeweg by the Koevlak entrance, is the main gateway to the park and has details about all the park's walking and cycling options, as well as its frequent educational excursions.

Elswout, one of the park's opulent estates

AT A GLANCE

Dune landscapes ▪ 14.6 square miles (37.8 sq km) ▪ Golden Age country estates ▪ European bison ▪ Thijsse's Hof botanical garden in Bloemendaal ▪ Extensive trails ▪ np-zuidkennemerland.nl

GERMANY

Most visitors think of Germany in terms of the great industries of the Ruhr Valley, stunning autobahns, and architecturally impressive cities such as Berlin and Düsseldorf. Yet its 16 national parks are among Europe's most diverse, offering a breathtaking range of scenic and experiential delights. There are few more inviting and accessible walks into woodlands than those of the Bavarian and Black Forest National Parks; the mountain parks of Berchtesgaden and Saxon Switzerland hit all the heights; and marine and shore habitats are protected and accessible to the public via the Wadden Sea parks of Hamburg, Lower Saxony, and Schleswig-Holstein Wadden Sea, as well as the Vorpommersche Boddenlandschaft park. Happily, several reserves still have the classic German scene of a fairy-tale castle rising out of the woods.

Opposite: Sunshine and shadow cast the Black Forest in a litany of light.

BAVARIAN FOREST
One of Europe's great forests made accessible

The domed tower of the Canopy Walkway offers spectacular winter vistas of snow-cloaked woods.

It's one of the great natural highs of western Europe, nature's answer to the thrill of a roller coaster ride. Billed as "the world's longest treetop trail," the Baumwipfelpfad takes visitors on a walk in the woods with a difference. The elevated walkway is strung across a series of angular wooden stilts that blend seamlessly with the rich array of beech, fir, and spruce trees of the Bavarian Forest National Park. It takes you up into the canopy level, so you really *can* see the forest for the trees.

The trail runs the best part of a mile (1.6 km) and rises to heights of 82 feet (25 m) above the forest floor. During the gentle ascent, as the path zigzags among leafy crowns, you get a crash course in the biosphere via a series of English-enabled informa-tion screens. The highlight comes at the end, with the dome-shaped observation tower. Then you ascend to the celebrated viewing platform held aloft by a giant spring—it's a showcase of German engineering, although most of the technology is tastefully concealed. A bridge from the treetop trail leads into the lower reaches of this amazing structure. Here, a walkway corkscrews 131 feet (40m) toward the clouds, affording a top-down view of the mighty firs within the dome's arched frame and panoramas reaching as far as the Alps in southern Bavaria. The path is open daily, year-round, and is espe-cially appealing in spring with the rising aromas of the reawakening for-est, and in winter, when snow cloaks the woods in serenity and silence.

COOPERATIVE PROTECTION

The Baumwipfelpfad is the cen-terpiece of the Bavarian Forest National Park, which sits along the border with Czechia. Opened in 1970 as Germany's first national park, it straddles the mountains along the border between Bavaria and Bohemia. On the Czech side is Šumava (Bohemian Forest) National Park, founded in 1991. The two parks are managed along complementary lines, with much cross-border cooperation, and together they protect the largest area of forest in central Europe. The understated motto of the German park is "Let nature be nature" and, nature indeed abounds in all direc-tions here, with streams, moors, fells, gorgeous lakes, and meadows interspersed with huge rock formations, as well as the beautiful Bavarian forests.

The park protects highland forests of mainly Norway spruce, mountain mixed forests of European silver fir, European beech, and spruce trees and, farther down in the valleys, streams, meadows, and spruce woods. Only a few remnants of ancient forest still remain. During the 1990s, a large-scale bark beetle infestation decimated much of the high-elevation forests, which resulted in an interventionist exception being made as the bark beetle was tackled in some areas.

Two peaks, the 4,281-foot (1,305-m) Grosser Falkenstein and the 4,767-foot (1,453-m) Grosser Rachel, rise above the raised bogs and bog lakes, but two lakes in particular define the park. The picture-perfect Rachelsee is a crystal clear lake that conceals many dark myths and legends beneath its mirrored surface. The lake was supposedly named after the devil's grandmother, Rachel. Legend has it that, upon the death of an evil woman who used to sail here, an ominous flock of black ravens accompanied her coffin across the lake. The Bavarian Forest abounds in such folklore. Stories of wolves and ghouls and handsome strangers with cloven hooves abound. *Achtung!* The devil is always somewhere in the details.

EXPLORING THE PARK

The Großer Arbersee is a glacial memento of the last ice age. A well-

A brown bear climbs a tree.

Eurasian Lynx

The stealthy and elusive Eurasian lynx was gone from Europe by the 19th century. Current populations here (mainly in Bohemia, Bavaria, and Austria) originate from animals reintroduced in Germany in the 1970s and in Czechoslovakia (today's Czechia) in the 1980s. Their stagnant numbers, a concern for conservation groups, are attributed to high mortality rates outside protected areas such as the Bavarian Forest and Šumava National Parks, caused mainly by traffic and poaching. The lynx competes for the same prey as humans—namely roe deer and red deer—giving hunters another reason to kill them. Since 2005, cross-border studies using GPS telemetry have given a broader understanding of the ecology and behavior of both the lynx and deer.

marked hiking trail circumnavigates this crystalline lake, and several small waterfalls and other scenic delights reward walkers. It's also an excellent spot for bird-watching. The capercaillie is the main avian inhabitant of the park, and among the more uncommon species are the white-backed or three-toed woodpecker and the pygmy owl, Europe's smallest. Some of the park's most important species, including 45 that are endemic, can be seen in wildlife enclosures. These locations give visitors a fine chance to watch boar, bear, wolves, wisent (European bison), and many other mammals. Tierfreigelände is one such sprawling area with a path devoid of visible barriers, and terrain designed to closely resemble the animals' natural habitat. Here, 40 species, including lynx and bears, roam freely.

For those interested in the forest's flora, a visit to the natural garden at the Hans-Eisenmann-Haus visitors center near Neuschönau is recommended in any season. The exhibits include more than 700 different plant species.

Cyclists get to explore more isolated regions along 124 miles (200 km) of biking trails. These connect with forests of the Šumava National Park in neighboring Czechia. A high level of fitness is recommended for those engaging on this rugged, mountainous terrain. A mountain bike is not necessary, though, as the Bavarian Forest National Park also has about 186 miles (300 km) of marked hiking trails. More than half of this forest is untouched by humans.

BERCHTESGADEN

Sheer rock faces, fabulous forestry, and an Alpine fortress with a dark past

The gateway to Berchtesgaden National Park is the Nationalpark-Haus, the interpretive center for the park, that offers information on the area's heritage, its varied wildlife, and its many choices of walks and more challenging mountain hikes and climbs. The garden of the Nationalpark-Haus offers stunning views of the park's sublime realm of protected landscape. An outer area of farmland and forest is managed under strict environmental regulations, while nature is allowed to take its course in the inner, core area. Within the park, you'll also find the fjordlike Königsee nestled in the shadow of the towering 8,900-foot (2,713-m) Watzmann, Germany's second highest mountain.

BERCHTESGADEN TOWN

The park's center point, the town of Berchtesgaden, is ringed by mountain peaks and overlooks a glorious valley. Stroll through its streets of old painted houses to the Schlossplatz. Opposite the arcaded building on the left are the church and prior's residence from the monastery, dating from the 12th century. The residence is now the Königliches Schloss, and from 1923 until 1933, was the home of Crown Prince Rupprecht, head of the deposed Bavarian royal family. The town's other attraction is Salzbergwerk, the underground saltworks, where you can don traditional miners' garb, and whiz underground on a slide, explore galleries and grottoes, then raft across a sparkling salt lake.

INTO THE PARK

At the information center, Dokumentation Obersalzberg, learn about Hitler's chalet on the Obersalzberg, now destroyed, and of the events of WWII around Berchtesgaden. Come spring, the four-mile (6.4-km) Kehlsteinstrasse, Germany's most spectacular mountain road, leads to Hitler's other chalet, the Kehlsteinhaus (Eagle's Nest), atop the Kehlstein, where the Alpine panorama is superb.

The classic Berchtesgaden experience is a boat ride on the Königssee into the heart of the mountains. Malerwinkel (Painters' Corner), is a picturesque landmark. An electrically powered boat takes you from the town dock to the lovely church of St. Bartholomew, where the captain plays the alpenhorn toward the wall of rock to create an echo. From here it's a two-hour walk up to the Ice Chapel at the foot of the east face of Watzmann. At the southern tip of the Königssee is a tiny lake, the Obersee, and the 1,542-foot (470-m) Röthbach waterfall.

FLORA & FAUNA

The Alpine landscape of Berchtesgaden includes montane and subalpine forests, mainly of larch, mountain pine, and spruce. Limestone peaks and highland moors give way to beautiful meadows where colorful springtime wildflowers include gentians, buttercups, orchids, pulsatilla, and Alpine rhododendrons. The edelweiss, of course, takes pride of place, which is apt, as *The Sound of Music* was filmed in these mountains. The current Alpine stars of the hillsides are familiar fauna— ibex, chamois, red deer—while lower down, marmots, capercaillie, and blue hares are the meadow's supporting cast; blue hares are actually white in winter and brown in summer. Watch too for Alpine salamanders, slick black lizards that live at elevations above 2,300 feet (701 m).

The Ostwand (East Face) of 8,900-foot (2,713-m) Watzmann Mountain is a challenge for mountaineers. There are hikes aplenty through this gorgeous park, including the scenic 3.7-mile (6-km) walk from St. Bartholomew to Eiskapelle, an ice cave at the foot of the Ostwand. If the day's hiking and Alpine views have left you weary, head for the Watzmann Therme, where spa and thermal baths are a treat for the feet and a meditative repose for the soul.

An Alpine idyll of mountains, chalets, and pastures

BLACK FOREST

A forest of myth, legend, and fairy tale

A walk in Black Forest National Park is like stepping into one of Grimm's fairy tales, where time falls away as you lose yourself in dark woods of pine, spruce, beech, and fir. Established in 2014, the park showcases these legendary woodlands that the Romans came upon 2,000 years ago and called the Silva Nigra (Black Forest). Time is very much on the minds of locals in the surrounds of this park, so during your stay try to visit the German Clock Museum in Furtwangen as well as the Schwarzwaldmuseum in Triberg with its displays of local costumes and crafts. The Black Forest Open-Air Museum is another must-see, for its collection of farm buildings and insight into local life.

Then it's time to take a drive along the Black Forest High Road (B500 or the Schwarzwald-Hochstrasse) leading into the heart of the Black Forest. Start in the spa town of Baden-Baden, where the Geroldsauer waterfalls soothe the mind, and then head for the mountain of Mehliskopf to choose among the several adventure sports available. Elsewhere, the Breitenbrunnen game reserve offers a chance for close encounters with red deer or wild boar. These woodlands are also known for their glacial, or cirque, lakes, none finer than Mummelsee; according to local legend, its darkened waters hide an underwater realm of a king and

Church bells and the river's flow mark time in the village of Schiltach.

his nymphs. Farther up the road, at Allerheiligen, a 2.1-mile (3.5-km) trail leads from the ruins of a Gothic abbey through a tree-lined gorge to a gorgeous waterfall. The Black Forest High Road ends at Freudenstadt, where you can relax with a beer or coffee in Germany's largest town square.

A WALK IN THE WOODS

The best way to experience the Black Forest, of course, is by foot, and a network of hiking trails vein the park. To get the lay of the land, a marked trail to the forest's highest elevation brings you to 4,898-foot (1,493-m) Grosser Feldberg, a block of granite and gneiss shaped by glaciers in the last ice age. The rewarding views reach as far as the Swiss Alps, and two chalets, the St. Wilhelmer Hütte and Todtnauer Hütte, offer rest on the way down.

From here you'll see other features that define these woodlands—heathered moorland, glacial lakes, and rivers such as the lovely Neckar.

Walking will bring you into habitats of red deer, pine martens, and avian inhabitants, including the rare three-toed woodpecker, the pygmy owl, and the Tengmalm's owl—the latter a small, shy creature with mottled feathering who uses woodpecker cavities for nesting.

Foraging in the park is popular, and your basket will soon fill with such berries and herbs as buckthorn, dill, bear's garlic, and mushrooms. There are many self-catering chalets for rent, or stay at the Nationalpark-Hotel Schliffkopf, a four-star wellness resort, and enjoy a spa and outdoor pool in the heart of this storybook woodland.

AT A GLANCE

An iconic forest ▪ 39 square miles (100 sq km) ▪ Magical lakes ▪ Woodland walks ▪ Forest foraging ▪ nationalpark-schwarzwald.de/en

EIFEL

A small natural preserve in an area once used for military exercises

Opened in 2006, Eifel National Park area encompasses the former Vogelsang Military Training Area, old training grounds of the Belgian Armed Forces, and the Dreiborn Plateau, terrain once used by NATO troops. These days the screech of jet planes has been replaced by the lazy flight of a black stork; the only tattoo heard is the *rat-a-tat-tat* of a middle spotted woodpecker; and the sight of marching squadrons or camouflaged soldiers is replaced by the industry of some 1,300 species of beetles and the quick slither of the wall lizard.

The landscape is largely deciduous and coniferous woodlands with a predominantly beech forest (the Kermeter) thriving in the maritime climate of North Eifel; lakes and streams irrigate the park, which opens occasionally into grassland. It is a delight for hikers, cyclists, or skiers, with 150 miles (240 km) of hiking trails. Some 65 miles (105 km) of these are also cycle paths, and skiing trails are groomed in winter. The Eifel Club issues a useful map, and you should *always* follow the wooden signs, especially those with colored bands that steer you clear of areas where land mines were previously planted. The four-day Wilderness Trail safely leads deep into this once militarized wilderness.

Four gates usher visitors into the park, each with a themed exhibit. Watch for spectacular narcissus meadows at the Höfen Gate, known as Bundesgolddorfes ("federal gold village"). Personable park rangers can guide you through this lovely national park.

AT A GLANCE

A reforested wilderness ▪ 41.3 square miles (107 sq km) ▪ The Wilderness Trail ▪ nationalpark-eifel.de/en

HAINICH

Protected park within a vast deciduous forest

The native beech forest of Thuringia is protected within Hainich National Park, itself part of the much greater Hainich, the largest contiguous deciduous forest in Germany. A superb walkway leads up into the canopy. This is accessible from the visitors center, in the spa town of Bad Langensalza.

The park styles itself as a "Primeval Forest in the Center of Germany," and populations of ash trees, hornbeams, maples, and lindens mix with the beech. The park is also

A park walkway skims the treetops.

a hothouse for fungi, and hosts wildlife including wildcats, bats, woodpeckers, and more than 500 types of wood beetles. Watch for the red and black stripes of the shield bug (aka the striped or minstrel bug) or the shining red bug whose color leaps out against the forest greens. The park also hosts 26 species of orchids and the maroon-blossomed Turk's cap lily.

The nearby town of Eisenach is worth a visit for Wartburg Castle, a fortification built high above the forests in the Middle Ages. Here, Martin Luther translated the New Testament of the Bible into German.

AT A GLANCE

The Canopy Walkway ▪ 29 square miles (75 sq km) ▪ Wartburg Castle ▪ Vivid insect species ▪ nationalpark-hainich.de/en

HAMBURG WADDEN SEA

A marine park within reach of the busy city of Hamburg

The Wadden Sea is the largest unbroken system of intertidal sand and mudflats in the world, and the whole region spans several national parks and belongs to three separate nations: Germany, the Netherlands, and Denmark. The smallest of the three German preserves, Hamburg Wadden Sea National Park lies 62 miles (100 km) from its parent city of Hamburg and just about eight miles (12.5 km) offshore in the Elbe estuary of the North Sea. A ferry from

section of the Wadden Sea, which is a UNESCO biosphere reserve. The unique position and climate of the Wadden Sea result in a wide range of transitional habitats.

VIBRANT BIRDLIFE

The salt marshes of the Wadden Sea are home to some 250 indigenous species, many attracted by the high concentrations of food at the mouth of the Elbe River caused by the influx of natural sediment. There are large

several million waders, geese, ducks, and gulls can be filling themselves, breeding, or resting within the park.

Unsurprisingly, the park is a huge draw for bird-watchers, but note that the eastern part of Neuwerk Island is the only area where visitors are welcome—and you must stay on pathways to avoid disturbing the breeding birds. Entry to Scharhörn Island is possible only with permission of the professional ornithologist who lives there. This same resident ornithologist is the only human visitor to nearby Nigehörn Island, which is part of the restricted Protection Zone II—he checks in on its bird populations once a year. If you do get to visit Scharhörn, bring binoculars to be able to gaze across to this elusive avian Shangri-la and study the birds of Nigehörn for yourself.

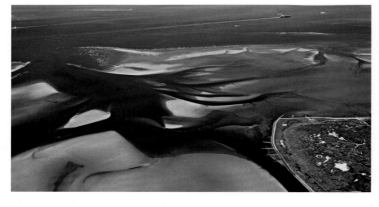

Neuwerk Island and the vital tidal mudflats at the mouth of the mighty Elbe River

Cuxhaven takes visitors out to Neuwerk Island, one of three islands in the park, along with Scharhörn and Nigehörn. Three German national parks—the other two being Lower Saxony (see page 101) and Schleswig-Holstein (see page 106)—protect the overall ecological area of the German

populations of common seals and gray seals, and the park is a key stopover point for migrating birds. Shelducks and eider ducks flock to the mudflats to feast on the rich array of easy pickings such as clams, mollusks, and sea snails. This unique smorgasbord means that at any time

Other activities within this watery national park include hiking the mudflats and combing beaches for tidal flotsam. You can also rent horses or cross the sands in a horse and carriage, but note that mudflat hiking and carriage crossings are only permitted in designated areas. Walking the salt marshes, viewing the seal colonies, and swimming are also popular, but check the tides and swim only in signposted areas. There are also Germany's other Wadden Sea parks: Lower Saxony Wadden Sea and Schleswig-Holstein.

(see page 101) (see page 106)

AT A GLANCE

Ferry ride to Neuwerk Island ▪ 53.1 square miles (137.5 sq km) ▪ Bird-watching paradise ▪ whc.unesco.org/en/list/1314

HARZ

A witches' altar awaits at the top of the storied Brocken.

The Brocken, at 3,747 feet (1,142 m), the highest of the Harz Mountains and Harz National Park, is recognizable from afar by its many communications towers and masts. But its influence is not just technological; the mountain's psychic power goes way back to medieval times, when it was believed to be a place of supernatural significance.

On the eve of May 1, witches are said to still gather on Brocken's craggy peak, where the festival of Walpurgisnacht was once celebrated by invoking the devil onto the bleak, windswept summit. Goethe immortalized these events in *Faust*. You don't have to dance with the devil to climb the hill, but you can save your feet some time in purgatory by taking the Brockenbahn, the steam railway operated since 1899. At the top, the weathered granite tors, known as Teufelskanzel (Devil's Pulpit) and Hexenaltar (Witches' Altar), tell their own stories.

Before you set out, the Harz National Park visitors center at the Brockenhaus can supply weather advice and maps. It also hosts three floors of exhibits on the history and wildlife of this historic mountain. The towerlike structure is a story in itself, with its dome containing listening devices from the communist era, and a fine observation deck offering panoramic views. The Brocken, on the border between East

A Brocken Railway train steams through a bewitched winter landscape.

and West Germany, was a restricted military area under the GDR and previously accommodated its own version of the Berlin Wall.

The national park today stretches from a low mountain range near Herzberg in the south, across the Harz massif to its northern slopes near Bad Harzburg and Ilsenburg. The natural forests of the Harz are mainly Norway spruce and rowan; as the Harz was partly deforested in the 19th century by ore mining, reforestation with fast-growing spruce was a practical decision in sustainable forestry.

LIFE BENEATH BROCKEN

Aside from the forests, the landscape runs the gamut of habitats: Reintroduced lynx now prowl again on boulders in the mountains' higher regions, having been exterminated 200 years ago; butterflies such as the cranberry fritillary flutter across the park's bogs and heaths; wildcats hunt here too; the spruce and beech forests fill with birdsong of ring ouzels or spotted nutcrackers. The wetlands and rivers host amphibians, reptiles, and fish species, including brown trout and fire salamanders, conspicuous by their vivid blue and yellow coloring. As you head for any of the park's summits, watch for the white and yellow flowers of alpine anemones or "Brocken anemones" as they are known locally. These wildflowers originate in Asia and supposedly arrived in Germany after a long, transcontinental trip, yet they are *only* found on Brocken Mountain. So maybe the devil or one of his witches summoned them hence!

AT A GLANCE

The Witches' Altar ▪ 95.3 square miles (247 sq km) ▪ Brockenbahn railway ▪ Brockenhaus visitors center ▪ Brocken anemones ▪ nationalpark-harz.de/en

HUNSRÜCK-HOCHWALD

A preserve of beech forests and slope bogs with an eye to the future

Male and female black woodpeckers swap incubation duty.

Stretching across nearly 40 square miles (100 sq km) of extensive beech woods, steep rocky outcrops, and rare slope or blanket bogs, Hunsrück-Hochwald National Park was established in 2015. It is the newest national park in a country that treasures and protects the great German outdoors.

Its philosophy, like many of its predecessors, is to "let nature be nature," allowing natural habitats to develop according to the hand of time and elements, rather than the hand of humankind. With this in mind, the forestry is left untouched so that woodpeckers, beetles, and other repossession specialists may avail of the fresh shelter that fallen trees, deadwood, and tree hollows offer. Black woodpeckers, black storks, and several species of bats all inhabit Hunsrück-Hochwald, and the woods also host one of the largest populations of wildcats in central Europe.

Black woodpeckers are probably the resident avians you are most likely to encounter on your travels. Recognizable by their vivid red-crested head, these crow-size birds with otherwise black plumage are also distinguished by their yellowy eyes. The woodpeckers' scary stare became a standard symbol of evil in many European fairy tales. And the birds' crazed, high-pitched calls don't help! Black woodpeckers are somewhat unnerving in being some of the few birds to have two very distinct calls: The first is a short high-pitched note, a loud, whistling *kree-kree-kree*, repeated only ever twice. Their second vocalization is a screechlike shrill made in mid-flight. Listen for both in the beech woods of Hunsrück-Hochwald.

EXPLORING THE PARK

A maze of hiking and cycle trails lead through the park: The Saar-Hunsrück Climb is a particular favorite with visitors as it ticks off many of the park's hot spots in four stages—an excellent way to enjoy rich flora and fauna as you take in placid lakes, idyllic valleys, and fine views. The Geierlay suspension bridge is a thrill for hikers. A 50-mile (80 km) national park cycle route also explores the park. Or you can join one of many educational tours led by park rangers, with subjects ranging from the park's rocks, moorlands, wildcats, and forestry, to the region's Celtic past.

The park intends to foster the interest of the next generation of German environmentalists; these children, it is hoped, will come of age by the time that the protected lands of Hunsrück-Hochwald National Park are fully restored to their natural state. This process of allowing nature to fully be nature again is estimated to take approximately 30 years.

JASMUND

Haunting white cliffs at East Germany's last national park

Germany's smallest national park is a little gem, tucked away on the Jasmund Peninsula in the northeast of Rügen Island. Jasmund National Park's main attraction is the six-mile (10-km) stretch of chalk cliffs called the Königsstuhl (King's Chair), which rise up some 528 feet (161 m) above the Baltic Sea. The park extends inland to embrace beech forests dating back to the 13th century, which grow on the chalky Stubnitz plateau, formed in the last ice age, as well as wild service trees. Jasmund occupies a poignant place in the history of conservation, as the final national park the government of East Germany designated before the fall of the Iron Curtain.

The park is also remarkable for the fragility of its landscape: The chalk cliffs constantly erode and wash away with storms. This King's Chair is no eternal throne.

EVOLUTION LESSON

The makeup of the chalk cliffs themselves is a lesson in evolution. They include fossils of sponges, oysters, and sea urchins frozen in time. The unique geological qualities of the landscape around the cliffs are also noteworthy. The woods of the Stubnitz contain many wet sinkholes, which began as dead-ice hollows during the ice age. Plants that thrive in this porous, marshy terrain include

black alders, European crab apple, yew, and a variety of orchids. A walk along the clifftops is a bird-watcher's delight, with white-tailed eagles and peregrine falcons among the predators that swirl over this Baltic coastline. House martins breed in the chalk cliffs, but, like kingfishers, they feed in the wet woodlands on the multitude of insects the swamp conditions foster. The kingfisher, despite its long bill and name, prefers land-based insects to the sushi-leaning menu that the park's bigger birds favor.

The park has many walks and cycle routes; the main hiking trail follows right along the cliffs in a lovely loop of just over five miles (8 km). Park rangers offer tours and excursions that highlight the area's rich history and culture. You can learn the legends of the Germanic goddess Hertha and the famous pirate Klaus Störtebeker, who is rumored to have buried treasure on Rügen Island. Visitors can also take a ride on Racing Roland, Rügen's narrow-gauge steam railway, visit the village of Vitt, or cast around the harbor of Sassnitz with its fishing museum. Art lovers will want to stop in at the Pomeranian State Museum in Greifswald to view works by Romantic painter Caspar David Friedrich; these images made the Jasmund Peninsula and its King's Chair known throughout Europe some 200 years ago.

Jasmund's chalk cliffs provide an ever evolving lesson in erosion on the Baltic.

KELLERWALD-EDERSEE

Amid dense forest rises a German castle.

Kellerwald-Edersee National Park nestles south of the Edersee lake amid the low-rolling Kellerwald hills. Its extensive beech forests, like many across Germany and neighboring countries, are now part of the UNESCO World Heritage site known as the Primeval Beech Forests of the Carpathians and the Ancient Beech Forests of Germany. This designation celebrates an ecosystem determined by many old-growth trees, the unique predominance of a copper beech species across central Europe, one found nowhere else in the world.

There are remnants of the primeval forests here, and the landscape is a magical mix of hardwoods and rocky slope forests, dry oak forests, bedrocks covered in mats of firewitch that bloom in a purple blaze, pure-water springs and creeks, as well as wooded meadow valleys. Forest bats love the deadwood stands, and wildcats hunt in these vibrant woods, as red deer graze the meadows. In the distance, Schloss Waldeck castle appears to rise majestically from the forests, and dramatically overlooks a lake in a classic German milieu.

The park's 20 hiking trails all start out from parking areas, and each is marked with an animal or plant symbol. Each loop should take about half a day, but the 43.5-mile (70-km) Urwaldsteig Edersee Trail is worth more time, as it goes deep into wild woods and on to the lovely lake of Edersee. The park also has four cycling routes, and e-bikes may be rented from the NationalparkZentrum.

AT A GLANCE

Schloss Waldeck castle ▪ Old-growth beech forests ▪ 22.1 square miles (57 sq km) ▪ Urwaldsteig Edersee Trail ▪ Edersee reservoir lake ▪ nationalpark-kellerwald-edersee.de/en/home

LOWER ODER VALLEY

A small cross-border park where fluvial wildlife thrives

The Lower Oder Valley National Park hosts Germany's only wetlands national park, a stretch of preserved lands that extends across the German border with Poland by a nature reserve on the eastern banks of the Oder River. The German park lies along the western banks, and performs a key environmental role: The flat western shore of the Oder has several levees that are opened regularly in winter and spring to control water levels and prevent flooding in populated areas. Excess water flows onto vast floodplains that remain submerged until April, when the dikes are reclosed and the water is drained.

The park's combination of fluvial and floodplain habitats, with some mixed deciduous woodlands and dry grasslands, provides ideal breeding and feeding grounds for many species of aquatic and woodland birds. The park sets aside a Special Protection Area (SPA) for them as part of a European Union initiative aimed at preserving vital habitats. The floodplains of the Lower Oder Valley offer a chance to spot menacing-looking black storks, aquatic warblers, and the corn crakes. Beavers and otters also thrive in the watery wilderness. Sturgeon have spawned here for millennia but are now threatened by poaching, pollution, and habitat loss due to dams; the park has started a preservation program with its Polish neighbor. The visitors center at Criewen has details on trails and wildlife activities.

AT A GLANCE

A cross-border wetlands park ▪ Avian sanctuary ▪ 41 square miles (105 sq km) ▪ Floodplains habitat ▪ nationalpark-unteres-odertal.eu/en

LOWER SAXONY WADDEN SEA

An ocean world revealed in the sands of Germany's northern coastline

Take a walk or a horse or carriage ride along the mudflats of the Wadden Sea and enter another world, the underwater realm of marine wildlife that lies exposed by ebbing tide. Then, wildlife from yet another realm descends from the sky, as thousands of birds come to feast along the exposed ocean seabed. Welcome to Lower Saxony Wadden Sea National Park.

The park encompasses the East Frisian Islands, mudflats, and salt marshes between the Bay of Dollart in the west and Cuxhaven in the east. For a marine park, the reserve incorporates a surprising range of habitats: mudflats, salt marshes, dunes, and the estuaries of rivers emptying into the North Sea. These rivers deposit nutrient-rich sediments and form large deposits in the Wadden's relatively still waters.

The majority of the park consists of vast, flat coastline that slopes in a gentle gradient down to the North Sea. Tides rinse this shelf twice a day, depositing sand, clay, and silt. Naturally formed dunes surround the coast, acting as breakwaters, and offering breeding grounds for avian inhabitants. The temperate climate enhances the rich biodiversity of the tidal landscape; the Wadden has been called the "larder" of the North Sea, as microorganisms such as diatoms (a group of algae) multiply in these nutrient-rich waters and serve as

Low tide brings carriage rides over the mudflats from Cuxhaven to Neuwerk Island.

food for larger animals higher up the marine food chain.

AVIAN ATTRACTIONS

The Wadden Sea provides unparalleled feeding opportunities for birds with each low tide exposing a sandy tray of rich pickings: snails, lugworms, mussels, and shrimp. The Wadden Sea is the realm of two northern European duck dynasties: Approximately 180,000 shelducks descend to spend their summer molting season here, as do some 200,000 eider ducks. Large populations of pied avocets and terns breed in the salt marshes, where sea holly and sea lavender bloom in summer months. Seals sun themselves along the sandbanks and dunes. Firmly rooted beach grass anchors these dunes against the winds of the North Sea.

When you enter this coastal wildlife world, remember to respect the park's quiet, intermediate, and recreational zones, and to follow the signs and paths designed to protect the wildlife. Back on terra firma, you can visit many cultural hot spots around the park's 11 islands: These include the lightship on Borkum, the fisherman's house museum on Norderney, the German Maritime Museum in Bremerhaven, and the old lighthouse on Wangerooge. See also Germany's other national parks, Hamburg Wadden Sea (see page 96) and Schleswig-Holstein (see page 106).

AT A GLANCE

Wadden Sea maritime habitat ▪ 133.5 square miles (345.7 sq km) ▪ Carriage rides across the sands ▪ nationalpark-wattenmeer.de/nds/overview-english

MÜRITZ

A landscape of lakes surrounded by old beech forests and lowlands

About halfway between Berlin and Rostock is one of Germany's best kept secrets, the Müritz National Park. The reserve, which opened in 1990, stretches over much of the Müritz lakeland. Apart from these lovely lakes, the park's landscape is mostly forestry with the rest a mix of terminal moraine (the rocky remains of a glacier), *sandur* (glacial plains formed by sediment deposits), and lowlands. Swamps and meadows add to the varied habitat that hosts a wide range of wildlife. Swedish hornless cattle, for example, have been grazing around Müritzhof since 1969 as part of a trial, with Gotland sheep being added in the 1980s.

WATCHING WILDLIFE

A stroll around these ancient beech forests will take you into the range of the park's population of red deer, whose stag fights culminate in late fall. A boat or canoe trip provides a good chance to spot many interesting birds from the water, including cranes, white-tailed eagles, or osprey. Other areas such as marshlands and meadows are better for spotting inhabitants such as the great bittern, reed warbler, redshank, greenshank, teal, garganey (a small duck), or the little stint. In the eastern part of the national park

Beech woods are part of this UNESCO World Natural Heritage site.

near Serrahn, you'll find several blinds from which to study wildlife in safety.

Since 2006, the Müritz Bear Sanctuary has worked with the national park to rehabilitate injured and neglected brown bears in an enclosure of 39.5 acres (16 ha). Currently, 18 brown bears live in the sanctuary and this is an excellent opportunity to experience this

The Müritzeum

This interactive, multimedia visitors center/museum is the starting point for any visit to Müritz. Here visitors learn about the landscape as well as observe 50 species of freshwater fish, crustaceans, and aquatic plants in Germany's largest freshwater aquarium. The Müritzeum hosts some 275,000 artifacts, including turtles, mollusks, insects, eggs, bird specimens, antlers, and a geological collection. Themed displays include the underwater world, birds, forests, the region's history, and the moorlands. The museum also examines the 1,000-year-old oaks at Ivenack, the fieldstone church, and the sociology of estate villages. For children, there is also an adventure garden and playground.

magnificent creature in close but safely regulated quarters.

TRAILS TO WANDER

A 410-mile (660-km) network of trails can take you through the park and along the shores of many of its 130 lakes. These paths are enhanced by boardwalks and observation towers, the most famous of which is the 180-foot (55-m) Käflingsbergturm. You can plot various routes according to your time and fitness level; one easy but scenic stroll is the 11-mile (18-km) route that takes you from Waren to Schwarzenhof. You walk along the shores of Lake Müritz to a fine lookout point at Schnakenburg; you'll pass Warnker See, which fills with noisy ducks and common and red-crested pochards in summer months; and then stroll on to the lovely lake of Rederangsee, where cranes can be seen (and heard) each spring and fall.

Müritz also has many cycle trails, and the park also organizes canoe tours that follow specific routes of interest. Canoeing trips on the Havel River are especially popular.

The Heinrich Schliemann Museum in Ankershagen is worth visiting for insight into the life and work of the well-known German archaeologist for which it is named. The beautiful old town of Waren is also rewarding for its many churches and historical buildings, and also for the Müritzeum.

Lakelands ▪ 123 square miles (318 sq km) ▪ Nature trails ▪ The Müritzeum ▪ Müritz Bear Sanctuary ▪ mueritz-nationalpark.de

SAXON SWITZERLAND

Sandstone monuments to nature's grandeur in a dramatic park

Mists swirl around Saxon Switzerland's strange rockscapes.

Some of the most memorable scenery in Germany is found in Saxon Switzerland National Park, close to the Czech border. Here, in the upper valley of the Elbe, 1,000-foot-high (305-m) sandstone cliffs have been eroded into fantastic shapes, forming a labyrinth of stone amid deep green forests. This is the Bastei ("bastion"), a series of stony fingers reaching skyward above the village of Rathen, at the heart of the Saxon Switzerland.

The Bastei is a great natural curiosity of weather-crafted sandstone cliffs, crags, and pillars towering above the curve of the Elbe River far below. This spectacle of stone is a crowd-pleaser and is best seen in late afternoon, when the groups have dissipated and ever reddening evening light on these rock formations makes for memorable photographs. Paths, viewpoints, and catwalks enable you to wander round the Bastei, protected by railings. As you cross the Basteibrücke—the amazing sandstone bridge between these rocks—to the partly reconstructed medieval castle of Felsenburg Neurathen, gaze out at the Saxony landscape, and you can be certain that this scenery is unlike anywhere else on Earth.

ROCKS, FLORA & FAUNA

These sandstone rocks rose up from the Cretaceous ocean. The cliffs, mesas, gorges, and spires of this "city in stone" are the result of more than 100 million years of work by the wind and waters of the Elbe River and tributaries as they flow into the North Sea. The eclectic mix of habitats in Saxon Switzerland is quite remarkable: Deep canyons fall away from plateau mountaintops; moors and plateaus are surrounded by primeval forests; and everywhere ferns, mosses, and lichens cling to rocky surfaces. The park also encompasses several microclimate zones due to its pronounced vertical divisions. At lower altitudes, wildflower-filled meadows offer a soft contrast to the hard rock protrusions.

Interestingly, the climate here is turned "upside down" by a phenomenon called climactic inversion.

Mixed montane forest is found at the damp, cool lower altitudes in shadowy gorges. This unusual climate has allowed two flowers normally found in tundra climates, the *gelbe veilchen* ("yellow violet") and the *sumpfporst* ("wild rosemary") to survive here since the last ice age.

The animals that make the park home are many: Peregrine falcons soar over the rocks and dive swiftly for smaller birds. Watch for the glaring orange eyes of the Eurasian eagle-owl on cliff ledges. In the forests, the adaptable lynx prowls for dormice and other prey; this shy, wildcat has evolved to blend into its habitat, changing its golden brown summer fur for a silvery winter coat.

WALKS & ACTIVITIES

The cultural high point of the park is the Königstein Fortress, a 13th-century citadel sitting high atop a table mountain, 853 feet (260 m) above the Elbe. This is Germany's largest castle and affords stunning views across Saxon Switzerland. Check out the Brunnenhaus with its endless well and Georgenburg, where many Saxon prisoners took their last breath . . . or wished they could. In the Second World War, it became a prisoner of war camp.

Just as the Romantic poets of England found their spiritual home in that country's Lake District, the Romantic painters of Germany flocked to Saxon Switzerland. The 19th-century Romantic landscape painter Caspar David Friedrich memorably captured the otherworldliness of the sandstone pinnacles and majestic mesas. Tourists followed this artistic colonization, and today large numbers of visitors threaten this delicately poised landscape. One objective of the park is to increase the protected area by limiting access to the wide number of hiking and climbing trails: There are currently some 250 miles (402 km) of hiking paths, 31 miles (50 km) of biking paths, and 755 climbing locations with around 12,600 possible climbing routes.

The rocks of the park make for great hiking with iron rung ladders leading you up and down mossy cliff faces in an intricate rocky maze. The Schrammsteinaussicht is a 3.7-mile (6-km), two-hour hike to the lookout point above the park's main rock formation, and involves a final ascent straight up a series of steel ladders and stairs. If you've got more time, you could take the Painters' Way, a 69.6-mile (112-km) circuit of the park via forest, gorge, and ladders, taking in some stunning hilltop castles along the picturesque route. Brace yourself for the endless one-way staircase called the Himmelsleiter (Heaven's Ladder), but the view once you get through this purgatory is divine. If you fancy a longer walk, Saxon Switzerland National Park borders Czechia's České Švýcarsko National Park (see page 342), and a hikers' border crossing was opened in 2003.

Following the great river as it winds its way through the heart of the national park, the Elbe Cycle Route offers another great way to see much of this spectacular landscape.

Saxon Switzerland is the home of free-climbing, which originated here in the mid-19th century. Today, schools enthusiastically teach the sport to newcomers. Free-climbing the sandstone spires is permitted in the park but strict rules apply, so make sure you've read up on them at the visitors center or online before you set out.

Basteibrücke (Bastei Bridge) leads through sandstone towers to a castle.

AT A GLANCE

Sandstone spires ▪ 36 square miles (93.5 sq km) ▪ Königstein Fortress ▪ Schrammsteinaussicht Trail ▪ A walk across the Basteibrücke ▪ nationalpark-saechsische-schweiz.de

SCHLESWIG-HOLSTEIN WADDEN SEA

A mudflat and ocean wildlife preserve on the North Sea

The Schleswig-Holstein Wadden Sea National Park was the first of Germany's three Wadden Sea parks, opening in 1985 (see also pages 96 and 101). Its area was expanded in 1999, making it also the largest of Germany's North Sea parks, covering an impressive 1,705 square miles (4,416 sq km). Although this is mostly ocean, the land habitats comprise salt marshes, sandbars, and dunes.

Plant life is scarce here, due to the harsh conditions, and eelgrass is the only flowering plant that thrives actually *in* the Wadden Sea. In 1930 much of the eelgrass in the Atlantic Ocean was destroyed by an epidemic, but it has since seen a slow regeneration here. Today the salt marshes host plants such as common salt marsh grass, sea aster, sea blite, and sea purslane in low-lying areas. The higher grounds enjoy more diversity, fostering plants such as the seaside centaury, red eyebright, and sea plantain.

Wide expanses of sand welcome walkers along the Wadden Sea.

THE BIG FIVE

A guided tour of the mudflats or salt marshes will give you a chance to spot the "big five" creatures of the Wadden Sea. These include the common seal, the grey seal, the harbor porpoise, and the white-tailed eagle, aka the sea eagle, the national bird of Germany. The fifth member, the European sea sturgeon, is now extinct in the Wadden Sea, but you can see this fish at the aquarium at the Multimar Wattforum National Park Centre in Tönning. The harbor porpoise is an interesting marine creature in that it is quite comfortable heading "inland" up freshwater rivers far from its saltwater habitat. Aside from the greater wildlife, look down in the mud for those small creatures indigenous to the mudflats: the eelpout, the sand goby, and the little fish that goes by the Latin name of *Myoxocephalus scorpius;* its many English names are far saltier, including shorthorn sculpin, goat sculpin, scummy, guffy, pig-fish, father-lasher, and horny whore.

ABUNDANCE OF ANIMALS

Altogether, the Wadden Sea sustains more than 3,000 animal species, including mollusks, sea stars, snails, and numerous mud creatures. Massive flocks of migratory birds use the rich ecosystem of the Wadden Sea in spring and fall as a stopping-off point for refueling on long migrations. Ducks make the most noise here: Aside from large numbers of shelducks and eider ducks, growing populations of barnacle geese (about 60,000) and Brent geese (about 84,000) now flock to the park's islands.

At certain times, you can visit Die Halligen islands in the midst of the mudflats. German author Theodor Storm described them as "dreams floating on the sea." As more than 66 percent of this preserve is permanently underwater, the park runs guided boat tours for visitors to observe marine wildlife in its natural habitat: Species are pulled from the ocean and returned after examination. The boat tours leave from harbors such as Büsum, Nordstrand, Dagebüll, Schlüttsiel, and from the islands of Föhr, Amrum, and Sylt.

AT A GLANCE

Mudflat walking ▪ 1,705 square miles (4,416 sq km) ▪ Island tours ▪ Germany's largest national park ▪ nationalpark-wattenmeer.de/sh/overview-english

VORPOMMERSCHE BODDENLANDSCHAFT

A coastline rich in biodiversity and scenic beauty

Situated on the coast of the Baltic Sea, Vorpommersche Boddenlandschaft National Park is another hidden gem tucked away in an oft overlooked corner of Germany. As the largest nature reserve on the Baltic coast, it comprises several peninsulas, islands, and lagoon shore areas, including the Darss Peninsula, the western coast of the island of Rügen, the islands of Hiddensee and Ummanz—along with several tiny islets in between—and numerous lagoons.

BIRDS & BODDEN

The shallow waters that wash these various land fragments provide a rich assortment of wildlife with a variety of habitats. The most frequent visitors are the thousands of migrating cranes and geese that use the park as a resting point. Each fall, approximately 30,000 cranes descend on the park in an amazing display of aviation and coordination. This is thought to be one of the largest roosting grounds for cranes anywhere in Europe. These waters also provide a welcome habitat for a variety of marine life, such as the Baltic herring that spawns in the park's shallow inlets. The differing salinity levels of the brackish water habitats of the Baltic and the *bodden*—shallow bays cut off from the Baltic Sea that contain a mix of saltwater and freshwater—affect this rich biosphere too.

TRAILS & TOURS

The park offers a variety of guided and independent walks that take visitors along the fascinating Baltic coastline and deep into its woodland. Guided tours also extend into Osterwald Forest on the Zingst Peninsula and Darss Forest, the largest unbroken area of woodland in the park. Numerous trails transect this most walkable of national parks, and those leading through Osterwald Forest bring you to several excellent vantage points, such as Pramort and Hohe Düne (near Rostock). Other trails bring ecologically curious hikers across historical salt marshes and into the habitats of birds and wildlife. The dune heathland and the Dornbusch area are well worth taking the time to explore.

Some 163 species of birds inhabit the park, and red deer and wild boar roam the oak and pine forests hereabouts. These and other creatures that inhabit the marshes and salt meadows of the park can best be seen from the aforementioned hilltop elevations of Pramort and Hohe Düne. Boat tours are also available to visitors hoping to spot marine life offshore.

Cultural attractions of the region include the Ahrenshoop artists' colony, the lighthouse and Natureum on Darsser Ort, the national park center on Hiddensee (the largest island in the national park and maybe the most peaceful as it is completely car free), and Stralsund Museum with its glittering exhibits of gold treasure.

Watery Vorpommersche Boddenlandschaft, also known as the Western Pomerania Lagoon Area

AT A GLANCE

Baltic Sea shorelines ▪ 310.8 square miles (805 sq km) ▪ Major crane roosting grounds ▪ Stralsund Museum
▪ nationalpark-vorpommersche-boddenlandschaft.de

SWITZERLAND

High within central Europe soars an iconic wonderland where cloud-shrouded dolomitic mountains, ancient glaciers, and rich forests have long lured those seeking peace and solace in nature. This a place of healing, where wildflower-carpeted meadows, spa towns, and crystal clear lakes have offered the wounded and war-weary a restorative respite in a country renowned for its neutrality. Since 1914, this apex of European scenic beauty has been the site of Swiss National Park, established to protect the continent's endangered wildlife. (Aside from Swiss National Park, Switzerland also has 18 official nature parks.) Within this national park, the Swiss leave the landscape and its fauna virtually untouched, so the human footprint is barely visible: No trees are felled, no grasslands cut, no wildlife hunted, no grazing permitted, no fruits or berries picked. Small wonder that this epic landscape typifies everything travelers envision when they hear the name "Switzerland."

Opposite: Alpine peaks loom over pasturelands in the canton of Bern.

SWISS NATIONAL PARK

A soaring Alpine wonderland of Europe's most dramatic wildlife and wildflowers

Enjoying the vista of peaks along the Val dal Botsch

Swiss National Park, located in the Western Rhaetian Alps of eastern Switzerland, was the first national park established in the Alps, and one of the earliest in all of Europe. Despite two world wars, mass industrialization, and the accelerated impact of global warming and climate change, this classic Swiss landscape has changed little in the last century. Sprawled within a remote part of the Engadin Valley in eastern Switzerland, the park touches on the Austrian and Italian borders. Glacier-capped mountains are the main event.

ALPINE EDEN

Opened in 1914 in an area centered on iron ore, lead, and silver mining, the park's main aim was conservation, particularly of the chamois, a goatlike species. Yet Swiss National Park has a laissez-faire policy of minimal management and interference with nature's rhythms. If a tree falls, it is left to rot, unless it is blocking a path. No dogs are allowed within the park, even on a leash, and hikers must stick to paths. The park hosts more than 600 plant species due to its variety of habitats and its range of altitude—from 4,593 feet (1,400 m) to 10,413 feet (3,174 m) at the summit of Piz Piscoc. Larch, Alpine alder, alpenrose, spruce, mountain pine, dwarf pine, and cembra pine all grow to great heights. The size of many trees lining the forest walking trails is proportionate to the towering mountains around them.

In June and July, the hillsides bloom in a riot of color, including many yellows (Alpine buttercup, yellow Rhaetian mountain poppy, mountain crowfoot, hawkweed), several whites (saxifrage, catchfly), reds (bearberry, primrose), and purples (spurred violet, gentian). Of course, there's also the delicate, white-blooming edelweiss, one of the world's most romanticized blooms ever since it was eulogized in *The Sound of Music*. The helpful visitors center in Zernez has the story of the park's flora, wildlife, and Alpine geology, as well as information on the numerous trails. The town also has a baroque church and a medieval castle, Schloss Wildenberg.

MILES OF TRAILS

Popular among the park's 50 miles (80 km) of marked trails is a three-hour hike from Zernez through Val Cluozza, where the Chamanna Cluozza mountain hut offers basic amenities for overnight stays. Built in 1910, it stands

6,175 feet (1,882 m) above sea level and accommodates up to 68 people. The chalet is open to hikers from late June to early October. The only alternative in the park for multiday hikers is the Hotel Parc Naziunal Il Fuorn, a 16th-century inn once frequented by smugglers and miners. The park's Naturlehrpfad (nature trail) starts and ends here and takes about four hours to enjoy.

Hikers should set out with a few local favorite foods in their backpacks, such as Bergkäse ("mountain cheese"), *salsiz* ("air-dried sausage"), *bündnerfleisch* ("air-dried beef"), and *nusstorte* ("caramelized walnut tart").

On the higher parts of many trails the park's notable wildlife make themselves visible, including chamois, marmots, and ibex. Listen for the whistle of marmots at Stabelchod and for the roaring ruckus of rutting stags in the Val Trupchun in fall. The Val Trupchun Trail, an easy three-hour hike from Scanfs, leads to this wild, wooded valley that is gloriously colored in autumn.

Ibex can be seen in particular around the lakes of Macun. They are recognizable by their distinctive curved horns with horizontally ridged notches, and are astonishingly agile and sure-footed rock climbers. Ibex thrive above 6,562 feet (2,000 m). This area is reached via a tough 10-mile (16-km) hike from Lavin to Zernez, which has fine views of the Bernese, Silvretta, and Ortler Alps and passes the plateau of Macun at 8,200 feet (2,500 m) looking down upon the sparkling lakes and tarns.

Alpine clough chase away a lammergeier, an act called "mobbing."

DIVERSE CULTURE

Besides wildlife, Swiss National Park also nurtures much Alpine culture within its mountain realm. You can hike up a craggy peak to the 17th-century ruin of Fortezza Rohan above the village of Susch, or drive over the Ofentalpass close to the Italian border where the early Christian town of Müstair hosts a Benedictine monastery, now a UNESCO World Heritage site. The park is one of the few places in western Europe where you'll hear four indigenous languages within a small area: Aside from German, French, and Italian, Romansch (a Swiss Romance language) is spoken in several villages of the Engadin Valley, including Guarda, Scuol, and Zuoz. These lovely towns are worth seeing in the razor-clear Alpine light for their sgraffito-decorated houses, oriel windows, ornately carved doors, and cobbled lanes. In Scuol, a town with 20 mineral springs, the Museum d'Engiadina (Museum of the Lower Engadin) gives insights into the history of the area.

Lammergeier

Swiss National Park broke its nonintervention policy to good effect with the reintroduction of lammergeiers (bearded vultures). This conservation initiative, a joint venture with the World Wide Fund for Nature (WWF), came about as lammergeiers had become extinct as breeding birds in the Alps in the late 19th century. They were reintroduced to the Stabelchod Valley in 1991, and in 2007—for the first time in more than 100 years—a chick was hatched into the wild in Swiss National Park. When fully grown, these fierce predators will have a wingspan of nearly 10 feet (3 m). They are also the punk rockers of the avian world, dying their feathers in ferric oxide–rich waters. Today, more than 100 lammergeiers once again circle the Alpine heights.

AT A GLANCE

Glorious Alpine scenery ▪ 65.7 square miles (170.3 sq km) ▪ Romansch-language Swiss cantons ▪ Growing lammergeier population ▪ Visitors center with exhibits in Zernez ▪ nationalpark.ch/en

The pristine wilderness of Swiss National Park

AUSTRIA

There are few more beautiful countries in Europe than Austria, and none more central for those traveling by road across the continental mainland. This compact nation shares its borders with seven European neighbors and its main river, the Danube, with nine other countries. The great river flows from its origins in the Black Forest mountains of Germany, through Austria, to its sea fall in Romania. The Danube crosses a couple of Austria's national parks, but it is the soaring Alpine landscapes that dominate the state's protected wildernesses. The mountains offer vital sanctuary at the heart of Europe's ever developing landmass to a range of species whose habitats have shrunk significantly over the last century. These include the chamoix, ibex, lynx, and griffon vulture.

Opposite: An Alpine mirror
in Kalkalpen National Park

DONAU-AUEN

Preserving the last major wetlands in central Europe

Located between the cities of Vienna and Bratislava, in Slovakia, Donau-auen National Park is a remarkable conservation success story that now preserves the Danube and its wetlands.

As the region industrialized in the 19th century, extensive engineering began to change the balance of the Danube landscape. Mankind dammed many side channels and felled much of the lowland forests. In the 1950s, a series

A backwater tributary of the Donau-auen, where wildlife thrives again

of hydroelectric power plants on the Danube further degraded the surrounding wetlands and riparian woodlands. In 1984, protesters won a court order to cease construction of a proposed power plant at Hainburg, downstream from Vienna.

Extensive studies revealed a diverse habitat supporting many species of fish. Twelve years later Donau-auen National Park was opened to preserve their river home, as well as the river islands, wetlands, floodplains, riparian forests, and meadows along this stretch of the Danube. This diversity of habitat now hosts about 50 species of fish, 100 species of breeding birds, 30 mammals, 8 reptiles, 13 amphibian species, and more than 700 species of plants. Add in countless insects and you have an amazingly diverse biosphere along this green ribbon connecting the two capital cities.

Some of the main characters in this fluvial sub-universe are the Danube crested newt, a tiny drag-onlike creature with crested back, distinctive orange coloring, and a white stripe along its tail, and the European pond turtle, which can live up to 100 years—so you may be spotting an animal that lived through both world wars. Also in evidence are the vivid blue- and orange-feathered Eurasian kingfisher and the Eurasian beaver, which thrives along the Danube's wooded banks. Look too for the male stag beetle with his "antlers" that are in fact its jaws. You might also spot an asp or a starlet, both now endangered, in the river's calmer waters.

The Danube's forests are split between softwood and hardwood riparian trees: Softwood species such as alder, willow, and poplar can live in areas of frequent flooding, whereas ash, oak, maple, and lime thrive on drier land. Endangered tree species such as the white willow and the black poplar are now grown here too, restoring essential habitat for beetles and birdlife.

The best way to see this park is, of course, by boat. While traveling past the thickly vegetated riverbanks, notice how many vines grow in this jungly water world. Look for traveler's joy, aka old man's beard, one of the few lianas found in central Europe. You'll spot it growing wild along woodland margins, recognizable by its creamy white, cottony fruit buds.

AT A GLANCE

One of Europe's favorite rivers ▪ 36 square miles (93 sq km) ▪ A biodiverse waterworld close to Vienna ▪ Riparian forestry ▪ donauauen.at

GESÄUSE

Three tiers of habitat layer the "roof garden of Europe."

The Enns River is the main artery of Gesäuse National Park; flowing through on its 158-mile (254-km) course from its origin in Salzburg to its meeting with the Danube, the Enns descends some 4,911 feet (1,497 m). This drop is a mark of the sheer majesty of the mountains that form the backbone of the park, the Gesäuse range within the Ennstal Alps. The dramatic glacial landscape of the mountains dominates Gesäuse National Park: The Hochtor and the Buchstein Massif are the high points, separated by the River Enns.

The park has three primary habitats: The towering limestone and dolomite rocks, capped by ice in winter, are the preserve of hardy plants such as sedge and dwarf shrubs, and of ibex and golden eagles; these give way lower down to Alpine meadows, where wildflowers thrive, and then to the green woods and pastures that are home to much of its wildlife.

The Alpine pastures host a diversity of fauna, and here local farmers work with the park to ensure that preservation is maximized in accordance with the agricultural priorities of the working farms. Eight Alpine pastures are presently farmed, using traditional methods.

The woodland habitat covers about 50 percent of the national park and it too is carefully managed; the park has steered away from the spruce-dominated com-

On the summit of Grosser Buchstein in the Ennstal Alps

mercial forests of the past toward a more diverse mix of spruce, fir, and beech for the future.

The flood zones of the riparian forest along the Enns still have old-growth forest, and higher up are the larch and Swiss stone pine woodland, which is several hundred years old. These mature stands attract the curious bird called the capercaillie, conspicuous by the male's metallic blue-green feathers and the red "rose" above the eyes of both cocks and hens.

SHARING NATURE'S BOUNTY

Along the Enns and Johnsbach Rivers, several bird and mammal species that suffered displacement with

the advent of 20th-century hydroelectric plants are now finding a safe haven within the park. Otters, once seen as fishermen's foes, are making a comeback, while common sandpipers find many gravel banks and islands in the rivers here on which to hide their eggs. Refugee fish species from the plants downstream include the brook lamprey and the bullhead.

For humans, trails vein the pastures, forests, and precipitous limestone peaks in Gesäuse, and mountain huts provide resting places for weary walkers. The Enns and other gushing river rapids offer fabulous white-water rafting opportunities. And of course, mountain and cross-country skiing are age-old traditions in Europe's Alpine realm.

AT A GLANCE

Protected Alpine habitat ▪ 42.5 square miles (110 sq km) ▪ The Enns River ▪ White-water rafting ▪ nationalpark.co.at

HOHE TAUERN

Ascend the Grossglockner Road into the awe-inspiring Austrian Alps.

The Krimmler Falls produce misty rainbows in summer and ice sculptures in winter.

Ask any Austrians in Hohe Tauern National Park to explain the *Alpenglühen* and you'll rarely get the same answer: Some say that the famous "alpenglow" is the reddish light on the mountains at dawn, some describe it as the shade of dusk; others will tell you it's the luminescence that follows the rain, painting rainbows amid the glacier-topped peaks. There are as many ways of seeing the light here as there are facets of nature illuminated by that same Alpenglühen in Austria's most spectacular national park.

Whatever the light, the sheer scale of this wilderness is a won- der to behold: There are 300 peaks in the park that rise majestically over 9,843 feet (3,000 m), includ- ing Grossglockner, Austria's tallest mountain at 12,460 feet (3,798 m). The Krimmler Falls are Europe's longest, roaring over three rocky tiers and cascading downward for some 1,247 feet (380 m), particularly dazzling when frozen in winter.

THE GROSSGLOCKNER ROAD

The Grossglockner Road that winds through the park is one of the world's great drives, an exhilarating experi- ence that takes you higher into an Alpine Eden with every switchback. The highest lookout point, Edel- weissspitze, at 8,435 feet (2,571 m), is the prelude to the Pasterze Glacier. As you ascend, colorful vistas below unfold: Tarns glisten in the sunlight; moorlands stretch across the Alpine plateaus with the white heads of cot- ton grass nodding their welcome; meadows of wildflowers blaze with the yellows and oranges of arnica and crowfoot, the pink of Alpine rho- dodendrons, and the Alpine white of the edelweiss. The higher peaks nur- ture *Saxifraga rudolphiana*, a rug- ged, cold-climate plant that thrives in rocky areas and whose bloom is a dramatic burst of five petals with a pinkish purple blush.

Although everyone should drive the Grossglockner Road, cyclists may prefer the 193-mile (310-km) Tauern Trail, starting in Krimml. This follows the Salzach and Saalach Rivers down to Salzburg and farther on to Passau. The park is, of course, a mountaineer's paradise, and if you plan to climb Grossglockner, you can take a path from Erzherzog Johann Hütte, cross over rock and ice, and then use the steel cable to help you safely up a ridge that leads toward the summit. It's not for beginners, and you can hire a local guide in Heiligenblut.

The Glacier Trail is an easier hike involving ice crossing. This hike is an imperative for anyone wanting to understand the intricacies of the ice fields that glaze the higher peaks of these granite mountains. This trail starts out at Glockner House (6,960 feet/2,121 m) and takes you on a four-hour loop across the Pasterze Glacier.

Elsewhere in the park, hikers can stop off for replenishment at the Matreier Tauernhaus, founded by the archbishop of Salzburg in 1207 and located on an old trade route over the Felber Tauern Pass. The lodge offers large wooden rooms, and has a climbing wall, a petting zoo, and an inn serving fresh fish and tasty *kasnocken* (cheese dumplings).

TIMELESS HOHE TAUERN

Fall is a particularly fine time to walk in the park, as the pine, spruce, and larch trees coat the hillsides in golden shades. The park is far

An Alpine marmot whistles shrilly.

enough south that walking can be enjoyed late in the year here, provided you take the right precautions and check the forecast before setting out. The Romans made Hohe Tauern the demarcation line to divide their northern and southern territories. It also served as a trade route,

and beasts of burden carried their loads along the Tauern Valley pass.

Another draw in times of old was the 15th-century Heiligenblut Church of St. Vincent set against the backdrop of the Grossglockner. The local legend of Briccius suggests that the glass vial in the church's tabernacle contains drops of the "Heiligen Bluet"—the holy blood—of Christ. The story is narrated via a set of paintings and continues to attract thousands of pilgrims to the church.

Today, the stunning mountain scenery of Hohe Tauern National Park is what attracts outdoor sports enthusiasts in equally large numbers these days: Adventurers seeking an adrenaline rush can engage in a wide range of park activities, such as climbing, canyoneering, whitewater rafting, wakeboarding, and for those who'd like to share some of Europe's finest Alpine views with a loved one, tandem paragliding. May the Alpenglühen be with you!

Animal Oddities

Covering an expansive area of about 717 square miles (1,856 sq km), Hohe Tauern National Park is the largest nature reserve in the Alps. The primary players of the park's vast ecosystem include the light-footed ibex that seem to dance daintily along the edges high in these rocky and often icy mountains. In winter, the males will fight fierce rutting duels for the affections of females. Chamois, like ibex, are best spotted in early dawn or late dusk. While you wait for a sighting of this goat-antelope, keep your eyes on the skies above for lammergeiers with their diamond-shaped tails and feathers dyed rusty red with mud. Or you might see the distinctive white head of a griffon vulture. On the moors, look for marmots' burrows and listen for their loud, strange whistling noise as it echoes around the clear Alpine air.

AT A GLANCE

The Grossglockner Road ▪ 717 square miles (1,856 sq km) ▪ A rest at the Matreier Tauernhaus ▪ Heiligenblut Church of St. Vincent ▪ The Glacier Trail ▪ hohetauern.at/en

KALKALPEN

Austria's Limestone Alps is a mountain park with a difference.

Spanning the Northern Limestone Alps mountain range in the state of Upper Austria, Kalkalpen National Park is characterized by its mountainous karst landscape and a subterranean labyrinth of more than 70 limestone caves and caverns. Four-fifths of Kalkalpen is covered by central Europe's largest area of forestry.

The trees within Kalkalpen are mainly spruce, fir, and beech, but more spruce and larch have been planted to replace the old-growth trees. If you spot any deadwood in the park, look closely for the microcosm of life that attaches to such fallen trees: You may see mushrooms, dormice, beetles, owls, or woodpeckers that have moved in; and look too for the lovely plush carpet of lichens or mosses that greet such new residents. You may even spot the rosalia longicorn beetle, with its distinguishing flat torso, long antennae, and blue-gray color marked with variable black spots. The Alpine longhorned beetle is thought to exist in significant numbers only in this park. Look also for Austria's rarest woodpecker, the white-backed woodpecker.

The canyons and karst springs of the Reichraminger Hintergebirge area are a thriving biosphere unto themselves, hosting more than 500 species of animals, including spring snails, beavers, and the native Danube river trout. The caves also warehouse bats by the thousand, including what are believed to be significant populations of two severely endangered species, the lesser horseshoe bat and the barbastelle.

EXPLORING THE PARK

On a clear day, a visit to the Wurbauerkogel, a 69-foot (21-m) tall panorama view tower near Windischgarsten is a must for stunning views of the jagged karst peaks. The park is crisscrossed with numerous hiking, mountain biking, and horseback riding trails, and in winter, snowshoe hiking and cross-country skiing is similarly tracked out. In the high Alpine pastures you may spot the elusive lynx stealthily hunting its prey, or members of the park's brown bear population.

The former Steyr Valley Railway, which passes through the park in the Molln area, is now part of the Steyrtal rail trail, aka the R8 Family Cycle Route, a 30-mile (48.1-km) bike ride that cleaves close to the River Steyr with swimming points, rest areas, mountain lookouts, and canyons along the way. The karst landscape is of course very popular for cavers, but the ice caves can be entered only with an approved guide, and are not for beginners.

Kalkalpen's Alpine forests cover a network of underground caverns.

AT A GLANCE

Central Europe's largest forest ▪ 80 square miles (207 sq km) ▪ Limestone mountains ▪ Villa Sonnwend park lodge ▪ Steyrtal rail trail ▪ kalkalpen.at/en/National_Park

NEUSIEDLER SEE-SEEWINKEL

A border wilderness shared with Hungary

A Eurasian spoonbill uses his long, ladled beak to catch a fish.

Birding With Experts

Neusiedler See-Seewinkel National Park offers excellent birding excursions with experts, in a range of options to suit all interest and mobility levels. Various viewing towers and blinds make for rewarding bird-watching safaris through a wealth of avian habitats. The fen that developed around the Hanság part of the Neusiedler See as it silted up is today home to rarities such as the great bustard, which defies all laws of gravity as the heaviest bird able to fly. The short-eared owl and the Montagu's harrier also breed here. The park's information center and its website have details of these multilingual expeditions.

Located on the eastern edge of the Alps and on the western edge of the Little Hungarian Plain, Neusiedler See-Seewinkel National Park is set in an area that for centuries was a neutral no-man's land separating the great powers of Europe. How apt that birdsong and bright wildflowers now fill the vacuum created by mankind's bellicosity.

The park was founded in 1993, following the opening of the bordering Hungarian Fertő-Hanság National Park (see page 396). The joint protected area now covers about 116 square miles (300 sq km), of which about 37 square miles (97 sq km) are the Austrian part of the park, and about half of which is a nature reserve zone, which means it is completely untouched by humans.

The sandy embankment on the east shore of the Neusiedler See has a unique range of flora and fauna, including the *Bembix rostrata,* an indigenous (and industrious) sand wasp that digs a separate burrow for each egg. The cuckoo wasp—an endangered species in Europe—uses the larvae of the *Bembix rostrata* to feed its own larvae. Scour the sands too for ant lion larvae, aka the doodlebug, that builds sand traps to catch ants and then throws loose sand into the pit from which the ant is trying to escape.

THE SEEWINKEL

The Seewinkel itself, a saline steppe lake located on the western part of the Little Hungarian Plain, covers part of the border between Austria and Hungary. It is one of the area's intriguing saline lakes, an extremely rare phenomenon on the European mainland, as plants that grow here, such as saltwort and sea purslane, are more commonly found along the continent's shorelines. The area cackles with birdlife: The avocet and the Kentish plover nest only in this part of Austria, and birds that find sustenance and shelter along the salty shores include the redshank, the black-tailed godwit, and the lapwing. Seagulls, terns, and herons stop here too as they migrate.

Look in the meadows for the lapwing, with its Mohawk-like spikes.

see page 396

AT A GLANCE

Saline inland lakes ▪ Five habitats ▪ 37 square miles (97 sq km) ▪ Birding safaris ▪ nationalpark-neusiedlersee-seewinkel.at

THAYATAL

A transnational park for the new millennium

Opened on January 1, 2000, Thayatal National Park is a forward-thinking conservation project that aims at protecting the wildlife and flora of this steep-sided river valley with its lush meadows, forests, and canyons. Since 1989, the Iron Curtain has been replaced by a green European thoroughfare for flora and fauna: The park shares its preservation mission with its Czech neighbor across the eastern border, the Podyjí National Park of Czechia (see page 343).

CROSS-BORDER COOPERATION

Many of both parks' fauna have benefited from this cross-border cooperation, extending as it has their habitats and protected areas. Chief among these is the black stork, a dramatic three-foot-tall (1-m) bird that pinches its raw fish meals between its long bill like a cowled monk using a set of red chopsticks. The arrival of the stork in mid-March from its wintering grounds in Africa signals the arrival of spring in the park. An early success for the national park was the surprising return of the wildcat: This extremely shy feline was spotted in Austria for the first time in several decades in Thayatal in 2007. The fish otter is a year-round park resident who catches its prey more convention-ally by ducking and diving in its river range. The dice snake (aka the water snake) also swims but takes occasional breaks to dry its golden scales in the sun.

RIVER, FOREST & MEADOW

The emerald lizard is another colorful resident, while the almost extinct noble crayfish still survives in the rock pools of the River Thaya. The park is named for this river and is one of the last seminatural valley landscapes in central Europe. As it meanders through the park, the river is banked by a rich mosaic of habitats. The dry grasslands atop rocky plateaus host many dwarf shrubs such as Scotch heather and a surprising number of rock-dwelling plants and bushes.

Most of the park is woodland, however, with its eastern side dominated by dry warm oak forests, while the lime and granite of its western side favor beech stands. The scarcer red pines, fir trees, yews, and juniper are indigenous to the region. The meadows are where the diversity of the landscape really shows its colors: Many rare species of flowers from southeastern Europe, the foothills of the Alps, and central Europe congregate in the small area of Thayatal in a glorious kaleidoscope of floral beauty. In spring and early summer, butterflies flutter their multi-hued wings while the sound of chirping grasshoppers and crickets fill the fields. This spectacle of nature's sound and vision can be easily accessed by the Thayatal's extensive network of hiking and cycling routes.

TRAILS & TOWN

Detailed information on trails of both Thayatal and the Podyjí National Park, across the border in Czechia, can be found in the "Hiking in the National Park" brochure, downloadable from the park website. A visitors center also provides extensive information on all activities, as well as exhibitions, a natural science laboratory, a café-restaurant, a gift shop, and a post office.

The park embraces a curious town, Hardegg, somewhat frozen in time due to its location at what was once the end of the Western world right at the Iron Curtain, bordering what was previously Czechoslovakia. The town is a sad example of how places with hard borders tend to empty in the absence of hope for the future. Hardegg's past is impressive, however: The town's castle, rebuilt at the end of the 19th century, is worth a visit, housing over a thousand years of central European history.

Burg Hardegg was an imposing castle, hard to breach.

AT A GLANCE

A cross-border nature reserve ▪ 5.1 square miles (13.2 sq km) ▪ Hardegg's hard-boiled history ▪ np-thayatal.at

NORTHERN EUROPE

NORTHERN EUROPE

Northern Europe stretches from Iceland in the Atlantic Ocean to Greenland farther north, down into Scandinavia and as far east as Lapland. The region's rugged landscapes are gripped for much of the year by the icy fingers of the Arctic Circle's climatic reach. Blasted by wintry blizzards and often sealed under snow and ice, only the stronger species survive. National parks here provide safe havens in all seasons for creatures great and small, from polar bears to reindeers to the arctic fox. For humans, the long dark winters bring stunning night skies sparkling over fjord landscapes and frozen forests, and visits to the farthest-flung parks are rewarded with nature's greatest light show, the northern lights.

Above: Ice and rock shape a winter wilderness at Kejser Franz Joseph Fjord, in Northeast Greenland National Park.
Previous pages: Northern lights dance above Þingvellir National Park, Iceland.

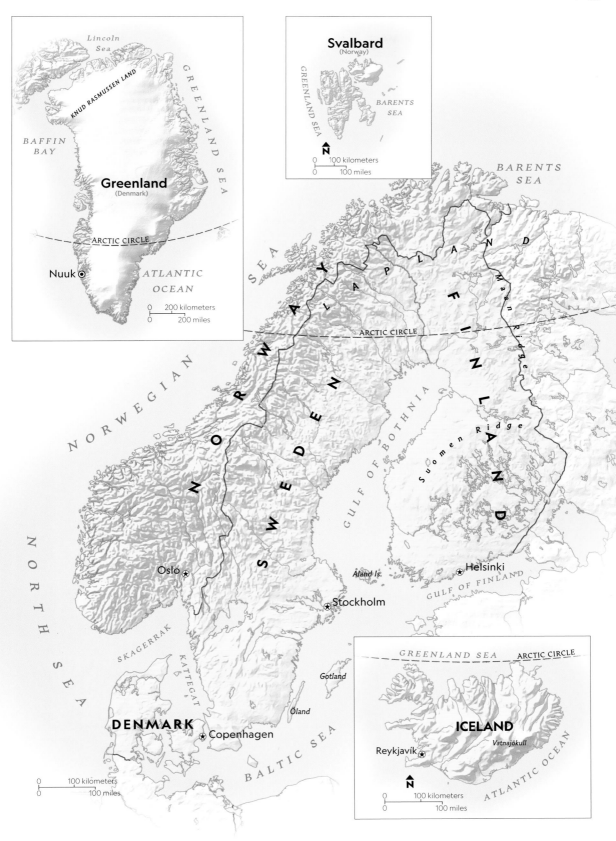

Lincoln
Sea

KNUD RASMUSSEN LAND

GREENLAND SEA

BAFFIN
BAY

Greenland
(Denmark)

ARCTIC CIRCLE

Nuuk ⊙

ATLANTIC
OCEAN

| 0 | 200 kilometers |
| 0 | 200 miles |

Svalbard
(Norway)

GREENLAND SEA

BARENTS
SEA

N

| 0 | 100 kilometers |
| 0 | 100 miles |

BARENTS
SEA

N O R W E G I A N   S E A

N   O   R   W   A   Y

L   A   P   L   A   N   D

ARCTIC CIRCLE

Maan Ridge

F   I   N   L   A   N   D

S   W   E   D   E   N

GULF OF BOTHNIA

Suomen Ridge

N   O   R   T   H   S   E   A

Oslo ✪

Åland Is.

Helsinki ●

Stockholm ✪

GULF OF FINLAND

SKAGERRAK

KATTEGAT

Gotland

Öland

DENMARK

Copenhagen ✪

B A L T I C   S E A

GREENLAND SEA   ARCTIC CIRCLE

ICELAND

Reykjavik ✪   Vatnajökull

N

| 0 | 100 kilometers |
| 0 | 100 miles |

ATLANTIC OCEAN

ICELAND

Iceland is the "Land of Fire and Ice," a cold,
steamy place where lava bubbles up and oozes
onto frigid, wintry icescapes. On this windblasted
North Atlantic island, the frozen, desolate plains
with their undercurrents of volcanic activity
long ago gave rise to legends of an underworld
of trolls and elves. These days, Iceland's roiling
geology is harnessed, and exported, for thermal
energy. Meanwhile, its dramatic national parks
have become year-round hot spots for millennial

ecotravelers. They are not disappointed: Iceland's subarctic climate fosters many
floral rarities with its vast temperature swings. Its mid-Atlantic location makes it a
halfway haven for migrating birds, and the dance of the northern lights is a timeless
spectacle to behold. The last decade has brought a huge increase in the number of
visitors who have thrilled to the sweeping waterfalls, gushing rivers, glaciers, and
ice caves of Þingvellir, Snæfellsjökull, and Vatnajökull National Parks.

Opposite: Öxarárfoss waterfall,
Þingvellir National Park
Above: A rift valley lake in Þingvellir

ÞINGVELLIR

A stunning glacial landscape, a continental rift, and an ancient seat of government

To claim that Þingvellir National Park is of monumental importance is no exaggeration. Geologically, the park straddles continents, lying where the North American and Eurasian tectonic plates meet in the rift valley that marks the crest of the Mid-Atlantic Ridge. Historically, Þingvellir links Iceland to its ancient democratic past.

The park embraces the site of the Alþing, the ancient parliament of the Viking commonwealth, which met here between 930 and 1798, when it moved 25 miles (40 km) southwest to Reykjavík (see sidebar). Þingvellir also played a large symbolic role in the Icelandic independence struggle, which culminated in nationhood in 1944. As the national burial ground of the small island state, Þingvellir is also considered Iceland's "holiest" place.

The national park, established here in 1930 to mark the 1,000th anniversary of the Alþing, also highlights and protects the rugged beauty of this small, enchanting island. Along with the waterfall at Gullfoss and the geysers of Haukadalur, Þingvellir is now part of Iceland's famous Golden Circle of environmental wonders. The modern Icelandic Parliament has even enshrined it in law, decreeing that the park would thereafter become "... a protected national shrine for all Icelanders, the perpetual property of the Icelandic nation under the preservation of parliament, never to be sold or mortgaged."

NATURAL WONDERS

A prime example of the plethora of natural treasures within this preserve is Þingvallavatn, the largest natural lake in Iceland, which laps the southern borders of the park. The lake covers an area of 32 square miles (83 sq km) and is more than 328 feet (100 m) deep. Its clear subarctic waters are home to no less than four different morphs of one species of fish, the arctic char, isolated here by shifting ground during the last ice age. Both the char and the brown trout caught in Þingvallavatn are among the largest in the world.

The lake's northern shore attracts divers to its Silfra fissure, one of a large number of such faults that characterize much of the park's landscape. They are surface evidence of the tectonic and volcanic activity rumbling beneath the Earth's crust hereabouts. These cracks are a result of the continental drift between the North American and Eurasian plates and include the main canyon of Almannagjá, which runs some 4.8 miles (7.7 km) on the west edge of the park. The Almannagjá gorge marks the western edge of the valley, while Heiðagjá gorge, on the east edge of Þingvellir, marks

The rift valley trail leads between the North American and Eurasian continents.

the eastern edge of the rift valley.

Walking the trail along the Almannagjá gorge is one of several highlights of a visit to the Þingvellir; as you stroll between the high lava walls separating the continents, consider the fact that should you return the following year, the plates will have shifted the local rocks by about 0.8 inch (2 cm). At Þingvellir, the continental plates are moving in opposite directions, breaking apart and causing the land between them to subside.

Several such trails lead through these imposing rocky valleys, many filled with water and ice. The bridge over one of these, at Nikulásargjá, was built for the royal visit of King Frederick VIII of Denmark in 1907. The deep fissure it spans is known today as Peningagjá, the Money Chasm, due to the tradition of throwing coins into the crystal clear spring water as you make a wish. On sunny days, the floor of the pool glitters with the wishes of thousands of visitors.

The Strokkur geyser erupts every 6 to 10 minutes beside the Hvítá River.

THE ALÞING

The focal point of the park is the Alþing (see sidebar), site of the Lögberg, the Law Rock, at a cliff overlooking the fields where great hordes of Vikings and Celts assembled each year. This is where speakers stood to address the gatherings and to recite the laws of the land. The exact location of the Lögberg is unknown, due to the ever changing surface geography of the rift valley over 1,000-odd years, but most Icelanders believe it to be

Alþing

Iceland's first settler, Ingólfur Arnarson arrived in 874, and the mix of Norse and Celtic settlers soon necessitated a unified law and a place to debate it. The Alþing, the legislative assembly and highest court of the Viking commonwealth was established here in 930—the name Þingvellir means "fields of parliament." Alþing was an open-air assembly, which began with the Law-sayer, reciting the laws at Lögberg (Law Rock). Then the goðar ("chieftains"), accompanied by their þingmenn (men of parliament), would deliberate and settle legal disputes. Today, Iceland boasts one of the world's highest numbers of female members of parliament, a fitting legacy of such open democracy.

in Almannagjá. Aside from the *lögsögumaður* ("Law-sayer"), any person attending the Alþing could argue their case from the Lögberg rock. Þingvellir National Park hosts some remains of the Alþing itself, fragments of 50 booths built from turf and stone.

Nearby, a darker history reveals itself at Almannagjá's Drekkingarhylur (Drowning Pool), where women convicted of adultery were drowned in sacks during the 16th and 17th centuries. The pool is one of many that swirl to the side of the Öxará River, which transects the national park and reaches its scenic high-water mark at the spectacular Öxarárfoss falls. The national park is enclosed by mountains on three sides, and is largely characterized by grass-covered lava fields.

The informative visitors center offers details of trails and important warnings on the park's changeable weather systems.

AT A GLANCE

Öxarárfoss waterfall ▪ Almannagjá's open-air parliament fields ▪ 35.8 square miles (92.7 sq km) ▪ Walk between continents at the Almannagjá gorge ▪ thingvellir.is/en

SNÆFELLSJÖKULL

Iceland's only coastal park, steeped in myths and legends

Traversing the glacier in Snæfellsjökull is one of Iceland's great adventures.

Snæfellsjökull National Park is named after Mount Snæfellsjökull, the glacier-capped summit rising 4,744 feet (1,446 m) over Faxa Bay, 75 miles (120 km) northwest of Reykjavík. The glacier, along with its surrounding Buðahraun lava field, is the main attraction. A sad sign of our times came in 2012, when the summit was ice free for the first time since records began. Mount Snæfellsjökull is an active volcano and the lava fields, caves, sea cliffs, and black-sand beaches all around bear witness to its influence on the landscape.

The Snaefellsnes Peninsula has inspired writers and artists for more than a millennium. Two novels in particular sealed its renown: Jules Verne's *Journey to the Center of the Earth* and Halldor Kiljan Laxness's *Under the Glacier.* In Verne's early science-fiction tale, a German geologist and his nephew descend into the volcano at Snæfells, guided by an enticing 16th-century Icelandic text: *Descend into the crater of Yocul of Sneffels, which the shade of Scartaris caresses, before the kalends of July, audacious traveler, and you will reach the center of the earth.*

Snæfellsjökull and its volcanic fields was also the setting for several Icelandic sagas—tales written by the island's original settlers. These stories told of battling trolls and wild seafarers. From this peninsula the first Europeans are believed to have reached the American continent, as evidenced by archaeological finds unearthed in Newfoundland, Can-

ada. Christopher Columbus supposedly stopped off here to seek the islanders' nautical advice.

Today's visitors to the Snaefellsnes Peninsula have a multitude of natural wonders to enjoy: The Saxholl mountain crater has an all-weather walkway to take you easily to the top.

Beyond the beautiful pebbled beach at Djúpalónssandur are strange sea rocks, the uniquely formed remnants of ancient basalt volcanic dikes. Off the beach's dramatic cliffs lies the mournful wreckage of the fishing vessel *Epine* that foundered here in 1948. The ghosts of the drowned are said to howl in the wind still. Among the living, large beach rocks have long been a test of Icelandic masculinity, but lifting them yourself is not advisable without good health insurance.

Elsewhere along this coastline, Londrangar and Svalthufa are the remains of a crater slowly eroded to its present form by the sea. Farmers refuse to make hay on Svalthufa hill, as it is said to be the domain of elves. Below the hill sits the famous Thufubjarg cliff, where, according to legend, the poet Kolbeinn Joklaskald had a lyrical duel with the devil that sent Satan back to hell.

SNÆFELLSJÖKULL'S WILDLIFE

Although Snæfellsjökull National Park is not particularly hospitable for most animal or plant life, a surprising number of hardy species survive here. Ytri-Tunga is a good beach for seal-watching. Both grey seals and harbor seals are seen here, the grey seals being more noticeable for their sheer size: These large mammals can grow to a length of up to 10 feet (3 m).

Look in the pools on the beach for smaller sea creatures including copepods, amphipods, and crabs. Out at sea, keep an eye out for the killer whales, minke whales, and porpoises that are often spotted around Snæfellsnes. Foxes may also be seen trotting across the lava fields looking for field mice, and mink comb the coast for food.

The birdlife is altogether richer, with many puffins and fulmars nesting in the park's cliffs. Large colonies of arctic tern nest in Arnarstapi, Rif, and Öndverðarnes. The lovely white tern with its black cap and red beak is easy to spot and beauti-

A wild horse stands before Kirkjufell (Church Mountain), shrouded in clouds.

ful to behold but beware of getting too near the nest of this very territorial bird. Terns winter the Southern Hemisphere in Antarctica, flying north to get the full value of the midnight sun during the Icelandic summer. These little birds have perfected a unique flight technique to enable them to make their astonishing annual round-trip of some 25,855 miles (40,000 km). Other migrant birds that stop here include the turnstone, brant goose, and robin. The cliffs along the coastline are alive with seabirds: Guillemot, Brunnich's guillemot, razorbill, fulmar, kittiwake, and shag all thrive along Iceland's west coast. The shag, a species of cormorant, can be spotted up close at Arnarstapi; look for its dramatic tuft of head feathers during mating season.

WALKS & ACTIVITIES

Cavers in particular enjoy the guided tour into Vatnshellir cave, an 8,000-year-old lava tube reaching 115 feet (35 m) below the earth. Participants get a flashlight and helmet, but need to dress warmly, and wear good hiking shoes. Songhellir (Cave of Songs) is another famous cave, known for its echo.

The park has many fine hiking trails including the 1.5-mile (2.5-km) Hellnar-to-Arnarstapi path leading past the caves of heroes of Iceland's sagas, and the dramatic sea arches that act as blowholes in stormy swells. A walk along Öndverðarnes at the peninsula's western tip brings you to the Skarðsvík beach with its ancient Viking grave and the Svörtuloft cliffs with their colonies of seabirds.

You can rent horses near the park at Lysuhóll and ride the beach on a stout Icelandic horse, bred from stock dating back to the 9th and 10th centuries.

VATNAJÖKULL

A vast world of ice belies the fire beneath the surface.

Many forces of nature went into the creation of Vatnajökull National Park, which embraces the Vatnajökull glacier and its surrounding lava fields. The rush of rivers, the gouging of glacial ice, and the explosive energy of Iceland's volcanic and geothermal netherworld have shaped a place of epic, desolate beauty. Here is every kind of landscape that the subarctic island of Iceland evokes: ice-capped mountains, calving glaciers, rocky canyons, vast ice sheets, geothermal springs, potent volcanoes, otherworldly ice caves, and strange basalt rock formations. Vatnajökull is now one of Europe's largest protected areas—covering approximately 14 percent of Iceland—and is proof positive of the island's commitment to environmental conservation.

CINEMATIC SCENERY

The otherworldly landscape around the park has proven irresistible to filmmakers eager to capture an alien or ancient atmosphere—so if parts of Vatnajökull make you feel like you're walking through a setting for *Interstellar* or *Game of Thrones,* then you probably are.

Vatnajökull is Europe's largest glacier outside the Arctic, with a surface area of 3,130 square miles

A dazzling crystal cave within the Breiðamerkurjökull glacier

(8,100 sq km), and at its thickest the ice cap reaches an incredible 0.6 mile (1 km) in depth. The park's other volcanoes of Askja, Kverkfjöll, and Snæfell loom large too, as does the volcanic table mountain of Herðubreið. In the northern part of the plateau stretches the glacial canyon of Jökulsárgljúfur, with the powerful Dettifoss waterfall roaring into its upper end. Farther north, the horseshoe-curved cliffs of Ásbyrgi are yet another example of the endless array of breathtaking scenery on display in this park.

THE VATNAJÖKULL GLACIER

Vatnajökull glacier is the star attraction of the park and the departure point for snowmobile and 4WD tours is at Skaftafellsjökull. From here visitors venture out onto the glacier's silent realm of ice. Getting up to these higher ice sheets of Vatnajökull requires expert guidance and some motorized horsepower, and the frozen core of the park is only open from July to September. Here, you tempt fate with the active volcano of Grímsvötn, which threw its last batch of ash sky-high in 2011, bringing much of Europe's air traffic to a halt.

DRIVES, HIKES & ACTIVITIES

The roads around the park offer many worthwhile drives, including the stretch of the Ring Road from

Skaftafell to Höfn that passes notable coastal attractions such as puffin colonies and icy lagoons.

Unless you're claustrophobic, a guided descent into one of the many ice caves of Vatnajökull is a must; the eerie light within the caverns and the blue and mint green shades make clambering through ice tunnels unforgettable.

An iconic Icelandic hiking trail is the two-day trek from Ásbyrgi to Dettifoss. This takes you into an elementally charged landscape, culminating at the immense falls of Dettifoss, awe-inspiring for their sheer power.

Watch on your walks for the thrilling sight of a herd of Icelandic reindeer. These beasts are the descendants of Norwegian herds imported in the 1770s. Close to the ocean, birdlife proliferates with puffins and pink-footed geese waddling along the shoreline. The nature reserve at Ingólfshöfði is a good place to study these comedic birds up close. Gyrfalcons and rock ptarmigans also survive in the harsh Icelandic climate.

At the end of an active day in the park, you may be offered the Icelandic delicacy of fermented shark. Be warned: It could just be the strangest taste you will ever experience. Make sure you have a shot of another national favorite, Brennivín (clear, unsweetened schnapps), ready to wash it down.

AT A GLANCE

Vatnajökull glacier ▪ Iceland's vast wilderness ▪ 5,460 square miles (14,141 sq km) ▪ Dettifoss waterfall ▪ Ice caves ▪ vatnajokulsthjodgardur.is/en

GREENLAND

The huge island of Greenland, located within the Arctic Circle, is a little-known anomaly in many ways. It is part of the Kingdom of Denmark; it has no cities, major or otherwise; and its only national park—Northeast Greenland National Park—is the world's largest, with no human inhabitants despite its vast area of 375,300 square miles (972,000 sq km). One of the largest protected land areas anywhere on our planet, it's also one of the least visited parks either in Europe or elsewhere on Earth. Yet the environmental health of this enormous and empty landmass, much of it covered in fast-melting glacial ice, will determine the futures of many far-flung coastal cities such as New York, Miami, Amsterdam, and even its own administrative capital of Copenhagen, more than 1,860 miles (3,000 km) away. Greenland's huge glacial ice mass now acts as the Earth's thermometer, indicating the health of a warming Earth and pointing to a forthcoming rise in sea levels that will demand practical and political remedies all across the globe.

Opposite: Expedition ships travel deep into Kejser Franz Joseph Fjord, amid ice floes and glacial mountains.

ARCTIC OCEAN

CANADA

Peary Land

KNUD RASMUSSEN LAND

King Frederick VIII Land

Northeast Greenland National Park

King Christian X Land

Zackenberg Research Station

GREENLAND SEA

BAFFIN BAY

Ittoqqortoormiit

Greenland
(Denmark)

King Christian IX Land

Denmark Strait

ICELAND

ARCTIC CIRCLE

King Frederick VI Coast

Nuuk

Davis Strait

ATLANTIC OCEAN

N

| 0 | 200 kilometers |
| 0 | 200 miles |

NORTHEAST GREENLAND

A frigid wilderness where Arctic wildlife thrives in the absence of humankind

Travelers can dogsled across the park pulled by a pack of Siberian huskies.

Imagine an Arctic Circle national park more than twice the size of California, much of it a wintry wilderness covered in ice. A place where humans are largely absent, where Darwinian evolutionary competition rewards the survival of the only the *very* fittest in some of the harshest conditions on Earth. This is what the Danish authorities saw when they nominated a huge area of Northeast Greenland as Denmark's first national park. This vast nature preserve covers more than one-third of this Arctic island and serves as a deep freezer for a large amount of the Earth's Arctic ice. Alarmingly, this deep-storage pantry has now started to feel the heat of global warming.

The interior of the park, part of the Greenland ice sheet, is edged by a composite fjord landscape: Long ice-free stretches of rocky shorelines run along Greenland's northern and eastern coasts and on Peary Land in the north. The park also includes King Frederick VIII Land and King Christian X Land.

Northeast Greenland includes both the highest parts of the Northern Hemisphere's largest ice cap and the world's northernmost area of land. Its jagged coastline meanders for more than 11,000 miles (18,000 km), and the remains of ancient Inuit settlements near the sea are evidence of humankind's presence here for thousands of years.

The park today has no permanent residents but hosts several military bases, scientific research stations, and weather stations. At Summit Station, located at the apex of the Greenland ice sheet, the United States' National Science Foundation operates under a permit from the Danish Polar Center to conduct year-round research on the ice sheet.

Zackenberg Research Station, located about 280 miles (450 km) north of Ittoqqortoormiit, is an important site for monitoring the effects of climate change. The station is located in a high Arctic climate zone that reacts earlier than other zones to shifts in global weather, and here, as elsewhere across the Arctic, recent findings have not been encouraging.

The fate of Greenland's huge glaciers, both in the southeast and here in the northwest, has long been viewed as a key determinant of sea levels worldwide. Alarmingly, recent studies have shown that Greenland's ice is melting even faster than scientists previously thought, with the pace of ice loss increasing fourfold since 2003. Enormous glaciers in Greenland are depositing ever larger chunks of ice into the Atlantic Ocean, where they melt. The figures are sobering: Greenland lost about 309 billion tons (280 billion metric tons) of ice per year between 2002 and 2016, enough to raise the worldwide sea level by .03 inch (0.8 mm) annually.

ICONIC ARCTIC WILDLIFE

In the absence of humankind, nature runs free here: An estimated 5,000 to 15,000 musk oxen roam the landscape. Healthy populations of polar bears and walrus are found near the coast. Other mammals include the arctic fox, the stoat, and the collared lemming, a rodent that turns completely white in winter. The shorelines are busy Arctic byways for a range of marine mammals, including ringed seals, bearded seals, harp seals, and hooded seals. Visitors looking from the decks of cruise ships along the park's coastline are likely to spot the "unicorn of the sea," the narwhal, with its strange protruding tusk, as well as the beautiful white beluga whale.

Birdlife in the park runs the full gamut of species of transcontinental migrants—great northern divers, barnacle geese, pink-footed geese, common eiders, king eiders, sanderlings, ptarmigans—including many that breed here. The skies swirl with gyrfalcons, snowy owls, and ravens all seeking to swoop on lemmings or arctic mice. For thousands of years, various Inuit cultures have survived in Greenland, living largely off the meat of the high Arctic animals they hunted. Today, hunters from Ittoqqortoormiit still venture into the national park, taking long dogsled trips across the snow and ice.

A HISTORY OF EXPLORATION

Look at the map of Northeast Greenland and a who's who of exploration history dots the landscape. The geographical place-names that honor the island's spirit of pioneering adventurers include Kaiser Franz Joseph Fjord, Kap Sussi, Peary Land, Teufelkap, and Påskenæsset. In 1822, William Scoresby , a Scottish whaler, was the first European to step onto the rocky terrain of Northeast Greenland.

The following year, the English captain Douglas Clavering met a group of Inuit on the southern side of the island that would later bear his name. He ill-advisedly demonstrated the firepower of a gun to the Inuit, who fled to the hills as if pursued by polar bears. In 1892, the American naval commander Robert Peary established that Greenland was an island. Peary, a frequent pioneer in pushing northward toward the pole, was awarded the Hubbard Medal by the National Geographic Society in honor of his groundbreaking 1905–06 expedition. In 1907, a three-man sledge team sponsored by Denmark completed the mapping of Greenland, charting the unexplored northeastern region that is now the national park. All three died in the effort, their harrowing tale recorded in the diary of Greenlander Jørgen Brønlund, found a year later. Groups of Danish and Norwegian trappers followed, and disputes over the rights to hunting grounds in Northeast Greenland were finally settled in the Hague in 1933, when Denmark was awarded sovereignty over all of Greenland.

Getting Around Greenland

The best way to visit Northeast Greenland National Park is by taking an expedition, either with a Greenland-based tour company offering expert-led treks across the wilderness, or on a cruise that navigates the fjord-indented coastlines. A smaller vessel is best for such environmentally focused travel, as the size of the ship will determine how close to the shore and how far up the fjords you will be able to explore. National Geographic Expeditions runs several cruises along these shorelines of Northeast Greenland. Once you get there, Greenland is an Arctic paradise for hiking, climbing, kayaking, diving, and wildlife and bird-watching—but always go with local experts who know the terrain, or you might find yourself face-to-face with a polar bear uninterested in being in your last-ever selfie.

AT A GLANCE

Greenland's huge glaciers ▪ 375,291 square miles (972,000 sq km) ▪ Narwhals and beluga whales ▪ visitgreenland.com/the-national-park

DENMARK

For a small archipelago country huddled on the cold shoulder of the North Sea, Denmark makes a large splash in European history. More than a thousand years ago the Vikings set out to the west in their longships to conquer islands including Britain, Ireland, and Iceland. When land was discovered farther north, the Danes sponsored the mapping of Greenland's Arctic wilderness in 1907. And when that great land-mass became theirs later in the 20th century, the people of Denmark created the world's largest national park in Northeast Greenland (see pages 138–9) in 1974. The four smaller parks in the homeland impress in other ways: Vadehavet (Wadden Sea) National Park concludes that great international coastline that strings together the dunes, islands, and salt marshes of the Netherlands, Germany, and Denmark. Mols Bjerge National Park encapsulates Denmark's history from Stone Age times to the present. The Icelandic sagas' connection to Skjoldungernes Land National Park reminds us of the pioneering spirit of this seafaring nation. And Thy's mossy woods and lovely coastlines must have warmed the hearts of those Vikings returning home.

Opposite: Undulating waves of blooming cross-leaved heath wash over Thy National Park.

MOLS BJERGE

A panoply of Danish landscape

Opened in 2009, Mols Bjerge National Park, in East Jutland, is named for the Mols Hills that rise in its heart, yet the park's landscapes are many. The windswept coastlines along the sea of Kattegat contrast with the central heathlands, and mossy forests of Kaløskovene in the west are at odds with the inlets, coves, and plains of glacial moraine in the south. The park reaches its apex at the Jernhatten ridge from where this varied land can best be appreciated. The ridge's height of 449 feet (137 m) makes it Himalayan in Danish terms, but it's a gentle hike offering fine vistas of the park's rolling Ice Age topography all around.

The national park embraces the town of Ebeltoft, along with several smaller villages. From here you can wander into the woodlands of Bjørnkær-Egedal Forest, the Ahl Plantation, and the small woodland of Tolløkke Wood, the only old-growth forest on the Ebeltoft peninsula. Here, deciduous trees, including beech, oak, ash, black alder, and willow, create a canopy allowing many plants to thrive in the shade of the forest floor. These include the white-flowered wood anemone, the purple early dog violet, and the yellow lesser celandine. Mols Bjerge is an incubator for plant life, and the park nurtures more than half

A purple-edged copper alights.

Mols Bjerge: The Human History

Stone Age granite barrows, dolmens, and passage graves litter Mols Bjerge, including a burial mound at Stabelhøje dating to the Bronze Age. The ruins of the 14th-century Kalø Castle are reached via a 1,640-foot (500-m) medieval road on a cobblestone embankment. Farther inland is the manor of Kalø Gods from the early 18th century, now a center for environmental education, and the hunting lodge of Jagslottet, built in 1898, and now the residence of the park secretariat. The old 18th-century farm houses of Øvre and Nedre Strandkær now house research and a visitors center.

of all Danish plant species. Common ivy climbs the trees, and the spotted woodpecker finds lots of hollowed-out trunks to call home.

The Ahl Plantation has a coastal forest of mountain pine, oak, and birch planted adjacent to its salt marshes in the 19th century. The green woodpecker thrives here, feasting on ant heaps in the forest. The park's northward shores attract foraging gulls and wading birds such as lapwing, curlew, oystercatcher, and ringed plover. Otters make their homes in the Stubbe and Lange Lakes in the northern reaches of the park. Wherever you walk, you may come across fox, hare, roe deer, and reptiles such as lizards and vipers.

The park has plenty of walking trails, one of the more bracing being a coastal stroll to the Jernhatten (The Iron Hat), a lookout onto the Kattegat sea. This cliff towers some 161 feet (49 m) above the waves. The trail also passes through the beechwood stands of Troldeskoven (Troll Forest) and onward to the hills of Hyllested Bjerge, the forest of Bagskoven, and down to the beach. If you can, bring a snorkel and the seafloor will be revealed to you as a stony reef with an extensive kelp forest known as the Blak. You may even be joined by some of the harbor porpoises that patrol this coast.

SKJOLDUNGERNES LAND

Denmark's newest park celebrates many ancient legends.

Skjoldungerne was Denmark's first royal dynasty, ruling from the royal seat of Lejre. Their domain, Skjoldungernes Land National Park, celebrates this ancient legacy as a national park.

The park's focal point is the jagged coastline around Roskilde Fjord, with inland landscapes of river valleys, meadows, lakes, marshes, and several woodlands, of which Bidstrup Forests is the largest. Its mix of hardwood and coniferous stands were granted to citizens by King Frederick III for sacrifices made during the Siege of Copenhagen of 1659.

Historical relics from the Stone Age and Iron Age are scattered throughout the park, alongside longhouses and stone ships built by the Vikings. These ancient stone ships were in fact burial sites, and their presence near the older burial mounds is a strong indication that Danes have considered this royal realm a sacred ground for millennia.

Begin your visit at Lejre Museum, which hosts a large Viking burial ship, the Margrethe Stone, and the unexcavated burial mounds of Grydehøj, Hyldehøj, Ravnshøj, and Harald Hildetandshøj. A few miles away is the 5,000-year-old Øm Passage Grave.

If you want to fully immerse yourself and your family in Danish history, the Maritimt Forsøgscenter (Maritime Research Centre) offers expert-led excursions on Viking ships. All who sign up will be expected to pull their weight in a voyage around the fjord and the preserved peninsula of Bognæs.

For landlubbers, many great trails cross the park, including a hike through Bidstrup Forests that is excellent for bird-watchers, and bike routes along the fjord. Another fine trail links the three natural landmarks of Særløse Overdrev, an ancient grassland still grazed by cattle; Bøllesø, an ancient excavated peat bog that hosts many amphibians; and the forest lake of Avnsø, where locals swim in the clear waters year-round.

Vikings & Icelandic Sagas

A visit to the Viking Ship Museum in the medieval city of Roskilde is a must-see for its five ancient ships, excavated from the fjord in 1962. In summer, you can learn the ancient Viking shipbuilding skills of carving and whittling in the museum laboratory. You can also volunteer to help sail a replica ship on the fjord. Here too, you'll learn of the Icelandic sagas, the oldest literature of Europe. From these seafaring tales, we know that Skjoldunge royalty reigned from this place known today as Skjoldungernes Land.

A replica of an ancient Viking ship sails the park's waterways.

AT A GLANCE

A legendary legacy ▪ 65.6 square miles (170 sq km) ▪ Roskilde Fjord ▪ The Viking Ship Museum ▪ eng.nationalparkskjoldungernesland.dk

THY

Mossy woodlands, deer herds, marshes, and surfing beaches

Downy birch trees and a green sheen of moss adorn the trails of Thy National Park.

Having inspired the world's largest national park in Northeast Greenland since 1974, the very Danish ideal of collective environmental responsibility finally came home to roost in northwest Jutland when Thy became the first national park on the Danish mainland. This was a fine choice of venue as its dunes, woodlands, and heath landscapes reflect much of the terrain of the overall Danish peninsula and islands. The park also cradles much of the flora and fauna found throughout the rest of this small northern country.

Thy stretches for 34 miles (55 km) along the windblasted coasts and dunes of western Denmark, some of which are covered by heaths and meadows. Conifer trees and marram grass were planted long ago to keep the sand in place, and red deer now graze around the coniferous forests. Small bogs, ponds, and lakes attract a vibrant birdlife, and limestone cliffs along the coastline are evidence that this area constituted the Littorina Sea in Stone Age times.

ENVIRONMENTAL ROLE

The national park fulfills a vital role that has long preoccupied Danish coast dwellers: to fight the drift of sands blown inland by the North Sea gales. Invasive flora can cause havoc to the dunes. Although deer are useful for grazing much of the excess vegetation, trees are sometimes uprooted, and controlled burning is carried out occasionally by park authorities to restore balance to the sandy heaths.

The dunes provide a rich ecosystem for a range of plants such as common heather, sand sedge, marram grass, black crowberries, and bell heather, as well as various lichens. Among the birds that breed in Thy's sandy heaths are the crane and the wood sandpiper. These find food in the multitudes of insects buzzing around the bogs and ponds, which are also inhabited by the natterjack toad and other amphibians.

Plants such as bog bilberry, bayberry, marsh gentian, cranberry, and sundew also thrive in the wetlands of Thy. Many edible plants grow in the park, including blackberries, sea buckthorns, or the sea kale often found on the beaches. The yellow flowering Scots lovage herb is protected, however, and if you see it growing in rocky crevices remember that its parsleylike leaves should not be picked.

In the north of the park lies the wildlife reserve of Hanstholm

Vildtreservat, which closes from April to mid-July, when the birds are breeding. Many rare or endangered birds are protected here, such as the European golden plover, which breeds nowhere else in Denmark—listen for its melancholy, extended whistle *plu-i-vii*.

Rare and endangered plants also thrive in the lakes and ponds of Hansholm Vildtreservat, including the water lobelia, quillwort, several species of chara, and the very rare slender naiad, a wispy water plant also known as Nodding waternymph.

Since 2009, several sightings of wolves have been reported around Thy and Hansholm Vildtreservat. Our lupine friends had not been seen in Denmark since they were hunted to extinction in Denmark in 1813. In fall 2012, a wolf carcass was found, thought to have strayed from the Lausitz region in Sachsen, Germany, and current numbers within the park are still uncounted. Farmers might demur, but the return of the wolf to such outlying parts of Europe as Thy is a success story for environmental cooperation across the continent.

THE HUMAN FOOTPRINT

The presence of humankind—from the Stone Age up to the modern Danish age of Roligan man (supporters of the Danish national football team)—is found in Thy. The park is dotted with dolmens, burial mounds, kitchen middens, and evidence of flint weaponry production. Bronze Age, Iron Age, Viking age, and medieval cultures are all visibly imprinted on the landscape, but a historic gap in the layers of history suggests that at some point in the Middle Ages the sands started to win the battle against agricultural land and the Danes moved inland, not reclaiming the landscape until the 19th century. From the 20th century, ugly German bunkers of World War II still scar the coastline as Thy was an important link in Hitler's Atlantic Wall, a bulwark against the Allied marine forces. In the true Danish spirit of recycling

Fireweed, a lure for bees and hummingbirds, lights up a meadow by night.

and remembrance, five of these huge concrete bunkers within the park have now been restored and converted into WWII museums or memorials.

WALKS & ACTIVITIES

Follow one of several hiking trails to the Hansholm Lighthouse. Built in 1843, this was once the world's most powerful lighthouse, and from here today visitors can enjoy its spectacular views over the northern part of Thy National Park and of the North Sea. Stay on the trail through the lighthouse garden next to the old coastal cliff, where you will gain a great view of Hansholm Nature Reserve and down along the dunes and coastline. Alternatively, take the yellow hiking trail that climbs steeply up the old coastal slope to Isbjerg, a tough workout, but worth it for the view. This is Hansholm's highest point of 184 feet (56 m)—high enough to appreciate the range of protected land and to peer down as far as Nors Lake to the south. The lake has a perfect bathing area, sheltered from the winds by woods and filled with crystal clear groundwater filtered through its limestone floor. As the lake is part of the nature reserve, sailing and windsurfing are prohibited. However, the beach at nearby Klitmøller is one of Europe's best spots for windsurfing and surfing. Surf schools will teach you how to ride the wild waves of the windy North Sea.

VADEHAVET (WADDEN SEA)

Tidal ebb and flow attended by multitudinous birdlife

It's a very elemental expedition, especially if you go barefoot: The cold saltwater of the North Sea washes around your ankles as the tide recedes and soon you're walking on a seafloor of silty brown sand—where you get a completely different kind of bird's-eye view. This is what 10 to 12 million birds experience as they wing in for dinner at the Vadehavet (Wadden Sea) National Park. On the menu tonight? How about some cockles for starters, with shrimp or crabs (if you can catch them) for the main course, and worms or sea snails for dessert? The mudflats of Denmark's west coast, in southwestern Jutland, are never short of marine delicacies, and multitudes of geese, waders, terns, and gulls stop here for their evening buffet and then go rest in the salt marshes or dunes nearby.

If you like bird-watching, you might never want to leave this national park. The numbers here are astonishing, and an avian cacophony usually greets visitors. Top billing goes to the park's undoubted star, the European starling. Walk close to the marshes around dusk in spring or fall, and you'll witness one of nature's great displays of synchronized flight. Hundreds of thousands of European starlings ebb and flow across the backdrop of a darkening sky in improvised formations that defy explanation. The wondrous waves of these agile little birds leave crowds gathered below open-mouthed in awe until they funnel down to rest in the marshes for the night. The Danes call this avian phenomenon *sort sol* or "black sky" but it's more like an invisible hand brushing a series of painterly strokes onto a fading canvas and erasing repeatedly.

WALKS & ACTIVITIES

This national park is very accessible, especially if you stay in the ancient town of Ribe, dating from A.D. 700. Ansgar, a missionary monk from Hamburg, founded the cathedral here in the Viking era, the first Christian church in Denmark. This oft disputed edifice is worth visiting for its amazing mishmash of architectural styles, which reflect its troubled history. The Wadden Sea Centre, six miles (10 km) southwest of Ribe, is a great place to get details of bird-watching, seal spotting, or mudflat tours. Check out the center's exhibition, styled as a journey through the Wadden Sea landscape from the perspective of the masses of migratory birds. In the off-season, try an oyster safari, when you can comb mussel beds for shellfish and shuck your own Pacific oysters, eating your fill with the salty sea breeze in your hair.

Always check the tides as there is a difference of 6.5 feet (2 m) between high tide and low tide. The park employs rangers to help you around the mudflats. They also lead guided five-mile (8-km) walks to the island of Mandø, where you can rent bikes for the six-mile (10-km) trail around the island. The mussel beds here are worth a visit and you can view the dikes and polders that are a reminder of Denmark's never ending battle with the North Sea. You're sure to spot some seals on the sandbanks too. You can take the easy way home after your day's exertions, with a bus from the visitors center to Mandø.

The island of Rømø has a causeway connecting it to the mainland, enabling visitors to drive over and rent horses for a ride on the beach or go kite buggying across the sands.

The park's other main island, Fanø, is a 15-minute ferry ride from Esbjerg. Here you can enjoy lunch at the thatched-roof inn called Sønderho Kro, which dates from 1722. Or stay the night in a room with a view of the Wadden Sea.

Back in Ribe, round off your visit with a guided Night Watchman Tour over the old cobbled streets and learn of the millennium-plus history of this charming town.

Greylag geese fly near Mandø Island, with Ribe Cathedral visible.

AT A GLANCE

Mudflat walks ▪ Oyster safaris ▪ 566 square miles (1,466 sq km) ▪ Ancient Ribe ▪ Birding ▪ eng.nationalparkvadehavet.dk

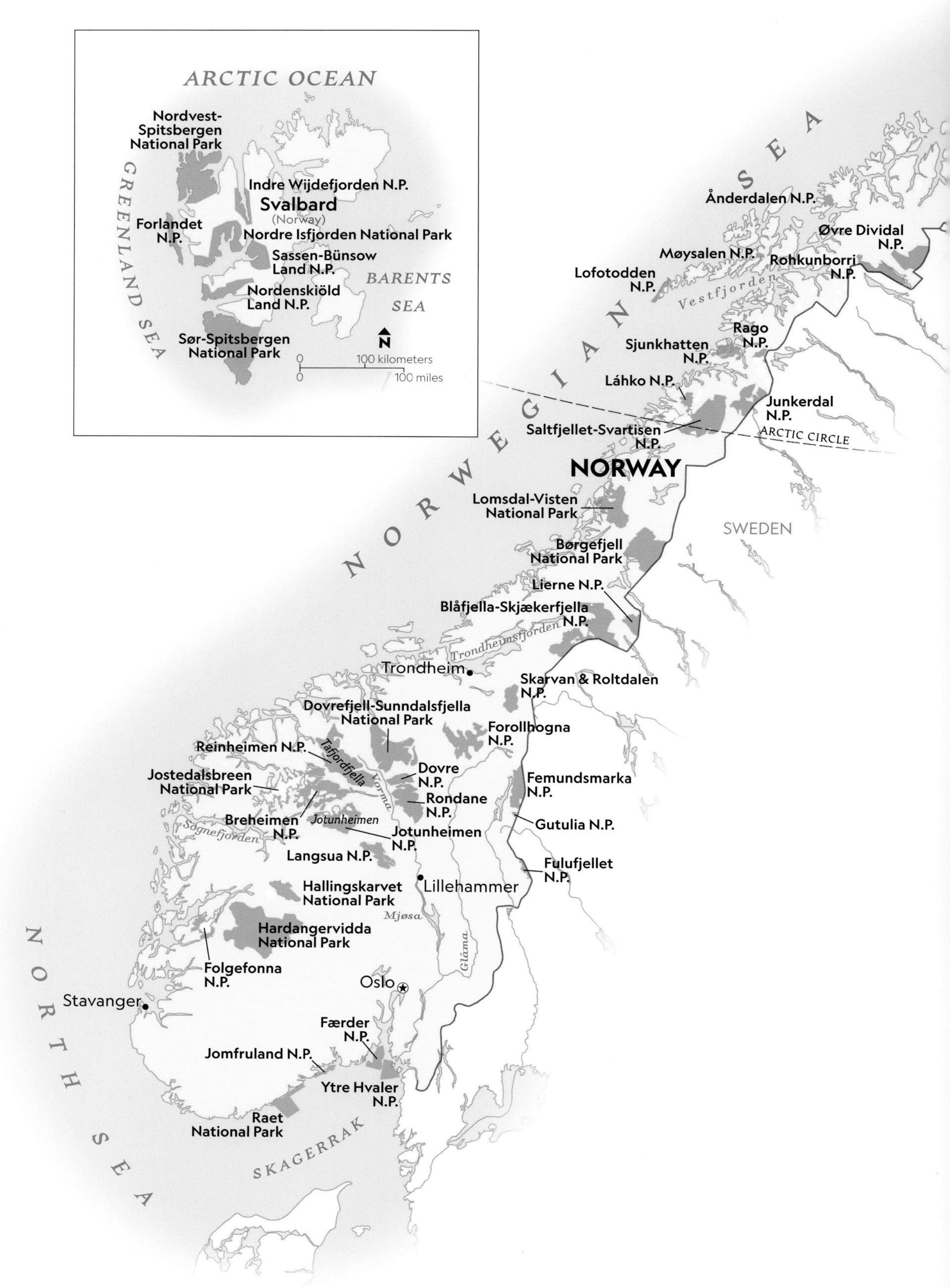

ARCTIC OCEAN

Nordvest-
Spitsbergen
National Park

GREENLAND SEA

Indre Wijdefjorden N.P.
Svalbard
(Norway)

Forlandet
N.P.

Nordre Isfjorden National Park

Sassen-Bünsow
Land N.P.

BARENTS
SEA

Nordenskiöld
Land N.P.

Sør-Spitsbergen
National Park

N

0   100 kilometers
0   100 miles

NORWEGIAN SEA

Ånderdalen N.P.

Øvre Dividal
N.P.

Møysalen N.P.

Rohkunborri
N.P.

Lofotodden
N.P.

Vestfjorden

Rago
N.P.

Sjunkhatten
N.P.

Láhko N.P.

Junkerdal
N.P.

ARCTIC CIRCLE

Saltfjellet-Svartisen
N.P.

NORWAY

Lomsdal-Visten
National Park

SWEDEN

Børgefjell
National Park

Lierne N.P.

Blåfjella-Skjækerfjella
N.P.

Trondheimsfjorden

Trondheim

Skarvan & Roltdalen
N.P.

Dovrefjell-Sunndalsfjella
National Park

Forollhogna
N.P.

Reinheimen N.P.

Tafjordfjella

Dovre
N.P.

Femundsmarka
N.P.

Jostedalsbreen
National Park

Breheimen
N.P.

Jotunheimen

Rondane
N.P.

Gutulia N.P.

Sognefjorden

Jotunheimen
N.P.

Langsua N.P.

Fulufjellet
N.P.

Hallingskarvet
National Park

Lillehammer

Mjøsa

Hardangervidda
National Park

Glåma

Folgefonna
N.P.

Oslo ✪

Stavanger

Færder
N.P.

NORTH SEA

Jomfruland N.P.

Ytre Hvaler
N.P.

Raet
National Park

SKAGERRAK

The mountains of Jotunheimen National Park offer hikers numerous memorable routes.

NORWAY

Situated at the top of Europe, the country of Norway, which translates as "the Way to the North," is a place apart. Much of the country lies within the Arctic Circle, and the resulting long summers of Midnight Sun are as discombobulating to many visitors as its long, dark winters. Then there is the nighttime solar spectacle of the northern lights. Add to this the sheer overwhelming beauty of much of the landscape, and visitors cannot help but be impacted. Fjords banked by mountains rise steeply and suddenly out of clear blue water all along the western coast of Norway, interspersed with spectacular waterfalls roaring down the rock cliffs. Including the fjords, Norway's coastline stretches for more than 12,500 miles (20,000 km), linking picturesque towns like a never ending string of pearls. Inland, a spine of mountains runs down this long, thin country, their presence giving rise to extreme weather systems. Marked trails and rudimentary overnight cabins are available in many parks by the Norwegian Trekking Association (Den Norske Turistforening, or DNT). The Svalbard Islands, an Arctic Ocean archipelago halfway between mainland Norway and the North Pole, is as far north as you can go in Europe, a remote icescape of glaciers, walrus, and polar bears. Norway's 47 national parks, seven of them in Svalbard, encapsulate all this beautiful wilderness as they lead you along the Way to the North.

ÅNDERDALEN

A Sami stronghold on Norway's second largest island

The original, indigenous people of Norway are the Sami a population whose herding grounds stretched from northern Norway across parts of Sweden, Finland, and into Russia. In Norway, they survived by fishing off northern coastlines, fur trapping, and seminomadic reindeer herding, the last of which they still practice. One stronghold of Sami culture is the island of Senja in Troms county. Ånderdalen National Park was established here in 1970, with a view to preserving the Sami legacy, as well as the landscapes they had lived off for centuries.

The park is an important calving and grazing area for semidomesticated reindeer, a tradition the Sami long ago embraced. Elk populations have increased over recent decades

Reindeer (Rangifer tarandus) *thrive on the island of Senja.*

too. The largest species of deer, called "elk" in Europe, is what North Americans commonly refer to as moose (with what are know as red deer in Europe a cousin to what is called elk in North America).

The park nurtures a wealth of smaller animals such as red foxes, stoats, hares, and two species of shrews, tiny mole-like creatures. Otters thrive in the rivers, which teem with trout, salmon, and char. Seals are a commonplace sight along the shoreline of the fjords.

The landscapes embrace many pine and birch forests, and many alpine plants grow in the relatively temperate climate. The national park has several trails around the island, a particularly fine trek being the 4.6-mile (7.5-km) walk to Åndervatnet Lake. This trail starts at the public parking lot across from Norwegian Wild campground, along Route 860 on the Senja's southern coast and takes you across marsh and woodland to this beautiful lake. Cabins and picnic resting areas are provided along many of the park's trail, and less than a mile past the lake, at Åndergammen, you'll find a restored traditional Sami hut.

The Sami

The indigenous Sami people have inhabited northwestern Norway for generations. In the 15th and 16th centuries, Norwegian farmers migrated north and began to colonize Sami lands, an expansion the Norwegian government later encouraged. The Sami—at the time reindeer hunters—soon switched to reindeer herding, leading them into a nomadic way of life as they moved their herds across northern Scandinavia. The advent of national borders constricted this migratory way of life, and the Sami have slowly become absorbed into modern Norwegian life. Although three Sami dialects are still spoken within the country, the language has started to recede, particularly in coastal areas, as the homogenizing effects of technology and globalization are felt. However, you may still hear one of these Sami dialects while traveling in Ånderdalen National Park.

AT A GLANCE

Fjord and forest landscapes ▪ 48 square miles (125 sq km) ▪ Senja Island ▪ Sami culture
▪ nasjonalparkstyre.no/Anderdalen

BLÅFJELLA-SKJÆKERFJELLA

Sami reindeer herds in one of Norway's largest remaining wildernesses

The third largest park in mainland Norway, Blåfjella-Skjækerfjella National Park contains several Sami settlements, gathering places, burial sites, and sacred places, all of which should be approached with respect. There are also some reindeer grazing areas where herds are tended; these are the Skjækerfjella and the Luru reindeer pasture districts. Centralized control of the national park areas has not always been met with complete approval of the Sami people, especially when land-use restrictions were implemented, and tensions between the Sami and authorities have simmered in the past in this northern stronghold of the Sami people.

EXPLORING THE PARK

The landscape of the reserve is a northern Norwegian mix of mountains, mountain plains, lakes, forested valleys, and marshes. The hunting and fishing grounds that long sustained the indigenous Sami now attract visitors to the park, who come to shoot ptarmigan, grouse, and other woodland birds, and to fish for brown trout and char in the clear mountain lakes. Elk (moose) hunting is also permitted in some parts. Like in many Norwegian parks, overnight stays are accommodated within a limited number of mountain cabins. The park's trekking association rents out these self-catering cabins (called Skjækerdalshytta) and some mountain farms (named Holden Fjellgård) for those planning multiday escapes into the wilderness. Several private owners also offer wooden rustic cabins such as those at Svartbakken Hytter, which are rudimentary with no electricity or running water—but obtaining freshwater in Norway has never been a problem. These accommodations offer basic self-catering shelter and access into the heart of wonderful countryside for hiking, fishing, and that most Norwegian of outdoor activities, cross-country skiing. Note that the hiking trails disappear in winter, and at any time of year, a visit to the national park visitors center is advisable for maps and other information before heading off into the great Norwegian beyond.

Blåfjella-Skjækerfjella has its own special place in the history of Norwegian forestry, as the region was the first to introduce the spruce tree to Norway. Areas of old-growth forest still exist in the valleys, but these are hard pines mainly. The rare arctic fox preys in the woods and the plains, as do brown bear, lynx, wolverines, and grey wolves. Elk (moose), roe deer, and red deer are among the larger animals of the park, which sustains four adjacent nature reserves: Arvasslia Nature Reserve, Berglimyra and Klumplifjellet Nature Reserve, Gaundalsmyra Nature Reserve, and Storfloa Nature Reserve.

Park lakes, such as Eldbekkskardvatnet, teem with trout and char.

BØRGEFJELL

Where the Sami herd reindeer and lakes teem with trout

A litter of curious arctic fox cubs take in their homeland of Børgefjell National Park.

The rugged and remote wilderness of Børgefjell National Park, opened in 1963, is mainly a nature reserve with a few tough trails. It is located in the extreme northern reaches of North Trøndelag and Norrland, and shares a border with Sweden. This park is for serious trekkers rather than casual hikers, and is a haven for those who want to spend several days fishing the lakes for trout or char. The scree-covered slopes and granite peaks of Kvigtinden (5,574 ft/1,699 m) and Jetnamsklumpen (4,964 ft/1,513 m) typify much of the subglacial moraine landscape here.

Birch-carpeted valleys, marshlands, and vibrant waterways are nature's stage for a cast of big-name predators: European brown bear, lynx, wolverines, and elk (moose) stalk the land, while golden eagles, rough-legged buzzards, and snowy owls hunt from the skies. The arctic fox, Norway's most endangered animal, is also on the prowl here, along with smaller mammals such as the red fox, the snow weasel, and the stoat. The bigger predators are a nuisance to the Sami herders who have kept reindeer in the area for at least 500 years. The park is also a reindeer border crossing for migrating herds

from Sweden. Several Sami cultural monuments are found in the park.

About 300 plant species are known to grow in Børgefjell, despite the stony soil. Anglers supplement their trout supper with some of the chanterelle and porcini mushrooms that sprout around the trails in late summer, or pick a nutritious dessert from the cloudberries, blueberries, and crowberries on the mountain slopes.

The isolated village of Røyrvik is the gateway to Børgefjell National Park, and maps of the park may be bought at the Tourist Information Office in Mosjøen.

AT A GLANCE

A rugged backcountry ▪ Trout lake fishing ▪ 559 square miles (1,448 sq km) ▪ Migrating reindeer herds ▪ wild-norway.com/destination/royrvik-borgefjell-national-park

BREHEIMEN

An archaeological mystery in a soaring mountain park

Breheimen National Park borders three other national parks but stands tall as a mountain preserve of towering peaks. Hestbreapiggan, Tverrådalskyrkja, and Holåtinden all rise within the park, which also encompasses the glaciers of Harbardsbreen, Spørteggbreen, and Holåbreen, vast reservoirs of ice nestled in the Norwegian heartland. With its barren mountains, huge glaciers, lush valleys, and working dairy farms, Breheimen is one of the most varied national parks in the country.

In the summer of 2011, the ice gave up a secret it had kept for more than 17 centuries. A well-preserved man's coat was found in a glacier that had melted due to climate change. The coat dates back to A.D. 300, making it the oldest piece of clothing ever found in Norway. The warmer weather caused by rising temperatures has provided archaeologists and museums with other opportunities to find artifacts dating back centuries. Many of these, including the coat, date back to Roman times and are on display at the Museum of Cultural History in Oslo. Other finds in the region include containers that may have been used as bags, a wooden spade, horseshoes, arrows, and several arrowheads. Humankind has inhabited this area since the Stone Age, leaving many cultural treasures behind; look in the Breheimen region for *stavkirke* or stave churches, dating back almost 1,000 years. These wooden churches, a curious mix of Christian and Norse design, are easily identified by their multiple roofs.

The park offers visitors opportunities for hiking, skiing, glacier walking, and summit tours with local experts. As in the country's other national parks, the Norwegian Trekking Association (DNT) maintains a series of well-marked trails and several self-serviced and staffed cabins within the national park.

Route 55 leads travelers across mountainous Norway on one of Europe's great drives.

AT A GLANCE

Harbardsbreen, Spørteggbreen, and Holåbreen glaciers ▪ 645 square miles (1,671 sq km) ▪ Marked hiking trails ▪ nasjonalparkriket.no/en/destinations/breheimen

DOVRE

The passageway to the north and the real Norway

Dovre National Park lies between the two larger and older parks of Rondane and Dovrefjell-Sunndalsfjella. From ancient times, Norwegians have seen Dovrefjell, the mountainous region around the park, as the borderlands between the southern and northern parts of Norway. This is where the Road to the North starts, leading to what some call the "real Norway." The road over the mountain has long been a well-known pilgrim trail.

Just as the English believe that their empire will fall when the Royal ravens fly away from the Tower of London, Norwegians believe the end of the world will occur when these great mountains fall. The expression *til Dovre faller* ("until the Dovre mountains fall apart") is still often heard, as it was in 1814, when the constitutional assembly at Eidsvoll declared itself "United and loyal until the mountains of Dovre crumble."

ANIMAL ENCOUNTERS

Like both its neighboring parks, Dovre is the home of wild Fennoscandian reindeer herds of Beringia origin. The park is also home to wolverines, arctic fox, and the real rock star of the park, impressive musk oxen. These

The male musk ox emits a strong odor during the seasonal rut.

huge beasts died out in Norway sometime during the last ice age, but were reintroduced from Greenland between 1932 and 1953. The herd continues to thrive in the cold and dry climate of Dovrefjell. Hikers can follow the marked Musk Ox Trail from Kongsvoll or Grønbakken, a stretch where sightings of these long-haired prehistoric mammals are plentiful. But always remember: If musk oxen feel threatened, they may attack. If you see them on or near a trail, give them a very wide (and slowly walked) berth, keeping at least several hundred feet between you and these beautiful but fierce animals.

Various large birds of prey such as the golden eagle, gyrfalcon, and rough-legged buzzard soar high among these rugged peaks, as do ravens (unlike their clipped-winged cousins in the Tower of London). The park's spectacular landscape consists of a multitude of plateaus and mountains, and most of the park lies above the tree line. With several peaks soaring above 5,577 feet (1,700 m), the scenery in the higher mountains is Arctic in character, with traces of permafrost. Yet here you can also find alpine flora thriving amid the calcareous rocks: These include several rare species, such as the wild grass *Poa lindebergii*, alpine harebell, and *Papaver radicatum*, a subspecies of arctic poppy, recognizable by its yellow flower and black stigma.

The Pilgrim's Route

Norway's best traveled pilgrimage takes you on a road that cuts through Dovre National Park. The Pilgrim's Route or *Pilegrimsleden*—also known as St. Olav's Way or the Old Kings' Road—takes believers from Oslo to Nidaros Cathedral in Trondheim, site of the medieval tomb of St. Olav. The Pilgrim's Route is approximately 400 miles (640 km), and it passes through several scenic parts of the park between Budsjord at Dovre and Fokstugu on Dovrefjell. This path has superb views of the valley of Gudbrandsdalen and three of Norway's best known mountain massifs: Jotunheimen, Rondane, and Snøhetta. The trail follows in the footsteps of the first king of Norway, the great Viking leader Harald Fairhair (850–933), who crossed Dovrefjell with an army of Norse warriors at the end of the ninth century.

Arctic mountains ▪ 112 square miles (289 sq km) ▪ Wild reindeer herds ▪ The Pilgrim's Route
▪ nasjonalparkriket.no/en/destinations/dovre

DOVREFJELL-SUNNDALSFJELLA

Norway's signature mountains beckon climbers, hikers, and skiers.

To the northwest in Dovrefjell-Sunndalsfjella National Park are contrasting landscapes of high peaks and waterfalls, with rolling mountains and dry climate to the east. At 7,500 feet (2,286 m), Snøhetta is the park's tallest peak, and the waterfall at Åmotan its longest cascade, falling some 512 feet (156 m). You can enjoy a fine view of Snøhetta and learn of the region's history and wildlife at the Norwegian Wild Reindeer Centre Pavilion at Tverrfjellet.

The park has similar flora and fauna to that of Dovre National Park (see page 155), including herds of wild reindeer. These timid creatures have roamed the mountains of Norway since the ice melted after the last ice age, and mankind has hunted and herded them ever since. The park was established in 2002, as an expanded version of the former Dovrefjell National Park, to preserve its alpine ecosystem, and to protect a vital habitat for the populations of wild reindeer in Snøhetta and Knutshø. Other key inhabitants of the park are arctic foxes. Although plentiful a century ago, these white-coated creatures went extinct here around 1990, but since 2010 a reintroduction program has proved successful.

The park has many hiking and biking trails, with cabins along the way. Climbing Snøhetta is a major draw—take the path from Hjerkinn to Snøheim or ask a guide at the visitors center for alternative trails. A guided musk ox safari is a popular excursion in summer.

FÆRDER

A coastal park close to Tønsberg, Norway's oldest city

Step into World's End, the visitors center for Færder National Park, one of two Norwegian marine parks. The rotunda provides panoramic views of this protected area, with its fjord landscapes, islands, rocks, and skerries. Færder encompasses much of the archipelago of Bolærne, as well as the 141-foot-tall (43-m) Færder Lighthouse and the ruins of Store Færder Lighthouse. The visitors center also aids with guided nature walks and boat trips.

The old-style lighthouse made of rocks

The park facilitates all manner of marine sports—including sailing, kayaking, rowing, kitesurfing, windsurfing, snorkeling, and diving. Kayaks can be rented at World's End, and boats at Sandøsund. Hikers should look for rare plants such as cow wheat, yellow horned poppy, and strawberry clover, with its distinctive pink blossoms. Vestbukta Bay on Vestre Bustein is the only place in Norway where sand timothy grows, but all kinds of mushroom and algae thrive in the national park. Look especially for the critically endangered Glanville fritillary butterfly.

FEMUNDSMARKA

Fishermen and falconers flock to the lakelands of eastern Norway.

Birch trees are mirrored in many of Femundsmarka's waterways.

The landscapes of Femundsmarka National Park are largely filled with marshes and lakes. This is fitting, as the park's name reflects its proximity to Femund, Norway's second largest natural lake. Canoeing and fishing are the major draws of this preserve, established in 1971 to protect the lake as well as the sparse pine and birch forests that run east to Sweden. When combined with the adjacent woodlands and lake areas on the Swedish side of the national park, Femundsmarka constitutes one of the largest wildernesses in southern Scandinavia.

FASCINATING FALCONRY

A habitat for many smaller birds, the park has also enjoyed a long history of falconry, a sport more usually associated with Asian and Arabian locales. Look for the areas marked as Falkfangarhøgda, or "falcon hunters' height." Falcons are magnificent, intelligent birds that can be trained to hunt the many rodents that inhabit the forests, such as voles.

Wild reindeer grazing is a common sight in the highlands. In summer, a herd of musk oxen roam the area along the Røa and Mugga Rivers, a splinter group from the herd in the Dovrefjell region. Other inhabitants of Femundsmarka include elk (moose), lynx, and wolverine, as well as brown bear. Wolves occasionally wander through these parklands too.

FINE FISHING

Freshwater fish are what most visitors come to pursue in these lovely lakelands, and the species they catch are many: Trout, perch, grayling, whitefish, burbot, and pike all thrive in these lakes. The lakes of Grøtåa, Mugga, Røa, and Rogen are particularly known for their trout. The Revlingsjøan lakes, and those of Røvollfjellet and Engerdal, are popular for ice fishing in winter.

Anglers should remember that permits are required to fish the lakes and rivers of Femundsmarka, and certain regulations apply, all of which can be found online or at either of the park's visitors centers in Røros at Doktortjønna or in Elgå. The rivers are protected from the start of September up to mid-November to facilitate spawning season, and in some areas, a minimum size for catches of certain species is imposed to protect the young. In Røa, for example, the minimum size for trout is 10 inches (25 cm).

The park has several good trails for hikers and many mountains that are worth climbing for their vistas of glacier-carved lakelands. The highest peak is in Storvigelen, standing at 5,121 feet (1,561 m), at the northern entrance of the park. In the south end of the park is Store Svukuen at 4,642 feet (1,415 m), Grøthogna at 4,596 feet (1,401 m), and Elgåhogna at 4,790 feet (1,460 m).

AT A GLANCE

Lakeland scenery ▪ 221 square miles (573 sq km) ▪ Femund Lake ▪ Freshwater fishing
▪ visitnorway.com/listings/femundsmarka-national-park/5349

FOLGEFONNA

Norway's glacial landscapes glitter in this pristine peninsula park.

Folgefonna National Park opened in 2005 to celebrate and protect the glaciers within the borders of this spectacular preserve on the southern shore of the Hardangerfjorden. Folgefonna is the name given to the peninsula that encompasses these natural wonders, and it is also the collective term for the three main glaciers, Nordre Folgefonna, Midtre Folgefonna, and Søndre Folgefonna.

GLACIAL LIFE

The higher reaches of the park are a harsh habitat for animals and plants, and, among avians, the glaciers remain the realm of ptarmigans—a gamebird in the grouse family. Golden eagles nest in the valleys and hunt the ptarmigans in the glacial heights. Meadow pipits also thrive above the tree line.

The forests are known mainly for their large populations of red deer, which are heavily hunted. Black grouse and capercaillie also inhabit the pine forests. Avalanches roaring down from the mountains leave many dead trees in the park, and these make ideal habitats for the distinctive white-backed woodpecker. Folgefonna is one of the last refuges in western Europe for this bird, the largest of the spotted woodpeckers. Their decline has caused much concern among Nordic conservationists. You'll recognize this rarity by the white bars across its wings and its reddish cap.

As much of the bedrock around the glaciers is acidic, only hardy plant species such as dwarf willow, common heather, three-leaved rush, and mountain birch survive here. Mossy mountain heather, rufine sedge, and arctic cotton grass are all found on the edge of the glaciers. Purple gentian and mountain queen are among the few flowers to bloom here. Lower down, however, organic farming produces tasty fruits, and berries and mushrooms are free to pick. Locals will tell you that Cistercian monks brought the first apple seeds to Hardanger in the 12th century. During the harvest season, you'll see fruit and berries for sale by the roadside. These stalls are often unattended (farmers are busy people), and transactions are conducted via a system that the Cistercians would have approved of . . . the old-fashioned honesty bowl.

EXPLORING THE PARK

The Folgefonn visitors center in the village of Rosendal offers interactive exhibitions on the park and on the aquatic life in the Hardangerfjorden. It also educates visitors on the Earth's water cycle, sustainable use of resources, and climate change. The park offers a range of expert-led "blue ice" trips across the glaciers, and many hiking trails (see sidebar), as well as activities such as glacier kayaking. The advice to visitors is to use common sense: The glacier ice is anywhere between 980 to 1,300 feet thick (300 to 400 m)—so dress for stress, not to impress. And as this area endures Norway's highest annual level of rainfall (216.5 inches/5,500 mm), bring your waterproof gear.

The water cycle: glaciers, lakes, falls, and rivers

Ancient Trails

Folgefonna National Park has many well-marked trails to explore, and on some, hikers follow in the footsteps of ancient Norwegians. Among these centuries-old pathways are the Keiserstien (Kaiser's Path), named after Kaiser Wilhelm who once walked here; and the Isstien (Ice Path), on which ice was transported down to a dock on the fjord, then transported on boats to supply refrigeration to coastal villages. Elsewhere, hikers follow well-trodden paths on which generations of farmers herded livestock up to higher summer pastures. Whichever trails you take, dress intelligently, and always check the weather forecast before setting out.

Spectacular glaciers ▪ 210 square miles (545 sq km) ▪ Ancient trails ▪ Last of the white-backed woodpeckers ▪ folgefonna.info/en

FOROLLHOGNA

An understated rolling landscape where wild reindeer reign

If you thought Norway was all dramatic mountains and fjords, Forollhogna National Park demonstrates the realm of Norwegian geography and geology that gives rise to the term "the gentle mountains."

Unlike many of its loftier Arctic counterparts, Forollhogna incubates extensive plant life and is an important range for wild reindeer. Large alpine valleys rise toward rolling hills, and centuries of agriculture have nurtured prosperous villages and mountain farms with pasture-

Wild reindeer migrate seasonally.

lands that are used only in summer months. The fall brings the sound of the reindeer hooves as they move down toward the valleys in search of fodder. This is one of Norway's most prolific populations of wild reindeer. Watch for majestic bucks with their magnificent antlers, standing proudly while guarding their herd.

The rich farming heritage of this region makes it a delightful place to village-hop if you are a food lover. Wander here and you'll discover guest farms and restaurants serving traditional Norwegian dishes, such as *kjøttkaker* (meat cakes and creamed vegetables) or *pinnekjøtt* (salted rib of lamb) produced from fresh, local ingredients.

AT A GLANCE

Rolling farmlands ▪ 410 square miles (1,062 sq km) ▪ Wild reindeer ranges ▪ Fine Norwegian food ▪ visitnorway.com/listings/forollhogna-national-park/3492

FULUFJELLET

A cross-border protection of the Fulufjället massif

Fulufjellet National Park is a small preserve located in Trysil, in the far east of Norway. Established in 2012, its eastern extremity overlaps the Swedish border, and the park mirrors the landscapes of Sweden's Fulufjället National Park (see page 198). Both parks preserve the Fulufjället massif. The geography here is dominated by bare mountains and valleys with dense old-growth forest. The heaths of brush, grass, and lichens are unique in Scandinavia's moun-

tains, a result of the absence of grazing reindeer.

The national park is located in an area of Precambrian sandstone, called Trysil sandstone, which has a deep reddish color and is rich in quartz. This rock weathers slowly and produces poor soil, so the plant life, outside of the forests, lacks the diversity of other Norwegian parklands and doesn't attract reindeer.

Practically all the woodland is coniferous Norway spruce and Scots pine. Large tracts of old-growth for-

est produce considerable amounts of deadwood. The west side of Brattfjellet has scattered pine trees of up to 350 years old. These woodlands resemble virgin forest and have a rich diversity of species, with many rare lichens and fungi.

Elk (moose) are common in Fulufjellet, but here the brown bear is king. Large numbers cross over from the parkland in Sweden, and Fulufjellet National Park is now a key habitat for expanding numbers of bears in Norway.

AT A GLANCE

A transborder park with Sweden ▪ The Fulufjället massif ▪ 32 square miles (82.5 sq km) ▪ Rich old-growth forest ▪ Growing bear populations ▪ regjeringen.no, trysil.com

GUTULIA

Norway's smallest national park has primeval forests with old-growth trees.

Established in 1968 to protect one of the last remnants of virgin forest in Norway and its surrounding landscape of rolling hills and bog, Gutulia National Park is a small wonder. It lies close to the much larger Femundsmarka National Park (see page 157) and the twin parks of Fulufjellet National Park (see opposite) and Sweden's Fulufjället National Park (see page 198) to the south. Gutulia has its own unique character and appeal nonetheless.

Although there is only one marked trail, you'll feel well off anyone's beaten path here. The landscape consists of lakes and old-growth forests, dominated by spruce, pine, and birch. Many of the spruce trees are hundreds of years old, and some pines are nearly 500 years old. Think about this: These trees have stood since Elizabeth I ruled England.

Friendly staff can arrange overnight stays in the park's cabins; bring your fishing rod and you might catch trout, grayling, perch, or pike. For dessert, fill a container with wild bilberries, cowberries, and cloudberries. You'll hear lots of birdsong: Birds such as the tree pipit and willow warbler breed in the upland woods. Redstarts, song thrushes, and dunnocks inhabit pinewood. Reed buntings live in the wet areas, while several smaller tarns and wet bogs form habitats for greenshanks and wood sandpipers. At night, don't be surprised to spy the big yellow eyes of a boreal owl.

AT A GLANCE

500-year-old pines ▪ Virgin forest ▪ 8.9 square miles (23 sq km) ▪ Vibrant birdlife ▪ visitnorway.com/listings/gutulia-national-park/2333

HALLINGSKARVET

An ethos of preservation and a Himalayan-inspired hike

Hallingskarvet National Park in central Norway spans the Hallingskarvet plateau and the high mountain region to the west of it. The Vargebreen Glacier is a focus of the preserve, as is the conservation of the wild stocks of Nordfjella reindeer that roam freely around the park. The highest peak in the park is Folarskardnuten, which soars to 6,342 feet (1,933 m) above sea level. The area's unique geological makeup and extreme climate facilitates the growth of several

Hallingskarvet offers great hiking year-round.

endangered species of plants such as whitlow grass and lanceleaf grape-fern.

The park has great trails for hiking in both summer and winter. The terrain goes from gently undulating moors in the south to the high plateau atop the Hallingskarvet. One classic trail takes you 1.8 miles (3 km) from Prestholt up to the summit of Prestholtskarvet at 5,594 feet (1,705 m), the last leg leading up a set of stone steps laid by Sherpas from Nepal. It will test your calf muscles, but the views across Hallingdal and Hardangervidda make it a rewarding climb.

AT A GLANCE

Vargebreen Glacier ▪ Protected plant life ▪ 174 square miles (450 sq km) ▪ Prestholt to Prestholtskarvet Trail ▪ miljodirektoratet.no

HARDANGERVIDDA

Breathtaking fjords, wildlife, and a classic train ride

The high plateau of Hardangervidda is Europe's largest mountain mesa, and a wilderness like none other on Earth. It is also the centerpiece of Norway's largest national park. Every visitor to Norway should cross this great elevated plain on the Oslo to Bergen Railway, to both experience one of the world's great train journeys and to witness the interior of this scenic Scandinavian country. If you have the time, ride the Flåmsbana railway from Myrdal down to Flåm and back up onto the plateau to gain a complete perspective of the sheer scale of Hardangervidda.

It's easy to imagine how this plateau served as an ancient trade route linking eastern and western Norway; the discovery of several hundred nomadic Stone Age settlements is evidence of how long this region has been inhabited. The vast plateau covers an area of about 2,500 square miles (6,500 sq km), and the average elevation is 3,600 feet (1,100 m). As the train travels across this seemingly endless terrain, gaze out on the barren, treeless moorland veined with rivers, lakes, and fast-flowing streams. All this land sits so high above the tree line, the climate here is Arctic. The park hosts the largest reindeer herd in Norway, which migrates across the plateau, moving from winter grazing lands in the east—where lichen is plentiful—to their breeding grounds in the plateau's more fertile west side. Their constant yet tenuous battle for survival was exposed on the night of August 26, 2016, when more than 300 wild reindeers, including 70 calves, were killed by lightning as they gathered in the grasses of the Hardangervidda plateau.

Another park resident not elsewhere seen so far south is the arctic fox. This fox is not a fussy eater, taking whatever is on offer—rodents, fruit, insects, or birds. Snowy owls too thrive in these cold elevations, unbothered by the lack of trees—they make their nests on the ground. Predators such as golden eagles, kestrels, and merlins swirl over the highlands of the park.

Grouse is the most common bird of Hardangervidda and is found everywhere, especially in the birch forests. The grouse has many foes.

Myriad rivers rush through the rocky landscape of this vast national park.

however—among them ravens, crows, and weasels. Foxes seek to steal the eggs and chicks, while falcons and eagles are always a threat. The grouse evades by camouflaging itself, changing its plumage according to the season.

Although the plain may look somewhat desolate out your train window, wild grasses, fungi, lichens, and mosses grow in the alpine climate in the east, and some alpine flowers even thrive in the west.

GEOLOGY

The mountain plateau landscape of Hardangervidda was largely formed by the erosion of mountains and accumulated organic matter, leaving it windswept and desolate. In the Tertiary period, 50 million years ago, a large land mount formed and deep fjords were carved out as a result of glaciers moving east. As the Ice Age continued, the great glaciers grew into one enormous ice cap that covered all of Scandinavia and northern Europe. The last great ice age ended about 75,000 years ago, and most of the glacial ice had melted off by maybe 8,500 years ago. The glaciers we see today formed around 1750, in a brief period of extreme cold.

The ice shaped the landscape and left sedimentary material in the form of moraines and eskers, long gravel ridges that are visible today in the eastern part of the park. In the park's west and northwest are large areas of hard, rocky outcrops without vegetation. These areas were the first to be exposed when the ice melted.

The Oslo to Bergen Railway train climbs to the high Hardangervidda plateau.

VISITOR ACTIVITIES

Eidfjord and Flåm are gateway towns to the park and the park has two visitors centers: the Hardangervidda Natursenter (Nature Centre) in the village of Øvre Eidfjord, and the Hardangervidda Nasjonalparksenter (National Park Centre) at Skinnarbu, near Møsvatnet lake. It's a huge park, with seemingly endless possibilities, so plan your days well, and if traveling by car, prepare to stop often for photos. The park has numerous cycling and hiking routes, several of which are torturously steep. Hardangervidda is a hiking paradise in summer, but consider only July and August as weather the rest of the year is so unpredictable. In the long winter months, ski trails cross all over Hardangervidda, with those around Geilo or Finse best for short treks. Always check the weather, as it can change in a heartbeat, and always head out in warm clothes, with a detailed topographical map and a compass. The park offers three-day crossings of the plateau, which are a great way to leave the crowds behind and really connect with this wilderness. You can also take guided walks to the glacier ice: The Hardangerjøkulen is a great four-hour, 8.5-mile (13.7-km) trek from Finse to the Blåisen Glacier tip of Hardangerjøkulen.

The Vøringsfoss to Kinsarvik Trail via Harteigen is a three-day hike to the mountain of Harteigen, which then descends the 616 stone steps of the Monk's Stairway to Kinsarvik; the 13th-century staircase is the only remaining physical trace of the English monks that founded the Opedal monastery.

The Norwegian Trekking Association maintains a series of excellent hiking paths and cabins connecting Hardangervidda from Haukeliseter and Mogen in the south to Finse in the north, Rjukan and Geilo in the east, and Eidfjord and Odda in the west.

AT A GLANCE

Arctic fauna ▪ Vøringsfoss waterfall ▪ 1,324 square miles (3,430 sq km) ▪ High mountain railway ▪ The Hardangerjøkulen Trail ▪ hardangervidda.com

Trolltunga (Troll's Tongue) cliff, Hardangervidda National Park

JOMFRULAND

A legendary island and surrounding seas make a magical maritime park.

Jomfruland National Park opened in 2016, and consists mainly of marine territories. The park also encompasses the islands of Jomfruland and Stråholmen; local legend has it that Jomfruland rose from the sea and was once inhabited by sea folk.

The park's land consists of dry meadows and open sandy areas, and those of Øitangen and Sandbakken host several rare plants and insects. You'll recognize sea holly, one of the Norwegian coast's rarest plants, by its leathery, waxy leaves. It grows in dry, sandy areas, and is extremely fragile. The endangered ant lion *(Myrmeleon bore)* and the maritime bee *(Osmia maritime)* both nest in the sand dunes. Higher up on the meadows, you'll find blushing waxcap among 10 rare species of fungi. In the protected area of Øitangen is a lush, old-wood forest. In springtime, the forest floor here is carpeted with white wood anemones, with the dead oak trees left to create habitat for a host of insects.

For centuries seaweed was used to fertilize these islands' fields. Rich in vitamins and minerals, seaweed was also used as a feed supplement for the islands' animals. Green grassy areas on otherwise stony beaches are evidence of seaweed harvest in an era before mass-produced agricultural fertilizer.

Look for saltstone headlands with fine, glacially polished gneiss rocks. In the center of Jomfruland stand two lighthouses, offering good vistas. In Øitangen, a bird station beckons to ornithologists.

Vikings named the island of Jomfruland for its composition, aur, *meaning gravel and coarse sand mixed with pebbles.*

AT A GLANCE

Maritime park ▪ Øitangen bird station ▪ 45 square miles (117 sq km) ▪ Jomfruland lighthouses ▪ jomfrulandnasjonalpark.no

JOSTEDALSBREEN

Glaciers and fjords make for a truly Norwegian experience.

Jostedalsbreen is mainland Europe's biggest glacier, and the focal point of this dramatic national park situated at the heart of central Norway's fjord country. The park lies near the towns of Fjaerland and Stryn, and between the popular fjords of Geirangerfjorden and Sognefjorden. Fjaerland is a great base if you're a book lover, as the town is full of bookshops. Also here is the Norwegian Glacier Museum, with interesting exhibits to get you up to speed on how glaciers shaped this land of fjords and other glacial goings-on. You can even touch 1,000-year-old ice.

Once out in the park, sheer rock walls, long ribbons of ice carving through valleys, and the famous fjords make this a quintessential Norwegian national park. Listen for groaning ice as it squeezes its way down the valley. The glacier, which grew for decades, is now shrinking with the effects of global warming, but its bulk still impresses: 309 square miles (800 sq km) of ice that is up to 1,970 feet (600 m) thick, with a highest point of 6,834 feet (2,083 m). The individual glaciers of Nigardsbreen, Briksdalsbreen, Lodalsbreen, Bøyabreen, and Supphellebreen are all part of the wider Jostedalsbreen ice sheet.

FLORA & FAUNA

Although brown bear and red deer roam this region, the animals go largely unseen, as much of this park is inaccessible to visitors. Also here are elk (moose). Look for the large antlers of the male; these

The glacier tongue of Briksdalsbreen

can spread nearly five feet (1.5 m). In fall, listen for the fierce antler duels of red deer stags resounding around the park. The glaciers are the main attraction here, but a hike or kayak through the fjords may yield sightings of foxes, hares, and squirrels on the shoreline.

WALKS & ACTIVITIES

Local tour operators offer hikes and glacier walks, and any of the towns' tourist offices will tell you the options. The shortest glacier hikes take an hour, but you can spend up to five hours on the ice, gazing down into its green-blue beauty. Nigardsbreen is one of the easier glaciers to hike, with a scenic boat ride across Nigardsvatnet lake as a prelude. Glacier hikes run April to September. During winter months, venture inside the Nigardsbreen Glacier to discover an icy blue underworld: This tour involves an hour-long hike to the tip of the glacier on skis or snowshoes, a warming winter meal at the mouth of the cave, then an unforgettable descent into a magical Norwegian realm of ice.

Kayaking in the fjords and the glacial rivers is popular, as it affords a good chance to appreciate the glacial behemoths from afar. Or try white-water rafting on the Jostedalselvi River. Campsites are plentiful, and several tour operators offer kayak and hiking combination trips that camp out near the glaciers. This allows for a memorable night listening to the ice groan as it makes its way, inch by inch down the valley. You'll also hear chunks of ice calving as they fall into the lagoon at the foot of the valley.

Visit the Breheimsenteret Glacier Center at Nigardsbreen for information on all aspects of Jostedalsbreen National Park.

AT A GLANCE

The five glaciers of Jostedalsbreen ice sheet ▪ 506 square miles (1,310 sq km) ▪ Glacier walks ▪ Breheimsenteret Glacier Center ▪ Norwegian Glacier Museum ▪ visitnorway.com/listings /jostedalsbreen-national-park/5160

JOTUNHEIMEN
The Norwegian Home of the Giants

Hikers on the Besseggen trail are rewarded with glorious views of Jotunheimen's mountain lakes.

Since 1862, this high-country wilderness has been known as Jotunheimen, or "home of the giants"; the Norse word for troll or giant is *Jötunn*. The great Norwegian poet, journalist, and romantic nationalist Aasmund Olavsson Vinje first used the term that year, and it still perfectly encapsulates the soaring, jagged peaks, hard gabbro rock massifs, green glacial valleys, and tumbling waterfalls of this soaring mountain kingdom. More than 250 peaks climb above 6,234 feet (1,900 m) in the national park, including northern Europe's two highest peaks: Galdhøpiggen at 8,100 feet (2,469 m) and Glittertinden at 8,087 feet (2,465 m). Here too is the Vettisfossen: At just over 900 feet (275 m), it is Norway's longest single-drop waterfall. Giant country indeed.

HISTORY & CULTURE

A worthwhile historical must-see just outside the park is Lom's 12th-century stave church, a medieval wooden Christian church building once common in much of Scandinavia. The name derives from the building's structure of post-and-lintel construction, a type of timber framing using load-bearing ore-pine posts, called *stafr* in Old Norse (or *stav* in modern Norwegian). Look for the crest with the original dragon's head, one of the few that survive in the country. These stave churches are a physical manifestation of that turning point in Norwegian history when the ancient Norse legends (such as these mountains of the giants) met with the early spread of Christianity to northern Europe. The Christian church adapted many native traditions, and it is easy to imagine persuasive early men of God praising his creative works in such a setting.

The greats of Norwegian literature have also found inspiration in this mountainous region. Henrik Ibsen's Peer Gynt took his treacherous ride down the "Gjendin ridge" on the back of a reindeer stag in Jotunheimen. These days, you can traverse this stunningly beautiful national park by means of the Sognefjellet Road (Rv55), the highest mountain road in northern Europe. Constructed by the unemployed youth of Norway in 1939, this magnificently scenic blacktop links Lom with Lustrafjorden and is one of the great European drives. Note, however, that the road is usually closed between October and April.

FAUNA, FLORA & FISHING

Jotunheimen National Park possesses a rich ecosystem that supports a host of wildlife, including reindeer, elk (moose), roe deer, martens, and Eurasian lynx. Also in evidence is the wolverine, a curious creature. This long and limber member of the weasel family has almost cute, bearlike looks that belie a fierce nature. The wolverine is perhaps the most all-consuming carnivorous link on the Jotunheimen food chain.

Because much of the park lies above the tree line, a majority of its flora is alpine: Hairy stonecrop, alpine catchfly, and alpine rock cress grow well at these higher altitudes. Glacier buttercups are everywhere, visible even high up near the summit of Glittertinden, almost a mile above the tree line. This is the domain of the eagle and the gyrfalcon, both of which ride the mountain thermals in search of prey.

Farther down, the forests of Bøverdalen and Utladalen contain a rich mix of mountain birch, mountain pine, black alder, elm, and hazel. The most alpine landscape is found in the western part of the national park, in the Luster and Årdal areas.

The park is one of Norway's peak destinations for the angling fraternity, and its pristine lakes and rivers teem with the most delicious trout you may ever taste.

WALKS & ACTIVITIES

Jotunheimen National Park offers some of the most scenic hiking anywhere in Europe—from short strolls to multiday hut-to-hut expeditions. The park is only accessible between May and late August, with hiking trails opening in mid-June.

Serious hikers will want to take on the Galdhøpiggen to the top of Norway: This 3.8-mile (6.2-km) hike starts at Spiterstulen and leads past glaciers and cirques to the summit at 5,709 feet (1,740 m). Another famous trail in Jotunheimen is the path to Vettisfossen waterfall. From Øvre Årdal, it travels 7.4 miles (12 km) up the Utladen Valley to the farm Vetti,

Glacier-carved valleys welcome visitors to the "home of the giants."

linking to skiing tracks leading to the stunning free-falling spectacle.

The hiking highlight within this national park (and maybe in all of Norway) is the trail along the narrow Besseggen ridge from Memurubu lodge to Gjendesheim lodge. Views to the south reveal the gorgeous green of Gjendevatnet lake (3,228 ft/984 m above sea level), while to the north you peer over Bessvatnet lake (4,504 ft/ 1,373 m above sea level). Here, you really are traversing the roof of Norway. The 14-mile (22.9-km) Besseggen trek is one of Norway's most popular trails, so expect lots of company.

If you like canine company, several husky operators also guide three- to five-hour dogsledding expeditions into the heart of the park. You can also ski in the summer months: The park's summer ski station sits at 6,070 feet (1,850 m) at the base of Galdhøpiggen. Close to here is the Mímisbrunnr Klimapark and Istunnel, a 230-foot (70-m) ice tunnel with an educational exhibition on the area's natural history and climate change.

The main visitors center for the national park is Norsk Fjellmuseum, located in Lom. The museum offers exhibitions on the park and can set you up with guides for any of the many outdoor activities the park offers. The shop also sells maps of the area and its many trails.

AT A GLANCE

Vettisfossen waterfall ▪ Arctic wildlife ▪ 444 square miles (1,151 sq km) ▪ Lom Stave Church ▪ Excellent skiing and hiking trails ▪ jotunheimen.com

JUNKERDAL

A wondrous landscape reflects the Sami belief in the souls of plants, animals, and places.

Junkerdal National Park is a plant lovers' delight, especially if you want to see rare arctic plants in the wild without going to the Arctic Circle. Opened in 2004, the park lies along Norway's border with Sweden. It offers mainly mountain and meadow landscapes, which foster a rich mix of both alpine and arctic flora, including rare white arctic mountain heather and white mountain saxifrage. Bullrush sedge, snow fleabane, and alpine arnica all thrive in this surprisingly southern habi-

Nordic cross-country skiing

tat. Look too for arctic bellflower and hairy lousewort.

The park's animal wildlife includes eagles, wolverines, lynx, and brown bears stalking the high-

lands, while elk (moose) and reindeer graze the meadows. Rare wetland birds nest here, among them the arctic loon and the long-tailed duck. The red-throated loon is easy to spot in breeding season, when the gray, nondescript bird acquires its namesake distinctive reddish throat patch. The loon's also quite a vocalist, having a range from cackles to long and short calls to wailing calls.

Junkerdal National Park is a Sami area, and the Sami still herd reindeer here.

AT A GLANCE

Arctic and alpine wildflowers ▪ 263 square miles (682 sq km) ▪ Rare aquatic birds ▪ Sami culture ▪ gonorway.com/norway/articles/698

LÁHKO

A karst wonderworld in Norway's marble region

Láhko National Park is a small park with a whole lot of geology. The Nordland region includes some of Norway's finest karst landscapes, and this park offers great caving opportunities. A highlight is Corbels Canyon, where glacial activity has sculpted a series of striated walls around the waters of this limestone valley. Corbels Canyon is a climb of some 1,903 feet (580 m), but worth it for its otherworldly rock formations and the chance

to see the region's famous Kalkspat marble—the same stone that was used to adorn much of the United Nations Building in New York. Rare plants thrive in the limestone landscapes as does charales, green algae that grows in freshwater and brackish environments such as the small pools that form in Láhko's porous limestone cavities. Local companies will take you skiing, hiking, kayaking, cross-country skiing, rappelling, and caving in the park.

The karst caves in Corbels Canyon

AT A GLANCE

Karst landscapes ▪ Caving opportunities ▪ 73 square miles (188 sq km) ▪ Corbels Canyon ▪ miljodirektoratet.no

LANGSUA

A hikers' delight rich in biodiversity

Nestled in central Norway between the valleys of Gausdal and Valdres, Langsua National Park is a small but accessible preserve of gentle landscapes with low mountains, lush mountain birch woodland, old-growth coniferous forests, rolling heathlands, and diverse wetlands. The park's two highest peaks are within the range of most hiking abilities, with Mount Skaget rising to 5,530 feet (1,685 m), and Mount Langsua's summit some 5,095 feet (1,553 m) above sea level.

The park offers plant lovers many trails to pursue: Look for the deep purple and somewhat hairy blossoms of the bearded bellflower, growing far north of its usual European habitats in the Alps and the Carpathians. In the park's lush birch forests, you'll also find purple patches where February daphne and moor-king lousewort thrive. Orchids of many colors complete the alpine picture.

The swamps and wetlands are thick with sedge in flower, including Finnmark sedge, and the peren-nial herb Oeder's lousewort. Snipes, marsh hawks, and cranes come to feast on the rich insect life. In winter, domestic reindeer graze the high ridges, watched over by the rock ptarmigan, while hares and willow ptarmigan are found in lower woods.

The park has many marked trails and DNT huts and cabins for overnighting nature lovers. Hunting and fishing permits, as well as maps and guided tour details, are available from Kittilbu Utmarksmuseum, the visitors center for Langsua.

AT A GLANCE

Gentle hiking ▪ 207 square miles (537 sq km) ▪ Old-growth coniferous forests ▪ Kittilbu Utmarksmuseum ▪ valdres.com

LIERNE

Ice Age Norway beckons outdoor adventurers.

Another mountainous national park with open woodlands located close to the border with Sweden, this small nature reserve provides protected habitat for lynx, wolverines, bears, and rare arctic foxes. Lierne National Park also has many elk (moose) and healthy beaver populations. This is dramatic Ice Age Norway, sporting unusual landscape forms such as ribbed moraines, drumlins, eskers, and meltwater channels. Several peaks rise more than 3,300 feet (1,000 m),

the highest of which is Hestkjøltoppen at 4,560 feet (1,390 m). There are also numerous wetland areas with large swamps attracting wildfowl on seasonal migrations. Other birds include osprey, who nest here, and the rare great snipe.

First stop should be Lierne National Park Centre in Nordli, a picturesque little village on the shore of Lake Laksjøn and a developing hub for adventure travel. Increased accommodations, a lakeshore café, restaurant, and a chic

chocolate boutique with lakeside terrace are all planned. Craft beer is also brewed locally, and a cottage industry harvesting fresh produce from field, forest, and lake currently thrives.

Lierne National Park is renowned for its good hunting and fishing, with plentiful trout and char in its lakes. The park also offers rich pickings of mushrooms and berries. Lierne Fjellstyre offers cabins and boats for rent within the park.

AT A GLANCE

Ice Age landscapes ▪ Climbing Hestkjøltoppen ▪ 129 square miles (333 sq km) ▪ Nordli's developing food scene ▪ visitnorway.com/listings/lierne-national-park/181623

LOFOTODDEN

Norway's new marine park is a coastal treat.

Lofotodden National Park was created in 2018 to protect part of the Lofoten Islands off Norway's northwest coast. As in many areas of Norwegian public life, the decision and the decision-making process were subjected to a healthy amount of debate in this highly democratic country. The process took more than 10 years, with substantial local opposition before Lofotodden Nasjonalpark became the country's 40th national park.

The protected area covers most of the northern coast of the island of Moskenesøya before wrapping around the western tip of the island, and includes many wild, rugged mountains and valleys. Property owners feared the loss of land-usage rights; locals also feared that the park will bring an unsustainable number of visitors to the archipelago, with its granite cliffs attracting climbers, fjords attracting anglers, and multicolored fishing villages attracting all-comers.

The area is rich in mountain flora and was one of the first regions to become uncovered at the end of the last ice age as glaciers moved eastward, meaning some of the oldest types of mountain vegetation can be found here. Among the many seabirds that make their homes in the park are colonies of black-legged kittiwakes. The park also contains evidence of human settlement dating back to the Stone Age. Cave paintings at Kollhellaren and Bukkhammerhola have been mesmerizing visitors since Stone Age Picassos painted them on the walls some 3,000 years ago.

AT A GLANCE

Maritime island and seascapes ▪ Ancient mountain flora ▪ 38 square miles (99 sq km) ▪ Kollhellaren and Bukkhammerhola cave paintings ▪ lofoten-info.no/nasjonalpark

LOMSDAL-VISTEN

A rich mix of varied landscapes

Located in Nordland county, this national park boasts perhaps the most diverse landscapes of any of Norway's preserves. The terrain within Lomsdal-Visten National Park ranges from steep-sided fjords with deciduous woodlands to coniferous forests, and from high mountain peaks to alpine meadows. The protected region also holds rich and varied geology, much of it concealed, with karstic terrain resulting in a subterranean labyrinth of caves, underground

Hiking here is mainly off trail.

rivers, and arches. The park has been a Sami stronghold from a time of hunter-gatherers up to their modern-day practice of reindeer husbandry, and remnants of their past are everywhere. Hikers will find trails only on the park's outskirts, so a map and compass are necessary. Remember too that rivers may swell dangerously during times of heavy rains and springtime snowmelt because much of the bedrock is unabsorbent gneiss.

AT A GLANCE

Northern wilderness ▪ Diverse Norwegian landscapes ▪ 425 square miles (1,102 sq km) ▪ Sami culture ▪ Karst caves ▪ lomsdalvisten.wordpress.com/information-in-english

MØYSALEN

A northern island's mountain beckons, bathed in the Midnight Sun.

The island of Hinnøya makes for challenging alpine climbs and hikes.

This national park is in classic fjord country, with high mountain peaks, the tallest of which is the 4,140-foot-tall (1,262-m) Møysalen mountain on the island of Hinnøya. Møysalen National Park, established in 2003 to preserve undisturbed coastal alpine landscape, embraces tracts of undisturbed birch forest, as well as many small fens and bogs.

Large-wing predators thrive here, feeding off rodents that infest the woodlands and shores: Golden eagles, white-tailed eagles, gyrfalcons, and peregrine falcons all circle in the mountain currents, awaiting their moment to swoop. The park is also home to several rare and endangered birds of prey, including kestrels, merlins, and rough-legged buzzards. The area around the Øksfjorden teems with elk (moose). Red foxes, stoats, and American mink all live off the park's various rodents and fish. The American mink is an invasive species, and a disruptor on the food chain, a carnivore that feeds on rodents, fish, crustaceans, frogs, and birds. Farmed for its extremely lucrative fur, its introduction onto mainland Europe has been linked to declines in the European mink, Pyrenean desman, and water vole populations.

The Møysalen is the focal point of the park, its name coming from an ancient legend of troll maidens who were petrified by the sun and turned into two smaller peaks Lille Møya (Little Maiden) and Store Møya (Big Maiden). The Møysalen (Maidens' Saddle) is the stone riding saddle of these two sisters, made by their troll father. The mountain has an alpine environment, with two glaciers by its summit including the Fonnisen glacier located just to the south.

WALKS & ACTIVITIES

Møysalen National Park and its surrounding nature conservation area offer many opportunities for hiking, but only experienced hikers should approach the alpine area itself. However, anyone can climb the mountain of Møysalen if accompanied by a guide arranged by the Møysalen National Park Centre. The guide will accompany you all the way up and across the glaciers near the summit. The ascent to the top and back takes about 10 hours, depending on fitness levels, and the scenic payoff is spectacular: From the summit of Møysalen, you can see all the way from Sweden to the Atlantic Ocean, from Bodø to Senja. The park website has details and prices for this adventurous challenge. Or choose a less demanding hike; the island has some excellent trails, and the park's northerly position means you'll benefit from the long hours of the Midnight Sun in summer months.

AT A GLANCE

Alpine scenery ▪ Climbing mighty Møysalen ▪ 20 square miles (51 sq km) ▪ Glaciers ▪ miljodirektoratet.no

ØVRE ANÁRJOHKA

A cross-border wilderness teeming with wildlife

The Anárjohka, a tributary of the Tana River and one of the park's many waterways, teems with fish.

Øvre Anárjohka National Park, located on the interior of the Finnmarksvidda plateau, shares a border with Lemmenjoki National Park in Finland (see page 252). Between them, these twin parks shelter extensive birch woods, pine barrens, bogs, and lakes, and constitute one of the largest wilderness areas in all of Scandinavia. There are few trails in this vast, unspoiled preserve, which also protects the largest remaining untouched pine forest in Norway.

Øvre Anárjohka is a park teeming with animal wildlife. In summer months, the main players here are elk (moose), which migrate to the cover of denser woodland areas outside of the park in winter. Park authorities have established 12 winter grazing areas for reindeer, and they are everywhere in the park during the long, sunless days until spring. Brown bears hibernate in their winter lairs, slowing their heartbeat down to almost crocodilian rates, yet able to awake in an instant and defend their territory, thanks to the amazingly recuperative qualities of their bile. Wolverines are occasionally seen passing through on the hunt for food. Red fox and stoat are among the other smaller predators that prowl the park.

Farther down the food chain are the lemmings, field voles, root voles, and northern water voles that frequent Øvre Anárjohka. The northern red-backed vole, a typical Siberian species, is a characteristic inhabitant of the national park. These rust-colored, slender little rodents make a small town of tunnels through the snow in winter. A few species of shrews also live in the park.

Fishing in Paradise

Øvre Anárjohka National Park is an anglers' paradise: Salmon, trout, three-spined stickle-backs, grayling, vendace, pike, perch, burbot, and minnows all thrive in abundant fluvial domains such as the Anárjohka river. The rarer arctic char is found in only one of the many lakes in the park. Which one? That's a fisherman's secret.

AT A GLANCE

A cross-border wilderness ▪ 544 square miles (1,409 sq km) ▪ Reindeer winter feeding areas ▪ Norway's largest untouched pine forest ▪ snl.no/Øvre_Anárjohka_nasjonalpark

ØVRE DIVIDAL

A remote Norwegian wilderness peering across Finland and Sweden

Between Setermoen and the Swedish and Finnish borders lies the lake-studded wilderness of Øvre Dividal National Park. No roads navigate out here, just a remote, semiforested, mountain wilderness with alpine peaks and lots of fresh Arctic air. The geology of the park makes it an attractive hiking spot, where several rivers have carved out ravines. The bedrock here consists of conglomerate, sandstone, and slate, and the rock formations on the banks of the Anárjohka river are particularly interesting. Around the park you will come across large rocks at unlikely locations. These were carried by the last glaciers to pass this way roughly 10,000 years ago, and deposited randomly at the end of the Ice Age. One red granite block that lies by the cairn on the summit of Jerta came from what today we know as Sweden.

FLORA & FAUNA

The lower forests have mainly pine trees, while higher up the mountain birch is common, and willow and dwarf birch dominate the open alpine tundra. Grey alder grows along the Divielva River. The ancient pinewood in Dividalen, with its twisted, stunted trees, looks straight from a fairy tale or *Game of Thrones*. You can eat mushrooms and berries here in fall—tasty cowberries (also known as lingon-berries) grow in abundance. Arctic rhododendrons flourish naturally in the park, giving a lovely purple hue to the meadows in springtime.

The park also hosts a rich array of wildlife, with brown bear, arctic fox, Eurasian lynx, and one of the largest wolverine populations in Europe. For centuries, the fearsome howl of wolves brought dread to Sami reindeer herders who live and migrate through this region. Although the Sami still herd their reindeer in the park, wolf sightings are few today, mainly just lupine predators passing through. Arctic foxes are also rare, making an occasional appearance (if you can spot them in the snow). The park's birds, however, are many and varied, including hawk owls, waxwings, longtailed skuas, parrot crossbills, and three-toed woodpeckers.

HIKES & ACTIVITIES

The marked hiking trail Nordkalott-ruta passes through Øvre Dividal as part of its 500-mile (800-km) trek crisscrossing the borderlands of Norway, Sweden, and Finland. The trail starts at Kautokeino, northern Norway, crossing international borders a total of 15 times before ending in the south in Sulitjelma (Norway) or alternately Kvikkjokk (Sweden). As well as Øvre Dividal, the Nordkalottruta passes through Norway's Reisa National Park (see page 179), and Sweden's Abisko (see page 192) and Padjelanta (see page 204) National Parks. The DNT maintains huts along the trail, as do park authorities in Sweden and Finland. If you visit Øvre Dividal in winter, a variety of local operators will take you dogsledding deep into the wilderness.

The bloom of a Carduus nutans, *aka musk thistle or nodding thistle*

ØVRE PASVIK

A small park with a big bear population

Characterized by Siberian-like taiga, the landscape of Øvre Pasvik National Park consists of flat, rolling hills with old-growth Scots pine forests, bogs, and fish-filled rivers and shallow lakes—perfect for bears. They have plenty to eat here; eight species of fish thrive in the park's waterways, including northern pike and European perch. The park also hosts lots of elk (moose), and the Sami cross through as they practice reindeer husbandry during winter. (The Skolts are the main Sami ethnic group in this part of Norway and Finland.) The birdlife in the park is unusual for Norway, and spotters will see rarities such as Siberian jays, pine grosbeaks, Bohemian waxwings, and whooper swans.

Øvre Pasvik is part of a multi-national vision of conservation, being the Norwegian component of Pasvik–Inari Trilateral Park. This includes Vätsäri Wilderness Area in Finland and the Russian part of the Pasvik Nature Reserve. The original vision for the park came from the Norwegian poet, Carl Schøyen, who proposed it back in 1936, but did not live long enough to see his dream reach fruition in 1970.

Many of the park's plants are typical of the Siberian taiga; it is one of only three locations in Norway for marsh Labrador tea. Lingonberry grows widely, along with common bilberry, bog bilberry, cloudberry, and some arctic raspberry. Alpine chickweed thrives on the steep cliffs at Revsaksskaret, along with white bluegrass and brittle bladder-fern.

Aside from bears (see sidebar), other mammals found in Øvre Pasvik include the red fox, stoat, least weasel, American mink, and European pine marten. Some intercontinental interlopers also inhabit the park: The raccoon dog, a close relative of the fox, is a species introduced to Europe from North America, and the Laxmann's shrew is a forest shrew more commonly found across northern Eurasia from the Baltic to the Sea of Japan, including Hokkaidō, Sakhalin, and the Korean Peninsula.

The park has no hiking trails, but fishing and hunting are permitted with a license. Be aware that this area shares borders with Finland and Russia, and military personnel are present. The visitors center is located at Svanvik.

Bear Country

This small preserve is the home of Norway's largest brown bear population. Its flat, rolling hills, old-growth forests with plentiful rivers, and shallow lakes provide ideal habitat for these cumbersome creatures. The ursine life is seasonal: Summer brings 60 days of Midnight Sun, and bears stock up for frigid winters when temperatures can drop to more than 40° below zero. Brown bears hibernate until spring, and two to four females have cubs in the protected area each year. Bears are also seen in transit between Russia and Finland.

Sunrise permeates the shallow waters of Lake Dagvatnet.

AT A GLANCE

Home of brown bears ▪ 46 square miles (119 sq km) ▪ A true wilderness with no roads or trails ▪ Reindeer husbandry ▪ Fine fishing ▪ nasjonalparkstyre.no/Ovre-Pasvik

RAET

A mainly maritime national park stretched along a remote coast

Opened in 2016, Raet National Park is mostly a marine park, and includes just three square miles (8 sq km) of land in the form of islands and coastal areas.

The park extends from the Valøyene islands off Grimstad along the entire Arendal coastal strip to Lyngør in Tvedestrand and encompasses all aspects of the beautiful Skagerrak coast. On coastal land you can walk through hardwood forests, and explore heaths, marshes, meadows, and bogs. Or take to the shores and the sea, diving deep into such marine habitats as mud plains, eelgrass meadows, and kelp forests. The landscape of this area is shaped by glacial movements from the last ice age, with long pebble beaches, mounds, ice-polished rocks, and vast stretches of glacial deposits. Hasseltangen and Søm-Ruakerkilen are part of a moraine ridge.

You can go trout fishing from the pier at the accessible Hasseltangen Recreation Ground. The same area has excellent bird-watching grounds, featuring a mix of habitats, with shallow inlets surrounded by beech woods, and moist farmland crisscrossed with reed-grown ditches, all habitats for geese, shorebirds, and several species of passerines, or perching songbirds. Søm-Ruakerkilen Nature Reserve, lying within the national park, is the most extensive and mature

The rocky shore at Hove, Tromoy, typifies the glacial Arendal coast.

beech forest in Southern Norway.

As you wander this coastline and the islands in springtime, look for the lovely sight of wild tulips growing in meadows and moors. This beautiful flowering bulb, the commodity that largely drove the Dutch Golden Age of the early 1600s, is thought to have come to the southern Norwegian coast by sail ships using soil for ballast, and has since become Arendal's flower.

BOATING, HIKING & BIKING

A good way to orient yourself to the lay of the land and the sweep of the sea is via a boat trip up the river Nidelva and out around the island of Hisøy. The M.S. *Nidelv* passes Torungen lighthouses, the Havsøy sound, and Merdø, leaving Merdø daily at noon on a leisurely two-hour cruise. If you want to explore farther out, the Osterøy

boat takes in the beautiful archipelago of Grimstad, with its many small islands and skerries, most of which can be easily accessed. The park and the Arendal coastline offer a wealth of beautiful sandy beaches: Spornes, just outside Tromøy, has the added advantage of a fine view toward the Skagerrak and a pebbled beach, ideal for beachcombing and examining the ice-smoothed gneiss rocks of the region. In addition, there are several good hiking trails in the area around Hove-Spornes. The park also has several great cycle routes, perhaps the most comprehensive of which being the 23-mile (37-km) Ebb & Flow Trail, which takes in an interesting combination of seashore, island views, and forestry interludes. The trail starts at the tourist information center in Grimstad.

AT A GLANCE

Coastal Southern Norway ▪ 234 square miles (607 sq km) ▪ Archipelago boat trips ▪ Ebb & Flow Trail ▪ raetnasjonalpark.no

RAGO

A brooding, barren wilderness with a melancholy mood

The small Rago National Park shares it borders with the Swedish national parks of Padjelanta (see page 204), Sarek (see page 205), and Stora Sjöfallet (see page 211). Together, they create an area of 2,085 square miles (5,400 sq km), making the combined parklands one of the largest tracts of protected land anywhere in Europe. The main attraction at Rago is the iconic Litlverifossen waterfall, spilling dramatically from an elevated mountain lake down a sheer rock face to the valley some 820 feet (250 m) below. It's a landscape straight from a Nordic saga of giants and trolls.

By Norwegian standards, this national park is somewhat barren. This is due to the poor quality of the soils and the harsh northern climate. However, two good anglers' lakes, Storskogvatnet and Litlverivatnet, lie within the park. Hardy Norwegian pine makes up most of the forestry stands, and several glaciers creep through the valleys of the southeastern part of the park.

The park benefits from the Sami legacy of domesticated reindeer, and wolverines stalk the woods. You'll also see many elk (moose) on your walks through the park. Willow ptarmigan—aka willow grouse—inhabit the woods and the moorlands, where you'll hear the full range of their vocalizations, from guttural chuckles to clucking sounds to the barking bravado of displaying males. Golden eagles that haunt higher grounds of this rugged northern wilderness are altogether more impressive avians.

AT A GLANCE

Rugged northern landscapes ▪ Litlverifossen waterfall ▪ 66 square miles (171 sq km) ▪ Willow ptarmigan ▪ Golden eagles ▪ gonorway.com/norway/articles/701

REINHEIMEN

A wilderness park with contrasting landscapes and fabulous fishing

Amid the peaks of western Norway, Reinheimen National Park encompasses much of the Tafjordfjella mountain range as well as the reindeer habitat in the northern part of the Ottadalen Valley. Wolverines, golden eagles, gyrfalcons, and ptarmigans are among the other inhabitants of this alpine ecosystem.

The landscapes contrast sharply within Reinheimen, from dramatic, sharply pointed peaks and knife-edge ridges in the west, to gently sloping plateaus, broad valleys, and slowly flowing rivers in the east. The park historically was a hunting grounds for wild reindeer, and many traces remain today of the practice, including pitfalls, mass trapping systems, bowmen's hides, and hunters' habitations. Trout fishing is popular in the park's well-stocked lakes, with lots of fresh trout and often char and grayling too. The park has an estimated 230 lakes and 112 miles (180 km) of water-ways, so a fishing license is money well spent. A few trails and hiking huts exist, but the park is largely wilderness.

The visitors center in Lom combines Reinheimen's information hub with those of Jotunheimen (see pages 168–9) and Breheimen (see page 153) National Parks at the interactive Norwegian Mountain Center. This self-styled gateway to the mountains provides information about hikes and guided tours in all three national parks.

AT A GLANCE

Alpine ecosystem ▪ 760 square miles (1,969 sq km) ▪ Wild reindeer hunting grounds ▪ Norwegian Mountain Center ▪ nasjonalparkriket.no/en/destinations/reinheimen

REISA

A watery oasis with some of Norway's finest salmon rivers

The Reisa River, famous for its salmon, winds through the park to the cascades of Imofossen.

Reisa National Park is a virtually untouched wilderness offering magnificent waterways with many splendid scenic hikes. Here too are some of Norway's best rivers for salmon fishing, including the Reisa. Several spectacular waterfalls, including Mollisfossen with a fall of 883 feet (269 m), flow into this fluvial thoroughfare.

The name of the river, Reisaelva, comes from the Norse word *rísa*, meaning "to rise." This river's water levels vary dramatically due of its large drainage basin, and it can become a torrent, especially during the springtime snowmelt. This main artery of the park remains frozen for most of winter and is ideal for skating, while in the summertime it welcomes via a hike on the riverside path, a boat trip, or a paddle in a canoe.

The area of Nordreisa has long been known as the "meeting of the three tribes," as the valley was a confluence of Norwegian, Kven, and Sami cultures. The remains of several tar kilns can be found in the valley, while rock art at Sieimma may be 3,800 years old. Farther up the valley, you can find remains of Sami *árran* (fireplaces) and pitfall trapping systems for reindeer.

Large Norwegian elk (moose) graze widely within the park, and wolverine and lynx patrol the higher grounds. An interesting visitor here is the harbor seal, who occasionally follows the Reisaelva River upstream from the coast.

Halti is the Reisa visitors center, where you will get good advice and tips about walks in the park.

AT A GLANCE

Mollisfossen waterfall ▪ Salmon rivers ▪ 310 square miles (803 sq km) ▪ Ancient cultural remains
▪ Halti visitors center ▪ reisanasjonalpark.no/en

ROHKUNBORRI

A mountainous wilderness teeming with wildlife and wildflowers

Rohkunborri National Park, located just south of Øvre Dividal National Park (see page 175), shares a border with the Swedish Vadvetjåkka National Park (see page 215). Rohkunborri encompasses parts of the Sørdalen Valley, and its deep

Sørdalen Valley beckons with its canyon, woodlands, and valleys.

canyon, surrounded by 4,920-foot (1,500-m) mountain walls, is a focal point of the park. Geavdnjajávri lake and the Rohkunborri mountain are other major attractions here.

The landscape varies from rich boreal deciduous forest to wetlands and bogs in the lowlands to alpine tundra in the higher reaches of the mountains. Brown bears, wolverines, and lynx all stalk the old birch woods, while the Sami herd their reindeer elsewhere in the park. Many lakes

teem with trout, burbot, perch, and pike. The char in Geavdnjajávri and Eartebealjávri are especially sizable. Lakes along the Sørdalen gorge and the Jordbruelva river are devoid of fish and host only rare crustaceans such as *Branchinecta paludosa* (a fairy shrimp) and *Lepidurus arcticus* (a tadpole shrimp), and also black zooplankton.

The snowy owl hunts in the woods while the gyrfalcon soars above the snowcapped mountain peaks. The wetlands around the birch woods and the alpine wetlands sit on calcareous bedrock and offer valuable habitat for wetland birds such as ringed plovers, red-necked phalaropes, dunlins, and Temminck's stints, whose name derives from a Dutch botanist

by way of Aristotle. Red-throated divers, black-throated divers, whooper swans, and numerous duck species all pass through the park, while scaups, long-tailed ducks, common scoters, and velvet scoters all nest in the wetlands.

The variety of plant life in the park is particularly rich: Three-leaved rush, a small reed (*Calamagrostis lapponica)*, and trailing azalea thrive on the open woodland floor. Abundant amid Sørdalen's birch woodland are wood crane's bill, meadowsweet, wood horsetail, field horsetail, and bilberry. Areas of grey alder–bird cherry woodland with extensive meadows of ostrich fern are also found in Rohkunborri. The rich lime bedrock fosters the growth of the arctic rhododendron.

EXPLORING THE PARK

The park is an outdoor lovers' paradise, and activities such as rock climbing, fishing, Alpine skiing, and hiking draw adventure seekers year-round. The Arctic Trail, which transects the regions of Sulitjelma and Kautokeino, also goes through Rohkunborri National Park, and visitors can spend a night at the Troms Rambling Association cabin at Lappjord before continuing onward to Abisko. A hike from Sørdalen to Lappjord offers superb views down into the Boldnoávži gorge and up to the snowcapped, glaciated mountains.

AT A GLANCE

Boldnoávži gorge ▪ Abundant birdlife ▪ 220 square miles (571 sq km) ▪ The Arctic Trail
▪ nasjonalparkstyre.no/rohkunborri

RONDANE

Norway's oldest park touches heaven and earth.

Rondane National Park embraces 10 mountains of more than 6,560 feet (2,000 m), the kingpin being Rondeslottet (the Rondane castle) at an altitude of 7,146 feet (2,178 m).

The park lies mainly above the tree line, where the climate is mild but relatively arid. White birch grow on the lower hills, but above the tree line the nutrient-deficient soil and rocks are covered by heather and lichen. Even higher, above 4,920 feet (1,500 m), nothing but the hardiest lichens grow on bare stones. One of the few flower species to survive at this altitude is the hardy glacier crowfoot, part of the buttercup family, found up to 5,580 feet (1,700 m).

In Rondane's deepest valley lies Rondvatn, a narrow lake filling the steep cavity between the large Storronden-Rondeslottet massif and Smiubelgen (the "blacksmith's bellows"). The central massif is also dissected by *botns:* flat, dead stone valleys below the steep mountain walls.

LITERARY LEGACY

The park is a vital habitat for herds of wild reindeer. It is estimated that about 2,000 to 4,000 of these nomadic animals roam about Rondane and the nearby Dovre region. The area is of huge cultural significance in Norway. Clear evidence exists on several high plains of reindeer traps, some dating back 3,500

The deep Nordic wilderness at dusk

years. Reindeer are known to have been hunted in the region up to the time of the Black Death. In 1867, Norwegian writer Henrik Ibsen set part of his play *Peer Gynt* in the mountains of Rondane, toward which the hero says in awe:

Tower over tower arises!
Hei, what a glittering gate!

The park has many unforgettable walking trails that can be hiked over several days going from hut to hut; a baggage delivery service is offered, so you can dine well on fine local produce if you plan ahead. Mysusæter is the gateway for many hikes in Rondane, including those to the mountains in the center of the park. Mysusæter is also the starting point for the multiday "triangle route," a five-day adventure into the heart of Rondane that includes a boat ride across Rondvatn lake.

Sollia Kirke

While in Rondane National Park, make time to explore the lovely Sollia kirke, one of Norway's best preserved and most beautiful baroque churches. This wooden church was built by Jon Jonsen in 1737. Prominent in its impressive interior, decorated by the Swedish Erik Walling, is the altar, a replica of the altarpiece created in 1700 for the Church of Our Savior in faraway Oslo. While the Sollia kirke now sits next to Route 219 at the start of Rondane's National Tourist Route, it was once quite isolated: The church was originally built after a pilgrim froze to death trying to attend Mass over the mountain in Ringebu. This followed a royal decree of 1720 that specified compulsory biannual Mass attendance for all citizens. Such remote chapels performed a key social as well as spiritual role in small rural communities.

AT A GLANCE

Ibsen's "glittering towers" ▪ The "triangle route" hiking trail ▪ 372 square miles (963 sq km) ▪ Sollia kirke ▪ nasjonaleturistveger.no/en/routes/rondane

SALTFJELLET-SVARTISEN

A diverse park with glaciers, fjords, karst caves, and activities for all

A visitor beholds the enormity of the Svartisen glacier

Encompassing a landscape shaped by ancient glaciers, Saltfjellet-Svartisen National Park is one of the largest parks in Norway, and may be its most diverse. As the name indicates, it includes Svartisen, the largest ice sheet in northern Scandinavia and the second largest glacier on mainland Norway. Covering 142 square miles (370 sq km), the glacier still covers a fifth of this dramatic park, with its tongues visible from the Kystriksveien Coastal Route.

This huge protected area ranges from the green but rugged Nordfjorden in the west, across alpine mountains and the never ending ice, down to gently sloping mountain plateaus and fertile valleys with mountain birch forests cut by sleepy rivers. In the east, there's another geographic surprise—the open fells of Saltfjellet with their great glacial sediments. These bleak, high moorlands of the Saltfjellet massif roll all the way to the Swedish border. A portion of this frontier is shared with the Vindelfjällen Nature Reserve in neighboring Sweden.

GLACIER & GEOLOGY

The Svartisen glacier forms the focal point of this national park. In many places, tongues of ice lap out from the huge ice sheet to form valley glaciers that can often be heard calving with a great groaning, crunching sound as ice tears itself away and falls into the water pools below. Svartisen itself consists of two glaciers, Vestisen and Østisen, which are separated by the valley of Vesterdalen. In a sign of our warming times, this valley recently became free of ice.

The glacier is a living phenomenon, constantly altering the landscape; one example of this is how outwash deposits of sand and clay shift constantly as streams of glacial meltwater change course. Much of this change, however, is hidden from human sight and takes place underground. The limestone bedrock in the central part of the park produces a typical karst landscape. For millennia the water has found its way down into fissures, carving out the subterranean rock and forming a labyrinth of tunnels and caverns, large and small. Some may be more than 350,000 years old.

Cavers looking for the most varied karst landscape should head to Pikhågan in Glomdalen. This spectacular karst area includes small marble pillars, fluted rock, springs and sinkholes, and small cavities and sculptures dissolved out of bedrock. The highlight is a marble rampart, a broad strip of light marble crossing diagonally over the entire valley.

FLORA & FAUNA

The calciferous bedrock of Saltfjellet-Svartisen supports a varied plant life, including several rare species such as the arctic rhododendron, which blossoms in a spectacle of springtime purple. Vast carpets of mountain avens spread across the valleys too, like a white-cotton picnic cloth dotted with yellow.

The rich limestone soils nurture some 250 plant species in Stormdalen, and the floors of the mountain birch forests prove a particularly rich incubator. The valleys of Tespdalen and Bjøllådalen also host a profusion of vegetation.

Given its range of habitats, it's not surprising that all the most popular animals of Norwegian park life inhabit Saltfjellet-Svartisen: The wolverine, Eurasian lynx, elk (moose), and arctic fox all live and breed here.

HISTORY & CULTURE

Hikers along the park's many trails may encounter some of the many legacies of Sami culture here. The traditional reindeer herding areas include an outstanding collection of Sami monuments as these native peoples were the first to hunt and trap wild reindeer in Saltfjellet. Today you can see traces of sacrificial sites, pitfalls, and fences for trapping that date from the ninth century. Domestic reindeer herding has been practiced here from the 16th and 17th centuries, centered mostly around the valley of Lønsdalen.

A visit to Bredekfjellet mountain farm gives a taste of the challenging lives of the later Norwegian settlers, who came to farm this northern land in the 19th century. This open-air museum is located an hour's walk from the E6 at Bjøllånes. The open farm is usually held in August and is a good excuse to take a hike up the mountain. Elsewhere in the park, you'll come across several long-abandoned valleys with old mountain farms and hay barns in the clearings of the birch forest—a reminder of hardships these pioneer settlers faced in this harsh northern land.

Remnants of several ancient pathways are likewise scattered throughout the park, including the old route from Rana to Salten. This ancient route was given new purpose when it was chosen for laying the telegraph line in 1867. A series of log cabins have long ago replaced the stone cabins built at the time of this communications breakthrough.

HIKES & ACTIVITIES

Along the park's many trails, visitors may arrange to stay at these log cabins and self-catering mountain huts, great for anglers taking advantage of the Midnight Sun as they fish for trout and char in the mountain lakes of Saltfjellet. Four major salmon rivers also originate in the national park, including Ranaelva. Elk (moose) and grouse are hunted in the valley, but remember to buy a hunting or fishing license to participate.

Cavers have a whole karst underground realm to explore in the park, and even casual visitors can take in the 13,780-feet long (4,200 m) limestone cave of Grønligrotta, complete with subterranean illumination to highlight 700,000 years' worth of water sculpting. On the 40- to 50-minute tour you view potholes, an underground creek and waterfall, and marvelous marble formations.

Maps and information are available from the tourist information center in Mo i Rana.

SEILAND

A pristine fjordland treasure with alpine peaks and rare plant life

The majority of the island of Seiland, and the two northernmost glaciers in Scandinavia (Seilandsjøkelen and Nordmannsjøkelen) are encompassed within the boundaries of Seiland National Park. This is coastal Norway at its finest, astonishingly green and lush, embracing majestic fjords. Melkelva, the milky meltwater river that emanates from Seilandsjøkelen Glacier, flows down rapids and waterfalls out into the sea in Store Bekkarfjorden.

The park's precipitous coastal cliffs offer nesting sites for many birds of prey. Bird-watchers may see such favorites as white-tailed eagles, golden eagles, gyrfalcons, merlins, kestrels, and rough-legged buzzards.

The national park offers exciting hiking terrain, from fjord coasts and coastal mountains to birch woods and lush, tall-herb meadows. Here too are mountainous terrain dotted with lakes and, of course, alpine peaks. The most suitable areas for walking are Store Bekkarfjorden, Bårdfjorden, and the Straumdalen valley. Note, however, that there are no marked trails or huts in this pristine wilderness park. But you may be rewarded by finding a macrocrystal zircon (a "Seiland diamond") here, thanks to the park's nutrient-rich, ultrabasic bedrock. This rich soil grows rare alpine plants in the mountains, such as low sandwort, spiked snow grass, and a rare subspecies of arctic poppy, *Papaver radicatum*.

Seiland offers ample outdoor activities year-round, including mountaineering, hiking, horse riding, skiing, and all kinds of water sports, including diving.

> **AT A GLANCE**
>
> Classic northern fjords ▪ "Seiland diamonds" ▪ 122 square miles (316 sq km) ▪ Pristine backcountry ▪ seiland-brygge.com/seiland-national-park

SJUNKHATTEN

A children's park welcomes all nature lovers who are young at heart.

Sjunkhatten National Park, located on a peninsula near the city of Bodø, is a park designed specifically for children. Paths are marked with signs and arrows, and the park publishes a rambling map for young visitors, showing hiking and ski trails.

Sjunkhatten's glacier-formed landscape encompasses Heggmovatnet lake, narrow fjords, lakes, wetlands, alpine peaks, corries, and moraines. The park's underground

The glacier-gouged landscape

is just as interesting, for both trolls and humans: The eastern part has marble belts, and limestone caves have karstic features formed by water erosion where children will learn the difference between a stalactite and a stalagmite. They can also follow a stream that suddenly vanishes only to reappear mysteriously farther on. Sjunkhatten's furry inhabitants are sure to charm, with possible encounters with lynx, otters, elk (moose), and the reindeer kept by the Sami. Whooper swans breed in the wetlands here, and are also park favorites.

> **AT A GLANCE**
>
> Norwegian children's park ▪ Underground exploration ▪ 161.2 square miles (417.5 sq km) ▪ Mapped and signposted trails to explore ▪ visitnorway.com

SKARVAN & ROLTDALEN

A gorgeous untouched wilderness lit by the northern lights

The terrain of Skarvan and Roltdalen National Park is one of mountain plateaus, wooded valleys, and extensive marshy areas. Its boundaries run east toward the Swedish border and embrace the Skarvan mountains. The park also protects a large spruce forest in the Roltdalen valley, a most valuable botanical asset with many trees more than 200 years old. The forest provides rich habitat for mosses, lichens, and fungi.

Skarvan and Roltdalen is also home to large populations of hare, ptarmigan, and forest birds. In addition, you may see some rarer species, such as arctic loons, greater scaup, chicken hawks, and lesser spotted woodpeckers. The old-growth forests shelter crested tits, coal tits, common tree creepers, three-toed woodpeckers, Siberian jays, and wood grouse, among others. Wetland birds thrive in the marshy areas here, including golden plovers, broad-billed sandpipers, and ruff and red-necked phalaropes.

Hiking in this park is formidable, and Trondhjems Turistforening maintains a network of hiking trails connecting Roltdalen to the trail network of the Nord-Trøndelag Tourist Association. Hikers may see the remains of dwellings, ironworks, Sami settlements, and catch pits for reindeer.

The Tydal Sami were formerly divided into three groups, one of

The park's waterways mirror the drama of Norwegian skies.

The Northern Lights

Wherever you are in Norway, your trip becomes magical once the northern lights begin their mysterious dance across the night sky. The cause of the aurora borealis gave rise to many mythologies throughout history. Many saw in them the souls of ancestors dancing. We now know that the spectacle is caused by solar flares leaping from the sun and firing electrical activity into the Arctic sky. Late September, October, February, and March are prime viewing times in Norway.

which had its home in Skarvan. They now live all together in the Essand reindeer grazing district, continuing their long symbiotic relationship with this great Scandinavian beast.

Along the banks of the Rotla River, you may come across signs of permanent settlement from before the time when the Black Death ravaged Europe. Today, there are just a few huts in the park, mainly on the outskirts of the central plateaus, so camping is a good option if you're venturing far into the wilderness. On a crystal clear night, you can cook a fresh fish supper on the campfire, then lie back in your sleeping bag and wait for the show of all electrical shows, the northern lights (see sidebar).

AT A GLANCE

Northern lights ▪ Sami reindeer grazing ▪ 170.5 square miles (441.5 sq km) ▪ Old-growth spruce in Roltdalen ▪ nasjonalparkstyre.no

STABBURSDALEN

Unspoiled wilderness in classic Norwegian backcountry

The small preserve designated as Stabbursdalen National Park protects the northernmost pine forest in the world. These forests grew in warmer times millennia ago, and have only survived in such sheltered valleys as Stabbursdalen, their twisted, gnarled forms evidence of a battle with cold, drought, and sterile soils that otherwise sustain mainly lichen and heather. The wetlands at Luobbal support birds such as black grouse and osprey, and hollowed pines provide a welcome nesting habitat

Reindeer roam Lapland's wilderness.

for goldeneye and goosander ducks.

The park's other landscapes encompass the barren mountains of Gaissene, open plateaus, and narrow ravines with scattered mountain birch stands. The Stabburselva river courses through the park with heady waterfalls and rapids and deep, still pools.

The Sami people have inhabited Stabbursdalen for centuries. While you can still see remnants of pitfalls where reindeer were once hunted, domesticated herds graze the park today. Visitors can hike and cross-country ski around the valley on marked trails—the Stabbursnes Naturhus and Museum has maps.

AT A GLANCE

Europe's northernmost pine forests ▪ 288 square miles (747 sq km) ▪ A wilderness without roads ▪ Stabbursnes Naturhus and Museum ▪ stabbursnes.no

VARANGERHALVØYA

Where mainland Norway meets the Arctic

This is where the far north truly starts. Welcome to the Land of the Midnight Sun and the northern lights, where bleak, desolate high plains stop suddenly, turning into cliffs dropping into the sea. Varangerhalvøya is the largest peninsula in Norway and the largest mainland area within the Arctic climate zone. But this is no Siberian tundra: Lime-rich bedrock and soil support rich pockets fostering rare species like the arctic poppy (*Papaver dahlianum*), field fleawort, and Svalbard snow cinquefoil. The alpine ecosystem includes domesticated reindeer, wolverines, and the endangered arctic fox. Steps were taken to reduce red fox numbers to restore balance to the biosphere.

Varangerhalvøya National Park's desolate landscape and Arctic skies give it a melancholy mood. The higher plateaus are dominated by stone fields completely lacking in vegetation. The ice cap laid down about three thousand circular moraines, or rounded glacial deposits, a phenomenon seen in only a few other places worldwide.

Although no marked trails exist, the park is suitable for skiing, hiking, and cycling, and unlocked huts are maintained in the interior. Salmon, sea char, and sea trout can be fished in several of the park's rivers, including the Vestre Jakobselva, Skallelva, and Komagelva. Around the water, look for two easily identified avian inhabitants of the park, the long-tailed skua and the red-necked phalarope.

AT A GLANCE

Arctic climate ▪ Alpine ecosystem ▪ 697 square miles (1,805 sq km) ▪ Salmon, sea char, and sea trout rivers ▪ nasjonalparkstyre.no/Varangerhalvoya

YTRE HVALER

A maritime park awash with history and alive with wildlife

Surveying the park's protected waters from the isle of Heia

Established in 2009, Ytre Hvaler National Park is mostly oceanic, covering the outer skerries of Oslofjord. The park's boundaries lie partly on the Norway-Sweden border next to Kosterhavet National Park (see page 202). Humans have lived here since the Bronze Age, and the park celebrates Norwegian coastal culture with sites including fishing boathouses and two fine lighthouses, Homlungen and Torbjørnskjer. Ytre Hvaler also protects the Tisler Reef, an important cold-water coral reef consisting mostly of Lophelia, the anemic branch of the coral family tree. This blanched translucent pink, yellow, or white coral thrives in the frigid depths of northern seas,

Shipwrecks

Ytre Hvaler is one of the great diving destinations in Norway; more than 50 shipwrecks lie strewn in its waters. The best known is the Danish frigate H.D.M.S. *Lossen*, lost in the Christmas Flood of 1717. Excavations have uncovered more than 4,300 artifacts, including butter, clay pipes, and game pieces. Since the heyday of Akerøya Fort (1682–1807), ships have perished on this dangerous coast, despite the lighthouses of Torbjørnskjer and Homlungen.

away from sunlight. Not surprisingly, diving is one of the park's most popular activities, especially with its profusion of shipwrecks (see sidebar).

The mud and silt of the shoreline are host to shrimp and Norway lobsters, as well as various species of bristleworms, sea stars, and mollusks. The dense kelp forest swaying in the shallows between Heia and Torbjørnskjer serves the same function as forestry on land. Fish, crabs, and several species of shellfish all thrive there, as well as various algae and anemones that grow on the seaweed. Large clams abound on the cliffs around Hvalerrenna.

If you go boating or kayaking in the waters between Heia and Torbjørnskjer, you'll pass a key pupping area for common seals. More than 12,000 eider ducks also gather in the park to molt.

Wintertime in Hvaler is prime season for kiters and windsurfers. The wind whips in from the southwest and great waves break at Ørekroken, a horseshoe-shaped cove and surfing mecca in Hvaler. The coastal trails along the park's many islands offer great hiking and local history; on Kjerkøya, for example, are Bronze Age cairns and an old quarry at Rødshuet. Look for the lovely yellow-horned poppy growing on pebble beaches, cliffs, and sand dunes.

AT A GLANCE

Diving at Tisler Reef ▪ 137 square miles (354 sq km) ▪ Torbjørnskjer and Homlungen lighthouses ▪ Island coastal trails ▪ visitnorway.com/listings/ytre-hvaler-national-park/5360

Svalbard Parks

Once you step onto the Norwegian archipelago of Svalbard, you've arrived at the outer reaches of Europe and you are about to walk into one of the last great wildernesses on Earth. This is a place etched into history by polar explorers, its latitude deep inside the Arctic Circle.

The Lindblad Expeditions ship National Geographic Explorer *in ice floes at Austfonna in the Svalbard archipelago*

Most visitors to Svalbard arrive by ship, as part of an expert-led and well-equipped expedition. National Geographic Expeditions runs several such voyages to this remote Arctic archipelago. Norway's most extreme national parks await, with their mythic landscapes of jagged peaks, glaciers, and frozen fjords, and their populations of polar bears, walruses, and teeming bird colonies. See miljodirektoratet.no for more information.

FORLANDET

Forlandet National Park encompasses the island of Prins Karls Forland and its ocean surrounds. On its western side are beaches and bird colonies, and in the east its steep glaciers meet the shore. A huge population of black guillemots will greet your arrival with their soft purring. Look, too, for seals on the rocks. At the bird reserves of Plankeholmane and Forlandsøyane, you'll see masses of common eider and barnacle geese; the park hosts six bird reserves in all. The historical human footprint on the island consists of remains from Norwegian and Russian hunters and whalers.

INDRE WIJDEFJORDEN

The steep fjord landscape of Indre Wijdefjorden National Park provides Svalbard with a green oasis of high Arctic steppe vegetation dominated by several exclusive species of grasses. These include Dane's dwarf gentian and false sedge. The climate here is moderated by the North Atlantic Current, which extends the Gulf Stream northward. The national park stretches along the archipelago's longest fjord, located on Spitsbergen's northern coast. Trapping cabins that once served the arctic fox fur trade are the only signs of any human life. The governor of Svalbard has a cabin at Austfjordnes that can be rented during the hunting season.

NORDENSKIÖLD LAND

Set on the island of Spitsbergen, Nordenskiöld Land National Park embraces the ice-free valley of Reindalen, which is washed by the river Reindalselva. The park is named after Finnish-Swedish explorer and geologist Nils Adolf Erik Nordenskiöld, whose expeditions to this island in 1858, 1861, and 1864 pushed the boundaries of Arctic cartography, geology, and botany. He found a land of moraines and rock glaciers, but also the lush vegetation of Reindalen, with its blanket of peat moss. Farther down, the wetland and delta of Stormyra is a vital grazing and calving area for Svalbard reindeer. The park's coast also protects huge numbers of breeding barnacle geese and common eiders.

NORDRE ISFJORDEN

Also on Spitsbergen, across the Isfjorden north of Barentsburg, Nordre Isfjorden National Park protects a rich ecosystem that is a result of regular inflows of warm, saline waters into the Isfjorden carried by the North Atlantic Current. These currents foster the growth of plankton, which then sustains large numbers of crustaceans. Fish species such as capelin and polar cod feed off these, and the fattened fish, in turn, draw seabirds and mammals to the fjord. Huge numbers of Brünnich's guillemot, little auk, Atlantic puffin, glaucous gull, and northern fulmar colonize the area. With so many nest eggs for plundering, arctic foxes lurk with hungry intent.

NORDVEST-SPITSBERGEN

On the far northwest of the Svalbard archipelago, visitors can experience the dreamscapes of those early explorers who raced to the North Pole at the Nordvest-Spitsbergen National Park. The remains of 17th-century whaling stations lie here, as do traces of Swedish engineer Salomon August Andrée's failed attempt in 1897 to reach the pole in a hydrogen balloon. This national park is still a hub of science and exploration: The research station at the gateway town of Ny-Ålesund studies the impact of global warming in the Arctic. Also of interest is the Mine Museum at Tiedemann's Tabak shop in town. Cruising inland, the stunningly beautiful Kongsfjorden and Magdalenefjord, and the walrus masses on Moffen Island are unforgettable. You are also likely to spy a heavy-set polar bear; weighing up to 1,590 pounds (720 kg), these animals are deceptively quick and agile as they hunt for seals, fish, and birds. In summer, you'll have

Svalbard's national parks provide vital habitat for polar bears.

24-hour daylight to enjoy all these natural Arctic wonders.

SASSEN-BÜNSOW LAND

Embracing glaciers, glacial valleys, and one of Spitsbergen's highest waterfalls, Sassen-Bünsow Land National Park lies on Spitsbergen. The sealer and whaler Hilmar Nøis built his Fredheim hunting station here. Just west of the park is the home of one of just three land mammals on Svalbard, the sibling vole—an animal confined to Grumant, a former Russian coal-mining settlement. Tempelfjorden is an important breeding site for ringed seals, whose pups abound on the ice in spring. Svalbard reindeer, almost hunted to extinction by 1925, now enjoy the protected grazing area of Sassendalen.

SØR-SPITSBERGEN

This national park spans the southern end of Spitsbergen and includes Wedel Jarlsberg Land, Torell Land, and Sørkapp Land. Sør-Spitsbergen National Park is glacier country, with much of the area capped with ice, and the remainder mostly tundra. The inland landscapes are mainly glacial with some protruding nunataks (exposed rocky ridges in the ice fields, aka glacial islands). Hornsund is vital for polar bears, and to help, the park protects the minimal grassy vegetation alongside freshwater ponds. The Isøyane Bird Sanctuary supports breeding populations of barnacle geese, common eiders, black-legged kittiwakes, and thick-billed guillemots.

Vadvetjåkka N.P.

Abisko N.P.

Padjelanta National Park

Stora Sjöfallet National Park

Torneälven

Gällivare

Sarek N.P.

Muddus N.P.

ARCTIC CIRCLE

Pieljekaise National Park

Storavan

Skellefteälven

Luleälven

Haparanda Skärgård N.P.

Ångermanälven

Björnlandet N.P.

S W E D E N

Indalsälven

NORWAY

Östersund

Töfsingdalen N.P.

Sonfjället N.P.

Skuleskogen N.P.

FINLAND

Fulufjället National Park

Hamra N.P.

G U L F   O F   B O T H N I A

N

0 — 50 kilometers
0 — 50 miles

Färnebofjärden N.P.

Garphyttan N.P.

Ängsö N.P.

Mälaren

Stockholm

Tresticklan N.P.

Tiveden N.P.

Hjälmaren

Tyresta National Park

Kosterhavet National Park

Vänern

Djurö N.P.

Gotska Sandön N.P.

Vättern

SKAGERRAK

Norra Kvill N.P.

Store Mosse National Park

Gotland

KATTEGAT

Bolmen

Växjö

Blå Jungfrun N.P.

Åsnen N.P.

Öland

DENMARK

Söderåsen N.P.

Dalby Söderskog N.P.

Malmö

Stenshuvud N.P.

B A L T I C   S E A

SWEDEN

Sandwiched between Norway to the west and Finland and the Baltic Sea to the east, Sweden is a land often overlooked in terms of its natural beauty and wintry wilderness. Like its Nordic neighbors, Sweden finds itself bathed in vastly different seasonal lights. The long dark winters give the landscapes of glaciers, mountains, forests, and tundra a brooding, melancholy mood; spring comes with a sense of relief and release, long celebrated in festivals; then, in summer, Sweden is awash with a surreal feeling of abundant liveliness as the midnight sun steals the night sky.

Sweden's national parks are an apt mix of the landscapes and landmarks contained within this diverse Scandinavian country. The parks range from the scenic Bohuslän coast, with its scattered islands and fishing villages of red weatherboard houses, to the north where the Sami heartland holds domesticated reindeer pastures and vast snow-covered plains. Sweden also has many tiny national parks, some less than one square mile (2.6 sq km) in area: This is a country where small is beautiful, and where there is always time to stop and smell the twinflowers (*Linnaea borealis*).

Intrepid hikers can traverse four of these national parks on the King's Trail, starting in Abisko National Park in the far north, and finishing on a nature reserve in Swedish Lapland, one of Europe's last true wilderness regions.

The red weatherboard houses of Ursholmen and Sweden's most westerly lighthouse at Kosterhavet National Park

ABISKO

The gateway to the King's Trail

The best way to see Abisko National Park is from atop the Alpine massif of Mount Kebnekaise, Sweden's highest mountain. The landscape below is dramatic, jagged, and huge—clearly carved by elemental glacial force at the time of the last ice age, some 10,000 years ago.

From this vantage point, too, you can see how the Tkäktjavagge Valley stretches out into the distance, with the vast lakes of Torneträsk and Akkajaure and the seemingly endless birch and spruce forests. Reindeer and elk (moose) roam this park, as do wolverine, foxes, and lynx, though they are less seen. Golden eagles and falcons prey on a host of wading birds. The region's microclimate brings relatively mild winters, and habitats include subarctic forests, alpine rivers, subalpine grasslands, and quaking bogs.

THE SAMI

The lands around Abisko are part of Sápmi, the historic hunting grounds of Sweden's northern Sami people that encompass large swaths of Norway, Finland, and Russia. The remains of their hearths and pit traps to catch reindeer may be found here, and though the Sami switched from hunting to herding centuries ago, they still move their reindeer along ancient migratory paths from lowland forests to summer pastures high in the mountains. Learn about nomadic Sami life and their reindeer husbandry at the Sami village of Rávtta, where you can ride a sleigh in winter, and even taste Sami dishes around an open fire in a traditional *lavvus* ("teepee").

King's Trail

Abisko is the northern gateway to the 275-mile (443-km) King's Trail (Kungsleden) in the very north of Swedish Lapland. The town of Abisko is just a 10-minute drive from the trailhead. Following the Kungsleden from Abisko Turiststation, you'll pass the rapids of the Ábeskoeatnu River, canyons, boglands, and small lakes. The trail climbs a mountain ridge before reaching a welcoming sauna at the Alesjauare cabin. Next is the Tjäkta Pass, rising to 3,773 feet (1,150 m) before you eventually reach the foothills of Mount Kebnekaise. After tackling Sweden's tallest mountain, head south out of the park and you're on the next part of the King's Trail, a month-long hike through Sweden's quiet wilderness at the roof of the world in Swedish Lapland. Taking the trail north to south keeps the warming sun in your face.

TRAILS & ACTIVITIES

A stay in the Ice Hotel, a winter wonderland built of ice blocks and decorated with ice sculptures, is a must. You get to sleep on beds of snow, covered by reindeer skins and army-issue sleeping bags. Skylights frame the northern lights overhead: Reds, greens, whites, and yellows streak across the sky in a mesmerizing display.

The park's Aurora Sky Station is one of the Earth's prime viewing spots for the lights: Chairlifts bring you to the lookout tower atop Mount Njullá between November and March.

The park mushes up lots of dogsledding expeditions, and crosscountry skiing is popular too. Climbing Mount Kebnekaise, Sweden's highest mountain at 6,909 feet (2,106 m), is a local challenge; the 12.4-mile (20-km) hike takes about 12 hours round-trip, and the views of the tundra from the summit are superb. A gentler hike is the 8.6-mile (14-km) Puddus Nature Trail, which takes you through a re-creation of a traditional Sami camp and a Sami sacrificial site, and also affords wonderful vistas of Lake Torneträsk.

Autumnal Abisko Canyon, with its walls cut by the River Abiskojåkka

ÄNGSÖ

Rare flora and wild fauna in the Stockholm archipelago

An island meadow of wild elder-flowered orchids

Ängsö National Park, located in the Stockholm *skärgård* ("archipelago"), is an island preserved in time, untouched by the technological effects of modern-day agriculture. In the 17th century, Ängsö was two separate islands, but the land rose in what was then a narrow sound and became the meadow of Stormier. Ängsö was established in 1909 and is today one of Europe's oldest parks, preserving a traditional farm landscape with flowering hay meadows and wooded pastures.

The park hosts a wealth of trees, shrubs, and flowers, including cowslip and the giant daisylike wood anemones. At the end of May, thousands of elder-flowered orchids bloom at the northern end of Långängen, and the whole meadow is a riot of purple and yellow. Other meadows in the park show their spring colors in dramatic displays; flowers include bird's-eye primrose, dwarf milkwort, lousewort, and snake's head fritillary. This last flower has many names, probably due to its oddly drooping blossom. To some it is the chess flower, or the frog-cup, or the guinea-hen flower, or the guinea flower; others know it as the leper lily, because its shape resembled the bell once carried by lepers; and to other floral enthusiasts it is the Lazarus bell or the drooping tulip.

A third of the national park is forestry of ash, birch, maple, and oak. Eagles and ospreys nest in Ängsö, their habitats protected from visitors in the nesting season.

The park has good hiking trails and is level and easy to get around. A park naturalist can meet you at the dock for a guided tour; tickets can be purchased on the boat. Note that the island has no shops or restaurants, so plan meals accordingly. You can hike on your own, but bring good hiking boots, as trails can be wet and rocky.

CROFTER LAND

Several crofter forests show the effects of agriculture up to the 19th century: Västerskogen, consisting of oaks and pines, is a fine example. The crofters were settler farmers who shared communal land to eke out a living within a township by means of small-scale food production. One such crofter was Adam Michelsson, who settled on Ängsö with his wife, Carolina, in 1857. A glade in the forest of Svartviken reveals the overgrown foundation of their house and the remnants of their paved cellar. The ruins stand as a monument to misfortune, as Adam disappeared one January night in 1864, probably falling through the ice and drowning, leaving his wife to raise their family single-handedly on this remote island.

AT A GLANCE

Island park with traditional farm landscape ▪ .65 square mile (1.68 sq km) ▪ Naturalist-guided tours ▪ Crofter forests and remnants ▪ nationalparksofsweden.se

ÅSNEN

A park of wetlands, forests, lakes, and lonesome islands

Åsnen National Park encompasses a lake archipelago with more than a thousand uninhabited islands and islets. The topography is varied, moving from old-growth deciduous forests with rare mosses, lichen, and fungi to lush coniferous forests with abundant lingonberry growth, to marshlands that host many bird species. Common goldeneyes and black-throated divers inhabit these lakes. The latter, also known as arctic loons, are recognizable by their distinctive gray-, black-, and white-striped plumage—it looks like these aquatic avians pulled on wet suits designed by Adidas. Other residents include white-tailed eagles,

The finely plumed black-throated diver

cranes, and osprey. Elk (moose) are the big mammals in Åsnen.

Activities in the park include canoeing and kayaking on the expansive waters, and pike fishing is especially good in Lake Åsnen.

Walking the park's well-tended trails is a treat. At the Trollberget entrance, a gap in the boulders is supposedly where trolls celebrated Christmas, and children can follow the Five-forest Kingdom Path from here. The Västra Torpaslingan trail takes you into swampland.

AT A GLANCE

Lakes and islands ▪ 7.3 square miles (19 sq km) ▪ Ancient beech forests ▪ Children's paths and nature trails ▪ nationalparksofsweden.se

BJÖRNLANDET

A small park with an ancient forest in a harsh northern climate

Deep in southern Lapland, and known for its large primeval forest, Björnlandet National Park protects a landscape of rolling mountain terrain broken by steep ravines and precipices. Large boulders and piles of rocks stand as evidence of the violent glacial movements that shaped this land. The harsh northern climate means that there is little fauna and flora of distinction aside from the ubiquitous reindeer (this is Åsele Sami country).

The pinewoods are marked by traces of earlier forest fires: Black charred stumps and "fire noises" in living pines are common throughout the entire region. These sounds express as faint hissing or popping—like popcorn crackling—noises that scientists have measured by way of microphones attached to the trees' trunks in times of heat and drought. The most recent great fire occurred in 1831, when wildfires swept through swaths of woodlands in much of

the north of Sweden. The fine pine stands and marshy spruce forests draped in lichen are dynamic, living ecosystems as well as environmental historical archives, an invaluable source of research into natural regeneration in woodlands. To explore, take the park's main hiking trail from Lake Ångsjön at the park's eastern boundary; it leads through the primeval forest and up Mount Björnberget, which at 2,241 feet (683 m) is a gentle climb.

AT A GLANCE

Virgin pine forests ▪ 4.2 square miles (10.8 sq km) ▪ Mount Björnberget Trail ▪ nationalparksofsweden.se

BLÅ JUNGFRUN

A legendary island of witches and wizardry

This tiny but spooky national park is centered around the island of Blå Jungfrun, or "Blue Maiden." It is a slate blue granite dome rising 282 feet (86 m) out of the Baltic Sea, home of black guillemots, white-tailed eagles, rock pipits, and various rare beetles. You can visit this island by tour boat from Oskarshamn or Byxelkrok, but you are not allowed to stay overnight, or to set fires.

The gnarled deciduous forest of the island's core is surrounded by bare rock toward the shore, with several caves. The stones, like the island, are the source of much superstition. Sailors of old started calling the island Blå Jungfrun, avoiding using its true name, Blåkulla, which they felt roused the wrath of evil spirits who dwelt there. According to the Catholic writer Olaus Magnus in 1555, witches would gather on the island each Maundy Thursday (Holy Thursday). There is also the remains of an ancient stone labyrinth, thought to have been used for ritualistic purposes.

Visitors to any national park should have the good sense to leave stones and natural artifacts where they belong, but at Blå Jungfrun you have an extra imperative. Not only is it illegal, but woe betides anyone who removes the water-rounded stones from the labyrinth or beaches here. Ancient legend decrees that anyone who steals a stone from the island will suffer from bad luck until it is returned. The mainland town of Oskarshamn annually receives stones back from former visitors to the park, often with accompanying letters in which the writers describe misfortunes and disasters that happened to them after they left the island.

Sunset on the coast of Oland, with the small island Blå Jungfrun (Blue Maiden) visible in the distance

AT A GLANCE

Witches' island in the Baltic Sea ▪ .76 square mile (1.98 sq km) ▪ Hardwood forest ▪ Stone labyrinth
▪ nationalparksofsweden.se

DALBY SÖDERSKOG

Sweden's smallest park protects broadleaf forest.

The tiny Dalby Söderskog National Park, measuring just 89.6 acres (36.2 ha), was established by the Swedish government in 1918, when this broad-leaved woodland was thought to be a unique remnant of primeval forest. This turned out not to be the case; the ground had previously been used as pasture. Today, the high levels of limestone and chalk in the soil produce an abundance of flora, and in springtime the forest floor is carpeted with color as the plants, including wood anemones, corydalis cava, gagea, and lesser celandine, burst into flower. Dalby Söderskog also contains a little mystery: A bank of earth surrounding parts of the park is speculated to be the ruins of an ancient Viking fort.

The forest itself is a lovely mix of deciduous trees: ash, elm, oak, and beech. There are also some beech forests in the southern and eastern parts of the park.

Interspersed throughout Dalby Söderskog's three distinct forests are common alder, apple, horse chestnut, lime, maple, and sallow. Needless to say, a walk in the woods of this small national park is accompanied by sounds of birdsong (and the rattle of woodpeckers) from start to finish. The Skryllestigen hiking trail, one of three paths in the park, runs for 2.1 miles (3.5 km) around the park from the Skrylle Naturum, also the visitors center.

AT A GLANCE

Broad-leaved forest ▪ Abundant forest flora ▪ .14 square mile (.36 sq km) ▪ Skryllestigen Trail ▪ nationalparksofsweden.se

DJURÖ

A remote lake park for adventurous souls

Established in 1991, Djurö National Park is another one of Sweden's many island parks, encompassing an archipelago of some 30 islands located on Sweden's largest lake, Vänern.

The islands are currently unoccupied, but humankind has long inhabited and hunted these waters; a lodge and an unmanned lighthouse can be visited in the park. The archipelago's abundant wildlife includes fallow deer and the park's wide range of winged inhabitants include ospreys, hobby, oystercatchers, and great black-backed gulls.

The park is largely water, and visitors to Djurö are responsible for their own transport—there is no ferry to the islands. Boats are available for rent on the mainland, and kayaking and canoeing are popular modes to explore the area from the water. Or you can contact park officials for a ride to the islands for a day or overnight visit.

A boat trip of five miles (8 km) takes you to the lake's nearest island from the mainland. Djurön Island has several natural harbors to dock at; the most frequently used is Malbergshamn on the north shore. A marked trail takes you on a circuit of the island, passing by the lighthouse and its residence, which you can rent. Fallow deer graze a large grassy glade at the island's heart. In contrast to the island's barren pine forest, the glade has several large oak trees and a lime tree.

AT A GLANCE

Lake archipelago ▪ Djurön Island ▪ 9.3 square miles (24 sq km) ▪ Djurön Island Trail ▪ Birdlife ▪ nationalparksofsweden.se

FÄRNEBOFJÄRDEN

A park Swedes cherish for its fishing lakes

Färnebofjärden National Park is situated close to the Limes Norrlandicus, an imaginary line marking the frontier between Sweden's north and south in terms of habitat. The park itself is transected by the river Dalälven, and water covers about 40 percent of Färnebofjärden.

The park has an interesting hydrology, crafted by the retreating glaciers of the last ice age; this left a wide floodplain over which the river courses in a series of rapids and wide bays (called *fjärdar*). The wetlands have given Färnebofjärden a rich biodiversity. Its coniferous, mixed, and broad-leaved forests are largely untouched due to its remoteness, and the rattle and hum of woodpeckers and owls is a constant sound track.

The biodiversity of this park, with its wetlands and drylands, and its northern and southern habitats, is reflected in the fauna. These include elk (moose), roe deer, red fox, and pine marten. Eurasian beavers have thrived in recent decades, and wild boar have been spotted in the last 10 years. The endangered Eurasian lynx, brown bears, gray wolves, and otter all find protection within Färnebofjärden, as does the very rare pond bat.

The area's rich acidic waters make it rewarding for anglers. The array of fish species here include the rare asp, carp, northern pike, European perch, zander, and grayling.

AT A GLANCE

First-class angling ■ 39 square miles (101 sq km) ■ Rich biodiversity on the Limes Norrlandicus ■ nationalparksofsweden.se

FULUFJÄLLET

Plunging waterfalls, bright-colored lichen, and primeval forests

This ruggedly scenic national park embraces the Swedish part of Mount Fulufjället, which towers 3,425 feet (1,044 m) above sea level; the Norwegian part of the massif is protected by Norway's Fulufjellet National Park (see page 160). The Fulufjället massif is a high plateau deeply carved by several rivers that flow into the river Dalälven. Sweden's largest waterfall, Njupskärs Vattenfall waterfall, is a dramatic focal point of the park, gushing some 305 feet (93 m) to earth. The central Sweden landscape offers both bare, rocky mountains where only lichen grows, and old-growth forests. The heathlands here, whose brush, grass, and lichens are unique in the Scandinavian mountains, are a result of the absence of grazing reindeers.

One of the world's oldest trees also stands in the park. Called Old Tjikko, the Norway spruce is thought to be approximately 9,550 years old.

The park's icon is the small and inquisitive Siberian jay, which thrives in the dense spruce swamp hereabouts. The visitors center is an attractive light-filled building, illuminated in summer with midnight sunshine. Here you'll find details of the park's many hiking trails (some 87 miles/140 km in all). The Kungsleden, or King's Trail (see page 192) passes this way.

Njupeskär, Sweden's highest waterfall at 305 feet (93 m)

AT A GLANCE

Njupskärs Vattenfall waterfall ■ Old Tjikko, a 9,550-year-old Norway spruce ■ 149 square miles (385 sq km) ■ The Kungsleden (King's Trail) ■ nationalparksofsweden.se

GARPHYTTAN

A small farm park of colorful meadows

The tiny Swedish national park of Garphyttan is packed into an area of less than one square mile. Although established in 1909, the hill farm with its deciduous forests and flowering meadows was in existence as early as 1857. These now spread over the southern slope of Kilsbergen ridge and down to the Närke plain.

The park has several loop trails, most running through the meadow areas. The 1.8-mile (3 km) Bergstigen path takes you farther afield, right to the top of Svensbodaberget mountain and broad views of the area. The 1.5-mile (2.4 km) Torpstigen Trail provides a good summation of the park's agricultural history, taking in the old Skomakartorpet (Shoemaker's Croft) with its refreshing spring. The regional hiking trail, Bergslagsleden, also runs through Garphyttan.

The initial philosophy of the park was to let nature grow freely over what was previously farmland, but as meadows became overgrown and inaccessible, authorities started to manage the land by cutting areas back. Each spring, the deciduous forest unfolds a carpet of blue anemones, wood anemones, hepaticas, and cowslips. Lilies of the valley are a strong thread in this landscape, with their bell-shaped white flowers and sweet scent. The song of the thrush is heard throughout the forest, and the rare dormouse is the unlikely kingpin of the park, resident here in great numbers. Garphyttan National Park is surrounded by Kilsbergen's coniferous forest.

AT A GLANCE

Farmland meadows and woods ▪ Svensbodaberget mountain ▪ .43 square mile (1.11 sq km) ▪ Bergslagsleden regional trail ▪ Bergstigen Trail ▪ nationalparksofsweden.se

GOTSKA SANDÖN

A remote island park in the Baltic Sea

Since 1909, Gotska Sandön (Gotlandic Sand Island) National Park has encompassed an uninhabited island in the Baltic Sea. The most isolated territory in the waters of Sweden, this is a remote, desolate, and barren place, yet it rewards intrepid visitors with a windswept beauty all its own.

In summer, the island is reached by boat service from either Fårö Island or Nynäshamn on the mainland, or by private transport. The landscape consists of sandy

Windswept isolation in the Baltic

beaches and dunes with dense pine forests. A large population of grey seals have colonized the island, with bats and mountain hares also present in large numbers. Rare insects, especially beetles, thrive in the forests, as do wild plants such as the Kashubian vetch (aka the Danzig vetch), which flowers in muted pink butterfly shapes. Several species of orchid also grow in this relatively warm oceanic climate.

Humans first inhabited Sandön in the 17th century, when sheep farmers settled. By the 18th century, the island's agriculture expanded to include crop and cattle farming.

AT A GLANCE

Wild island sandscapes ▪ Rich beetle life ▪ 17.3 square miles (44.9 sq km) ▪ Kashubian vetch blossoms ▪ Seal colony ▪ nationalparksofsweden.se

HAMRA

Hike through ancient forests and tranquil boglands.

Hamra National Park is another small Swedish gem, lying in an undulating landscape of primitive rock, rolling mountains, a river, and ancient forests. Hamra is a great place for a walk in the woods, where a series of well-maintained trails traverse untouched forest, with wooden walkways over swamps and streams, and a railed walkway leads up to an observation tower over the park's swamp area. Another good vantage point is in the old-growth forest overlooking Svansjön lake.

A large part of the park is a contiguous swamp consisting of marshes, brooks, tarns, quagmire, and pine-covered islets. The Svartån River

Fringy bogbean loves wet soil.

teems with fish and small aquatic fauna. In winter, a well-tended snowmobile track runs along the Svartåmyran swamp, or you can book a dogsledding tour. The oldest part of the national park has one of the few virgin forests in central Sweden; this takes about one hour to see via the Virgin Forest Loop.

Other loop trails include the Swamp Loop, crossing a forest that burned in 2009 but has since regrown. Watch out for black grouse and cranes that inhabit the wetlands.

> **AT A GLANCE**
>
> Virgin forests ▪ Svartåmyran swamp ▪ 5.3 square miles (13.8 sq km) ▪ Svartån River ▪ The Hamra Trail ▪ nationalparksofsweden.se

HAPARANDA SKÄRGÅRD

A rising island archipelago in Bothnian Bay

Close to the Finnish border in Bothnian Bay spreads Sweden's northernmost archipelago. A portion of these hundreds of islands are protected by Haparanda Skärgård (Haparanda Archipelago) National Park. These include the two main islands of Sandskär and Seskar-Furö, ringed by several smaller islands and reefs. In geological terms, these islands are babies, having emerged in the last 1,500 years as the seabed of the bay rose due to postglacial rebound after the last ice age. The

land continues to rise about .33 inch (8.5 mm) a year, so the islands are steadily expanding.

Tour boats go to Sandskär from Haparanda harbor in Nikkala—you can reserve tours and cabins at the Haparanda tourist office. In the Gulf of Bothnia, you'll see ringed seals that nest in the pack ice covering the bay from December to May. The gulf's low salinity levels and brackish water attract perch and lavaret, as well as sea species such as herring. On Sandskär, dense knotty

forests of pine or aspen trees grow. Here you can walk over dry juniper moors, and through rich birch groves with the lovely scents of lesser butterfly orchids or lilies of the valley to entice you along. You may see occasional island-hopping elk (moose) or reindeer (they walk across the ice in winter), and the woods are filled with myriad birds, such as black grouse, willow grouse, wrynecks, and pied flycatchers, the latter looking like short, fat magpies with their black-and-white plumage.

> **AT A GLANCE**
>
> Bothnian Bay archipelago ▪ Ringed seal colonies ▪ 23.1 square miles (59.8 sq km) ▪ Myriad birdlife ▪ nationalparksofsweden.se

KOSTERHAVET

A watery refuge for seals and rare marine species

Sunset over the waters of Kosterhavet National Park

Sweden's only exclusively oceanic park, Kosterhavet National Park is a national marine park composed of the waters and shorelines around the Koster Islands in the Skagerrak sea. Kosterhavet borders the Norwegian marine park of Ytre Hvaler (see page 187) and is home to Sweden's largest colony of harbor seals. The Kosterfjorden runs some 660 feet (200 m) deep with a relatively low temperature of 41° to 45°F (5° to 7°C) and a high salinity. Divers who brave the cold waters here can observe the brachiopod, sponge, and coral larvae brought in by Atlantic currents. Of the 6,000 marine species that have been identified in Kosterhavet, more than 200 are found nowhere else in Sweden. Plaice, cod, and sea trout breed in the shallower waters closer to shore, but these waters are not protected from commercial fishing, and northern prawn and Norwegian lobster are caught in large numbers here. The park also plays host to many seabirds, such as arctic terns and skuas.

Koster Boats depart year-round from Strömstad for the 45-minute trip to the islands, taking you across the archipelago and over the Koster fjord's deep trench.

The excellent Naturum Kosterhavet visitors center, near Ekenäs jetty on (Syd-Koster) South Koster Island, offers maps and information on the park, as well as an aquarium, interactive activities, and a microscope that allows you to examine your own beach discoveries. You can even dip your hand into the touch tank to feel some of Kosterhavet's marine inhabitants. Among the activities offered are kayaking, hiking, snorkeling, bird-watching, and angling.

AT A GLANCE

Skagerrak sea and shorelines ▪ 150 square miles (388 sq km) ▪ Naturum Kosterhavet visitors center ▪ Diving and snorkeling ▪ nationalparksofsweden.se

MUDDUS

A brooding park in the northern region of Lapland

Apart of the UNESCO World Heritage Laponian area, Muddus National Park spans landscapes of old-growth forests, expansive boglands, and deep ravines. The park is also home to Sweden's oldest known pine tree, a weather-toughened, seasoned survivor of more than 700 winters in the cold north of Sweden. This tree is known to have withstood a forest fire in 1413.

Muddus is unusual for its range of mires and wetlands. Bryophytes such as liverworts and mosses grow on the rich fens in abundance. The park's boreal climate nurtures mainly woodland birds such black grouse and hazel hen, as well as northerly types including the Siberian jay and Siberian tit. Whooper swans, bean geese, and black-throated loons all cause a cacophony on the lakes in summer, while cranes, sandpipers, and snipes all thrive in the marshy boglands. Reindeer and elk (moose) are a common sight for hikers in the park, but arachnophobes beware: The spruce and pine forests and shallow lakes of the region mean that the park is crawling with spiders of many species.

The Naturum Laponian Visitor Centre on Viedásnjárgga point by Lake Láŋas serves the entire Laponian World Heritage site in a superbly crafted building. Its circular design allows it to collect snow, which enhances its shape. The Naturum has tours, maps, and information on the park's trails; it also offers lectures and exhibits on the Sami way of life.

AT A GLANCE

UNESCO World Heritage Laponian area ▪ Rich spider life ▪ 190.5 square miles (493 sq km) ▪ Sami stronghold ▪ Naturum Laponian Visitor Centre ▪ nationalparksofsweden.se

NORRA KVILL

A tiny national park with a famous leafy neighbor

In southeastern Sweden, tucked away in backcountry that most people pass by, is a small forest park. What makes Norra Kvill National Park notable is that a couple of kilometers from its borders, within the same forested area, rises the world-renowned Rumskulla oak, Europe's largest English oak, with a circumference of some 46 feet (14 m). The oak is estimated to be about 1,000 years old. As you venture out to touch this ancient giant of the Swedish woods, consider that the Vikings were marauding their merry way across a terrified Europe when this seed took root. The park is also home to pine trees more than 350 years old.

To wander in this small park is to revisit the continent the way it must have looked before we all used motorways to bring home our Ikea wooden furniture to construct. Giant imposing trees, fallen trunks alive with woodpeckers and insects, and massive boulders strewn about make Norra Kvill a most primeval-looking forest. In the midst of this wilderness is a lovely small lake, Stora Idegölen, delightfully decorated with water lilies and bogbean like a miniature Monet masterpiece in the middle of nowhere.

Hikers should know in advance that the park is very inaccessible, with rough terrain and footbridges and rope handholds leading up to the overlook Idhöjden. The paths are identified with red and blue ground markings.

AT A GLANCE

Remote forestland ▪ .44 square mile (1.14 sq km) ▪ Stora Idegölen lake ▪ Rudimentary trails ▪ nationalparksofsweden.se

PADJELANTA

The largest of Sweden's national parks with the country's most remote point

Padjelanta is Sweden's largest national park and part of the UNESCO World Heritage Laponian area. The park is set in the heart of the native Sami lands and includes three villages of settled Sami who bring reindeer to graze in Padjelanta in the summer, at the traditional communities of Stáloluokta, Árasluokta, and Sállohávrre.

The park has mostly alpine landscapes comprising a vast plateau around the two vast lakes of Vastenjávrre and Virihávrre. Most of Padjelanta is above the tree line, which means that few trees survive the harsh climate. A variety of plants thrive in the chalk-rich bedrock, such as the dwarf mountain cinquefoil with its attractive bouquet of yellow flowers. The birdlife around Padjelanta's mountains and lakes is particularly rich, and includes European golden plover, meadow pipit, northern wheatear, Eurasian dotterel, and whimbrel.

Padjelanta is as far away as you can get from traffic in Sweden: The south-eastern bay of the Rissájávrre lake is some 29 miles (47 km) from the nearest road, and it takes half a day just to hike from here to the park. The best known trail is the 87-mile (140-km) Padjelantaleden (Padjelanta Trail) that runs between Kvikkjokk in the southeast and either Vaisaluokta or Änonjalme beneath the Áhkká massif in the north. The Sami maintain cabins that are well spread along the trail. Skiing is popular in winter, but remember that trails disappear in the snow, so bring a map and a compass.

> **AT A GLANCE**
>
> Remote Swedish wilderness ▪ Scenic Virihávrre lake ▪ 766 square miles (1,984 sq km) ▪ Padjelanta Trail ▪ nationalparksofsweden.se

PIELJEKAISE

A mountainous walking ground along the King's Trail

Pieljekaise National Park consists largely of birch woods traversed by the Kungsleden hiking trail (see page 192). Also known as the King's Trail, this renowned pathway continues into the nearby Vindelfjällen Nature Reserve, one of the largest protected areas in Europe. Keep an eye out for solitary elk (moose), which can reach a shoulder height of 6.9 feet (2.1 m). Their hooves act as snowshoes to carry their considerable heft—males (known as bulls) can weigh up to 1,874 pounds (850 kg).

Cloudberry is a spring delight.

This is a place of valleys filled with lush birch forests as well as desolate wilderness higher up in the Arjeplog mountains. The national park takes its name from its highest peak, which stands some 3,733 feet (1,138 m) above sea level. The Sami call this mountain Bieljijgájse, meaning "ear mountain," as the two peaks of the mountain look like an ear in profile.

On the north end of the park, near Jäckvik, a rest cottage with a stove awaits weary walkers; the key to another refuge, Pieljekaise cottage on the Kungsleden, can be rented from shops in nearby Jäckvik and Adolfsström.

> **AT A GLANCE**
>
> Birch forests ▪ 59.2 square miles (153.4 sq km) ▪ Pieljekaise mountain ▪ The Kungsleden (King's Trail) ▪ nationalparksofsweden.se

SAREK

A remote magic mountain kingdom in one of Europe's great wildernesses

A male älg (aka moose), largest of all the deer species

Opened in 1910, Sarek National Park in northern Sweden is one of the oldest national parks in Europe, and one of the most remote. Sarek adjoins two other national parks, Stora Sjöfallet to the north (see page 211) and Padjelanta on the west (see page 204). This is high mountain country composed of mountain peaks, valleys such as Rapadalen, and high plateaus. The park has six of Sweden's 13 peaks over 6,600 feet (2,000 m), as well as about 200 peaks over 5,900 feet (1,800 m). Sweden's second highest mountain is here too: Sarektjåkkå, standing at a height of 6,854 feet (2,089 m), is a popular challenge for mountaineers. There are also about 100 glaciers throughout the park. The delta of the Rapaätno river provides one of Sweden's loveliest views, as does the summit of Mount Skierfe, with an impressive vista of that glacial trough valley covered in ice. The park is veined by several rivers, the most notable of which is the Rapaätno river, which empties into Lake Laitaure.

WILDLIFE & FLORA

Due to its different altitudes, the park has several zones; the subalpine zone of old-growth birch forests hosts shrew, vole, reindeer, and brown bear, as well as a host of birch-favoring birds, including the willow warbler, the common redpoll, the yellow wagtail, the northern wheatear, and the bluethroat. Gyrfalcons and golden eagles also nest at these altitudes, while predators such as merlins and rough-legged buzzards reside higher up on the cliffs. Up in the alpine zone, wolves, wolverine, and arctic fox prowl the meadows, where plants such as mountain avens, purple saxifrage, velvetbells, alpine pussytoes, and alpine veronica bring color to the hillsides. The humid zone also hosts a rainbow of plants, including northern Labrador tea, Goldilocks buttercup, St. Olaf's candlestick, common self-heal, and common marsh-bedstraw. The birdlife is likewise multitudinous with common cranes, wood sandpiper, and short-eared owl all common at lower altitudes, while Eurasian teals, Eurasian wigeons, greater scaups, red-breasted mergansers, sedge warblers, and common reed buntings are all often seen in the Laitaure delta and around Pårekjaure Lake.

Hiking in the park can be hazardous for the inexperienced, and a guide is recommended. There are no cabins in the park. The Kungsleden trail (see page 192) passes through the eastern section, from Saltoluokta to Kvikkjokk. The Padjelanta Trail (Padjelantaleden), stretching from Kvikkjokk to Akkajaure, runs along the western edge at Tarraluoppal, where the Tarraluoppal cabin is located just outside the park.

AT A GLANCE

Remote mountain topography ▪ Climbing Sarektjåkkå ▪ 760 square miles (1,970 sq km) ▪ The Kungsleden (King's Trail) ▪ nationalparksofsweden.se

SKULESKOGEN

A rocky park of uplifting geology, biodiversity, and wilderness trails

Skuleskogen's rough, rocky peaks reward with fine vistas.

Verdant valleys, old-growth spruce forests, Baltic coastal landscapes, beautiful lakes, and geological intrigue that points to oceanic origins—Skuleskogen National Park offers visitors a little bit of everything. Here is Sweden in microcosm, encapsulated in a relatively small park that covers the eastern section of the Forest of Skule. The park's topography is very rough and rocky, with many peaks rising directly from the sea. The highest of these is Slåttdalsberget, which runs to 920 feet (280 m) above sea level.

Along the rocky shoreline, adventurers will also thrill to the exploration of many deep crevasses and caves, typical of Sweden's High Coast along the Baltic Sea. These crevasses are, in fact, small valleys *(sprickdal)*, the most impressive of which is Slåttdalskrevan, measur-ing 130 feet (40 m) deep, 660 feet (200 m) long, and 26 feet (8 m) wide. Also look for the Trollporten (Trolls' Door), a small crevasse known for the large rock lintel that rests across the top. Enter with caution!

THE HUMAN FOOTPRINT

Despite the fact that the Skuleskogen forest was the scene of large-scale logging during the latter half of the 19th century, much of the woodlands within the national park has the pristine sense of a primeval forest. Many of the trees growing here now are more than a century old. This shows the value of protection, as the region exhibits many other traces of humankind's presence throughout the ages, including numerous Bronze Age funerary cairns still evident along the ancient coastline. Later, from medieval times onward, the forest was mainly used as pastureland. Then came the countrywide logging activity that claimed forestry all over Sweden from the middle of the 19th century.

This forest is now in the process of restoring its own biodiversity, regenerating much important fauna and flora in the absence of humans. Several endangered species, such as the lichen *Dolichousnea longissima*, grow in abundance in the cool, moist forests of Skuleskogen. You'll see this lengthy lichen hanging like great strings of blanched candy floss from the trees. This stringy lichen is the world's longest, mea-suring several inches, and is commonly known as old man's beard or Methuselah's beard lichen. The ragged old man's beard has become the park's symbol, an appropriate development for a place that has ceased being groomed by human intervention.

Skuleskogen is located on the northern border of the range of many plant species. This means that several deciduous tree species grow in the park, such as the little-leaf linden, the common hazel, the guelder-rose, and the Norway maple.

The park is also home to many mammals, including Eurasian lynx, endangered brown bear, red fox, European badger, European pine marten, elk (moose), Eurasian bea-ver, grey seal, and muskrat. Smaller mammals, such as the Eurasian red squirrel, American mink, and stoat thrive here too. The forest fills with birdsong of, among many others, the Siberian jay, three-toed woodpecker, red-throated loon, and greenish warbler.

EXPLORING SKULESKOGEN

Skuleskogen's geological and biological richness led to the park's inclusion with the rest of the High Coast in 2000 in the UNESCO World Heritage List. Today, the park attracts some 20,000 visitors annually, with its principal attraction being the 131-foot-deep (40-m) crevasse of Slåttdalskrevan. This is easily accessible by numerous hiking trails, including the Höga Kustenleden, which runs along the entirety of the High Coast.

This is a rocky terrain so wear good hiking footwear or boots in spring, summer, and fall, and skis or snowshoes in winter. Skuleskogen has six cabins that are open year-round, but you must bring along sleeping bags, cooking utensils, and other supplies.

Geology on the Rise

Skuleskogen is a region on the rebound. Most of this land was under the sea less than 10,000 years ago, when the ice sheet that had blanketed it melted. The melting of such a mass of ice relieved the land of a huge weight that had been pressing it down, allowing the ground to rise up, or rebound. This lifting has continued ever since, with the current rebound speed measuring .31 inch (8 mm) a year. This postglacial rise will eventually turn the island of Tärnättholmarna into a peninsula. The main rock in Skuleskogen is Nordingrå granite, making the park part of the Nordingrå massif. This crumbly granite has a bright red color and erodes easily.

The Naturum visitors center is located at the foot of Skuleberget mountain, at the center of the High Coast World Heritage site. Here, helpful staff will provide information for your visit to Skuleskogen and other destinations in the High Coast World Heritage site. In summer, the Naturum arranges guided tours of the national park.

The park also has several interesting trails of varying lengths, including the half-mile (0.8-km) Nylandsruten trail leading to a fine vantage point on the southeastern slope of Nylandsruten mountain. From here you'll enjoy great views of the park and of the Skags lighthouse to the northeast, the Trysunda nature reserve to the east, and the Ulvöarna islands to the southeast. Below this skullcap mountain, the Swedish sky is mirrored on the waters of Svartjärn tarn.

A slightly longer walk is the 1.6-mile (2.7-km) Skrattabborrtjärn Trail that brings you to the ruins of a collection of summer dwellings known as Norrsvedjebodarna. Up until the turn of the 20th century, people spent the summer here tending livestock. Today, a log cabin with six wide beds is open to visitors year-round. From Skrattabborrtjärn, you can hike farther east in the direction of Slåttdalen and the Slåttdalsskreva crevice, a distance of about 2.17 miles (3.5 km). Here you walk over high rocky ground through a typically sparse flat-rock pine forest. On a clear day, you can also take in a panoramic view of the entire High Coast archipelago.

Elevated trails lead through the park's woodlands.

AT A GLANCE

Unique geology ▪ Methuselah's beard lichen ▪ 11.8 square miles (30.6 sq km) ▪ UNESCO World Heritage Listed ▪ Höga Kustenleden trail ▪ nationalparksofsweden.se

SÖDERÅSEN

A small national park with an interesting geological foundation

Söderåsen National Park is based around Söderåsen, an elongated bedrock ridge in southern Sweden intersected by several fissure valleys. The long, deep gorge by Skäralid is especially dramatic— a plunging rift valley with perpendicular cliffs that envelop the Skärån River below. The focal point of this small park, however, is the circular shape, thought to resemble the single eye of the Norse god.

LIFE IN THE PARK

The landscape of the park is that of scree-covered high rocks, vibrant waterways, and lush deciduous forests of beech, oak, and ash. The area is also rich in mushrooms, insects, water creatures, and mosses.

Söderåsen lures hikers with several fine forest walks.

viewpoint Kopparhatten located on Söderåsen at a height of 660 feet (200 m). Aside from the view, this highest point in the park is close to several deep ravines that cut through the ridge, exposing walls of up to 300 feet (90 m). Another geologic point of interest in Söderåsen is Odensjön, or Oden's Lake. This small glacier lake, in what may be a volcanic crater, has a diameter of 490 feet (150 m); the name Oden may have been conferred due to its

Birds and bats thrive among the old-growth trees, and several rare beetles find habitats in dead trees slowly decaying in the forests.

The flora is extremely varied for such a confined area; you'll find species such as hollow wort and tall meadow-rue. The wonderfully named enchantress's nightshade is found here too; its genus name comes from the enchantress Circe of Greek mythology, and the specific designation is derived from Lutetia,

the Latin name for Paris, which was sometimes referred to as the "Witch City" back in Roman times. Despite this pedigree, this simple, tannin-rich plant is not poisonous.

As with many Swedish parks, the hiking trails are well kept, with many wooden pathways designed to maximize access for disabled visitors. The main path is a 2,625-foot (800-m) nature trail with information signs guiding around Skärdammen pond in Skäralid.

A longer trail is the Liakroksrundan loop, leading to the plateau atop the ridge. This trail goes through tall beech forest and past croft ruins, taking you along the edge of Skäralidsdalen, with great views of the park from Kopparhatten and other points.

The Naturum visitors center here has plentiful nature information on the park and its many educational activities. The park also offers a network of fine cross-country biking trails with plenty of hills for great views and a powerful workout. Or saddle up and go for a ride through the woods on powerful Haflinger horses, with comfortable Western saddles. The Rönne Å River provides a nice variety of gentle streams, fast rapids, and abundant wildlife in leafy green forests for canoeists to enjoy. The park runs a tour that starts in Rögnaröd/Djupedal and finishes at the canoe center in Ljungbyhed.

AT A GLANCE

Kopparhatten observation point ▪ 6.2 square miles (16.2 sq km) ▪ Skäralid fissure valley ▪ Liakroksrundan trail ▪ nationalparksofsweden.se

SONFJÄLLET

A beautiful Swedish wilderness filled with life

Located in central Sweden, Sonfjället National Park contains dramatic mountains strewn with large boulders, vibrant rivers and lakes, and an extensive forest area. Yet despite its scenic setting, Sonfjället is all about the animals, as Swedes come here to see the large populations of resident bears, as well as several herds of elk (moose). Wolves and lynx also prowl these woods and meadows for plentiful prey. The park is named after the mountain Sonfjället, which climbs some 4,193 feet (1,278 m) above sea level. Its great (and usually snowcapped) peak seems to dominate the area of Härjedalen and its denizens the way that Mount Fuji pervades the consciousness of Tokyo and its surrounds. It is always there, bathed in Swedish sunlight, casting and catching shadows at twilight, sparkling in the sunrise, or visible 24/7 for an eye-watering eternity under summer's midnight sun.

Within the park are lots of marked, well-kept summer trails, catering to all visitor needs, from short child-friendly trips to day-long expeditions along the mountaintop. The park's helpful guides will assist you in plotting a course to suit your activity level. Cairns or posts delineate the summer trails, which mainly start from Nyvallen, Nysätern, or Dalsvallen. Cabins can be rented privately; you can inquire at the visitors center. If you've come to see bears or other animals, you can book activities such as bear or beaver safaris at Dalsvallen. The Hede tourist office also arranges guided tours, scouting for bears, and lodging.

Swedes have a long tradition of spending summers in the mountains to tend animals on higher pastures. At the Nyvallen *fäbod*, a group of summer dwellings where people live while tending cattle, you can learn about the fäbod life in the cabin, enjoy a guided tour (for a fee), and even taste traditional fäbod food such as cheese and smoked goat meat.

Sonfjället's rock faces, forests, and waterways host myriad wildlife.

AT A GLANCE

Swedish wildlife ▪ Sonfjället mountain ▪ 40 square miles (103 sq km) ▪ The fäbod life ▪ nationalparksofsweden.se

STENSHUVUD

A simple Swedish park makes a mountain out of a small hill

Swans add to the mystique of Stenshuvud, a small hill shrouded in legend.

Stenshuvud, a little hill in the southeastern corner of Sweden, has since 1986 been one of the country's national parks.

This mound rises 318 feet (97 m) above the level of the Baltic Sea, which is visible from its peak. In olden times, seafarers used the hill as a landmark. From the hilltop, what you see below is mainly broad-leaved forest, especially European hornbeam, a species that usually favors a lofty elevation of about 600 feet (183 m). The landscape also encompasses heaths, meadows, and swamps. The park's mild climate, tempered by the Baltic, incubates some unusual Swedish wildlife, such as the hazel dormouse, European tree frog, and agile frog. You won't miss the male Eurasian golden oriole in the forest: His plumage is a vivid canary yellow with jet-black wings. Several types of orchids grow wild in the meadows, as does the very rare barren strawberry. Below the hill sits a gorgeous, tree-lined beach that is popular for swimming. Close to the top of the hill are the remains of a ruin of a fifth- or sixth-century fortress. According to local folklore, the hill got its name ("Sten's head") from a giant living in the nearby cave of Giddastuan.

The park's Naturum visitors center offers guided tours on Sundays during spring and autumn, and daily during the summer. North of the hill is the Hällevik arboretum, which is on the park's orange trail. This is planted mainly with Asian and North American coniferous trees and cypresses, many dating back to the end of the 19th century. The yellow trail takes you all the way around the mountain, a hike of about 2.5 miles (about 4 km).

AT A GLANCE

Spectacular view from Stenshuvud ▪ Eurasian golden oriole ▪ 1.5 square miles (3.9 sq km) ▪ nationalparksofsweden.se

STORA SJÖFALLET

Waterfalls and reindeer in a land between lakes

Stora Sjöfallet, meaning "great waterfall" in Swedish, takes its name from the five majestic waterfalls that cascade into Lake Lánas. The preserve's first name, Stuor Muorkke, refers to the Sami label of "land between two lakes." Stora Sjöfallet National Park was formed to protect the waterfall and its source lakes, but soon after its opening in 1909, its map was redrawn to generate hydroelectric power. The waterfall, known as Stuormuorkkegårttje in the Sami language, remains.

Today, the national park encircles the dam-regulated Áhkkájávrre reservoir. The park also encompasses alpine mountains, glacial mountain heaths, mountain birch slopes, and primeval pine forests. To the north, its boundary is the deep Dievssávágge, regarded by many as the most beautiful valley in Sweden. Rising in the southwestern corner of the national park is the majestic Áhkká massif and its glaciers. The Áhkká mountain is also known as "the Queen of Lapland."

This park encompasses grazing lands for the Sami villages of Sirges and Unna Tjerusj. A Sami communtity (*sameby* in Swedish) is not a village in the traditional sense of the word, but rather an economic and administrative unit engaged in reindeer husbandry. In summer, the herds graze in the lush mountain valleys that stretch all the way to the Norwegian border. As a protectorate of the Sami culture, the national park is part of the Laponian area, which is a UNESCO World Heritage site.

AT A GLANCE

Dievssávágge valley ▪ Áhkká mountain ▪ 493 square miles (1,278 sq km) ▪ Sami reindeer ranges ▪ UNESCO World Heritage site ▪ nationalparksofsweden.se

STORE MOSSE

Sweden's Big Marsh—a hallowed haven for birds

Located right in the heart of the largest boggy grounds south of Lapland, Store Mosse (Big Marsh) National Park is a magnet for many species of birds. The marshlands also provide unique protected habitats for other animals and plants. A 40-foot (12-m) bird-watching tower, with wheelchair access, overlooks Lake Kävsjön and the marshland, while the park's Naturum visitors center supplies binoculars and telescopes to watch birdlife from panoramic windows

facing Lake Kävsjön. From here visitors can look onto the "sea of sphagnum," as the center evocatively describes the vast quagmire outside its doors.

Cranes can regularly be seen foraging around their nesting area in the Stora Gungflyet (Large Quagmire). This is a fen area along the southern side of Lake Kävsjön, a blanket of entangled roots and other half-submerged or floating vegetation.

During the winter, national park

rangers feed the golden eagles and white-tailed eagles, and visitors can observe these predators from a vantage point near the feeding station along the Kittlakull–Östra Rockne gravel road.

The park has more than 25 miles (40 km) of walking trails to explore, and three cabins are open for those wishing to stay in the park overnight. Guided tours are available to visitors all through the summer, as well as guided snowshoe tours on the bog.

AT A GLANCE

Bird-watching tower ▪ Eagle feeding ▪ 30.3 square miles (78.5 sq km) ▪ Stora Gungflyet ▪ Birdland walking trails ▪ nationalparksofsweden.se

TIVEDEN

A small park with an outlaw past

In southern Sweden's Tiveden forest area, a region carved by glaciers, lies Tiveden National Park. This is wild, hilly, and rugged country, notable for the giant boulders at Stenkälla, the Trollkyrkobergen mountains, and the swimming area at Vitsand.

The park has nine marked hiking trails and three entrances; the easiest loop is the Mellannäsrundan trail, which runs for just over a mile (1.9 km), starting south of the Ösjönäs entrance. This takes you out onto the Mellannäs headland, a rolling esker. You'll also pass by the secluded woodland lakes of Stora Trehörningen and Lilla Trehörningen.

For a good overall sense of the park's geography and geology, take the 4.1-mile (6.7-km) Oxögabergsrundan trail. This demanding path leads into Tiveden's mossy, wet spruce forests and marshy valleys and on through capercaillie forests. You'll pass through Stigmanspasset, a typical rift valley, for a close-up view of faults formed millions of years ago by the continental shift. Another interesting geological outing is the 1.7-mile (2.8-km) trail up to Junker Jägare's boulder, an enormous rock deposited by the inland ice about 10,000 years ago. This is named after the legend of Junker Jägare (Squire Hunter), a young man who loses his beloved. On

your walks, look for foxes, badgers, and martens, as well as for scarab beetles in the deadwood. Listen, too, for the winnowing sound of a boreal owl.

The old-growth forests of Tiveden are unusual for the region, which was heavily logged in the 19th and 20th centuries. The woodlands are now being left to evolve naturally, and it's easy to imagine the outlaws who took refuge in the park's rift valleys from the Middle Ages onward.

The park offers guided and themed tours in summer, and arranges cycling, canoeing, fishing, cross-country skiing, and horse-riding activities.

A park trail leads past the still waters of Stora Trehorningen lake.

AT A GLANCE

Bandit country ▪ Vitsand swimming area ▪ 7.7 square miles (19.9 sq km) ▪ Oxögabergsrundan trail
▪ Junker Jägare's boulder ▪ nationalparksofsweden.se

TÖFSINGDALEN

A remote and desolate wilderness of forests and rocky hills

There are no trails in Töfsingdalen National Park, but intrepid visitors can climb Hovden Mountain (2,930 feet/893 m) for a lay of this rough land, or relax by a forest lake and feel light-years from civilization.

This park is inaccessible by car, located miles from the highway, a remote area of primeval pine forests, lush spruce woods, and fields filled with glacial boulders. Töfsingdalen lies in the Långfjället nature reserve next to the Rogen and Femundsmarka wilderness areas, which are all part of Gränslandet, the borderlands between Sweden and Norway. The park includes the reindeer grazing land of the Idre Sami group.

Bears, wolverines, and elk (moose) also live here, while golden eagles nest on rocky precipices or in old pine trees. The adult eagles remain on the mountain in winter, while young eagles migrate south. You'll recognize a young bird by the white markings at the base of its tail and under its wings. At three years of age, the tail turns dark brown. Smaller birds that thrive in the woods include black grouse, Siberian jays, and ptarmigans; the boulders are preferred habitat of wheatears and ravens.

Spruce thrive along the Töfsingån river, growing to several feet in circumference. The woodlands are covered in the rare, intensely yellow-green wolf lichen. By the river's largest waterfall, you'll find ostrich fern, whorled Solomon's seal, and one of the Dalafjällen mountains' rarities— the white-and-yellow flowers of pond water crowfoot.

AT A GLANCE

Hovden Mountain ▪ Desolate backcountry ▪ 6.2 square miles (16.15 sq km) ▪ Gränslandet borderlands ▪ nationalparksofsweden.se

TRESTICKLAN

A rift valley landscape preserved in southern Sweden

Tresticklan National Park was established in 1996 to protect the rift valley landscape and one of the few remaining areas of old-growth forest in southern Scandinavia. The park's highest point for a view of its lake-dappled landscape is the Orshöjden, which stands at 905 feet (276 m).

The park's sparse, barren pine forests are covered with lichen, and everywhere you'll step across flat rocks blanketed in moss. High mountain ridges run in a north-south direction, with swamplands and narrow lakes in between. Elk (moose) and roe deer stalk the park, and the area is known for its high wolf numbers. Birdlife is also plentiful, with deadwood inhabitants including the crested tit, great tit, pied flycatcher, redstart, great spotted woodpecker, black woodpecker, and common goldeneye. The European robin, chaffinch, willow warbler, and tree pipit are often seen too, as are the willow tit, goldcrest wren, and siskin. Several rare insects breed in the dead trees, including *Etorofus pubescens*, which is recognizable by its black head and antennae and bright orange body.

The park has several trails for visitors to walk, the most comprehensive being the Orshöjdsleden trail. From the high point of Orshöjden, this follows old paths to pass Kleningen Lake, the Lilla and Stora Pylsan tarns, and, farther on, the Ekedrågen croft, one of the last inhabited crofts in the area.

AT A GLANCE

Rift valley landscape ▪ Old-growth pine forests ▪ 11.1 square miles (28.9 sq km) ▪ Orshöjdsleden trail ▪ nationalparksofsweden.se

TYRESTA

A small oasis of nature just outside Stockholm

The Tyresta National Park and Nature Reserve have a rift valley landscape with several lakes and one of the largest areas of untouched forest in southern Sweden. The park provides a beautiful recreation space for citizens of the nearby capital; Stockholm is just 12 miles (20 km) away. Its lovely coniferous old-growth forests include pine trees up to 400 years old, dating from the great days of the Swedish Empire. The park also has deciduous broad-leaved forests, open arable land, and several historical buildings. In the fertile valleys, spruce stands are more prevalent than pine, with trees towering up to 100 feet (30 m).

As well as its forests, Tyresta has many bogs and marshes, where plants such as marsh Labrador tea and sweet gale thrive.

The park is home to a wealth of wildlife, and weekend walkers from the city stroll past roe deer in the Tyresta forests, as well as elk (moose), ermine, and weasel. Foxes were afflicted by fox mange in recent years but are making a good recovery. Several varieties of bats breed in the area, and Tyresta's 112 bird species include European robins, willow warblers, chaffinches, the lesser spotted woodpecker, Eurasian three-toed woodpecker, capercaillie, and the spotted nutcracker. Walkers by the lakes in the park will hear the characteristic call

A high brown fritillary butterfly alights on a purple thistle flower.

of the black-throated diver, a whistling song that has been transcribed by the human hand as *oooéé-cu-cloooéé-cu-cloooéé-cu-cluuéé.*

The human footprint has been left on this area since at least the 14th century: On the mountain north of Stora Stensjön lake are remnants of an ancient castle. From this vantage point, you get a fine view of the lake and dense forests. The Naturum House visitors center in the village of Tyresta offers talks and guided tours year-round.

Walking in Tyresta

Tyresta has several trails, all superbly maintained with elevated wooden walkways across marshy areas. The Primeval Forest Trail gives you an excellent overall view of these woodlands, starting at the visitors center in town. On this 1.5-mile (2.5-km) walk, you will venture through a typically untouched Tyresta forest of tall pine trees and small swamps, with information boards to explain the growth process and the plants and wildlife around you. On many of the trails you'll also find fireplaces stocked with wood, and in winter the park sets ski tracks. If you venture an hour south of the visitors center, you'll come across the area of forest damaged in the fire of August 1991. Here you can see how the forest regenerates and how wildlife reclaims the blackened trees.

Old-growth pine forest ▪ Rift valley landscape ▪ 7.7 square miles (20 sq km) ▪ Primeval Forest Trail ▪ nationalparksofsweden.se

VADVETJÅKKA

A taste of Swedish wilderness inside the Arctic Circle

Sweden's most northerly park, Vadvetjåkka National Park encompasses desolate alpine country northwest of Torneträsk lake. The park is named for Mount Vádvečohkka, which towers over the area. Vadvetjåkka is a key part of the summer grazing land for reindeer of the Talma *sameby*, a Sami village. To the south of the mountain spreads a large delta area, as well as lakes and thickets of willows and marshes. Most of the park's landscape consists of bare mountain areas located above the tree line.

This national park also has an interesting underground: Some of Sweden's deepest limestone caves are found in the park's western areas, amid a karst labyrinth carved out by flowing subterranean water. The largest cave here is about 1,312 feet (400 m) long and 460 feet (140 m) deep.

FLORA, FAUNA & TRAILS

The climate within Vadvetjåkka is affected by its proximity to the Atlantic. The moisture that gathers over the ocean and blows in across the mountains brings clouds and swirling mists, and large amounts of precipitation. This rainy climate supports abundant flora, which is also nurtured by Vadvetjåkka's calcareous bedrock. Plants that thrive here include mountain avens, purple saxifrage, and Scandinavian primrose.

Also found is the uncommon narrow-fruit braya, a pretty white blossoming plant that exists only here, in Greenland, and in parts of Canada.

Large predators such as brown bears, lynx, and wolverines stalk the woods. In the delta you'll see elk (moose) and many birds, including teal, greater scaup, widgeon, sedge warbler, and Hornemann's redpoll, a subspecies of the arctic redpoll.

Vadvetjåkka National Park is extremely remote and without trails. One way to visit is to hike from the parking lot at Kopparåsen ridge, in Abisko National Park (see page 192). This trail runs for approximately six miles (10 km) to a bridge that leads you into Vadvetjåkka.

The northern wilderness of Vadvetjåkka beckons dedicated hikers.

AT A GLANCE

Desolate alpine wilderness ▪ 10.2 square miles (26.3 sq km) ▪ Deep limestone caves
▪ nationalparksofsweden.se

NORWAY

Lemmenjoki National Park

Urho Kekkonen National Park

Saariselkä

Inari

Porttipahta Reservoir

Lokka Res.

Pallas-Yllästunturi National Park

Pyhä-Luosto National Park

Oulanka National Park

SWEDEN

ARCTIC CIRCLE

Rovaniemi

Riisitunturi National Park

Kemijoki

Simojärvi

Syöte National Park

Hossa National Park

Bothnian Bay National Park

FINLAND

RUSSIA

Oulu

Oulu

Rokua N.P.

Oulujärvi

Hiidenportti N.P.

Tiilikkajärvi N.P.

Patvinsuo N.P.

Pielinen

Salamajärvi National Park

Koli N.P.

Nöytiäinen

Vaasa

Lappajärvi

Pyhä-Häkki N.P.

Petkeljärvi N.P.

Southern Konnevesi N.P.

Kolovesi N.P.

Orivesi

GULF OF BOTHNIA

Kauhaneva-Pohjankangas N.P.

Linnansaari N.P.

Lauhanvuori N.P.

Helvetinjärvi N.P.

Leivonmäki N.P.

Seitseminen N.P.

Isojärvi N.P.

Saimaa

Tampere

Kokemäenjoki

Päijänne N.P.

Päijänne

Bothnian Sea National Park

Puurijärvi-Isosuo N.P.

Repovesi N.P.

Torronsuo N.P.

Liesjärvi N.P.

Valkmusa N.P.

Kurjenrahka N.P.

Nuuksio N.P.

Sipoonkorpi N.P.

Gulf of Finland National Park

Turku

Åland

Archipelago N.P.

Teijo N.P.

Helsinki

Ekenäs Archipelago N.P.

GULF OF FINLAND

N

0   50 kilometers
0   50 miles

ESTONIA

FINLAND

For many, Finland is a Scandinavian afterthought, unfairly grouped together with its Nordic neighbors, Norway and Sweden—an opinion without appreciation for all this beautiful country has to offer. For Finland is a wilderness wonderland, a sparsely populated landscape of remote, peaceful lakes and vast forests alive with wildlife and birdsong. There are the great parks such as Oulanka, where the famous Karhunkierros hike leads into a mixed biosphere of Arctic, Siberian, and northern European habitats.

Others parks are all about the ocean, including two by the Bothnian Sea. Wherever you venture, Finland sends out a seductive siren call to solitude. For although the quirky Finns might invite you to share a sauna (a sacred Finnish ritual of relaxation, reflection, and regeneration), or come to a wife-throwing contest, ultimately they believe in giving everyone their own space. And Finland has wide-open spaces in abundance; the Sami reindeer herders have traversed these lands for centuries, under the light of the midnight sun in summer and the dazzling light show of the northern lights in winter. It is fitting that the national animal is the bear, a rugged survivor who is happiest when left alone to live a life of contentment in the woods.

A wilderness cabin in Riisitunturi National Park, in Finnish Lapland, is a night sky delight—the perfect place to witness the northern lights and enjoy the constellations.

ARCHIPELAGO

This Finnish archipelago has more islands that any other such grouping worldwide.

Beaches ring green elevations on the numerous islands of Archipelago National Park.

Archipelago National Park covers a vast swath of islands in southwest Finland. The park includes much of the Archipelago Sea on the eastern side of the Åland Islands and south of the Korpo, Nagu, Pargas, and Kimitoön main islands. It also includes the UNESCO Archipelago Sea Biosphere Reserve, which incorporates the rest of the islands in the Åboland archipelago. The varied landscapes range from the larger historically agricultural islands with their rustic pastures and villages, to windswept and desolate rocky islets.

The archipelago historically nurtured a traditional self-sufficient way of life, where much of the fertile ground was used to graze cattle. The woodlands were cleared and burned to create meadows, where many indigenous species of birds, plants, mushrooms, butterflies, and beetles flourished. However, when the crofters (small-holding farmers) started to leave here in the 1900s, the traditional pasturelands and meadows began to disappear. To protect these precious habitats, the national park now ensures that the tradition of grazing by cattle and sheep is continued; camps of volunteers have taken on the traditional role of the communal village.

Many of the islands, islets, and skerries within the archipelago are privately owned, but visitors are free to move around by boat except in certain protected areas, and camping and fire building are limited too. The park's two main visitors centers provide all information and guidelines; these are the Blue Mussel visitors center in Kasnäs on the island of Kimitoön, and the Korpoström Archipelago Center on the island of Korpo. Shuttle ships run to the national park islands of Holma, Jurmo, and Berghamn from the ports of Prostvik and Pärnäs on Nagu and Kasnäs on Kimitoön.

The archipelago, also referred to as Skärgårdshavets, is a divers' paradise, and Stora Hästö in Korpo offers an underwater trail for divers and one for snorkelers in shallower water. Off the island of Dalskär is another undersea trail with seven statues, six made by schoolchildren and one by artist Armi Nurminen. Buoys and ropes guide scuba divers and snorkelers along the underwater trail, which lies at a depth of about 10 feet (3 m).

Several of the islands also offer nature trails with excellent views or access to cultural sites. The Björkö Trail, for example, leads to the lovely lake of Insjön, while on Högland, the highest island of the Archipelago, a trail takes you to a lookout tower and an old crofter's cottage. Örö island's trails explore artillery posts, barracks, and defense points, and the Yxskär Trail introduces you to the endemic plants and birdlife.

FAUNA & BIRDLIFE

Among the 25 mammals recorded within Archipelago National Park are the more common species of the common shrew, pygmy shrew, mountain hare, bank vole, red fox, raccoon dog, and elk (moose). Gray seals are increasing in numbers here, while ringed seal numbers are dropping. The sea teems with a wide variety of fish such as Baltic herring, European perch, northern pike, common roach, bream, European flounder, fourhorn sculpin, and the very ugly viviparous eelpout.

Archipelago is home to some 132 types of birds, so don't take a trip to the islands without bringing binoculars to spot arctic tern, black guillemot, common redshank, common sandpiper, common whitethroat, Eurasian oystercatcher, Eurasian rock pipit, European herring gull, goosander, great blackbacked gull, great cormorant, or hooded crow. On the islands themselves you might spy the mute swan, mallard, tufted duck,

The Human Footprint

Humans have lived on this Finnish archipelago since the Late Stone Age (2000 to 1300 B.C.), attracted by plentiful Atlantic cod and other fish. Archaeological remnants of Iron Age (500 to 1150 B.C.) agriculture are common. The park has some 40 burial mounds or "barrows" from the Bronze and Iron Ages, most at elevations with sea views, and some containing jewelry or weapons. The colorful Finnish name for these cairns roughly translates to "Devil's sauna stoves." On Korpo, the village island of Jurmo is known for its mysterious "monk rings," four stone circles thought to be built by medieval Franciscans on fishing trips. By the Middle Ages, half of the Archipelago's villages were already settled.

red-breasted merganser, ruddy turnstone, white wagtail, meadow pipit, northern wheatear, thrush

nightingale, or lesser whitethroat. Keen bird-watchers look for some of the rarer birds that nest around the archipelago, such as the white-tailed eagle, the arctic skua, lesser blackbacked gull, Caspian tern, Eurasian eagle-owl, barred warbler, common raven, and the lovely canary yellow icterine warbler.

An interesting subplot of nature developed within the park in the 1990s, when mink were found to be overrunning many nests and decimating bird numbers. After the authorities initiated the removal of the vermin, studies showed an immediate uptick in populations of many avian species, including the tufted duck and the velvet scoter.

Aside from bird-watching and hiking trails, Archipelago National Park offers a wide range of activities, from chartered sailing to exploring islands in rented kayaks. Voluntary work camps encourage visitors to engage with the environment of this unique place, and the park organizes cycling trips, sells fishing permits, and gives advice on where to ski and skate on the ice in winter.

Rocky shorelines and forested hills abound.

AT A GLANCE

Archipelago islands ▪ 193 square miles (500 sq km) ▪ Burial mounds ▪ Högland historic trail ▪ nationalparks.fi/archipelagonp

BOTHNIAN SEA

A long ribbon of islands stretched on an aquatic blue canvas

Bothnian Sea National Park is not for landlubbers: About 98 percent of its surface area consists of water—that's just 5.7 out of 352 square miles (15 of 912 sq km). The park is located in Finland's southernmost corner, where the land is still "rebounding" from being weighed under in the last ice age.

This string of islets and islands in the Bothnian Sea are rich habitats for many birds. The park's star avian, the goosander, is the symbol of the park. This diving bird is perfectly adapted to the park's seascapes with its grebe-like body, longish neck, elongated head, and strong beak, which is curved into a hook perfect for diving for small fish, clams, and shellfish. You'll recognize its gravelly rattle, and the male by his dark green head, while the female's head turns from white to henna red at the throat. Other waterbirds of interest are the common eider, greylag goose, greater scaup, and arctic skua. Preiviikinlahti Bay in Pori is the best place for bird-watching. Also in Pori, the Ark Nature Centre showcases exhibits on the flora and fauna of the Bothnian Sea.

Many of the islands offer trails to wander, such as the path through the boulder fields and forests of Enskeri Island and the Säppi Culture Trail, which explores the life of lighthouse keepers. Säppi Island's lighthouse, dating from 1873, is one of several in the park; another is the Isokari Island lighthouse, completed during the reign of Tsar Nicholas I in 1833, when Russia ruled Finland. Another historic island, Katanpää, was once home to convicts, soldiers, and sailors. This was where Tsar Nicholas II built military fortifications in the 1910s, just before Finland gained independence.

A winter sunset on the Bothnian Sea: Most of the park is maritime area between Finland and Sweden.

EKENÄS ARCHIPELAGO

An archipelago seascape at Finland's southwest tip

Ekenäs Archipelago National Park is mostly composed of small rock islets in the open sea, and the surrounding waters of the Gulf of Finland. The park protects aquatic birds that nest around the islands' shores, a mandate that extends to banning the use of motorboats near the bird islands from April to July. The park itself can only be accessed by boat, and a water taxi service ferries visitors across this aquatic preserve.

ISLAND DELIGHTS

The park's largest island is Älgö: Walk out to the gorge valleys to take in the shadowy spruce forests and light pine forests. You'll also find wetlands and three small lakes, Storträsket, Näseträsket, and Lillträsket. The shallow and sheltered bays on the eastern side of Älgö are typical of the whole inner archipelago. Älgö in Swedish means "Elk Island," and although elk (moose) can be seen here, white-tailed deer are more common. On the larger islands, you'll also come across the Eurasian badger and the hare. Off the islands of the southern part of the park, visitors often witness grey and ringed seals sunning themselves on the rocks. Jussarö, the park's second largest island, has old-growth forest on its western side with nature trails, and the remnants of old mines on its eastern side. There are many other wooded islands to explore where the range of birdlife is a major draw, with majestic white-tailed eagles

Boats bob in Ekenäs Harbor.

(aka sea eagles) the predator kings of the archipelago. The park runs boat excursions to the main points of interest, and kayaking around the smaller islets and islands is very popular.

The Ekenäs Nature Center, housed in a waterfront edifice built in the 1840s, has educational displays on the changing nature of the Baltic Sea and the western Uusimaa archipelago. The interactive exhibits for children let them listen to underwater sounds, admire a fisherman's hut, search for invasive species in a dry aquarium, and learn about life in the wetlands. The center also has information and maps on marked trails on the islands of Älgö, Modermagan, and Jussarö. The 2.9-mile (4.7-km) Jussarö Trail

takes you past mine shafts from the mid-1800s, and on to an old-growth forest of tall pines and spruces, a very rare mix of trees for a coastal island. There is also an observation tower along the way, giving fine views of the island.

BIRD-WATCHING

Ornithologists should head for the bird-watching towers along the nature trail on the island of Älgö and in Lotsstuberg on Jussarö. Each spring, several Arctic migratory birds can be spotted in the park. The park's signature species is the common eider, and you'll recognize this large sea duck by the male's distinctive black-and-white plumage, its green-tinged head, and its large, wedge-shaped bill. Eiders feed near the shore, diving to the seabed for their main source of food, blue mussels. Eiders live long lives and can reach up to 30 years of age.

Thousands of other seabirds nest on the park's smaller islets, their species including red-breasted merganser, great cormorant, tufted duck, and several types of gulls.

The archipelago's plant life is typically coastal, but some rare and threatened plants flourish here, such as the heath sedge, marsh spike-rush, and common beaked sedge.

The water vegetation includes some rare species too, and the park is a popular destination for divers and snorkelers in the summer months.

AT A GLANCE

White-tailed eagles ▪ 20 square miles (52 sq km) ▪ Ekenäs Nature Center ▪ Jussarö nature trail
▪ nationalparks.fi/ekenasarchipelagonp

GULF OF FINLAND

A bird-watcher's coastal paradise with a storied past

To the east of Ekenäs Archipelago National Park (see page 221) lies the tiny coastal Gulf of Finland National Park. Although it shares similar landscapes with its larger neighbor, here the small islands and islets host mainly pine trees. Many of the desolate rocky islands have shorelines of *rapakivi* ("crumbly") granite that drops off abruptly into the sea; this rock splits apart in a sharply cubical way.

The Gulf of Finland is home to many species of aquatic birds. The most common are goosanders and tufted ducks, but also nesting on these protected islands are razorbills and black guillemots, among others. Charter boats and water taxis are available, and springtime is a great time to visit huge flocks of migrating arctic geese and waterfowl on their way northeast. The bird-watching tower on Ulko-Tammio Island is an excellent place to watch this winged spectacle.

Ulko-Tammio also has a fine 1.8-mile (3-km) nature trail that introduces the park's flora and fauna and the region's history of fishing, smuggling, and seal hunting. The shorter 1-mile (1.6 km) trail on Mustaviiri focuses on the park's ecosystems and the area's cultural heritage.

Mustaviiri is also host to a mysterious stone labyrinth and a tiny World Heritage site: one of the original station points of Struve Geodetic Arc, a chain of survey triangulations that helped determine the exact size and shape of our planet. You'll also find much World War II lore throughout many small, lively villages in the park.

AT A GLANCE

Island landscapes ▪ 2.6 square miles (6.7 sq km) ▪ Ulko-Tammio bird-watching tower ▪ Ulko-Tammio Nature Trail ▪ nationalparks.fi/gulfoffinlandnp

HELVETINJÄRVI

Hell's Lake and Hell's Hole beckon adventurous hikers.

Spanning the wild forests of the Tavastia region, Helvetinjärvi National Park (Hell's Lake National Park) protects the deep gorges and much rugged scenery formed by faults cleaving through the bedrock. The most impressive of these is the dramatic Helvetinkolu (Hell's Hole) cleft at the southeastern end of Helvetinjärvi. The rugged cliffs around the lake and the Helvetinkolu gorge are geological features created millions of years ago, and they

The park's gorges are strenuous hikes.

make for excellent hiking in the spring and summer months. However, the park warns that sections of the trails are challenging due to differences in elevation, and huts are provided for rest. The 2.4-mile (4-km) Helvetistä Itään Nature Trail from Kankimäki to Helvetinkolu, is a worthwhile hike, taking in spruce forest, bright pine forests, a rugged gorge, a waterfall, bog landscape, and a 200-step staircase to a campsite and hut.

AT A GLANCE

Helvetinjärvi lake ▪ Helvetinkolu gorge ▪ 19.2 square miles (49.8 sq km) ▪ Helvetistä Itään Nature Trail ▪ nationalparks.fi/helvetinjarvinp

HIIDENPORTTI

Portal to a vibrant Finnish wilderness

Many of the coniferous trees of Hiidenportti National Park are more than 100 years old; cutting for timber ceased here at the start of the 20th century. The park—today a mixed landscape of canyons, mires, and dry forests—gets its name from the steep-cliffed gorge Hiidenportti, or "Hiisi's gate." This evokes the legend of a goblinlike being escaped into the wilderness.

Several large carnivores also prowl here, including brown bear, wolverine, and lynx, while the gray wolf is a transient visitor. The North American beaver, introduced to Finland in 1937, finds rich habitat in the Porttijoki river. The reindeer in the park are likely wild forest reindeer *(Rangifer tarandus fennicus)*, a subspecies reintroduced in the 1970s. These are taller, longer-limbed, and straighter horned than their reindeer cousins *(Rangifer tarandus tarandus)*.

The great grey owl, the world's largest, is the symbol of the park. This huge bird measures between 24 and 33 inches (61 to 84 cm), and tends not to move in the presence of humans. Look for it well camouflaged in the woods and stay still yourself to study this impressive creature.

The capercaillie and hazel grouse are the most plentiful fowls in the park, while rarer species include bean goose, crane, osprey, and red-flanked bluetail.

The park has about 19 miles (30 km) of trails, with boardwalks over the marshes. The Hiidenkierros trail leads you down into the Hiidenportti gorge, and up steps to the far cliffs.

> **AT A GLANCE**
>
> Hiidenportti gorge ▪ 17.3 square miles (45 sq km) ▪ Great grey owl habitat ▪ The Hiidenkierros trail ▪ nationalparks.fi/hiidenporttinp

HOSSA

A place far away, in a land beyond time

The village of Hossa is known for the oldest rock paintings in Northern Finland, dating back from 1500 to 2500 B.C. The name Hossa is from the old Sami word *Huossa* meaning "a place far away." The Värikallio paintings, on a cliff at Somerjärvi lake, will transport you to such a realm. Discovered in 1977 by skiers, the imagery includes 60 figures, many of them human images with triangular heads and one with horns. The Julma-Ölkky canyon

The Värikallio rock paintings

lake has a smaller painting on its walls and a vaultlike rock fracture, Pirunkirkko (Devil's Church), where a legendary shaman cast his spells.

Hossa National Park has about 56 miles (90 km) of marked trails to lead you through the ridges, pine forests, mires, and lake-dotted terrain formed in the last ice age; kettle ponds created by receding glaciers are everywhere. The trailhead of the 100-mile-long (162-km) Eastern Border Hiking Trail is here, and the park also offers canoeing, mountain biking, and great lake fishing.

> **AT A GLANCE**
>
> Värikallio rock paintings ▪ Pirunkirkko (Devil's Church) ▪ 34.7 square miles (90 sq km) ▪ Eastern Border Hiking Trail ▪ nationalparks.fi/hossa

ISOJÄRVI

A vibrant woodland ecosystem in central Finland

Isojärvi National Park, located in central Finland, has a landscape largely made up of Scots pine and Norway spruce forests and bogs. The park takes its name from the lake Isojärvi. All the park's lovely lakes and rivers are rich habitat for North American beavers, whose tree felling and river damming is evident everywhere. Beavers became extinct in the mid-1800s because of hunting for furs. In the 1930s, European beavers were successfully reintroduced to Finland.

On the rocky shores of Isojärvi you'll hear the distinctive whistling song of the black-throated diver, one of several bird species that nest around the small forest lakes, including the red-throated diver.

Sphagnum moss runs riot along the shores of these lakes, and swamps spread into the woodlands. The old-growth forest at Latokuusikko is one of the most interesting for flora: This is spruce-dominated forest typical of central Finland. Here spruce trees can tower 100 feet high (30 m), alongside smaller aspens and little-leaf lindens. Decaying wood is abundant, and many shelf fungus species develop on the dead trunks. Elsewhere around this herb-rich forest you'll find bird cherry, the European meadowsweet, ostrich fern, subarctic ladyfern, and lesser butterfly orchid.

There are two nature trails and several loop trails, most of them starting at the Heretty or Kalalahti park-

Lakes and pine forests are the classic Isojärvi landscapes.

Cabins & Crofts

The park's buildings offer interesting historic insight: Heretty cabin, now a museum, was built for local loggers in the winter of 1946–47, housing up to 40 men, a housekeeper, and helper. You can visit the stables, a building for drying cones, and the sauna. Huhtala Croft, in the northwest of the park, is a fine example of this traditional farm type with its storage buildings, sauna, straw-storage shed, and outhouse for elders. Wuori-Huhta farm dates back to the 1700s.

ing lots. The 2.1-mile (3.5-km) Heretty Nature Trail circumnavigates Kannuslahti bay on Kurkijärvi lake. Signs along the way tell the history of logging and the forest's ecosystems. The 1.8-mile (3-km) Lortikka Nature Trail gives you a good introduction to the area's geology and topography. The trail between the cabins of Heretty and Lortikka (see sidebar) was laid out for cycling in the 1950s, and survives today as a 2.5-mile (4-km) mountain bike path. Canoeing and boating are popular park activities: The narrowness of Isojärvi lake—12.5 miles (20 km) long—makes it ideal for canoeing. Rowing boats can be rented from the Heretty café in Kalalahti bay.

Isojärvi lake ▪ 7.3 square miles (19 sq km) ▪ Lortikka Nature Trail ▪ Heretty cabin museum ▪ Huhtala Croft ▪ nationalparks.fi/isojarvinp

KAUHANEVA-POHJANKANGAS

Elevated walkways and a tower make this a perfect park for birders.

Kauhaneva-Pohjankangas National Park consists mainly of swamp areas, raised bogs, and mires—a unique landscape that is part of the southwestern region of the Suomenselkä watershed. The soil here is mostly turf, and the bedrock is composed of porphyric granite. Much of the park sits some 525 to 581 feet (160 to 177 m) above sea level. The windswept bogs stretch westward along a medieval route, the unpaved Kyrönkangas summer road, that heads north through the pine forests of Kyrönkangas.

RAISED BOGS

The large raised bog of Kauhaneva, together with Kampinkeidas Mire to its northwest, forms a vital swamp complex. Raised bogs are mires where turf has grown higher than the surrounding mineral soil. The center is often several feet higher than the edges, resulting in hummocks. Raised bogs are low in nutrients, and hence these hummocks remain largely barren, because they only receive nutrients with the rainwater. Some sphagnum moss and sparse tortuous pines can grow on them.

BIRDING

Birds, and bird-watchers, flock here in the springtime as the woods and marshes fill with birdsong. The park has a 3.1-mile (5-km) hiking trail that follows part of the medieval Kyrönkangas road: A 1.2-mile (2-km) boardwalk loop takes you to an observation tower on the north side of Lake Kauhalammi, an excellent place from which to pick out your favorite feathered friends in the wetland, such as cranes, whooper swans, gulls, and waders. The bird-watching tower is located close to Nummikangas campfire site and affords great views over the raised bog of Kauhaneva.

A wood sandpiper looks for food.

A walk along the Kauhaneva Mire is likely accompanied by a host of birds, such as herring gulls, little gulls, yellow wagtails, and European golden plovers. Other avian species found in the park include whimbrel, the common redshank, and common greenshank. Black-throated divers and red-throated divers also nest here.

By far the most common wader in the mire of Kauhaneva is the wood sandpiper. The sandpiper's population has declined in recent years and the species has been declared regionally endangered in southern Finland. Listen for its rhythmical *liro-liro-liro* mating call in the open mires in late spring and early summer. Another avian species to look for is the European nightjar, especially in the light pine heath of Pohjankangas. This bird's hypnotic churring can be heard on the bright summer nights when the midnight sun makes for endless days across Scandinavia. The nightjar, however, is extremely hard to spot due to its superbly camouflaged coloring. Likewise, the morning song of the common redstart can begin at midnight in the summer—listen close.

Pohjankangas is part of the esker landscape of Western Finland. Here, the forests are dry and consist of barren pine heaths. All along the ground is a carpet of reindeer lichen and big red stem moss, augmented in places by spurts of wild heather, and the vivid red fruits of lingonberry and bearberry shrubs.

The park has several biking trails, and National Bike Trail no. 44, marked with brown signs, goes through Kauhaneva-Pohjankangas. This runs partly along the medieval Kyrönkangas road and links the park to Lauhanvuori National Park.

AT A GLANCE

Lake Kauhalammi ▪ Medieval Kyrönkangas road ▪ 22 square miles (57 sq km) ▪ Pohjankangas pine heaths
▪ nationalparks.fi/kauhaneva-pohjankangasnp

KOLI

A magic mountain and landscape steeped in Finnish history

The white quartzite hill of Koli, like the village below it of the same name, has a long and interesting heritage. This treeless peak was a sacrificial site in Finnish folklore, and it inspired a Romantic art movement in the 19th and 20th centuries, becoming a symbol of Finnish nationalism. The American writer Kurt Vonnegut wrote wistfully about the wild frozen blueberries that he tasted on the slopes of Koli. Today, the pasturelands of Koli are preserved by Koli National Park, stretching across the forested hills on the western shore of Lake Pielinen, in eastern Finland.

AGRICULTURAL HERITAGE

The traditional agricultural heritage is kept alive in the practice of slash-and-burn cultivation, whereby fields are cyclically slashed, burned, and recultivated, with hay cut yearly. Traditional Finnish breeds of cattle (*kyyttö*) and sheep graze in the meadows of Koli, and mowing helps regenerate these flora-rich fields. Look for rare flowers, such as moonworts or stiff-straw mat-grass. The landscapes of Koli vary widely with the higher rocky, rugged terrain contrasting with the fells and meadows of lower ground, and dense forests of old spruces and birches on valley slopes. In the forests, watch for the Siberian flying squirrel, which flings itself from tree to tree.

The Koli Nature Centre Ukko near the top of Koli has details on all hiking and skiing trails within the park. The favored destination for visitors is the Ukko-Koli vantage point with its sweeping view over Lake Pielinen; you can take the ski lifts up in summer. Two good trails to get the lay of the land and its cultural significance are the 1.6-mile (2.6-km) Paimenen Polku (Shepherd's Trail) and the 1.8-mile (3-km) Koli Cultural Environments Circle Trail.

Koli also has many caves to explore, such as the 112-foot-long (34-m) Pirunkirkko cavern. Two ski resorts operate in Koli National Park: Loma-Koli for families and Ukko-Koli for more advanced downhill skiing.

Sunrise over Lake Pielinen in an area steeped in Finnish folklore

KOLOVESI
A vital lake habitat for an endangered Finnish species

Early morning mists rise above the lakes and forests of Kolovesi.

Kolovesi National Park, located in eastern Finland, protects vital lake habitat of the critically endangered Saimaa ringed seal (see page 231). The area's rugged landscapes, shaped by the last ice age, are typified by craggy cliffs rising dramatically over the narrow lake channels that form part of the vast labyrinth of the Saimaa lake system. This makes Kolovesi a paddlers' paradise for both canoe and kayak. Birds such as Eurasian eagle-owls and common ravens nest on the cliffs, and red fox, lynx, and Eurasian badger all prowl between the boulders.

SUMMER TRAILS

Kolovesi is a summer park, not suitable for wintertime outings. The park has two trails. The 2-mile (3.3-km) Nahkiaissalo Nature Trail in the Selkälahti area traverses dif-

Old-Growth Forests

Kolovesi is filled with old-growth forests, mainly of spruce and pine. These provide rich habitat for many rare species of forest dwellers. Look closely at the deadwood for rarities such as hole nesters, beetles, shelf fungus, and coral tooth fungus, a white growth that looks like it belongs in the ocean. Birds that live in the old forests include the greenish warbler and the wood warbler, as well as threatened species such as the black-throated diver, the red-throated diver, the lesser black-backed gull, the northern hobby, and the red-breasted flycatcher.

ficult terrain as it takes you through old-growth forests (see sidebar). Alternatively, the 2.3-mile (3.8-km) Mäntysalo Trail at the northern end of Mäntysalo Island explores the forests of Kolovesi. These vary from old-growth mixed-wood stands to cultivated forests. This trail has even more challenging terrain, so wear good boots and bring sturdy rain gear. Listen in these forests for the enchanting whistle of the yellow- and black-feathered Eurasian golden oriole, which has all the lovely intonations of a flute.

CAVE PAINTINGS

Several significant rock and cave paintings have been discovered in the area: A painted figure on the steep side of Ukonvuori Hill represents a hunter who once stalked these lands. Others show elk (moose), a source of meat for Stone Age hunters. The paintings date back about 5,000 years. There are further rock paintings on the sides of Havukkavuori and Vieruvuori Hills close to the park.

The park offers excellent boat excursions to the Joutenvesi Nature Reserve, located between Kolovesi and Linnansaari National Parks along the Heinävesi water route. Here you may spot a rare Saimaa ringed seal, catch sight of nesters such as a common tern, or hear the distinctive deep *wo-ho . . . woho uhwo-ho,* of the Ural owl, as a western honey buzzard or an osprey loom overhead.

AT A GLANCE

Old-growth forests ▪ 8.9 square miles (23 sq km) ▪ Saimaa ringed seal ▪ Nahkiaissalo Nature Trail ▪ Heinävesi water route ▪ nationalparks.fi/kolovesinp

KURJENRAHKA

A vibrant patchwork of raised bogs and old-growth forests

A winter sun lights the way for a well-wrapped day on the trails.

Kurjenrahka National Park, in southwest Finland, consists mainly of bog and primeval forests, some of which have been untouched for more than 150 years. These were purchased in the early 1800s by two manor houses; the estates cleared much of the forestry before selling the lands to the government toward the end of the 19th century. Fortunately, isolated islands of forest in the middle of inaccessible mires remained unlogged. Pukkipalo old-growth forest is one of the park's best examples. Here, old spruces, dead standing barkless trees, and decaying wood on the forest floor make ideal habitat for hole-nesting birds as well as many species of insects. Look here for such rare and threat-ened moths as straw belle, and butterflies including the Freija fritillary. These woods also host rare fungi such as *Fomitopsis rosea* and *Amylocystis lapponica*.

Although some of these mires were drained under private ownership, many ditches have now been blocked up again to allow the mires to return to their origin state. This allows plants to grow on the hummocks (higher and dryer patches) of the raised bogs of Kurjenrahka, Lammenrahka, and Vajosuo. This vegetation includes marsh tea and sparse tortuous pines, and sphagnum moss grows in abundance. The park takes its name from Kurjenrahka Mire, a raised bog divided by forested islands.

WILDLIFE

Kurjenrahka is home to many bird species, a safe oasis on which to nest as it is inaccessible to land-based predators. Watch for stately cranes using their long legs to wade through the marshes while they croon their familiar *kruu, kruu*. Other avian residents include the northern hobby, common kestrel, grey-headed woodpecker, and woodlark. The Eurasian lynx also resides in Kurjenrahka, while brown bears have been known to wander through the park, as have gray wolves.

The park is located close to the historic town of Turku, and offers visitors more than 186 miles (300 km) of marked hiking trails; ski trails cover the silent snow-covered marshes in winter.

AT A GLANCE

Raised bogs and old-growth forests ▪ 11 square miles (29 sq km) ▪ more than 186 miles (300 km) of trails ▪ nationalparks.fi/kurjenrahkanp

LAUHANVUORI

A haven for rare plants and wildlife in western Finland

The landscapes of Lauhanvuori National Park are mainly pine forests, spring brooks, and swampy lakelands. The park's high point is the 758-foot (231-m) hill of Lauhanvuori. Because this glacial moraine was once an island in the middle of Ancylus Lake, its summit has retained its soil and nutrients, unlike the barren hillsides lower down.

You can get a fine panoramic view of the park from the viewing tower on Lauhanvuori hill, right across the forested lowlands stretching off to the faraway Gulf of Bothnia. From here it's possible to see how extensive boulder fields and banks formed along ancient shorelines as the glaciers melted since the last ice age. The largest of these is the half-mile-long (800-m) Kivijata stone field. On a clear day, you can also see the tallest chimneys of the towns of Kristiinankaupunki and Kaskinen, some 37 to 43 miles (60 to 70 km) away.

The top of Lauhanvuori hill is the starting point of one of the park's several hiking trails, the 1.6-mile (2.6-km) Rantapolku Nature Trail. This leads visitors on an educational exploration of the geology, vegetation, and history around the hill.

As you come down the hill, look for Aumakivi rock, a huge boulder. This is a typical Tor formation, where erosion has stripped away the surface layers, leaving just the core of the granite exposed. On the lower slopes of Lauhanvuori hill, you'll notice how the bedrock changes from sandstone to granite.

MARSHY LIFE

The marshlands hum with life in the summertime, with cranes *kruuing*, willow grouse hiccupping out in their accelerating call, and capercaillie going through their strange "lek" courtship song and dance. The park is working together with the World Wide Fund for Nature to help restore the

Finnish forest's reindeer population here, hunted to extinction in the 20th century. Lauhanvuori also contains a small area of fen, a watery oasis of rare plant life where you'll find *Succisa pratensis,* brown beak sedge, carnation sedge, moor rush, and Scottish asphodel

A stoat checks if the coast is clear.

thriving alongside many rare species of mosses.

The winters are the longer months in this northerly park, and the well-maintained cross-country trails in Lauhanvuori make for great skiing. The Metsähallitus visitors center has information on all hiking and skiing trails, as well as biking trails, including one that connects Lauhanvuori with Kauhaneva-Pohjankangas National Park (see page 225).

Leprosy Lake

The lakes of Lauhanvuori are famous for salmon. But one of them, Spitaalijärvi, has the odd title of Leprosy Lake. Legend has it that, since medieval times, the lake's waters were known to act as a cure-all for ailments and diseases, including leprosy. The curative water was even transported to Russian aristocracy up until the October Revolution of 1917 signaled an end of Russian rule in Finland. Despite the superstitions, the effects of this particular water may have a scientific explanation: The lake's water is high in acidity; to this day, its pH value is about 4.7.

Lauhanvuori Hill ▪ 20.4 square miles (53 sq km) ▪ Cross-country skiing trails ▪ Spitaalijärvi (Leprosy Lake) ▪ nationalparks.fi/lauhanvuorinp

AT A GLANCE

LEIVONMÄKI

A small park with esker landscapes, brimming with wildlife

The lovely Leivonmäki National Park in central Finland is one of the country's smaller parks, but its protected areas of swamplands, esker forests and ridges, and the shores of Rutajärvi lake make it a rewarding place to visit. The park has a wealth of trails, many with elevated boardwalks over the swamps. The Harjunkierros (Esker Trail) is a strenuous 2.8-mile (4.5-km) hike with some steep hills to bring you onto an esker formation—a ridge over what was once a glacial tunnel—which the path follows. You'll also take in the lakes of Iso Pirttilampi, Erijärvet, and Ruta-järvi. In addition to the intriguing esker landscape, visitors experience the light pine woods that typify the park. Listen for birds such as the goldeneye and the European night-jar, whose song is compared to the whirling sound of a spinning wheel. The nesting birds of Rutajärvi lake include the black-throated diver, whooper swan, great crested grebe, and red-necked grebe.

In the northern part of the national park lies a wilderness called Syysniemi, where visitors will find esker forests, old-growth spruce forests, and spruce bogs. The trees here can be up to 130 years old. Many raptors and wood-peckers inhabit these old-growth forests, and owls nest in hollowed-out trees. The small Siberian flying squirrel may be spotted doing its trapeze act through the trees, and along the river you can see much evidence of the otter.

AT A GLANCE

Esker forests and ridges ▪ 11 square miles (29 sq km) ▪ Siberian flying squirrels ▪ The Harjunkierros (Esker Trail) ▪ nationalparks.fi/leivonmakinp

LIESJÄRVI

A small but intoxicating taste of the lake highlands of Häme

Small is beautiful in Finland, and that applies to Liesjärvi National Park. Despite its size, the park has more than 25 miles (40 km) of shoreline, and is covered by dense forests (mostly spruce), and small, tree-covered mires. Cowberry and blueberry heaths are common. The landscape represents a thin sliver of the lake highlands of Häme, with its spruce mires, ridges, and lakes. At Korte-niemi Heritage Farm you can try your hand at traditional Finnish

Lakes are Liesjärvi's main draw.

agricultural work or wander along old crofters' paths.

Hikers enjoy the park's 19 miles (30 km) of marked trails, including the mile-long (1.5-km) Ahonnokka Nature Trail through old-growth forest. At the end of Cape Ahon-nokka, you'll get a fine view of Lies-järvi lake. You can also walk out along Kyynäränharju, a low sandy ridge that separates the Liesjärvi and Kyynäräjärvet lakes.

The park is filled with wood-peckers: The black woodpecker, the great spotted woodpecker, the three-toed woodpecker, the grey-headed woodpecker, and the lesser spotted woodpecker all nest here.

AT A GLANCE

Lake highlands of Häme ▪ Korteniemi Heritage Farm ▪ 8.5 square miles (22 sq km) ▪ Ahonnokka Nature Trail ▪ nationalparks.fi/liesjarvinp

LINNANSAARI

A lakeland kingdom for several endangered species

A female Saimaa ringed seal (Pusa hispida saimensis) *basks at sunset on a rock in Lake Saimaa.*

In southeastern Finland, there is a lake kingdom where a special mammal reigns. This is Linnansaari National Park, where the critically endangered Saimaa ringed seal is king. The Saimaa's realm lies in Lake Haukivesi, part of the greater Saimaa lake system, which at approximately 1,700 square miles (4,400 sq km) is Finland's largest.

The Saimaa is a subspecies of ringed seal exclusive to Lake Saimaa, and is now thought to number about 400. They have lived and evolved in isolation for about 9,500 years, after being sep-arated from their ringed brethren as the land rose after the last ice age. For years, fishermen hunted the Saimaa, seeing them as com-petition for the Saimaa salmon (a subspecies, also endangered), but they've been protected now since 1955. The seals need ice cover to breed, so they are now falling vic-tim to climate change.

The park islands have deciduous forests of birch, aspen, and alder, bare rocks covered in lichen, and open meadows. The endangered white-backed woodpecker thrives here. Linnansaari has more herb-rich forests than any other Finnish national park, a source of habitat for additional endangered species such as the lime hawk moth, and the beautiful checkered blue butterfly.

On Linnansaari island, the area around the old croft is now ben-efiting from the reintroduction of the slash-and-burn agriculture that was practiced from the 1500s up to the 1930s. You can study this and other natural and historical aspects of Linnansaari on the 1.2-mile (2-km) Linnonpolku nature trail, one of several through this vibrant park.

AT A GLANCE

Saimaa ringed seal ▪ 14.6 square miles (38 sq km) ▪ Slash-and-burn agriculture ▪ Linnonpolku nature trail ▪ nationalparks.fi/linnansaarinp

NUUKSIO

Lakes and forests beckon just 19 miles (30 km) from downtown Helsinki.

Just a short bus or car ride from Finland's capital is an oasis of forested hills and serene lakes. Nuuksio National Park comprises the westernmost part of the Nuuksio lake highlands, a peaceful, contemplative place of escape for weekend walkers and nature lovers. If the invention and use of the sauna is a large part of the Finns' reputation for being calm, their collective proximity to nature must be another contributing factor. Even the name Nuuksio denotes serenity, coming from the word "swan" *(njukca)* in the Sami language; a Finnish schoolteacher coined it in the 1930s.

A flying squirrel (Pteromys volans)

HIKING THE FOREST

Nuuksio has a total of eight marked hiking trails. In addition, there are 19 miles (30 km) of biking trails and 13.6 miles (22-km) of horse-riding trails. Skiing routes also crisscross the park when the snow and ice come. The 1.6-mile (2.7-km) Kaarniaispolku nature trail is an interesting loop that takes in old-growth forests, marshland, and bared rocky landscapes. The 1.2-mile (2-km) Nahkiaispolku nature trail educates hikers on the efforts being made toward forest restoration in the park. Finally, the Haukankierros trail leads to high rocky ground from where you can look over Brook Myllypuro Valley.

Lower down, under the cliffs, the dense spruce forests are cool,

The History of Kattila

In the park's Kattila area, by Lake Kaitlampi, you can tour a curious functionalist mansion. Eljas Erkko, owner and editor of *Helsingin Sanomat* newspaper, bought Kattila farm in 1934, to found a communal rest home for his workers. His rural Eden was shattered, however, when a snake bit and killed his wife. Erkko sold the farm to the Alsano cooperative, owned by a Bible researchers' society, in 1935. A religious sect called Hartelalaiset benefited from the rest home; their baths can still be visited in the basement.

damp, and darkened by the canopy. The brook hollows are rich in nutrients, and here the park's vegetation is at its most luxuriant: You'll find alpine currant, the sweet-smelling European honeysuckle, mezereon, and trees such as hazel and littleleaf linden in abundance. In spring, the ground rolls out its carpet of blue and white as the liverleafs and the wood anemones burst into flower. And in the dells you'll hear the birdsong of blackcaps and red-breasted flycatchers, among many other nesting species. Endangered species inhabiting the park include the European nightjar and the woodlark.

FLYING SQUIRRELS

The other flying creatures in the park are less expected: Great squadrons of Siberian flying squirrels fling themselves from the pine and spruce trees here, and these furry acrobats, smaller than common squirrels, are the emblem of Nuuksio National Park. Flying squirrels inhabit the boreal mixedwood forests of North America and Eurasia, and their dwindling European populations are spread from Finland across the Baltic countries eastward to Siberia and the Pacific Ocean. These nocturnal rodents move by gliding from tree to tree, using a flap of loose skin that connects their back and front limbs. Amazingly, the Siberian flying squirrel can glide up to 250 feet (75 m). Small wonder that they can be found as far afield as Hokkaido, in northern Japan.

Nuuksio Lake highlands ▪ Siberian flying squirrels ▪ 20 square miles (53 sq km) ▪ Kattila farm ▪ Nahkiaispolku nature trail ▪ nationalparks.fi/nuuksionp

OULANKA

Arctic, European, and Siberian nature in Finland's fast-flowing park

Few places on Earth offer the triptych of natural habitats that Oulanka National Park combines—a biosphere of Arctic, European, and Siberian flora and fauna.

The park is transected by Finland's greatest hiking trail, the 51-mile (82-km) Karhunkierros (Bear's Ring). This trail offers hikers a dazzling spectacle: whitewater rapids, roaring waterfalls, five swinging river bridges, and the 84-mile (135-km) Oulankajoki river with its dramatically carved gorges and boreal forested banks. The thick Scots pine woods are filled with eagles, woodpeckers, and red-breasted flycatchers.

Oulanka's biodiversity is a result of the calcium-rich bedrock and wide variations in temperatures between the low river valleys and the high rising fells. This nurtures a variety of rare and endangered species, including the lovely calypso orchid, a pale pink flower that thrives in the meadows. Between April and September, you'll see plenty of brown bear, who come for the rich pickings on offer in the park, including brown trout. In late summer, the park abounds with bilberries (similar to blueberries but darker and smaller) as well as mushrooms, both attracting many *Homo sapiens*.

Riverbeds and alluvial meadows are home to many rare species of butterflies like the violet copper. Most meadows are managed in a traditional manner, and the Sami herd reindeer in the park. Rare birds such as Siberian jays and capercaillie thrive in the herb-rich forests of Oulanka. Endangered species including lynx and wolverine also make their home here, along with elk (moose).

A great way to see the park is along its two famous canoe routes: The first, for experienced adventurers, takes you along an eight-mile (13-km) stretch of fast upper rapids; the second is a gentler ride along 15.5 miles (25 km) of the lower river. The Oulanka Visitor Centre has information on all hikes and activities, and details on cabins available to hikers throughout the park.

Winter at Myllytupa gorge and lodge house

AT A GLANCE

Oulankajoki river ▪ White-water rapids and canyons ▪ 104 square miles (270 sq km) ▪ Unique biodiversity ▪ Karhunkierros (Bear's Ring) trail ▪ nationalparks.fi/oulankanp

Oulanka National Park supports Arctic, European, and Siberian flora and fauna.

PÄIJÄNNE

A small park of archetypal Finnish esker landscape

Tiny Päijänne National Park comprises a series of islands in the southern parts of Lake Päijänne in southern Finland.

This is esker country, formed by glaciers moving through this region at the end of the last ice age, gouging out the long hollow tunnels above which esker ridges now sit. Here you can take a boat or rent a kayak to enjoy the pristine waters of Lake Päijänne, coming to land on the sandy shores of the lake's myriad islands that were formed along the ridge. Geologically, the park has two distinct island landscapes. The islands with sandy shores are part of longitudinal esker systems, running south to north; other islands consist of rock and moraine, which is typical of the hilly Päijänne region.

ESKER ISLANDS

Pulkkilanharju ridge, in the southeast of the park, is a long chain of esker islands, popular with hikers, as the nature trail here offers fine views of the lake. Kayakers favor the rocky cliffs around the islands of Iso Lammassaari and Haukkasalo, which rise steeply out of the pristine waters of Lake Päijänne.

The focal point of the park is the large esker island of Kelvenne, known for its many kettle holes, formed when blocks of trapped ice melted in the ground forming marshy hollows. The resultant mires are small pine bogs, with a few open fens. Here, the lovely scent of the white-flowering marsh tea plant fills the air in spring. On the esker ridges, the nutrient-rich soils support dry herb-rich forests. These are mainly pine or spruce stands, with some deciduous trees including birch, aspen, and lush growths of littleleaf linden.

In spring the floor of these

A lesser black-backed gull

herb-rich forests blossoms into a patchwork of hepatica, lily of the valley, wild strawberry, fly honeysuckle, and mountain currant bushes. Vetches thrive in the rich soils, alongside the delicate purple shades of the cinnamon rose, and the lovely reds of mezereon. In the shadier glades, look for herb Paris, or true lover's knot.

You'll probably notice dramatic ospreys circling Lake Päijänne, but look carefully at the gulls that might follow your boat too: These are no ordinary seagulls, but probably lesser black-backed gulls, a subspecies that has been adapted as the emblem of Päijänne National Park. Their black wings are artfully edged with white feathers, and although declining throughout Finland, numbers of this indigenous species have remained steady at this location. Merlin and northern hobby also nest here.

EXPLORING THE PARK

The park offers a wealth of hiking trails, canoe and boating routes, and well-maintained ski routes in winter. The 1.2-mile (2-km) Pulkkilanharju Nature Trail leads you along an esker ridge with fine lake scenery; one steeper slope is climbed with stairs, while boardwalks take you over the marsh terrain. The Kelvenne Island Trail runs the five-mile (8-km) length of the island through mostly dry pine forests, from Kirkkosalmi in the south to Likolahti in the north. The trail climbs the esker in parts, and the going can be rocky, so good hiking shoes are advisable.

The lake, with steep and pronounced underwater ridges, is also a diver's delight. In the west of the park, toward Haukkasalo, you will find impressive underwater cliffs and crevices.

PATVINSUO

Marshlands filled with birdsong and lakes teeming with fish

Patvinsuo National Park is a place of marshes, slash-and-burn areas, and fine examples of old-growth forests. Patvinsuo has several viewing towers overlooking the marshlands, which are good vantage points for springtime viewing of the flocks of feeding, breeding birds that descend on the park. From the Teretinniemi tower you can observe myriad swamp birds including meadow pipits, western yellow wagtails, and waders such as common greenshanks and whimbrels.

The park has some 50 miles (80 km) of marked hiking trails, offering walks through lovely old-growth forests such as Autiovaara, which was untouched for more than a century. You'll hike past impressive large aspens as well as spruce trees covered with beard lichen and several old pine stands.

Another Patvinsuo attraction is the pristine Suomunjärvi lake, located in the northeast of the park. Here you'll find 15 miles (24 km) of white-sand beaches wrapped around the lake, which has 10 islands and a labyrinth of inlets. You can fish for your supper of vendace, perch, or pike. The Suomunkierto circle trail, one of several in the park, goes around the lake and takes you through pine forest. Afterward you can relax in Suomunjärvi's lakeside sauna. Saunas have deep roots in Finnish history: "From olden times," writes Pirkko Valtakari, a former Finnish Sauna Society official, "children were taught to behave in the sauna as if in a church."

AT A GLANCE

Old-growth forests ▪ 40.5 square miles (105 sq km) ▪ Suomunjärvi's lakeside sauna ▪ Suomunkierto circle trail ▪ nationalparks.fi/patvinsuonp

PETKELJÄRVI

A historic slice of 20th-century Finnish history

Located in eastern Finland, the tiny Petkeljärvi National Park sits atop esker ridges and a key fault line of Finnish history: The park preserves fortifications, some renovated, dating from what is known as the Continuation War. That conflict was fought by Finland and Nazi Germany against the invading Soviet forces of the U.S.S.R. from 1941 to 1944. Today the landscape mostly consists of light Scots pine forests, and Petkeljärvi, along with nearby Patvinsuo National Park

(see above), belongs to the UNESCO North Karelia Biosphere Reserve.

Watch here for black-throated divers. An emblem of the park, adult black-throated divers have plumage like no other bird, with shades of black, gray, and white in stripes and perfectly symmetrical spots. It looks as if they are wearing a designer wet suit, and they live up to their outfit with an ability to dive for hundreds of feet at a time.

Petkeljärvi has several partially restored battle structures from

World War II (including the Winter War between Finland and the Soviet Union from 1939 to 1940) at Petraniemi cape. The remains of wartime horse shelters can be found at Joutenjärvi lake. Fierce fighting took place at Oinassalmi sound near the park. During this war, the Russians took heavy losses as the nimble skiers of the Finnish forces left the Soviets reeling in unmapped forest lands where they were ill equipped to fight in the harsh winter conditions.

AT A GLANCE

World War II fortifications ▪ 2.3 square miles (6 sq km) ▪ Black-throated divers ▪ Esker ridges ▪ nationalparks.fi/petkeljarvinp

PUURIJÄRVI-ISOSUO

A vital swampland habitat for insects in southeast Finland

As eradication of many of Earth's insect species continues apace, it is more vital than ever that we provide habitat for the planet's smaller creatures. So the small area of protected swamplands that make up Puurijärvi-Isosuo National Park is vital to a world where pesticides and fertilizers are taking a huge toll on the insect world. The park encompasses Puurijärvi lake and the pristine alluvial shores of the Kokemäenjoki river. The waters of lush Puurijärvi lake brim with sedges, common reeds, and horsetails. On its fertile shores, flood meadows and wet bushlands provide further habitat for insects and the many birds they attract.

The four-spotted chaser (Libellula quadrimaculata) *with its dotted wings*

RAISED BOGS

The mires of Puurijärvi-Isosuo are part of coastal Finland's raised bog region. Their barren centers, consisting mainly of sphagnum moss-covered turf, stand several feet above the luxuriant, wet edges. In summer, mires are abloom with colorful bog rosemary, marsh tea, and cloudberry. On the park's boardwalk trails, you can examine carnivorous plants such as round-leaved sundew and great sundew.

FLYING VISITORS

Out on the lake's open waters, you'll see yellow water lily, whose leaves provide food for insects such as water striders and water lily leaf beetles.

Look for the four-spotted chaser (aka the four-spotted skimmer), a dragonfly that is the fiercest predator of the insect world, whose sharp jaws devour all in its path. Fossils of dragonflies date back to the Carboniferous period, some 300 million years ago. The wingspan of the largest of these was some 27.5 inches (70 cm) wide, making them the largest flying insects ever recorded. The wingspan of the average dragonfly in Puurijärvi-Isosuo National Park is a more modest three inches (8 cm). The four-spotted chaser's long, flat, and triangular body is yellow-brown and hairy. Its name comes from the spots midway along all four of its translucent wings.

Among the butterflies and moths that inhabit the marshes are the wonderfully named northern grizzled skipper, the straw belle, and the streaked wave.

Puurijärvi lake and the mires around it are one of Finland's top sites for birds: The mires of the national park abound with meadow pipit and yellow wagtail. The many wader species nesting here include the European golden plover and the wood sandpiper. On Isosuo mire you'll likely spot the great grey shrike and the red-throated diver. In addition, Puurijärvi lake is a vital stopover for migrating waterbirds: In spring, hundreds of whooper swans and bean geese make an amazing avian spectacle on the lake.

Three marked trails take you to the bird-watching towers in the park. The tallest, Kärjenkallio tower, is 59 feet (18 m) high.

AT A GLANCE

Vital insect habitat ▪ Puurijärvi lake ▪ 10.4 square miles (27 sq km) ▪ Four-spotted chaser ▪ Bird-watching towers ▪ nationalparks.fi/puurijarvi-isosuonp

PYHÄ-HÄKKI

A classic ancient Finnish woodland

Trees grow, mosses spread, and nature takes its course, regardless of history or the politics of humankind. Take Pyhä-Häkki National Park, planned in the late 1930s but stalled by World War II. Located in central Finland, the park protects old Scots pine and Norway spruce copses, most of which were planted when Finland was still under Swedish rule in the 1700s. By the early 1800s, these trees were in Russian territory, not that they cared. A century later, Finnish intellectuals were agitating for a homeland where the virgin forests of Pyhä-Häkki could be a *national* park. The pine and spruce kept growing regardless, joined by other tall species such as silver birch, downy birch, Eurasian aspen, and black alder. Having survived 400 years of history and several forest fires, the giants of Pyhä-Häkki still stand tall. The only comparable remnant from the human world in the park is the old croft at Poika-aho, whose residents probably told their children tales of the trolls and elves as warnings not to wander too far into these old woods.

The dead standing trees make ideal hosts for many bird species. Hole-nesting birds include the national park's emblem bird, the black woodpecker, as well as the great spotted woodpecker and the three-toed woodpecker.

In Yellowstone's Wake

In 1912, a portion of Pyhä-Häkki Crown Park was protected from "all land and forest use." A national park was proposed in 1938, but WWII broke out, and the plan was delayed until 1956. For centuries, a footpath in Pyhä-Häkki led visitors to a famous ancient pine. When two trails for the new park were planned, Yellowstone National Park, opened in 1872, was used as a model, and Pyhä-Häkki became a small-scale Scandinavian version of the American park. The Big Old Tree, seeded in 1518, died in 2004, but still stands in Pyhä-Häkki.

Accompanying the woodpeckers' rattling, you'll hear the lovely songs of birds such as common treecreeper, goldcrest, pied flycatcher, and chaffinch. The dead trees also support an amazing array of fungi.

Bogs compose the other half of the park, inhabited by birds such as common crane, wood sandpiper, and greenshank. In the sandy heathland forests, you might spot capercaillie, black grouse, hazel grouse, and red grouse. In summer, along the trail's boardwalks, look for lizards, toads, and European vipers. The park's 12.4 miles (20 km) of trails take you to natural wonders such as the prosaically named Big Old Tree (see sidebar), a famous pine that dates from 1518.

Many forest lakes form some ice throughout much of the Finnish year.

AT A GLANCE

Old-growth forests ▪ 5 square miles (13 sq km) ▪ Boardwalk trails ▪ Ancient pines
▪ nationalparks.fi/pyha-hakkinp

REPOVESI

A reclaimed Finnish forest thrives close to Helsinki.

The Lapinsalmi suspension bridge, a memorable part of a Repovesi hike

Once an intensively logged commercial forest, the now pristine pine and birch lands of Repovesi National Park have long since replaced the angry growl of the chain saw with the sound of birdsong. The park, located just a few hours northeast of the populous city of Helsinki, is now home to many bears year-round. Eurasian lynx, elk (moose), many owl species, and several galliformes also inhabit Repovesi.

In Finnish folklore, the northern lights are referred to as "fox fires" as the fur of an ancient fire-fox was believed to have sparked as it brushed up against the fells of Lapland, igniting the night sky with shimmering color. The fox is the symbol of the park, and you'll likely see this russet canine hunting at dawn or at twilight. But he is not exclusively a carnivore: Foxes also eat berries and plants.

The Koukunjoki river courses through the park and its connected waterways, supporting a variety of aquatic wildlife including the red-throated diver. This bird migrates to Repovesi in April or May to nest along the mire-like shores of small lakes and ponds. The extremely loud call of red-throated divers during mating season may startle hikers around Olhavanlampi pond; here the "long call," often voiced in a male/female duet, really resounds off of cliffs.

The cliffs of Repovesi were shaped by movement of the Earth's crust, the Ice Age, and erosion. At Olhavanvuori Rock the cliff face shows evidence of the shifting glaciers. On the north side of the Lapinsalmi chasm, two rock types meet. To the north, the rock is hard granite typical of central Finland; on the south side is the world's largest deposit of rapakivi, called Vyborg rapakivi, a very rare rock.

The Olhavanvuori hill is popular with climbers, and taking the Kultareitti water taxi route is a good way to see a sweep of the park. Repovesi has 25 miles (40 km) of hiking trails, including the popular 3.1-mile (5-km) Ketunlenkki (Fox Trail).

AT A GLANCE

Repovesi's restored forests ▪ Olhavanvuori Rock ▪ 5.8 square miles (15 sq km) ▪ Kultareitti water taxi ▪ The Ketunlenkki (Fox Trail) ▪ nationalparks.fi/en/repovesinp

ROKUA

A small geological gem and a UNESCO global geopark

The tiny Rokua National Park is located on the southern side of Rokuanvaara Hill in central Finland, where old pine forests grow in their natural state, untouched by the interfering hand of humankind. Rokua is also a UNESCO global geopark, and a small geological wonder. Within its rather tight confines, the park preserves a host of glacial formations representative of a wide swath of the ice-sculpted landscapes of Finland.

BURIED ICE

The unique and diverse landscape of Rokua was formed when Rokuanvaara Hill rose as an island out of the sea after the last ice age. Consisting mainly of sand, the island was subsequently sculpted by water and wind. The forests have since absorbed the sand dunes blown inland, but this is a sandy park. From the beach embankments, created by ice and waves, we can now read what the water levels were at various postglacial stages of the Baltic Sea. Look in the esker ridges for steep-sided *suppa* holes, places where large blocks of ice were once buried in the sand during the Ice Age. Syvyydenkaivo, the "well of depths," is the deepest suppa hole in Finland.

Among the other glacial landforms found in the park are drumlins (from the Irish word *droimnín* or "smallest ridge"), elongated hills in the shape of a hump or a half-buried egg formed by glacial ice acting on underlying moraine. Also seen are kettle holes, which are shallow, sediment-filled bodies of water formed where blocks of ice were left buried by retreating glaciers or draining floodwaters,

Lichens create a colorful tableau.

and subsequently melted. Terminal moraines, the end points or snouts of a glacier, are easily spotted as where the glacier's accumulated debris is dumped in a heap. And then there are the eskers, or ridges, formed above a glacially formed ice tunnel. The park's focal point is Rokuanvaara Hill, part of a 12.4-mile-long (20-km) and 3.1-mile-wide (5-km) esker and sand dune formation that rises above a flat expanse of mires.

FLORA & FAUNA

Rokua's fauna and flora are those of a typical barren forest with low biodiversity. The rarest of these, found on the slopes of suppa holes and on steep southern hillsides parched by the sun, include creeping thyme, shaggy mouse-ear hawkweed, fragrant Solomon's seal, and the uncommon spring-sedge. Many threatened butterflies that feed on thyme and hymenopteran plants are also found in Rokua.

The absence of reindeer from the area for at least 150 years has allowed the lichen on the barren sandy heath to grow uninterrupted. At Rokuanvaara Hill, the ground is covered in beautiful bright-white reindeer lichen, which gives the landscape a slightly mythical appearance. You'll feel like you're walking through a woodland straight out of *Lord of the Rings*.

Rokua, one of Finland's smallest national parks, has old-growth forests with plenty of stout old pines and dead but standing, barkless trees. These are traversed by many of the marked trails that run throughout the Rokua area and the national park. You can travel from Oulu to Rokua along the Tar Route Hiking Trail. Hikers often spot the spotted flycatcher, tree pipit, or willow tit. The male common redstart is noticeable for its colorful orange-and-red plumage and its slightly mournful vocalization, often heard early on bright summer nights.

AT A GLANCE

Rokuanvaara Hill esker ridge ▪ 3.4 square miles (8.8 sq km) ▪ Barren forest ▪ Rare plants ▪ Tar Route Hiking Trail ▪ nationalparks.fi/en/rokuanp

SALAMAJÄRVI

Walk through an unspoiled wilderness with a diverse ecosystem.

Summer in Salamajärvi is a time to explore the park's many mires.

The Peura Trail, one of Finland's most interesting, traverses 71 miles (115 km) through the rugged Suomenselkä watershed of central Finland. The landscapes along the way encompass mires, inhabited backwoods forests, and secluded lakes. At the heart of this famous Finnish trail, you'll enter Salamajärvi National Park. Here, the diversity of the mire ecosystem (see sidebar) can be studied up close on boardwalks across marshy wetlands. (Note that during spring floods, some boardwalks may be submerged.) In winter, the trail becomes a ski route.

Within Salamajärvi National Park, there are smaller nature trails, including Lasten luontopolku (Kids' Nature Trail). This mile-long (1.4-km) loop round Hepolampi pond explores the mires and forests—home to fair-ies and gnomes—and the insects of the lakes. The 4.3-mile (7-km) Pahapuron Lenkki trail to Risuperä takes in an old tar pit, old-growth pine forests, and the Church Stone, a boulder on an old pilgrims' route. If you have time, the 37-mile (59-km) Hirvaan Kierros trail takes in most of the park's landscape, including the impressive Heikinjärvenneva fen, the tar pits at Pakokangas, the lake scenery at Jyrkkäniemi, the birdlife of Iso-Valvatti wetland, and the old-growth forests along Koirajoki river.

You may see wild forest reindeer, a rare subspecies of the native breed. Elk (moose) may also be spotted on your hikes, and at Heikinjärven-neva, you can climb the observation tower to spy common snipe, jack snipe, wood sandpipers, and common greenshank in the mire. Look for the hilarious brightly colored head tuft of mating male ruffs, which look like wigs.

Mire Ecosystems

The marshy mires of Salamajärvi National Park are microcosmic worlds within themselves, a realm of hummocks (dry islands) and hollows (wet puddles). The biodiversity of these mires makes them a key habitat for insects and birds. The mires nurture cotton grass, arctic cloud-berry, and many dwarf shrubs such as bog rosemary, as well as sphagnum mosses. Sedges also thrive in the waterlogged flanks.

Mires are vital habitat for many threatened species such as yellow marsh saxifrage.

Finland protects its mires proudly, because no other European country except Russia enjoys such a variety of mire ecosystems. Raised bogs have completely disappeared from many parts of central Europe and aapa mires (also called Finnish fens or peatlands) do not form in more southerly climes.

AT A GLANCE

Mire ecosystems ▪ 24 square miles (62 sq km) ▪ Heikinjärvenneva fen ▪ The Peura Trail ▪ Hirvaan Kierros trail ▪ nationalparks.fi/en/salamajarvinp

SEITSEMINEN

The ancient forests and bogs of the Suomenselkä watershed

The Suomenselkä watershed landscape is a mix of upland and lowland coniferous boreal forests, the higher grounds dominated by towering stands of Norway spruce and Scots pine, while the lowlands, in stark contrast, are covered by sphagnum swamp and bog areas with stunted Scots pine and shrublike Norway spruce.

Parts of Seitseminen National Park, situated on this watershed, allow access to some of Finland's most ancient forests. The prime old-growth forest is Multiharju, where 400-year-old shield bark pines grow. Eskers run from north to south in the park, the highest of which is Seitsemisharju on the western edge of the park rising to 722 feet (220 m) at Rappumänny-nmäki. The park also has cultural curiosities such as the Kovero Farm, a tenant homestead established in 1859, and now an exhibit of the hard life of a Finnish crofter.

About half of the park consists of mires, and these are home to a wealth of wildlife: Black grouses, common cranes, whooper swans, wood sandpipers, and northern willow grouses all feast on the fenlike smorgasbord of fish and insects. In the old-growth forests, look for hole nesters such as Eurasian pygmy owls, Ural owls, three-toed woodpeckers, red-breasted flycatchers, and the Siberian flying squirrel. The symbol of the park is the ubiquitous pine marten, a nocturnal weasel.

Seitseminen Nature Centre has details of the park's 37 miles (60 km) of marked trails and 28 miles (45 km) of skiing routes. The 1.2-mile (2-km) Saari-Soljanen nature trail is a good introduction to the diversity of mire habitats, while the Harjupolku (Esker Trail) takes you 3.2 miles (5.2 km) out along the Seitsemisharju Esker.

Seitseminen's swampy marshlands host a variety of wildflowers.

AT A GLANCE

Seitsemisharju Esker ▪ Saari-Soljanen nature trail ▪ 17.6 square miles (45.5 sq km) ▪ The Kovero Farm ▪ Pine martens ▪ nationalparks.fi/en/seitseminennp

SIPOONKORPI

A rich avian habitat twitters loudly east of Helsinki.

In southern Finland, a patchwork of spruce forest and swamplands spreads eastward from Helsinki. Ensconced in a landscape of rolling fields and picturesque villages, Sipoonkorpi National Park is a serene green oasis for city folks. Many flock here in late summer and fall to fill their picnic baskets with nature's bounty of wild mushrooms and berries. The park also hosts many rare plant species, including dog's mercury and fumewort, which grow in the herb-rich forests.

The small Byabäcken River flows through Sipoonkorpi toward the shores of the Gulf of Finland. The wood grouse, lynx, and grey-headed woodpecker all take refuge in its valley. Thrush nightingales sing by the brook, while the grey-headed woodpecker and the ortolan bunting nest here. The spotted nutcracker lives on the forest's fringes, and other birds you'll see and hear on the trails include the greenish warbler, the red-breasted flycatcher, and the three-toed woodpecker.

The European eagle-owl is the park's symbol and thrives in Sipoonkorpi's rocky forests. You'll recognize this, the largest of all owls, by its plumage speckled with yellowish brown and black, by its thick, projecting "eyebrows," and not least by its orangey red eyes. A declining population of this bird across northern Europe has edged closer to threatened status.

The 3-mile (4.8-km) Sotunki Kalkinpolttajan Nature Trail will give you a good walk in these bird-filled woods.

AT A GLANCE

Herb-rich forests and swamplands ▪ 7.1 square miles (18.5 sq km) ▪ Byabäcken Valley ▪ Sotunki Kalkinpolttajan Nature Trail ▪ nationalparks.fi/en/sipoonkorpinp

SOUTHERN KONNEVESI

The rocky realm of the osprey

Imagine you're out kayaking on one of Finland's largest and loveliest bodies of water, Lake Konnevesi. Like other boaters and canoeists, you've spent the day paddling through a maze of islands in the south of the lake, along the east coast of the mainland. This is a dramatic glacial landscape, with smooth glaciated rocks and vertical rock walls of steep canyons shaped by ice and wind. You peer into the pristine waters of the lake and spot

a large specimen of the brown trout that thrive here, when suddenly, he appears! A huge osprey swoops at high speed from the rocky cliffs and with incredible agility lifts the large fish from the lake . . . then wings it back to his lair. This is Southern Konnevesi National Park, realm of this magnificent bird.

The park is also a great place to hike, with multiple trails as well as canoe and boating routes. Many of the hiking trails are challenging due

to steep hills and rocky terrains. The Kalajan Kierros trail, for example, is 2.8 miles (4.6 km) long but may take half a day. This trail takes you to the top of Kalajanvuori hill, which rises 252 feet (77 m) above a lovely pond below. The reward for the stiff climb is a magnificent view of the lakes and old-growth forests of the park.

A wide-winged osprey swoops and strikes for his fish supper.

AT A GLANCE

Lake Konnevesi ▪ Osprey country ▪ 5.8 square miles (15 sq km) ▪ The Kalajan Kierros trail
▪ nationalparks.fi/en/southernkonnevesinp

SYÖTE

A maze of trails leading through northern old-growth forests

If you want to disappear into the magical world of Finland's old-growth forests for a day or two, the lovely log cabin–style Syöte Visitor Centre is an excellent place to plan your escape. Grab a warming coffee—this is the Arctic north of Finland—and enjoy the educational exhibitions and films on the backwoods of Syöte National Park and how humans have fared there. Then, don a pair of snowshoes, or good hiking boots if it's summer, and go explore these beautiful spruce woods for yourself.

One of Finland's larger national parks, Syöte protects a chain of old-growth forests, some of which are high-altitude woodland. These offer several rare species vital habitat for survival in this northerly part of the country.

The limestone cliffs around Kouvanjärvi lake rise out of the water almost vertically, and are thus best seen from a canoe or kayak. Several threatened species of mosses are worth looking out for on the rocks here, including the almost featherlike moss species *Pseudoleskeella papillosa, Encalypta brevicolla, Encalypta rhaptocarpa,* and *Platydictya jungermannioides.* Although these long Latin names are instantly forgettable, these lovely green growths on a backdrop of limestone are worth preserving: The bright green spleenwort is probably the easiest to spot, due to its long fern leaves.

Alpine saxifrage and the Haller's Bartramia moss are additional threatened rock vegetation that thrive around the lush lakeshores. Also along the water's edges are fine examples of scree rock fields, which have been created by frost breaking the rocks.

OLD-GROWTH FORESTS

Most of the park is covered by a chain of old-growth forests in their natural state, although some areas have suffered natural forest fires and some were historically subjected to slash-and-burn agriculture (see sidebar). These formerly deciduous woods have evolved into spruce-dominated old forests, with plenty of dead trees left standing in their midst. These provide homes for all the usual suspects who choose hollowed-out trees as their nesting places, including Siberian flying squirrels and beetle species such as *Pytho kolwensis* and

A moose and her calf emerge from the forest to forage the Syöte moorlands.

Pytho abieticola. The golden eagle and the merlin are two of the larger winged predators seen here, and their smaller avian cousins include the red-flanked bluetail, and the chiffchaff, a leaf warbler that gets its name from its distinctive and repetitive sound.

Nesting birds in the park tend to be northerly types, including the white-tailed eagle, Siberian Jay, Siberian tit, and black woodpecker. In addition to Siberian flying squirrels, the mammals of the park include the brown bear, wolverine, Eurasian lynx, wolf, and European otter. The park also has many elk (moose). The park's streams teem with brown trout, so a fishing license is a good buy.

TRAILS & ACTIVITIES

The wild wooded hills, placid lakes, and marshland of Syöte provide great opportunities for many activities. You can cross-country ski through magical snow-cloaked forests, or pedal up hills and down dales along the park's many fine mountain biking routes. Syöte National Park unspools approximately 76 miles (122 km) of marked trails, providing a choice of day trips depending on your fitness, or if you're a serious hiker, many options for multiday treks.

Most of the trails are in the Syöte area, while the National Hiking Route, the UKK Trail, transverses both the Syöte and Maaselkä areas. As this is northern terrain, subarctic conditions apply in winter, and snowshoes or skis are essential to get around the trails. The visitors

Winter coats the trees of Syöte.

Syöte's Mires

About a quarter of Syöte is covered by mires, swampy ecosystems based on peat. The best aapa mires (ridged mires that follow the slope of the terrain) in the park are at Jaaskamonvaara Hill, Päätuore-Ahmavaara Hill, and Salmitunturi fell. Boardwalk paths provide access to explore the diversity of mires situated in the depressions between the hills, on the slopes, and on the upper areas. The largest mires are often only forested around the edges and have not been drained, making this is an ideal place to experience these wetlands in their natural state. In the aapa mires, look for greater pond sedge, a threatened plant with a yellow speared bloom, and on higher fens, see the protected marsh saxifrage with its bright yellow blossom.

center can direct you to local enterprises that offer equipment rental.

A good picnic trail for day hikers is the 1.3-mile (2.1-km) Vattukuru Nature Trail, open year-round, which leads through the flora and fauna of the old-growth forest; the landscape varies from slope bog to lush riverbanks to spruce forests. Watch overhead in Vattukuru ravine for the fabulous Siberian flying squirrels. The 0.6-mile (1-km) Huippupolku trail explores Finland's southernmost fell on the summit of Iso-Syöte fell, a lookout point that offers splendid views. Anglers should take the 0.6-mile (1-km) Kellarilampi Nature Trail to the gorgeous Kellarilampi pond, where a lean-to offers shelter from the elements. You can also climb the Pytkynharju Esker for great park views.

Probably the best views of all are at the pinnacle of the 1.2-mile (2-km) Pyhitys Trail, at the top of the highest wooded hill in Syöte National Park. The vistas out over the wilderness and Kostonjärvi lake are excellent, and on the slopes you will come across rocks that the Sami people used as sacrificial altars. In ancient times, these hunter-gatherers asked for better luck in hunting and fishing by sacrificing some bounty of the forest and lake to their gods. On the longer, overnight trails, the park offers many day-trip huts as rest stops for hikers. The log cabin sauna at Ahmatupa in the heart of the park is a wonderful place to soothe your weary body and refresh your soul.

AT A GLANCE

Kouvanjärvi lake ▪ Siberian flying squirrels ▪ 115 square miles (299 sq km) ▪ Syöte's mires ▪ Kellarilampi Nature Trail ▪ nationalparks.fi/en/syotenp

TEIJO

A eutrophic fen amid the pine forests of the south coast

Most national parks in Finland, especially in the north, bear little trace of the human footprint aside from the reindeer enclosures of the Sami people. Teijo National Park, located in southwest Finland is different: In Teijo you'll encounter several historical industrial areas, including a former ironworks area in Kirjakkala. These ironworks were fueled by local timber, and many of the log houses built here in the 1800s have now been renovated to their original state.

An early spring sunset on icy Matildanjärvi lake

EUTROPHIC BALANCE

Teijo National Park is also remarkable for its eutrophic fen, a well-nourished marshland that has become overly enriched with minerals and nutrients, which induce excessive growth of plants and algae. Once this abundant plant life decays, the dissolved oxygen is depleted, particularly in shallow waters. This type of fen is extremely rare in southern Finland. The multitude of plants this enriched fen supports include broadleaved cotton grass, dioecious sedge, common yellow sedge, cotton deer-grass, and marsh arrowgrass.

The fens are surrounded mainly by stands of young pine and herb-rich forests, where deer and elk (moose) abound. Other aquatic landscapes to be enjoyed in Teijo are the seashores and lakes, some of them dammed, which teem with freshwater fish such as salmon and trout.

Teijo's Ironworks

The iron foundries of Kirjakkala, Teijo, and Mathildedal in Halikonlahti Bay showcase Finland's great iron-producing age. The ironworks in Kirjakkala has been renovated and is operational to give visitors a taste of an industry dating back to 1686. Klaus Fleming, who bought the foundry in 1729, after crop failure and the Great Northern War, built a powerhammer, an ore mill, and workers' houses here. Jaokob Kijk, who owned Teijo and Kirjakkala in the 1770s, built a rococo-style manor, and Robert Bremen added a church in 1830. Viktor Zebor Bremer constructed a calcining kiln, charcoal furnaces, a mill, and a rectory in Teijo between 1844 and 1859.

In Jeturkasti and Miilunummi, the rocky fields show the ancient shores of the Baltic Seas.

The symbol of Teijo is the grey-headed woodpecker that inhabits many of the groves, mixed forest, and aspen stands in the park. You'll recognize this species by the male's bright yellow forehead and by its distinctive fading call of *ki-yoo ki-yo ki-yo ki-yo*. If you're a good mimic, you can even lure a mating male out of hiding and, if successful, you'll be able to say you speak a little avian Finnish.

The park has about 31 miles (50 km) of hiking trails: The 2.8-mile (4.6-km) Ancient Jeturkasti Trail gives a good cross section of the park landscapes, taking in pine forests and rocky high grounds, and bringing you across a small mire on boardwalks. You'll also see the ancient shoreline of the Baltic at the stone field of Jeturkasti. Fishing and canoeing are also popular within the park.

AT A GLANCE

Eutrophic fen ▪ Grey-headed woodpecker ▪ 13 square miles (34 sq km) ▪ Teijo's ironworks ▪ Ancient Jeturkasti Trail ▪ nationalparks.fi/en/teijo

TIILIKKAJÄRVI

A mix of southern and northern landscapes

Tiilikkajärvi is a fascinating lake, surrounded by beaches, and dissected by esker capes. The lake is the focal point of Tiilikkajärvi National Park, which hosts a wealth of birdlife, including the northern species of brambling and rustic bunting that nest in the park's forests. The yellow wagtail thrives on the marshlands, along with the whimbrel, a large wader whose name mimics its distinctive call; you'll also recognize it by its long, crescent-shaped bill.

You're likely to spot the black-throated diver around Tiilikkajärvi lake, and the little ringed plover on its beaches. Other species you might see in the park include the lesser black-backed gull, willow grouse, bean goose, Eurasian golden plover, and Siberian jay.

The many lovely lakeshores include the beautiful beach of Venäjänhiekka (Russian Sands), named for the 1595 Treaty of Teusina that divided these lands between Sweden and Russia. Look for the crown and cross symbolizing the two countries on the old border stone on the esker ridge in Tiilikkajärvi lake. Here too is the Tiilikanau-

tio tenant farm that was occupied until the start of the 19th century. Deserted until the 1920s, it serves as a reminder of the past, complete with remains of a pit where ore from the lake was melted into iron.

The park has about 12.4 miles (20 km) of marked trails. The 4.3-mile (7-km) Uiton kierto trail takes you around Sammakkojärvi lake, and the hilly sections reward with good views of the lakes Sammakkojärvi and Autiojärvi. Two bridges arch over the water, before boardwalks lead you across the mires and through the dry, birdsong-filled forest.

An old cabin is a reminder of previous times in the region.

AT A GLANCE

Tiilikkajärvi lake ▪ Esker ridge capes ▪ 13 square miles (34 sq km) ▪ Russian Sands beach ▪ Uiton kierto trail ▪ nationalparks.fi/en/tiilikkajarvinp

TORRONSUO

A fine example of a raised bog

The thick raised bog of Torronsuo welcomes myriad birds.

In southwest Finland you'll find a national park focused around a typical raised bog—a thick plateau of turf with its center rising above its edges. The turf layer is one of the thickest in any Finnish mire, in places extending to up to 39 feet (12 m). This is Torronsuo National Park, a small preserve where bird-life and butterflies take wing in this specialized habitat.

Torronsuo hosts many rare species, including birds usually found much farther north, such as the northern pintail, the great grey shrike, and the ruff. The willow grouse may be spied at the edge of the mire, while the spotted crake can occasionally be seen and heard, recognizable by its distinctive and repetitive *hwuit, hwuit* call.

The Kiljamo bird-watching tower offers fine views over the vast open bog, a great vantage point for spotting migrating cranes and geese in spring and fall.

A diversity of mire plants grow in Torronsuo: Among abundant bog plants such as heather, marsh tea, and bog bilberry, look for tangles of crowberry and cranberry. The butterflies alighting on such plants include Freija fritillary and Frigga fritillary.

The park offers visitors two boardwalk trails: The first is the 0.9-mile (1.5-km) loop around the island of Kiljamo. This trail offers insight into the open middle parts of Torronsuo mire, as well as the pine bogs and diversity of islands with small patches of herb-rich forest. The other option is a 1.8-mile (3-km) trail over the mire, through forests, and on to the old quarry of Härksaari, where quartz and feldspar were once mined. In winter, the frozen, snow-covered bog becomes a wider maze of cross-country skiing trails.

Geology of Torronsuo

The Torronsuo area has been widely known for its quartz deposits since the 1700s, and for its rare minerals, such as pegmatite, since the start of the 1800s. Of the 60 pegmatite minerals found in the area, 15 were discovered for the first time in Finland here in Torronsuo. Sukulatite, named for the nearby village of Sukula, was first discovered in this area. In 1862, the famous geologist, mineralogist, and Arctic explorer A. E. Nordenskiöld made an expedition to this area to study its tantalum mineral deposits, a rare and highly corrosion-resistant metal with the symbol Ta and atomic number 73.

AT A GLANCE

Ombrotrophic raised bog ■ 9.8 square miles (25.5 sq km) ■ Spotted crake ■ Kiljamo bird-watching tower ■ nationalparks.fi/en/torronsuonp

VALKMUSA

Finland's swamp varieties condensed into one small park

If swamps are a signature landscape of the Finnish wilderness, particularly in the north, it is extraordinary that more than 30 different swamp types can be categorized in a very concentrated area of southern Finland consisting of less than seven square miles (17 sq km). Valkmusa National Park is like the theme park of Scandinavian swamps.

The mires in the park are Munasuo, Valkmusa, Kananiemensuo, and Mustanjärvensuo. Munasuo mire is Finland's largest coastal hummocked raised bog, thick with a wealth of mosses and with a center raised higher than its edges. Munasuo mire is edged with wet mires hosting peat moss, spruce mires, and pine mires. Kananiemensuo mire has retained its wilderness-like appearance, and is a fascinating mix of multiple mire types. Clearly visible in the mix are two raised bogs and an aapa bog. The center of Kananiemensuo is extremely damp.

BIRDLIFE & BUTTERFLIES

Given the diversity of plant and insect life in this concentrated preserve, the park attracts a rich diversity of birdlife. Northern species such as the whimbrel, willow grouse, and rustic bunting nest easily in these marshlands alongside their coastal aviary brethren such as the common redshank and the common pochard. Osprey, crane, and geese are among the bigger birds nesting in the park.

Six pairs of western osprey are known to make their homes here in safe environments with open views, and they are prepared to fly long distances in search of food; the closest fishing grounds are on the Gulf of Finland. But that's a short hop for a bird that flies to southern Africa each winter and makes the return journey in spring. During the breeding season, you can usually hear and spot the ospreys from the boardwalks or viewing platform at Simonsaari.

Many rare and endangered species of butterflies flutter across these fens. The symbol of Valkmusa National Park is *Idaea muricata,* a moth that is commonly known as the purple-bordered gold. This is one of nature's most beautiful miniature masterpieces, with a wing pattern of gold flourishes on a purple base, variable yellow spots that are sometimes distinctive, sometimes fused, and an outer crossline that is blue-violet, slightly wavy, and edged with a thin band of jagged purple. With such an imaginative appearance, *Idaea muricata* deserves a more memorable moniker, that is, if this glorious but endangered species can survive our era's insect apocalypse.

The swamps of Valkmusa can be crossed on marked routes over boardwalk trails. The main hike through the park is the Western Oasis Trail, a 1.5-mile (2.5-km) loop that starts at the Simonsaari parking lot. This hike will bring you through most of the various types of boglands in Valkmusa National Park, including the ombrotrophic raised bogs. Bring binoculars and a camera as a nature observation tower is located along the trail, from where you can look onto the vast array of mires.

Boardwalks lead hikers across Valkmusa's diverse swamplands.

Lapland's National Parks

Fanned out above the Arctic Circle, Lapland's preserved lands form the crown of Finland's parks system. Snowcapped mountains; deep, ancient forests; and vast, untamed wildernesses beckon you north into six Lapland national parks, the wintry terrain of bears, lynx, and arctic fox.

Northern lights (aurora borealis) shimmer and swirl over Bothnian Bay.

In Lapland, you can dogsled from lodge to lodge deep into parks such as Lemmenjoki and Riisitunturi, ending each day in a wood-heated sauna. You can experience the ancient reindeer-hunting culture of the Sami people, spending evenings tasting local fish and game around a roaring fire, while the aurora borealis flares overhead. The Sami have inhabited these harsh northern latitudes since the last ice age and are the only indigenous people within the European Union. They revere the reindeer, and with good reason: These sturdy Arctic animals have provided their families with meat, milk, and hides for centuries, while their bones and antlers are still crafted into tools and weapons. The Sami have about 1,000 words to describe reindeer appearance and behavior.

Finland's Lapland parks are reminders that national parks can preserve Europe's many cultures as well as its threatened fauna and flora. The Sami now fear that their region is under threat from global political and economic interests keen to exploit Lapland's natural resources and open up Arctic shipping routes to Asia. The Sami worry that the building of a proposed new railway to the EU's first Arctic port, in Norway, will provide mining and logging companies with the infrastructure to venture farther into the wilder, untouched parts of Lapland.

BOTHNIAN BAY

Only about 0.97 square miles (2.5 sq km) of this marine park's 61 square miles (157 sq km) is on land, mainly consisting of bay islands formed by postglacial rebound. Although the landscape is in flux, a strong fishing culture has prevailed in the bay area for centuries, and the seas offer diverse ecosystems to explore. Look for grey seals, ring seals, and arctic terns, and for Siberian primrose on the shore meadows of the bay. There's an underwater trail for divers and a nature trail for hikers, but the park is somewhat inaccessible, and boating to the islands is only recommended for experienced sailors. *nationalparks.fi/bothnianbaynp*

LEMMENJOKI

If Lapland is the crown of Finland's park system, Lemmenjoki is the jewel in the crown, a vast wilderness of forests, fells, and bogs, stretching all the way to the Norwegian border. This is backcountry of dazzling, sometimes disconcerting light, where the scenery of the heavens above is as remarkable as the landscapes of the river valleys and forests. The northern lights dance their way across these skies all winter, while in summer the midnight sun bathes the land in a seeming eternity of ethereal light. The Sami heritage is at its strongest here, in lands far from the southerly capital, where these indigenous people have hunted, then herded, their reindeer for generations. The Lemmenjoki river veins the park, and leads to one of its scenic highlights, the Ravadasköngäs waterfall. This is a great canoe route, with spectacular scenery to admire. The park has numerous trails and shelter huts: The 10-mile (16-km) Joenkielinen Trail passes the Joenkielinen Fell.

The park's emblem is the lonesome wolverine, which you won't spot too easily, but you might smell its presence: There's a reason native Finns call it "skunk bear." *national parks.fi/lemmenjokinp*

PALLAS-YLLÄSTUNTURI

Pallas-Yllästunturi National Park covers some 394 square miles (1,020 sq km), much of it a chain of fell landscapes. The highest fell, Taivaskero, rises 2,648 feet (807 m) above sea level in the center of the park. Other landscapes are prime-val forests that stretch across the hills and various types of muskeg, moss bogs with acidic soils typical of Arctic and boreal areas. The park has around 220 miles (350 km) of hiking trails, and many mountain biking trails. The most popular is the 34-mile (55-km) Hetta–Pallas Trail, which takes you high into the fells. Look for the black-and-white snow bunting bird, and the pincushion flower. *nationalparks .fi/pallas-yllastunturinp*

PYHÄ-LUOSTO

In 2005 Finland's oldest park, Pyhätunturi, was merged with the protected lands of Luosto, to form the country's newest park. The landscape is of old-growth forests with 200-year-old pines, wetlands, and the 12 peaks of the tunturi line. The tunturis are remnants of Alp-like mountains, formed billions of years ago; the highest peaks are Noitatunturi, standing at 1,772 feet (540 m), and Ukko-Luosto at 1,686 feet (514 m). Trails and ski routes are plentiful, including the 6.2-mile (10-km) Karhunjuomalampi Trail, which takes in the park's most famous sights: the Pyhänkasteen-putous waterfall, Isokuru gorge, and Uhriharju ridge. *national parks.fi/en/pyha-luostonp*

RIISITUNTURI

The remote park of Riisitunturi is a mountainous area with many swamplands, especially sloping bogs on the hillsides. The only wilderness hut in the park is located near the twin peak of Riisitunturi Mountain, some 1,527 feet (465.3 m) above sea level. The 2.6-mile (4.3 km) Riisin Rääpäsy Trail gives an oversight of the Kitkajärvi lakes, Ikkunalampi pond, hanging bogs, and the Riisitunturi fell. *national parks.fi/en/riisitunturinp*

URHO KEKKONEN

Expect to see Sami herding their reindeer in this huge Lapland park of 985 square miles (2,551 sq km), named after a late president and prime minister of Finland. The Suomujoki river flows through the north of the park. Highlights of this vast wilderness are the Kiilopää fell, the Aittajärvi lake along the Suomu-joki river, and the remote fell of Korvatunturi, famous among Finns as the home of Father Christmas. This is the heart of Lapland; look to the skies for golden eagles circling by day, and the aurora borealis dancing by night. *nationalparks.fi/ en/urhokekkonennp*

Winter sunrise lights a familiar vista of snow-covered trees in the frozen Lapland wilderness.

SOUTHERN EUROPE

SOUTHERN EUROPE

From the Iberian Peninsula, home to two great empires—to the island of Malta, a crossroads of culture, and eastward to the cradles of European civilization in Italy and Greece—southern Europe is a tapestry of history. Rich threads of religion are found in national parks such as Portugal's Peneda-Gerês and Spain's Picos de Europa; the drama of geology defines Italy's Etna and Vesuvius; and mythology and ancient civilization are stitched into Olympus, Parnassós, and Sounio in Greece. Throughout southern Europe you'll experience a rich brew of cultures that swirls around the Mediterranean Sea: Cowboys on the plains of Doñana; the culinary and wine subcultures of every regional park in Italy; and the contemplative life of Parnitha in Greece with its 13th-century Byzantine monastery, and of Prespes with its medieval hermitages. Both saints and sinners have long sought an escape into nature from the bustling Mediterranean trade routes and city settlements of southern Europe.

Above: Santa Maria Assunta, Alta Murgia National Park, Italy
Previous pages: Garajonay National Park, Spain

PORTUGAL

Portugal is a long, coastal country bathed in rich Atlantic light, forever facing westward onto the Atlantic Ocean that beckoned to its earliest adventurers. In the country's golden age of exploration, the horizon was a mysterious edge that your ship might disappear over, never to be seen again. Thus, Portugal's westernmost point of Cabo de São Vicente at Sagres became known as the End of the World, and the music that later came to define the Portuguese soul was one of eternal sadness and longing for a homeland left behind. Fado music, according to one expert, mourned "the presence of an absence."

So it's somewhat apt that the country's one national park—the Peneda-Gerês National Park—is located in a desolate, inhospitable landscape of granite mountains, an emptiness where the lonesome song of fado would not be out of place. The howl of the wolf and the whistle of Atlantic winds, however, are nature's music in this northerly park. The park's rugged peaks and river valleys are a hikers' delight. And remember, this small country has many natural parks, protected landscapes, and reserves to explore too; and Portugal's lush volcanic islands in the Atlantic—Madeira and the Azores—are also excellent places to hike.

Opposite: The waterfalls of Arado, near Gerês in Peneda-Gerês National Park

PENEDA-GERÊS

Remote villages, Iberian wolves, and golden eagles

Espigueiros, *raised granite granaries, built to store crops for the villagers of Lindoso*

Portugal has only one national park, which curls around the border with Galicia in Spain. The horseshoe-shaped Peneda-Gerês National Park protects the remote, traditional villages of the Norte region, as well as much threatened flora and fauna. A partnership with the adjacent Spanish national park of Islas Atlánticas (see page 272) embraces a wider protected habitat. Most of the Peneda-Gerês infrastructure is concentrated in a buffer zone that encircles the spectacular, elevated core region.

The park borders stretch between the towns of Castro Laboreiro in the north and Casdas do Gerês in the south, an area traversed by the Ríos Lima, Homem, and Peneda. Four mountain ranges (*serras*), rich in granite and schist, are the spine of the park, creating a series of peaks and valleys edged with undulating foothills. The highest peak, Gerês in the Serra do Gerês, climbs to 5,046 feet (1,538 m). The ancient megaliths (particularly around Castro Laboreiro and Mezio) and strange granite formations are more impressive.

FLORA & FAUNA

Peneda-Gerês is on the cusp of the Mediterranean and northern European biosystems, giving it a diversity of flora and fauna. Plant life here is most vibrant in April and May, which is also peak hiking time in the park. But be warned—this is the wettest part of Portugal.

The hills of the Serra da Peneda form a barrier to the passage of hot and wet air masses coming off the Atlantic, which results in Portugal's highest rainfall. Hikers should always dress or pack for the possibility of wet weather. The rainfall has the effect of nourishing the park's luminous green meadows, which local long-horned *barrosão* cattle greedily munch. Several species of oak dominate the lower hills, with an interesting mix of other trees, such as English oak, cork oak, butcher's broom, maple, and Portuguese laurel. Shrubbery in these lower hills includes bilberry, strawberry tree, and European holly. Natural and man-made fires have been a huge threat to the forestry of Portugal in recent years.

Higher elevations have typical moorland vegetation, including seas of vibrant yellow gorse, heather, broom, pine, and fir trees. In wooded areas, look for the wild Gerês lily, endemic to the park.

Inhabitants of the park include Spanish ibexes that come across the border from Galicia, wild boars, otters, foxes, and raptors such as golden eagles and European honey buzzards. The park shelters an impressive 200 species that are threatened or protected. These include three species of bat: the greater horseshoe bat, the lesser horseshoe bat, and the Mediterranean horseshoe bat. Other species that find sanctuary are the Iberian shrew, the European pine marten, the wildcat, the gold-striped salamander, and the snub-nosed viper. Roe deer, which are a symbol of Peneda-Gerês, are prolific park dwellers, especially along the outskirts of the park.

NOSSA SENHORA DA PENEDA

An unexpected sight in such a raw, craggy setting and dwarfed by a sheer granite cliff is the lovely sanctuary of Nossa Senhora da Peneda, a graceful baroque building with a zigzagging stairway inspired by the church of Bom Jesus do Monte in nearby Braga. The long flight of steps is flanked by 14 chapels, each representing a major event in the life of Christ. The sanctuary was inspired by a reported vision of the Virgin Mary by a local shepardess in the 13th century. If you visit around September 7, you will witness one of Portugal's most sacred pilgrimages. The sanctuary is in the most rewarding northern part of the park, where you will discover the traditional rural lifestyles that the park protects—despite the population's ongoing drift to the cities.

THE SUBMERGED VILLAGE

To get a real sense of the ancient rural customs of the Norte region, visit the town of Terras de Bouro, just outside the southwest corner of the park. Its ethnographic museum, Museu Etnográfico de Vilarinho da Furna, reveals the traditional life once enjoyed in Vilarinho das Furnas, a village that was submerged by the Vilarinho das Furnas dam on the Río Homem in 1972. Building stones were saved to construct the museum. During years with low rainfall, the village ruins stands above the water.

An interesting footnote to the flooding of the village is the Garrano (or Minho horse), a breed of small equine that were ancestors of the Galician pony and Andalusian horse. These now live in the wild, but are a gentle breed with no fear of humans. This is because for a long time this breed was raised on the farms of Vilarinho das Furnas.

The park is filled with history: Roman Geira, a Roman road, crosses the region, and stretches of the road along the Río Homem are still preserved, along with several Roman bridges. The town of Soajo is also worth visiting for its Ladeira medieval bridge, its raised granite granaries, and its Castro Laboreiro breed of dogs.

Walking in Wolf Territory

There are few more wildly invigorating sounds in all of nature than the plaintive cry of the wolf in the wilderness. Especially when you are camping. You can get up close with the wild and untamed in Peneda-Gerês National Park by tracking one of its rarest residents, the endangered Iberian wolf (*Canis lupus signatus*). One- to eight-day expeditions into the wilderness are offered with Ecotura (Lugar do Queimadelo, Castro Laboreiro, Melgaço, *ecotura.com*). Knowledgeable guides lead small groups along centuries-old shepherd paths and known wolf trails, searching for wolf tracks and pointing out the ancient traps once used to catch these elusive and much feared creatures. The tour explains the importance of wolves to this northern region and their miraculous ability to survive extinction despite man's efforts (until recent years) to be rid of them. Guide and owner Pedro Alarcão suggests that the best time to visit is in September and October, when the likelihood of spotting a wolf is greatest.

AT A GLANCE

The Church of Nossa Senhora da Peneda ▪ 271.3 square miles (702.9 sq km) ▪ Wolf tracking ▪ The Roman Geira ▪ Museu Etnográfico de Vilarinho da Furna ▪ natural.pt/portal/en

SPAIN

Anyone who goes looking for the heart of Spain is tilting at windmills as foolishly as Don Quixote. Spain has many hearts. This country is a potpourri of regions, each as distinct in character and landscape as the Basque Country of the Pyrénées is from the cowboy country of Doñana's sand dunes. Spain's national parks span this diversity: Garajonay lures you into lush forest repose off the coast of Africa; the Atlantic Islands of Galicia cackle with prolific birdlife along gorgeous shorelines; Picos de Europa soars to Cantabrian heights alive with exotic mountain wildlife; and the Sierra Nevada has even higher peaks, the backdrop to photos of La Alhambra in Granada, the highpoint of Spain's Moorish architecture.

Opposite: Stone on stone—Tella village in Ordesa and Monte Perdido National Park

AIGÜESTORTES I ESTANY DE SANT MAURICI

The park of winding waters hits all Catalonia's highs.

The park offers some of the best hiking—on paths old and new—in the Spanish Pyrénées.

The only national park in Catalonia is located in the heart of the Pyrénées and embraces all the main ecosystems to be found in the Catalan Mountain region.

Aigüestortes i Estany de Sant Maurici National Park—the name translates as "winding streams and lakes of St. Maurice"—is a scenic mix of glacial lakes, waterfalls, and rushing streams, spiked by towering granite peaks with flanks clad in fir and pine forests. On the high pastures, carpets of spring wildflowers roll out in spring.

The park has a variety of alpine vegetation due to its wide range of altitudes. The lower valleys host European deciduous forests with pubescent oak, European ash, beech, or common hazel being the predominant trees. Former meadows and pasturelands that humans historically farmed are now usually covered with grasslands and shrubs, dominated by secondary forests with Scots pine.

Mountain pine forests reign from about 4,920 feet (1,500 m) to above 6,560 feet (2,000 m). Mountain pine can survive the long, hard winters of the High Pyrénées at altitudes up to 7,875 feet (2,400 m). At this height, only hardy plants such as alpenrose and blueberry thrive.

The crystalline lake of Estany de Sant Maurici is among the most popular scenic spots within this park of many natural, cultural, and historical highlights. The inviting trail connecting the villages of Espot and Boí leads past this glacial lake, which owes its existence to the impenetrable granite rock of these mountains. Another highlight in this area is the spectacular Estret de Collegats, a narrow gorge gouged by the torrential Noguera River, where you'll see the Roca de l'Argentina, a rock face dripping with icy stalactites.

At the spa town of Caldes de Boí, on the west side of the park, hikers can rest their weary feet in hot springs. Reproductions now replace the unique frescoes that once graced the walls here; they were painstakingly moved to Barcelona's Museu Nacional d'Art de Catalunya. More history awaits in the town of Taüll, where the lovely churches of Santa Maria and Sant Climent are worth visiting for their Lombard-style bell towers that rise against a backdrop of verdant meadows and craggy peaks. In winter, this area becomes the realm of skiers at the Boí Taüll resort, which reaches 8,060 feet (2,457 m). The steep-sided valley known as Vall de Boi has the most impressive group of Romanesque churches in the world, their tall slender towers pointing heavenward from the valley floor. These UNESCO-listed churches were built between the 11th and 14th centuries.

HEADING FOR THE HILLS

But it is when you leave the town and head into these hills that the true magic of this park begins to reveal itself: You might come across horses wearing cowbells, or embark on a quixotic search for the legendarily named Estany Perdut (Lost Lake) and Agujas Perdut (Lost Mountains). Perhaps you'll find the century-old bonsai pine tree growing out of a rock near the Estany Llong, or seek out the famous 600-year-old, 20-feet-thick (6-m) black pine that has stood here since Columbus set sail from Spain in August 1492. Because of the park's high altitudes—its tallest peak is Pic de Comolaforno at two miles (3 km)—many of the park's trails are only open in spring and summer. Between May and June, the streams are at their fullest, and colorful

wildflowers begin blossoming in June and July.

Even in summer the weather is changeable, so head out prepared. The park's trails are well marked, and the longer routes have refuge huts; the Espot-Boí trek is about 15.5 miles (25 km) and takes about nine hours to complete. The Marmot Trail is a particularly picturesque hike, leading past the Cavallers dam and finishing at Estany Negré (Black Lake), while the Estany Llong trail takes you into the inner realms of the park along the Aigüestortes plateau.

To get a sense of the history of

The Pyrenean highlands, wrapped in the frigid cloak of winter

these mountains, take the Camins Vius (Living Paths). This route travels along traditional valley paths, most dating back to medieval times and some even older, through the villages surrounding the park, passing through Alta Ribagorça, Vall d'Aran, and Pallars Sobirà.

The park hosts many creatures

to look for on your hikes: Among its avian inhabitants are capercaillie, rock ptarmigans, golden eagles, griffon vultures, and bearded vultures. The bearded vulture is the common name for the brownish black-feathered lammergeier, an impressive indigenous bird with a wingspan of almost 10 feet (3 m). Walkers in the woods might also spot the black woodpecker or the red-billed chough.

The park's mammal species include Pyrenean chamois, stoat, alpine marmot, and fallow deer. The relatively small roe deer (about 3 feet/1 m long) were introduced to the park during the second half of the 20th century.

Although the park is not exactly aslither with amphibians, look for the well-camouflaged Pyrenean brook salamander, and especially for the *Vipera aspis,* a poisonous snake that should not be provoked. The lakes and rivers teem with brown trout.

AT A GLANCE

Estany de Sant Maurici (lake) ▪ 54.4 square miles (141 sq km) ▪ Vall de Boi Romanesque churches ▪ Camins Vius (Living Paths) ▪ Espot-Boí trail ▪ spain.info/en

ARCHIPIÉLAGO DE CABRERA

A mix of Mediterranean Sea and Balearic Islands

An often overlooked Spanish jewel adrift between Europe and Africa, Archipiélago de Cabrera National Park preserves vast colonies of birds and marine wildlife. If you want to brave it out to Isla Cabrera—just over an hour by boat from Majorca—you'll need to plan ahead. The park has restricted access, and the islands are still used by the Spanish military. The marine ecosystem here is unique, with meadows of *Posidonia oceanica* nurturing many species of marine fauna. The seas around the islands teem with cetaceans including sperm, pilot, and fin whales, as well as dolphins. A 14th-century castle and local lighthouse are open to the public, and a small visitors center offers details on trails and diving permits.

The park embraces the Balearic Islands and well-preserved coasts.

Calcareous island and pristine seabeds ▪ 38.7 square miles (100 sq km) ▪ Exclusive diving ▪ Cabrera castle and lighthouse ▪ Bird colonies ▪ seemallorca.com/sights/reserves/cabrera-archipelago-maritime-terrestrial-national-park

CABAÑEROS

A mountain wilderness in the Spanish heartland

In the mountains of Toledo, in central Spain, is the largest surviving area of Iberian-Mediterranean forest. Bracketed by the Rios Estena and Bullaque, and reaching into the Sierra del Chorito and de la Miraflores mountain ranges, this is the beautiful Spanish wilderness of Cabañeros National Park.

Cabañeros protects vital habitat for such a wide range of animals, many of them endangered, that it has been called the Serengeti of Spain. Some 276 species of vertebrates live here, including the elusive European otter. The otter's sleek brown fur is often paler on its underside, covering a long lithe body, thick tail, and short legs. This thick layer of short fur traps a layer of air to insulate the otter, who spends much of its life in the water. A powerful swimmer thanks to its webbed feet, it can close its small ears and nose while diving, and locate prey using its sensitive whiskers.

Other park inhabitants include wild boar, red deer, and fallow deer. The park also attracts the critically endangered Iberian lynx, which was reintroduced to the Toledo mountains.

Birdlife in the park includes the black stork, the threatened Spanish imperial eagle, and the Eurasian black vulture, which stands at nearly four feet (1.2 m) with a wingspan of up to 10 feet (3.1 m).

Points of interest are a Paleozoic site where Ordovician fossils have been found and the cabins of coal miners *(carboneros)*, which gives the park its name.

Iberian-Mediterranean forest ▪ 158 square miles (409 sq km) ▪ Ordovician fossils on Paleozoic site ▪ The Serengeti of Spain ▪ spain.info/en_US

CALDERA DE TABURIENTE

A stunning geological phenomenon in the Canary Islands

Another of Spain's island parks, this intriguing preserve centers around the large caldera on La Palma in the Canary Islands. A caldera is a type of geological sinkhole that results when a large, cauldron-like hollow forms following a volcanic eruption. As large quantities of magma erupt outward, structural support for the crust above the magma chamber degrades rapidly and the ground collapses downward into the semi-vacated magma chamber, leaving a huge depression at the surface. The Caldera de Taburiente collapsed approximately two million years ago, following the eruption of a massive shield volcano of about 12 miles (20 km) in diameter; a similar geological event occurred at Iceland's Bárðarbunga volcano from 2014 to 2015. The volcanic ash generated by this recent eruption and collapse grounded most of the airplane flights across western Europe.

HITTING THE HEIGHTS

The Caldera de Taburiente is about 6.2 miles (10 km) in diameter, and its walls reach 6,560 feet (2,000 m) over the inner base. The pinnacle is the Roque de los Muchachos on the northern wall, at 7,960 feet (2,426 m), which can be reached by road. An observatory close to the summit has telescopes for sweeping views of the entire caldera. If you don't want to climb to the summit,

La Cumbrecita, located lower down in the southeastern section of the rim, affords another fine view into the caldera. To the southwest you'll see where the caldera opens out to the Balearic Sea through a riverbed called Barranco de las Angustias. A popular attraction for hikers within the park is the beautifully hued Cascada de los Colores, a waterfall with mineral-stained walls.

Caldera de Taburiente National Park is host to a large forest of Canary Island pine, a subtropical pine species that does not survive frost. Some vital stands of the endangered Canary Islands juniper are also found in the park.

HISTORY IN THE MAKING

This caldera has two claims to historical fame: When the Spanish conquered the Canary Islands in the 15th century, the indigenous people of the archipelago, a branch of the Guanches known as Benahoaritas, used the great bowl as a fortress making their last stand. The invading Spaniards were unable to breach the natural fortification, and they finally broke the siege by luring the Benahoarita leader out on the pretext of peace talks. In 1815, German geologist Christian Leopold von Buch visited both the Caldera de las Cañadas and the Caldera de Taburiente on a trip to the Canary Islands. After comparing the two, he became the first scientist to distinguish between calderas of volcanic and erosional origins, also introducing the term "caldera" to the geological lexicon.

Roque de los Muchachos rises high above the island of La Palma.

AT A GLANCE

Caldera landscape ▪ Canary Island pine forests ▪ 18.1 square miles (46.8 sq km) ▪ Roque de los Muchachos Observatory ▪ Cascada de los Colores ▪ reservasparquesnacionales.es

DOÑANA

A rich biosphere surprises in Spain's sandy southwest.

Las Marismas, the delta where the Río Guadalquivir flows into the Atlantic, is the focal point of Doñana National Park. With its marshes, shallow streams, and vast sand dunes, Doñana often looks like a scene from *Lawrence of Arabia*, and with good reason as the film was partly shot here. Although the camels have long since disappeared—released into the wild after filming—the area now hosts a national park whose cast of animal characters is epic: Thanks to

White storks (Ciconia ciconia) *cluster in a tree at sunset.*

its great range of ecosystems, this park is home to thousands of European and African migratory birds, Spanish red deer, wild boars, Egyptian mongooses, and endangered species such as the Spanish imperial eagle and the Iberian lynx. The lynx is the star attraction: Doñana is one of only four Spanish colonies of the world's most endangered wildcat, and the Acebuche breeding center has established a successful captive breeding program.

HORSES, HORTICULTURE & HISTORY

The park's other beloved beasts are two indigenous horses—the marsh horse and the Retuerta, which dates to 1000 B.C. A strong ranch culture persists in Andalusia, and cowboys are often seen driving wild horses across Doñana's plains.

The reptiles and amphibians that thrive in these marshes and dunes include the western cowl snake, Montpellier snake, Carbonell lizard, ocellated lizard, Iberian newt, and the chameleon. The park's birdlife is legendary, embracing some 360 species: the purple heron, Egyptian vulture, Bonelli's eagle, Montagu's harrier, flamingo, Spanish sparrow, Audouin's gull, Cetti's warbler, black-bellied sandgrouse . . . the list goes on and on.

This who's who of Europe's birds and mammals is attracted by the park's rich flora, which thrives in the mild, typically Mediterranean climate. Cork, oak, and pines are plentiful, and maritime juniper grows in abundance alongside roses and shrubs. Some of the 875 species indigenous to Doñana include oleander, sea wallflower, sweet saltwort, prickly tumbleweed, camarina, and labiérnago, a woody plant that thrives amid oak. The constant southwest wind gradually buries the coastal plants and trees in sand, forming an ever evolving ecosystem in these transdunes.

The area has a rich history dating back to 1262, when King Alfonso X established a Real Cazadero (a royal hunting preserve) in the Las Rocinas forest. In the 16th century, Alonso Pérez de Guzmán, seventh duke of Medina Sidonia and commander of the Spanish Armada, established a country retreat here for his wife; the house was renovated later as a palace. The park's modern-day equivalent, Acebrón Palace, was built in the 1960s by Luis Espinosa Fondevilla as a residence and hunting lodge. It now serves as a visitors center.

AT A GLANCE

Acebuche Iberian lynx breeding center ▪ 210 square miles (543 sq km) ▪ Acebrón Palace ▪ Spanish cowboy culture ▪ andalucia.org/en/natural-spaces/national-parks/donana/

GARAJONAY

A magical forest park on a legendary Canary Island

Imagine a wooded parkland so enchanting that it is named after a pair of legendary lovers. Picture a path through a canopy-shaded mass of moss-covered trees; then daydream of a vast swath of floral color along the forest floor as if it were a cathedral filled with Arabian carpets. This is something like the experience of walking in Garajonay National Park.

Located in the center and north of the island of La Gomera, one of the seven main Canary Islands, this gorgeous park was declared a World Heritage site by UNESCO in 1986. It takes its name from the rock formation at the highest point on the island, some 4,879 feet (1,487 m) above sea level.

The woodlands are the finest

The hiking trail near El Cedro passes fine hillside plant life.

remaining examples of Canarian laurisilva, a humid subtropical forest that once covered most of southern Europe, but is now only found in the Azores, the Madeira Islands, and Garajonay. The rare plants hothoused in this habitat include Azores laurel and Canary laurel. The laurisilva valleys in the north of the island consist of subtropical rainforest where the large laurel trees reach above the canopy. Birds and bats proliferate in the shady forest undergrowth, including two breeds of pigeons native and restricted to the Canary Islands, the laurel pigeon and Bolle's pigeon.

The national park offers a network of 18 footpaths; on hikes look for indigenous species such as the Gomeran lizard and the Gomeran skink, as well as the stripeless tree frog.

The Legend of Gara & Jonay

The tale of the doomed lovers Gara and Jonay is Spain's version of Romeo and Juliet, set on the island of La Gomera. During the festival of Beñesmén, a common practice for young maidens was to gaze into the waters of Chorros del Epina to see their future. But when Princess Gara of Agulo did so, her reflection turned to flames. The wise man Gerián warned her that fire and water could not mix. Soon Jonay, son of a king from Tenerife (with an active and fiery volcano), arrived and the two fell in love. But when their betrothal was announced, the volcano Teide erupted in fury and the parents broke the match in fear of this omen. Jonay returned to Tenerife, but swam back to La Gomera by night to be with his beloved. A search was ordered, the lovers were trapped on a mountain, and they took their own lives.

AT A GLANCE

Canarian laurisilva forests and valleys ▪ 15 square miles (40 sq km) ▪ UNESCO World Heritage site ▪ Guanche culture ▪ reservasparquesnacionales.es

Doñana National Park, within Spain's cowboy country

ISLAS ATLÁNTICAS DE GALICIA

A wild Atlantic island archipelago with a grievous history

Galicians, like Catalans, Basques, and most other regional groups in Spain, consider their territory a land apart. So Islas Atlánticas de Galicia Maritime-Terrestrial National Park is a source of great pride. The park comprises the archipelagos of Islas Cíes, Ons, Sálvora, and de Cortegada—much of its area being maritime. The three islands of Islas Cíes—Monteagudo (Sharp Mount), del Faro (Lighthouse), and San Martiño (Saint Martin)—are granite mountains once part of the Galician mainland and now marooned in the Atlantic. The park's walking trails circle the shores of these islands and of Isla Ons. Take the 4.3-mile (7-km) Monte Faro trail for the steep switchback climb to the lighthouse.

The main landscape is laurel forest, the same laurisilva type of subtropical forest that dominates Garajonay National Park (see page 269). The seas here are especially fertile, with more than 200 species of seaweed and many more of shellfish, corals, and anemones. Whales, orcas, and dolphins bask in the waters. The rocky shores are alive with seabird colonies, including seagulls, razorbills, and European shags. Look for the almost extinct Iberian guillemot with its black head and white front.

The islands have had a rough history. Occupied since the Iron Age, their yield of Roman ceramics establishes them as one of the westernmost outposts of empire. Monastic orders settled here in the Middle Ages, but the islands' strategic value as launching sites for attacks on the mainland meant little peace was to be had in medieval times. Later, when pirates used the archipelago as a base to attack ships returning from the New World, the islanders up and left. In 2002, the massive oil spill from the MV *Prestige* oil tanker decimated many shorelines, killing much birdlife in the park.

Nosa Señora beach on Islas Cíes, part of the Atlantic Islands of Galicia

AT A GLANCE

Laurisilva subtropical forest ▪ 32.7 square miles (84.8 sq km) ▪ Seabird-watching on Islas Cíes ▪ Monte Faro trail ▪ iatlanticas.es/html/index3af1.html

MONFRAGÜE

A historic Iberian refuge for raptors

For centuries, three walled cities in the western Spanish province of Cáceres provided citizens with shelter from the perils of life in the Middle Ages. Today, at the center of the triangle formed by those citadels of Plasencia, Trujillo, and the city of Cáceres, sits Monfragüe National Park, a place of refuge for many of the big bird species endangered by our modern age.

As the crow flies, the park runs east to west along the valley of the Río Tajo, the longest river in the Iberian Peninsula. The valley has been gouged from a long mountainous ridge, and the rock face on its western side is known as the Peña Falcon (Falcon Rock). On the valley's eastern side rise the remnants of the Castle of Monfragüe, craggy medieval ruins that are now the aerie of the griffon vulture. These fearsome predators nest here in the hundreds, far surpassing the local human population. Yet this has been a much inhabited region: Caves in the area have prehistoric paintings from the Copper, Bronze, and Iron Ages. The Romans coined the name Monfragüe, meaning "lush mountain." The park's location close to the Ruta de la Plata (Silver Route) means the remains of Roman roads, bridges, fountains, and gravestones are common. The castle of Monfragüe was constructed in the ninth century, with five towers and two perimeter walls.

The Tagus flows below Peña Falcon and the ruins of the Castle of Monfragüe.

It was later destroyed by Napoleon's forces in the Spanish war of independence between 1807 and 1814.

RAPTOR REFUGE

In 2003, UNESCO recognized Monfragüe as a biosphere reserve; it became a national park in 2007. The story of this park is one of reclamation. Just as the birds have reclaimed the castle keep, the land has now been preserved on their behalf after two man-made decimations of nature. In the 1960s, the Río Tajo was dammed, altering its course through the park. Then in 1970 came a brutal reforestation with nonindigenous eucalyptus and pine for an aborted paper industry; much of the vital thickets of the Mediterranean forest were wiped out.

The park now preserves remaining habitats of extensive dense scrub, small oak woodlands, and cliff and rock faces for multitudes of raptors. Monfragüe boasts one of the world's highest concentrations of imperial eagles, large numbers of griffon vultures, and several pairs of Spanish imperial eagles, golden eagles, and Bonelli's eagles. Observation blinds along the course of the Río Tajo help visitors admire these impressive creatures as they swoop for prey.

Other breeding birds in the park include black storks, Eurasian eagle-owls, azure-winged magpies, and white-rumped swifts. While your eyes will be mainly on the sky in this park, keep an eye out for Iberian lynx and wild boar on the ground.

AT A GLANCE

Castle of Monfragüe ▪ Raptor-watching ▪ 69 square miles (179 sq km) ▪ Río Tajo bird-watching blinds ▪ Griffon vultures ▪ Spanish imperial eagles ▪ reservasparquesnacionales.es

ORDESA & MONTE PERDIDO

A soaring Pyrenean park in the heart of Basque Country

The Ordesa Valley and the Lost Mountain: Who could resist such a mysteriously named landscape? The Basque region of the Pyrénées has long been a riddle, wrapped in a vast mountain range. Just what is this stateless nation? How can a cultural identity span two countries, Spain and France? Even the language, *Euskara*, is unrelated to all other European tongues, and continues to confound linguists. This is a place apart.

Ordesa and Monte Perdido National Park is located in the Pyrénées of Huesca province, Aragon, and since 1997, it has been part of the UNESCO Ordesa-Viñamala Biosphere Reserve. It is also part of the cross-border Pyrénées–Mont Perdu World Heritage site.

This elevated park has a diversity of biospheres, stratified by altitude: Between about 4,900 and 5,580 feet (1,500 to 1,700 m), extensive forests of beeches, silver firs, pines, and oaks dominate the landscape, mixed with stands of birches, ashes, and willows. At higher elevations, up to 6,550 feet (2,000 m), mountain pine prevails. Bushes of boxwood are found up to 5,900 feet (1,800 m). In the higher meadows, the hardier wildflowers that color the mountains in spring include earleaf bellflower (purple

The Gradas de Soaso cascades, Ordesa Valley

bells), Pyrenean violet (yellow stamen), and long-leaved butterwort (long green leaves). The snow-white edelweiss is the symbol of the park.

PYRENEAN FLORA & FAUNA

Many animals and birds inhabit this mountain wilderness. The Pyrenean chamois is a goat-antelope with a russet-brown coat, dark eye patches, and superb mountain climbing skills. This indigenous species was nearly hunted to extinction in the 1940s, but thrives today in the Pyrénées. The alpine marmot, boar, and Pyrenean desman (a tiny water mole with a scaly tail) survive in the wooded areas of the park's lower levels, as does the beautiful royal owl. Predators such as the golden eagle, bearded vulture, and griffon vulture nest high up in craggy limestone peaks.

Ordesa and Monte Perdido National Park has protected many species of flora and fauna throughout the years, as did its park predecessor, Ordesa Valley National Park, dating back to 1918. However, perhaps the park's most cherished inhabitant, the *bucardo* or Pyrenean ibex, went extinct in January 2000, in spite of preservation efforts—another reminder of humankind's incursive effects on the habitats of so many of Earth's species. When you wander high in these hills and watch a griffon vulture swoop for

food with its awe-inspiring nine-foot (2.8-m) wingspan, it's easy to conclude that *Homo sapiens* is the most invasive species of all.

HIKING TRAILS

Fortunately for nature lovers, these remote and daunting Pyrenean mountains have resisted a heavy human footprint over the course of centuries. This was the rugged landscape of smugglers and bandits, who regularly crossed the borders between Spain and France. To visit a lovely Pyrenean village such as Tella today is to step back in time. The national park allows only 1,800 visitors in at one time, so a sense of space and timelessness prevails within its mountainous confines. Hiking trails are plentiful, and many are challenging to even the fittest of walkers; the Circo de Soaso is one such challenging nine-mile (15-km) hike that takes you through the Ordesa Valley and onward to a beautifully scenic waterfall called the Cola de Caballo (Horsetail Falls). The somewhat longer Balcón de Pineta Trail leads you up to the Pineta Balcony, where you'll enjoy stunning vistas of the mountains and the glacier. Many of the trails in Ordesa and Monte Perdido start from the tranquil village of Torla, which is the gateway to the national park and includes the beautiful and historic San Salvador church, which dates back to the 13th century.

AT A GLANCE

Pyrenean peaks ▪ 60.2 square miles (156 sq km) ▪ Pyrenean chamois ▪ Balcón de Pineta Trail
▪ Circo de Soaso trail ▪ ordesa.net

PICOS DE EUROPA

A soaring park of rugged limestone peaks

The impressive limestone massif of the Picos de Europa straddles the regions of Asturias, Cantabria, and Castilla y León in northern Spain. These "Peaks of Europe" soar to more than 8,500 feet (2,600 m), and their subterranean karst landscapes include some of the country's most interesting cave networks.

The Picos de Europa was Spain's first national park and is inhabited by the full gamut of Spanish wildlife: Cantabrian brown bears, Pyrenean chamois, Iberian wolves, and royal eagles are among the park's prime attractions. Grouse, wild boar, and deer are plentiful too, and you'll also see plenty of cattle grazing the meadows here. In local restaurants, game and organic veal are on most menus, while the local cheeses made from the milk of grass-fed cows are varied and delicious. Try the Cabrales, a pungent blue cheese traditionally wrapped in sycamore leaves and left in limestone caves to ripen. This should be washed down with some strong local cider, poured into the glass from a great height—to aerate it—as tradition demands.

Much of the park is at altitudes high enough to look down on clouds, and even its lower areas feel a world away from modern. Long isolated by its rim of peaks, the string of valleys known as Liébana successfully repelled Romans, Arabs, and French invaders. Flowing through it, the Río Deva has carved out a spectacular gorge, the Desfiladero de la Hermida. Craggy, eroded limestone peaks rise above,

The Basilica of Santa María la Real of Covadonga at dusk

while the boulder-strewn torrent of the Deva rushes through its floor, teeming with salmon and trout.

The easiest way to get the most spectacular views of the park is to take the Fuente Dé cable car up the sheer rock face to a lookout at 6,060 feet (1,847 m). The ride whips you up 2,470 feet (753 m) in just four minutes. From a café at the top, you can take a 1.8-mile (2.9-km) trail leading to the Puerto de Aliva, a remote stomping ground for bear, chamois, and the Cantabrian capercaillie, the largest member of the grouse family and a protected species. Look too for the lammergeiers throughout the park—the bearded vulture is making a comeback after a recovery program that began in 2002. You may also see an Iberian wolf, another threatened species; they are not looked on kindly by local farmers and are often shot to protect livestock.

HISTORY & CULTURE

Liébana has many lovely churches and hermitages worth visiting, especially Nuestra Señora de Lebeña, a 10th-century Mozarabic structure. The region's most important religious site is the monastery of Santo Toribio de Liébana, built in the eighth century to honor the fragment of the True Cross of Christ (supposedly) brought here from Jerusalem. A large gold-plated cross contains the holy relic in the Capilla del Lignum Crucis (Chapel of the Wood of the Cross).

On the Asturian (western) side of the mountains, the most historic site is the Cangas de Onís, Spain's first Christian capital 1,300 years ago and now a major canoeing hub.

One of the high points (literally and figuratively) of Picos de Europa National Park is a visit to the Covadonga, site of the Visigoth leader Pelayo's famous victory over the Moors in A.D. 722. This major pilgrimage site is a picturesque mountain sanctuary on the northern flanks of the Picos, where

Pelayo began the Christian Reconquest (Reconquista). A statue of the legendary hero stands in front of the 19th-century basilica. Inside the adjoining Museo de la Virgen are offerings to the Virgin of Covadonga, including a diamond-studded crown. Pelayo's sarcophagus is in the neighboring cave, the Santa Cueva, alongside a much venerated statue of the Virgin, patron saint of Asturias.

HIKES & ACTIVITIES

The Picos de Europa National Park is a hikers' and cyclists' heaven, with excellent mountain trails and well-maintained roads with little traffic. The lively market town of Potes is a center for climbers, mountain bikers, canoeists, and hikers, with several specialist equipment shops and many guides who will take you through the mountains. Potes sits at the crossroads of four valleys where the mild climate nurtures the outlying cherry orchards and vineyards. The warm, friendly restaurants are a great way to get a flavor of the local mountain cuisine, serving sausages, cheeses, cheesecakes, and delicious milk-based desserts.

The park offers a multitude of trails to choose from, with the Garganta del Cares being the most popular. This 6.2-mile (10-km) hike takes you through spectacular rocky gorges along the Río Cares, up steep paths, across bridges, and through tunnels that exemplify the limestone karst landscape of the area. The trail is best walked from north (Poncebos

in Asturias) to south (Caín in Castilla). Plenty of attainable mountain peaks are also worth climbing, such as the Naranjo de Bulnes (Orange Tree of Bulnes).

You can take a kayaking expedition down the Río Sella from Arriondas, or canoe along one of the ravines or out onto one of the

park's many lovely glacial lakes, such as Enol or Ercina. These lakes have good trails around them, and the hair-raising road of Mirador de la Reina leading up to them is a memorable drive or cycle. The park's three visitors centers have maps and information on all trails and guided hikes.

The Cares gorge trail is one of Spain's great hikes.

AT A GLANCE

Limestone massif ▪ Lammergeiers ▪ 250 square miles (646.6 sq km) ▪ Garganta del Cares trail ▪ Shrine of Santa Cueva de Covadonga ▪ parquenacionalpicoseuropa.es/english

SIERRA DE GUADARRAMA

Granite mountains offer elevated escape from Madrid's summer heat.

Slicing through the border between Madrid and Castilla y León, this 62-mile-long (100-km) range of granite outcrops, streams, and oak and pine forests attracts masses of Madrileños in summer. The Sierra de Guadarrama National Park protects the 11 different ecosystems found in the Guadarrama mountains, including the only instances in Iberia of high Mediterranean mountain. The park also provides vital habitat for 13 endangered species. The lower slopes of these jagged granite peaks are bearded with forests of Scots pine and oak, while its meadows nurture dramatic yellow blazes of *piorno,* or Spanish broom, as well as juniper plants with their blue-black "berries" that are actually cones.

The hills of the Sierra de Guadarrama are filled with deer (red, roe, and fallow), wild boar, wild goats, badgers, weasels, wildcats, foxes, and hares. Great raptors such as the Spanish imperial eagles and Eurasian black vultures circle the skies in search of prey. In recent years, a pack of wolves was spotted in the park after a 70-year absence from this region. This is not a welcome development for the Sierra's traditional farmers, who graze livestock in the meadows.

The mountains are beloved by hikers and climbers; the park's highest peak is Peñalara, at 7,970

A female Iberian ibex (Capra pyrenaica) *in her native habitat*

Shepherds' Legacy

Although agriculture has faded in these mountains, the remains of shepherds' cabins are still found in the mountaintops, alongside sheep-shearing stations and the brick chimneys of old sawmills. Up until the mid-20th century, it was common to encounter the summer migration of a herd to the high Sierra de Guadarrama, and you can still hike a number of pathways that follow these ancient cattle trails.

In spring and summer, the villages throughout the park still host traditional rural festivals celebrating livestock and pilgrimages.

feet (2,429 m). Other scenic high points include the Puerto de Navafría pass and the La Morcuera and Siete Picos mountain ranges. On your hikes, you'll pass glacial cirques and lakes, and granite rock fields. Hiking in the spring, when meadows are in flower, is particularly rewarding, whereas the mountains in winter offer plenty of skiing and snowboarding opportunities. The slopes of Valdesquí and Puerto de Navacerrada are easily reached and are suitable for family winter activities. Sierra de Guadarrama National Park has other adventure activities such as canyoneering, horse riding, and zip-lining. Cycling is especially popular: Bike rental shops are plentiful, and the four visitors centers supply maps of the park's best trails and roads.

AT A GLANCE

Granite mountain peaks ▪ Climbing Peñalara ▪ 131 square miles (339.6 sq km) ▪ Village festivals ▪ 11 ecosystems ▪ parquenacionalsierraguadarrama.es/en

SIERRA NEVADA

The snow-cloaked mountains that frame Granada's Alhambra

Gaze up from the heat-hazed plains of Andalusia and you'll see two incongruous sights: the miracle of Moorish architecture that is Granada's Alhambra, and behind it, the snowcapped peaks of the Sierra Nevada.

The mountains of Sierra Nevada National Park shelter glacier lakes, such as the stunning Laguna Altera, as well as stark tundra landscapes. The Iberian ibex is the mammal most adapted to this high-altitude geography: With its short legs and flexible hooves, this wild goat navigates the rocky heights with ease. Look for the curved horns of males.

Lower down are pine forests, the realm of badgers, beech marten, and mountain lions. The park boasts more than 2,000 botanical species, including the snow star, which grows in rocky crevices and resembles a white starfish when in flower. Butterflies such as the rare Nevada blue and the Glandon blue thrive here. Hoopoes show their flashy plumage, and among the birds of prey soaring above the rocks are golden eagles and Bonelli's eagles. The clue to spotting a Bonelli's eagle is identifying this brown- and white-feathered bird's yellow feet.

Las Alpujarras, a hub of villages on the sierra's southern slopes, retains much of the Arabic influence of its original settlers, the followers of Boabdil, last Islamic ruler of southern Spain. Boabdil fled across the sierra in 1492 when the Christian armies of the Reconquista recaptured Granada.

The park offers great skiing at Europe's most southerly ski area, which has 85 downhill and cross-country runs open for a ski season lasting from November to April. Other park activities are horse riding, mountain biking, and paragliding. Hiking trails through this high-altitude park are gloriously scenic, many winding through the villages of Las Alpujarras. Take the GR7 from Lanjarón to Pampaneira for an excellent 12.4-mile (20-km) hike. Mountaineers come here to climb two of Spain's highest mountains, Pico de Mulhacén (11,420 feet/3,481 m) and Veleta (11,128 feet/3,392 m).

The ski resort of Pradollano sparkles after a heavy snowfall.

AT A GLANCE

The Villages of Las Alpujarras ▪ 333 square miles (862 sq km) ▪ The GR7 national hiking trail
▪ andalucia.org/en/natural-spaces/national-parks/sierra-nevada/

TABLAS DE DAIMIEL

A bird-watcher's gem of floodplains wetlands

Wooden walkways lead over the park's protected wetlands.

The smallest of Spain's national parks, Tablas de Daimiel is a bird-watcher's delight. The park consists mainly of floodplain wetlands on the La Mancha plain, a mainly arid area of central Spain. Plans are afoot to expand the nature reserve to incorporate surrounding dryland farming areas; it is hoped this will improve management of the area's water resources, and thus increase protection of the wetlands. La Mancha has a long history of water issues, stretching back to the time of its famous windmills, built to pump water rather than to torment Don Quixote.

The Tablas de Daimiel has a long tradition of waterfowl hunting and in 1966 the Tablas became a national hunting reserve. Migratory and nesting birds are well served by two types of water: The Guadiana supplies freshwater, while its tributary the Río Gigüela is brackish.

The long list of birds that stop in here mid-migration include the purple heron, grey heron, little egret, black-crowned night heron, and red-crested pochard. Look for the Slavonian grebe, aka the horned grebe; its name comes from the large patches of yellowish feathers located behind the eyes, which resemble horns and are raised and lowered at will.

Aquatic residents of the park once included large stocks of European freshwater crayfish, but these were overfished by locals and today are almost extinct. Other indigenous species such as the barbus, the common carp, and the chub are now under threat from invasive northern pike. Watch for mammal residents such as the European polecat, red fox, otter, and water vole as you walk the park's wooden trails.

AT A GLANCE

La Mancha floodplain wetlands ▪ 11.7 square miles (30.3 sq km) ▪ Ríos Guadiana and Gigüela ▪ lastablasdedaimiel.com

TEIDE

A Martian landscape on a Spanish island

Is there life on Mars? Well, look first to Tenerife, where the environmental and geological conditions of Teide National Park are so similar to the red planet that researchers come here to plan for interplanetary travel.

The park is centered on Pico de Teide, Spain's highest mountain at 12,198 feet (3,718 m) high and one of the world's highest volcanoes. The aboriginal Guanches of the Canary Islands believed the Teide to be the gateway to hell.

The park also encompasses Cha-horra, another high volcanic mountain, with a peak of 10,285 feet (3,135 m). The unique volcanic landscape of Teide National Park led to its status as a UNESCO World Heritage site. You can get a good overview from the Observatorio del Teide, located on the east side of the Teide.

The lava on the flanks of the Teide has weathered to a thin but nutrient- and mineral-rich soil that hosts many plant species. Canary Island pine forests cover the middle slopes of the volcano; Canary Island cedar and Canary Island pine grow at higher altitudes. The rich soils nourish several indigenous plants including Teide white broom, which blooms in a white-and-pink flower; the Canary Island wallflower, which has white-and-violet flowers; and the Teide bugloss, whose red flowers form a pyramid up to nine feet (3 m) high.

Three endemic reptile species are also found here: the Canary Island lizard, Canary wall gecko, and Canary Island skink.

AT A GLANCE

Volcanic landscapes ▪ 73.3 square miles (189.9 sq km) ▪ Endemic reptiles ▪ Observatorio del Teide ▪ webtenerife.com

TIMANFAYA

Lanzarote's active Timanfaya (Fire Mountain)

The island of Lanzarote, in the Canary Islands, is host to another of Spain's volcanic parks. Timanfaya National Park consists entirely of volcanic soil as its namesake volcano, around which the park centers, is still active. The surface temperature in the core ranges from 212 to 1112°F (100 to 600°C) at a depth of about 43 feet (13 m). Pour a drop from your water bottle as you hike up the hill here (you can also take a camel!) and watch it steam as it hits the ground.

The infernal influence pervading this national park is witnessed in its symbol, the statue "El Diablo" by César Manrique.

A Canary Island camel ride around Lanzarote's "Fire Mountain"

AT A GLANCE

An active volcano ▪ 19.7 square miles (51 sq km) ▪ "El Diablo" statue by César Manrique ▪ A camel ride to the volcano ▪ spain.info/en_US

AUSTRIA

SWITZERLAND

P

S

Stelvio
National Park

Val Grande
National Park

L

Lake
Maggiore

Dolomiti Bellunesi
National Park

SLOVENIA

Gran Paradiso
National Park

Lake
Guarda

•Milan

Po

A

CROATIA

FRANCE

Genoa•

A

Appennino Tosco-Emiliano
National Park

P

Cinque Terre
N.P.

Florence•

P

SAN
MARINO

LIGURIAN

SEA

E

Capraia

Foreste Casentinesi,
Monte Falterona
& Campigna N.P.

Archipelago Toscano

Monti Sibillini
National Park

Portoferraio•

N

Gran Sasso &
Monti della Laga
National Park

Elba

Tiber

ITALY

Giglio

N

Corsica
(France)

Arcipelago Toscano
National Park

•Rome

I

Majella
National Park

Gargano
National Park

ADRIATIC   SEA

Asinara
N.P.

Arcipelago
di la Maddalena
National Park

Abruzzo, Lazio & Molise
National Park

Circeo
N.P.

N

E

Alta Murgia
National Park

SARDINIA

Gulf of Orosei
& Gennargentu
National Park

Naples•

Vesuvio
N.P.

Cilento, Vallo di Diano & Alburni
National Park

S

Appennino Lucano-
Val d'Agri-Lagonegrese
N.P.

TYRRHENIAN

SEA

Pollino
National Park

Sila
National Park

•Cagliari

Calabria

IONIAN

SEA

M
E
D
I
T
E
R
R
A
N
E
A
N

Reggio
di Calabria•

•Palermo

Aspromonte
National Park

Etna
Park

S I C I L Y

•Catania

S E A

Pantelleria

Isola di Pantelleria
N.P.

N

0   50 kilometers
0   50 miles

ITALY

Italy has created many of the world's great works of art, literature, and architecture. It has also administered to some of the greatest empires of the ancient and medieval world, and it has developed one of the world's finest cuisines from the fruits of its fertile fields and plentiful seas. And then there's its fabulous fashions. So even first-time visitors to this land have already been beguiled by its culture and history. Yet what awaits is a country with a medley of landscapes as surprising and varied as any in the world.

Go to Gran Paradiso National Park in the northwest and you'll discover Graian Alpine landscapes that equal those of Austria or Switzerland. Dolomiti Bellunesi National Park offers its own unique mountain wilderness in the northeast while Etna on Sicily and Vesuvius National Park outside Naples showcase the geological drama of volcanoes. In central Italy, Abruzzo, Lazio and Molise National Park is a surprising wilderness of bears and wolves nestled in the Apennine Mountains. Then there are the island preserves, such as Arcipelago Toscano and the tiny Isola di Pantelleria, nearer to Tunisia than mainland Italy, not to mention Sardinia's pair of parks. Cinque Terre with its necklace of picturesque cliff-side towns strung out along the Ligurian coast presents coastal Italian culture, and Pollino protects the vast forests of the deep south. This endlessly diverse country is as rich and varied in natural beauty as it is in culture, history, and culinary delights.

Cavoli beach on Elba in the Tuscan Archipelago National Park

ABRUZZO, LAZIO & MOLISE

Man and nature coexist high in the Apennines.

The ancient village of Barrea overlooks Lago di Barrea in the Abruzzo region of the park.

Often just called Abruzzo National Park, the majority of this park is located in the Abruzzo region, much of it high in the Apennine Mountains. Since its inception in 1922, this preserve has provided key habitat for indigenous species such as the Italian wolf, the Abruzzo chamois, and the Marsican brown bear. Much of the protected area consists of beech forest, with scatterings of silver birch and black pines. Above the level of the beech tree forests, the high mountain stony grounds are now planted with stands of Swiss mountain pine, allowing a whole new ecosystem to develop. Above the forests, chamois live alone or in small groups.

In the lower-level forests inhabitants include the European polecat, Eurasian otter, and two species of marten: pine marten and beech marten. The reintroduction of deer and roe deer to the park and the return of wild boar have opened up new food chains, expanding habitat for the park's traditional carnivores.

THE BEAR STORY

Chief among these carnivores is the Marsican brown bear, a park success story. The bear's habitat has continually shrunk as development in the Abruzzo region continues apace, and poaching has taken its toll on this valuably pelted creature. Their numbers have rebounded in recent years though, and 100 bears are now estimated to live in the park.

The Marsican bear, now the official symbol of Abruzzo National Park, is often referred to as the Abruzzo brown bear. It has a calm temperament, with no aggression toward humans. Male Marsicans are larger than most other brown bears, with a weight of around 480 pounds (217 kg). The Marsican bears' seasonal hibernation is also unusual: Unlike other bears who enjoy a single winter-long slumber, this bear wakes intermittently, which makes their resurgence in the spring less lethargic. Marsican bears have lent their name to *pan dell'orso* (bear bread) and other local foods. Their presence brings much ecotourism to the Abruzzo region, although conflicts with shepherds and honey farmers are still reported.

Abruzzo brown bears are shy creatures, and easier to spot within the park are the red fox, mountain hare, least weasel, European mole, and western European hedgehog.

Other mammals on the lower end of the park food chain are the snow vole, edible dormouse, wildcat, and crested porcupine.

BIRDLIFE

The golden eagle is probably the park's prime avian predator. Other raptors that find rich pickings in the forests and fields of Abruzzo include goshawks, peregrine falcons, Eurasian buzzards, and kestrels. Keep an ear open at night for several species of owl, such as the little owl, barn owl, or tawny owl. Higher up on the rocks and cliffs, you might see red-billed chough, partridge, and white-winged snowfinch. In the streams of the park, aquatic avians such as grey wagtails and white-throated dippers are often seen.

The park's extensive beech tree woods are desirable habitat for the park's most flamboyantly feathered bird, the Lilford white-backed woodpecker. This large bird (10 inches/25 cm tall) sports white bars across its wings, and a white lower back. The male has a distinctive red crown, the female a black one.

HISTORY & HIKING

The park's landscapes are a mix of the gentle slopes that typify the Apennines and several more dramatic Alpine peaks. The park is veined by the Fiume Sangro river, with several tributaries. This is karst country, so the waters often duck underground only to resurface at the base of a valley. The park abounds with interesting features such as glacial cirques in the upper valleys, large morainic deposits of stones along the valleys, caves, fractures, and dolines (large sinkholes created by the collapse of the limestone underground). Although much of the park's rock is porous and calcareous, in the Camosciara-area dolomite rock is predominant; this waterproof rock enables water to flow freely over the surface, creating several picturesque waterfalls and water pools. The park's flora is rich and diverse with about 2,000 species of plants, not to mention numerous musks, lichens, algae, and mushrooms. Watch for the park's most beloved flower, the rare lady's slipper, a beautiful yellow and black orchid.

The park's many trails offer a variety of hiking challenges. One recommended trail is the six-hour Valico Passaggio dell'Orso hike. This takes you into the heart of the park, along the Upper Sangro to the Valle di Fondillo, nestled in the Serra delle Gravare mountains.

Abruzzo National Park is also filled with a host of picturesque villages where you can sample the local culture and cuisine of the Apennines. Gioia dei Marsi and Lecce ne' Marsi are worth a visit for the remnants of their ancient Marsi civilization, much of which an earthquake wiped out in 1915. Other charming communities are Villavallelonga, in the basin of Fossato di Rosa; Bisegna in the Giovenco Valley; and Scanno in the Tasso Valley. Many medieval features have been preserved in these places, with narrow, winding streets and tall, vertical buildings taking you back in time. The village of Pescasseroli hosts the park's main museum and visitors center.

A shy doe is startled at the edge of the wood.

AT A GLANCE

Apennine Mountains ▪ 191.8 square miles (496.8 sq km) ▪ Marsican brown bear ▪ Valico Passaggio dell'Orso trail ▪ parcoabruzzo.it

ALTA MURGIA
A southern park in the land of trulli

The southeast of Italy, down toward the heel of the boot, is an often overlooked region. The poor rural area of the Alta (High) Murgia has long lived in the shadow of the industrial north, glamorous Rome, and the Mediterranean islands of Sicily and Sardinia to its southwest. In 2004, the opening of Alta Murgia National Park in Apulia started to change this perception. The park's headquarters is in the walled town of Gravina in Puglia, where you'll find the main visitors center.

The Murgia Ceraso is a karst plateau, which means that winter rains drain through the soil into fissures in the strata of limestone bedrock and flow through underground watercourses into the Adriatic Sea. Much of the landscape of rolling hills and ridges is punctuated here and there with dolines (collapsed karst sinkholes) and other types of enclosed depressions characteristic of karst territories. The largest of these are found near Altamura, the impressive Pulicchio and Pulo dolines, which measure respectively more than 328 feet (100 m) and 230 feet (70 m) in depth. Over the course of several millennia, the landscapes of Alta Murgia National Park have been shaped by erosion. The canyon of Gravina in Apulia, for example, slopes down toward Matera and Bradano, marking the southwestern border of the park.

Castel del Monte, the citadel built by Emperor Frederick II

LAND OF STONE

The park lies in trulli country: A *trullo* is a traditional Apulian dry stone hut with a conical roof. This style of construction is specific to the Valle d'Itria, in the Murgia Ceraso area of Apulia. Trulli were generally constructed as temporary field shelters and storehouses, or as permanent dwellings by small proprietors or agricultural laborers. The golden age of trulli was the 19th century, especially its final decades, which were marked by development of a wine-growing culture throughout the region.

Alta Murgia National Park is filled with other interesting stone architecture, and any visit should incorporate the 13 towns around it and their many attractions: The archaeological sites in Botromagno, Gravina in Puglia; the stone and tufa architectures of the historical town centers, including Norman castles; the Romanesque-style cathedrals of Altamura, Bitonto, and Ruvo di Puglia; and several museums including Museo Fondazione Ettore Pomarici Santomasi in Gravina in Puglia and the State Archaeological Museum in Altamura. The park also holds many rock churches and *jazzi*, architectural structures created for sheep breeding.

In addition, this area boasts the richest paleontological field in the world: Thousands of dinosaurs' tracks were found in an abandoned quarry between Altamura and Santeramo.

A great way to experience Alta Murgia is to take a day to cycle or walk the Jazzo Rosso–San Magno–Castel del Monte, a cycle/pedestrian trail. This runs for about 40 miles (65 km) through the heart of the park.

AT A GLANCE

Trulli stone houses ▪ 261.5 square miles (677.5 sq km) ▪ World-renowned paleontological sites ▪ State Archaeological Museum ▪ Jazzo Rosso–San Magno–Castel del Monte trail ▪ parks.it/parco.nazionale.alta.murgia

APPENNINO LUCANO-VAL D'AGRI-LAGONEGRESE

A mountain reserve in a spiritual setting

In the southwestern region of Basilicata lies a mountain realm enclosed by some of the highest summits of the Lucanian Apennines. The national park of Appennino Lucano–Val d'Agri–Lagonegrese also incorporates the upper valley of the River Agri.

Opened in 2007, the park's proximity to Pollino National Park (see page 310) and Cilento, Vallo di Diano and Alburni National Park (see page 294) extends the total area of protected habitat. This park spans a wide array of biotopes due to its variances of altitudes—Monte del Papa stands at 6,578 feet (2,005 m), while Murgia di Sant'Oronzo is a mere 984 feet (300 m). The biospheres range from the dense beech woodlands of the mountains to white poplar forests to woodlands alternating with pastures and meadows.

Amphibians found within the national park include the widespread Italian newt, the yellow-bellied toad, and the spectacled salamander, which is only found in this region. This species is recognizable by the four toes on its hind feet (rather than the five normally found on other salamanders and newts), and by its pinkish red underside on the legs and tail. Crustaceans found in the park include the river crab and the European freshwater crayfish—important indicators of the water quality. Otters live off these crustaceans and the plentiful fish stocks around lovely Lake Petrusillo.

THE HUMAN FOOTPRINT

Much of the landscape has been cultivated over the years, and the historical human footprint in the park is evident at the archaeological site of Grumentum, the most important Roman town of ancient Lucania and one of the best preserved Roman sites in Italy. The nearby Archaeological Museum of the region, who is celebrated at the monastery of Santa Maria Orsoleo. The monastery also hosts a museum outlining the spiritual significance of Basilicata.

The region is renowned for its fine food products and culinary specialties. While visiting the park, try some strong Canestrato di Moliterno cheese, or any dish based on Sarconi beans. Wash down these treats with a local wine, such as a Grottino di Roccanova or a Terre dell'Alta Val d'Agri.

Meadows mesmerize with red poppies in Val d'Agri, Basilicata.

of the dell'Alta Val d'Agri is also worth a visit. The park has numerous churches of historical significance, many located in the villages of Viggiano and Sant'Arcangelo, the religious heart of Basilicata. The best known religious icon is the Black Madonna, patron saint

Appennino Lucano–Val d'Agri–Lagonegrese National Park has a choice of trails running through its undulating hills and mountains; information is available from the main visitors center of Masseria Crisci, located on the shores of Lake Petrusillo.

AT A GLANCE

Lucanian Apennines ▪ 266.4 square miles (689.9 sq km) ▪ Canestrato di Moliterno cheese ▪ Masseria Crisci visitors center ▪ parks.it/parco.nazionale.val.agri

APPENNINO TOSCO-EMILIANO

At the crossroads of Italy's famous culinary traditions

Few regions in the world offer the hungry gourmand a more attractive vacation than the fertile landscapes of Appennino Tosco-Emiliano in north-central Italy. In 2001, the Italian government decided that protecting the land that produces much of the country's delicacies and promoting its wonders to the world would be a fine idea: Thus, Appennino Tosco-Emiliano National Park was inducted into the country's impressive park system. Located in the heart of an area noted not only for its natural beauty but also for its local fine-quality food products and handicrafts, this foodies' fantasia is now a national park that spans the regions of Massa and Carrara, Lucca, Reggio Emilia, and Parma.

The park is split into two regions, Emilia-Romagna and Tuscany. This gives it two distinct climate zones and dramatic biodiversity: You'll find olive trees, holly oaks, vineyards, and warm springs on the park's south side, in Lunigiana and Garfagnana. On the north side, in Reggio and Parma, grasslands, fir trees, and ample snowfall define the landscape. The park is dominated by the soaring summits of Alpe di Succiso, Monte Prado, and Monte Cusna, as well as lakes and high mountain meadows and grasslands. In Emilia, the strange cylindrical rock formation of Pietra di Bismantova dominates the hori-

In autumn the park hosts the World Mushroom Championship.

Taste the Terroir

Appennino Tosco-Emiliano National Park lies between the Po Plain, the Cisa and Forbici passes, and the Luni Sea—a historic crossroads of gastronomic traditions. Great Italian produce such as Parmesan cheese and Parma ham are world-renowned, but a visit here unearths fine local and traditional cuisines. Certain treats, such as *testaroli* (an ancient pasta from Etruscan times), Parmesano Reggiano, and the park's famous chestnuts, are sure to surprise. Recipes here are passed down for generations. In fall, the park welcomes mushroom hunters who seek out the finest fungal delicacies.

zon with its vertical walls rising over half a mile (1,047 m) above the plains. The rock consists of a type of limestone, yellowish calcarenite over a marl basement that once sat on the seafloor.

A WEALTH OF LANDSCAPES

The Appennino Tosco-Emiliano National Park protects a variety of environments, ranging from the pasturelands that produce some of Europe's finest dairy products, to bilberry moorlands that have inspired some famous pies, to the most inaccessible Apennine Mountain peaks. Lakes, waterfalls, and well-stocked streams make it a fine hiking prospect, especially when one can encounter wildlife such as wolves, mouflon, roe deer, and golden eagles along the trails. Many of these pathways, along with mountain passes and the park's historic roads, such as La Via Francigena and La Via del Volto Santo, have been traversed by traders, pilgrims, armies, and smugglers for centuries.

Today, anglers come to fish the rivers and lakes, hikers find a wide variety of landscapes to ramble across, and food lovers from around the globe come to savor some of the finest local delicacies that northern Italy has to offer (see sidebar). The Appennino Tosco-Emiliano National Park is a mouthful in more ways than one!

AT A GLANCE

Dual north/south landscapes ▪ 88 square miles (228 sq km) ▪ World-class Italian cuisine ▪ World Mushroom Championship ▪ parcoappennino.it

ARCIPELAGO DI LA MADDALENA

Sardinia's maritime park boasts golden (and pink) beaches.

The coast of Sardinia is one of the Mediterranean's loveliest marine environments, so where better to locate one of Italy's finest marine national parks. Arcipelago di La Maddalena National Park encompasses some 112 miles (180 km) of coastlines as well as all the islands and islets within the region of La Maddalena. The territory of the national park will also represent a key element of the proposed international marine park planned to embrace Bocche di Bonifacio, the stretch of sea between Sardinia and Corsica. Of the islands and islets the park presently protects off the coast of Gallura, only La Maddalena island has a significant human presence. The rest are either deserted or scattered with small settlements, such as in Caprera and the Santa Maria Islands.

The flora of the park has all the characteristic Mediterranean coastal abundance you'd expect. Inland you can walk across heaths filled with juniper, phillyrea, lentisk, myrtle, heather, broom, rock rose, and euphorbia (aka spurge); the sandy and salty areas host Mediterranean saltbush, and sand-loving vegetation. The wind, strong sun, arid ground, poverty of the soils, and altitude of Sardinia give rise to several indigenous plants: Look for the Phoenicean juniper, also called Arâr, which grows in several locations around the park including in Spargi, Caprera, Budelli, Santa Maria, and on La Maddalena.

ARCHIPELAGO LIFE

La Maddalena Archipelago is home to many amphibians, reptiles, and mammals; it also hosts several colonies of nesting marine birds. Many trans-Saharan migratory birds stop off here on their travels too. Among the nesters are the Audouin's gull, the single endemic seagull species of the Mediterranean; the Mediterranean subspecies of the European shag also flocks to the park in the tens of thousands. Watch for peregrine falcons hunting and fishing in the park too. The seas abound in vertebrates, and pods of dolphins are a regular sight, as are fin whales.

One of the most interesting quirks of nature in the park is its famous pink beach. This is located on Budelli Island, one of the most beautiful islands anywhere in the Mediterranean. Spiaggia Rosa ("pink beach") gets its color from the high percentage of bioclasts (skeletal fragments of bryozoans with a pink color) in the sedimentary formation of its sands. These bioclasts originate mostly in the *Posidonia oceanica* meadows on the seabed and are transported to the beach by coastal currents. These sea meadows are now protected from boats' anchors to preserve the beach, which first gained world fame thanks to the 1964 film by Michelangelo Antonioni called *Il Deserto Rosso*.

Cala Coticcio beach on the northeast part of the island of Caprera

AT A GLANCE

La Maddalena Archipelago ▪ Bocche di Bonifacio ▪ 77.7 square miles (201.4 sq km) ▪ The pink beach ▪ parks.it/parco.nazionale.arcip.maddalena

ARCIPELAGO TOSCANO

A biodiverse Mediterranean archipelago steeped in history

The Tuscan Archipelago is a strange place, as Napoleon Bonaparte found out (see sidebar), caught between the devil and the deep-blue Mediterranean Sea. In geographic fact, this string of islands lies between *two* seas, the northerly islands are in the Ligurian Sea, while the southerly islands float on the Tyrrhenian Sea. As the largest marine park in Europe, Arcipelago Toscano National Park spans the whole archipelago, protecting some 219 square miles (567 sq km) of seas and about 69 square miles (178 sq km) of island habitat. The island of Elba forms its central point, but the protected area includes the other Tuscan Archipelago islands of Isolas del Giglio, Capraia, di Montecristo, Pianosa, di Giannutri, and di Gorgona. The highest point in the park is Monte Capanne, rising 3,343 feet (1,019 m) above sea level on Elba.

Mankind has long looked upon these isolated islands as ideal for incarceration. In 1858 Pianosa was developed as agricultural penal colonies. As political unrest in mainland Italy fomented in the second half of the 19th century, this quickly went from being a holding place for low-risk prisoners and petty criminals to becoming a top-security prison with a reputation for severity. In the late 1990s, the islands' prisons were closed and the archipelago instead dedicated to preservation of nature.

NATURE & MANKIND

The islands of the Tuscan Archipelago have always been an impor-

Capraia, the most northwesterly island of the Tuscan Archipelago

tant shelter and migration corridor between mainland Italy and the Sardinian-Corsican islands to the south.

This "between two worlds" geography has seen the development of extremely specialized fauna and floral species. The remote islands host colonies of seabirds, such as shearwaters and seagulls, including the rare Audouin's gull, an endemic Mediterranean species. The Mediterranean monk seal is spotted intermittently, with its numbers now believed to be less than 700 individuals.

These islands have very individual geological formations: Isola Capraia is a volcanic island, while Giglio and Elba are mainly granitic. The presence of iron in the archipelago attracted settlers from prehistoric times on, as evidenced by

Elba's iron mines, worked up to the 20th century. Minerals have been exploited on the island since 1000 B.C., when people called Ilvates came from the region of present-day Liguria (the name Elba is derived from Ilva). The Etruscans and later the Romans accelerated the process of iron extraction here. Likewise, the island of Pianosa, settled since prehistoric times, has remnants from the Neolithic and Copper Ages as well as maritime dwellings from the Roman period.

Mankind has shaped the vegetation on the islands and the original ilex (oak) woods only survive in some parts of Elba, which is dominated by densely growing evergreen shrubs, a biome called Mediterranean maquis, typical of the region. This type of vegetation produces a thick and tangled landscape of strawberry trees, buck-thorns, mastic trees, Phoenician junipers, myrtles, rosemary, and lavender. Keep a lookout, too, for the delicate purple flowers of the *Linaria capraria*.

MEDITERRANEAN VEGETATION

The Mediterranean climate and the islands' isolated geography mean that the vegetation that survives here is mainly evergreen plants with leathery leaves protected by a robust and hardly impermeable epidermis. There are also plants with extremely reduced leaves that sometimes become thorns, or those without leaves altogether, such as brooms. The common self-heal grows here too, a tasty herbaceous plant that can be eaten in salads.

Only a few copses of the old-growth holm oak forests remain. The climate and high grounds of Elba nurture mainly chestnut tree woods, and on the mountains you will find some European yew and hop hornbeam stands.

The national park hosts a wide variety of marine life and seabirds. The seas around the islands offer a range of habitats, and whales and dolphins are spotted off the shores of the archipelago. The variety of the coastlines also encourages great biological diversity. From the beaches of Elba to the rocky cliffs of western Capraia, a wide array of vegetable and animal species thrive in the marine ravines along these coasts. If diving in the waters, look for the sea lily, a creature with frondlike ten-tacles that resembles a plant. This marine invertebrate animal fixes itself to the sea bottom by a stalk.

ENDEMIC SPECIES

Arcipelago Toscano National Park hosts quite a number of endemic species, that is, animals that are found only in this area. These include the citril finch, the Sardinian tree frog, the Tyrrhenian painted frog, and the leaf-toed gecko, the latter a lizard with a divided, expanded adhesive pad at the distal end of its toe, resembling a ginkgo leaf. This incredible creature is almost impossible to spot due to its uncanny camouflage that blends seamlessly into its arid Mediterranean surrounds.

Rabbits and martens provide plenty of prey for larger predators higher up the food chain on the archipelago. Although the wild boar of the Maremma were hunted to extinction at the beginning of the 19th century, a reintroduction scheme initiated 30 years ago failed when the central European boar ran amok on Elba, destroying many of the endemic species and agricultural crops of the island.

A creature with a much gentler footprint that is worth seeking out on the islands is the southern white admiral. This somewhat misleading moniker belies a beautiful butterfly whose wings are a deep turquoise blue with a stripe of white spots, while its underside has the same pattern but with orange-red instead of blue. You'll find this winged wonder feeding on herbaceous and arboreal flowers around the islands.

The park's four visitors centers have information on the many hiking and cycling trails in the park, as well as other activities available throughout the Tuscan Archipelago.

Napoleon on Elba

The strategic desirability of Elba as well as its penal colony has ensured a long and tortuous history for the island, but it is mainly known for one of its many reluctant inhabitants, Napoleon Bonaparte. The French emperor was exiled here following the Treaty of Fontainebleau, arriving at Portoferraio on May 3, 1814. He kept a personal guard of 600 men and was made sovereign of Elba, although French and British ships patrolled its seas.

Napoleon carried out a series of economic and social reforms on Elba for 300 days, before he escaped to France on February 26, 1815. Today, you can visit his main residence of Villa dei Mulini, much of it the emperor personally designed, including the small theater. The Villa di San Martino, a secondary residence, has several 19th-century prints of Napoleon and antique furniture in its fine frescoed rooms.

Mediterranean maquis vegetation ▪ Island archipelago ▪ 288.3 square miles (746.6 sq km) ▪ Endemic species ▪ Napoleon's residences ▪ parks.it/parco.nazionale.arcip.toscano

ASINARA

Sardinia's forgotten island of secrets and delights

Little Asinara is Sardinia's forgotten island, set off its northwest tip. Lesser known than the larger island of Sant'Antioco hugging Sardinia's southwestern shore, narrow Asinara's indented coast rings a wide swath of habitats, making it a logical location for a protected area.

Asinara National Park now plays host to many Mediterranean indigenous species of flora and fauna, but its history is somewhat darker. The island was long known as Isola del Diavolo (Devil's Island), due to its historical role as a quarantine location, and as a prisoner camp during World War I. Even more recently, the island was one of Italy's highest-security prisons during the 1970s, when the Red Brigade terrorized the mainland. It also housed the big players of the Cosa Nostra in the fight against organized crime. Today, you can visit the prison at Fornelli to get an idea of the life of these notorious guests. Prisoners created the front gardens. The establishment of Asinara National Park in 1997 ushered in a brighter future for the island.

These days Asinara's inhabitants encompass 80 species of terrestrial vertebrates, including several endangered species. Among the park's endemic species are the three-toed skink, a scaled reptile, and the greater white-toothed shrew. Sardinian-Corsican

A walkway leads to La Pelosa beach on Asinara island.

species include the Sardinian barn owl, and the wren, the spotted flycatcher, and the cirl bunting all thrive here. Among the rare species that find refuge on the island are the tiny pygmy keeled lizard, the mouflon, Hermann's tortoise, and the European leaf-toed gecko. On marshy lands, look for the Tyrrhenian painted frog.

Bird-watchers should look for the Barbary partridge (streaked white-and-red legs and red beak), Cory's shearwater (a large seabird 18 to 22 inches/45 to 56 cm in length), and the Manx shearwater (a slow flier on stiff wings with few wing beats).

THE WHITE DONKEY

The star of this Sardinian show, however, is the Asinara white donkey, a lovable little donkey that

looks like a stuffed toy, due to its reduced dimensions. The adult donkey is about three feet (1 m) high. The head of this mini-donkey is somewhat quadrangular, and centuries of insular isolation has left this beast with a short neck, strong limbs, a white coat, but not very resistant feet. They are not a great advertisement for evolution, given their dislike of the strong Sardinian sunlight and unsteady gait in bright places. Look this donkey in the eye and you'll see partial pigmentation of its iris, which is a pinkish light blue.

The park has four visitors centers, including one at the prison in Fornelli, another at the Loggerhead Sea Turtle Recovery Center in Fornelli, and one at the Sea Center in Cala Reale, which has excellent exhibits on the island's marine life.

AT A GLANCE

Sardinia's Devil's Island ▪ Asinara white donkeys ▪ 288.2 square miles (746.5 sq km) ▪ Loggerhead Sea Turtle Recovery Center ▪ parks.it/parco.nazionale.asinara

ASPROMONTE

A dramatic mountain habitat in southern Italy

High in the southern slopes of the Calabrian Apennines, on the tip of the toe of Italy, great predators swirl on the Mediterranean winds that sweep across these mountains. Peregrine falcons, eagle-owls, goshawks, short-toed eagles, and even rare Bonelli's eagles—all ride the upsweeping air currents, looking down on forests of beech trees, silver firs, black pines, downy and Hungarian oaks, and chestnut trees, or surveying the Mediterranean maquis for prey. This is Aspromonte National Park, located close to the Mediterranean Sea yet rising to 6,414 feet (1,955 m) at its high point of Montalto (High Mountain). The granitic-crystalline mountains here resemble a giant rock pyramid pointing out of lush lower lands that stretch down to the sea.

The park's landscape is veined by several watercourses, and roamed by wolves. Despite the altitudes of the mountains, the lower reaches of the park nurture rare plants that thrive in the heat, such as the tropical European chain fern. These lower areas are evergreen, with olive trees, citrus fruits, and typical Mediterranean vegetation such as broom, strawberry tree, mastic tree, and myrtle. Higher up you'll find shade under chestnut trees, and higher still, stands of maples, ash, and black and Neapolitan alders. The

The Griko Influence

Many civilizations have traversed the mountains of Aspromonte, but visit any village within the park and you'll notice a distinct Greek influence. You might even hear the Griko language spoken among some of the elders of the Griko or Grecanici people, the ethnic Greek community of southern Italy who have handed down their traditions of skilled craftsmanship through generations.

Many Calabrian agricultural and pastoral tools are made from wood, such as cheese molds, collars, and spoons. The area's rich woods also produce fine musical instruments, including tambourines as well as bagpipes made from the root of Calabria's arboreal heather, which is considered among the world's most resonant wood for this purpose. Gerace is a hub for lace making and ceramics, both centuries-old traditions brought from Greece.

park's vast woodlands are home to many birds: Look for the black woodpecker while hiking the massif. Also inhabiting these woods, feeding on dormice, is the wildcat. This cat is bigger than its domestic feline brother, with thick, gray-black fur, striped on its sides, and a short tail with alternating dark and light rings.

Palizzi, a Greek-speaking village of Bovesia, southern Italy

AT A GLANCE

Calabrian Apennines ▪ Granite peak of Montalto ▪ 247.7 square miles (641.5 sq km) ▪ Griko villages
▪ parks.it/parco.nazionale.aspromonte

CILENTO, VALLO DI DIANO & ALBURNI

History, nature, and culture at a southern Italian crossroads

Travelers to the Cilento coastal district can take boat tours around its coves and into its karst caves.

Located in the southern Italian province of Salerno, in Campania, this sweeping park encompasses much of three distinct regions: the Cilento (a coastal area), the Vallo di Diano (a valley), and the Monti Alburni (a mountain range).

Cilento, Vallo di Diano and Alburni National Park protects not just vital habitat for flora and fauna, but also the cultural and historical treasures of the Campania region. The park was opened in 1991 to protect the territory of Cilento from building speculation and mass tourism. In 1998, it became a UNESCO World Heritage site with the aim of preserving the ancient Greek towns of Paestum and Velia, as well as the Padula Charterhouse.

The park's protected area also includes most of the Cilentan coast and the central forest area of Pruno, stretching from the Tyrrhenian coast to the foot of the Apennines in Campania and Basilicata, and including Monte Cervati and Monte Gelbison in the Alburni Mountains, and the coastal landmarks of Monte Bulgheria and Monte Stella.

Cilento has a mixed landscape incorporating gently undulating hills covered with green and ash-colored olive groves that overlook the blue Tyrrhenian Sea. Here you'll find fast-flowing streams, chestnut and ilex tree forests, and small hillside towns clinging to the steep cliffs.

Slightly inland and to the south you'll find the lunar landscapes of karst geology, formed from the calcareous rock of the inner and southern mountain ranges. Don't miss the Grotte di Castelcivita, a karst cavern complex also known as the Spartacus Caves, thanks to the local legend of the Roman gladiator sheltering in the caves on his march from Brundisium to the Battle of the Silarus River, close to Castelcivita. Today, the caves are laid out for visitors to explore in a series of galleries, saloons, and tight passages: The Castle Room, Crocodile Room, Vegetable Rooms, and Pagoda are a few examples. The named features created by the caves' glorious stalactite and stalagmite formations include organ pipes, spaghetti, and a stunning pool of diamonds.

FLORA & FAUNA

The park offers fine hiking through its rich mix of landscapes. Along the trails you'll come across about 1,800 different species of plants and trees. Look in particular for the symbol of the park, the *Primula palinuri*, which is only found among certain stretches of the southern Campania and Basilicata coastlines. This beautiful primrose plant grows amid coastal rocks and blossoms in bell-shaped drooping flowers of an intense yellow-gold color set atop a thick rosette of fleshy leaves.

The multitude of biodiverse environments within this sprawling park means that many creatures find suitable habitat here: On the summits and high mountain cliffs nest golden eagles, swooping down to the high mountain grasslands in search of their prey of choice, rock partridge and mountain hare. Other birds of prey that inhabit the park include peregrine falcons, lanner falcons, ravens, and choughs.

THE HUMAN FOOTPRINT

Mankind has found shelter amid the karstic features of Cilento since the Middle Paleolithic Age (500,000 B.C.), and archaeological finds trace human presence here throughout the Neolithic and Metal Ages. Tools have been found in the coastal caves between Palinuro and Scario and in the Castelcivita Caves.

The park includes three sites of major cultural significance. Velia was the birthplace of the philoso-

The ruins of Paestum include three Doric Greek temples.

phers Parmenides and Zeno, as well as the Eleatic school of which they were a part. Velia was the Roman name for this ancient city of Magna Graecia on the coast of the Tyrrhenian Sea, founded by Greeks as Hyele circa 535 B.C. Paestum is a major Greek city of Magna Graecia, along the same coastline. The ruins of Paestum are famous for their three ancient Doric Greek temples, dating from about 600 to 450 B.C., which are very well preserved. The city walls and amphitheater are largely intact, and the bottom of the walls of many other structures remain, as do paved roads. The site is open to the public, and contains a national museum that also houses the finds from the associated Greek site of Foce del Sele.

Finally, the Padula Charterhouse is a large Carthusian monastery located in the town of Padula, within the national park. The monastery is the largest in Italy, and its history spans 450 years. The prin-

cipal parts of the buildings are in baroque style. This large monastery and its grounds are a World Heritage site.

The park's five visitors centers have details on how to get to these sites of interest as well as maps and information on the many trails throughout the region. Cilento, Vallo di Diano and Alburni is located at a crossroads of several ancient trails; it is also at a key point along the Southern Apennines, at the heart of the national trail network. The park has devised a series of excellent hikes to help you explore the park's many facets, with such enticing names as the Antece Mystery and the Cave of St. Michael the Archangel, In the Realm of the Otter, and the Ghost Castle (Capaccio Castle). The Coast of the Mermaids trail gives you ancient legends *and* a visit to the spectacular modern aquarium called the Museum of the Sea in Pioppi.

AT A GLANCE

Coastal, valley, and mountain landscapes ▪ Grotte di Castelcivita ▪ 699 square miles (1,810.4 sq km) ▪ Paestum ▪ Velia ▪ Padula Charterhouse ▪ parks.it/parco.nazionale.cilento

CINQUE TERRE

A unique coastal landscape in need of constant protection

The Cinque Terre (Five Lands) is one of Europe's supreme landscapes, a unique combination of distinct communities with a remarkable social and historic heritage. Its stunning environment artistically blends the Ligurian Sea, plunging cliffs, and mountainous hinterland with extraordinary vineyard terraces and 5,000 miles (8,000 km) of drystone walls of the man-made landscape.

The Cinque Terre refers to the quintet of tiny seafront villages that dot this national park, built in medieval times high up the cliffs to defy pirates. Their streets are a maze, twisting and turning every which way to confuse potential invaders. They certainly confuse modern drivers, and parking is infamously impossible. A leisurely stroll along the village-to-village trails is much easier, or better yet, take a boat and enjoy the spectacle of color that the villages display.

The attractions of all five villages are similar: intimate pebbly beaches, tiny coves, crisp white local wines, romantic seafood restaurants, and the quaint huddle of pastel-colored houses. The largest beach is at Monterosso, but Manarola is for many the most attractive village. Corniglia, situated high above the sea, is the smallest of the Cinque Terre, a farming rather than fishing community, but with a long pebble beach good for walking.

HIKING, BIKING & DIVING

The park's visitors centers have details on all the trails, including the famous Via dell'Amore (Path of Love) between Manarola and Riomaggiore, along which you can (metaphorically) walk a mile (1.6 km) in your loved one's shoes. The park offers some 30 other hikes, including the classic Sentiero Azzurro trail along the coast. On these trails you can enjoy the sight and smells of blossoming poppies, jasmine, and violets as you thrill to the old-world buzz of bees and the flutter of colorful butterflies. The citrus scent of the lemon orchards combined with sea breezes is an aroma that will linger long in your memory.

Serious cyclists should try the 94-mile (151-km) GranFondo route through the park. Or head into the sea: Diving expeditions with local operators are richly rewarding, exploring undersea canyons and caves, and enjoying the underwater company of stingrays, lobsters, and scuttling crabs.

A FRAGILE LANDSCAPE

The Cinque Terre is a landscape under threat: Only a small portion of the area remains under cultivation now, following the drift from agriculture and subsistence farming in the 1950s—and the terraces for vines and olives that were the work of centuries have crumbled in little under a generation. Once isolated villages are now prey to mass tourism and its inherent problems. Hikers on the celebrated trails between the Cinque Terre villages—Manarola, Vernazza, Monterosso, Riomaggiore, and Corniglia—can contribute to coastal erosion.

Many local organizations, however, are addressing these challenges by inviting volunteers to join programs aimed at restoration and preservation of this treasured landscape. You can help local masons still skilled in the art of drystone walling repair terraces above the villages. Or pick and carry grapes on the steep slopes, thus helping preserve a unique system of agriculture in decline due to the labor-intensive approach necessitated by the terrain. In 2011, storms battered this coast and rivers of mud poured down the hillside, devastating Monterosso and Vernazza. The damage to the terraces has been repaired, but the danger to these five pearls in this Ligurian coastal necklace is ever present.

Opposite: Boats and buildings pile high in Riomaggiore harbor.

AT A GLANCE

Cinque Terre medieval villages ▪ 14.9 square miles (38.6 sq km) ▪ Via dell'Amore (Path of Love) ▪ Sentiero Azzurro trail ▪ parconazionale5terre.it/Eindex.php

CIRCEO

Five distinct habitats in one unique park

In 1934, the Pontine Marshes were shrinking fast due to extensive drainage works. Then the dictator Benito Mussolini took the advice of Senator Raffaele Bastianelli, a doctor with his finger on the pulse of Italy's environment, and ordered the preservation of the last remnants of the wetlands. Circeo National Park now embraces a strip of coastal land from Anzio to Terracina, including a section of forest on the mainland of San Felice Circeo, and the island of Zannone. Originating from a dark period of Italian history, this small preserve provides a lasting legacy of conservation.

In a relatively small area, Circeo National Park spans a diverse array of five distinct habitats.

THE FOREST

The park's wooded area is the largest plain forest in Italy. This once great woodlands is the last remnant of the ancient Selva di Terracina that occupied the central province of Latina. The forest, today known as the Selva di Circe, sweeps down toward the coast of San Felice Circeo, and covers an area of about 8,155 acres (3,300 ha). This is dominated by Turkish oak, fraxinus, and English oak, as well as typical Mediterranean trees such as holm oak, bay laurel, and cork oak. The woods are transformed in the fall by the emergence of *piscine* ("swimming pool") landscapes, whereby rainwater inundates the forest floors, turning it into marshland. The flooded floors cultivate a maquis shrubland, with plants such as hawthorn, blackthorn, wild apple, pear, and strawberry trees. Look in these woods for the heathlike erica shrub, with its delicate pink flowers amid green pine-like leaves. The berry vegetation attracts many animals, including wild boar, European badger, fox, weasel, green whip snake, viperine snake, and Triturus newt. Look too for land and marsh Testudo, a threatened genus of tortoises.

THE PROMONTORY

The focal point of the park is Monte Circeo, also known as the Promontory of Circeo, a Mesozoic limestone-dolomite massif standing at 1,774 feet (541 m). The humid climate of its northern slopes hosts vegetation varying from thick shrub of holly oak in higher reaches to manna ash, European hop hornbeam, downy oak, and Italian oak lower down. The undergrowth here includes erica, broom,

The still waters of Sabaudia Lake reflect the mountainous landscapes of Circeo.

and strawberry tree, giving way to a vast stretch of cork oak wood where the promontory descends to the plain below.

The promontory's southern slopes enjoy a milder climate that nurtures the usual Mediterranean rock vegetation such as holm oak, Phoenician juniper, euphorbia tree, myrtus, and rosemary. Amid the rocks, look for the colorful flowers of various thistle-like Centaurea plants.

As you walk the trails around the Promontory of Circeo, watch too for a host of wildlife, including European badger, wild boar, and beech marten, and keep an eye to the skies for the predators that favor high rocks, such as peregrine falcons and common kestrels.

As you'd expect for a limestone region, the coastline at the base of the promontory has many caves of interest: In 1939 a skull of *Homo neanderthalensis* was found in the Grotta Guattari; the Grotta delle Capre (Goats' Cave) and the Grotta Breuil are also worth a look. It's unknown what the Neanderthal people who inhabited the cave made of this landscape, but the strangely shaped Promontory of Circeo has since spawned many legends of heroes, gods, and witches.

THE LITTORAL DUNE

The park includes a 13.6-mile-long (22-km) coastal sand dune, forming a half-moon shape from the limestone cliffs of Monte Circeo up to Capo Portiere. This fine-sand strip, a unique protected environment, hosts a thin hinterland of maquis

A Historic Park

Circeo National Park has a huge human footprint, with archaeological and architectural evidence of history everywhere. Neanderthal man inhabited the park's caves, including the Grotta Guattari and Grotta Breuil. The Roman Age, both imperial and Republican, is preserved in great works of engineering such as the port-channel of Torre Paola and the thermally heated residence of Domitian's Villa. The Villa also gave up several artistic treasures, such as Kessel's *Apollo and the Faun with Concert Flute*.

At the peak of the promontory sits the Ara di Circe, a platform thought to be an altar to Circe, the ancient goddess of sorcery. Elsewhere, there are ancient thermal baths at Torre Paola, Villa del Pereto's old farm, and the Necropolis of Cala dei Pescatori, a group of 10 sepulchres—all clues to how mankind has lived, and died, in this region for millennia.

shrubland, where European badgers, foxes, lizards, and several species of beetles make their homes. Farther inland, prickly juniper and mastic thrive, along with trees such as maritime pine and holm oak.

THE HUMID AREA

Adjacent to the coastal dune is a humid lagoon environment. This is formed by a string of four coastal lakes—Paola, Caprolace, Monaci, and Fogliano—and by the wetlands that flood in fall.

These are what remains of the Pontine Marshes. A vast range of wildlife still thrives here, thanks to the intervention of Dr. Bastianelli: Aquatic birds such as egrets, cranes, geese, skylarks, and curlews, as well as rare species such as the marsh turtle are all nurtured by these wetlands. Other animals residing in the humid area include wild boar, fox, crested porcupine, wild weasel, and hedgehog. The lakes and marshes are connected to the sea by a series of canals.

ZANNONE ISLAND

The small, uninhabited island of Zannone is part of the Ponziano Archipelago, and was added to Circeo National Park in 1979. Zannone, covered with oak and holm oak forests, is the only island in the archipelago to have kept its original vegetation cover, including strawflower, mastic, myrtus, broom, euphorbia, and bay laurel. The island is accessible by boat from Ponza, and the Zannone Trail will take you to the Benedictine monastery that was built in A.D. 504, and abandoned three centuries later due to constant raids by Saracen pirates. The park has similar cultural and nature trails for hikers and cyclists throughout all five of its habitats.

The Promontory of Circeo ▪ Humid area wildlife ▪ 32.6 square miles (84.4 sq km) ▪ The Zannone Trail ▪ parks.it/parco.nazionale.circeo

DOLOMITI BELLUNESI

Where the towering Dolomites nurture agriculture, forestry, and culture

The Dolomites are a mountain range unto themselves, extremely rich in water resources, which propagate a profusion of wildlife and wildflowers. So it was fitting when these beautiful and biodiverse mountains were declared a UNESCO World Heritage site in 2009.

Dolomiti Bellunesi National Park sits broadly between the Cismon River and the Piave River, the Maè Valley and the Agordo Valley. The park's territory is richly irrigated with peaks of Alpi Feltrine, Monti del Sole, Schiara, Talvena, Pramper, and Spiz di Mezzodì.

Lower down, the forests are mainly of broad-leaved trees (hornbeams and oaks) and pines. The rich pastures and alpine meadows of the park host a multitude of flora, notably rhododendron, edelweiss, and Carduus, a purple-flowering plumeless thistle. Mammals inhabiting the woods and meadows are marmot, stoat, marten, roe deer, and red deer.

The massive bulk of Monte Pelmo, part of the Dolomite range

springs, swamps, and streams, many of them carving out deep canyons.

The mountain ranges here are high-altitude, karst rockscapes with forested and rock-covered slopes that provide homes to mountain species including chamois and mouflon. Raptors such as northern goshawks, kestrels, and golden eagles make their homes high in the rocky

BATS & BIRDS

The karst landscape gives bats plenty of dark, damp caves in which to breed, and the many species that flap about the park include the greater mouse-eared bat, common pipistrelle, and Daubenton's bat.

The woods attract multitudes of birds, as Dolomiti Bellunesi is located along the corridor of many migrations. As you hike in these forests, expect to hear the *whoo* of owl species such as the Eurasian pygmy owl, boreal owl, tawny owl, and Eurasian eagle-owl. Also echoing will be the birdsong of hoopoe, Corvidae, corn crake, black redstart, and white-winged snowfinch. And watch for the red crown of the black woodpecker as he taps out his tattoo on deadwood of the forest. Higher up, you might spot rock ptarmigan and rock partridge, and the colorful wallcreeper, all prey for the park's raptors.

The wet, marshy areas also play host to a multitude of reptiles, including Alpine newts, Italian crested newts, fire salamanders, Alpine salamanders, yellow-bellied toads, mountain frogs, and European and green toads. Beware especially of *Vipera ammodytes,* the most dangerous European viper due to its large size, long fangs, and toxic venom.

The park has few human inhabitants, but includes some precious historical sites: These mountains are filled with medieval hospices (lodgings), churches, fortifications, old towns, and tiny Alpine villages. The Charterhouse of Vedana, dating from 1456 is particularly worth visiting. The park's many visitors centers can point you in the right direction to these sites or give information on the park's many thematic trails, such as the Route of the Hospices and the Forgotten Mountain.

AT A GLANCE

Dolomites mountain peaks ▪ Karst landscapes ▪ 12.3 square miles (32 sq km) ▪ Route of the Hospices ▪ Forgotten Mountain Trail ▪ dolomitipark.it/en

Mount Etna

The Fire Mountain of Mount Etna is the focal point of this Sicilian regional park and one of the most active volcanoes anywhere on Earth, in a state of almost continuous eruption for half a million years.

Broad-shouldered Mount Etna looms over the Sicilian village of Cesarò.

Although this is not a national park, a visit to Etna is a worthwhile addition to any Italian itinerary. The park is a history lesson written in lava, from recent flows still raw to remnant rock from ancient eruptions that have long since been covered by forests of pine, beech, and birch. The park extends from the summit of the volcano to the towns surrounding it.

Mount Etna is the highest active volcano in Europe, standing menacingly at about 10,925 feet (3,330 m). Like any volcano, its height is somewhat fluid, changing whenever volcanic material accumulates during eruptions and crater walls subsequently collapse.

Etna's activities date back as far as 1500 B.C. Some 200 eruptions have been documented throughout history, and most have taken a relatively light toll—approximately one hundred deaths have been caused by the volcano. But the threat to lives and livelihoods is constant;

in 1928 Etna destroyed the town of Mascali. Volcanic activity can also be beneficial to mankind, leaving a geological legacy of rich soils as evidenced by Etna's lower slopes, planted with terraced vineyards and groves of oak, apple, chestnut, and hazelnut trees. Olive and pistachio groves also thrive here.

The slopes of the volcano, once roamed by wolves, are now inhabited by Sicilian foxes, martens, wildcats, porcupines, bats, and mice. These small mammals help sustain the spectacular birds of prey swirling around its higher reaches, such as peregrine falcons and golden eagles.

VISITING THE PARK

When visiting the park, make time to take in the horseshoe-shaped Bove Valley, an ancient volcanic caldera of cliffs, gullies, and lava formations covering some 14 square miles (37 sq km). The walls of this large basin tower some 3,280 feet (1,000 m) high.

The park's Citelli–Serracozzo Trail affords good views of the valley.

To get a big-picture view of the park, take the three-hour train ride on the Circumetnea line, which leaves from Borgo metro station in Catania and circles the entire mountain. Jeep tours to the mountain's northern side can be booked from Catania, Taormina, Giardini Naxos, and Letojanni. On the south side, cars and buses run from the park's headquarters in Nicolosi to the Rifugio Sapienza high on the mountain. From this alpine hut, cable cars and jeep buses climb higher toward the summit and guides lead climbs—though not into the restricted area near the active craters.

Cavers can explore some 200 local caverns carved out by volcanic lava. Over the centuries, Sicilians used these as sacred burial chambers and as cold cellars to store foods in the hot Mediterranean climate. For more information, visit *parks.it/parco.etna*.

FORESTE CASENTINESI, MONTE FALTERONA & CAMPIGNA

A forest park of understated treasures in north-central Italy

This diverse national park straddles both sides of the Apennine watershed between Romagna and Tuscany, extending around the long ridge, and descending steeply along the parallel valleys of the Romagna side and more gradually on the Tuscan side, with its gentler slopes. The park is filled with many natural and cultural treasures. These include the Campigna forests of white fir, the beech woods of Badia Prataglia, Castagno d'Andrea's lovely chestnut woods, and the scenic Acquacheta waterfall, made famous by Dante's *Divine Comedy*. Also of note are the picturesque hill town of La Verna and the monastic sites of Camaldoli and Chiusi della Verna.

WILDLIFE & WOODLANDS

With such a varied range of woodlands, it's not surprising that Foreste Casentinesi, Monte Falterona, and Campigna National Park is home to a who's who of Italian wildlife. The park hosts a healthy population of Apennine wolves, whose numbers continue to grow. Wild boars, red foxes, martens, Eurasian badgers, fallow deer, red deer, and roe deer all roam the forests here, where the wide eyes of barn owls and tawny

Opposite: Fall colors adorn a waterfall in the Casentinesi forest.

owls oversee this rich Italian tapestry of fauna, and common buzzards and eagles are among the larger birds of prey.

The sheer diversity of its forests is what makes this park special. The Camaldoli area features woods of hornbeams, turkey oaks, and sessile oaks. In some of the park's rockier places you'll even find the last remaining stands of rare cork oaks. The flora within this fecund park includes over 1,000 herbaceous species, and botany aficionados should head to the Monte Falco-Falterona massif for the widest sampling of these. Alternatively, a visit to the Valbonella Botanical Gardens near Corniolo brings many of them together under one roof.

PARK TRAILS & SITES OF INTEREST

Among the park's many intriguing sites is the famous Acquacheta waterfall, its waters tumbling over a 230-foot (70-m) sandstone cliff face. Upstream is the medieval village of Romiti, built on the ruins of the hermitage of San Benedetto in Alpe. Here Dante took refuge during his exile from Florence. The park has a fine nature trail of 2.8 miles (4.5 km) running through the valley called La Valle e la Cascata di Dante.

Another short trail, Alberi e

Bosco, takes visitors around the Camaldoli monastery. This was built sometime after the year A.D. 1000 as a hostel to replace the castle of Fontebuona; it later became the monastery of the Camaldoli monks. Here the cloisters and the Church of St. Donnino and Ilariano, with their paintings by Vasari, are well worth a visit, as is the ancient chemist's shop with alembics, mortars, stoves, and precious manuscripts.

The clifftop town of La Verna is another must-see: Located high on the steep southern wall of Monte Penna, the famous Franciscan sanctuary, situated in a silent, gloomy wood where the saint spent most of his hermitic life, has long been a draw for Italian pilgrims. In A.D. 1224, the miracle of the stigmata was recorded at La Verna, an event commemorated by believers to this day.

The park's multiple visitors centers offer exhibits on everything from the roe deer population to astronomy. Probably the best way to appreciate the wealth of woodland and culture here is to hike the seven-stage trail from the lake at Ponte di Tredozio to La Verna. This 62-mile (100-km) Sentiero delle Foreste Sacre (Path of the Sacred Forests) takes in many of the forests, valleys, and towns of this diverse park.

AT A GLANCE

Diverse woodlands ▪ Acquacheta waterfall ▪ 142 square miles (368 sq km) ▪ La Verna ▪ Sentiero delle Foreste Sacre trail ▪ parks.it/parco.nazionale.for.casentinesi

GARGANO

One of Italy's lesser visited parks is a gem of the southeast.

The waterfront of Vieste, a coastal town on the Adriatic Sea

The Gargano is the spur of the Italian boot, an elevated peninsula jutting out into the Adriatic Sea from the Puglia plains. The national park that bears its name embraces Monte Gargano, the Foresta Umbra (Shadow Forests)—a protected enclave of wild and ancient woodlands cloaking the interior—and the Isole Tremiti, an archipelago of attractive islands off the coast. Along the park's coastlines are a string of cliffs, coves, white-sand beaches, fishing villages, and small resorts.

Inland, the sunbaked southern valleys are rich in flora and wildlife. The Foresta Umbra is mainly Mediterranean and Aleppo pines, with some trees more than 500 years old. The promontory of Monte Gargano is inhabited by roe deer and many woodpecker species; among those tapping are two extremely rare subspecies, the lesser spotted woodpecker and Lilford's woodpecker. In recent decades, the park has worked hard to increase awareness about forest fires in an effort to preserve these birds' habitats. Lakes Varano and Lesina on the north coast also host large bird populations including cormorants, pochards, and red-breasted mergansers.

Gargano has one of the richest variety of orchids in Europe, with more than 60 varieties. Much of the land toward the shore is Mediterranean maquis, from the ground atop the great karstic plateaus, pockmarked with dolines, all the way to the steep cliffs overhanging the sea.

The four Isole Tremiti continue the karstic theme, with many coastal blowholes and caves to explore. The main islands of San Nicola and San Domino can be reached by ferry or hydrofoil in summer, leaving from Manfredonia, Vieste, and Peschici. Diving here is first-rate and you can also hike several trails to historic sites such as San Nicola's ninth-century Benedictine abbey, Santa Maria a Mare.

AT A GLANCE

Monte Gargano ▪ 456 square miles (1181.4 sq km) ▪ Bird-watching at Lakes Varano and Lesina ▪ Islands of San Nicola and San Domino ▪ parks.it/parco.nazionale.gargano

GRAN PARADISO

Italy's first national park rises to all the heights.

Italy's elevated Eden in the Graian Alps began in 1856, as the royal hunting reserve of Victor Emmanuel II of Savoy. In 1920, he gave it to the state, and three years later it was declared Italy's first national park. Today, Gran Paradiso spans the regions of Piedmont and the Valle d'Aosta, and protects the majestic scenery on and around the 13,232-foot (4,061-m) Gran Paradiso massif.

The landscapes in the park are a patchwork of high mountain wilderness, meadows, and dulcet valley floors. Year-round snow and glaciers shroud its inner peaks, from which fast-flowing streams plunge into flower-strewn pastures and forests of larch, fir, and pine.

HIKING IN GRAN PARADISO

Hiking through the park reveals a wonderland of waterfalls, deep-carved valleys, and pastoral villages. The park is best approached from the Valle d'Aosta to the north, driving southward on one of the trio of roads that cleave the major valleys on the park's northern flanks—the Val di Rhêmes, Val Savarenche, and Valle di Cogne.

These roads offer amazing views and the chance to pick up many hiking trails. The Valle di Cogne has the added appeal of the castle at Aymavilles and, if you take a short detour, the tiny village of Pondel that is famed for its third-century B.C. Roman bridge and aqueduct. A short trail from the lovely little slate-roofed village of Lillaz takes you to the Cascata di Balma, one of Gran Paradiso's many dramatic waterfalls.

One of the park's most popular trails starts at the busier village of Valnontey and leads to the Vittorio Sella mountain refuge (trail 106/36), then back via the Lago di Lauson (trail 39) and Sella Herbetet refuge (trail 33). This hike can take up to a day; look above for birds such as Eurasian eagle-owls, Alpine accentors, and golden eagles. In Valnontey, you can also visit the Giardino Botanico Alpino Paradisia, where many of the park's wild Alpine plants can be admired, including high meadow plants such as wild pansies, martagon lilies, and alpenroses.

As you hike, you'll likely see the *stambecco* (alpine ibex) stepping sprightly over the high rocky ground. Virtually extinct elsewhere in Europe, numbers are healthy here—the park hosts about 5,000, and the species has thrived here since 1821. Recently arrived wolves, however, may curb their population in future years. Numbers of the antelope-like chamois are also considerable, as are those of marmot, a small furry mammal whose piercing warning whistle is commonly heard on trails. The Valnontey walk has almost guaranteed sightings of the ibex and chamois. Gran Paradiso itself is one of the easier 13,120-foot (4,000-m) peaks to scale in the Alps, but you will need a guide.

A sure-footed alpine ibex (Capra ibex ibex) *surveys his mountain domain.*

GRAN SASSO & MONTI DELLA LAGA

A spectacular Apennine park dotted with ancient hillside villages

The sun sets over Santa Maria della Pietà Chapel, high in the Apennines.

Located primarily in Abruzzo, at the heart of the Apennines, this mostly mountainous wilderness is leavened with alpine plains.

Even if you are heading north or south to hike one of Italy's better known parks, you can drive through this vast preserve, which is well worth a detour for its scenery alone: It is transected by the Strada Maestra del Parco (Grand Highway of the Park), which runs between the Gran Sasso d'Italia mountain peak and the range known as Monti della Laga. The highway connects Montorio al Vomano with Amiternum, ascending the Vomano Valley up to the Capannelle Pass in the Apennines, at 4,265 feet (1,300 m); it then winds down toward the archaeological site of Amiter-num, and eastward toward L'Aquila.

The park's focal point is the Gran Sasso massif, which rises vertically over the vast pastures of the Campo Imperatore. The Calderone Glacier lies just beneath the tallest peak, the Corno Grande, and is Europe's southernmost glacier. On the north side of the mountain lies the Monti della Laga chain, where thousands of migratory birds stop on the shores of Lake Campotosto. This area is bearded by woods of beeches, firs, turkey oaks, and chestnuts.

FLORA & FAUNA

A mix of continental and Mediterranean climates provides biodiversity of habitats for many species of flora and fauna; among the park's 2,000 plant species are several that grow exclusively in Gran Sasso and Monti della Laga, such as the Abruzzo edelweiss. This hardy white plant of the daisy family thrives in rocky limestone places from 5,905 to 9,845 feet (1,800 to 3,000 m). It is distinguishable from its common Germanic cousin by its thicker, hairy white leaves that protect it from the cold.

As you hike through the park, look for rare creatures such as the Abruzzo chamois, as well as wolves, Marsican brown bears, roe deer, wildcats, and wild boars. Birds such as golden eagles, white-backed woodpeckers, and goshawks ply the skies. Whenever you wander near an alpine meadow in these hills, seek out the incredibly beautiful Apollo butterfly; its gray-white wings, dotted with black spots and red dots on its front and back wings (respectively) make this threatened butterfly easy to identify.

EXPLORING THE PARK

The park is an equestrian's heaven, with more than 125 miles (200 km) of horse trails. Canoeing, mountain biking, and hiking are popular too, and the winter months bring out aficionados of Alpine skiing, ski mountaineering, and cross-country skiing. The 3.7-mile (6-km) Santo Stefano di Sessanio–Rocca Calascio Trail leads you to a stunning 10th-century hilltop castle fortress and to Santa Maria della Pietà, an octagonal 17th-century church.

AT A GLANCE

Apennine mountain landscapes ■ 545.6 square miles (1,413.3 sq km) ■ Calderone Glacier ■ Santo Stefano di Sessanio–Rocca Calascio Trail ■ parks.it/parco.nazionale.gran.sasso

GULF OF OROSEI & GENNARGENTU

A sparkling island park on the east coast of Sardinia

The Gulf of Orosei and Gennargentu National Park basks in the Sardinian sun, its protected mountains and bay providing a wealth of habitat for many Mediterranean creatures. Here the Sardinian wildcat hunts for rodents such as the garden dormouse and the (very loud) greater white-toothed shrew. Another indigenous species, the Sardinian fox, may be seen seeking out martens and weasels in the steep green ravines that divide Monti del Gennargentu's jagged limestone peaks. Amid these mountains the horned mouflon rambles on higher grounds, overseen by griffon vultures, golden eagles, Bonelli's eagles, and peregrine falcons.

The juniper, holm oak, and olive woods are alive with the sounds of the great spotted woodpecker, while the seas off the coast teem with Mediterranean monk seal, fin whales, sperm whales, and passing pods of dolphins.

The park is also home to a truly beautiful creature, the Corsican swallowtail butterfly. Its yellow-and-black wings look like a study in sepia, until you notice its bright blue and red circular markings in the center of its back wings.

MOUNTAIN REALM

The park is named for the Gennargentu mountain range, the large massif in central-southern Sardinia. The highest peak in Sardinia, Punta La Marmora stands at 6,017 feet (1,834 m) and lies within the boundaries of the national park. These mountains are of huge geological significance, as their rocks are among the oldest found anywhere in Europe, weathered into smooth shapes over many millennia. Rock types of the Gennargentu include schist, limestone, and granite.

Nestled in the mountains are the only ski resorts on the island: on Monte Spada, Bruncu Spina, Separadorgiu, and S'Arena. In summer, the national park offers a range of excellent hikes, but be warned, the Sardinian sun is deceptively strong, even in the cooler air of elevated mountain trails, so wear a protective hat and plenty of sunscreen.

GULF OF OROSEI

The other part of this lovely isolated park is the Gulf of Orosei, which offers an array of gorgeous sandy beaches with turquoise Mediterranean waters lapping through coastal limestone features such as sea arches and cavernous caves. The diving in these clear waters is superb, and boat trips run from the park around the coast. One of the finest beaches is the last one along the gulf, the Cala Goloritzè. Along the cliffs at its southernmost end, you'll find strange limestone formations. Chief among these is the daunting Monte Caroddi or the Aguglia, a 486-foot-high (148-m) spire of rock that presents an irresistible challenge to climbers. The splendid 2.1-mile (3.5-km) Cala Goloritzè Trail from the Altopiano del Golgo takes you to this beach. Also worth the effort is the Cala Fuili to Cala Luna Trail, a 2.4-mile (4-km) hike through Mediterranean *macchia* and woods to the ravine-backed crescent of Cala Luna. Or hit the road: The coastal drive from the Gulf of Orosei to Baunei is one of the Mediterranean's finest road trips.

Cala Mariolu beach in Sardinia's Gulf of Orosei

AT A GLANCE

Mediterranean mountains ■ Gulf of Orosei to Baunei drive ■ 282 square miles (730 sq km) ■ Bronze Age tombs ■ Cala Fuili to Cala Luna Trail ■ sardegnaturismo.it/en/node/14480

ISOLA DI PANTELLERIA

A volcanic island between Europe and Africa

The island of Pantelleria, closer to Tunisia than to Sicily or mainland Italy, is a rich mix of nature and history. Situated at a crossroads between two continents and their very divergent cultures, the island fuses southern and northern influences in a distinctly Mediterranean medley.

The landscape is volcanic: Coastal features are shaped by wind and sea erosion, while the land has been sculpted by numerous eruptions over the last 50,000 years.

The rich volcanic soils of this westerly outpost of this Sicilian-administered island have ensured that agriculture and viticulture have long thrived here, for crops from either the African or European continent. The distinctive *dammuso* wall and field terracing, using the plentiful volcanic rock, and the breeding of Pantelleria goats (a subspecies) and of short, white-faced Pantelleria donkeys are threads in the island's environmental story. As for wildlife, the narrative is similarly

caught between two worlds: You'll come across exotic storks just as often as you'll hear the call of birds that straddle the Mediterranean and the Maghreb, such as the zitting cisticola (aka the streaked fantail warbler) or the western yellow wagtail.

The park's only visitors center is part of the Volcanology Museum of Khaggiar, located in Punta Spadillo within a restored World War II military structure. The park has many fine trails that will give you the lay of the island.

AT A GLANCE

Volcanic island landscape ▪ *Dammuso* walls ▪ 25.3 square miles (65.5 sq km) ▪ Volcanology Museum of Khaggiar ▪ parks.it/parco.nazionale.isola.pantelleria

MAJELLA

A hikers' heaven in the Italian heartland

The calcareous Majella massif rises in the Abruzzo region to a peak of 9,163 feet (2,793 m) at its high point of Monte Amaro. Majella National Park offers hikers more than 310 miles (500 km) of trails that sweep through largely untouched Apennine valleys and mountains, with a wealth of wildlife. In particular, Majella hosts 11 or so packs of Apennine wolves, 17 of which are monitored with GPS collars. The Abruzzo chamois was reintroduced to the high

Medieval Pacentro

slopes in 1991, Marsican brown bears inhabit the beech forests, and golden eagles hunt from the high aeries.

A visit to the cave paintings of Grotta Sant'Angelo and Grotta del Cavallone is a must, and the white stone castle of medieval Pacentro is unforgettable. The Maurizio Locati Visitor Center, in Lama dei Peligni, has exhibits on chamois and archaeology in the park, a reconstruction of a Neolithic village, and botanical gardens.

AT A GLANCE

Apennine highlands ▪ 242.6 square miles (628.3 sq km) ▪ Apennine wolves ▪ Cave paintings ▪ Maurizio Locati Visitor Center ▪ parks.it/parco.nazionale.majella

MONTI SIBILLINI

A mythical landscape between heaven and earth

Monte Vettore looms over the wide expanse of the Fosso dei Mergani at sunrise.

In central Italy, in a landscape known in medieval times as the realm of demons, necromancers, and fairies, Monti Sibillini National Park points to the heavens. The park reaches its peak at 8,123 feet (2,476 m) where snowcapped Monte Vettore scrapes the sky. Here, time seems to stand still: The wolf's howl echoes across the ages as golden eagles and peregrine falcons swirl above icy mountain vistas as they did in ancient times. Here, too, plants such as the Orsini fritillary, narcissus, and alpine aster color the slopes each spring like a blessed rebirth.

On the side of these hills lie fortress towns that have changed little since the Middle Ages. Here the defensive nature of the Italian psyche—the idea of what we have, we hold—is writ small in fortified hillside villages. These towns had thick walls with towers and entrances around main buildings such as the church, the palace, and the square; they were built high up to deter outsiders. Italy was, until the late 1800s, a land of many kingdoms.

Today, the Sacred Slope is a focal point of the park; among the ancient monasteries and abbeys scattered about is the birthplace of San Benedetto, in Norcia. Schools of learning blossomed in religious establishments during the Renaissance, including at the Abbey of Sant'Eutizio in Preci, where the surgical school's reputation soon spread across Europe. The region drew many into the ascetic life, and hermits headed for the isolation of high summits to meditate.

Today, Italians come to ski, ride horses, mountain bike, hang-glide, paraglide, and rock climb, and to visit ancient settlements such as the fortress town of Montefortino.

AT A GLANCE

Monti Sibillini landscape ▪ 269.2 square miles (697.2 sq km) ▪ Fortress town of Montefortino
▪ The Sacred Slope ▪ parks.it/parco.nazionale.monti.sibillini

POLLINO

A favorite Apennine mountain park of Italian hikers

Monte Pollino towers some 7,375 feet (2,248 m) above sea level in the south of Italy. This famous peak and the huge national park that protects it form the high mountainous instep of the Italian "boot." Pollino National Park straddles the regions of Basilicata and Calabria, and is one of Italy's largest national parks. It embraces both the Pollino and the Orsomarso massifs, which are part of the southern Apennine Mountains, and climbing to any of its summits will put the waters of the Tyrrhenian and the Ionian Seas on your horizon. The highest mountain in the park is the Serra Dolcedorme, topping off at 7,438 feet (2,267 m) in height.

The region is utterly wild and majestic and embraces the traditional ways of the rural south. Until recently, this was a place largely unknown to outsiders.

ANCIENT PAST

The park offers a wide range of diverse landscapes with high snow-covered mountains, areas of dolomitic rocks, morainic deposits, glacial cirques, and many scattered gorges and caves. In addition, many slopes lower down are covered with large swaths of beech tree forests. Throughout this vast nature preserve you'll find evidence of humankind's historic footprint, with paleontological sites such as Grotta del Romito and Valle del Mercure, as well as archaeological sites dating back to Greek colonization.

This is also a place of much cultural and religious significance, with sanctuaries, monasteries, castles, and historic towns that are like time warps to a medieval era, such as Laino Castello. The park is home to several ethnic-linguistic minorities of Albanian origin that have lived here since the 16th century. These were refugees from the era when the Ottomans conquered Albania, people belonging to Orthodox groups who fled their country and settled in Basilicata.

Just to the east of Monte Pollino lies Sibari, site of the ancient Greek colony of Sybaris, home to the high-living Sybarites, from where we get the English word "sybaritic," which is used to define people who are "self-indulgent." Only one percent of the huge archaeological site, which is 20 times larger than Pompei, has been excavated. Sibari and its small museum can be visited daily. If this peek into Greek history puts you in the mood to indulge in some southern Italian cuisine and fine wines, a host of towns throughout the park will oblige with fine rural fare. These include San Paolo Albanese, a small Albanian village that was founded around the 16th century, and Latronico, a small enchanting village with three beautiful churches—the Church of Saint Egidio, the Church of Saint Michael, and the Church of Saint Nicola.

EXPLORING THE PARK

The village of Terranova di Pollino is a good base for exploring these hills, while the seaside town of

Moss-covered beech forests are a delight to hike.

Maratea is a favorite among beach-goers. Above all, this park is a hikers' heaven. The summit of Monte Pollino is a great hiking destination for its attractive views and wildlife and bird-spotting opportunities. Among the spectacular array of southern wildlife here are Italian wolves, roe deer, and European otter. The forest dormouse, a small brown rodent with a bushy tail, also inhabits the woods of the park, providing a useful meal for the many raptors that prey in these parts.

Hikers who venture up into the rocky hilltops will be rewarded with the company of some of the most spectacular birdlife anywhere on the Italian Peninsula: Golden eagles and peregrine falcons swirl through the rarified mountain air, while lower down you might spot some interesting avian oddities such as a lanner falcon feeding on smaller birds and bats. Also seen is the Egyptian vulture, a white scavenger sometimes known as the Pharaoh's chicken, recognizable by its vivid orange face, contrasting underwing pattern, and wedge-shaped tail that makes it easy to spot in flight as it rides thermal updrafts during warmer hours of the day. Egyptian vultures are also unusual in that they use tools: They feed on the eggs of other birds by dropping large pebbles on them.

Look too for the orange underbody and black-and-white wings of the red kite, and the black-eyed, hard stare of the raven. Wander through lush beech, chestnut, and turkey oak woods and you might

Pollino's Natural Wonders

In the higher areas of the Pollino and the Orsomarso massifs, you can find a rare arboreal leftover from the last great ice age: Bosnian pine trees, symbol of the national park. Known for its decorative purple cones, this hardwood pine is also found in Bosnia and Herzegovina, Montenegro, Croatia, Bulgaria, Albania, North Macedonia, Serbia, and northern Greece. These hardy trees thrive at altitudes of 4,920 to 8,200 feet (1,500 to 2,500 m).

The park hosts what many experts consider to be the oldest tree in Europe, a Heldreich's pine estimated to be 1,230 years old. This puts its initial sprouting at about the same time that King Pepin of Italy was busy conquering Istria on the Adriatic, and around the same year that the *Anglo-Saxon Chronicle* recorded the first appearance of Vikings in England.

The Calda, the park's famous springs of sulfurous and magnesian water, may not prolong your life quite so long, but are worth a visit. Celebrated for their curative powers since ancient times, they now operate as a modern thermal spa, Terme Lucane.

spot an Apennine wolf, Orsomarso roe deer, or the destructive work of the black woodpecker, if not his distinctive crown. This shy fellow has a habit of hiding behind trees when humans approach.

The park is a geological dreamscape, mainly made up of Dolomitic rocks, and hiking in these hills and valleys reveals many interesting features: calcareous ramparts, tectonic fault walls, karst caves, swallow holes, morainic deposits, glacial cirques, glacially deposited boulders, and "timpes" or gorges of volcanic origin. Floral relief is at hand, however. The downward part of the park's many trails reveal gentle landscapes of cultivated cornfields, of wild pear trees, hollies, blackberry bushes, mistletoes,

hawthorns, brooms, thistles, and flowers like violets, poppies, peonies, and orchids.

In the thick, impenetrable mountain woods of beech, chestnut, and turkey oak, you'll find a rich undergrowth of mushrooms, fruits, and aromatic herbs. On these hills, you can slake your thirst in springs of cold, clear water that gush down to fill the gorges of Torrente Raganello, Fiume Lao, and Fossato di Rosa.

Among the most enchanting paths are those that lead to the summits of Dolcedorme, Serra di Crispo, and Gole del Raganello, as well as the trail leading to the Pollino plains. The visitors centers also offer information on mountain biking, horse riding, canoeing, and rafting in the park.

AT A GLANCE

Pollino and Orsomarso mountain landscapes ▪ 743.5 square miles (1,925.6 sq km) ▪ Europe's oldest tree ▪ Terme Lucane in the Calda ▪ parks.it/parco.nazionale.pollino

SILA

A delightful national park with a magical cuisine

Deer roam the park near Cecita Lake.

If you like fresh food straight from the field, forest, or freshwater stream, head for Calabria.

There you'll find the lovely southern wilderness of Sila National Park, a focal point for a feast of fine southern produce (see sidebar). The park is also a great place to hike in the Mediterranean sunshine and enjoy some of the cleanest air in Europe. Thirty-one trails lead to many points of interest.

A VAST FOREST

The Sila refers to the vast forested plateau deep in the interior of Calabria with an average elevation of over 3,300 feet (1,000 m). The park has a couple of mountain hikes that are none too strenuous: Botte Donato stands at 6,325 feet (1,928 m), in Sila Grande, and Monte Gariglione is an even easier climb at 5,787 feet (1,764 m) in Sila Piccola.

The Sila's forests are mainly beech, especially in higher areas, and pines on lesser slopes and plateaus. In Sila Greca, stands of oaks (mainly turkey oak and *farnetto*), are mixed with maple, ash, and other deciduous trees. In the Catanzaro you'll walk through chestnut groves and holm oak stands mixed with cork oaks and Mediterranean pines. Leafy black alder trees line many of the park's waterways.

An important legacy of the park is the forest of Fallistro, which now has its centuries-old giant pines protected against the extensive logging that the area endured for centuries. These wildwoods are beautiful to walk through when filled with birdsong. As author Enrico Massetti says,

"today the forest may not be primordial, but it certainly feels like it."

Sila has gained recognition for successful reintroduction of its park symbol, the wolf, which was hunted to extinction by 1970. The growth in numbers is not without controversy, however, as farmers have seen their livestock attacked.

The park has several educational museums, including the Olive Oil and Peasant Society Museum, a must for chefs interested in how generations of Calabrians got those special tastes into their southern cuisine.

Sila Cuisine

Sila National Park embraces many small towns where centuries-old traditions and recipes live on in delightful local cuisine. No winter visitor here should omit a taste of *mpanata*, a soup made with ricotta, hot whey, and hard bread. This can also include cheese, anchovies, capers, and olives. While hiking in the park, look for delicious berries, chestnuts, and Sila porcini mushrooms, all of which make delicious snacks. Before you head out, pack some *nduja*, a soft, spreadable spicy sausage, spread on *pane di Cerhiara*, a bread from Pollino, or any locally baked bread.

AT A GLANCE

Mediterranean mountain trails ▪ 284.5 square miles (736.9 sq km) ▪ Old-growth forest of Fallistro ▪ Rustic Italian cuisine ▪ parks.it/parco.nazionale.sila

STELVIO

A soaring Alpine park welcomes winter sports lovers.

High in the Alps, looking north toward Europe and south toward Italy, is a winter wonderland, Stelvio National Park. It protects a prime slice of Alpine wilderness straddling two regions, Trentino-Alto Adige/Südtirol and Lombardia. This is a mountain playground with lots of skiing opportunities and almost 1,000 miles (1,600 km) of marked hiking trails. The town of Bormio is a good base from which to explore the park's many villages and scenic highs, and the Valtellina around Bormio has several spas offering the local therapeutic thermal and mineral waters. The Valle dello Zebrù to the east offers spectacular valley hikes with equally beautiful views.

The park's landscapes run the full Alpine gamut—from majestic ridges to lush forests to high green pastures crossed by streams springing from perennial glaciers.

WILDLIFE & WILDFLOWERS

The many animals who make their home here include chamois, alpine ibex, roe and red deer, wild boar, red foxes, Alpine marmots, and Eurasian badgers. The forested areas teem with hazel grouse, ravens, carrion crows, great spotted woodpeckers, black woodpeckers, western capercaillie, and nutcrackers, while Eurasian dotterels ply the park's waterways. On higher grounds, golden eagles, buzzards, lammergeiers, and golden eagles patrol the skies. Keep an eye out too for the magnificent European eagle-owl, who can grow to a height of 30 inches (75 cm) with a wingspan of 74 inches (188 cm). This mottled black- and tawny-feathered owl is also distinguishable by its pointed ear tufts.

The park's meadows are a joy to hike in spring, when the floral carpet is rolled out with a multitude of colorful wildflowers. These include wolfsbane, white genepì, alpine aster, bright yellow globeflower, deep-orange tiger lily, mountain violet, crowberry, and the glorious pink shades of rhododendrons.

The castle of Castelbello greets spring in the Venosta Valley.

VAL GRANDE

A small mountain park with many hidden delights

True to its name, the Highland cow grazes the park's upper meadows.

In the highlands of the northern Italian region of Piedmont sits the small wonder that is Val Grande National Park. This park, on the border with Switzerland, lies within the delta of the Po River. Its landscape is wild and unpopulated, characterized by snowcapped peaks and three defining valleys: Val Vigezzo in the north, the Cannobina Valley in the northwest, and the Val d'Ossola in the southwest. Most of the park is densely forested, lower Val Grande mainly with chestnut trees, while beech is most widespread in the upper regions, along with some spruce and silver firs. Higher up in the Alpine grasslands, rare floral species thrive, including Alpine columbines and Alpine tulips.

Hikers in these mountains may spot chamois, roe deer, and deer. Lower down, the red fox trots through the woodlands, also the realm of badgers, beech martens, hedgehogs, and dormice. The tiny shrew is further down the food chain but makes quite a racket for its size, using echolocation to navigate its way. Birdlife is rich and varied with black grouse, dippers, and golden eagles sharing the same airways. Walkers on all park trails should keep an eye out for dangerous vipers.

HISTORY IN THE PARK

The lovely Lake Maggiore in the southeast is popular with hikers and trout anglers. Aging hippies who hear strains of their favorite songs here in late July/early August are not suffering flashbacks—the music will be coming from the Spirit of Woodstock Festival held in Armeno to the south. Americans in particular may also recall the lake's name from the escape by boat of the hero and heroine in Ernest Hemingway's novel *A Farewell to Arms*. The novel's title is an apt reminder of why the park lost its human population in the years after 1944, when Nazi troops decimated the remains of the Italian resistance in the area. Following this roundup, the Alpine communities of summer herdsmen and woodcutters abandoned Val Grande. Today, the physical scar of World War II's Cadorna Line consists of the ruins of a series of military forts built against an Austrian-German attack arriving through Switzerland.

The park has several visitors centers and two museums, dedicated to water and soapstone. One visitors center is in the historic 14th-century Castle of Vogogna, where military enthusiasts will particularly enjoy a permanent exhibition of tin soldiers from the 5th to the 21st century.

The authorities maintain a number of nature trails throughout the park but advise that most expeditions into this unpredictable Alpine wilderness should be accompanied by an authorized guide. Mountain huts are available for rest and recuperation. An interesting hike called "Living on the Slope" follows an old mule trail through the town of Premosello and continues uphill to Colloro to explore how summer herders lived.

AT A GLANCE

Piedmont's Alpine peaks ▪ 58 square miles (150 sq km) ▪ Castle of Vogogna ▪ Living on the Slope Trail ▪ parks.it/parco.nazionale.valgrande/Eindex.php

VESUVIO

Site of one of history's most explosive natural disasters

Vesuvio. Vesuvius. The very name evokes calamity, sorrow, and an ancient terror that this region has long lived under. The catastrophic eruption of Vesuvius in A.D. 79 famously buried and preserved the Roman towns of Pompei and Herculaneum, freezing many citizens in a mold of lava. Visitors still flock to Pompei to view these strange volcanic mummies. The volcano is dormant—at least for now. The most recent eruption was in 1944, and the next one's just a matter of time.

MONTE SOMMA

Vesuvius National Park, southeast of Naples, is centered on the active volcano. Visitors can hike the trail to its most ancient—and now inactive—crater of Monte Somma.

Somma-Vesuvius is a classic example of a fenced-in stratovolcano consisting of two different morphological structures: the Somma caldera and the Great Cone of Vesuvius. The semicircular Somma caldera reaches its highest point of 3,714 feet (1,132 m) at Punta Nasone: This is all that remains of the ancient volcano, which was active for nearly 300,000 years. A large depression, Valle del Gigante, is divided into Atrio del Cavallo and Valle dell'Inferno. This represents the inner part of the ancient caldera, within which you can observe the most recent Great Cone of Vesuvius. The natural wall of Somma is well preserved in its northern section, and its crater edge is characterized by a series of minisummits, called *cognoli*.

FLORA & FAUNA

Despite the somewhat desolate landscape around Vesuvius, the mineral-rich volcanic soils of the park nurture more than 600 plant species, including Spanish broom, Scotch broom, and Etna broom, as well as several species of colorful orchids. The slopes of Vesuvius are drier than those of Monte Somma and are partly reforested, but much of the dense vegetation now consists of Mediterranean maquis; the wetter slopes of Somma are characterized by mixed woods.

A surprising array of animals live within this small national park: The rare oaken mouse resides here along with the dormouse, beech marten, fox, and hare.

Birdlife too is a rich affair: Among the species that nest in the shadow of the volcano are the buzzard, kestrel, peregrine, hoopoe, turtledove, and great spotted woodpecker. Migratory birds from the southern Sahara include pied flychatchers, redstarts, wood warblers, bee-eaters, and nightjars. Among the reptiles that bask on the volcanic rock are the colored green lizard, the western whip snake, and the disk-fingered gecko.

Unless you are driving, the easiest way to the 4,189-foot (1,277-m) summit of Vesuvius is to reserve a package tour at the Circumvesuviana desk at Napoli Centrale rail station, which includes the train to Ercolano Pompeii Scavi and the bus to the volcano. Wear sturdy shoes for the 20-minute hike to the crater.

The Great Cone of Vesuvius, located between Naples and Pompei

AT A GLANCE

Somma-Vesuvius volcanic mountains ▪ 28 square miles (72.5 sq km) ▪ The crater of Monte Somma ▪ Nine hiking trails ▪ parks.it/parco.nazionale.vesuvio

MALTA

There are many national parks in Europe that are considerably larger than the entire archipelago of Malta. Yet few islands have been as fiercely sought after as these three tiny isles comprising just 122 square miles (316 sq km), to the south of Sicily. Malta's strategic significance is due to its location at the entrance to the eastern Mediterranean Sea. Throughout the centuries, most of Europe's larger empires have fought over this rocky ground for the right to moor their trading and warships in ports such as Valletta and St. Julian's and in inlets such as Birżebbuġa.

The island's many invaders and occupiers are stitched into the islanders' DNA, which is a heady brew of Arabic, Sicilian, Norman, Spanish, Italian, and English. The fortified capital of Valletta was built by the crusading Knights of Saint John and it is close to where modern-day visitors find Malta's main national park, Ta' Qali. This is very much an urban park, and you'll have to go farther afield to encounter the impressive Maltese falcon, or to enjoy world-class diving amid the reefs, shipwrecks, and sea caves of Malta's extensive coastlines. Two nature parks, one in the northwest and one in Qawra await intrepid travelers (see page 319).

But head for Ta' Qali to find your bearings on your first day, download some *għana* folk music (typically slow rhythmic singing), and maybe grab a ricotta-filled *pastizza* ("pastry wrap") from a vendor. Then start making plans to explore Malta's three historic islands, and follow in the footsteps of emperors, pirates, knights, and sultans.

Above: The medals on an Order of Malta veteran show the ubiquity of the George Cross in Maltese culture.
Opposite: An aerial view of Ta' Qali National Park

TA' QALI

A city park in the middle of the Mediterranean

The park's sweeping entrance invites visitors with the sound of the central fountain's waters.

Ta' Qali is the only European national park set on an old military base. The preserve is located at Attard in central Malta, on the site of the former Royal Air Force airfield and barracks where British warplanes were based between 1943 and 1950. In the mid-1950s, Ta' Qali became unused ground until the park and other attractions filled the wide-open spaces: Ta' Qali also hosts a national football stadium, a crafts village, and a popular national vegetable market, known locally as the Pitkalija.

HISTORY OF TA' QALI

Shortly before World War II, RAF Ta Kali was built as a military aerodrome for Britain's Royal Air Force (RAF). With this move, the British became the latest in a long line of foreign armies to recognize the strategic importance of Malta at the Mediterranean confluence of Europe, Asia, and Africa. The base was operational throughout the war and continued to be used as an RAF airfield up until the mid-1950s, later as a center that was used for joint training operations.

These days Ta' Qali is first and foremost central to the Maltese people as a recreational area. Fans will troop out in the thousands to support the national soccer team, as the tiny island takes on the might of European powerhouses. Many citizens of Valletta make the six- or seven-mile (11-km) trip west to enjoy a picnic in the sun or take in a summer's evening concert in the Greek amphitheater. In 2011, a new U.S. Embassy was opened across from Ta' Qali National Park.

Today, model aircraft owners use the runways where real jets used to land and take off, and artisans of the crafts village house studios in the converted military huts and outbuildings. One *can* still view real airplanes here by visiting the Malta Aviation Museum. The museum has exhibits on aircraft engines, models, and uniforms as well as a rebuilt Spitfire Mk IX and a Hawker Hurricane Ila.

FLORA OF TA' QALI

Ta' Qali National Park hosts a wide variety of ornamental plants and trees, beautifully laid out in formal Italian gardens with a hint of Arabic design. The park's gardeners care for both indigenous and nonindigenous floral species. Approach Ta' Qali through the main entrance, where a circle of planters with flowering plants surround a central fountain. Depending on the season, the annuals on display include pansies, geraniums, celosias, and marigolds. Then let the paths bring you down trellis-covered tunnels with *Plumbago auriculata* blooming in white and blue, surrounded by planters of the spiny *Carissa macrocarpa*.

A gate opens onto the Formal Garden, where a great variety of indigenous and nonindigenous ornamental tree species can be enjoyed. Small tracts of Mediterranean woodland have also been re-created in the park by mixing indigenous tree species. Here you can amble through the piney Syracusa Grove and other shady areas. Next, climb the stairs to the top of the main gate for a fine view of the park.

Opposite the main entrance, in a large space known as the Kite Area, more floral beauty awaits visitors with plantings including a mix of indigenous Sandarac gum trees and olive plants.

The Formal Garden is a fantasia for any botany enthusiast or gardener: You can spend hours admiring trees such as Aleppo pine, stone pine, Sandarac gum, and Mediterranean cypress. The medley of Mediterranean trees within the park includes bay laurel, holm oak, chaste tree, African tamarisk, common jujube, southern nettle tree, Judas tree, European dwarf palm, and Spanish broom.

Nonindigenous ornamental trees are also planted in this most democratic of parks: You can admire plants such as *Lagunaria patersonii*, more commonly known as Norfolk Island hibiscus, primrose tree, or cow itch tree. Here too is *Erythrina variegata*, a native of Africa and India, aka tiger's claw, Indian coral tree, or sunshine tree. Among other imports are the flowering *Washingtonia filifera*, also called desert fan palm or California fan palm, and *Washingtonia robusta*, a Mexican fan palm.

This plethora of plant life reflects Malta's long history of adapting outsiders and mixing many cultures.

FAUNA OF TA' QALI

The park's wide variety of plant life has given rise to a welcoming range of habitat for much of the islands' birds, bees, insects, and reptiles.

Strollers in the park will have birdsong year-round: Resident birds here are the Sardinian warbler, Spanish sparrow, zitting cisticola, and collared dove, the latter recognizable by the collar of black feathers on the back of its neck. In summer the spotted flycatcher breeds in Ta' Qali, while the short-toed lark can be seen in open fields around the park. Hopes for a brighter European future are on the wing when one reflects that these fields where jets once roared are now filled with the sounds of doves and larks.

The end of autumn always heralds the arrival of several wintering bird species: Robins, stonechats, white wagtails, and common starlings can all be seen foraging for insects. Goldcrests and firecrests frequent the coniferous groves in winter, as do blackcaps.

In spring and fall, look for the hoopoe, which can usually be observed feeding on the ground. In spring, woodchat shrikes perch on lookout posts seeking insects; you'll know them by their black-and-white plumage with chestnut-colored head. A memorable sight during spring and fall migration season are the flocks of night herons descending to roost in pine groves in the early hours of morning.

Indigenous reptile species in the park include geckos, western whip snakes, Maltese wall lizards, and Mediterranean chameleons. Mammal species include the Etruscan shrew and Algerian hedgehog. Watch as you walk for butterflies such as painted ladies and the lovely swallowtail butterfly. And don't forget to watch for the lobed agriope, the largest spider in Malta.

Malta's Nature Parks

Il-Majjistral Nature and History Park takes its name from Malta's northwest wind and protects the stretch of coast from Golden Bay to Il-Prajjet and ix-Xaghra l-Hamra. It also embraces historical and archaeological sites including British military architecture and ancient tombs. You can take guided snorkeling tours from the sandy beach at Golden Bay. Along Majjistral's karstic plateaus you'll see endemic plants such as Maltese spurge, Maltese sea chamomile, and Maltese pyramical orchid, and watch for the Mediterranean chameleon blending into the landscape.

Salini National Park is a masterfully re-created area of rural green space at the southern tip of Qawra: The government has landscaped this reclaimed land, building rustic walls and planting forests of Aleppo pine, Mediterranean oak, bay laurels, and other tree species for future generations to enjoy.

Maltese urban park ▪ The Formal Garden ▪ .13 square mile (.34 sq km) ▪ Syracusa Grove Walkway ▪ Mediterranean chameleons ▪ msdec.gov.mt/en

GREECE

Greece is the cradle of European civilization—a country blessed by the gods, and a wellspring of art, philosophy, architecture, and democracy. This is the home of Mount Olympus, Delphi on Mount Parnassós, and the Temple of Poseidon, all now enshrined in national parks. Greece itself is a monument, a sun-soaked testament to the beauty of nature, with deep-blue skies, forested mountains, white-sand beaches, and islands strung like pearls across the turquoise waters of three seas. The 12 Greek national parks are a medley of landscapes that are among the least explored in Europe; and everywhere you go, you'll meet the Greeks, a most civilized people who may also be the most hospitable in the world.

Opposite: Shipwreck Beach, Zákynthos National Marine Park

AÍNOS

A legendary mountain shrouded in myth and history

Mount Aínos, the tallest mountain on the Ioanian island of Kefalonia, rises some 5,341 feet (1,628 m) above the turquoise-blue Ionian Sea. The mountain and its surrounds are protected by Aínos National Park, a dolostone and limestone bedrock covered by thick forests of indigenous Greek (Cephalonian) fir and black pine. These grow between elevations of 2,300 feet (700 m) and 3,940 feet (1,200 m). The forests thrum with wildlife, but look especially for the semiwild ponies *(Equus caballus)* that graze the meadows around the woodlands.

Mount Aínos overlooks the Kefallonián coast and the Ionian Sea.

VIEWS FROM ABOVE

The views from the top of Mount Aínos on clear days make the long slog up the trail worthwhile, with rewarding lookouts encompassing the northwestern Peloponnese and Aetolia, and the islands of Zakinthos, Lefkada, and Ithaca. Near the top, keep your eyes open for a glimpse of the rare Cephalonian violet that only grows here among the rock crevices on the peaks of Mount Aínos. Circling overhead may be such birds of prey as short-toed snake eagles, lanner falcons, and European honey buzzards.

The park has several trails, many of them starting at the Environmental Center of Aínos. The easiest of these is the Chionistra Trail, a circular hike of 3.8 miles (6.1 km) that rewards with several spectacu-

lar vistas. A more strenuous trek is the Kissos–Petasi–Nyfi–Megas Soros–Kissos trail that has some steep climbs along the way. This loop hike is about 5.3 miles (8.6 km) in length and can take up to five hours, and you should allow some time to explore the Petasi and Nyfi caves. At the summit of Aínos await fine panoramic views of the neighboring peaks of Kroukoumpia and Olympus, as well as the islands in the south Ionian Sea and the western parts of the Peloponnese. Wear good hiking boots, as this trail has dirt roads and rocky stretches.

CAVES & CIVILIZATION

The northern part of these partly limestone mountains offers many caves well worth exploring. The most dramatic cavern on the island is perhaps Spii Melissani, the site of an underground saltwater lake, which is

illuminated by shafts of natural light where the roof of the cave has fallen. The name translates as "purple cave," but it is usually a deep blue. Boats can take you into this mysterious and somewhat haunting place, once thought to be a sanctuary to Pan.

Modern civilization has left its mark on the ancient mountain: A highway across these hills connects the southwestern to the eastern part of the island, meaning you can drive almost to the top. A sanctuary to Xenios Zeus—the Greek god of hospitality—once welcomed travelers to the crown of Mount Aínos (Megas Soros), where animals were sacrificed to the genial Greek god; today, several television and cell phone towers occupy the summit. Approximately 3,000 to 4,000 people live on the slopes of Aínos, and all will still welcome you, cell phone in hand or not.

AT A GLANCE

Legendary mountain vistas ▪ 11.8 square miles (30.4 sq km) ▪ Spii Melissani cave ▪ Kissos–Petasi–Nyfi–Megas Soros–Kissos trail ▪ foreasainou.gr/en/

ALÓNNISOS & NORTHERN SPORADES

An unspoiled Greek island hosts a small species-specific marine park.

The hilly, wooded island of Alón-nisos is one of the lesser visited of the Sporades group—good news for diving enthusiasts heading to Alónnisos and Northern Sporades National Marine Park. This small preserve was created in 1992, mainly to protect the endangered Mediterranean monk seal. Less than 800 of these creatures survive worldwide, and about 30 are thought to breed here on the tiny islands around Alónnisos. Fishing is banned in certain areas to deter the local fishermen who have long regarded the seals as competitors for diminishing fish stocks. If anyone offers to take you out to the seals, you should refuse—monk seals are extremely shy creatures, easily disturbed.

Other wildlife pass through this national marine park, from multitudes of migrant birds to pods of dolphins. Look for the Eleonora's falcon, with its distinctive sooty brown and black plumage.

In addition to the sea area, the marine park embraces the island of Alónnisos, six smaller isles (Peristera, Kyra Panagia, Nisida Gioura, Psathoura, Piperi, and Skantzoura), as well as 22 uninhabited islets and rocky outcrops. The islands' landscapes are made up of mainly Mediterranean conifer-ous forest and macchia vegetation.

Numerous yachts now visit Alónnisos, as many of the islands around the protected area offer good harbors and gorgeous isolated beaches, such as Kyra Panagia, as well as great snorkeling amid lovely offshore sea grass beds of *Posidonia oceanica*.

Alónnisos itself consists mainly of the small port of Patitiri, the attractive restored old town of Alónnisos high above it, and a few scattered traditional villages. This is the real Greek islands, undeveloped, unspoiled, and protecting wildlife that has long thrived here, but is now under threat.

The endangered Mediterranean monk seal mostly seeks refuge in inaccessible caves.

AT A GLANCE

Marine preserve of Mediterranean monk seal ▪ .87 square mile (2.2 sq km) ▪ Snorkeling ▪ Old town of Alónnisos ▪ alonissos.gr/en/marine-park/overview.html

OETA

A mountain refuge for wildlife, on a peak where a Greek hero sacrificed his life

Mount Oeta is a legendary mountain located in central Greece, standing at 7,060 feet (2,152 m) above sea level. In Greek mythology, Oeta is famed as the scene of Hercules's death, and tales of witches and crones still haunt these hills.

About a quarter of the mountain was declared a national park in 1966. Oeta's northern side consists of steep and inaccessible terrain that descends to the Spercheios Valley, forming a series of deep gorges and waterfalls, including the spectacular Kremastos waterfall, a popular scenic beauty spot. To the east, Oeta is bordered by the gorge of the Asopos River. By contrast, the southern slopes of Mount Oeta are gently sloped and easier to climb. The national park embraces two wildlife refuges: Skasmeni Frantzi–Dyo Vouna on the northeastern slopes, and Oiti–Pavliani on the southeastern side.

WATCHING WILDLIFE

The forests of the national park include black pine stands, and provide rich habitat for a wide range of animals such as roe deer, wild boar, and the endangered Alpine newt. Larger mammals passing through this mountainous and wooded terrain include brown bears, wolves, and wildcats. The Balkan chamois lives in the rocky highlands. The old-growth forests are particularly hospitable to woodpeckers: Other birds you might see (or hear) as you walk in the woods include the misnamed grey-headed woodpecker (he's actually quite colorful), the white-backed woodpecker, and the Syrian woodpecker, himself a bold and colorful spectacle of red, black, and white.

A stream courses through the woods of Pavliani.

Preserved mountainous forests ▪ 27 square miles (70 sq km) ▪ Balkan chamois ▪ Karst caves ▪ oiti.gr

OLYMPUS

A pinnacle of ancient mythology and home of the Greek gods

Mount Olympus takes hikers into the realm of the gods.

It is apt that the home of the gods became Greece's first national park (1938). Mount Olympus, the highest Greek mountain, is made all the more dramatic by the way the short mountain range that it belongs to rises sharply from a flat plain. It is less than 12 miles (19 km) from the top of Mount Olympus to the shore of the Aegean Sea.

The national park is home to European wildcats, badgers, jackals, and wild boar. Birds of prey give the climb to the summit a certain epic quality as they swirl above snowcapped peaks. Some 1,700 plant species grow in the meadows and forests lower down. The forests are a fragrant mix of oak and beech woods, stretches of Macedonian fir, stands of rare Bosnian pine, and a centuries-old rare yew grove near the Monastery of St. Dionysus.

WHERE THE GODS MEET

The pinnacle of the Olympus range is referred to as either Mount Olympus or Mount Mytikas. The ancient Greeks called Mytikas "Pantheon" and revered it as the meeting place of the deities. The 12 gods were believed to have lived in the alpine ravines, which Homer described as the mountain's "mysterious folds."

Mytikas, standing at a daunting 9,571 feet (2,917 m), was not scaled by mortal man until 1913; of course, the mountain has been a playground of the gods since the beginning of time. This was the site of the Battle of the Titans, when the 12 Greek gods led by Zeus defeated the Titans, immortal deities descended from Gaea and Uranus. In this mythic conflict, the wild forces of nature were tamed by the gods, who introduced a new kind of civilization to the world.

Today, you can reach the apex of the gods if you are reasonably fit and plan ahead. The hike takes the best part of a day, so you must spend a night on the mountain either camping or staying (by reservation) at one of the two mountain refuges. It's best to make the trek with a local guide and to consult with the park visitors center in planning your adventure. The base for approaching the mountain is the busy village of Litochoro. As you stand at the summit, consider the mountain's honored place in classical Greece, a mythical status passed down through millennia, across Western civilization.

You are also standing on the spot where the notion of sport was born. The village of Dion, on the mountain's flanks, was a Macedonian holy city where King Archelaus (r. 414 to 399 B.C.) held nine days of games to honor Zeus. Today, Dion houses an important archaeological site and an archaeological museum, where much of the region's rich classical history is displayed.

AT A GLANCE

Climbing Mount Olympus ▪ Village of Dion ▪ 92 square miles (238 sq km)
▪ olympusfd.gr/en

PARNASSÓS

The center of the ancient Greek world

Behind Delphi (see sidebar) rise the dramatic Parnassós Mountains. The highest point of this limestone range is the 8,061-foot (2,457-m) Mount Parnassós. According to Greek mythology, this mountain was sacred to Dionysus, Apollo, and the Corycian nymphs, and was home of the Muses. In antiquity, Parnassós was known as Mount Lykaio, or Wolf Mountain. There are not too many wolves on the mountain today, as roads make the top easily accessible, and skiers, hikers, and mountain bikers flock here now. Nearby Gerontovrachos, or Old Man's Rock, looms slightly lower at 7,989 feet (2,435 m). Parnassós may have been revered in ancient Greece, but its rich deposits of bauxite led to systematic mining since the end of the 1930s, which caused ecological damage to part of the mountain.

EXPLORING THE PARK

Much of this lush mountain landscape is now protected by Parnassós National Park, which opened in 1938. The park covers the mountainous region between Delphi, Arachova, and Agoriani. The landscape is dominated by forested slopes of Cephalonian fir, with stands of oak and black pines, alpine valleys, bare cliffs, and

In the hills of Delphi, the Sanctuary of Athena Pronea remains.

moraines. Lower down, you can walk through gorgeous meadows abloom with colorful alpine flowers in the spring. Endemic flora species protected within the park include the Cephalonian fir tree and the Parnassian peony, a lovely pink flowering plant.

The 3.5-mile (5.6-km) Path of the Kahal Canyon (starting from Tithorea) is a particularly good trail to take if you want to experience

Delphi

The Greeks saw Delphi as the center of the world. The ancients flocked to this site on the southern slopes of Parnassós to question the oracle on the seventh day of the month, a tradition going back 3,000 years. The oracle, or Pythia, was usually a woman over 50 deemed to be given powers of prophecy by the god Apollo; the Pythia's words were interpreted by her attendee priests. The Rock of the Sibyl, where she was consulted, is marked on the Sacred Way leading to the fourth-century (B.C.) Temple of Apollo. Above the temple is the Roman theater, and beyond that the stadium where the Pythian Games were held. Delphi's museum is a treasure trove of local finds.

some of the park's springtime floral finery. The path leads onward to an exquisite dilemma: whether to go to the impressive cave of Odysseas Androutsos or to brave a longer, steeper hike to the great summit of Parnassós. The Muses on the road not taken might call you back another day.

Although an occasional wolf makes a visit, driven down by harsh conditions on the mountains, this is home to less fearsome wildlife, including badgers, foxes, squirrels, and wild boars. The mountain airways are also patrolled by many different birds of prey, such as vultures and golden eagles.

The Parnassós Mountains are particularly popular with skiers, and the Greek season runs roughly from December to April, depending on snow conditions. The Parnassos Ski Center, located close to Delphi, boasts 25 marked ski runs and about 15 cross-country ski routes of 22 miles (36 km) in combined length.

The park has many historic towns and settlements aside from Delphi, such as the charming hillside village of Parori, perched 500 feet (150 m) up the eastern foothills of Parnassós. Wander around to admire its stone houses, narrow cobbled streets, and fine tiled roofs before visiting its traditional threshing floors, medieval tower, and the fascinating frescoes in St. Theodore Church.

AT A GLANCE

Legendary Greek mountain preserve ▪ 58 square miles (150 sq km) ▪ Delphi ▪ Path of the Kahal Canyon trail ▪ onparnassos.gr/en/location/ethnikos-drimos-parnassou

PÁRNITHA

Protecting vital habitat from the march of "progress"

Mount Párnitha is a densely forested mountain just north of Athens. Its summit, known as Karabola, rises some 4,636 feet (1,413 m) above sea level. This mountain and its surrounding peaks now constitute Párnitha National Park. Its landscapes are varied, with mountain peaks, steep gorges, streams, and plateaus. Long ridges extend from east to west, with 16 summits rising 3,300 feet (1,000 m) or more. Notable among the many cavernous features in this karst landscape are Ntabelis cave on the mountain range's limestone southern side, and the cave of Panas, in Keladonas's gorge, dedicated to the worship of the god Pan and the nymphs.

Above 3,300 feet (1,000 m) the slopes of Mount Párnitha are covered with Greek fir, grasses, and shrubbery. Below this are forests of Aleppo pine, as well as macchia and phrygana (a type of low, soft-leaved scrubland). Red deer forage here, just as they did in ancient times, according to writers of Greek antiquity. The parklands nurture about 1,000 species of plants.

These forests, however, are often threatened by fire, due to human negligence and Greece's dry summer heat. A huge fire in 2007 claimed 80 percent of the rare Greek fir and Aleppo pine forest; it also killed 150 red deer, pushing it higher up the list of endangered species. Scientists estimated that it will be at least a century until the forest recovers, but with climate change, this may be an optimistic assessment.

AT A GLANCE

Aleppo pine forests ▪ Karst landscapes ▪ 96.5 square miles (250 sq km) ▪ Hiking trails and lodges ▪ parnitha-np.gr/welcome.htm

PINDOS

A mountain park perfect for offtrack wilderness hiking

The Pindus Mountains range from Greece's northern borders west to the Ionian Sea and east into North Macedonia. Within this area, Pindos National Park protects the Balkan and black pine forests that have covered these mountain slopes for thousands of years. This is the home of Greece's remaining European brown bears and European silver wolves, both endangered species. Other wildlife include deer, wild boar, wildcats, and chamois. On the trails you might see dice snakes, and nose-

Pindos: A gateway to fine hiking

horned vipers too, so tread carefully.

The skies are alive with goshawks, Egyptian vultures, golden eagles, imperial eagles, and griffon vul-

tures. This is rugged and potentially treacherous mountain backcountry, so hiring a guide is advisable. The ultimate challenge for experienced hikers is Mount Smolikas, which at 8,459 feet (2,578 m) is Greece's second highest peak after Mount Olympus. You'll need to reserve the mountain huts in advance and bring camping gear. The small town of Konitsa, a few miles from the Albanian border, is a popular hub for walkers; its old bazaar and Turkish quarter are particularly interesting.

AT A GLANCE

Pindus Mountain forests ▪ 26.7 square miles (69.1 sq km) ▪ Climbing Mount Smolikas ▪ Konitsa's old bazaar ▪ pindosnationalpark.gr/en

PRESPES

A vital pair of lakes that are part of a tri-nation parks system

In the northwestern corner of Greece lie the lovely Prespa lakes, two freshwater bodies of water shared by Albania, Greece, and North Macedonia. Greece has the lesser share, owning just 14.05 square miles (36.4 sq km) of the total surface area of 68.07 square miles (176.3 sq km). The lakes offer a range of rare habitat for birdlife, being the highest tectonic lakes in the Balkans, at an elevation of 2,798 feet (853 m).

Dalmatian pelicans are among nature's heaviest flying creatures.

The Great Prespa Lake is divided between all three countries, while the Small Prespa Lake is shared only between Greece and Albania. All three countries have dedicated national parks to the preservation of the lakes (see pages 439 and 448), so the reality is that these waters lie beyond national boundaries and are ruled by Mother Nature, with a little help from the three states on their shorelines. In Greece, this protected area is known as Prespes National Park.

The two lakes, scenically framed by rolling mountains, are separated by a sandy islet of alluvial sediment, and reed beds decorate large stretches of shoreline. The waters nurture extensive beds of aquatic plants such as hornworts, water milfoil, and pondweed rooted in the depths, with large leaves taking in oxygen on the surface.

The lakes and their surrounding forests provide rich habitat for

Prespes' Birds

Prespes' 1,200 pairs of Dalmatian pelicans attract most of the avian paparazzi around these lakes. Their worldwide population of just 10,000 to 20,000 are all that survive of a species that once numbered millions. The pelicans usually reside here year-round, but in harsh winters they fly south to Corfu. You can spot many other birds in these waters, such as herons, cormorants, egrets, geese, and the only population in Greece of the rare goosander (look for its red bill). Keep an eye to the skies for raptors such as golden eagles, short-toed eagles, booted eagles, and lanner and peregrine falcons.

over 200 species of birds, the most exotic of which are two species of pelicans—white and Dalmatian. If you can get close as they feed, you can marvel at the strange evolutionary quirk that resulted in these birds' large beaks that scoop up fish from the lake. The lakes also host the largest colony of Dalmatian pelicans in the world (see sidebar). Prespes' inland location and elevation has resulted in 80 percent of its fish being endemic: These include the Prespa spirlin, the Prespa bleak, the Prespa trout, and a subspecies of roach.

The area has many interesting churches, monasteries, hermitages, and rock paintings dating from the 10th century: Visitors can, for example, view the ruins of the 10th-century island Church of St. Achillius built by Tsar Samuil on Agios Achillios.

AT A GLANCE

International lake parklands ▪ 126 square miles (327 sq km) ▪ Dalmatian pelicans ▪ Church of St. Achillius ▪ visitgreece.gr/en/nature/forests/prespes_national_park

SAMARIÁ

A stunning gorge landscape on the island of Crete

Hikers descend the Samariá gorge in central Crete.

The Farángi Samariás (Samariá gorge), on the island of Crete, has been a national park since 1962. Due to its unique geology, it is also a UNESCO world biosphere reserve. Samariá National Park was established to preserve the habitat of the rare kri-kri (Cretan ibex). Once common throughout the region, they were probably introduced to Crete in Minoan times. Today their range is restricted to the park and an island off the shore of Agia Marina.

The now abandoned village of Samariá lies just inside the gorge; both the village and the gorge derive their names from the ancient church of Óssia María.

The gorge was created by a small river running between the White Mountains and Mount Volakias. The dolomite beds here have been fractured by glacial action and karstic stress, which is particularly marked around the best known (and most photographed) part of the gorge, the stretch called the Gates. Here, the sides of the gorge close in to a width of only 13 feet (4 m) and rise to a height of almost 980 feet (300 m).

EXPLORING THE PARK

The national park is well regulated for the protection of this gorge and its habitat, opening from May through mid-October. Most visitors take the trail from the Omalos plateau all the way down to the shores of the Libyan Sea at Agia Roumeli.

From this small village, you can sail to the nearby village of Sougia. This strenuous trek is 10 miles (16 km) long, and starts at an altitude of 4,100 feet (1,250 m). It takes five to seven hours, and good hiking shoes are a must. The distance through Samariá National Park is eight miles (13 km), but it's 1.8 miles (3 km) farther to Agia Roumeli from the park exit.

If the hot Crete sun is making you lazy, you can cheat and just walk from Agia Roumeli to the Gates, and back. Whichever way you go, look for rare wildflowers and herbs such as the Cretan maple and orchids, for vultures and eagles, and, of course, for the kri-kri, whose home you are walking through.

AT A GLANCE

Dolomite karst landscape ▪ 18.7 square miles (48.3 sq km) ▪ The kri-kri (Cretan ibex) ▪ Omalos plateau to Agia Roumeli Trail ▪ samaria.gr/en/home-2-2

SOUNIO

The national park of Greek history is capped with the Temple of Poseidon.

Perched 200 feet (61 m) on the headland of Ákra Soúnio (Cape Sounion), the great Temple of Poseidon stands as a monument to the Greek Golden Age. This is the jewel in the crown of a wonderful park that celebrates history as much as it protects nature for future generations. The temple is dedicated to Poseidon, god of the sea, and it stands tall on Cape Sounion, a promontory at the southern tip of the Attic peninsula, with fine views of the Aegean Sea on three sides.

COLUMNS, CAVES & CIVILIZATION

The Temple of Poseidon was built from 444 to 440 B.C. at the behest of the Athenian statesman Pericles, who also rebuilt the Parthenon in Athens. The temple was constructed out of gray marble mined just a few miles away at the quarries of Agrileza. Of the original 34 columns, 15 still stand to their full height. At the column nearest the entrance, you might spot the carved initials of the English Romantic poet, Lord Byron, who visited here in 1810. The temple was built on the ruins of a previous place of worship, destroyed in 480 B.C. by Persian troops during Xerxes I's invasion of Greece. Like nature, civilization is a cycle of life, death, and rebirth. The Temple of Athena, goddess of wisdom and warfare, is located nearby, about 1,000 feet (300 m) farther up the hill.

The ancient ruins are but the core of Sounio National Park, which stretches north up the coast of Attica from this southernmost cape of Sounio.

The landscape of the park is trifold: The majority of the area is covered in Mediterranean pine forest, maquis covers both the inland and coastal areas, and the rest consists of arid

The Temple of Poseidon overlooks the Aegean at Cape Sounion.

brushland. Holm oak are prevalent in the arboreal maquis, where intensive grazing by livestock and wild animals controls the environment. Throughout the park, old mines and numerous places of archaeological and paleontological interest abound. As the early Roman statesman Cicero (106–43 B.C.) wrote, "wherever you set your foot, you encounter some memory of the past."

This maxim also applies to nature: The park is riddled with caves and other karstic formations, and these cool limestone cellars have acted as conservatories for all kinds of ancient fossils for centuries. These include plant samples of marine pine and black pine, as well as animal curiosities from the past such as the spalax mole rat and the brown bear, both of which are long extinct in Greece.

Cape Sounion is renowned for its sunsets, which result in breathtaking bloodred and fiery orange skies, but the best way to avoid throngs of sightseers is to arrive early in the morning. Dawn over Sounio can be quite beautiful too, as a new light rises once again over this place of ancient civilization.

AT A GLANCE

Temple of Poseidon ▪ Temple of Athena ▪ 15.4 square miles (40 sq km) ▪ Mediterranean pine forest
▪ visitgreece.gr/en/nature/forests/sounio_national_park

VÍKOS-AÓÖS

Deep gorges and a place of holy retreat deep in the Pindus Mountains

The Pindus Mountains stretch from the northern borders of Greece west to the Ionian Sea, south to Metsovo, and east into North Macedonia. This mighty mountain range encompasses two national parks, the second longest gorge in Europe, and several of the highest peaks in Greece. The Víkos-Aóös National Park protects the area around Mount Tymfi and the Víkos gorge. This is glorious hiking country, with mountain terrain crisscrossed by ancient intra-village trails, dense coniferous and deciduous forest, and karst caves and canyons. The clifftop monastery of Agia Paraskevi, overlooking the Víkos gorge, is unforgettable.

VÍKOS GORGE

The park's prime attraction is the spectacular Víkos gorge, which runs for seven miles (11 km). The gorge is located on the southern slopes of Mount Tymfi, between the villages of Víkos and Monodendri. In places the walls of the gorge rise 3,117 feet (950 m) sheer from the ground, while elsewhere they open out to flower-filled meadows. At the right time of the year, hikers can swim in the Voidomatis Potamos river. You can walk the length of the gorge in a day, if you're reasonably fit. Bear in mind that this is a remote wilderness, so you may not pass a soul on the trail in early and late summer. Remember too that this is karst country, with porous rock, and water can be hard to come by in summer. Be prepared, check the visitors centers for forecasts, and let someone know where you are headed. In winter, the gorge may be impassable; likewise, in April and May, when the mountain snows melt, trickling rivers become torrents. The park is one of the last Greek sanctuaries for brown bears, so make noise if you're walking alone. Look in the forests for cool-climate plants such as Scot's elm, nettle-leaved bellflower, horse chestnut, and large-leaved linden.

AÓÖS GORGE

The Aóös gorge is carved into Mount Tymfi, which rises to 8,192 feet (2,497 m) at Gamila peak, on the northern periphery of the park. This gorge is close to the town of Konitsa, where the Aóös Potamos river passes through channels in the mountains of Tymfi, Trapezitsa, and Flampouro. As you hike look for wolves, foxes, wild horses, and roe deer. The Aóös gorge is six miles (10 km) long and has numerous stone single-arched bridges from the 17th to 19th centuries, as well as ancient monasteries. There are four villages inside the Víkos-Aóös National Park, and nine more near its borders. All are sparsely populated. Historically, all the villages of the region were connected by a system of slate or cobblestone paths.

VILLAGE TRAILS

North of Ioannina, toward the Albanian border, lies the region of Zagoria. Forty-six Zagorian villages are linked by a network of ancient paths that make for ideal hiking. In spring, these dirt trails become carpeted with wildflowers. The trails are narrow, and bridges along the way have bells to alert crossers of strong winds. These bridges were originally built by traders who crossed the region in spring when flooding was common. One of the best preserved is the triple-arched Kalogeriko Bridge, near Kipi.

The Zagorian villages in the area are worth exploring for their distinctive limestone houses with slate roofs and walled yards. These *archontika* were built in the 18th and 19th centuries, mainly with money earned abroad when the ruling Ottoman Turks, who governed from Ioannina 31 miles (50 km) to the south, gave Zagoria autonomy, allowing the retention of wealth. Some of these manors have now been restored as museums or guesthouses.

The sheer walls of the Víkos gorge on Mount Tymfi

AT A GLANCE

Víkos gorge ▪ Kalogeriko Bridge ▪ 49 square miles (127 sq km) ▪ Zagorian village trails
▪ visitgreece.gr/en/nature/forests/vikos_national_park

ZÁKYNTHOS
Protecting maritime habitat, especially for the loggerhead turtle

This aerial view shows the underwater rock shelf around the island of Zákynthos.

Located south of Kefalonia (and connected to it by ferry), the island of Zákynthos (also called Zante), is popular for its idyllic white-sand beaches and its lovely capital, but the island's chief claim to fame is its unique amphibious inhabitant, *Caretta caretta*, otherwise known as the green loggerhead turtle. The Zákynthos National Marine Park was opened in Laganas Bay in 1999, to protect the habitat of this sea turtle.

Zákynthos is the principal nesting site in the Mediterranean for these creatures and the first national park established for their protection in the region. The nesting habitat in the bay comprises six separate beaches: Gerakas, Daphni, Sekania, Kalamaki, Laganas, and Marathonissi islet. This combined protected tract of beach runs about three miles (5 km) in length, with Sekania being rated among the world's highest loggerhead nesting concentrations.

Apart from these nesting areas, the park embraces the wetland of Keri Lake and the two small islands of Strofadia, which are located 31 miles (50 km) south of Zákynthos. Aside from the beaches, the park's landscapes embrace a variety of habitats including sand dunes, *Posidonia oceanica* beds, submarine growths of the critically endangered sea daffodil, and several submerged reefs.

The park has the usual cast of migrating Mediterranean seabirds: wild swans, swallows, kingfishers, and seagulls. Another interesting mammal that swims in these waters, although they play second fiddle to the loggerheads, is the critically endangered Mediterranean monk seal, which resides in numbers along the west coast of Zákynthos. Bottlenose dolphins are often spotted from the beaches or from boats. On land, you'll find many frogs, tortoises, iguanas, and soft water snakes; while on the island trails you might see porcupines and wild rabbits.

LOGGERHEAD TURTLES
Turtles have nested in Laganas Bay for thousands of years, but following the influx of tourists to Zákyn-

A loggerhead turtle in Laganas Bay, off Zákynthos Island

thos and the Greek islands in the 1960s, they had human competition for the lovely, soft, gold sand in which they lay their eggs. Although the turtles came ashore at night to lay their eggs, during the day their nests were being destroyed by spikes of beach umbrellas. At nighttime, the lights and music of increasing numbers of bars and discos further disturbed and disoriented these timid creatures. They also had the misfortune to nest on prime development land.

Fortunately, the authorities took steps to protect the turtles to some extent, with stretches of the 8.5-mile (14-km) beach being fenced off from tourists. Local people have also realized that the turtle is a tourist attraction, even if hardly any visitors ever see them—most people just buy the T-shirt or the fridge magnet.

ZÁKYNTHOS TOWN

The island's capital, Zákynthos town, suffered severe damage in the 1953 earthquake that roiled the region but has since been rebuilt in a mostly successful attempt to recreate the original style. It has an attractive waterfront with plenty of small, colorful fishing boats alongside the large interisland ferries. Behind the waterfront are some fine shops (filled with loggerhead memorabilia), which are colonnaded to protect shoppers from the strong Greek sun of summer and the rain in winter. The buildings show the influence of the Venetians, who ruled here from 1484 until 1797, and who referred to the island as Fiore di Levante (Flower of the East).

One building that did survive the earthquake (locals believe it was divine intervention) was the grand cathedral, built in 1925 and dedicated to the island's patron saint, Agios Dionysios (1547–1622). Interestingly, the church and chapel at the 16th-century monastery of Moni tis Panagias tis Anafonitrias, where St. Dionysios was the abbot for the last years of his life, also survived the earthquake. The monastery is on the northwest end of the island and is a popular stopover on organized tours of Zákynthos. The saint's bones are kept in a silver coffin in the cathedral in Zákynthos town, and his vestments are kept in the chapel of Agios Nikolaos sto Molo, at the far end of the harbor on Plateia Solomou.

The Turtle's Tale

Caretta caretta reaches Zákynthos in summer, having traveled thousands of miles across the Mediterranean. The female goes ashore at night to dig large nests in the soft island sand with her back fins. Into these she places 120 small eggs about the size of ping-pong balls. She then returns to the ocean, leaving a trail in the sand. After 40 to 60 days, the eggs begin to hatch. The nascent loggerheads remain for a few days in their warm nest as their bodies take shape. Nature's GPS—the natural instinct of geographic memory—leads them back to the sea, where their migratory, amphibious life begins. They may return as adults to breed and nest on the same protected beach of Zákynthos, where their journey began. Alas, just one in a thousand will survive as they encounter many perils, most of them man-made.

EASTERN EUROPE

EASTERN EUROPE

The Iron Curtain long defined the western limits of eastern Europe. No longer. Since 1989, not only birds and badgers range from Germany to Poland, from Finland to Russia, but nature lovers too. Stunning national parks, long forbidden, are now within reach: Anyone with a passport can easily explore the eastern wildernesses of Tusheti in Georgia, the Carpathian parks of Ukraine and Romania, and Pirin in Bulgaria. Much of Europe's east is defined by mountains; Albania has its "accursed mountains" around Valbonë Valley, Poland has its Tatras, and the Low Tatras and the Slovak Ore Mountains dominate Slovenský Raj (Slovak Paradise) National Park in Slovakia. The land boundary with Asia is the line tracing Russia's Ural Mountains from the Arctic Ocean south to the Ural River and Caspian Sea. This line continues along the crest of the Caucasus Mountains between the Caspian and Black Seas.

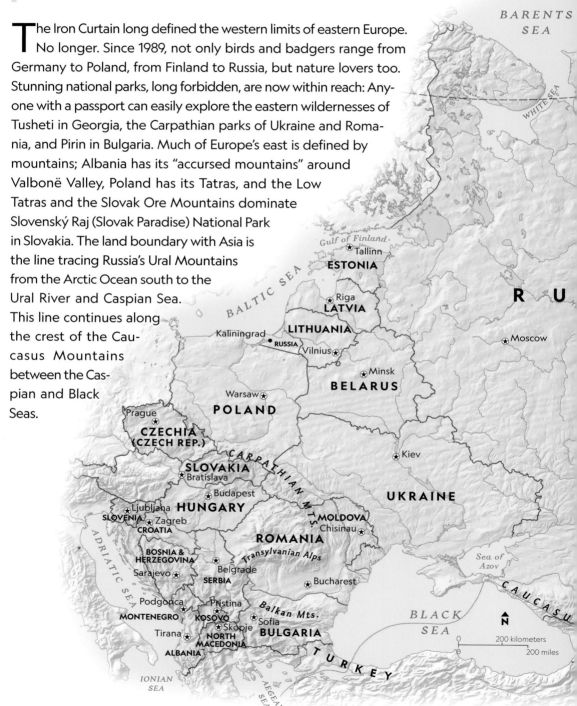

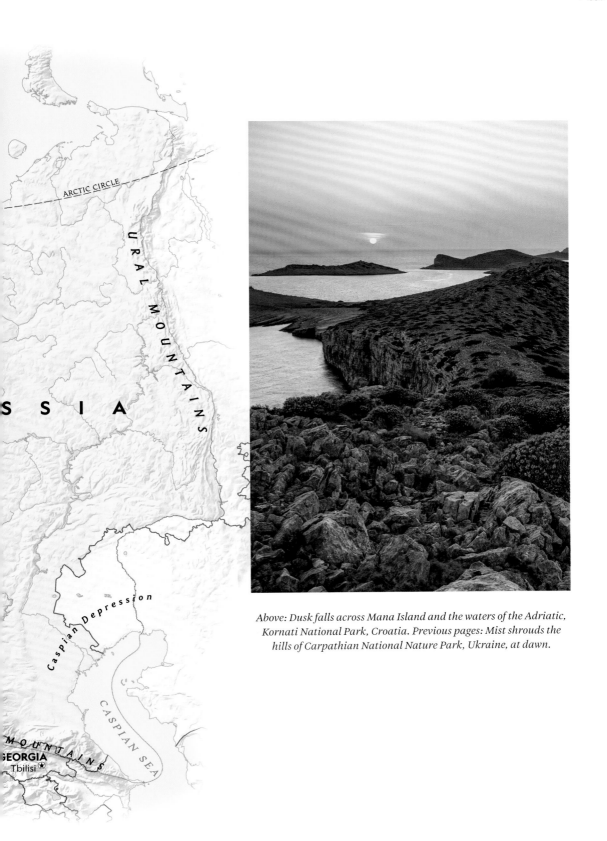

ARCTIC CIRCLE

URAL MOUNTAINS

SSIA

Caspian Depression

MOUNTAINS

GEORGIA
Tbilisi ✱

CASPIAN SEA

Above: Dusk falls across Mana Island and the waters of the Adriatic, Kornati National Park, Croatia. Previous pages: Mist shrouds the hills of Carpathian National Nature Park, Ukraine, at dawn.

CZECHIA

Visitors to Czechia—as the Czech Republic is now known—arrive with images of Prague's "thousand spires," cobbled streets, towering medieval castle, and beautiful bridges seared into their imaginations. Yet the rest of the country is an equally charming realm awaiting discovery. Most Czech towns are laid out with a central square, perfect for sipping coffee or a pilsner lager, one of this land's many gifts to the world. This square often doubles as a marketplace, overlooked by a main church and a brightly decorated town hall. Out in the countryside, a pastoral paradise awaits hikers.

Landscapes are varied: To the north, mountains rise high, covered by woods and spangled with resort towns. In the southern parts of Bohemia and Moravia, the terrain takes the form of rolling hills along with plains dotted with lakes that have for centuries been used to farm fish, and lots of vineyards. National parks such as České Švýcarsko and Šumava are crisscrossed by trails and filled with bizarre geological formations, ruined castles, fast-flowing rivers, deep gorges, and stands of primeval forest. These parks are ideal for mountain biking, hiking, and canoeing, while skiing, snowboarding, and skating in winter provide outdoor fun.

Opposite: The Vranov nad Dyjí Chateau towers above Podyjí National Park.

ČESKÉ ŠVÝCARSKO

A labyrinth land of rock in a region called Czech Switzerland

The fascinating geological wonderland known as České Švýcarsko (Czech Switzerland) got its name from the Swiss Romantic artists who visited in the 1770s. The national park—to the east of the Elbe River—runs adjacent to Germany's Saxon Switzerland National Park (see pages 104–105). Between Hřensko and Česká Kamenice, the hills are pierced by small valleys packed with well-kept villages of half-timbered cottages.

Hidden in the woods are the cliffs, rock pillars, and sandstone formations that give the areas around Jetřichovice and Hřensko a unique sense of drama. Eons ago, volcanic rock surfaced here to form fissures, canyons, and other rock oddities. Unfortunately, air pollution has hastened their erosion, but the park now protects them from development, as well as the park's flora and fauna, such as an outstanding array of ferns.

The lovely village of Hřensko sits in a gorge edged by overhanging rocks, and features quaint Germanic cottages. At the end of a three-mile (5-km) hike from here into the woods, you'll find Pravcicka Brána, the largest sandstone arch in Europe, some 85 feet (26 m) across and 68 feet (21 m) high. Farther on, the tranquil town of Mezná is a hub for hikers, and from here you can return by boat to Hřensko.

The park has many gorgeous walks, taking in medieval stone castles and churches; the visitors centers in Hřensko and Jetřichovice have details. One trail particularly worth taking is Edmund's gorge (aka Kamnitz gorge), a rock ravine near Hřensko.

AT A GLANCE

Sandstone landscape ▪ Pravcicka Brána natural arch ▪ 30.5 square miles (79 sq km) ▪ Edmund's gorge trail ▪ npcs.cz/en

KRKONOŠE

High bog landscapes within the legendary Krkonoše Mountains

Krkonoše National Park is nestled in north-central Czechia within the Krkonoše Mountains, the highest range of the country. This park borders Karkonosze National Park in Poland (see page 352). The pinnacle of Krkonoše is Snow Mountain, which, at 5,259 feet (1,602 m), is the highest mountain in Czechia. These mountains are home to 165 species of birds, so as you walk up near Krkonoše's peat bogs, look for black grouse or fan-tailed capercaillie. The 1,300 species of flora found in the park include many rare trees and other plants that thrive in the unusual elevated peaty pastures characteristic of the area.

Though once visibly damaged by acid rain caused by heavy industry of this northern region, the park is bouncing back, and now nurtures several organic farms. Since medieval times, these "Giant Mountains" have inspired terror, especially in the German and Italian prospectors who began mining operations here in the 16th century. This fear was personified by the supernatural giant Krakonoš, blamed for everything from forest fires to avalanches.

Today, the mountains host the ski resort of Vrchlabí, just outside the park, which also has a regional museum featuring local arts and crafts. Just inside park boundaries is the quiet, small spa town of Janské Lázne.

AT A GLANCE

Krkonoše Mountains ▪ 212.2 square miles (549.7 sq km) ▪ Elevated peat bogs ▪ Janské Lázne spa town ▪ krnap.cz/en

PODYJÍ

A South Moravian park of regional and international significance

Wild horses were brought from England to graze invasive plants.

When the walls—both physical and psychological—came down across Europe in 1989, nature was a winner. The administrations of many wildernesses were expanded and made easier by the prospect of cross-border cooperation. Countries whose borders had made up eastern Europe's "Iron Curtain" now opened their doors to nature. As the winds of change swept Czechoslovakia, Podyjí National Park was established in 1991, to preserve vital biome in South Moravia. The lush forests along the Dyje River Valley extended eastward to the protected woods of Thayatal National Park across the border in Austria (see page 122).

Podyjí National Park has undulating hills, but no significant peaks; the highest point is 1,782 feet (543 m), and its rich array of habitats cover forests, grasslands, arable land, shrubland, and wetlands. The Dyje River meanders for 25 miles (40 km) through the densely forested valley cutting the Českomoravská vrchovina uplands, and the park authorities now oversee the careful balance of ecosystems with a mix of conservation, research, forestry, and agriculture.

EXPLORING THE PARK

The park offers a range of fine hiking trails, with plenty of history to enjoy along the way. You can trek to the ruins of Nový Hrádek castle, or cross the border into "Austria's smallest city" to view Hardegg Castle, and then hike out to the deserted village of Umlauf inside the park to view the 12 fishermen's huts and ponder the hard lives lived there. Or hike to the dramatic 12th-century Vranov nad Dyjí Chateau, perched high on a forbidding clifftop and now beautifully renovated in the baroque style. Another option is the climb up Šobes hill, one of the oldest vineyard trails in Czechia.

WATCHING WILDLIFE

You'll have plenty of foliage to watch for while hiking these trails. Podyjí is host to 77 species of plants, which include oak woods, hornbeam, beech, and alder. Perennial plants include cyclamen, mullein, and pasqueflower, with its beautiful light purple flowers and yellow stamen. The upper plateau was logged in the 19th and 20th centuries, and now consists of grasslands. Along the park's rivers, you'll see reed beds or willow shrubs, and elsewhere you can enjoy the colorful spectacle of some of the numerous species of orchids that thrive in Podyjí.

The park is also home to the Syrian woodpecker (look for its black, white, and red plumage) and the barred warbler. Watch in the woods and wetland for some of the park's many reptiles, including tree snakes and green lizards.

AT A GLANCE

Southern Moravian forests ▪ 24 square miles (63 sq km) ▪ Vranov nad Dyjí Chateau ▪ Šobes vineyard trail ▪ nppodyji.cz/en

ŠUMAVA

These Bohemian forests are the Czech patch of the "Green Roof of Europe."

The Bohemian forests of the southwestern Czechia are a continuation of Germany's Bavarian forests, making an extensive range of woodland, including non-native spruce varieties and remnants of primeval forests. This area is now partly protected by Šumava National Park.

The landscapes here are plateaus in the west with dramatic peaks and canyons, the rolling hills of the Trojmezenská mountain massif, and the Vltava alluvial plain in the south. Šumava retains remnants of primeval mountain forest, and its glacial lakes, mountain bogs, and raised bogs are largely unpopulated. This means that, especially in winter, you'll have many of the park's hiking and skiing trails to yourself.

WATCHING WILDLIFE

Aside from the cry of the reintroduced wolf (see sidebar), you might hear the soft footfall of red deer in the park, or spot rare northern lynx, which have been successfully reintroduced since the 1980s; a population of 80 individuals now roams Šumava. Elk too have returned to the southern part of the park. Although no bears live here any longer, a fine hike is the aptly named 8.6-mile (14-km)

Eurasian lynx (Lynx lynx) are impervious to Czechia's snows.

Bear Trail through the Šumava Mountains.

Birdlife is plentiful in the park, with the higher altitude of the Šumava forests attracting alpine birds that typically frequent more northerly European mountains. While out on the trails, look for the capercaillie, which breed in the upland forests; the grouse, which inhabits the moors and open wetlands; and the hazel grouse, which is seen throughout the park.

These forests are a mix of silver birch, beech, fir, spruce, and often elm and sycamore. Šumava's beech stands are home to the Ural owl and the white-backed woodpecker, while the spruce forests provide rich habitat for birds such as three-toed woodpeckers, boreal owls, and ring ouzels.

The Wolf Howls Again

By the end of the 20th century, wolves that were once plentiful in South Bohemia had been hunted to extinction. Šumava National Park is now undertaking a program to try to reintroduce these magnificent wild creatures into this beautiful wilderness where, especially in wintertime, their poignant howls seem to belong. A new, purpose-built woodland enclosure has been built at Srní for a breeding wolf pair that have taken to the park. An elevated wooden walkway transects this area, allowing hikers to enjoy close encounters of the lupine kind.

THE HUMAN FOOTPRINT

Although many of the forests feel like virgin territory, glassmaking in the region has had a major impact on Šumava. The industry goes back to the mid-14th century in the Vimperk and Horní Planá areas, and the practice of glassmaking expanded in the 16th century. Although the glassworks were small businesses, their effect on the forests was significant, as the heating of even a small kiln for glassblowing required a lot of cut wood.

From 1475 to 1849, Šumava also had many gold and silver mines, which were protected by castles, many of which still stand today. As you wander through this lovely wilderness, it can feel like a land deserted, a place apart. History bears out that feeling: After World War II, most of Šumava's German-speaking dwellers were expelled, and the area morphed into a deserted zone along the Eastern Bloc border. Today, thanks to the presence of the national park, its future looks a lot brighter.

Primeval Bohemian forests ▪ Northern lynx ▪ 262.8 square miles (680.6 sq km) ▪ The wolf walkway ▪ The Bear Trail ▪ npsumava.cz/en

POLAND

Poland's lands stretch from the Baltic Sea to the Carpathian Mountains, but its cultural influence is global. Despite repeated invasion and occupation, Poland's national identity and its people have persevered in the face of adversity as great as any in European history. Many Poles left their homeland, but their homeland never left them. Pope John Paul II (Karol Józef Wojtyła) returned to bolster the struggle against Soviet influence; Joseph Conrad (Józef Konrad Korzeniowski), the Polish sailor turned English novelist writing in his third language, railed against Russian occupation throughout his life in exile. You'll realize why when you experience the tranquil bucolic beauty of places such as Białowieża, Bieszczady, and Wolin, where European bison roam free, or where a hike into the Tatras helps crystallize the pride the Polish people take in their homeland.

Opposite: Sunset lights the trail to Morskie Oko Lake, Tatra National Park.

BABIA GÓRA

The woods of southern Poland protected and cherished

In south Poland, along the border of Slovakia, lies the woodlands of Babia Góra National Park. The vast majority of this park is forested, and the variety of elevations provide several different habitats for flora and fauna. The lower forest belt, up to 3,775 feet (1,150 m), is mainly planted with Carpathian beech trees, fir trees, and a mix of fir and spruce species. The subalpine belt, from 4,560 feet (1,390 m) up to 5,415 feet (1,650 m), has dwarf pine thickets and shrubs such as bilberry, while the alpine belt, above 5,415 feet (1,650 m), features grassland pastures long used for grazing.

Some 105 species of birds inhabit these rich woodlands, including several varieties of woodpeckers and eagle-owls. Animals such as deer, lynx, wolves, and bears roam the mountains here, where insects, including several indigenous species of beetles, thrive in the deadwood of fallen trees.

The park embraces the northern side and part of the southern side of the Babia Góra massif. Diablak, its highest summit, stands at 5,659 feet (1,725 m) and is the highest peak of the Orava Beskids mountain range, a section of the Western Carpathians. If you climb it, be forewarned: The locals call it "the Mother of Bad Weather." The area of Babia Góra is also a UNESCO biosphere reserve, with just 20 residents. The national park offers guided tours in a variety of languages; its main visitors center is in the village of Zawoja.

AT A GLANCE

Polish mountain forests ▪ 13.1 square miles (33.9 sq km) ▪ Diablak Mountain (aka Babia Góra) ▪ Orava Beskids mountains ▪ bgpn.pl/en

BIAŁOWIEŻA

Bison, history, and mystery within old-growth forests

Białowieża is a wilderness that has been torn apart by history, yet blessed with a bounty of natural beauty. At the turn of the 20th century, during the Russian Partition of Poland, a Palace Park was founded around the tsar's home in Białowieża. Today, you can visit that historic manor house from 1845, as it has been refurbished and now serves as the Centre for Nature Education. Although the national park was opened in 1932, in the wake of World War II the forest was divided between Poland and Belarus in the Soviet Union. Today, it is known as the home of the European bison and incorporates the Bison Breeding Centre. It is also a UNESCO World Heritage site.

In addition to protecting 800 of these magnificent beasts, the park's inner zone offers a chance to walk in primeval forests that have remained largely untouched for eight centuries. Visitor groups are limited to 20 people, each led by an expert guide, and as you walk through these ancient, moss-floored forests, you'll be steeped in nature's sweetest silence. The presence of pygmy owls in these woods is a rare treat.

At the visitors center in Białowieża, in the Museum of Nature and Forest, you can climb the observation tower for a fine view of the park. This multimedia museum explains local plants, animals, and birdlife, and multilingual guides are available.

AT A GLANCE

Primeval European forest ▪ Bison Breeding Centre ▪ 58.8 square miles (152.2 sq km) ▪ Abundance of lichen and moss species ▪ UNESCO World Heritage site ▪ bpn.com.pl

BIEBRZA

Poland's largest national park is a vast expanse of teeming wilderness.

In northeastern Poland, Biebrza National Park encompasses a range of habitats, from oak-hornbeam forests, wild meadows, and pasturelands to a large area of marshes. It also protects unusual barchan dunes that take on vegetative cover to form perches, or protruding domed hills. The park's southern extreme is located along the Biebrza River, a waterway best known for the vivid wildlife that lives within the peat bogs and marshes of its floodplain. The park's northern boundary is near the Belarus border.

The preservation focus of the park are its marshes. Biebrza protects a vast swath of relatively untouched fenlands with a unique variety of plants, rare wetland birds, and animals such as elk and beavers. A multitude of birds come to feed, nest, and rest in these Biebrza wetlands and in the Narew River Valley. The park contains the Red Marsh Nature Reserve, whose birch and dwarf trees offer an alternative habitat to the riparian morass of the river. This wooded landscape provides homes for a host of animals including the marsh deer, roe deer, and several packs of wolves. Rare predators such as white-tailed eagles, golden eagles, and lesser spotted eagles circle the skies above the Red Marsh.

The park has several nature trails; stop by the visitors center in Osowiec-Twierdza, within the grounds of the 19th-century Osowiec Fortress, for more information.

AT A GLANCE

Biebrza marshes and wetlands ▪ Red Marsh Nature Reserve ▪ 228.6 square miles (592.2 sq km) ▪ Osowiec Fortress visitors center ▪ biebrza.org.pl

BIESZCZADY

A timeless place in nature, part of UNESCO's East Carpathian Biosphere Reserve

Imagine a dark green forest that has, in the words of the poet Andrew Marvell, the power to annihilate "all that's made / To a green thought in a green shade." Such is the power of the Edenic garden of Bieszczady National Park, located in the far southeast corner of Poland, on the borders of Slovakia and Ukraine. This green haven is 80 percent forests and embraces the Polish pinnacles of the Bieszczady Mountains. Wildlife abounds—bears, wolves,

Dawn light in the pine forest

wildcats, boars, otters, lynx, and 100 or so European bison roam this range. The park is also home to the largest Polish population of Aesculapian snakes. The species' common name, *Aesculape* in French, refers to the classical gods of healing (Greek Asclepius and Roman Aesculapius), whose temples the snake was encouraged to enter. Watch for these harmless brown reptiles as they slither up the great trees of Poland's healing green garden.

AT A GLANCE

Remote forest wilderness ▪ Bieszczady Mountains ▪ 112.7 square miles (292 sq km) ▪ Aesculapian snakes ▪ European bison ▪ bdpn.pl

BORY TUCHOLSKIE

Well-maintained boardwalk trails deep in the heart of the Tuchola Forest

This small park in the northern region of Poland is located deep in the heart of the Tuchola Forest, Poland's largest woodlands. Bory Tucholskie National Park is also the centerpiece of UNESCO's Tuchola Forest Biosphere Reserve. Aside from the protected forests, Bory Tucholskie is characterized by a string of forest lakes, meadows, and peatlands. The park centers around an area known as Seven Lakes Stream.

The Tuchola Forest region is a glacial landscape, carved out by the Scandinavian Glacier. Like parts of northern Germany toward the Baltic Sea, the area is characterized by sandy plains, and punctuated by dunes and long, narrow lakes. This is Poland's prime angling country, with more than 20 lakes in the park hosting 28 species of fish such as whitefish and gwyniads. Among the more pristine lakes are those around the villages of Wielkie Gacno, Nierybno, and Gluche. Anglers might also spot the European beaver in the park's waterways. Yachting is popular on Lake Charzykowy, and the park offers visitors a network of bicycle and hiking trails. Among them, the Kaszubski Trail leads from the historic city of Chojnice to the small village of Wiela.

The park is a heaven for birdwatching, with some 144 species; cranes inhabit the wetlands and eagle-owls haunt the woods. Although the symbol of the park, the wood grouse, has faded from the Forest District of Klosnowo, park authorities plan to reintroduce this bird.

AT A GLANCE

Tuchola Forest ▪ 17.8 square miles (46.1 sq km) ▪ Lake Charzykowy ▪ The Kaszubski Trail ▪ pnbt.com.pl/en

DRAWA

White-water rapids within the woodlands of the Drawsko Forest

Nestled within the massive Drawsko Forest, on the Drawsko Plain, lies this preserved area of woodlands and waterways. Drawa National Park takes its name from the fast-flowing River Drawa, which runs for 25 miles (40 km) through the park's boundaries. The park's landscapes encompass the deep valleys of both the Drawa and Plociczna Rivers, as well as the vast waterways that vein their peripheries, fanning out into a series of channels, lakes, and peat bogs. This plains countryside undulates considerably, with elevations varying by 100 feet (30 m) within the space of less than half a mile (0.4 km). The highest summit of 350 feet (106 m) is located near Martew Lake.

The fast pace and white-water rapids of the River Drawa attract kayakers. Visit little Lake Czarne, which is a meromictic lake, meaning that its layers do not mix—creating a saltier lower level, the phenomenon famously observed in the Black Sea. Interesting fish species in the lakes here include brook lamprey, salmon, trout, and Baltic vimba.

Many of the trees in Drawsko are older than 80 years with some 400-year-old oak trees also present. The forests are a nursery for more than 210 species of mushrooms, and watch on the trails for animals such as roe deer, red deer, wild boar, beavers, and occasional elk (moose) and grey wolves.

AT A GLANCE

Drawsko Forest landscapes ▪ 43.7 square miles (113.4 sq km) ▪ Drawa and Plociczna Rivers ▪ Salmon, trout, and Baltic vimba fishing ▪ Hiking and kayaking trails ▪ dpn.pl/en

GORCE

A highland park crossed by trails and a wide array of interesting fauna

Cross-country skiing trails lead high into the Beskid Mountains.

Gorce National Park sits within the Gorce Mountains, which are part of the Western Beskids, at the western end of the great Carpathians. The Gorce range is dramatized by the many arched peaks and river valleys carved into its landscapes. The highest of these peaks is Turbacz at 4,300 feet (1,310 m). Alpine and subalpine plants flourish on the meadows, and forests—mainly of spruce, beech, and fir trees—cover about 95 percent of the park.

The Beskid Mountains are a hospitable habitat for a wide range of creatures. Birds of prey include the honey buzzard, goshawk, and a variety of owls—the eagle-owl, Ural owl, and tawny owl among them. Game birds are plentiful, including hazel hen, black grouse, and capercaillie. Wander the trails and you'll also come across black storks, nutcrackers, ravens, and rock pipits.

The park has its share of large predators too: Wolves, lynx, and brown bears all hunt here, while red deer, roe deer, and wild boar rummage in the forests. The woods are alive with the common dormouse, fat dormouse, and forest dormouse. Many amphibians prosper here too: The spotted (or fire) salamander is the park symbol, and newts, European toads, and yellow-bellied toads all inhabit the park. Reptilians include sand lizards, blindworms, adders, and grass snakes.

The park visitors center in Poręba Wielka has details on hiking and skiing trails. While there, ask about Gorce's folk architecture, especially Jaworzyna Kamienicka's unique chapel, built in 1904 by Tomasz Chlipała, aka Bulanda, a legendary local folk wizard.

AT A GLANCE

Gorce Mountain landscapes ▪ 27.1 square miles (70.1 sq km) ▪ Hiking and skiing trails ▪ Bulanda's wizard chapel ▪ zpppn.pl/gorczanski-national-park-en/park

KAMPINOS

An escape into the forest wilderness just a few miles from Warsaw

A mist-shrouded marshland. The dawn twitter not of cell phones but of birdsong. Early risers say *cześć* ("hello" in Polish), and it would be easier to imitate the sound of one of this park's black storks, eagles, or grey herons than repeat the greeting; so, a nod and a smile suffice. Cyclists whiz by on the 124-mile (200-km) Kampinos Cycling Trail; there's a 224-mile (360-km) horse trail too. Kampinos National Park sits on the outskirts of Warsaw, and though 70 percent of the park is pine for-

Forest trails beckon Varsovians.

ests, the landscape also mixes sand dunes, meadows, and swamplands. The park's symbol is the elk (moose), but bikers and strollers may also see such endangered species as elk, beaver, and lynx, all of which have been reintroduced. The trails are rich in history too, leading to tombs of patriots from the 1863 anti-Russian uprising, cemeteries for WWII soldiers and resistance fighters, and at Żelazowa Wola on the park's outskirts, the manor house birthplace of composer Frédéric Chopin.

AT A GLANCE

Warsaw area park ▪ Historic sites ▪ 148.8 square miles (385.4 sq km) ▪ Żelazowa Wola manor house ▪ Kampinos Cycling Trail ▪ zpppn.pl/kampinoski-national-park-en/park

KARKONOSZE

A hikers' high mountain paradise with a wealth of wildlife

Few parks in Europe are more welcoming than Karkonosze: Visitors can avail of some 69.5 miles (112 km) of hiking paths, 10 ski lifts, and 12 guesthouses. The information center in Jelenia Góra will point you in the right direction whatever your reason for visiting this most accommodating of Polish national parks.

Karkonosze National Park sits in the Karkonosze Mountains of southwest Poland, along the border with Czechia. The neighboring Czech Krkonoše National Park (see page 342) extends the preserved area southward. This elevated park rises in the highest part of the Sudetes Mountains, which are themselves the highest part of the Bohemian Massif. Most of the park is mountain forests, lovely to walk through; these open out occasionally onto vistas of glacial lakes and cirques, steep rocky slopes, and peat bogs that shimmer with the movements of migratory birds, insects, amphibians, and fish. The graceful Szklarka waterfall,

surrounded by beech trees, is well worth the walk.

The highest peak is Śnieżka at 5,256 feet (1,602 m); this forms a triangle with the twin peaks of Śnieżnik and Ślęża that is traced by the challenging Red Hiking Trail. Hikers will enjoy landscapes teeming with wildlife, including the park's main attraction, mouflons, wild sheep brought here from western Europe at the start of the 20th century. The park also hosts several packs of gray wolves.

AT A GLANCE

Karkonosze Mountains ▪ 21.5 square miles (55.7 sq km) ▪ Bohemian Massif landscapes ▪ Tri-peak Red Hiking Trail ▪ zpppn.pl/karkonoski-national-park-en/park

MAGURA

Stroll through nature and history in the Magura Wątkowska highlands.

If you find yourself in southeast Poland, close to Slovakia, head for the village of Krempna and step inside the visitors center of Magura National Park; you have just escaped the modern world. The park covers the main part of the upper basin of the Wisłoka River, and consists mainly of forests. Here Scots pine dominate the foothills, and beech woods prevail above 1,740 feet (530 m), with some stands of fir and pine.

The focal point of the park is the Magura Wątkowska massif, with its highest peak, Wątkowa, standing at 2,779 feet (847 m). The Wisłoka River courses through the area, showcasing some picturesque ravines for hikers and kayakers. Throughout, you can observe a rich array of wildlife that includes 137 species of birds, including endangered species such as the eagle, eagle-owl, and delicately striding stork, unmistakable with its long stout orange bill. The park also hosts many endangered mammals, including lynx, wildcats, wolves, otters, and the cosmopoli-

tan brown bears that roam back and forth across the borders of Poland and Slovakia.

Humans too have left their mark: A ninth-century stronghold at Brzezowa, on the Walik mountain was built by the Wislanie tribe, and you'll see many wooden Orthodox churches, built by the Slavic Lemkos. In Olchowiec, you can visit a tiny museum of Lemko culture. World War I cemeteries are scattered about, as well as a burial ground for 1,250 Jews killed by the Nazis at the Halbów pass in 1942.

The Catholic church in Huta Polańska, destroyed in World War II and rebuilt in the 1990s

AT A GLANCE

Magura Wątkowska massif ▪ 75 square miles (194.3 sq km) ▪ Greek Orthodox churches ▪ World War I cemeteries ▪ magurskipn.pl/en/index.php

NAREW

A panoply of birds in the Narew Valley of northeast Poland

The waterways of Narew National Park host a wealth that is far out of proportion to its small size. Among the 179 species of birds present here are wetland inhabitants such as bitterns, marsh harriers, terns, spotted crakes, ruffs, and great snipes. Endangered birds breed here too, such as the aquatic warbler. Pride of place goes to the marsh harrier, the park's symbol, which nests in the dense reed beds. You'll recognize the female by her brown plumage with pale head, while the male sports a brown-and-gray tail and gray-black wings.

Narew National Park follows a 22-mile (35-km) stretch of the Narew River. The landscape is a swampy valley surrounded by moraine hills. The Narew is a braided river, with a network of channels separated by small, often temporary, islands called braid bars. This changing landscape creates several riparian area ecosystems, depending on the season and the level of the water table. Most of the Narew vegetation is characterized by tussock grasses with surrounding black alder and white willow forests.

The park's variety of habitats thus include marshes and reed beds as well as forests and meadows on higher ground. This brings a variety of mammals into the park including elk (moose), otter, and a healthy population of some 260 or so beavers.

The visitors center in Kurowo can direct you to the park's watery trails and to the hiking and cycling trails on its outskirts.

> **AT A GLANCE**
>
> Narew River Valley ▪ Extensive aquatic birdlife ▪ 28.4 square miles (73.5 sq km) ▪ Narew hiking trail ▪ Textile Workers' Walking Trail ▪ poland.pl/tourism/national-parks/narew-national-park

OJCÓW

A karst landscape and the enchanting village of Ojców

At the bottom of the scenic Prądnik Valley sits a tiny village that acts as the gateway into the Kraków-Częstochowa Upland. This is Ojców, heart of Ojców National Park, the smallest of the 23 national parks in Poland. Here, time slows and the past is ever present in a landscape of castles, caves, dramatic rock formations, and mysterious monadnocks.

The park's landscapes—topographically and underground—are those of a soluble karst bed-

Castle Pieskowa Skała, near Krakow

rock. Two rivers, the Prądnik and Saspówka, have carved out valleys with limestone cliffs, ravines, and more than 400 caves. The larg- est, Łokietek's Cave, is 1,050 feet (320 m) deep. The area is noted for its strange rock shapes, such as the gravity-defying Hercules' Club, an 82-foot (25-m) limestone column, and the White Hand rock—weathered stone that mimics fingers. More than 5,500 species live here, including many beetles and butterflies. Watch for the sleek ermine, and the 15 bat species that hibernate in the caves. The Renaissance castle at Pieskowa Skała is located on the scenic Trail of the Eagles' Nests.

> **AT A GLANCE**
>
> Village of Ojców ▪ Kraków-Częstochowa Upland ▪ 8.2 square miles (21.4 sq km) ▪ Pieskowa Skała castle ▪ Trail of the Eagles' Nests ▪ zpppn.pl/ojcowski-national-park-en/park

PIENINY

A brooding landscape alive with history and wildlife

This small national park has 21 miles (34 km) of hiking trails, and here in Pieniny National Park you walk in history's wake. In 1280, the Polish princess Kinga founded a monastery at Stary Sącz. Later the Czorsztyn Castle was built on the southern side of the Dunajec Valley. The Hungarians built a castle called Dunajec that now belongs to Poland and is called Niedzica. You can scale the peaks of Sokolica and Trzy Korony for fine views of the Pieniny and Tatra Mountains, or take an adventure downriver on a wooden raft.

Pieniny National Park protects vital woodlands in the heart of the Pieniny Mountains in the southernmost part of Poland. On the Slovak side of the mountains sits a twin park of the same name (see page 386).

The Pieniny karst mountain landscape has many limestone caves and cliffs. Dramatic rock walls rise up vertically from the Dunajec River. The highest peak, Trzy Korony (Three Crowns), soars 3,221 feet (982 m) above the forests and man-made meadows that host 640 kinds of mushrooms. On hiking trails, you may spot the lynx, as it soft-paws its way through the long grass or springs through the higher rocky grounds. Take extra care to avoid the venomous common European adder. Among other creatures to look for are the otter, along the banks of the Dunajec; the rare wallcreeper bird, in the limestone cliffs; and in the meadows, seek out the rare and beautiful Apollo butterfly, with its distinctive red spots.

AT A GLANCE

Pieniny karst mountain landscape ▪ Niedzica Castle ▪ 9 square miles (23.4 sq km) ▪ The Apollo butterfly ▪ Lynx ▪ pieninypn.pl/en

POLESIE

Vibrant wildlife belies the dark stain of history in this swampy park

Polesie National Park is located in eastern Poland in the historical region of Polesie. The topographical landscape of this small area consists of four former peat bog preserves, wetlands, and tundra-like forests. However, it is the dreadful historical significance of what happened on these marshlands that gives the park its real resonance. The area of Polesie is infamous for a "Jewish reservation"—a concentration camp complex—that the Nazis established here in 1939 after their invasion of Poland. Adolf Eichmann was given the task of removing all Jews from German-occupied lands. Within less than two years these marshlands would be the scene of dreadful large-scale atrocities. In these woods Hitler's "final solution" was implemented: Hundreds of thousands of Jews were murdered as part of Operation Reinhard. Today, these lands protect vital wildlife, and visitors can reflect on the horrors of mankind's worst instincts as they walk through the park.

Polesie: A place for reflection

AT A GLANCE

Swamp and bog wetlands ▪ Insurgent camp trail ▪ 37.7 square miles (97.6 sq km) ▪ Educational museum ▪ Turtle ponds ▪ Mietiułka biking and nature trail ▪ zpppn.pl/poleski-national-park-en/park

ROZTOCZE

A small park with a history of captive-breeding conservation

In east central Poland, a small park protects Roztocze, a land notable for its 112-mile (180-km) spine of hills. Today, the densely forested up-and-down landscapes of Roztocze National Park provide rich habitat for animals such as wolves, beavers, red deer, and European badgers, as well as birds including eagles, storks, and woodpeckers. The park also protects more than 400 ancient trees, including some of the largest firs in Poland, which grow up to 150 feet (50 m) high.

This legacy of conservation dates back to the 16th century when Jan Zamoyski, a Polish nobleman, created a zoo in the area called Zwierzyniec. Then deer, lynx, boars, wildcats, and tarpans were fostered in an enclosed area in the Bukowa Góra mountains. The zoo closed at the turn of the 19th century, but its modern-day successor, a nature reserve, lives on in the village of Zwierzyniec and in the surrounding mountains.

The national park is today best known for its program for breeding Polish koniks, the indigenous horses descended from wild forest horses called tarpans. Koniks have been bred in Roztocze since 1982, and they graze on 445 acres (180 ha) of parklands, with supplementary feeding in winter. The folks at the visitors center in Zwierzyniec will tell you where to see the koniks, and give you details on the five hiking paths and one cycling trail in the park. When out walking, look out for the poisonous European adder.

AT A GLANCE

Roztocze forest landscape ▪ 32.7 square miles (84.8 sq km) ▪ Konik horses ▪ Nature hiking trails ▪ roztoczanskipn.pl/pl

SŁOWIŃSKI

A Baltic coast park protects a fast-evolving landscape.

Słowiński National Park is located on the Baltic coast, between Łebsko and Rowy. The park's northern boundary stretches across 20.2 miles (32.5 km) of shoreline; this coast and the Słowiński wetlands lying slightly inland are protected by the park. The area, once a Baltic Sea bay, has evolved into a series of sand dunes, which creep inland at a rate of 10 to 33 feet (3 to 10 m) a year. These advancing dunes reach heights of up to 100 feet (30 m). The lakes of Łebsko and Gardno were once bays too, but are now isolated by the movement of dunes. Several rivers, including the Łebsko and the Łupawa, vein these waterways. The forests of Słowiński consist mainly of pine trees, surrounding several types of peat bogs.

The park offers some 87 miles (140 km) of hiking trails. You can climb observation towers to spot migrating birds that rest within these remote swamplands, including white-tailed eagles, eagle-owls, ravens, swans, and various kinds of ducks. Among the mammals you might encounter on the trails are deer, wild pigs, and the raccoon dog, an oddity of nature that looks like a cross between a fox and a raccoon.

The park is named after the Slavic people known as the Slovincians, a Kashubian tribe, who once lived in this swampy marshland at the edge of Lake Łebsko. To learn more, visit the village of Kluki, where there is an open-air museum that celebrates Slovincian history and culture.

AT A GLANCE

Słowiński wetlands ▪ Baltic sand dunes ▪ 71.8 square miles (186.1 sq km) ▪ Bird-watching observation towers ▪ Raccoon dogs ▪ zpppn.pl/slovinski-national-park-en/park

STOŁOWE MOUNTAINS

A labyrinth of fascinating sandstone formations on the Czechia border

Stołowe Mountains National Park sits on Poland's western border with Czechia, amid summits sometimes known as the Table Mountains, part of the Sudetes range. The forests here are mostly spruce, introduced at the turn of the 19th century to replace beech and fir forests that had been cut.

The topography of Stołowe features notable rock formations whose shapes have inspired their fanciful names, among them Kwoka (Hen), Wielblad (Camel),

Among Błędne Skały (Errant Rocks)

and Glowa Wielkoluda (Giant's Head). Also scattered across the park are many rock labyrinths, the result of millions of years of erosion on this porous sandstone landscape.

The park's trails total 62 miles (100 km) in length, leading to places such as the "Rocky City" atop Szczeliniec Wielki, at 3,015 feet (919 m). Hiking the park's forests takes you into the realm of red deer, wild pig, hedgehogs, and reptiles such as lizards and adders.

AT A GLANCE

Stołowe Mountains forest landscapes ▪ Sandstone labyrinths ▪ 24.4 square miles (63.3 sq km) ▪ Glowa Wielkoluda rock formation ▪ pngs.com.pl/index_gb.html

ŚWIĘTOKRZYSKI

A forested park in central Poland with a distinctly spiritual feel

Świętokrzyski National Park, in central Poland, protects the highest ridge of the Świętokrzyskie (Holy Cross) Mountains—the Łysogory—and its two highest peaks: Łysica at 2,008 feet (612 m) and Łysa Góra (Bald Mountain) at 1,952 feet (595 m). It also encompasses the eastern part of the Klonowski Ridge and part of the Pokrzywianski Ridge. Forests cover the vast majority of the park, and Świętokrzyski is famous for its trees, with 674 specimens protected as natural monuments. Most

of the forests are pine and beech, with scattered fir stands along with some mixed oak-fir forests. An area of endemic Polish larch can also be found in Chełmowa Góra, the nature reserve on the slopes of Chełmowa Mountain, which was the first protected area within Świętokrzyski. The park authorities have in recent years planted about 1,300 reintroduced yew trees to the area.

Visitors to the park should make an effort to see the 12th-century Benedictine Holy Cross Abbey,

located on the summit of Łysa Góra. This hosts the oldest example of Polish writing in existence–*Kazania Świętokrzyskie* (the Holy Cross Sermons). Łysa Góra also has a stone embankment, piled with quartzitic sandstone boulders, which has long been a site of religious rituals.

The park's visitors center in Bodzentyn has details of all hiking trails. Watch for the common shrew, the rarer pygmy shrew, which is Poland's smallest mammal, and the water shrew.

AT A GLANCE

Central Polish religious landscape ▪ 29.4 square miles (76.2 sq km) ▪ Benedictine Holy Cross Abbey ▪ Shrews ▪ Łysa Góra sandstone embankment ▪ zpppn.pl/swietokrzyski-national-park-en/park

TATRA

Where eagles circle above serrated mountain peaks

Meadows of purple giant crocus (Crocus tommasinianus) *are a spring joy.*

One of Europe's great untamed wildernesses soars where two mountain ranges meet, the High Tatras and the Western Tatras on Poland's southern border. Tatra National Park has scenery that takes the breath away: Its 23 glacial lakes are crystalline mirrors of the changing skies above, framed mostly by forests of spruce, European beech, and silver fir.

The Tatras Mountains are more than 65 million years old, formed by retreating glaciers that left behind a beautiful landscape of jagged peaks, sharp-cut valleys, and silt-covered moraines. Underground, you can delve into an intricate labyrinth of 650 caverns with karst curiosities to delight even the most experienced cavers.

HUMAN HISTORY

The human footprint goes deep in these hills: Herding flocks to the hilltop meadows has been a summer ritual for centuries here. Mining and ironworking depleted the forests throughout the 18th and 19th centuries, while ethnic Góral or highlander communities have nurtured a culture of traditional folk music, cheesemaking, and distinctive wooden architecture. The Góral culture was traditionally passed on in oral stories, as this ethnic group spread across southern Poland, northern Slovakia, and the region of Cieszyn Silesia in the Czech Republic. Their mountain culture is celebrated each August in Zakopane's Festival of Highland Folklore when horse-and-carriage parades sweep through the town and much festivity ensues. The town is also where you'll find the park's main visitors center.

Authorities have taken steps to learn the lessons of the past, so when the ski industry took off in Zakopane, slightly north of the park, in the latter half of the 20th century, certain slopes within its bounds remained protected. In 1992, the Polish Tatras park was twinned with Tatranský National Park (see page 389) across the Slovakian border, forming a UNESCO biosphere reserve. The Tatra Mountains form a natural border between Poland to the north and Slovakia to the south, and the neighboring countries have been partners in conservation efforts since the early 20th century.

TRAILS & ACTIVITIES

Tatra National Park has multiple hiking, horseback riding, and skiing trails to pursue, and peaks of every degree of difficulty to climb. The bare rock peak of Świnica (or Svinica in Slovak—it means swine either way) is an ascent of 7,549 feet (2,301 m). A marked trail leads to the summit. Triple-peaked Rysy gives the options of a central peak of 8,212 feet (2,503 m); a northwestern summit of 8,199 feet (2,499 m); or a southeastern climb of some 8,114 feet (2,473 m). Or you can simply take the lazy way and hop aboard the popular cable car to the lookout at Kasprowy Wierch, where sweeping views of these rugged mountain landscapes await. The summit station is situated next to the highest meteorological observatory in Poland at 6,519 feet (1,987 m).

In winter, you can take your choice of the mountain slopes between the shorter Dolina Gąsienicowa skiing trail and the longer pistes of Goryczkowa. One word of warning though: You will be fined for wandering off-piste in these dangerous mountains, where avalanches are always a possibility.

Hiking to glacial lakes, such as Morskie Oko, is a treat, especially in springtime when the meadows fill with wildflowers. Plants to look for include edelweiss and the stemless white-flowering carline thistle. Spring in the Kościeliska Valley brings fields of purple giant crocus.

The Five Ponds Valley Trail is a demanding 15.5-mile (25-km) loop that takes in Morskie Oko, as well as the waterfalls of Wodogrzmoty Mickiewicza and Wielka Siklawa, the park's highest at 230 feet (70 m). Along the way, you might spot wolves, bears, or lynx, all of which still find refuge here in the Tatras. Watch too for the Tatra chamois in the rocky highlands, and marvel at their hoofed agility. There are only about 250 of this local subspecies of the goat-antelope in the park. Red deer haunt the woods with their fleeting presence, pursued by lynx and wolves. Hunting wolves was banned in Poland in 1998, and the populations have since bounced back to sustainable numbers. The fate of the golden eagle has not been so fortune-blessed, and Tatra National Park is one of the last refuges in Poland for this majestic bird. Other trails on which to explore this beautiful wilderness include the 8.6-mile (14-km) Kościeliska caves circuit from Kiry to the karst subterranean underworlds of the Mroźna and Mylna caves, and the 8.6-mile (14-km) Lenin Trail from Kuźnice to Hala Gąsienicowa that takes in the wooded Boczan ridge.

Wherever you roam in Tatra National Park, always take three precautions: Check the weather forecast, as conditions on the mountains can change in the time it takes to say *piękny dzień* ("beautiful day" in Polish); inform someone of where you are going and when you'll be back; and finally, do as all good Polish hikers do, and pack plenty of *kabanosy*, the local air-dried sausage that is perfect for a long day out on the trails.

Kasprowy Wierch (Kasper Peak) in the Western Tatra Mountains

AT A GLANCE

Tatras Mountain landscapes ▪ 81.7 square miles (212 sq km) ▪ Kościeliska caves ▪ The Lenin Trail ▪ zpppn.pl/tatra-national-park-en/park

WARTA MOUTH
Wetlands for birds and accommodations for bird lovers

Warta Mouth National Park also goes by the name Ujście Warty, with the Polish word *ujście* indicating the termination of a river at another river rather than the sea. The park runs along the lowest stretch of the Warta River, and runs as far as its confluence with the River Oder, which delineates the Polish–German border. Its swampy landscape and plentiful muddy waters and marshlands make it a perfect bird sanctuary.

The floodplains of the Warta, especially the Northern Polder, provide habitat for a host of migrating and nesting birds. Some 245 species of birds are found here, including several species of ducks. Among the 26 endangered species that are protected in the park are the aquatic warbler, corn crake, godwit, Eurasian crane, great bittern, little bittern, and black tern, which is known in England as the blue darr. (Is he black or is he blue? It might have something to do with the more northerly light shining on his feathers. Or the bespectacled eyesight of the bird-watcher.) Beavers and otters are the main mammals in this aquatic park.

The main visitors center of the park is located in the village of Chyrzyno, and there you'll get details of the park's hiking and cycling trails as well as two nature trails. The park also offers a small lodge with rooms and a guesthouse for larger groups.

AT A GLANCE

Swampland bird sanctuary ▪ Guest accommodations ▪ 31 square miles (80.3 sq km) ▪ Bird-watching nature trails ▪ zpppn.pl/warta-river-mouth-national-park-en/park

WIELKOPOLSKI
A peaceful oasis for hikers in lakeland

Wielkopolski National Park (or the National Park of Greater Poland) sits about nine miles (15 km) south of Poznań. The park embraces part of the Poznań Lakeland as well as parts of Poznań's Warta gorge. The flat landscape was shaped by glacial activity, resulting in several tunnel-valley lakes. The most beautiful of these is Góreckie Lake, with its two islands. Also of note is Skrzynka Lake, partly covered by a thick layer of peat bogs. Trout,

Old oaks are protected in the park.

pike, and eel inhabit these waterways. Huge, glacially deposited rocks include the protected natural monument Głaz Leśników. Most of the forests are composed of pine trees, with some old oaks, and these woods host vast numbers of beetles and spiders, as well as black woodpeckers. Buzzards are the main avian predator.

Drop into the visitors center in the village of Jeziory for details of the seven park trails, then try to visit the 17th-century wooden church in Łódź, or one of the churches in Komorniki, Puszczykowo, Stęszew, or Wiry.

AT A GLANCE

Lakeland park ▪ 29.2 square miles (75.8 sq km) ▪ 17th-century Łódź church ▪ Hiking trails ▪ zpppn.pl/wielkopolska-national-park-en/park

WIGRY

An anglers' dream in one of Poland's most secluded backwaters

If you like fishing, welcome to paradise. Encompassing parts of both the Masurian Lake District and the Augustów Primeval Forest of northeastern Poland, Wigry National Park is named after Lake Wigry, the largest of the park's many lakes. Others worth flinging a line out into include Pierty, Leszczewek, and Mulaczysko. The Masurian chain of lakes, some interlinked by canal, begins 150 miles (240 km) northeast of Warsaw and stretches nearly to the Kaliningrad

Lake Pierty: Anglers' heaven

(Russian) and Lithuanian borders. In these waters, you'll find 32 species of fish, including pike, lake trout, European catfish, brown trout, and the indigenous crayfish. Your only competition will be an occasional friendly fellow fisherman, who might offer you a beer, or an industrious European beaver, who won't have the time. Carry on fishing, admiring the endless array of lakes with shores lined with fir forests, and peat bogs rising behind them.

AT A GLANCE

Lake and peat bog landscapes ▪ 58.2 square miles (150.8 sq km) ▪ Masurian lakes ▪ Superb fishing ▪ wigry.org.pl/index_en.html

WOLIN

An island park that hosts a population of European bison and a multitude of birds

Wolin National Park is located at the mouth of the Oder River on the island of Wolin, close to the German border. The park's attractions include the sea cliffs of Gosań and Kawcza Góra, which overlook the Bay of Pomerania, and a wisent (European bison) sanctuary. The landscape of the park incorporates nine miles (15 km) of cliffs that rise up to 312 feet (95 m) above the Baltic Sea. This is a landscape in flux: With coastal erosion, the cliffs recede approximately 30 inches (80 cm) every year.

Moraine hills dominate the interior. The vegetation of the park is varied for a saline and sand environment. More than 1,300 vascular plant species have been recorded on Wolin Island, with many rare and protected species among the plants used to anchor the sand dunes, such as sea-beach sandwort, lyme grass, sea rocket, spiny saltwort, and several saltwater plants.

The steep slopes of the cliffs are overgrown by common sea buckthorn. The park hosts more than 230 bird species: White-tailed sea eagles, aquatic warblers, and red-breasted flycatchers all breed here, and many waterfowl stop over during spring and fall migrations. The eagle-owl has been reintroduced recently so look for this magnificent predator's distinctive ear tufts. Watch too in the park's beech forests for the stag beetle, with its crablike claws.

AT A GLANCE

Baltic coastal landscape ▪ 42.2 square miles (109.3 sq km) ▪ Sea cliffs of Gosań and Kawcza Góra ▪ European bison sanctuary ▪ wolinpn.pl

LITHUANIA

Lithuania is one of Europe's most surprising countries. Its people are worldly rule-breakers who enjoy life, come what may. Here you will find a Hill of Crosses, as well as a park filled with sculptures of Soviet-era leaders (the famous Grūtas Park, nicknamed Stalin World). Capital city Vilnius is beguilingly baroque and bohemian. Lithuania's national parks are likewise filled with history and mystery and, sometimes, the shock of the new: In Curonian Spit National Park, you'll visit Witches' Hill, if you dare; Trakai, with its stunning redbrick island castle on Lake Galvė, is Europe's only historical national park; while Dzūkija National Park welcomes with its futuristic, dome-shaped glass visitors center. The landscapes of the five national parks of this small Baltic state range from shifting sands and white beaches to lush, forested lakelands to castle-populated hills. Surprising Lithuania has it all.

Opposite: A field of water lilies float before Trakai Island Castle, Trakai Historical National Park.

AUKŠTAITIJA

In the heart of Lithuania's lake district

When the sun sets on Lake Lūšiai (Wild Cat Lake) in Palūšė, you might see the silhouette of a stork on a rock as twilight reels into darkness. Come back 12 hours later and you may spot a white-tailed eagle emerging from a hunting foray in the forests, the swooshing sound of the great predator's wings carried across the surface of the lake, shrouded in early morning mist. This is Lithuania's lake district, the site of Aukštaitija National Park, Lithuania's first national park, established in 1974 under the name Lithuanian SSR National Park. It was renamed in 1991, when the Soviet era was over and the opening of the country's four other parks heralded a new era in conservation.

THE LANDSCAPES

About one-fifth of the national park is strictly protected; you can only visit the Trainiškis Wildlife Sanctuary and Ažvinčiai Forest Reserve if accompanied by a park ranger. Most of the park's landscape is covered with forests, mainly of pine, spruce, and deciduous trees. Some of these trees are more than 200 years old, planted in an age when the Russians, Prussians, and Habsburgs all sought control of Lithuania. The planters may be long gone, along with the Soviets, but these glorious trees still stand tall.

The park's many lakes make it a popular destination for kayaking, boating, fishing, and water sports. Some 126 lakes nestle among the woods and hills, interconnected by an extensive waterway of rivulets and streams. The largest of the lakes is Lake Kretuonas with an area of 3.2 square miles (8.29 sq km). Also here is Lake Tauragnas, the deepest lake in Lithuania, with a depth of 198.5 feet (60.5 m). A quirk of nature occurs on one of Lake Baluošas' seven islands, where a small lake sits upon a lake island—only in Lithuania!

The River Žeimena veins the park for 13.6 miles (22 km), providing a shoreline for fine trails; another trail leads up to Ladakalnis hill, a national geomorphological monument. You can climb this to get an excellent view of six of the park's lakes and join the locals who leave stones by the oak tree as an offering to the goddess Lada.

Aukštaitija is famous for its biodiversity—59 percent of all plant species in Lithuania can be found within park boundaries, including 64 separate species of plants. Eight species of fungus also grow here, and 48 species of bird make their homes in the park, including the golden eagle.

THE HUMAN FOOTPRINT

Human life abounds here too, with 116 villages in the park inhabited by about 2,300 residents. The main village of Palūšė is worth visiting for its beautiful old church, built in 1750 and thought to be the oldest surviving wooden church in Lithuania. Stripeikiai is the park's oldest village, famed for its Lithuanian Museum of Ancient Beekeeping. Honey farmers, or apiarists (or sometimes even apiculturists), have been reaping honey and wax from bee yards for many centuries in Lithuania. Stop by the village of Ginučiai to view the workings of its famous 19th-century watermill.

Some 45 burial sites within the park date from the 4th through 12th centuries A.D. and feature hundreds of burial mounds. These tumuli are usually surrounded by a ring of stones or a shallow ditch. The ancient Lithuanians were buried with objects they might need in the afterlife—jewelry, tools, guns, and even horses to spirit them safely through the underworld. The park also has several ancient *piliakalnis* ("fortification mounds"), such as the Taurapilis mound on the southern shore of Lake Tauragnas. The visitors center, located in the village of Palūšė, has information on all activities and trails, including the wooden sculpture trail around Lake Lūšiai that highlights aspects of Lithuanian folklore.

This working windmill adorns Lithuania's first national park.

AT A GLANCE

Trainiškis Wildlife Sanctuary and Ažvinčiai Forest Reserve ▪ 156.6 square miles (405.7 sq km) ▪ Taurapilis mound ▪ Wooden sculpture folklore trail ▪ aparkai.lt/en

CURONIAN SPIT

A long tail of sand curling into the Baltic Sea

The Curonian Spit is a 60.8-mile-long (98-km), curved, sand-dune strip separating the Curonian Lagoon from the Baltic Sea coast. Its southerly section lies within Kaliningrad Oblast, part of Russia; its northerly portion (running 32.3 miles/52 km) extends within southwestern Lithuania. Both countries protect their dunes as national parks. The spit was formed with a glacial moraine as its foundation; winds and sea currents deposited sufficient sand to raise these dunes above sea level. Curonian Spit National Park has the tallest moving sand dunes in Europe, with an average height of 115 feet (35 m). Dune ridges, wetlands, meadows, and pine forests are also part of the landscape.

The spit's German settlers were ousted after World War II by the Soviets, who changed many place-names. Following the breakup of the Soviet Union, many German descendants of former inhabitants have returned to vacation on the Curonian Spit, especially at Nida.

Hikers will relish the Baltic breezes along the trails, and you might try kitesurfing. Look for the huge granite sundial on Parnidis dune, which is also a calendar and a seasonal measure of solstices and equinoxes. Vecekrugas dune gives 200-foot-high (60-m) views of the spit. There are also platforms for bird-watchers to view the 10 to 20 million birds that pass through in spring and fall, herons and cormorants among them. Look, too, for the wild boar with its surprisingly dainty hooves.

AT A GLANCE

Baltic moraine and dune landscapes ▪ 102 square miles (264 sq km) ▪ Vecekrugas dune ▪ Bird-watching platforms ▪ nerija.lt/en

DZŪKIJA

A brooding lake and forest preserve

Dzūkija National Park preserves the pine forests and picturesque villages of Dzūkija, a cultural region in southern Lithuania, and encompasses a significant area around the banks of the Neman River. It is the country's largest national park and enjoys a more continental climate than most of Lithuania. The mainland dune massifs located in Marcinkonys, Lynežeris, Grybaulia, and Šunupis are its most significant landscapes, along with the country's largest swamp,

Dusk descends on Neman's riverbanks.

the Čepkeliai marsh, located south of Marcinkonys, where the park's visitors center is located. Near the Ūla River and within the park lies the village Zervynos, which dates back to 1742; today, this serves as a living history site, with 48 homesteads providing insight into rural life in the 18th and 19th centuries. Eight of these homesteads, along with 32 other buildings, are now preserved as national ethnographic monuments. The Saint Petersburg-Warsaw Railway runs through the village, which is also renowned for beekeeping: Two old pine trees with hollows for bees are preserved as natural monuments.

AT A GLANCE

Mainland dune massifs ▪ Pine forests ▪ 212.4 square miles (550 sq km) ▪ Zervynos ethnographic village ▪ Čepkeliai marsh ▪ wigry.org.pl/dzukija.htm

TRAKAI

Keeping the past alive for future generations

The redbrick gothic castle of Trakai, in its fairy-tale lakeside setting, is a must-see for every traveler to Lithuania. Trakai Historical National Park opened in 1992, to protect the intriguing community of Trakai, some 15.5 miles (25 km) west of Vilnius, and the forests, lakes, and villages in its surrounds.

The park encompasses hill forts, castles, manors, villages, and isolated farmsteads. All are connected to a citadel that was fiercely defended throughout a tumultuous

Trakai reflects a multiethnic history.

history. The multiethnic town of Trakai evolved to embrace Lithuanians, Karaites, Tatars, Jews, Russians, Germans, and Poles. Along-side a largely Catholic congregation, Orthodox, Muslim, Jewish, and Karaite communities flourished in Trakai too.

The park runs guided tours of the Užutrakis Manor Estate, which tell the story of the Tyszkiewicz family. The tours also take in the 198-acre (80-ha) Užutrakis Park, with an introduction to its flora and fauna. Nature lovers may also tour the Varnikai Botanical-Zoological Reserve, which highlights the park's wildlife and rare plants, mosses, and lichens.

AT A GLANCE

Historic city of Trakai ▪ 32 square miles (82 sq km) ▪ Užutrakis Manor Estate ▪ Varnikai Botanical-Zoological Reserve ▪ seniejitrakai.lt/news

ZEMAITIJA

A Cold War strategic site amid a rustic backwater of lakes and forests

A gentle hike around the 2.4-mile (4.1-km) Šeirė Educational Nature Path near Plateliai is an excellent introduction to many of the delights of Zemaitija National Park. Along this route you'll observe Šeirė forest, the Gaudupis Mire, and perhaps some local birds such as the black stork or the corn crake, as well as wildlife such as lynx and otters. This national park is set on the Samogitian highlands, just 28 miles (45 km) from the Baltic Sea. Lake Platelių is the largest of several lakes in the park.

From the town, Cold War history buffs should head for Plokštinė missile base, a massive underground site constructed by the Soviets in 1960 at the height of tensions between the superpowers. The base is located near the village of Plokščiai in the sparsely populated Plokštinė forest. This site constituted the Soviet Union's first nuclear missile base, built mainly to accommodate underground R-12 Dvina ballistic medium-range missiles as close to the West as was then possible. In 2012, some 23 years after the fall of the Soviet Union, a Cold War Museum was opened at the site, and visitors from both sides of the old Iron Curtain can now descend into one of the four existing silos and ponder the strange subterranean lives of those who lived with their fingers on the keys of nuclear Armageddon. It's interesting, too, to wonder at which Western cities the missiles maintained here were once trained upon.

AT A GLANCE

Samogitian highlands landscape ▪ Šeirė Educational Nature Path ▪ 83.8 square miles (217.2 sq km) ▪ The Cold War Museum at Plokštinė missile base ▪ zemaitijosnp.lt/en

LATVIA

Latvia is the quiet, young country at the European party, the unassuming guest who turns out to be a fascinating character with a riveting story to tell. The country is sandwiched in the middle of the Baltic triplets, reborn in the 1990s, with Lithuania to the south and Estonia to the north. Onion-domed Orthodox cathedrals are everywhere in this once Communist-ruled country, and in the capital, Riga, you'll discover Europe's finest examples of art nouveau architecture, colorfully decorated along cobblestone streets. As you move into the countryside, there are pine forests, caves, trails, and Soviet bunkers to explore at Gauja National Park, not to mention the magnificent Turaida Stone Castle. Alternately, you can walk across the great bog of Ķemeri, as well as enjoy the glorious Latgale Lakelands at Rāznas National Park. And you'll still have the desolate Baltic seashores along the Courland Peninsula to relish, where Cape Kolka at Slītere National Park has the haunted feel of the end of the world. Everywhere you go in the country, you'll find a variety of landscapes from isolated beaches to broad-leaved forests, boggy wetlands to boreal woods, all filled with fascinating Baltic flora and fauna.

Opposite: Trails in Ķemeru National Park take visitors across three types of wetlands, with a multitude of wild plants and wildlife to enjoy along the way.

GAUJA

Pine forests, medieval castles, and myriad activities

If you've ever wanted to fly like a bird, your dream can take memorable wing on the zip lines at Gauja National Park. Soar high above the pine forests, then experience free fall at the Aerodium wind tunnel near Sigulda. Or bungee jump in Sigulda from 140 feet (43 m) above the Gauja River. Or hike to Eagles' Cliffs on the Gauja River for authentic avian action. This is a park with an array of activities: Cavers can descend into subterranean nirvana at Gutmanala, the Baltic's largest grotto. Speed seek-

The knights' stronghold in Sigulda

ers can ride down the Sigulda luge and bobsled track. Hikers or kayakers can travel to admire an array of massive rock outcrops, including the Kuku Cliffs on the Gauja River, the sandstone and dolomite of Zvartes Rock and Kaubju Ridge on the Amata River, and the sandstone of the Anfabrika Cliffs along the Ligatne River.

Gauja is Latvia's largest national park, and it follows the valley of the Gauja River. Scattered about are medieval castles. Prime among these is Turaida Stone Castle, situated within a museum reserve where you can look from medieval ramparts or stride like a knight of old along verdant hiking trails.

AT A GLANCE

Pine forests and medieval castles ▪ 354.2 square miles (917.4 sq km) ▪ Adventure activities
▪ The Amata Geological Trail ▪ latvia.travel/en/sight/gauja-national-park

ĶEMERU

A park of forests and lakes amid a great bog

Located just west of the city of Jūrmala, Ķemeru National Park is a place of natural therapy within an area renowned for spa resorts. The park today protects landscapes where natural mineral springs and mud baths gained an international clientele that flocked to its resorts, spas, and sanitoriums. Ķemeru has natural sulfur springs, due to its sublayer of gypsum and soil bacteria forming hydrogen sulfide gas, which dissolves in the water.

Here, the Great Ķemeri Bog is the focal point of a mire wilderness that stretches for miles, with a network of wooden boardwalks constructed across the marshlands to serve hikers throughout the park. The area features all three types of wetland—fens, transition, and raised bogs. Many plants thrive in the bog, especially mosses and orchids. Watch as you hike above the waters for a wide variety of rare species, such as native snails and mussels, storks,

and otters. The wetlands are home to birds such as common cranes, while raised bogs provide vital habitat for wood sandpipers and European golden plovers. As you cross the bogs, you can feast on several edible berries that grow wild here, including cranberries, crowberries, cloudberries, and blueberries. Nature trails start at Lake Slokas, Forest House, and Lake Kanieris, and are an excellent way to learn about the wetlands of Latvia.

AT A GLANCE

Great Ķemeri Bog ▪ 147.3 square miles (381.6 sq km) ▪ Boardwalk trails and observation towers
▪ Natural sulfur springs ▪ latvia.travel/en/sight/kemeri-national-park

RĀZNAS

A lakeland park protecting some of Latvia's most cherished natural resources

Within the historical and cultural region of Latgale gleam the Latgale Lakelands, among the loveliest in eastern Europe. In 2007, Rāznas National Park was established to protect these extensive waterways, mainly Lake Rāznas, the second largest lake in Latvia, and its environs.

Lake Rāznas itself covers an area of 22.2 square miles (57.5 sq km), and is often referred to as the Latgale Sea on account of its sandy beaches. Rāznas is a great place to rent a boat and head out for a day's fishing. If it's chilly,

take a flask of Latvia's famous Black Balsam, the 45-proof national liquor sure to calm the shivers. Out on this well-stocked lake, you might even witness some industrial fishing with nets. Should you find yourself here in wintertime, be adventurous, bundle up, and try your hand at ice fishing.

You can also climb to the top of the 814-foot (248-m) Mākoņkalns hill next to Lake Rāznas to view the preserved ruins of the stone Volkenberg Castle, built by the Livonian Order in the 13th century.

Valuable ecosystems of deciduous forests that nurture many rare species of plants are found on several of the 30 or so islands dotting Lake Eša Ezers. Throughout the lakelands, reed beds and rushes are alive with wildlife, and the seminatural grasslands around the lakes are cultivated by the park authorities to nurture local fauna.

The Latgale region is culturally Russian, home to a large population of ethnic Russians, especially in the main city of Daugavpils. There is also a significant Polish minority.

SLĪTERE

Latvia's smallest park is a coastal treasure with a haunted feel.

Follow the Northern Kurzeme Peninsula out to the point of Cape Kolka, at the end of the Irbe Strait, and you will soon find yourself at the southern exit of the Bay of Riga. Slītere National Park covers much of this desolate cape and about 39 square miles (101 sq km) of the Baltic Sea. On land, the Zilie Kalni, or Blue Hills, are covered with broad-leaved forests, and park trails offer superb views of the peninsula, as does the Slītere Lighthouse. The River

Green light pervades the forest.

Irbe follows the coastline toward the sea, and its brown brackish waters constantly shift the sandbanks in the estuary. In late fall, watch for brown trout migrating upriver to spawn. Millions of birds pass over Slītere, such as the bar-tailed godwit on its way south from the northern tundra in fall, and the great grey owl that migrates here from Russia. Swamp turtles, wolves, lynx, and copperhead snakes all inhabit this appealing national park.

ESTONIA

Estonia may be geographically linked to its Balkan siblings to the south and Russia to the east, but its people have always gone their own way. Consider that ancient Estonians were among the last Europeans to be Christianized, following the Livonian Crusade of the 13th century. They also refused to cede their notoriously difficult language through centuries of occupation by Sweden, Nazi Germany, and the Soviet Union. In the 21st century, Estonia was the first democracy to hold an election online. The country's five national parks evoke a proud pagan land that refuses conquest or colonization: Lahemaa National Park, a land of bays and manor houses, is one of Europe's largest; Karula is a preserve of forests, lakes, and marshes; Matsalu is one of Europe's best bird-watching destinations; Soomaa has its own "fifth season," when the forests turn into lakes; and remote Vilsandi is an island park in the wilds of the Baltic Sea.

Opposite: Vilsandi Lighthouse, built in 1809, welcomed home generations of the nation's seafarers.

KARULA

Estonia's smallest park is a natural gem in the south.

The park's towers afford views of rolling hills and blue lakes.

Climb to the top of the 100-foot (30-m) Rebasejärve Tornimähi Observation Tower and you'll enjoy a fine panorama of Karula National Park: On a clear day, all around you, you'll see blue lakes and densely forested rolling hills with myriad shades of green.

This is a legendary landscape, filled with stories of fairies, ghosts, and witches alleged to dwell around the area woods, lakes, and ancient stone burial mounds. The park's focal point is Ähijärv, a large and peaceful lake surrounded by woodlands and reed beds. Locals have considered this place sacred since pagan times.

The flora of Karula is particularly varied, and includes several species listed as endangered in Estonia such as the Baltic orchid, mezereon (with its vivid red berries), and the daisyleaf grape-fern. This latter plant is as delicate as it is rare, and also goes by the names chamomile grape-fern and matricary grape-fern.

As you hike through these beautiful parklands, watch for a host of threatened species, such as the pond bat, the lesser spotted eagle, and the distinctive black stork, easily identified by his white underplumage, thick black "jacket," and long red bill (and legs). The park's many meadows provide ideal habitats for butterflies, bumblebees, bees, and beetles. Birds that thrive in such open landscapes include the Eurasian skylark and the corn crake. You might also spot several of the park's larger mammals such as elk (moose), lynx, or polecats.

THE HUMAN FOOTPRINT

Look too for the human footprint: Karula National Park has more than a hundred farmsteads, many dating back several hundred years. This is an area of dispersed settlement, with farmsteads scattered between the hills. The farm buildings are generally log structures, typical of those built throughout Latvia in the early 20th century.

The park strives to protect these human settlements and to preserve the village architecture, the traditional way of life, and the Võro dialect that evolved here over the course of several centuries.

The visitors center by Lake Ähijärv has maps for the park's many trails. Ask also about the smoke saunas in the park. Saturday is locally called *puulpäiv*, meaning "half day," as people work only until midday; the rest of the day is dedicated to heating and enjoying the sauna, where meat is still smoked. For Estonians, a sauna is a sacred place, and a smoke sauna is believed to cleanse not only the body, but also the soul.

AT A GLANCE

Karula hills ▪ Lake Ähijärv ▪ 47 square miles (123 sq km) ▪ The Ähijärv Trail (2.3 miles/4 km)
▪ loodusegakoos.ee/where-to-go/national-parks/karula-national-park

LAHEMAA

Bog boardwalks, empty beaches, forest walks, and manor houses in the land of bays

If you camp in the beautiful bay of Lahemaa these days, you are pitching your tent on beaches that the Soviet military once covered in military hardware and barbed wire. Yet somehow, in 1971, the canny Estonians convinced their occupiers that this place would be ideal for the U.S.S.R.'s first national park, *nyet?*

The park landscape is Estonia writ small: coastlines indented with peninsulas and beautiful bays, plus an interior of pine forests, lakes, rivers, and bogs. Picturesque villages dot the park amid gently rolling hills that encourage the laziest of cyclists to explore. In the wilds, bears and lynx roam, while beavers busy themselves making their river lodges. The park also preserves the manor houses and estates of the Baltic-German aristocrats who once called Lahemaa home. Käsmu celebrates a host of legendary sea captains from this nation of sailors, and the art museum of Viinistu showcases contemporary Estonian artists. The visitors center at Palmse has details of all museums, trails, and activities.

In spring and fall, the aptly named Beaver Trail travels a 0.6-mile (1-km) walkway past beaver dams on the Altja Oja River. The Viru Bog Trail takes you across the marsh to a viewing tower, while the Oandu Old-Growth Forest Nature Trail is a 2.9-mile (4.7-km) loop through virgin forest. On the latter, signs point out where animal activities have left their mark, such as bear claw marks and bark eaten by elk (moose). Winter is particularly attractive in this park, when people (and mosquitoes) dissipate, the seas freeze, and snow rolls out its white carpet for hikers who brave the windy shorelines and frigid forests.

Wooden walkways and bird-watching towers make these bogs a nature lover's delight.

AT A GLANCE

Lahemaa's varied landscapes ▪ 280 square miles (725 sq km) ▪ Aristocratic manor houses ▪ Oandu Old-Growth Forest Nature Trail ▪ kaitsealad.ee/eng/lahemaa-national-park

MATSALU

A bird-watcher's marshland paradise

Migrant barnacle geese (Branta leucopsis) *rest and forage at a roost site in Matsalu Bay.*

Matsalu National Park is one of the key staging grounds for migratory birds in Europe. Flocks of birds fill these Baltic skies, sweeping over the vast marshlands. Dissociate yourself from your human perch on the bird-watching tower for a moment and you can envisage this scene in medieval times, in pre-Christian times, or even when the primeval forest was taking root.

Some 282 species are known to make landfall here, and in spring or autumn few places are better to be than on one of the park's seven bird-watching towers, such as those at Haeska, Keemu, or Kloostri. In spring, more than two million waterfowl pass through Matsalu, including about 1.6 million long-tailed ducks. Other avian spectacles include the arrival of tens of thousands of beautiful Bewick's swans, or greater scaups, or common goldeneyes. One of nature's great predators, the rare white-tailed eagle, takes wing here too.

The national park encompasses Matsalu Bay, the lower course of the River Kasari, coastal reed beds, wooded meadows, flooded meadows along the River Kasari, coastal pastures, and about 50 islands. The park's visitors center, in the renovated Penijõe Manor near Lihula, offers an educational exhibition on all the area's avian activity. You can also book a local guide through the park. If you're heading out for a long day on the trails, pack some local *verivorst* ("blood sausage") and ask your local host to put some Vana Tallinn (a local syrupy liquor) in your coffee flask as a warming pick-me-up.

AT A GLANCE

Wooded wetlands ▪ Prime bird-watching ▪ 187.7 square miles (486.1 sq km) ▪ Nature trails and observation towers ▪ kaitsealad.ee/eng/matsalu-national-park

SOOMAA

Discover a host of flora and fauna within a land of bogs.

If you're looking for a *haabjas*, a traditional dugout canoe, head for the quiet backwater of Soomaa, where they are still crafted by hand. Soomaa National Park is located in the wilderness between the cities of Pärnu and Viljandi in southwest Estonia. A range of elevated boardwalk trails lead into this "land of bogs." The 3.1-mile (5-km) Riisa Trail heads to Riisa bog, and the 2.7-mile (4.5-km) Ingatsi Trail leads to an elevation of 26 feet (8 m) onto the raised bog of Kuresoo; both have watchtowers from where you can study the birdlife below, including tundra swans, cranes, and about 100 pairs of whimbrels. Predators such as golden eagles, merlins, and Montagu's harriers stalk the skies. Many mammals also inhabit the park, including roe deer, wild boar, lynx, wolf, and brown bear. If your sense of musicality stretches beyond birdsong, be sure to take the Hüpassaare Study Trail, a 3.1-mile (5-km) hike through several habitats, including the Kuresoo bog, with a stopover at the museum of Mart Saar, a famous Estonian composer.

Soomaa protects raised bogs, floodplain grasslands, biologically diverse glades, wooded meadows, and a variety of forests. The area is widely known for its great annual flood or the so-called "fifth season," when the spring runoff from melted snow or heavy rains floods the lower forests, turning them into Baltic bayous, and cutting off many roads.

AT A GLANCE

Soomaa raised bogs ▪ Riisa Trail ▪ 139 square miles (359 sq km) ▪ Soomaa's "fifth season" ▪ kaitsealad.ee/eng/soomaa-national-park

VILSANDI

Marking Estonia's long history of taking to the seven oceans

Estonia is a seafaring nation, and its shipbuilders and sailors are widely celebrated on the national stage. So it's particularly apt that Vilsandi National Park is a maritime park embracing the islands and waters of the Baltic Sea. The park includes part of the island of Vilsandi, several smaller islands, adjacent parts of western Saaremaa (Estonia's largest island), as well as the Harilaid Peninsula on Saaremaa. The westernmost point in Estonia—Nootamaa Island—is also located within the bounds of the park.

Vilsandi National Park is a celebrated bird reserve with a highly sensitive ecosystem. Saaremaa is visited biannually by many migratory birds, such as barnacle geese and Steller's eider, two of the more than 247 species of birds that breed and nest on these grounds. Eider ducks flock here in great numbers, matched only by the number of Finnish tourists who visit the region for the positively balmy southern weather (comparatively speaking). Like the birds, the Finns are attracted to the coves, capes, and many coastal islands. The vegetation is characterized by coastal plants and includes several species of orchids and juniper bushes. The national park has several hiking trails, one of the best of which is the 3.1-mile (5-km) path leading from the tip of the Kuusnõmme Peninsula across a couple of islets to Väike-Vilsandi.

AT A GLANCE

Baltic Sea island landscapes ▪ Bird migration point ▪ 92 square miles (238 sq km) ▪ Kuusnõmme Peninsula Trail ▪ kaitsealad.ee/eng/vilsandi-national-park

BELARUS

Belarus has a cold reputation that belies a warm, friendly heart. The Soviet-style architecture of the country's capital, Minsk, and the fallout from the Chernobyl disaster have left most outsiders with a not altogether positive image of this centralized state. Yet Belarus is a beautiful land of fairy-tale castles, fabulous forests, languorous rivers, and lakes aplenty; here, weekends are still spent as in centuries past: at the *dacha* (country house), and the *banya* (Belarusian bathhouse). Visit the national parks and you'll see Europe's only wild bison at Europe's oldest wildlife refuge (Belavezhskaya Pushcha), or drift through the country's several aquatic wildernesses: the swampy marshlands of Pripyatsky National Park, the Braslav Lakes, or the vast waterways of Narochansky National Park.

Opposite: The morning mists rise in Braslav Lakes National Park.

BELOVEZHSKAYA PUSHCHA

A protected forest with Europe's only wild bison population

Adjacent to the Polish border, Belovezhskaya Pushcha National Park is part of UNESCO's Białowieża Forest World Heritage site, the last primeval part of the vast woodlands that once covered the European plains. Białowieża National Park (see page 348) on the Polish side extends this protected forestry, and you can hike or cycle across the border without a visa (but take your passport).

Back in Belarus, you can visit the Eco Education Center, where exhib-

Wild boar forage in the park.

its at the Museum of Nature explain the park's harsh history: The Napoleonic Wars and both World Wars took a heavy toll on these forests of old ash, pine, and silver fir. Today, the park embraces large meadows where bison graze. The Belovezhskaya Pushcha hosts several rare grass plants, and smaller creatures include wolves, lynx, otters, greater spotted eagles, cranes, and long-tailed tawny owls. In spring, watch in the forests for the loud song and dance of the mating male wood grouse, who spreads his lovely blue-black tail out like a fan and struts and sings at the top of his voice in an impressive Jaggeresque performance.

AT A GLANCE

Cross-border protected parkland ▪ 579.4 square miles (1,500.6 sq km) ▪ Primeval forests ▪ Eco Education Center and Museum of Nature ▪ npbp.by/eng

BRASLAV LAKES

A string of lakes nicknamed the Blue Necklace of Belarus

Braslav Lakes National Park hosts a unique ecosystem and protects a total of 30 lakes along with a large expanse of mainly pine forests. The three largest of these lakes are Dryvyaty, Snudy, and Strusta, and others are worth visiting for their rich ecosystems. The southern part of the park preserves a landscape of lowlands covered with coniferous-deciduous forests, with different types of bogs occupying much of the surrounding areas. The

park also encompasses several beautiful forest lakes, including Bohinskaye. The woodlands of Borunsky, Belmont, Boguinsky, and Druiskaya Dacha make for fine hiking and cycling, amid mixed forests of pine and fir trees. In its northern section, the park runs along the Latvian border.

Several rare species inhabit the park, including the badger, lynx, brown bear, and swan. Elegant swans, once rare in this area, now grace the Braslav Lakes in healthy

numbers. Other species to observe here include the black stork, common crane, silver seagull, willow grouse, and dunlin.

The numerous lakes of Braslav are an anglers' delight, where a rich mix of pike, perch, bream, whitebait, tench, and whitefish are seemingly there for the taking. As you wander the trails, watch for myriad animals, including boar, roe deer, squirrel, brown and white hare, fox, raccoon, wolf, marten, otter, and mink.

AT A GLANCE

Braslav Lakes countryside ▪ Bohinskaye forest lake ▪ 267 square miles (691 sq km) ▪ Excellent angling ▪ braslavpark.by/en

NAROCHANSKY

A lake district destination for birds and humans

The lovely Naroch Lake District embraces Narochansky National Park, which pulses with wildlife at the heart of the region. Popular with passing birds, this is also the largest resort region of Belarus, where holiday-makers come to enjoy picturesque lakeside towns, clear lake waters, and the region's healing mineral springs.

Large reservoirs line the basins of the Neman River and Western Dzvina River. The rivers Stracha, Narochanka, Vuzlyanka, and Sviritsa course through the park, feeding 43 lakes, of which the most popular are Lake Narach, Lake Myastra, and Lake Batorino. Pine and birch groves cover almost half the park, and the moist landscape fosters a wide array of mosses, lichens, fungi, and algae.

Watch for rare and protected plants, including Belarus's most beautiful orchid—lady's slipper. European red deer, wild boar, elk (moose), and roe deer all roam the woodlands; raccoon dogs, badgers, martens, minks, otters, beavers, and muskrats are other Naroch inhabit-ants to watch for on the trails. You'll find plenty of birds of interest too, including bitterns, common cranes, and the magnificently clawed osprey. This latter bird is a keen fisher; witness a skilled catch and you'll understand its various avian aliases—this large predator is also known as the sea hawk, the river hawk, and the fish hawk. Ospreys have a large menu to choose from in this national park: pike, roach, perch, bream, crucian carp, silver bream, and ruff all ply these vast waterways.

AT A GLANCE

Naroch Lake District ▪ Diverse wildlife ▪ 360 square miles (933 sq km) ▪ Pine and birch forests ▪ belarus.by/en

PRIPYATSKY

Protecting an ecosystem of wildlife and ancient cultural traditions

Pripyatsky National Park protects forested landscapes around the Pripyat River. Much of the park consists of turf swamps that are host to 51 species of mammals, including about 100 European bison, elk (moose), wild boar, badger, and lynx. The extensive floodplain in the Pripyat Valley comprises varied landscapes: rivers and streams, forested and non-forested peatlands, freshwater wetlands, transitional mires, raised bogs, and ponds within seasonally flooded agricultural land. The inundated oak

The Pripyat River veins the park.

woods are beautiful to kayak through during spring floods.

Pripyatsky also preserves the rich folk traditions and cultural identity of the Polesie people. You can witness their history on a farm estate tour, where ancient traditions and crafts are explained. The park also hosts the annual Polesie's Call Festival, when choirs and singers perform Polesie songs and craftsmen demonstrate ancient skills. The festival also has fishing contests, boat racing, fairs, and several days of general merrymaking. The visitors center in Lyaskavichy has information on the park and the festival, and includes a nature museum.

AT A GLANCE

Pripyat River floodplain ▪ Turf marshlands ▪ 320.4 square miles (830 sq km) ▪ Polesie's Call Festival ▪ belarus.by/en

SLOVAKIA

Slovakia is one of eastern Europe's overlooked treasures, a stunning land that has held fast to its traditions in the face of globalization and membership in the European Union. In the last century, the identity of Slovakia's Slavs has been tethered first to Hungary, then to the Czechs; who could blame them if they suffer the syndrome of always playing second fiddle on the international stage. Yet in terms of national parks, Slovakia is second to none. The High Tatras and Low Tatras mountain parks are heaven for hikers and skiers, the Pieniny National Park offers all the hiking and history of its Polish counterpart, and the Malá Fatra and Slovenský Raj National Parks are stunning wildernesses, with cliffs, caves, and canyons to explore. Plus there's Veľká Fatra, offering a foretaste of the vast Carpathian forests farther east. Everywhere in Slovakia, Gothic cities, rustic villages, and stately castles are never far away.

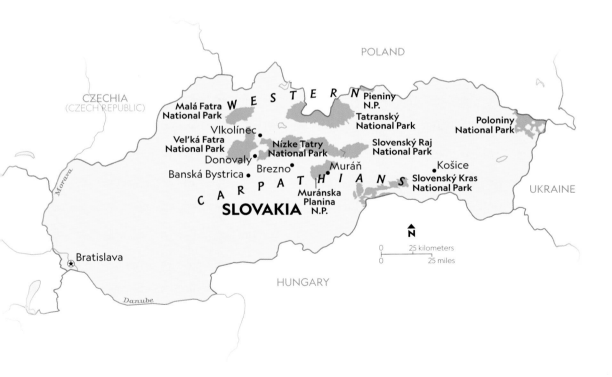

Opposite: A chamois (Rupicapra rupicapra) climbs the heights of Tatranský National Park.

MALÁ FATRA

A mountainous park with a wealth of natural and cultural high points

The park's high mountain trail offers 360-degree views of Malá Fatra.

Set in the Western Carpathians in northwestern Slovakia, Malá Fatra National Park offers challenging and adventurous mountain hiking, where level trails quickly become steep canyon ascents by ladder. Most of the park's trails start at Terchová, where chairlifts and cable cars take walkers and skiers up to the mountain.

Malá Fatra's hills are covered with mixed beech forests, and higher up with fir and spruce. Pinewoods and meadows beckon hikers to higher altitudes, where spring's colorful carpets of wildflowers include vivid violet-blue gentians, bright yellow mountain cowslips, pink sweet williams, and round-leaved sundews that look like red-tinged sunbursts. In particular, look for the plant lovers' delight that is the lady's slipper orchid, with its shoe-shaped flower pouch to trap pollinating insects. The fauna is equally diverse: Golden eagles soar high, eagle-owls haunt the woods, and black storks stalk the waters. The latter is easily spotted with its long, red legs and bill, and its impressive wingspan of about 60 inches (152 cm). The black stork is a shy bird, unlike his more sociable white relative, but standing at over three feet (102 cm), he cannot help standing out. Brown bears, lynx, wildcats, and wolves all prowl these highlands, while beech marten and otters ply the wooded riverbanks.

The park has a variety of appealing destinations for hikers: The calcite formations of Kryštálová jaskyňa (Crystal Cave) sparkle subterraneously within Malý Rozsutec mountain; Šútovo waterfall tumbles some 125 feet (38 m); and Strečno Castle is a reconstructed medieval marvel. Or, you can climb the park's highest peak of Velký Kriváň (5,607 feet/1,709 m).

AT A GLANCE

Western Carpathian mountain landscapes ▪ 87.3 square miles (226.3 sq km) ▪ Kryštálová jaskyňa (Crystal Cave) ▪ slovakia.travel/en/national-park-of-mala-fatra

MURÁNSKA PLANINA

Slovakia's karst region with fine hiking over its limestone and dolomite plateau

Welcome to karst country: The terrain of the Muránska Planina National Park is rugged and rocky, so bring your best boots. The focal point is the massif of the Muránska planina range, a limestone and dolomite plateau with karst formations edged by steep ravines. A local guide is advisable, as the plateau is a labyrinth of abysses, caves, sinkholes, karrens, and springs. Note that for safety reasons, the 300 or so caves are not open to visitors. The park does offer 186 miles (300 km) of trails, and the town of Muráň, with its rock-top castle ruins, is a good place to start.

Look for wild horses, and the pink flowers of *Daphne arbuscula*, the park's endemic plant.

A Slovakian sunset on Nizna Klakova meadow

AT A GLANCE

Limestone and dolomite landscape ▪ 82.2 square miles (213.1 sq km) ▪ Muránska planina mountains ▪ slovakia.travel/en/national-park-of-muranska-planina

NÍZKE TATRY

Mountain hikes and spectacular karst caves in the Low Tatras

The central part of Slovakia is a landscape carved by water, due to its porous rock base of limestone and dolomite. The country's largest park, Nízke Tatry National Park (the Low Tatras) protects this cavernous landscape of long valleys, deep canyons, and steep rocky cliffs. These mountains are swathed in dwarf pine forests and grasslands, while the lowlands are cloaked in woods of beech, spruce, larch, and maple. The hiking here is excellent: Reaching the peaks of Chopok (6,640 feet/2,024 m) and Ďumbier (7,063 feet/2,043 m) are challenging treks with rewarding views of the Tatras and beyond. Both have chalets near their summits. The visitors center in Donovaly has details of these and other popular hikes, such as the trail between Chopok and Čertovica.

The park's karst caves are intriguing, and several are worth visiting: Demänovská jaskyňa slobody (Demänovská Cave of Freedom) features a series of large domes, the largest being the aptly named Great Dome, measuring 134.5 feet (41 m) high, with a length of 246 feet (75 m), and a width of 115 feet (35 m). Bear's Passage Cave got its name from bear bones found there. Other caverns of note include Demänovská ľadová jaskyňa (Demänovská Ice Cave), Bystrá, Važecká, and Jaskyňa mŕtvych netopierov (Cave of Dead Bats). The mammal inhabitants of Nízke Tatry include bears, lynx, wolves, and marmot.

AT A GLANCE

Karst subterranean landscapes ▪ 281.1 square miles (728 sq km) ▪ Demänovská Cave of Freedom ▪ slovakia.travel/en/national-park-of-nizke-tatry

PIENINY

A wonderful concentration of the great Slovakian outdoors

There are few better ways to spend a summer's day than drifting downriver on a raft; especially when that river is the Dunajec, and the lovely countryside you're floating through is the region of Zamagurie, with its green shady forests, dramatic mountain peaks, and fields of fresh-cut hay. This is all encompassed in the tiny Pieniny National Park set along the border with Poland. The visitors center in the village of Červený Kláštor will point you toward the

A plte (raft) plies the Dunajec River.

trails, some of which lead to lookout points in the Haligovské skaly limestone outcrops, others to Pieniny's many caves. Then there's the

wildlife—the park boasts some 766 species of butterflies, 99 species of mollusks, and more than 200 species of vertebrates. Look for otters along the river, or lynx hunting in the woods. The gentle river raft tour is 8.7 miles (14 km) long and takes around 1 hour and 45 minutes. Your *pltník* ("raftsman") is also your knowledgeable guide to the park, and the *plte* ("raft") holds up to 10 people. So go ahead, release your inner Huck Finn, and drift down the Dunajec.

AT A GLANCE

Zamagurie countryside ■ Rafting on the Dunajec River ■ 8.1 square miles (21 sq km) ■ slovakia.com/national-parks/pieniny

POLONINY

A wealth of wildlife amid Slovakia's finest old-growth forests

Across the border from the Bieszczady National Park in Poland (see page 349), Poloniny National Park is the southern portion of the East Carpathian Biosphere Reserve. Set in northeastern Slovakia, Poloniny embraces the Bukovské vrchy mountain range, which is also located on the Ukrainian border. The park takes its name from the Eastern Slovak word *poloniny* ("alpine meadows"), which are common on the main ridge of the mountains.

Forests, mainly of beech and fir, cover much of the park, which also boasts the highest concentration of old-growth forests in Slovakia. These forests nurture some 800 species of fungi and 100 lichens endemic to Poloniny. The woods and streams crawl with amphibians, reptiles, mollusks, insects, and spiders, and some 819 species of butterfly take wing in Poloniny. Among the animals to watch for are Eurasian lynx, bear, and a small herd of wisent (European

bison) that was reintroduced to the national park in 2004.

The park's main hiking trail starts from the villages of Nová Sedlica, Runina, Topoľa, and Uličské Krivé. Several cross-country skiing trails also span the hills. An excellent hiking trail connects several wooden churches from the 18th century in Topoľa, Uličské Krivé, and Ruský Potok. Another focuses on Stužica, one of the Primeval Beech Forests of the Carpathians UNESCO World Heritage site.

AT A GLANCE

Bukovské vrchy mountains ■ European bison ■ 115 square miles (298 sq km) ■ Heritage and nature trails ■ slovakia.travel/en/national-park-of-poloniny

SLOVENSKÝ KRAS

A karst underworld beneath a rocky mountain region with a unique biosphere

The name for the Slovenský Kras Mountains translates as "Slovak Karst," signaling the area's abundance of caves—712 of which are recognized as a UNESCO World Heritage site. These are the Slovak Karst caves, which along with the Aggtelek Karst caves in Hungary, spread out over a total area of 138,000 acres (55,800 ha), straddling the Slovak-Hungarian border. There are few finer karst cave regions in all of Europe.

The stunning Baradla-Domica Cave complex stretches 13 miles (21 km) long, with about a quarter on the Slovak side. Visitors to Slovenský kras National Park can descend more than 5,600 feet (1,700 m) into its frigid, humid depths, as humans did as long ago as 5000 B.C. The system's vast limestone passages are rich in speleothems, the spires of secondary mineral deposits typical of limestone or dolostone caves.

Also accessible is the Gombasek Cave, known as the Fairy-tale Cave, such is its beauty. This cave is also used as a sanatorium for "speleotherapy," an experimental approach to airway diseases. Its constant temperature of 48°F (9°C), humidity of 98 percent, and favorable microclimate are thought to benefit breathing. Another cave worth visiting is the small (1,000 feet/300 m) Ochtinská Aragonite Cave near Rožňava. This is one of just three caves worldwide with aragonite deposits, form-

Climbers scale the famous rock wall of the Zadielska Valley.

ing bright, white branches of acicular crystal that reflect light with a sparkling effect.

The park has many highlights aboveground too, including the Zádielska tiesňava gorge, reached via a relatively demanding loop hike from Zádiel. This trail along the Zádielská planina plateau is dotted with information panels explaining the region's geology, plant and animal life, and history.

AT A GLANCE

Slovak Karst region ▪ Baradla-Domica Caves ▪ 133.6 square miles (346 sq km) ▪ Zádielska tiesňava gorge trail ▪ slovakia.travel/en/national-park-of-slovensky-kras

SLOVENSKÝ RAJ

A wondrous national park that lives up to its name of "Slovak Paradise"

Hikes in Slovenský Raj are a cross-country adventure.

If you like your hiking on the epic side, then welcome indeed to paradise, Slovenský Raj National Park. The deep canyons of the Hornád River include Prielom Hornádu, which takes four hours to cross as you navigate 7.5 miles (12 km) of climbing irons and ladders pinned to rock faces. Hiking the Suchá Belá gorge is just as adventurous, involving a 2.4-mile (4-km) clamber over moss-covered rocks, an ascent of a steep wooden stairway, footbridges, clinging to cliff chains, and getting very, very wet. Whatever trail you take, you'll encounter sweeping forests of beech, spruce, fir,

and pine, and watch cascades of crystal clear water tumbling over limestone cliffs. You'll also trek into the realm of creatures such as wild boar, wildcats, and wolves. If you're blessed, you may get a heaven-sent sighting of a brown argus butterfly with its beautiful black and amber markings. Or you could spot a very rare saker falcon, diving for prey from the rocky heights of the Low Tatras or the Slovak Ore Mountains. Fit hikers should climb to the park's most spectacular lookout, the Tomášovský Výhľad (Tomášovský's View). Havrania Skala (Raven Rock), at 3,783 feet (1,153 m), offers

another fine panoramic view. The park's highest peak is Predná Hoľa at 5,069 feet (1,545 m).

Beneath your feet, a whole netherworld of karst caves beckons: Chief among these is the UNESCO-listed Dobšinská Ice Cave. Enter near the village of Dobšiná on the north slopes of Duča hill, and descend into a subzero grotto where columns of glistening ice rise from glaciated floors. Warm air cannot percolate here, so your breath is Siberian frigid as you tramp your way through this "hell frozen over" under Slovak Paradise.

AT A GLANCE

Slovak mountain landscapes ▪ Tomášovský Výhľad lookout ▪ 76.3 square miles (197.6 sq km) ▪ Dobšinská Ice Cave ▪ slovakia.travel/en/national-park-of-slovensky-raj

TATRANSKÝ

The great mountains of central Europe

High in the Tatras Mountains of northern Slovakia, a Tatra chamois uses rubbery hooves to climb a rocky peak, and survey his realm: His is a landscape of snow-capped summits, tarns, cascades, and caves at the heart of central Europe. Here in Tatranský National Park, this endemic subspecies of goat-antelope thrives in times of peace. Tatra chamois numbers were at all-time lows during Europe's two great wars; today, they are at historic highs, following a 21st-century preservation push. The

The Tatras brood over spring meadows.

majestic Tatras form a natural border between Slovakia and Poland to the north, and both countries have long cooperated to protect these peaks and their flora and fauna. The Slovakian park has about 375 miles (600 km) of hiking trails and 16 bike trails, taking you into the chamois' world, one shared with alpine marmots, lynx, and brown bears. Look also for three-toed woodpeckers in forests of spruce, Scots pine, Swiss pine, and larch. The highest peak is the 8,711-foot (2,655-m) Gerlachovský Štít.

AT A GLANCE

Tatra Mountain landscapes ▪ Gerlachovský Štít ▪ 284.9 square miles (738 sq km) ▪ UNESCO biosphere reserve ▪ Tatra chamois ▪ spravatanap.sk/web/index.php/en

VEL'KÁ FATRA

Hiking, biking, skiing, and all varieties of tree hugging

Vel'ká Fatra National Park protects most of the Greater Fatra Range, which is part of the Outer Western Carpathians. Within the park are many well-preserved Carpathian forests, mostly of European beech, as well as ridgetop cattle pastures dating back to the 15th to 17th centuries when Romanian tribes settled these hills. There are also remnants of Scots pine forests, and the Harmanec Valley has possibly the richest concentration of Irish yew trees in Europe.

The mountains' granite bedrock has few outcrops but the limestone and dolomite rocks create a ruggedly attractive terrain known locally as Bralná Fatra. Karst features are plentiful, with a vast subterranean aspect to the park only being open to visitors at Harmanec Cave. This is a stalactite cave of dark gray Gutenstein limestone, which contains several domes, such as the White Gothic Dome, so called for its chemically clean white calcite roof. The caves' stable temperature makes them

ideal hibernation dens for bats, and 10 species have been identified, including the greater mouse-eared bat and the lesser mouse-eared bat.

Vel'ká Fatra is home to wildlife including brown bears, grey wolves, and Eurasian lynx. At the end of a long day on the trails you can head to the spa and aquapark of Turčianske Teplice. Just outside the park, the folk architecture village of Vlkolínec, a UNESCO World Heritage site, is worth a visit for a taste of the lives of early settlers in these mountains.

AT A GLANCE

Vel'ká Fatra Mountains ▪ Harmanec Cave ▪ 155.8 square miles (403.5 sq km) ▪ Vlkolínec World Heritage site ▪ slovakia.travel/en/national-park-of-velka-fatra

HUNGARY

You'll find as much zest and flavor in the 10 national parks of this wonderfully diverse central European country as you'll taste in the Hungarian national dishes of *paprikás csirke* (paprika chicken) or *gulyás* (beef goulash). A few of the main ingredients: cowboys on the Nagy Magyar Alföld (Great Alföld) prairies herding wild horses; labyrinths of limestone caves; salamanders slithering across arid rocks; the beautiful Badacsony region, inspiration of painters and poets; the Bükk Mountains rising in the northeast; the Danube and Dráva floodplains; a capital national park within Budapest; lovely Lake Fertő, third largest in central Europe; marsh tortoises of Lake Kolon; the shifting sand dunes of Fülöpháza; the great bird flocks of Körös-Maros; and the new environmental watch posts of Orség National Park. This appetizing array of indigenous riches is laid out for you in the Carpathian Basin, right in the heart of Europe. How you cook them is up to you.

Opposite: A breeding pair of European bee-eaters (Merops apiaster) in Kiskunsag National Park

AGGTELEK

A subterranean karst wonderland beneath a wildlife-packed wilderness

Hungary's Aggtelek Karst region is home to the largest stalactite cave in Europe. The Baradla Cave runs for 11 miles (17.7 km) under the Aggtelek National Park; an additional five miles (8 km) of this spectacular cavern lies in Slovakia, there known as Domica (see page 387). The Baradla-Domica cave system has been a destination for centuries known for its speleothems, the accreted formations within limestone or dolostone caves. In Hungary, the cave has a natural entrance at Aggtelek, at the foot of a high white cliff overlooking the village. The varying depths and mineral makeup of the rock produces spectacular passages of different-colored stalactites and weirdly shaped deposits.

The dramatic subterranean Baradle cave system

Aggtelek National Park protects a total of 280 caves. Some of these caverns are known for their therapeutic air, such as the Peace Cave, which acts as a sanatorium for asthma sufferers.

As varied as the caves belowground are the animals that inhabit the park above. The fire salamander is one of central Europe's most colorful creatures, its black body striped with yellow (sometimes red) blotches. The salamanders live in the park's limestone hills and hide in fallen leaves and around mossy tree trunks. The European copper skink is another common curiosity, a lizard also known as snake-eyed skink or juniper skink. It looks like a cross between a snake and a lizard. Look too for *Saga pedo*, one of Europe's largest insects. This wingless bush cricket has a body of up to 4.7 inches (12 cm) long.

On the even larger side, Eurasian lynx, gray wolf, and wild boar all stalk these forests, and red deer are plentiful. The mountains are home to winged predators such as the common buzzard and the rare eastern imperial eagle, which the monarchy of Austria-Hungary once adapted as its heraldic animal. Elsewhere, your hikes will be accompanied by the birdsong of white-throated dippers, Eurasian bullfinches, hazel grouse, common kingfishers, red-backed shrikes, Old World swallowtails, and scarce swallowtails.

The park offers guided zoological, botanical, and ecotours through picturesque villages and forests, meadows, and hills.

Hucul Horses

If you're equestrian minded, visit the park's Manor House Hucul Riding Centre. There, you'll learn about this small, stocky horse with great endurance, originally from the Carpathian Mountains, and sometimes called the Carpathian pony. The Hucul Riding Centre offers a range of activities, including riding lessons for children, trekking, horse-and-carriage tours, and the Shadow Ranger Tour. The International Hucul Horse Races and International Farrier Competition is held in August. The park maintains a herd of more than 200 horses and can be visited year-round.

AT A GLANCE

Aggtelek Karst landscapes ▪ The Baradla-Domica cave system ▪ 76.8 square miles (198.9 sq km) ▪ Manor House Hucul Riding Centre ▪ UNESCO World Heritage site ▪ anp.hu/en

BALATON UPLANDS

A wondrous natural tapestry of six distinctive landscapes

The six landscapes of Balaton Uplands National Park consist of the northern shores of Lake Balaton, the Tihany Peninsula, the Pécselyi Basin, the Káli Basin, the Tapolca Basin, the Keszthely Mountains, and the wetlands of Kis-Balaton.

Lake Balaton is a freshwater lake and the largest lake in central Europe. Its mountainous northern shores are striped with vineyards. The Tihany Peninsula is protected for its ecological and historic value: The Benedictine Tihany Abbey was founded here in 1055 by András (Andrew) I, who lies in its crypt. The church was rebuilt in baroque style in 1754. The last Habsburg emperor of Austria, Charles I, was briefly held prisoner here.

Gently sloping hillsides, wide mountain plateaus, and flat highlands with karstic features dominate the Pécselyi Basin. The Káli Basin and Tapolca Basin, together with the Keszthely Mountains, are collectively called the Badacsony district. For centuries, poets, novelists, and painters flocked to this verdant region in search of inspiration. The dolomite bedrock of this forested area nurtures a distinctive ecosystem of plant and animal life typical of the Transdanubian Mountains. These lovely lands are now protected by the national park.

The Kis-Balaton is an expansive wetland habitat, known for its waterfowl. You can take guided tours of all six landscapes, and be sure to visit the water buffalo reserve at Kápolnapuszta.

AT A GLANCE

A rich mix of landscapes ▪ Tihany Abbey ▪ 220 square miles (569.7 sq km) ▪ Kápolnapuszta water buffalo reserve ▪ bfnp.hu/en

BÜKK

A huge range of flora and fauna in Hungary's highest mountain range

Bükk is a Hungarian treasure, and the country's largest national park. The park's vast landscapes, with many oak, beech, and hornbeam forests, offer rich habitat for a wide array of flora and fauna: Some 90 species of nesting birds call Bükk home, and every species of bat indigenous to Hungary hangs out in the park's karst caves. White-backed woodpeckers rattle around Bükk's forests, while gray wagtails lurk near streams (look for their vivid yellow underplumage).

Above, many species of raptors menace the skies, including hawks, eagles, and falcons.

In spring, meadows here erupt in a riot of wildflowers such as daylily, insect-trapping lady's slipper, wolfsbane, and northern dragonhead, with its tall stems and lovely cluster of purple blooms. Insects and reptiles creep and crawl, among them the blind ground beetle, the alpine Capricorn beetle, and the spotted salamander. In meadows look for the surreal beauty of the purple-edged copper butterfly. The big mammals of Bükk include lynx, wildcat, mouflon, wild boar, deer, and wolves.

The park has well-signposted trails for hikers and cyclists and is on the National Blue Trail. Worthwhile day trips include the UNESCO World Heritage site of Hollókő, a preserved Palóc village, and Szilvasvárad, worth visiting for its karst waterfall, trout ponds, and the National Lipizzaner Stud, home of Hungary's famous horses.

AT A GLANCE

Bükk Mountain range ▪ National Blue Trail ▪ 166.5 square miles (431.3 sq km) ▪ ieger.com/bukk-national-park.html

DUNA-DRÁVA

A tale of two rivers runs through the most fluvial national park in Europe.

The Duna-Dráva (Danube-Drava) National Park is dedicated to giving both its named rivers safe passage through landlocked Hungary to the Black Sea; the Drava is a tributary of the Danube that joins the great river near Osijek.

The park protects the floodplains lying along the Danube, from the mouth of the River Sió to Hungary's southern border, and all of the Hungarian section of the River Drava. The landscapes of these vast floodplains are rich in plant and insect life, an abundance that attracts rare bird species to the Lower Danube floodplains. This is also one of the most prolific fish-breeding areas along the Danube. The sandbars of the Danube consist of rough sand, so when water levels are low, the habitat is arid. Purple willow bushes thrive here. Along the dead channels, at banks covered by silty sand, white willow trees grow, with their distinctive silvery leaves. Forests of oak, ash, and elm thrive on the high floodplain, their rich undergrowth sheltering protected woodbine and wild grape. The many herbs that prosper in these habitats include the checkered lily, with its pinkish brown-spotted flower. Deer herds roam the woods.

The Drava is one of the most unspoiled rivers in Europe, and hosts many unique species. Danube salmon, zingel, grayling, and ship sturgeon all inhabit these waters. Little tern, little ringed plover, and common tern nest on the river's gravel bars. Species endemic to the park areas include the Hungarian hawthorn plant, which produces an edible large black berry, and the Drava caddis fly.

Traditional Life

A visit to the Taplós-Góga Exhibition Sector in Gemenci is a wonderful opportunity to meet and interact with people employed in the traditional tasks of farming and maintaining the floodplain, which have been observed for centuries. The skills on display include fishing, beekeeping, and tending orchards; you'll also get within touching distance of grazing Hungarian grey cattle, the Hungarian Racka sheep, and indigenous breeds of poultry. In addition, you'll learn about the region's *fok* culture, whereby floodwaters were used to capture fish and to hydrate hay fields and orchards via artificial canals, or foks. The maintenance of these foks required high levels of expertise and long hours of hard labor.

SOUTHERN GREAT PLAIN

In the Southern Great Plain region, the wetland forests of Gemenci are worth visiting; Gemenci's gorgeous floodplain forest is a fine place to hike. These woods are interwoven with artificial channels known as *foks,* which were an integral part of traditional floodplain management. You'll find the largest populations of black storks and white-tailed eagles in Hungary in the Gemenci wetlands.

Perhaps the best way to see Gemenci is to take a ride on the narrow-gauge Forest Train. At certain stops—Malomtelelo, Nyéki Holt-Duna, Bárányfok—you can hop off to wander one of the history or nature trails. Alternatively, take a boat ride down the Danube, starting from Mohács or Baja. Walking trails include the National Blue Trail, which passes through Gemenci; for cyclists, the levees alongside the Danube are open as trails. The flat landscapes of the Great Hungarian Plain region make for easy cycling.

You can also visit the Mohács Memorial Park that marks the Battle of Mohács held here in 1526, when the Hungarian Army was annihilated by the invading Turks. Some 16,000 Hungarians, including their king, Louis II, were killed in the bloody battle.

The Danube's woods and rich floodplains nurture many deer.

Danube and Drava floodplains ▪ Southern Great Plain ▪ 189.1 square miles (490 sq km) ▪ Taplós-Góga Exhibition Sector ▪ ddnp.hu

DUNA-IPOLY

Embracing the riverside habitats of the Danube and the Ipoly

One of the most interesting mix of habitats in any of the national parks of Europe is manifested in this amazing conglomeration of preserved areas. Duna-Ipoly National Park encompasses the floodplain of the River Ipoly, a tributary of the Danube, as well as areas in the capital city of Budapest and several surrounding counties. The park protects several rare and endangered species found only within its environs. In addition, the park's floral delights include the alpenrose, and the red helleborine; its extensive birdlife stretches from great predators such as eastern imperial eagles, short-toed eagles, and saker falcons to the common mallard. Greater mouse-eared bats come out at night, and there is no shortage of insects to feed upon along the banks and floodplains of the rivers. These include caddis flies and mayflies—both, of course, good lures for anglers who stalk these riverbanks. The Danube and the Ipoly are stocked with fine brown trout and other central European staples, but endemic to these rivers is the schraetzer, or striped ruffe, a species of perch native to the Danube Basin.

The park also hosts a wealth of karst caves, and you don't even have to leave Budapest to explore Szemlő-Hegyi Cave. This cavernous maze has been called the city's underground flower garden due to its floral-like hydrothermal karst formations. The natural thermal water that once filled this cave is now diverted to fill the pools of Budapest's Szent Lukács Bath.

AT A GLANCE

Danube and Ipoly river habitats and floodplains ▪ 232.9 square miles (603.2 sq km) ▪ Karst caves ▪ Szemlő-Hegyi Cave ▪ dinpi.hu

FERTŐ-HANSÁG

A transborder lake park with exceptional ecology, beauty, and serenity

The third largest lake in central Europe, Lake Fertő is a continental salt lake. It is also a shapeshifter: Due to shallow water levels and the prevailing winds of northwestern Hungary, the size and contours of the lake have changed significantly over time.

Fertő-Hanság National Park is also a fine example of cross-border environmental protection: It was opened in conjunction with the Austrian Neusiedler See-Seewinkel National Park (see page 121), and both parks are on the shorelines of Lake Fertő, called Lake Neusiedl in Austria.

The lake provides habitat for a rich array of avian residents and migrants, including great egrets, purple herons, common spoonbills, and greylag geese. During the migration season, sandpipers descend here in multitudes. Rare species are often spotted in the park too, such as the red-breasted goose, the white-tailed eagle, and the hen harrier. Anglers frequent the lake for its stocks of weatherfish, northern pike, and ziege, aka sabre carp. Hikers on the meadows that run west of the lake can admire several rare plants such as the yellow lady's slipper, fly orchid, the Hungarian iris, and pygmy iris. The steppes to the east of the lake are rich in sea aster and herbaceous seepweed.

Fertő-Hanság National Park has two visitors centers: the Egret Castle in Sarród and the István Csapody facility in Fertőújlak. Both offer accommodation.

AT A GLANCE

Twin park of Austria's Neusiedler See-Seewinkel National Park ▪ 91 square miles (235.8 sq km) ▪ Rich lake ecosystems ▪ ferto-hansag.hu/en

HORTOBÁGY

Cowboys, buffalo, and wide-open plains in Hungary's eastern prairies

In terms of color, the hoopoe (Upupa epops) *bird goes out on a limb.*

The *puszta* are the flat grassland prairies and marshes of eastern Hungary, where cowboys rounding up endangered Przewalski's horses are as common a sight as buffalo roaming over dusty plains. This is Europe's Wild East. Hortobágy National Park protects the pastoral legacy of centuries of breeding and herding traditions.

The Great Hungarian Plain stretches across the eastern half of Hungary and here the *csikósok*, skilled rancher, still rides. Herdsmen learn and demonstrate the horse-riding techniques of their ancestors, and visitors can stay in herdsmen's inns that have retained their age-old character. The legends and folklore of these plains cowboys are celebrated at the Hortobágy Herdsman Museum.

WHAT TO SEE

The place to see all this tradition in action is at the Máta Stud Farm, where you'll watch the csikósoks round up long-horned grey cattle and see the indigenous Mangalica swine (a woolly pig) and shaggy-fleeced Racka sheep. Then comes the awe-inspiring display of horsemanship. The csikósoks' skills include the "puszta five" where a cowboy stands astride five galloping horses.

The landscapes of alkaline pasturelands, meadows, and wetlands give the plains an inevitable flatness; traditional T-shaped sweep wells dot the horizon. But the puszta has plenty of variety. The park has been a stopover point to some 135,000 migrating cranes in late September and October of peak years. You can catch these winged multitudes at Tisza Lake, just west of the park, where you'll spot some 160 avian species, such as nesting geese. At the Hortobágy Bird Park you can visit injured birds and orphaned chicks as they are nursed back to a return to the wild. Out on the prairies, watch for one of the heaviest flying birds on Earth, the great bustard, who takes wing in a labored flutter of its striped russet plumage. Watch too for the bright hoopoe with its colored crown of feathers that resembles a Mohawk haircut.

To get a sense of the park's marshlands, visit the Hortobágy Great Fishponds, where you can walk the footpaths or take the narrow-gauge railway that winds around these teeming wetlands.

In summer months, the park runs safaris on the Great Plain, given by knowledgeable guides. From the comfort of a Land Rover, you wind through the home of the puszta's wild horses and maybe spot a rare white-tailed eagle. Then watch the sun set on the golden fields of ryegrass. After sundown, the park offers stargazing walks, in what is one of Europe's prime Dark Sky sites.

AT A GLANCE

The *puszta* and Great Hungarian Plain ▪ 288.8 square miles (748 sq km) ▪ Hortobágy Bird Park ▪ Máta Stud Farm ▪ hnp.hu/en

KISKUNSÁG
Environmentally fragile landscapes in a patchwork of protection

A meadow of poppies (Papaver rhoeas) *stretches across the* puszta *area.*

Like several of Hungary's preserves, Kiskunság National Park is a quilted patchwork of protected environments—in this case, seven disjointed units scattered around the Pannonian Basin between the Danube and Tisza Rivers.

Chief among these is the Kiskunság's *puszta*, where annual events celebrate the traditional pastoral life and cattle-breeding customs of Hungary's past. The best place to explore Kiskunság's environmentally fragile area, and see its famous horse herds put through their paces, is at the small town of Bugac, on a sandy steppe 18.6 miles (30 km) southwest of Kecskemét. The park's main visitors center, the educational House of Nature, is located in Kecskemét.

Nature lovers will head for the alkali lakes of the Little Cumania, near Fülöpszállás and Szabadszállás. These serve as temporary home for tens of thousands of migratory birds, including avocets, geese, and black-winged stilts. Lake Kolon, near the town of Izsák, protects the rare marsh tortoises; visitors can only observe these ancient creatures on guided tours, and not at all during hatching season. An excellent vantage point of the lake and its environs is from the 413-foot-high (126-m) sand hill of Bikatorok (Bull's Throat). The lush landscape is rich in flora and fauna: The open waters are covered with water lily and pondweed, and the rare nettle (Urtica) grows in the reed beds. Nine orchid species and Siberian and blue irises thrive in the marsh meadows.

As well as the alder woods along the fens, remnants of the former oak-ash fen woods line the Danube near Páhi. Around these lakelands, the shifting sand dunes of Fülöpháza are blown by the strong winds of the central plains of Hungary.

AT A GLANCE

Kiskunság's *puszta* ▪ Birdlife of Little Cumania lakes ▪ 220 square miles (570 sq km) ▪ Fülöpháza's sand dunes ▪ knp.nemzetipark.gov.hu

KÖRÖS-MAROS

A mosaic of landscapes forms an environmental picture of Hungary's southeast.

Another patchwork park of many landscapes, the Körös-Maros National Park illustrates the diversity of this corner of Hungary. The park's protected areas embrace the Kis-Sárrét swamp as well as the plains of Fáspuszta and Mágorpuszta. Birds are the focus of the wildlife protected here, and the reserve at Dévaványa is a refuge for the great bustard, one of the heaviest flying birds. Tens of thousands of plovers, cranes, and ducks rest and nest at Lake Fehér near Kardoskút, a bird-watcher's paradise during fall migration. The park protects several local species, including the *búbos banka,* a subspecies of hoopoe recognizable by its pale pink body color and its distinctive crown of feathers, which it raises like a Mohawk haircut. Watch along the steppes for the purple blooms of *agárkosbor,* a protected species of green-winged orchid, and for the delicate brown and cream-colored wings of the rare large *szikibagoly* butterfly. Tired hikers might want to head for the spa town of Gyula. The park's visitors center, in the small town of Szarvas, has an exhibit on the park's flora and fauna. Two other exhibitions to note are the Kardoskút Museum, which explores the ecology of Lake Fehér (White Lake, Hungary's largest saltwater lake) and the evolution of local landscapes; and the Vésztő-Mágor Historical Exhibition, which highlights the Mágor Mounds, Neolithic to Bronze Age finds, and the ruins of a 12th-century monastery.

AT A GLANCE

Dévaványa bustard reserve ▪ Kardoskút Museum ▪ 193.5 square miles (501.3 sq km) ▪ Vésztő-Mágor Historical Exhibition ▪ kmnp.hu

ŐRSÉG

A place of sweeping hillside forests and meadows

This southwestern region of Hungary acquired the name Őrség, which means "watch post" from the defensive strategies of the Magyar. These embattled early agriculturalists built a network of watch posts across this much contested region to thwart potential invaders from medieval times onward. For centuries, the Magyars shaped this landscape by farming on small holdings and maintained harmony by sustainable practices such as crop rotation. Today, Őrség National Park preserves this lovely landscape from the desirous attentions of property developers and the 21st century's most invasive species, *Homo touristicus.*

Őrség is located at Hungary's westernmost point, close to the Austrian and Slovenian borders where thick forests, rolling hills, glorious meadows, and rich farmlands still characterize the landscape. The park offers bird-watchers well-maintained trails to pursue the area's rich birdlife; cycling and horse riding are other popular park activities. The marked trails link many of Őrség's villages, including Őriszentpéter, Szalafő, Velemér, and Pankasz. These attractive settlements have maintained their centuries-old agrarian traditions, with several featuring local pottery works that go back generations. The open-air ethnographical museum at Szalafő-Pityerszer is a great place to view traditional Őrség architecture.

AT A GLANCE

Őrség agrarian landscapes ▪ Village-to-village hiking trails ▪ 170 square miles (440 sq km) ▪ Szalafő-Pityerszer Ethnographical Museum ▪ orseginemzetipark.hu

SLOVENIA

The "land of the Slavs" could equally be called "land of the trees" or "land of pagan legends." Tiny Slovenia is one of the greenest, most densely forested countries on Earth, where a rural people still celebrate three-headed mountain gods, and a pagan appreciation of nature persists. Yet this is a thoroughly modern society. Slovenia has historically been the crossroads of Slavic, Germanic, and Romance languages and cultures. The country sits at the meeting point of four major European geographic

regions: the Alps, the Dinaric Alps, the Pannonian Plain, and the Mediterranean (via its short Adriatic shoreline). Slovenia's national park is located at the confluence of these, where Alpine snow lingers on Mount Triglav long into spring, yet where a warm Mediterranean breeze will bring friendly Slovenians flocking to the trails to enjoy one of eastern Europe's loveliest landscapes.

Opposite: Lower Martuljek falls in Triglav National Park
Above: The alpine ibex (Capra ibex) *in Triglav National Park, one of his many domains.*

TRIGLAV

The crowning peak of the Julian Alps towers over a park of folkloric legends.

Climbing in the Julian Alps is rewarded with views of Europe east and west.

Triglav means "three-headed," a reference both to its three peaks, and also to the highest Slavic deity, the three-headed Triglav who had his throne on the summit of his namesake mountain. From here, he was believed to rule over the three kingdoms of heaven, earth, and the underworld.

Triglav National Park is Slovenia's only national park, located in the northwest of the country, on the southeastern part of the Alpine massif. The park centers around Mount Triglav, the highest peak of the Julian Alps and Slovenia's tallest mountain, which soars to a height of 9,396 feet (2,864 m). It is a national symbol, featured on Slovenia's coat of arms and flag.

Green valleys radiate from Mount Triglav, hydrating two large river systems with their sources in the Julian Alps: the Soča and the Sava, flowing to the Adriatic and Black Sea, respectively. Forests of beech and spruce cloak much of the park while belowground numerous springs carve out a labyrinth of caves from the limestone rock undergirding much of the park.

Triglav's Wildlife

While enjoying the adrenaline rush of Triglav's rivers, rocks, and canyons, it's easy to overlook the park's array of wild creatures as they largely give humanity a wide berth. In the beech and oak forests, tread lightly and you may see badgers, red foxes, or martens. Wander the meadows filled with gentians and geraniums, and watch for the black-and-white-striped face of a badger digging for earthworms. When exploring the Soča and its tributaries, note that they teem with trout; look for endemic Soča trout, and also for the speckled colors of rare marble trout. Also rare, white-throated dippers dive in Triglav's waterways. Higher up, marvel at the surety of foot of high-climbing mountain goats, alpine ibex, and chamois. Some 84 bird species fly Triglav's skies, including the golden eagle, who, like the colorful wallcreeper, nests high in rock cliffs.

Waterfalls are a favored destination for hikers here; Peričnik cascades for 171 feet (52 m) from a hanging valley into the glacial Vrata Valley, while Savica falls some 256 feet (78 m) high from a karst spring. Much of its water flows from a karst basin around Black Lake, which lies 1,640 feet (500 m) higher. When this overflows in spring, the whole rock face can become awash with cascades. Glacial lakes such as Bohinj, horseshoe-shaped glacial valleys, and boulder-burdened moraines complete the geological drama that is Triglav National Park. The folkloric drama is another story: one that involves a golden-horned chamois kicking up all this rocky rubble to bury its treasure high on Mount Triglav.

CENTER FOR ADVENTURE

Whatever the mythology, the modern-day reputation of the park as an adventure-sports destination is legendary. The karst landscape is a carved-out playground for kayaking, caving, and canyoneering. You can climb 148-foot (45-m) Parabola waterfall, rappel rocky cliffs, or take a canyoneering expedition to Fratarica. The Soča River offers excellent white-water rides from 446-foot-high (136-m) Boka falls. In winter, the pistes of Vogel, on the southwestern shore of Lake Bohinj, are particularly fun to run, or take an even more scenic route on one of the cross-country trails through this glorious park. Cycling is easy around the lakes, but better still is hiking the Julian Alps: Try

The Tolmin gorges offer rocky adventure and breathtaking trails.

the 15.5-mile (25-km) Soča Trail following this lively river from its source through the verdant Trenta Valley to Bovec. Or hike the wooden boardwalks of the Vintgar gorge for an easy 2.4-mile (4 km) stroll.

AT A GLANCE

Julian Alpine landscapes ▪ Karst caves and gorges ▪ 340 square miles (880 sq km) ▪ Peričnik and Savica waterfalls ▪ Rafting the Soča River ▪ tnp.si/en

CROATIA

The small yet stunning country of Croatia stretches along the northeast Adriatic coast and reaches inland to the Danube. Long a part of Yugoslavia, it now has many neighbors: Slovenia and Hungary to the north, Bosnia and Herzegovina as well as Serbia to the east, and Montenegro to the south. Croatia is blessed with the Dalmatian coastline, exceptional medieval towns, and wonderful national parks. The lakes and waterfalls of Plitviče, the limestone crags of Rožanski Kukovi, the gorge of the Krka River, the wetlands of Kopački Rit, the sea cliffs of Kornati—all are enshrined in parks of rare beauty.

Opposite: Red sea stars (Echinaster sepositus) *are among the sights awaiting divers in Kornati National Park.*

BRIJUNI

Exotic inhabitants amid an archipelago of Adriatic islands

The Brijuni Islands are a group of 14 small islands in the North Adriatic Sea, separated from the west coast of the Istrian Peninsula by the narrow Fažana Strait. The main isles are Veliki Brijun Island, just two square miles (5.2 sq km) in area, and the smaller Mali Brijun. These scenic destinations are popular with vacationing Croatians and are embraced within Brijuni National Park. The archipelago lies about two miles (3 km) off the mainland and can be visited on tours departing from Fažana, north of Pula. You can also book excursions in Poreč, Rovinj, or Pula, where the park's visitors center is located. These outings include travel to and from the islands and a guided tour around Veliki Brijun. Brijuni island landscapes are mainly macchia, meadows, and holm oak and laurel forests.

BRIJUNI PAST & PRESENT

The Brijuni Islands have many Roman and Byzantine remains worth visiting. By the late 19th century, the grouping was overgrown and rife with malaria. In 1893, Austrian businessman Paul Kupelwieser purchased the archipelago and converted the islands into a series of luxury health resorts. These boasted fine hotels, a zoo, and an ostrich farm. General Tito had a summer home on the islands from the late 1940s onward, where he entertained dignitaries and

Roman villa ruins in Verige Bay

celebrities. He also imported tropical plants and animals, resulting in the hundreds of deer that still inhabit the islands, as well as blue antelope, mountain zebras, and Somalian sheep. Other exotic animals, no longer in evidence, were given as gifts: Nilgai antelopes, zebu cattle, and Asian elephants were donated as gifts from India, while plains zebra and mountain zebra were given by Guinea; waterbuck came from Ethiopia.

When Croatia gained independence in 1991, four hotels on Veliki Brijun Island were reopened, as well as the safari park that housed the animals given to Tito. Within the safari park an ethno park protects the domestic island species. Istrian ox (descendants of aurochs), Istrian sheep, donkeys, and goats are all nurtured here.

Out on the trails you'll come across animals roaming freely, the legacies of Kupelwieser and Tito: Chital deer, fallow deer, European hares, and mouflons were all introduced to Veliki Brijun in the early 1900s.

The islands are a haven for birdlife, with smaller islands that host nesting grounds for gulls, sea swallows, and cormorants. The Brijuni Islands also host key seasonal habitats for northern bird species, especially around Saline. This damp area contains three marshy lakes with a fenced area of ornithological preservation. Its largest lake is overgrown with hospitable reed beds.

The national park includes the seas around the Brijuni archipelago. These are key hatching grounds for many northern Adriatic marine organisms. The park protects clams and mollusks such as the pen shell and the date shell, and sea turtles and dolphins can be spotted in Brijuni's waters. Divers will also see endemic plants, such as black tang (a seaweed), Jadranski bračić (an algae), and Jadranski ciganin (a tunicate), as well as an abundance of sponges, shellfish, sea urchins, and crustaceans.

AT A GLANCE

Adriatic archipelago ▪ Exotic animal safari park ▪ 13 square miles (33.67 sq km) ▪ Roman and Byzantine ruins ▪ np-brijuni.hr/en

KORNATI

Idyllic Adriatic islands protecting delicate marine ecosystems

The Kornati archipelago is located in the northern part of Dalmatia, running for about 22 miles (33 km) and encompassing some 140 islands—some large, some tiny—in a sea area of about 124 square miles (320 sq km). The Kornati takes its name from the plural form of the largest island in the group, Otok Kornat. Geographically, the islands are divided into two groups: the Gornji Kornati (Upper Kornati), closer to the mainland, and the Donji Kornati (Lower Kornati), which mostly face the open Adriatic in the southwest. Kornati National Park protects the Donji Kornati, which comprises 109 islands, along with their marine surrounds. This includes the island of Kornat and its satellite islets. The park's main visitors center is in the town of Murter, on Murter Island, which is connected to the mainland by a drawbridge in Tisno.

STORIES IN STONE

The landscape of most of the Kornati Islands is karst limestone that originally arose from sediment from the sea. So take a sharp look at the stones for numerous fossils of ancient crustaceans and fish. All around the archipelago, you'll find typical karst formations. The effects of wind, rain, and sea on this porous rock result in bizarrely shaped sea stacks, cave systems, elevated rock flats, and dramatic crowns (cliffs).

The foliage of the park is mainly sparse maquis. A tough variety of grass prevails, but more notable are the prevalence of many scented and medicinal herbs, such as sage, feather grass, and the daisylike *Xeranthemum*, which makes spring a fragrant time of year. Olive trees make up about 80 percent of the land under cultivation, along with vineyards, figs, orchards, and vegetable gardens. The Kornati Islands were thought once to be covered with forests of Mediterranean holm oaks, but open fires and Venetian shipbuilders took their toll; today, the sole remnants are found around the bay of Telašćica.

KORNATI WILDLIFE

The wildlife is limited to the smaller island habitats, where multitudes of gulls nest. Other inhabitants include the Dalmatian wall lizard and ring-necked snakes. Some 69 varieties of butterfly flutter across the archipelago, and amphibians and rodents are plentiful. The main action is under the waves though, where scuba divers find a wonderworld of colorful algae, sponges, and coral, including the endangered red coral. The noble pen shell (or fan mussel), a large species of Mediterranean clam, is protected within these waters.

Many visitors to the park are sailors, but hikers, cyclists, and stargazers are well served too. As the Irish writer George Bernard Shaw wrote "On the last day of the Creation, God desired to crown his work, and thus created the Kornati Islands out of stars, tears, and breath."

Looking south to the myriad Kornati Islands

AT A GLANCE

Adriatic islands ▪ Karst limestone landscapes ▪ 124 square miles (320 sq km) ▪ Superb scuba diving ▪ np-kornati.hr/en

KRKA

A river park of waterfalls, wooden walkways, and wondrous wildlife

The Krka River carves a deep gorge on its way from its source at the base of Dinara, descending over a series of spectacular waterfalls before reaching the Adriatic near Šibenik. Krka National Park now protects much of this watershed. You can take a boat upriver from Skradin to the base of the falls, from where you can walk the area on wooden boardwalks. The cascade beds are made of travertine, limestone deposits made over millennia. The most impressive cascades are those at Skradinski Buk

The island monastery of Visovac

and Roški waterfalls, where the river plunges into Lake Visovac.

Within park borders, a Franciscan monastery stands on the island of Visovac, and the old 19th-century water mills can also be visited. The Roman military camp at Burnum, with its amphitheater and Praetorian ruins, is worth seeing. Near Skradin is Bribirska Glavica, an Illyrian and Roman hilltop site with ruins from Roman and medieval times, and great views of the park.

An interesting inhabitant of the pools of Krka is the newtlike olm, a pink-bodied, blind, subterranean amphibian that lives only in the dark, cave waters of southeast Europe.

AT A GLANCE

Krka River watershed ▪ 42 square miles (109 sq km) ▪ Limestone karst gorges and falls ▪ Burnum Roman military camp ▪ np-krka.hr/en

MLJET

Lakes, fine walks, and impressive forests within a historic park

Mljet is one of the larger Adriatic islands off the Dalmatian coast. Mljet National Park includes the western part of the island, the two saltwater lakes of Veliko Jezero and Malo Jezero, Soline Bay, and a span of sea 1,640 feet (500 m) wide from the most prominent cape of Mljet. The focal points of the park are the two lakes, and the villages of Govedari, Polače, and Pomena. Large tracts of the park are covered with luxuriant Mediterranean forest, including large stands of Aleppo pine. The 12th-century Benedictine monastery on the island of St. Mary was used as a hotel in the Tito era. A ruined Roman palace stands at Polače, and at Babino Polje you'll discover two pre-Romanesque churches. Mljet was historically home to the Illyrians, and the remains of their hill forts are found here. The Romans arrived in 35 B.C.

Mljet has very easy hiking trails. Head up the road behind the national park office in Pomena, then turn right down a marked woodland trail to the shore of Malo Jezero, the smaller of the two lakes within the park. Following the footpath around either shore leads to the point where the two lakes meet, the channel between them spanned by a small bridge (Mali Most). You can rent canoes or bikes at the small beach. A longer hiking route, the Mljet hiking trail, covers nearly half the length of the island.

AT A GLANCE

Adriatic island park ▪ Lush Mediterranean forests ▪ 20.8 square miles (54 sq km) ▪ Mljet hiking trail ▪ Roman ruins ▪ mljet.hr

PAKLENICA

A park for serious hikers, mountaineers, cavers, and canyoneers

The rock walls of Paklenica challenge Europe's climbers.

If clinging for dear life to a vertical rock wall is your thing, head to Paklenica National Park. This realm is well known for the dramatic canyons of Velika Paklenica and Mala Paklenica, as well as a host of weathered and wonderful karst rock formations. In particular, Manita Peć cave features stalagmites, stalactites, and numerous bat species. The park is accessed from the town of Starigrad, with a national park office and the start of the hiking trails at the entrance to the gorge of Velika Paklenica.

THE VELEBITS

The Velebit Mountains, Croatia's most extensive mountain range, hosts the country's most extensive long-distance footpath, the Velebitski Planinarski Put (VPP). This trek runs 62 miles (100 km) along the spine of the Velebit Mountains, from the village of Oltare in the north to Paklenica National Park in the south. There are huts and shelters along the trail, but carry plenty of water when hiking these arid limestone hills.

The whole Velebit range has since 1977 been classified as a UNESCO world biosphere reserve, and contains two Croatian national parks, Paklenica in the south, and Sjeverni Velebit (see page 413) to the north. There are plenty of challenging peaks to climb, the highest being Vaganski (5,764 feet/1,757 m), and some good rock climbing routes in Paklenica.

While you're hanging off that cliff, look for soaring short-toed eagles and falcons that make their aeries high in the karst mountains that define this landscape. In the beautiful black pine forests far below, if you walk softly, you might see roe and red deer that inhabit this lovely park. Other residents include grey wolves, wild pigs, chamois, and rare capercaillie. But watch out along the trails for the nose-horned viper (known locally as *poskok*), Europe's most venomous snake. A rarer creature that you may be lucky enough to spot here is the brown bear, found in small numbers in Croatian mountain regions, especially Velebit and Gorski Kotar. Attacks on humans are extremely uncommon, and the bears tend to give people a wide berth. Note that hunting bears is still legal in Croatia, and the annual quota is based on population figures supplied by hunters.

The Mala Paklenica Educational Center has exhibits on endangered birds of prey and details of the excellent hiking and cycling trails that crisscross the park. You can also get advice on safe caves to explore while avoiding the area's particularly deep sinkholes.

AT A GLANCE

Dramatic karst country ▪ Velika Paklenica and Mala Paklenica gorges ▪ 36.6 square miles (95 sq km) ▪ Mala Paklenica Educational Center ▪ paklenica.hr

PLITVICE LAKES

Croatia's most famous natural monument celebrates the serenity of water.

Autumn frames Plitvice's blue-and-white waters in fiery shades.

The walkers' wonderland of Plitvice Lakes is the oldest and largest of Croatia's national parks, established in 1949 and declared a UNESCO World Heritage site in 1979. The focal point of the national park is a series of 16 emerald and turquoise-colored lakes, flowing into each other over a series of travertine falls. The lakes descend roughly 425 feet (130 m) over about five miles (8 km), before flowing onward as the Korana River. These lovely lakes are set amid lush vegetation and dense beech forest. The park is home to a host of wildlife, including black storks, brown bears, rare Eurasian lynx, and deer. In the waters, you'll see European pond turtles, and listen in the woods for the Eurasian eagle-owl's deep territorial *ooh-hu*.

WATERY WALKS

A network of well-marked trails and wooden boardwalks and bridges run for 11 miles (18 km) through the park. Plan to arrive early to avoid summertime crowds that descend on the park, which can number 4,000 visitors a day. The walkways are especially beautiful when cloaked in fall foliage, and the whole park takes on a magical ice kingdom appeal in times of winter freeze-outs. Trails are clear and easy to follow, and you can get around most of the lakes in a day, though taking two days to wander at a leisurely pace is even more rewarding.

The lakes at Proscansko and Kozjak are the largest among the 12 upper lakes. Head to the scenic Labudovac waterfall, which is more than 65.6 feet (20 m) high, at Okrug-ljak Lake, and the Cave Garden below. Other trails worth taking are to the peaks of Oštri Medveđak (2,917 feet/889 m) or Tupi Medveđak (2,848 feet/868 m), which are connected by 700-year-old beech forests. Another trail leads to the Turčić summit (2,628 feet/801 m) along a five-mile (8 km) karst track shaded in parts by spruce woods. This will lead to great views of the Veliki Slap waterfall and Kozjak Lake.

For a prime view of Plitvice Lakes, climb to the top of the stairs next to the 250-foot (76-m) Veliki Slap waterfall. For the best overall hiking experience, the 13-mile (21-km) Čorkova Bay Trail takes you through the large forests, brimming with wildlife and plant life; listen for the tattoos of busy woodpeckers. At the ticket office or visitors center, you can buy a detailed map of the park and its trails (Nacionnalni Park Plitvika Jereza Tourist Map: scale 1:50,000). Make sure you stay on the marked trails to avoid damaging this treasured environment.

GEOLOGY OF PLITVICE

Travertine (chalk rock also known as tufa) is a porous sedimentary rock formed through the precipitation of calcium carbonate from the area's rocks and rivers. The mineral also forms deposits on mosses, leading to their gradual petrification over time. The mosses you'll see in Plitvice—mainly *Cratoneuron,* but also *Bryum*—form into the rocky surfaces, and are evident growing on the travertine barriers and waterfalls. The rock is also packed with algae and various forms of bacteria, so everything you see in these waters is in a state of growth or decay.

Beneath the water you will see pale, ghostly tree trunks and branches, which are undergoing a similar process as the mineral-rich waters of the region deposit calcium carbonate on them. These can make lovely studies in decay, if you're a photographer with a knack for experimentation with filters and delayed

Walkways allow a close look at the falls and the park's plants.

exposure. Keen plant lovers should keep a watch for unusual plants; several species do not grow outside the national park, and you can obtain a list at the visitors center.

The formation of travertine is an ongoing process. Four hundred years ago Kozjak Lake was actually two lakes, but the accrual of continual deposits on the lake beds raised the water levels, submerging the travertine barrier between the lakes. The old barrier is still visible beneath the surface.

History & Legend

Like many other places in Croatia, local legend has spawned its own, more poetic version of the creation of Plitvice Lakes than the prosaic millennia-long story of rocks and water. According to folklore, during the course of a terrible drought locals prayed to the infamous Crna Kraljica, or Black Queen, who answered their prayers by unleashing spectacular rainstorms that flooded the entire area and created these lakes. Another dark storm descended in 1991, when Serbian militia occupied the park headquarters, and the subsequent standoff and shoot-out with Croatian police resulted in the first deaths of Croatia's Homeland War (1991–1995). The park was spared the worst excesses of the conflict, though troops occupied area hotels, which were later used to house refugees.

Travertine lakes and waterfalls ▪ Veliki Slap waterfall ▪ 114 square miles (295 sq km) ▪ Čorkova Bay Trail ▪ np-plitvicka-jezera.hr/en

RISNJAK

A small park amid the legend-filled mountains of Gorski Kotar

Risnjak's moody mountain woodlands provide cover for shy wildlife.

The long arc of mountains called Gorski Kotar is a densely forested region that is home to many rare species. Risnjak National Park lies in the north of this range. The peaks of Risnjak (5,013 feet/1,528 m) and Snežnik (4,938 feet/1,505 m) dominate the preserve, which has a maze of well-marked hiking trails with scattered mountain huts. Detailed hiking maps are available at the visitors center.

The park is home to brown bears, grey wolves, and Eurasian lynx, although all are shy creatures that stay well out of sight. More visible to the average hiker here are red deer, roe deer, and chamois. The main access point to the park is just outside the village of Crni Lug, and several trails radiate from the visitors center here. An alternative entry point, from the village of Gornje Jelenje, will leave you with a shorter hike up Risnjak peak.

CAVES, PEAKS & GORGES

The small village of Fužine is worth visiting for the Vrelo Cave, just outside town. This 984-foot-long (300-m) cavern is richly spiked with stalactites and stalagmites, but check the weather, as the cave is often flooded after heavy downpours. While in Fužine, try the regional food, which features dishes of local game, frogs' legs, and a homemade cheese called *skripavac*.

The north face of the mountain of Klek (3,875 feet/1,181 m) has long lured climbers, but you can also attain it on a relatively easy six-mile (9.5 km) trail that starts from the train station in Ogulin. That town hosts an annual Fairytale Festival in June, and the area has a rich legacy of witchcraft: Local legend has it that witches still gather on the summit of Klek. The town of Skrad, near the Slovenian border, has a spectacular narrow gorge—in places just 6.5 feet (2 m) wide—appropriately known as Devil's Pass.

Ogulin was the birthplace of Ivana Brlić-Mažuranić, Croatia's greatest fairy-tale writer. The Ivanina Kuća Bajke (Ivana's Fairytale House) is an excellent interpretive center with interactive displays and explanations in English. Also worth visiting is Ogulin's imposing 16th-century castle perched on the edge of Đula's Abyss—a steep gorge into which, according to legend, the noblewoman Đula threw herself when her love was slain in battle.

AT A GLANCE

Gorski Kotar mountains ▪ 24.5 square miles (63.5 sq km) ▪ Vrelo Cave ▪ Đula's Abyss ▪ Ivanina Kuća Bajke (Ivana's Fairytale House) ▪ np-risnjak.hr/en

SJEVERNI VELEBIT

A hiking and climbing treasure in the northern karst Velebit range

Croatia's most extensive mountains, the Velebit range stretches for more than 70 miles (114 km) down to Paklenica at its southernmost extreme. Its impressive karst landscapes, which lure climbers from all around Europe, run from the southern parts of Velika Kapela in the north, in the Kvarner region, south to the twin gorges of Velika Paklenica and Mala Paklenica. The northern section is preserved as Sjeverni Velebit National Park, and the whole of the Velebit range has been classified as a UNESCO world biosphere reserve since 1977. It is also protected as a nature park, with Paklenica National Park (see page 409) serving as a conservation counterweight on the range's southern side.

HIKER'S HEAVEN

The Velebit Mountains offer stunning hikes along lush forests and impressive limestone formations (including the specially protected reserves of Hajdučki and Rožanski cliffs), with an opportunity to see plenty of wildlife and flowers, including several species endemic to the park.

Croatia's finest long-distance trail starts out in Sjeverni Velebit. The Velebitski Planinarski Put (VPP) runs for some 62 miles (100 km) along the spine of the range, from the villages of Oltare in the north to Paklenica National Park in the south. Its northern section, the superbly engineered Premužičeva Trail, is the finest hiking passage anywhere in Croatia. The trail was the brainchild of forester Ante Premužić, who built it in 1933. From its various peaks, you will get magnificent views of the Adriatic Sea and many islands such as Pag, Rab, Goli Otok, Prvić, and Krk, as well as excellent vistas into the continental side of Croatia. You'll also come across many abandoned summer lodges, once used by the Velebit's shepherds and cattle farmers. These ruins and the crumbling stone walls are all that remain of a long-lost local population.

Walking the full length of the VPP requires planning and commitment as the route takes about 10 to 12 days to complete. You will need to carry your own sleeping bag and food, although you will find accommodation in a series of staffed and unstaffed mountain huts and shelters run by the two parks. Be sure to carry enough water for each day's trek, as springs are few and far between in the porous rocks of this limestone country. Some of the southern parts of the route come close to areas that still have land mines from the Homeland War, so take particular care in keeping to the proscribed route. Hiking maps are essential for safely trekking the VPP.

The northern Velebit Mountains are best explored from the mountain hut PD Zavižan, which can be reached on foot from the villages of Gornja Klada, Krasno, and Oltare.

Fine trails link the limestone peaks of Sjeverni Velebit.

AT A GLANCE

Velebit Mountains ▪ Karst country ▪ 42 square miles (109 sq km) ▪ Velebitski Planinarski Put trail ▪ np-sjeverni-velebit.hr

BOSNIA & HERZEGOVINA

Most travelers know the Bosnia and Herzegovina of Sarajevo, the "Jerusalem of the Balkans" with its cultural buzz and bohemian café culture. Or they think of a slowly healing land, elegantly symbolized by Mostar's reconstructed Stari Most (Old Bridge). Yet, this heart-shaped gem of a country has many hidden facets. You can visit the Tekija (dervish lodge) nestled in the cliff face at Blagaj, or seek out Orthodox monasteries in mountainous retreats. You'll hear the muezzins' call to prayer from Bosniak minarets as you soak up history in the medieval Bosnian capital of Jajce. Or head into the country and visit the gorgeous cascades of Kravica falls on the Trebižat River, or the sweeping falls of Martin Brod in Una National Park. The long-protected forests of Kozara National Park await hikers, as do the staggering mountains of Maglić, Volujak, and Bioč, celebrated in Sutjeska National Park.

Opposite: The massive fractal walls of the Tjentiste War Memorial commemorate the 1943 Battle of the Sutjeska in Sutjeska National Park.

KOZARA

A national forest protected by Tito, with a history of resistance

The green fingerprints of Yugoslavia's former president Josip Broz Tito are widespread around the Balkans. Kozara National Park was first protected under Tito as a national forest in 1967. These woodlands stretch between four of Bosnia and Herzegovina's main waterways—the Una, Sava, Sana, and Vrbas Rivers. No doubt the nature-loving general liked the fact that Kozara's dense forests and hilly meadows came to be known as the "Green Beauty of Krajina."

The Yugoslav Partisan Memorial

As in Tito's time, Kozara is still a popular hunting ground, with 64.5 square miles (167 sq km) of the park open to hunters in search of deer, pheasants, foxes, boars, hares, and ducks.

Elsewhere, you can hike a network of trails, cycle, or enjoy a morning gathering herbs in the meadows. As you listen to the peaceful cooing of a turtledove, reflect that just a few decades ago, Tito and his Partisans fought for this ground by resisting the Nazi occupation. A WWII monument, memorial wall, and museum can be reached on the Mrakovica Trail, a 2.7-mile (4.4-km) loop that also takes in beech and fir forests.

AT A GLANCE

Forest park landscapes ▪ 69.5 square miles (180 sq km) ▪ World War II memorial ▪ Hiking, cycling, and skiing trails ▪ Mrakovica Trail ▪ npkozara.com

SUTJESKA

A mountain park of historic significance and rare dramatic beauty

Bosnia and Herzegovina's oldest national park, Sutjeska, protects the country's highest peak of Maglić, which soars majestically to a height of 7,828 feet (2,386 m) on the border with Montenegro.

In addition, Sutjeska embraces the Perućica Nature Reserve, which preserves one of the last remaining primeval forests in Europe. The park is also known as the site of the Battle of Sutjeska, which raged from May 15 to June 16, 1943, when Tito's Partisans broke out of their encirclement by the Nazis, despite heavy losses. Several memorials at the northern edge of the park commemorate the victory.

This is landscape of stunning vertical drama: The park extends from Pivska Mountain in the east, along the courses of the rivers Piva, Drina, and Sutjeska, to Zelengora Mountain in the west. It includes the giant mountains of Mala Lelija, Volujak, and Bioč, as well as Maglić, all of which rise above 7,500 feet (2,286 m). Everywhere you hike, breathtaking views steal your oxygen: The Skakavac falls cascades some 246 feet (75 m) from a small mountain creek, almost hidden amid the forest's concealing cloak of beech, black pine, and spruce. Golden eagles, grouse, peregrine falcons, and rock partridge all thrive in these forest highlands, as Balkan chamois, bears, wild boar, wolves, mink, martens, and wildcats stalk the land.

AT A GLANCE

Maglić Mountain ▪ Perućica Nature Reserve ▪ 67.5 square miles (175 sq km) ▪ Skakavac waterfall ▪ Battle of Sutjeska memorial ▪ npsutjeska.info/eng/home

UNA

Walls of waterfalls await intrepid travelers in western Bosnia.

The fluvial beauty of the Štrbački Buk waterfall is Una's main draw.

The focal point of Una National Park is the stunningly beautiful Štrbački Buk, an 82-foot (25-m) waterfall along the Una River, located on Bosnia and Herzegovina's border with Croatia. The park encompasses the valley of the River Una, the canyon of the River Unac, a tributary of Una, and the orographic slopes of the Pljesevica, Grmeč, and Osječenica Mountains that feed these rivers with vast volumes of freshwater.

You should also take time to visit the more sedate, but no less lovely Milančev Buk falls at Martin Brod.

The International Una Regatta kayaking competition starts here, but the park offers less competitive visitors a wealth of other outdoor pursuits. These include rafting, fishing, cycling, hiking, and camping along its well-maintained trails. And if you've ever wanted to try bungee jumping without the cord, then leaping from the city bridges in Bihać and Bosanska Krupa is a local pastime that might appeal. At least to some.

LONG HERITAGE

This national park is rich in his-tory: The Roman fort of Milančeva Kula and the hermitage of Rmanj, a Serbian Orthodox monastery dedicated to Saint Nicholas in Martin Brod, are both within its boundaries. The 16th-century Ostrovica Castle towers over the village of Kulen Vakuf; this hilltop stronghold is worth seeing for its purveyance of Ottoman-Turk power over the province of Bosnia.

Note that if your name is Una (or presumably Oona, too), you pay no admission. So bring your ID, Una: This national park belongs to you.

AT A GLANCE

Štrbački Buk and Milančev Buk waterfalls ▪ 76.4 square miles (198 sq km) ▪ Ostrovica Castle ▪ Rmanj Monastery ▪ nationalpark-una.ba/en

SERBIA

Few countries on Earth are more welcoming than Serbia. That may be because this landlocked nation at the crossroads of eastern Europe has so many neighbors: Hungary and Romania to the north, Bulgaria and North Macedonia to the south, Bosnia and Herzegovina as well as Croatia to the west, and Montenegro to the southwest. The Serbs see Albanians as neighbors too, via the disputed territory of Kosovo. Serbs are friendly to a fault, fun-loving, and festive. If too much *ćevapčići* (grilled kebab) and *rakija* (fruity firewater) give you the Belgrade blues, head to the national parks of Djerdap on the Danube, Tara with its jaw-dropping Drina River canyon, or Fruška Gora and Kopaonik, mountain retreats in a land where monasteries have long been yin to the cities' yang.

*Opposite: Tara National Park
is the zenith of Serbian wilderness.*

DJERDAP

Djerdap (meaning "whirlpool") protects Europe's longest gorge.

Djerdap National Park stretches along the Danube from the medieval Golubac Fortress to the dam near Novi Sip. The star turn is the Djerdap gorge, the famous Iron Gate that cuts through the southern slopes of the Carpathians for 62 miles (100 km). At Gospođin Vir, the river's depths reach 269 feet (82 m), while the cliffs in Kazan rise to heights of almost 1,000 feet (300 m). The terrain is a karst spectacle of mountainous rock cut with caves, pits, springs, and

The 14th-century Golubac Fortress

lakes. The building of power plants to harness the river has come at a cost to some plant life, such as the Djerdap's tulip. But the greenery along the banks still features Turkish hazel, European yew, largeleaf linden, downy oak, and European holly. The park's 15 indigenous Balkans plants include Pančić's maple and species of heartsease, wild thyme, and meadow fescue. Bear, lynx, wolves, jackals, white-tailed eagles, owls, black storks, and more recently, Dalmatian pelicans, frequent the park. The park's many historic sites include the prehistoric Lepenski Vir, which has stone sculptures and altars.

Djerdap gorge ▪ Karst landscape ▪ 246.2 square miles (637.8 sq km) ▪ Dalmatian pelicans ▪ Historic sites ▪ npdjerdap.org

FRUŠKA GORA

The "Serbian Mount Athos" protects centuries of monastic life, wineries, and wildlife.

Fruška Gora National Park comprises a 50-mile (80-km) stretch of mountainous preserved lands that have historically been blessed with a distinctly religious flavor. Many monasteries were built here between the 15th and 18th centuries to preserve the traditional Serbian faith of Christianity and safeguard Serbian manuscripts from the invading Muslim Turks. The cloistered life of 16 of these hermitages continues to this day, and visitors can witness the austere life of the monks.

Little is sequestered about Fruška Gora's other tradition, wine, and the region's many small wineries will welcome you with popping corks, a traditional toast or two, and the standard three-kiss Serbian greeting—in this Christian landscape, much of your time will be spent turning the other cheek! Vineyards were originally planted here by the Romans in the second century A.D., and you can taste for yourself how Fruška Gora's Rieslings and sparkling wines have

come a long way since Marcus Aurelius first ordered the growing of grapes.

Fruška Gora's highest peak is Crveni Čot, standing at 1,768 feet (539 m). Today, its rolling hills and linden, oak, and beech forests make for fine hikes and off-road cycling for those who seek adventure in the Serbian outdoors. The area is sprinkled with picturesque villages, among them the baroque Sremski Karlovci, which acts as a gateway to the national park.

Rolling hillsides ▪ Monastic sites ▪ Wineries ▪ 102.9 square miles (266.5 sq km) ▪ Sremski Karlovci village ▪ serbia.travel/nature.621.html, serbia.com

KOPAONIK

A soaring mountain park rises high and wide near the southern border.

Serbia's largest mountain range, the Kopaonik, straddles its border with Kosovo. The highest point here is Pančić's Peak, which soars to a height of 6,617 feet (2,017 m). The central part of the Kopaonik plateau has been protected as a national park since 1981. Kopaonik has a subarctic climate with short, fresh summers and long, cold winters with abundant snowfall. The snow lasts from November to May, which means the park shares these mountains with the huge Kopaonik ski resort.

Kopaonik National Park is situated on the mountain plateau of Suvo Rudište, directly below which lies the Samokovska River Valley, with rapids, falls, and gorges excellent for adventure sports. A popular hike leads to Jelovarnik falls, which cascade over stepped rock for 100 feet (30 m). The mountains are cloaked in forests of Balkan beech, fir, spruce, yew, maple, pine, and oak. You'll also trek through woods of willow, poplar, common hornbeam, durmast oak, and turkey oak. Look for the ancient "Fir of One Hundred Elbows" in Samokovska Reka.

Kopaonik hosts 175 species of birds, including protected woodpeckers, rock partridges, redbacked shrikes, and woodlarks. Hikers should seek the endemic Balkan postman butterfly, whose uniform consists of orange wings with brown tinges, and a darkened dot on each upper wing. After hiking you can visit the Jošanička Banja spa, whose thermal waters reach temperatures of 190°F (88°C).

AT A GLANCE

Kopaonik Mountains ▪ Samokovska River Valley ▪ 46.7 square miles (121 sq km) ▪ Jelovarnik falls ▪ panacomp.net/kopaonik-national-park, serbia.com

TARA

A stunning canyon park of vast proportions

You could quite happily sit for hours at the outlooks in this dreamlike park. Then there's the surreal Lonely House on the Drina River, perched midstream on its own mini-clifftop. The sense of dramatic beauty continues as you make your way down the Drina River Canyon, where the sheer scale of the rock walls seems positively Tolkienesque. Tara National Park, set in the Dinaric Alps, is the very pinnacle of Serbian wilderness. Drina's canyon is the third

The vertiginous Drina River canyon

largest of its kind in the world and makes for adrenaline-pumping white-water rafting. For calmer waters, try kayaking on Tara's two lakes, Perućac and Zaovine. As you roam along the scenic trails, you'll walk through the home of endangered brown bears as well as foxes, lynx, and otters. The park provides woodland habitat for more than 130 species of birds, and a wide range of Balkan flora—more than 1,000 species—including the rare Pančić spruce.

AT A GLANCE

Dinaric Alpine landscapes ▪ Drina River Canyon ▪ 85 square miles (220 sq km) ▪ Perućac and Zaovine Lakes ▪ nptara.rs/en

MONTENEGRO

Among hikers, the small country of Montenegro is Europe's best kept secret. In its native language, this nation is called Crna Gora, or Black Mountain, a hint at its dramatic terrain. To watch sunrise or sunset over the glacial mountains of Durmitor National Park is a lesson in humility for humankind. Small wonder that the watchwords of Montenegro's code of chivalry are *"Čojstvo i Junaštvo,* Humanity and Courage." Few of this warrior race personified that credo better than Petar II Petrović-Njegoš, the 19th-century national hero whose mountaintop mausoleum you can hike to in Lovćen National Park. Since 2006, this has been an independent country, its citizens free to worship in the ancient Orthodox monasteries that cling to its cliffs, or at the Albanian mosques in numerous towns, or simply to hike high into the grandeur of nature to be closer to whichever deity they choose.

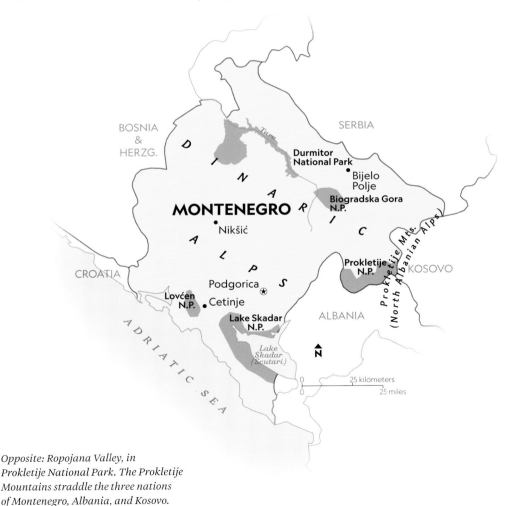

Opposite: Ropojana Valley, in Prokletije National Park. The Prokletije Mountains straddle the three nations of Montenegro, Albania, and Kosovo.

BIOGRADSKA GORA

Mountains, lakes, and some of the last virgin forests in Europe

Biogradska Gora is one of the last untouched temperate rainforests in Europe, located in central Montenegro between the rivers Tara and Lim. Ridges, verdant pasturelands, and five high-altitude glacial lakes at 5,970 feet (1,820 m) or more make hiking here a delight. Shepherd's huts provide a place to rest at various points as trails lead to heady peaks, many more than 6,560 feet (2,000 m) high. Head for the virgin forest of Biogradska Gora, with Biogradsko Lake at its heart.

Shepherds have tended the highland meadows for many centuries.

The lake is edged with ancient European beech, sycamore maple, juniper, and European ash, many more than five hundred years old. Three species of trout make these lakes attractive lures for anglers.

AT A GLANCE

Virgin temperate rainforests ▪ 20.8 square miles (54 sq km) ▪ Biogradsko Jezero (lake) ▪ nparkovi.me/en

DURMITOR

Embracing soaring peaks, virgin forests, and plunging canyons

Durmitor National Park encompasses the Durmitor Mountain massif and three breathtaking canyons, including that of the wild Tara River, home to Europe's deepest gorge at 4,265 feet (1,300 m). Waters from Black Lake gush below the Durmitor massif to the upper canyon valley of the River Komarnica. The park landscapes sparkle with the glinting of its many glacial lakes.

Durmitor is densely forested with deciduous and pine forests—including one of Europe's last virgin stands of black pine, near Crna Poda. These towering trees are more than 400 years old, witness to Montenegro's history of Adriatic pirates, Ottoman Turks, Venetian plunderers, and Yugoslav communists. In summer, many of the park's high pastures host grazing sheep and cattle owned by the 1,500 or so farmers living on these lands and by others from the village of Zabljak.

You can reach the plateau in the Dinaric Alps via a network of trails, with three overnight shelters to help you rest: a hut, a refuge, and a bivouac. The massif has 50 peaks above 6,560 feet (2,000 m). Due to the dramatic differences in altitude, Durmitor enjoys both Mediterranean (in the valleys) and alpine microclimates. While hiking the lower slopes, you can pick blueberries and wild strawberries, but keep watch for wolves, wild boars, brown bears, chamois, and eagles.

AT A GLANCE

Dinaric Alpine landscapes ▪ 131 square miles (339 sq km) ▪ Durmitor Mountain massif ▪ Summer pastures ▪ nparkovi.me/en

LAKE SKADAR

Southern Europe's largest lake nurtures multiple mollusk, fish, and bird species.

A classic karst lake, Skadarsko Jezero (Lake Skadar) lies on Montenegro's border with Albania. In Montenegro, Lake Skadar National Park protects steep mountains, island monasteries, and floating fields of water lilies. The Albanian section is protected as a nature reserve.

An interesting characteristic of Skadar's water balance are the high volumes of freshwater that surge up from below, through karstic springs. These can be a danger to swimmers, producing sudden unexpected jets and freezing whirlpools. These springs tend to occur on the bays around the southern and southwestern shores, where the shorelines are rocky, barren, and steep. On the lake's northern side, an enormous swamp attracts multiple birdlife, its boundaries shifting as water levels fluctuate.

Boating and fishing are popular in the park. You can also visit the small islands, including Beška, which has two churches, and Grmožur, which houses a former fortress. Near the mouth of Rijeka Crnojevića, divers can explore the wreck of the steamboat *Skanderbeg*, sunk by Partisans in 1942. The ghostly boat rests 36 feet (11 m) below the surface.

FRESHWATER HABITAT

Lake Skadar National Park is a unique biosphere and a well-known hot spot of freshwater biodiversity.

Skadar enjoys quantities of freshwater from karstic springs.

Skadar is one of Europe's largest bird reserves, hosting some 270 species. These include some of the last Dalmatian pelicans in Europe, as well as multitudinous flocks of pygmy cormorants, seagulls, and herons. Bird-watchers arrive here in spring and fall, armed with binoculars, cameras, and flasks of *loza* (grape brandy) to stake out the migrant masses as they descend from the skies. Anglers also gravitate to this well-stocked lake for its carp, bleak, and trout. Of the 34 native fish species, 7 are endemic to Lake Skadar.

The lake is also host to a highly diverse range of mollusks. Many of the 50 or so species of freshwater snails found in the lake basin are endemic. Lake Skadar is also inhabited by five species of gastropods, and it is a hot spot of gastropod evolution. The lake is also a nurturing incubator for crustaceans, with about 17 amphipod species thriving in the Lake Skadar watershed, 10 of them found only here.

Park authorities are increasingly aware of new threats to this fragile aquatic biosphere from hypertrophication (overenrichment of the water, resulting in algae bloom and other blights), water pollution, and sand and soil displacement. Future generations will need to carefully choreograph the delicate dance between enjoyment of this fertile resource and its ruination.

AT A GLANCE

Karst lake landscape ▪ A main European bird-watching site ▪ 142.9 square miles (370.1 sq km) ▪ Wreck of the *Skanderbeg* steamboat ▪ visit-montenegro.com

LOVĆEN

A fitting pinnacle for a national hero in his country's spiritual homeland

It's a long, long way up. As on many of Montenegro's mountains, here on Mount Lovćen you feel closer to the realm of the gods than the world of mortal men. So this is a fitting resting place for a mere mortal who became a Montenegrin legend—high in the heavens, looking down on his beloved land and the strangers who come to admire rather than to plunder, pillage, or occupy.

the inspiration for the name of the country itself: Crna Gora (Black Mountain), was first mentioned in 1276, referencing Mount Lovćen, which at the time was covered in dense, dark forests.

Mount Lovćen rises from the Adriatic Basin, overlooking the long, twisting bays of Boka Kotorska and the coastal town of Kotor. The mountain has two imposing

Hiking and Nordic skiing are popular park activities.

HISTORY & CULTURE

Lovćen National Park protects the nation's history and culture as much as its dramatic landscapes. As you hike its trails, you'll come across old houses and cottages in *katuns,* summer settlements of cattle herders. The park also offers a glimpse of the aristocratic side of Montenegrin history: Take the long and winding road uphill from Kotor to the village of Njeguši and you'll find yourself at the birthplace of Montenegro's royal family, the House of Petrović-Njegoš. Here, you'll also find the country's best *pršut* (smoke-dried ham) and *sir* (cheese).

The steps to the mausoleum of poet-patriot Petar II Petrović-Njegoš

Montenegrin patriarch and patriot Petar II Petrović-Njegoš (1813–1851) asked to be buried here at the summit of Jezerski Peak as his dying wish, a wish finally granted in 1971.

Mount Lovćen lends its name to its attendant national park in southwestern Montenegro. It is also

peaks: Štirovnik, which soars to 5,738 feet (1,749 m) and Jezerski Peak, which stands at 5,436 feet (1,657 m) above the deep-blue Adriatic. These are rocky mountains, covered with scree, and the landscape is marked by numerous fissures, pits, and deep depressions.

On Jezerski Peak, the second highest point in the park, sits the mausoleum of Petar II Petrović-Njegoš. Its foundations were built into 20 feet (6 m) of mountain rock. Njegoš was a bishop-prince *(vladika),* a poet and philosopher whose works shaped much of Serbian and Montenegrin literature, and inspired the fight for independence from the Ottoman Empire. You can reach the mausoleum by the road from Cetinje, but bring your hiking shoes; 461 steps lead up to the monument. This is a fitting tribute to this national hero whose epic poem was called *Gorski vijenac (The Mountain Wreath).*

PROKLETIJE

Jagged peaks, medieval mosques, and abundant wildlife

A long and winding road leads through the magnificent scenery of the remote Grbaja Valley.

The Prokletije Mountains are a massive, sprawling expanse of wilderness in southeastern Europe, where the borders of three countries—Montenegro, Albania, and Kosovo—meet. This giant range is the southernmost—and highest—part of the Dinaric Alps. Because of its remoteness, this startlingly beautiful and rugged landscape is a surprise to most of the hikers, cyclists, and birders who discover the hills in the summer months.

This is classic mountain massif wilderness filled with jagged alpine peaks, many over 6,560 feet (2,000 m), as well as stony gorges, sweeping river valleys, glacial lakes, fast-running streams, underground aquifers, mineral-water wells (Ali-Pasha's springs), and glorious meadows of blooming wildflowers. The park is rich in fauna, with wolves, brown bears, lynx, wild boar, and chamois all occupying its diverse ecosystem. Golden eagles, snake eagles, and peregrine falcons ply the skies.

The human historic footprint is large here too: Several old mosques date from the 15th to the 18th centuries, such as the Redzepagic Mosque in the town of Plav. Aging churches dot the landscape too, including the Church of St. Brezojevica in Plav and the Church of St. Balic in Gusinje.

In 2009, when Prokletije National Park was declared Montenegro's fifth national park, it became the third national park in the Prokletije Mountains, joining Thethi (see page 442) and Valbona Valley (see page 445) National Parks in Albania. Montenegro, Albania, and Kosovo are now ambitiously planning to create a tri-nation park across the entire region, to be called the Balkans Peace Park. It's certainly a better name than the one historically given to this ominous mountain range, the Accursed Mountains. Small comfort that this refers to their difficult environments rather than to any curse. The trails are spectacular but not always well signposted. The mountaineering society in Plav can recommend local guides.

AT A GLANCE

Prokletije Mountains ▪ Dinaric Alpine landscapes ▪ 61.7 square miles (160 sq km) ▪ Region of national parklands ▪ nparkovi.me/en, balkanspeacepark.org

KOSOVO

Kosovo is Europe's newest country, declaring independence in 2008. The Kosovans suffered dreadfully in the fierce ethnic war of the 1990s, but now strive to turn a new page of history. This multiethnic nation has chosen to participate in a proposed transnational Peace Park, to be shared with Albania and Montenegro as its symbol of hope for a better future. The land of Kosovo is sacred to many, not least to neigh-

boring Serbs, who contest its independence. Yet inside Serbian Orthodox monasteries protected in Kosovo by NATO, such as Dečan and Gračanica, monks go about their age-old traditions of making cheese and honey, and praying for lasting peace. Likewise, Muslims answer the call to prayer at Sinan Pasha Mosque in Prizren, where the Kalaja Fortress reminds travelers that this land has long been embattled. High in the rugged peaks of Bjeshkët e Nemuna and Sharri National Parks, many Kosovans find a sense of serenity that has eluded their nation throughout much of its history. As the poet Rumi wrote: "Out beyond ideas of wrongdoing and rightdoing, there is a field. I'll meet you there."

Opposite: The roads of Sharri National Park twist around the northern Šar Mountains. Above: The park's many hiking trails lead high into these scenic peaks.

BJESHKËT E NEMUNA

All-day walking trails through sheer snow-peaked mountains and glorious valleys

The "Accursed Mountains" punctuate the borders between Montenegro, Albania, and Kosovo.

Bjeshkët e Nemuna National Park is located in western Kosovo, along the borders with Albania and Montenegro. This is dramatic mountain country, with glacial lakes, dense forests, and soaring alpine peaks. As everywhere in this storied land, churches and other cultural and historical sites lie scattered throughout the valleys.

The rocky peaks within this park are part of the Prokletije Mountains, the southernmost outposts of the Dinaric Alps. Rising to an elevation of 8,714 feet (2,656 m), Gjeravica is the highest peak in Kosovo.

Many species of plants and wildlife thrive in these mountains, due to the wide differences of elevations here and the rugged topography of the landscapes. Large mammals that stalk this wilderness include wildcats, chamois, roe deer, wolves, as well as several rare or endangered species such as lynx, imperial eagle, and capercaillie.

You'll see signs of brown bears when you hike in the park: Look for claw marks on oak trees that dominate the lower woods. Up to 2,625 feet (800 m), you'll walk through lush forests of Italian, Austrian, and Cornish oak; at the next level, the beech forests prevail, including stands of silver fir, sycamore, European flowering ash, and Bos-

nian pine. The mixed oak forest zone comes next, mainly cloaked in silver fir, Norway spruce, and European hornbeam. Higher again, the dark coniferous forest zone has mainly Bosnian pine, Norway spruce, and Macedonian pine.

Stands of fir forests are planted above this, and once you reach the shrub zone that extends up to 6,725 feet (2,050 m), you will walk among meadows of grass, moss, lichen, and herbaceous plants, including wood cranesbill, wild strawberry, willow, and forget-me-not. Welcome to the roof of Kosovo, with wonderful views of the country stretching below.

AT A GLANCE

Prokletije mountain landscapes ▪ Six altitudinal growth zones ▪ 243.4 square miles (630.4 sq km) ▪ Excellent one-day hiking trails ▪ parksdinarides.org

SHARRI

Dramatic peaks, wondrous wildlife, adventurous hiking trails, and great skiing

Sharri National Park, in south-eastern Kosovo, centers around the northern Šar Mountains, a range that extends into north-eastern Albania and northwestern North Macedonia. The locals know the main peak as Šara. The park's stunning range of terrain is a delight to adventurous souls. Here, you'll hike through glacial and periglacial landscapes on trails that climb to rugged alpine peaks past lakes, creeks, bogs, and broad-leaved forests. You'll view cirques, moraines, great rock deposits, "tundra mosaic" deposits of silt, caves, and many karstic features.

PLANT LIFE

An amazing array of plants grow in this park, even at its rocky, elevated peaks. In all, some 1,800 plant species thrive here including, on Šara, 18 species found nowhere else. These mountain woods also nurture the endemic Macedonian pine and whitebark pine trees. Here too is the alpenrose, a rugged, pink-flowering bloom that grows even on the stonier heights of the Šar Mountains. Other perennials you'll see along the trails include white blossoming King Alexander's yarrow, Nikolić's silene, and the pink-flowering Šar carnation.

In this part of the world, things get politicized, even when you're talking botany: So when exploring the heights of Sharri National Park, have a good look for a rugged rock bloomer called Natalie's ramonda, identifiable by its mint-like, rounded crenate evergreen leaves, long purple-red stem, and delicate lilac-blue flowers. This is a relic species, one that went extinct from most of Europe during the last ice age and yet today grows as an endemic species in several gorges in Kosovo, Serbia, North Macedonia, and Greece.

This green caterpillar will transform into a "night butterfly" or moth.

This asterid has been chosen as the Serbian symbol for Armistice Day. That this of all flowers was chosen by the fearsome warriors of that country, Kosovo's northerly neighbors, as a symbol of the Serbian Army's struggle during World War I perhaps has something to do with its tenacious ability to thrive in the rockiest, harshest terrains at altitudes higher than most such plants. Natalie's ramonda sprouts from rocks at an angle, allowing rainwater to run off the surface of its leaves. It can resist exposure and winter temperatures as low as 5°F (−15°C). This is a true Balkan survivor species.

ANIMAL LIFE

The animal species prowling the park include the rare Balkan lynx, the largest European cat. Only 100 of these stealthy felines survive in the entire Balkans region. The European pond turtle and Hermann's tortoise, Europe's two freshwater turtle species, also live on Šara. Other wildlife include bears, chamois, wolves, roe deer, and many bird species. The park also protects about 720 sure-footed chamois.

AT A GLANCE

Šar Mountains terrain ▪ Balkan lynx ▪ 206.4 square miles (534.6 sq km) ▪ Natalie's ramonda ▪ European pond turtle and Hermann's tortoise ▪ parksdinarides.org/en/park/national_park_sharri/

ALBANIA

Like a European Cuba, Albania is a land where the past seemed to get stuck on pause for several decades. This was bad news if you lived in a grim communist tower block in Tirana in the 1970s or 1980s, but thankfully, the future has been on fast-forward since the 1990s, following the fall of the Iron Curtain. Yet the feeling of time standing still has been beneficial in terms of conservation and preservation of the environment. This means you can go to Berat and step back into an Ottoman-era town of whitewashed houses stacked stylishly on the hillside. Or visit the mountaintop town of Gjirokastër, with its imposing castle and elegant Ottoman mansions. Everywhere you can spread your wings across the stunning natural wonders of this "land of the eagles." Start by riding the cable car from Tirana up to Dajti National Park. Cross the Katiu Bridge and get healed at the Benja thermal waters in Bredhi i Hotovës-Dangelli National Park. Or take a boat out onto the great lake of Prespa, and watch for brown bears fishing or flocks of white pelicans socializing. You can also commit to one of Europe's great hikes, the glorious mountaintop trek between Valbonë and Thethi, and see two of Albania's finest national parks in one unforgettable day.

Opposite: Valbona Valley National Park, northern Albania

BREDHI I DRENOVËS

A tiny national park celebrates a famous European tree species.

One of the smallest national parks you'll find anywhere in Europe, Bredhi i Drenovës National Park is situated six miles (10 km) from Korçë, on the side of Morava Mountain in eastern Albania. Here you can walk among old forests dominated by the European silver fir, a tree that can grow to heights of up to 200 feet (60 m). This is one of the great mountain trees of Europe, flourishing on hillsides from the French and Spanish Pyrénées north to Normandy; east across the Alps and the Carpathians, Slovenia, Croatia, Bosnia and Herzegovina, Montenegro, and Serbia; and south to Italy, Bulgaria, and northern Greece, as well as here in Albania. In the United States, this triangular-topped, green-needled species has long been grown as a Christmas tree.

The park woodlands are also rich in beech and black pine trees. The lower part of the park is covered in hazelnut trees. Bredhi i Drenovës's rich fauna includes the famous Bozdoveci bear, a rare Albanian subspecies. The national park also has several interesting rock formations, such as the Stone of Capi, the Cut stone, the Zhombrit's Pyramid, and the Cave of Tren. Within its small parameters, you'll also find the Lenies Lakes and the Karstic Cave, both of which the Albanian government has declared natural landmarks. Natural springs such as those of Shëngjergj, Plaka, and Pllica will slake the thirst of hikers in this small, rustic park.

AT A GLANCE

European silver fir forests ▪ The Bozdoveci bear ▪ 3.9 square miles (10.3 sq km) ▪ Zhombrit's Pyramid ▪ akzm.gov.al

BREDHI I HOTOVËS-DANGELLI

Protecting and celebrating the Hotova fir tree

A green wilderness of rolling hills, lush forests, and dramatic peaks, Bredhi i Hotovës-Dangelli National Park is named for the Hotova fir. But the park's landscapes are not all forests; much of the mountainous terrain comprises sharp limestone and sandstone deposits, carved out by rivers into valleys, canyons, and gorges. This remote mountainous region makes for fine hiking. The deep, narrow Lengaricë Canyon, near Petran, is worth exploring for its many caves

Forests carpet the mountain folds.

and thermal springs such as Banjat e Bënjës. The landscape also makes for exciting rafting; the Vjosë River is the main waterway, flowing through Përmet before ending its journey at the Adriatic Sea. The park is home to wildcats, roe deer, wild boars, Eurasian otters, and brown bears. The old-growth forests host barn owls, sparrow hawks, Egyptian vulture, kestrel, and lanner falcons. This is a wilderness that shouldn't be wandered into lightly. Check the weather, be prepared, and consider hiring a local guide. The Katiu Ottoman Bridge and the healing waters of Benja thermal pools should be left until the end of your travels.

AT A GLANCE

Remote mountainous landscapes ▪ 132.7 square miles (343.6 sq km) ▪ Lengaricë Canyon ▪ Katiu Ottoman Bridge and Benja thermal pools ▪ akzm.gov.al

BUTRINTI

A park of rare historic richness and ecological diversity

Butrinti National Park in southern Albania has a hilly landscape with freshwater lakes, wetlands, salt marshes, open plains, reed beds, and the islands of Ksamil.

The park hosts more than 1,200 different animals and plants, many of which live in the protected lake and lagoon of Butrinti. Golden eagles prey overhead, while golden jackals and grey wolves hunt these lands. Marine life spans such visitors as striped dolphins to the endangered Mediterranean monk

The Roman theater

seal that inhabits certain caverns. The wetlands are resting and nesting grounds for a wealth of birdlife: Look for the great black cormorant

with its yellow bill. Park reptiles include the Balkan green lizard and the Aesculapian snake.

Butrinti is a UNESCO World Heritage site because of its architectural ruins, spanning 2,500 years of history. The Castle of Ali Pasha Tepelena lies on a tiny island in the Vivari Channel. There's also a Roman theater, a Dionysian altar, an aqueduct, temples of Minerva and Asclepius, the Lion Gate, and a baptistery— monuments from the Greek, Roman, and Byzantine eras are all found here.

AT A GLANCE

Butrinti Lake and lagoon ▪ Archaeological ruins ▪ 36.3 square miles (94.2 sq km) ▪ Extensive wildlife and birdlife ▪ expoaus.org/butrint-national-park-uso12

DAJTI

A mountain park of forests and wild animals just outside Tirana

Dajti National Park in central Albania lies just 25 miles (40 km) west of the Adriatic Sea and 16 miles (26 km) east of Tirana. The park has an extremely fragmented, rugged topography that hosts a diversity of ecosystems. However, Dajti is under modern-day duress of deforestation partly because of the effects of climate change. Forest fires have become a major worry in summer months as wildfire crews remain on standby for a repeat of a recent Dajti Mountain immolation

that burned large areas near the summit.

The park centers around the Dajti massif, which rises to 5,292 feet (1,613 m). Climbers of Dajti get stunning views of the city of Tirana and of the surrounding Skanderbeg Mountains from the peak nicknamed the Balcony of Tirana. Lake Bovilla, located to the northeast of Brar, is a gorgeous green, with steep cliffs and a canyon. Elsewhere, you can hike to the prehistoric Pellumbas

Cave located in the Skorana gorge. Another worthwhile trek is to the Shëngjini waterfalls, near the village of Shëngjergj.

Dajti's varied inhabitants include wild boars, Eurasian wolves, red foxes, European hares, brown bears, and wildcats. In the lower parts of the mountains the vegetation is scrub with extensive stretches of heath, myrtle, and fragaria. Oak trees dominate the higher areas along with scattered beech stands.

AT A GLANCE

Skanderbeg Mountain landscapes ▪ 113.4 square miles (293.8 sq km) ▪ Shëngjini waterfalls ▪ Prehistoric Pellumbas Cave ▪ akzm.gov.al

DIVJAKA-KARAVASTA

An avian sanctuary along the Adriatic coast

Karavastasë Lagoon spans an area of 16 square miles (42 sq km).

This is *the* Albanian park for birds and bird-watchers. The vast Divjaka-Karavasta is a rich wilderness, teeming with wildlife and lush vegetation. The park is located in western Albania, sprawling across the Myzeqe Plain directly inland from the Adriatic Sea. The terrains of these flatlands provide every variety of avian habitat, spanning wetlands, salt marshes, coastal meadows, floodplains, woodlands, reed beds, forests, and estuaries.

The park mainly protects the lagoons of Godulla and Karavastasë and the estuaries of Shkumbinit and Semanit. The Karavastasë Lagoon is a vital marine bird sanctuary in the Mediterranean. It is separated from the Adriatic by a large strip of sand, the sediment discharged by the rivers Shkumbinit and Semanit. The islands in the lagoon offer vital conservation

Dalmatian Pelicans

The Dalmatian pelican is the iconic bird of Divjaka-Karavasta National Park. This huge creature inhabits the lagoon of Karavastasë, its only coastal breeding site in the Adriatic. The park is now home to 5 percent of the entire population of this globally endangered species. The pelicans nest only on the lagoon's islands, safe from disturbance. At the start of the 20th century, more than 250 pelican pairs were counted; the current count is about 53. Hunting in the park is now forbidden; the birds can partly thank American author Jonathan Franzen for this, as he highlighted lax local rules in an essay for the *New Yorker*.

habitat. The endangered Dalmatian pelican (see sidebar), collared pratincole, little tern, and many other breeding birds of the park nest on these islands safe from predators and human disturbance.

This largely coastal park enjoys a Mediterranean climate, with hot summers and relatively dry winters; its location makes it a key Adriatic hub for the migrating millions of birds on their way between Europe and Africa.

Illyrian deciduous forests cover much of the park, and these woodlands and the scrub around them are hunting and foraging grounds for animals such as the red fox, golden jackal, and roe deer. Watch for otters in the park's waterways too. The forests contain a mix of deciduous and coniferous trees, including junipers, willows, oak, alder, elm, and ash. Much of the park's forests grow in the northern corner of Karavastasë between the sandy beaches and the estuary of Shkumbinit. Watch on the trails for the two strains of pine that stand out within this protected woodland: the Aleppo pine and the stone pine, whose edible pine nuts have long been used to flavor dishes throughout the Mediterranean. In the wetlands and swamps, an abundance of algae and dense phanerogam grasses grow, while the dunes are held in place by several salt-tolerant grass species.

AT A GLANCE

Adriatic coastal bird habitats ▪ Karavastasë Lagoon ▪ 85.8 square miles (222.3 sq km) ▪ Dalmatian pelicans ▪ akzm.gov.al

KARABURUN-SAZAN

A marine park lures divers to discover the wonders beneath the Adriatic.

Albanian landscapes hit all the high notes of Dinaric Alpine beauty, a magnificence that extends to the depth of the Adriatic shelf and the aquatic world just beneath the offshore waves. Karaburun-Sazan National Marine Park, along the southwest coast of Albania, encompasses both the Karaburun Peninsula and Ishulli i Sazanit (the island of Sazanit).

Karaburun-Sazan is home to a vast array of landforms including mountains, caves, islands, bays, cliffs, canyons, and rocky coastlines. Hiking here is challenging, but the wildlife is spectacular: Golden jackals, wildcats, chamois, roe deer, badgers, and otters all inhabit the park. Out at sea, you might spot dolphins and seals, including the rare Mediterranean monk seal. Loggerhead sea turtles, green sea turtles, and leatherback sea turtles all swim in the waters of this park.

Karaburun-Sazan is also a divers' paradise, with ruins of sunken Greek, Roman, and World War II ships lying within reach in these turquoise waters. A world of lush underwater fauna, steep cliffs, and gorgeous giant blue caves await divers. But be aware that the marine park is situated close to an Albanian military base, and permission may be required to dive in certain places. Hiring a professional local diver as a guide is a smart idea. Also, many roads are inaccessible and you can only reach remote parts of the park by boat or long, cross-country hikes.

AT A GLANCE

Karaburun Peninsula ▪ Coastal karst landscapes ▪ 48.5 square miles (125.7 sq km) ▪ Spectacular diving ▪ Mediterranean monk seal ▪ akzm.gov.al

LLOGARA

A coastal park along the "Albanian Riviera" in the sun-soaked southwest

Like much of the Albanian coastline on the Adriatic and Ionian Sea, Llogara enjoys a mild Mediterranean climate that results in dense forests of pine, oak, and fir trees growing atop its limestone and dolomite landscapes. Llogara National Park stretches along this shoreline, shadowed by the Ceraunian Mountains. The lovely drives high above these coasts afford vistas of the shoreline that have given Llogara the reputation of an "Albanian Riviera." The park's

Llogara lies in the Ceraunian hills.

terrain also encompasses alpine meadows, vertical rock faces, and steep cliffs. You'll walk through Bosnian pine, black pine, Bulgarian fir, silver fir, and ash stands, with the chance to spy a griffon vulture, golden eagle, or a chamois anywhere in this coastal wilderness. Qafa e Llogorasë, the mountain pass of Llogara, at 3,369 feet (1,027 m), marks the watershed between the Adriatic and the Ionian Seas. This is a park for all seasons: The snow-topped peaks lure skiers in winter while its Ionian coastline beckons hikers, cyclists, and divers all summer.

AT A GLANCE

Ceraunian mountain landscapes ▪ 3.9 square miles (10.1 sq km) ▪ Adriatic and Ionian coastlines ▪ Llogara mountain pass ▪ akzm.gov.al

LURË-MOUNT DEJËS

Two Albanian wildernesses combine in a newly protected national park.

The remote darkness of Lurë dramatizes night skies.

Welcome to the mountains of Kunora e Lurës and Dejës, home of Lurë-Mount Dejës National Park. The woodlands here are rich in European beech, silver fir, black pine, red pine, and Bosnian pine. The park is famed for the Field of Mares, a meadow with a painter's palette of wildflowers and coniferous trees. Another prosaically named feature worth seeking out is the Lake of Flowers, a glacial lake that fills with white water lilies, coaxing you into a Monet painting on a hot summer's day. Here you are in the realm of brown bears, Eurasian lynx, wolves, pine martens, and capercaillie, among a multitude of other wildlife.

DEFORESTATION THREAT

The trees of the remaining old-growth woods range from 150 to 200 years old: These trees have stood through a period of history when the Albanian Renaissance first raised the idea of liberation from Ottoman rule in the early 19th century through to the declaration of independence in 1912. The trees continued to grow at the time when many Albanians found themselves left outside the new nation's borders, with a population split between Montenegro and Serbia in the north and east and Greece to the south. King Zog I oversaw the first republic until Mussolini's Italian forces invaded in 1939 and Hitler's Nazis followed in 1943. The trees matured as the state then went through four and a half decades of communism. The fall of the Berlin Wall left them prey to free-market loggers who saw their chance to make fast cash in eastern Europe's changed economic landscape. When Albania's economy opened up in the 1990s, illegal loggers moved in. Deforestation and forest fires decimated vast ecosystems, and an estimated 50 percent of woodlands in what was then Lurës National Park were destroyed during this "eastern European Wild West" period. Since 2014, the government has launched a controversial rehabilitation, and in 2018 Lurës National Park and the adjacent Zall-Gjoçaj National Park combined under the name of Lurë-Mount Dejës National Park. It contains within its confines a surprisingly wide range of biodiversity and habitat.

ALBANIA'S NIGHT SKIES

The remoteness of this park in central Albania gives it an advantage shared by many other parks in this largely undeveloped country: The night skies here, unadulterated by light pollution, are stunning. While you visit, spend at least one night stargazing. Your nocturnal musings might be accompanied by the howling of wolves. Brown bears, lynx, foxes, wild boar, deer, and other large beasts also inhabit Zall-Gjoçaj. The mighty golden eagle, proud national symbol that adorns the Albanian flag, circles the skies above here.

AT A GLANCE

Kunora e Lurës and Dejës Mountains ▪ 78.1 square miles (202.4 sq km) ▪ The Field of Mares ▪ Old-growth forests ▪ Golden eagles ▪ Night skies ▪ parksdinarides.org/en/park/

PRESPA

Protecting the great lakes of Prespa with a park of vast avian habitats

Prespa National Park lies on the tri-nation border shared with Greece and North Macedonia, and embraces Albanian sections of the Great and Small Prespa Lakes. The lakes are surrounded by the mountains of southeast Albania and include habitats of small islands, extensive freshwater wetlands, salt marshes, meadows, reed beds, and dense forests. The park also protects the island of Mallograd, which has many caves inhabited by wildlife and a circular cliff.

These mountain lakes are situated between 2,790 and 2,950 feet (850 to 900 m) above the Adriatic Sea, and some 490 feet (150

m) above Ohridsko Ezero (Lake Ohrid). Prespa waters pass through underground channels composed of karst, and emerge from springs into this lower lake. The mountain of Mali i Thatë separates Great Prespa from Lake Ohrid. Locals cultivate a popular mountain tea that thrives on the limestone rock here; order a *caj mali* ("mountain tea") and get a taste of the park.

Brown bear and gray wolves roam here, and Balkan lynx use this preserve as a corridor to get to Shebenik-Jabllanicë National Park (see page 441) on the other side of Lake Ohrid. But our feathered friends are by far this park's main

wildlife attractions: Some 270 species feed or breed here, with white pelicans and Dalmatian pelicans being the stars of the show, taking advantage of the peaceful wetlands for their noisy, gregarious gathering, like an avian white night dinner party.

On the darker side, the park hosts more than 25 species of bats in its extensive caverns. The Treni cave is home to the largest population of long-fingered bat in Europe. Amphibians in the wetlands include European pond turtles, yellow- and black-shelled Hermann's tortoises, fire salamander, and various frogs.

A farming family makes hay in late afternoon summer sunshine.

AT A GLANCE

Great and Small Prespa Lakes ▪ 107.1 square miles (277.5 sq km) ▪ Treni's bat cave ▪ *Caj mali* ("mountain tea") ▪ akzm.gov.al

QAFË SHTAMA

A spectacular mountain pass links two Albanian towns.

Brown bears' range has shrunk across much of Europe, but the population remains strong in Qafë-Shtama Pass.

A dramatic pass has long linked the towns of Krujë and Burrel, giving travelers a chance to pause at an elevation of 4,100 feet (1,250 m) and take in the views. Since 1996, Qafë-Shtama National Park has enshrined this route—known locally as the Qafë-Shtama. The park itself sits at the edge of the mountain chain north of Tirana, about 15.5 miles (25 km) east of Krujë.

The road leading to the park entrance travels through the Vaja Canyon, carved out by the Lumi i Drojës (Lumi River) to depths of more than 2,133 feet (650 m). Like with much of the landscape in the land of the eagles, a legend accompanies this canyon. Local folklore has it that after the siege of Krujë in 1450, 90 young virgins from the town threw themselves to the bottom of the canyon to avoid falling into the hands of the invading Turks. Albanians still take great pride in the heroism of their forebears during the siege. The Skanderbeg Museum in Krujë commemorates this event.

The landscape travelers experience here today is one of spectacular mountain terrain, with pine forests, several small lakes, and reservoirs that feed cities and towns nearby. The black pine trees reach heights of up to 65 feet (20 m). Illegal deforestation is a widespread concern in Albania, a threat to this rich habitat for brown bears, wolves, foxes, and various birds.

Qafë-Shtama National Park is fast becoming one of the more popular hiking destinations in Albania. This small park is home to a historic water source called Burimi i Nënës Mbretëreshë (Queen Mother's Spring). The crystalline waters of this natural spring are renowned for their curative properties, so fill up your canisters for a day on the trails.

AT A GLANCE

Qafë-Shtama Pass ▪ Skanderbeg Museum in Krujë ▪ 7.7 square miles (20 sq km) ▪ Burimi i Nënës Mbretëreshë (Queen Mother's Spring) ▪ akzm.gov.al

SHEBENIK-JABLLANICË

A park of majestic landscapes and wonderful wildlife diversity

Shebenik-Jabllanicë National Park is a soaring mountainous wilderness in eastern Albania, along the border with North Macedonia. This dramatic park encompasses most of the connected mountain massifs of Shebenikut and Jablanica. Shebenik-Jabllanicë has many peaks over 6,560 feet (2,000 m), the highest being Maja e Shebenikut at 7,392 feet (2,253 m). Jablanica's long mountain ridge rises higher than 6,560 feet (2,000 m) for about 31 miles (50 km)—at its center stands its highest peak, known as Black Stone, at 7,405 feet (2,257 m). Hikers in the park find a range of breathtaking landscapes to enjoy, including glacial lakes, deep-cut valleys, dense coniferous and deciduous forests, and attractive Alpine meadows and pastures.

Some of the park's most ruggedly dramatic scenery is found in the eastern extremes of Albania, where the retreating glaciers of the last ice age produced their most lasting sculpture works. Here, happy hikers will find no less than 14 glacial lakes, the highest at elevations between 4,920 and 6,230 feet (1,500 to 1,900 m) above sea level.

Visitors to the park will also come across several cirque glaciers in both mountain ranges, nestled within depressions on the eastern-facing sides of many mountains. Two rivers course through the park, the Qarrishtes and the Bushtrices.

The parklands, and their parallel wilderness across the border in North Macedonia, are one of the few remaining habitats of the Balkan lynx, a subspecies of the Eurasian lynx and the largest wildcat in the Balkans.

The remoteness of these mountains provides vast swaths of undisturbed habitat for a variety of other endangered species, including brown bears and grey

The park's peaks present many challenges to mountaineers.

wolves. Other inhabitants of note are the least weasel, beech marten, stoat, and European badger. Bats are a largely invisible presence throughout the Balkans, but they are everywhere: A total of 18 species are known to live in these hills, where cool caves for hibernation are never too far away. The park's pastures, forests, and scrublands provide rich insect-hunting grounds for the greater horseshoe, lesser horseshoe, and Mediterranean horseshoe bats, whose yellowish white and somewhat translucent-looking fur gives this last species an albino appearance.

The forests here also contain a number of rare and endemic species of plants and fungi. These dense woodlands have beech, fir, Bosnian and Macedonian pine, and oak trees, as well as species such as purple willow, Norway maple, silver birch, and silver fir in the northern slopes of the mountains. High in the mountains, golden eagles circle outward from their rocky aeries, the symbols of a proud nation; the elegant peregrine falcon has similarly elevated tastes in real estate. In the woodlands, the rare capercaillie and the hazel grouse forage for food.

AT A GLANCE

Shebenikut and Jablanica massifs ▪ 130.9 square miles (339.2 sq km) ▪ Majestic Maja e Shebenikut Mountain ▪ Balkan lynx ▪ akzm.gov.al

THETHI

A hikers' heaven high in the Albanian Alps leads to a village lost in time.

If Albania is eastern Europe's best kept secret among backpackers, then Thethi National Park is the 21st century's Shangri-la. This mountain village set in the Albanian Alps has a backdrop straight out of an epic Romantic poem or a landscape artist's vision of Eden.

You can now drive here on a new asphalt road from Shkodër, one that has opened this long-mysterious enclave to the outside world. But a word to the wise: Don't attempt to drive to Thethi on your own. The last few miles are still a dirt road that winds with heart-stopping turns along a cliff-side, so this is not a drive for the inexperienced or the faint of heart. Much easier to ride in one of the local jeeps and minibuses that make the run daily from Shkodër.

Alternatively, you can take a day to hike from Valbonë (see sidebar). What you find on arrival is a tiny village nestled in a valley surrounded by imposing mountain walls of rock. The village is the focal point of Thethi National Park, a protected area that extends into some of the most stunning scenery in Europe, all accessed via a series of hiking trails. These include the 12-mile (19.3 km) trek to a beautiful pool known as the Blue Eye, which takes you through mountains and canyons, and the slightly more difficult hike to Valbonë Peak of around the same distance. The

hike to Grunas waterfall is equally scenic. Like most of the Albanian Alps, Thethi National Park is dominated by limestone and dolomite rocks, and its most prominent features are karstic, such as the Grunas Canyon and the southern Maja e Arapit (Wall of Arapi), one of the

Valbonë to Thethi Hike

One of the great hikes anywhere in Europe is the six- to seven-hour trek across the Albanian Alps between the villages of Valbonë and Thethi (also spelled "Valbona" and "Theth"). Standing at 5,771 feet, (1,759 m), the Valbonë Pass leads you to a mountain path in the west, whereupon you leave Valbona Valley National Park and enter the remote realm of Thethi National Park. You won't need a guide, as the signs are clear, and the walk is relatively easy with just a few steep climbs and descents. The majestic beauty of the Valbonë River Valley and the descent through beech forests to the mythic village of Thethi makes for one memorable day. Small shacks serve drinks and snacks along the way, or stop and fill your canister with fresh mountain water from the bluest rivers you'll ever see.

highest rock faces in the Balkans.

Thethi is another world. Soaring rocky peaks, plunging valleys, gushing rivers of crystal clear water, dramatic waterfalls, and dense forests set the stage for wildlife's drama: Golden eagles and lesser kestrels circle above on the lookout for smaller birds such as nuthatch, red-backed shrike, capercaillie, and rock partridge. The rivers teem with brown trout, while grey wolves, lynx, chamois, and brown bear roam the landscape. The forests range from lower levels of Austrian oak, hornbeam, and flowering ash, to higher stands of beech, silver fir, and sycamore. Once you reach the alpine floor, above 6,233 feet (1,900 m), your olfactory senses are tickled by aromas of herbaceous plants such as juniper, willow, alpine bluegrass, alpine aster, and bird's-foot trefoil, with its vivid yellow-and-red flowers.

One of the other great joys of staying in a mountain guesthouse here or in the Valbonë Valley is coming back to the hearty cuisine of rural Albania. The roast lamb is delicious, and everywhere you'll be offered *byrek*, layered pastries filled with cheese, potato, or shredded meat. Albania is a feast for both the eyes and the stomach.

The River Thethit gushes through the Albanian Alps.

Albanian Alpine landscapes ▪ Thethi village ▪ 10.1 square miles (26.3 sq km) ▪ Hiking Valbonë to Thethi across the Valbonë Pass ▪ akzm.gov.al

TOMORRI MOUNTAIN

One of the most important protected areas in Albania

Tomorri Mountain National Park in southern Albania lies in the central and higher portions of the Tomorr massif. The area's karst landscapes are a mix of woodlands and scrub that sit atop its limestone bedrock. The park is named for Mount Tomorr, one of the Pindus Mountains, which rises some 7,930 feet (2,417 m) between the Osum and Tomorrica Valleys.

Mount Tomorr as seen from the historic city of Berat

lurk in these woods and highland meadows, including wolves, foxes, wild boars, roe deer, and wild goats. Look too for golden eagles and sparrow hawks riding the thermal uplifts of these dramatic mountain peaks, and the several species of owl that inhabit the woods. These avian raptors feed on the park's smaller mammals such as the forest dormouse and wood mouse.

The forests of the park hold diverse species of deciduous and coniferous trees as well as wildflowers, including European beech, Bosnian pine, Turkish hazel, linaria, great yellow gentian, autumn crocus, Greek whitebeam, and European mistletoe. Great mammals

This national park offers various sports, including hiking on the massif. In recent years, the park has developed and maintained a number of challenging hiking trails, maps of which can be downloaded from its website. The terrain of this national park is jagged and cav-

ernous, and hiring local guides is highly recommended. Horse and donkey riding, skiing, and canoeing through the Osum Canyon are also popular pursuits within the scenic parklands.

Travelers should remember that Mount Tomorr is a sacred site. Christians climb it on Assumption Day (August 15) to honor the Virgin Mary, and the Bektashi, a Sufi dervish order, honor Abbas ibn Ali here during a pilgrimage in late August. Abbas ibn Ali is the half brother of Muhammad, and he is buried here on Mount Tomorr 3,940 feet (1,200 m) above sea level. Every August thousands of Bektashi pilgrims ascend the mountain for a week, to celebrate their most important holiday of the year. The roads from the surrounding valleys leading to Mount Tomorr become an endless line of vehicles for many miles as the Bektashi make their pilgrimage to this sacred place.

The mountain is also steeped in local folklore. Albanian legend relates how Tomorri came into existence. The people of the region believed that Tomorr was a giant who challenged and fought another giant named Shpirag for the hand of a beautiful young woman. The two dueling giants killed each other, and on hearing the news, the forlorn young woman cried for days and eventually drowned in her own tears while creating the river of Osum.

AT A GLANCE

Pindus Mountains ▪ Karst landscapes ▪ 100.8 square miles (261 sq km) ▪ Osum Canyon canoeing ▪ August religious pilgrimages ▪ akzm.gov.al

VALBONA VALLEY

"Accursed Mountains" that are a rich blessing to hikers and adventurers

The Valbonë River cuts through the distinctive karst terrain of the valley with its rich woodlands.

Valbona Valley National Park is a European wilderness so primeval that mountains are still traversed by foot or horse or donkey. The trails here are rudimentary, but as more travelers come to this stunning mountain park, infrastructure is improving. The town of Shkodër, with its warm and welcoming guesthouses, is the base camp for your Albanian Alpine adventure: The Koman Ferry brings visitors down the scenic valley of the Drin (or Drim) River, traveling through a series of stunning gorges before leaving you at the town of Fierzë. Next, a minibus brings you up to the village of Valbonë, from where these limestone and dolomite mountains are yours to roam; or you can strike out on the one-day hike to Thethi (see page 442).

The park encompasses the Valbonë River and the surrounding karst terrain with its alpine landscapes, glacial springs, and lively waterfalls. The valley has forests of Austrian, Balkan, Bosnian, and Scots pine, while the riverbanks are lined with growths of grey alder, olive willow, and goat willow.

If you want to hit the heights, Jezercës is the highest peak, standing at 8,838 feet (2,694 m) above the Adriatic Sea. Throughout the park, trails take you through the habitats of wolves, jackals, foxes, and Eurasian lynx. As may be expected, the karst caves are aflap with many bats. Watch for wild boar that can be angry creatures if provoked. If you take the Gjarpëri Trail, a longish 10-hour hike, you might spot brown bears feasting in some of the valley's abandoned orchards. But remember, even the cutest bears don't do selfies. Other trails worth pursuing are the Rosi Mountain Trail, a full-day trek to a peak in neighboring Montenegro, which also takes in two beautiful glacial lakes. If you've less time, the Çerem Trail gives a good overview of the valley along the western bank of the Valbonë River, with some rocky patches to navigate.

AT A GLANCE

Albanian Alpine terrain ▪ Valbonë River and Valley ▪ 30.8 square miles (80 sq km) ▪ The Çerem Trail ▪ akzm.gov.al

NORTH MACEDONIA

"Long live the Republic of North Macedonia," tweeted the newly named state's leader in 2019. This historic country could finally look forward to not looking back. Neighbor Greece could rest easy that neither the name of their great northern province nor the land itself would be appropriated. North Macedonia, at the heart of the Balkans, is a nation now happy to

absorb all, and not intent on conquering the Earth, as in the time of the greatest Macedonian, Alexander the Great. A Slavic Orthodox majority lives side by side with Albanian, Serbian, Turkish, and Jewish minorities in a peaceable Balkan mosaic that is enhanced by small groups of Vlachs and Romany. In a practical and symbolic gesture toward a greener future for all, 200,000 Macedonians planted two million trees on their inaugural National Tree Day in 2008. At the death of Alexander the Great in 323 B.C., a seer predicted that the land where he was laid to rest "would be happy and unvanquishable forever." We still don't know where the man who first put Macedon on the map is buried; but the new land of mountains, lakes, dense forests, and sacred sites remains for future generations to enjoy.

*Opposite: Great white pelicans on Lake Macro Prespa, Pelister National Park
Above: The remote mountains of North Macedonia are popular destinations for hikers and climbers.*

GALIČICA

A place of diverse natural habitats and profound religious importance

Tucked away amid the Galičica Mountains in southwestern North Macedonia, the lovely Galičica National Park embraces most of the area between Ohrid and Prespa Lakes. Mount Galičica forms the focal point of the park, with the area's main village being Elšani, located on Lake Ohrid.

Galičica hosts a rich array of fauna and flora in its mountains, lakeside landscapes, and some 130 dense forests. The island of Golem Grad, on the western side of Lake Prespa, is worth exploring for its unusual plants and many species of birds, including rare pelicans. Eleven endemic plants grow on Mount Galičica, and the park is home to 10 species of amphibians, 18 reptile species, 124 types of birds, and 18 mammal species. Many of these can be seen along the park's extensive network of hiking and mountain biking trails.

The region also has a deeply religious past. St. Bogorodica Zahumska is a church that can be reached only by taking a boat from Trpejca or Ljubanista villages. It was built on a rocky beach along Lake Ohrid in 1361, and is worth seeing for its medieval architecture and its fresco of Mary feeding the baby Jesus. The large stone complex of St. Naum Monastery was rebuilt in the 16th century at the other end of the lake with Mount Galičica as its backdrop. This key pilgrimage site was founded around 910 by the saint. The monastery is set on a plateau over Lake Ohrid right next to the Albanian border, so be careful not to wander into the military zone.

AT A GLANCE

Galičica Mountains landscape ▪ 88 square miles (227 sq km) ▪ Ohrid and Prespa Lakes ▪ Golem Grad island birding ▪ galicica.org.mk

MAVROVO

A panoply of picturesque villages among the mountains

The village of Mavrovo is the center point of this large park that embraces the lake and region of the same name. Mavrovo National Park's landscapes of gorges, pine forests, karst fields, and waterfalls attract hikers and skiers from Skopje and beyond. The country's tallest peak, the 9,068-foot (2,764-m) Mount Korab, has lately become popular with hikers from all over Europe.

Mavrovo National Park embraces many cultural sites within its

The sunken church of St. Nicholas

impressive sweep, including St. Jovan Bigorski Monastery, founded by the monk John in 1020 and known for its intricately carved iconostasis. The Elen Skok bridge on the river Mala Reka celebrates the legend of a famous local deer. The old mosque in Rostushe is of interest for its recently restored minaret, built with the same limestone as was used for the reconstruction of the St. Jovan Bigorski Monastery in a symbolic act of the multifaith nature of North Macedonia.

AT A GLANCE

Mount Korab ▪ Major ski resort ▪ 278.7 square miles (721.8 sq km) ▪ Mavrovo Lake ▪ St. Jovan Bigorski Monastery ▪ npmavrovo.org.mk

PELISTER

A park of many altitudes, with elevated lakes and a diversity of habitats

The Big Lake, higher of the twin tarns known as Pelister's Eyes

Pelister National Park is located in the Baba Mountain massif, which gives the protected area a wide range of altitudes, varying between 3,041 and 8,533 feet (927 and 2,601 m) above sea level. This, in turn, makes for a broad diversity of habitats for the park's flora and fauna.

Among the floral rarities found in Pelister is the five-needle pine molica, *Pinus peuce*—or Balkan pine. This rugged tree grows mainly on higher grounds (between 3,280 and 7,220 feet/1,000 and 2,200 m) around the Balkan Peninsula, but its ability to withstand subfreezing temperatures and severe winter winds has allowed it to thrive as far north as Punkaharju in eastern Finland.

EXPLORING THE PARK

Hikers in Pelister are walking through a wilderness that is home to a diverse range of wildlife: Brown bears, wild boars, and roe deer forage for food in the forests, while birds nesting in the woods include partridges and owls. Higher up, red-billed choughs make their home in the rocky peaks and cliffs, alongside several species of eagles, which circle over meadows in search of rabbits or field mice. Other sure-footed residents of the craggy granite peaks are stags, chamois, and wolves whose howls provide an evocative call of the wild through these mountains, especially in winter.

Pelister is also known for its two tarns, or mountain lakes, known locally as Pelister's Eyes. The Big Lake sits at 7,277 feet (2,218 m) above sea level, while the Small Lake lies at 7,150 feet (2,180 m).

Throughout Pelister waterways, you'll find an endemic creature, the Macedonian Pelagonia trout. But anglers should throw back this beautiful fish. Poaching and overfishing have driven the Macedonian Pelagonia trout to the verge of extinction, despite conservation efforts the North Macedonian government imposed, including a 10-year fishing ban up to 2014. In 2018, scientists and fishermen teamed up to initiate artificial breeding for this endangered species unique to this part of North Macedonia.

Several hiking trails, such as the children's, historical, and Stone River trails, start from the Hotel Molika, about a mile and a half (2.5 km) from the park's visitors center. These trails lead along mountain meadows, past tarns and springs, and high into the Baba Mountains, while also taking in many of the national park's historic sites of interest. Pelister is known for its excellent skiing in winter, but it is a remote wilderness. The best way approach is from Bitola, through the villages of Trnovo and Magarevo. The trails are rudimentary, and good hiking boots are recommended.

AT A GLANCE

Baba Mountain massif ▪ Macedonian Pelagonia trout ▪ 66.2 square miles (171.5 sq km) ▪ Mountain hiking trails ▪ park-pelister.com/en

BULGARIA

Bulgaria is a land where the past is proudly preserved and natural beauty highly valued. This is apparent in the wide array of architectural styles you'll witness throughout the country's cities, towns, and delightful 19th-century Revival-era villages. Bulgaria's many Orthodox monasteries were maintained through eight centuries of Ottoman rule, and the same careful curation has been applied to the country's landscapes in Bulgaria's parks system. From snowcapped Balkan peaks to Black Sea beaches, parks have long been beloved by Bulgarians. As the country integrates its future into the European Union, the traditions of the past are preciously preserved: Pastoral ways of life are kept alive at Central Balkan National Park; Ottoman administrative buildings are protected along with the glacial lakes and wildlife of Pirin National Park; and antique architecture and wilderness are equal parts of the allure of Rila National Park.

*Opposite: The Seven Rila Lakes form a
fluvial necklace in the Rila Mountains.*

CENTRAL BALKAN

A stunning mountain park in the heart of Bulgaria

Central Balkan National Park lies at the center of the country's famous mountain range. The highest peak in the range is the 7,795-foot (2,376-m) Botev Peak. This mountain was previously known as Yumrukchal (meaning "primary peak" in Ottoman Turkish), but was renamed in honor of Bulgarian poet and revolutionary Hristo Botev in 1950. A total of 20 of the park's peaks reach altitudes of 6,560 feet (2,000 m) and over.

The park encompasses nine nature reserves covering about one-third of its territory. Since 2017, the ancient beech forests within all these park reserves have been included in UNESCO's Primeval Beech Forests World Heritage site.

The park hosts an astounding 2,340 species and subspecies of plants, including the protected edelweiss, snowdrop, yellow mountain lily, and Stara planina primrose. Here, too, sharp eyes may see the endangered Transylvanian campanula, starry lady's mantle, Kerner's thistle, and Stefchov's stonecrop. Woodlands occupy 56 percent of the total area, consisting of centuries-old forests of beech, spruce, fir, hornbeam, and durmast oak. Parkland inhabitants include Balkan chamois, wolves, martens, and otters; bats such as Geoffrey's bat, barbastelles, and Schreiber's bats; and birds such as imperial eagles, corn crakes, and ring ouzels.

The Central Balkan terrain includes large high mountain meadows, vertical rock faces, cliffs, deep canyons, and waterfalls, making it a favored hiking destination.

AT A GLANCE

Central Balkan Mountain terrain ▪ Botev Peak ▪ 276.6 square miles (716.6 sq km) ▪ Primeval beech forests ▪ visitcentralbalkan.net/-2.html

Bulgaria's Nature Parks

Few countries protect their cherished natural and cultural heritages as well as Bulgaria. Aside from three national parks, the country has 11 nature parks and 55 nature reserves, all overseen by the Ministry of Environment and Water. Many lie within the national parks. The first nature park within the entire Balkan Peninsula was Vitosha Nature Park, established in 1934. All of Bulgaria's protected areas are part of the Natura 2000 network of protected areas within the European Union. (See *parks.bg/ en/parks* for more information.)

Belasitsa Nature Park protects the northern slopes of Belasitsa Mountain in southwestern Bulgaria. **Bulgarka Nature Park** embraces rich beech forests and vital Balkan fauna on the northern slopes of the Balkan Mountains.

Persina Nature Park, named after the island, protects a wetland area along the Bulgarian side of the Danube. **Rila Monastery Nature Park** spans a huge western area of the Rila Mountains, embracing forests, meadows, alpine areas, and 28 glacial lakes. It is part of the Rila National Park (see page 454). **Rusenski Lom Nature Park** protects the canyon of the Rusenski Lom, the last significant tributary of the Danube. **Sinite Kamani Nature Park** covers the "Blue Stones" around the town of Sliven.

Shumensko Plato Nature Park is located in the Shumen Plateau, the highest of the Danubian Plain. The park encloses the Bukaka Reserve Forest, and shelters beech woods, the Shumen fortress, and cave monasteries. **Strandzha Nature Park** (aka Stranja Nature Park) is the largest protected area in Bulgaria, spanning a territory of 448 square miles (1,161 sq km) in the Strandzha massif. **Vitosha Nature Park** protects the Vitosha Mountains, the dramatic backdrop to Sofia. **Vrachanski Balkan Nature Park** hosts valuable flora and fauna in northwest Bulgaria. And finally, **Zlatni Pyasatsi Nature Park** stretches along Bulgaria's Black Sea coast covering shore terrain and forests of moss-capped oak, Hungarian oak, swamp white oak, and hornbeam.

PIRIN

Ancient pine forests, glacial lakes, and rocky peaks: Bulgaria's call of the wild

High-altitude camping on the Kamenitsa ridge

Wild weather is common in the Pirin wilderness. These mountains are named for the thunder god Perun, whose storm clap no doubt caused many a catastrophic avalanche, whose high winds still carry mighty eagles and falcons, and whose breath has long swayed the ancient trees of the primeval forests of Pirin National Park.

The park's most famous tree is the Baykuchevata Macedonian pine, a thousand-year-old legend that probably inspired the same kind of awe and respect as the thunder god. For medieval pagan worshippers, sacred trees like this were believed to be rooted in the underworld of the dead, their trunks being the earthly living part, and their branches stretching toward the heavens.

The park, also part of a UNESCO World Heritage site, is filled with such natural treasures. Here you can camp beside, and swim within, gorgeous glacial lakes carved out of the soaring limestone peaks. Dramatic canyons drop from plateaus, exposing sheer-faced granite walls, and on clifftops you might spot a golden eagle's nest, or watch the swoop of a peregrine falcon, or spot the vivid black, white, and red plumage of a wallcreeper. Along rivers, look for the Eurasian otter, especially in the waterways around the Banderishki Lakes. Jackals, bears, mountain goats, and Hermann's tortoises also inhabit this vast and varied wilderness.

OUT & ABOUT IN PIRIN

Trails lined with simple hiking huts, through ancient pine forests, lead toward snowy "marble" peaks and vistas of more than 100 peaks of 6,560 feet (2,000 m) that really do make you feel like you've reached the realm of the gods. Take in scenic forest and mountain paths along the six-mile (10-km) hike from the Prevalski Lakes to the Popina area at the southwestern edge of the park.

Bansko is the gateway town to Pirin National Park, just 1.2 miles (2 km) outside the park entrance. Several hotels in its vicinity have saunas and spas to ease aching muscles from a day on the trails. You can rent mountain bikes and take a chairlift in the eastern part of the park, which will drop you off near the start of several thrilling descents. If you're feeling adventurous in the winter months, hire a local guide and head for the lake of Popovo, especially by night, when the snow glistens spectacularly in the moonlight and you may hear that evocative sound of the eastern European wilderness, the howl of a wolf.

AT A GLANCE

Pirin Mountains ▪ The Baykuchevata Macedonian pine ▪ 154.4 square miles (400 sq km) ▪ The Prevalski to Popina trail ▪ whc.unesco.org/en/list/225

RILA

Where a remote monastery has kept the faith through centuries

Hikers who seek out the higher grounds of Rila discover rich mountain meadows and wildlife.

Rila National Park, the largest national park in Bulgaria, is located in the central and highest regions of the Rila Mountains. The park protects a variety of rare and endangered wildlife species, as well as historic Orthodox religious sites. Some of the largest rivers in the Balkan Peninsula originate in Rila, which is derived from the Thracian word *roula,* meaning "lots of water."

Due to this abundance of water and moisture on its mountain terrain, Rila National Park is a veritable moss kingdom. A total of 282 moss species of all ecological groups have been identified, carpeting the woods in a soft green that is particularly beautiful when morning light filters through the trees, or at night when the gloom of twilight descends on the park.

THE SEVEN RILA LAKES

The Seven Rila Lakes are one of the many geographical delights of Rila, a group of glacial lakes, elevated between 6,890 and 8,200 feet (2,100 and 2,500 m) above sea level. Each lake is named for its most characteristic feature: The highest is Salzata (The Tear) due to its deep crystal clear waters. The next one down is called Okoto (The Eye) because of its almost perfectly oval form. This is the deepest cirque lake in Bulgaria, with a depth of 123 feet (37.5 m). Babreka (The Kidney) has the steepest shores. Bliznaka (The Twin) is the largest by area. Trilistnika (The Trefoil) is irregularly shaped with low shores. The shallowest lake is Ribnoto Ezero (Fish Lake) and the closest to sea level is Dolnoto Ezero (Lower Lake), where waters from all the higher lakes gather to form Dzherman River.

FLORA & FAUNA

The most abundant of Rila's many plant species occur on the higher grounds of mountain meadows. The Bulgarian or Balkan endemics are most beautiful among them, such as the Rila cowslip, Rila rhubarb, and lady's mantle. In all, the park hosts about 57 species that are found only in Bulgaria or the Balkans.

Rila National Park has the highest peak of the Balkan Peninsula, the Musala, which rises to 9,596 feet (2,925 m) above sea level. The mountain is a good case study of the typical division into altitudinal zones that define the ecosystems of the park's mountain terrains. Musala has four distinct vegetation zones: beech, coniferous forest, subalpine, and alpine. The subalpine forests are mainly planted with coniferous species, chiefly dwarf pine, a coniferous shrub, as well as some Siberian juniper. In the alpine zone, small shrubs such as blueberries and grassy willows predominate. Up in the alpine meadow, you'll find endemic plants such as amethyst fescue, Rila rhubarb, and others.

In a park named for its fluvial abundance, it's no surprise that five species of fish, 20 species of amphibians and reptiles, 48 species of mammals, and 99 species of birds all inhabit or migrate through this wilderness. Twenty-four of these vertebrate species are listed as nearly extinct. Many chamois and the sole high mountain population of European ground squirrel inhabit the higher grounds, while capercaillie, hazel grouse, rock par-

Rila Monastery

The Rila Monastery dates from the 10th century and has since played a major role in the development of Bulgarian spirituality, art, and culture, and in the preservation of national traditions during the five centuries of Ottoman rule. This majestic monastic site nestles within the folds of the Rila Mountains at a height of 3,763 feet (1,147 m). It was founded by St. Ivan Rilski, who lived as a hermit in a place now called the White Cells, where he is buried. Rila Monastery's role in the Bulgarian National Revival of the 18th and 19th centuries lent this place a special significance as the spiritual home of the nation itself. Traditional skills fostered by the monks, such as wood-carving, icon painting, and printing, were all valuable ways to spread ideas of nationhood. The clapper still summons the monks for service each day, more than a thousand years since Ivan's arrival.

tridge, and European pine marten all live in the forests. In the trees, too, listen for the hooting of boreal and Eurasian pygmy owls. Large predators such as bears and wolves also stalk the woods. Rila National Park is known as the home of some of the most viable populations of predatory birds in Europe. High mountain inhabitants include the wallcreeper, the alpine chough, and the alpine accentor.

The Orthodox Rila Monastery is among the array of park architecture.

AT A GLANCE

Rila Mountains landscapes ▪ Musala Mountain ▪ 312.9 square miles (810.4 sq km) ▪ Rila Monastery ▪ The Seven Rila Lakes ▪ rilanationalpark.bg/en

ROMANIA

Romania is an eastern country more Mediterranean in culture and language than its Slavic surrounds would suggest. The people are passionate, gregarious, and always open to life's great adventures. It's a shame then that their reputation has so long been defined by an Irishman's tale of a Transylvanian count. Of course, a visit to Nicolae Ceaușescu's monstrous Palace of the Parliament in Bucharest brings a realization of Romania's all-too-recent, real-life horror story, and the damage done to the national psyche by that life-draining tyrant. Yet venture out into this big, beautiful country and you'll realize that Romania has much to draw travelers: a vast swath of the Carpathian Mountains; the white-beach coastlines of the Black Sea; river cruises along the Danube Delta; train rides through Transylvania's bucolic scenery; and the legendary lakes and peaks of Retezat National Park

Opposite: The gorges at dawn, Cheile Bicazului-Hașmaș National Park, Transylvania

BUILA-VÂNTURARIȚA

An invitation to go wild in Romania's Southern Carpathians

A hike in the highlands of Buila-Vânturarița takes you on an Alpine adventure into the Căpățînii Mountains.

Buila-Vânturarița National Park protects the local Căpățînii Mountains, part of the Southern Carpathians. The park embraces the 8.6-mile-long (14-km) calcareous crest, dominated by the two massive peaks that give the mountain its name: Buila Peak, which stands at 6,066 feet (1,849 m), and Vânturarița Peak, at 6,184 feet (1,885 m). Over the course of time, the Bistrita, Costesti, Cheia, and Olanesti Rivers have carved spectacular gorges and cascades into the mountain.

Twenty caves are hidden in the steep mountainsides of the national park, some of which have been declared protected areas, including the Cave of Bat (St. Gregory the Decapolite). Others are Arnăuți, Clopot, and Pagoda Cave.

The park embraces a range of attractions, including hermitages and a UNESCO site, the Trovanti Museum Natural Reserve in the village of Costesti. Here can be seen a series of strange sedimentary formations known as "the stones that grow." Wilderness landscapes include the rich forests of Călinești-Brezoi and Valea Cheii, nature reserves such as Rădița-Mânzu, and Mount Stogu, a popular hangout for brown bears and many bats.

This is wolf country, and on a winter's night you may hear many a piercing howl. The park also hosts large numbers of chamois, lynx, deer, and boar. In the forests and meadows, look for fine flora such as sweet william, king's roses, yew trees, dwarf mountain pines (at higher altitudes), and junipers.

AT A GLANCE

Căpățînii Mountains landscape ▪ Buila and Vânturarița Peaks ▪ 16.1 square miles (41.6 sq km) ▪ The Trovanti Museum ▪ Bat caves ▪ buila.ro

CĂLIMANI

A rich combination of flora, fauna, and stunning mountain walks

This is the place to spot much of Romania's best wildlife, and to appreciate some of its most interesting geology. As you hike through the Swiss stone pine and juniper woods of Călimani National Park, you venture into the realm of some rare and endangered species including brown bear, deer, lynx, elk (moose), wildcats, wild boar, roe deer, and badgers. Wolves prowl the highlands and forests, where tree martens are a common sight. On Călimani Mountain's western side, the rare-in-Romania black grouse makes its home in cedar and juniper forests.

The park protects the volcanic Călimani Mountains in the Eastern Carpathians. The Călimani boasts the highest massif in the Romanian volcanic chain, the Pietrosul Peak, which stands at 6,896 feet (2,102 m). Natural erosion of the volcanic plateau has led to the formation of several unusually shaped rock features, chief among them the Twelve Apostles, Red Stones, and Nefertiti geological reserves. These are all favored destinations for hikers and climbers in the park. Other popular pursuits in Călimani are cross-country skiing, mountain biking, horseback riding, and bird-watching. Hiking in spring is richly rewarding with a host of wildflowers in bloom on meadows, including alpine leek, narcissus anemone, and the beautiful purple rosettes of mountain soldanella. In juniper tree forests or in volcanic soils, you'll find the rosebay rhododendron.

AT A GLANCE

Călimani Mountains ▪ Twelve Apostles, Red Stones, and Nefertiti rock formations ▪ 100 square miles (258.9 sq km) ▪ romaniatourism.com/park-national-calimani.html

CEAHLĂU

The Olympus of Romania has fauna, flora, and rock formations of epic scale.

The Ceahlău massif stands at 6,257 feet (1,907 m) high, supporting watercourses and dam lakes, and hosting an impressive concentration of flora—more than 2,000 flower species thrive in Ceahlău National Park.

The limestone rock formations of Dochia and Cusma Dorobantului, and the Duruitoarea waterfall are among the many attractions in this park, bounded to the east by the Bistrita River and Lake Bicaz, and to the south by the Bicaz River. If the beauty of the landscape doesn't light up your imagination, then the strange rock formations certainly will. These have inspired a whole canon of local legend: The Dochia rock formations are believed to represent a mean old woman called "Baba" who arrived on Ceahlău Mountain to feed her sheep. Deceived by the sunny days of early spring, she disrobed, slowly shedding all her nine sheepskin coats. When a late frost fell, it turned both her and her animals into ice, which over the years has transmogrified into the stones now among the park's most popular sites.

Romanians have a special reverence for mountains, and Ceahlău was considered to be the sacred mountain of Zalmoxis, the ancient deity of the Dacians. On this holy ground today, you'll find the three-toed woodpecker and wallcreepers, who, along with ravens, nest high in rocky peaks.

AT A GLANCE

Ceahlău massif ▪ Legendary rock formations ▪ 29.7 square miles (77 sq km) ▪ Hiking, skiing, bird-watching ▪ romaniatourism.com/park-national-ceahlau.html

CHEILE BICAZULUI-HAȘMAȘ

Canyons, lakes, and the Hășmaș Mountains form a thriving habitat.

The national park of Cheile Bicazului-Hașmaș protects several significant geological features including Cheile Bicazului (Bicaz Gorge), a deep canyon dug by the Bicaz River; Lacu Roșu (Red Lake), a natural dam lake; and the Hășmaș Mountains. The park was established in 1990, just as Romania was emerging from the long shadow of Nicolae Ceaușescu and decades of communist rule.

The landscapes of this national park consist of spruce forests mixed with beech on the mountain slopes, vast highland pastures, and peaks with subalpine vegetation. Specific to this region is the endemic plant that goes by the Latin name of *Astragalus pseudopurpureus,* a beautiful purple bloomer with fernlike green leaves.

Rarities that thrive in these mountain meadows include juniper, pyramidal bugle (which resembles a purple pagoda more than a pyramid), barren strawberry, and the wonderfully scented daphne. Protected plants are the insect-trapping yellow's slipper, edelweiss, vibrant red *Nigritella rubra,* and the yew tree.

Cheile Bicazului-Hașmaș shelters an equally impressive array of fauna. Watch for the Apollo and *Polygonia* comma butterflies, two of nature's winged wonders. The viviparous lizard and smooth snake are among reptilian representatives of a vast food chain. Golden eagles are top of the avian pile, looked up to by lesser feathers such as Ural owls, rock buntings, and Old World grouse. Red deer, wild alpine goat, bear, lynx, and wolf are among the park's many mammals.

Red Lake reflects the Suhardul Mara massif and the spruce and beech forests of this Transylvanian park.

AT A GLANCE

The Bicaz Gorge ▪ Red Lake ▪ 25.4 square miles (65.7 sq km) ▪ Kayaking and fly-fishing
▪ romaniatourism.com/park-national-bicazului-gorges-hasmas.html

CHEILE NEREI-BEUSNITA

Easy wilderness hiking in southwest Romania

Cheile Nerei-Beusnita National Park is located in the south of the Aninei Mountains, and transected by the Nera and Beu Rivers. Its main trail follows the Nera River gorge (Cheile Nerei) between Șopotu Nou and Sasca Română, a route of 14.1 miles (22.7 km) that takes about nine hours. The landscapes are a hikers' delight of waterfalls, canyons, caves, cirques, and ravines. This is a remote Edenic garden, but watch for snakes. The poisonous European adder slithers here across the rocks and cliffs.

A fairyland of waterfalls and moss

As the park's trails traverse gorges, wetlands, and forest lakes, you'll mostly see amphibians, birds, bats, and vipers. Here too are green lizards, smooth snakes, and fire salamanders, as well as the Eurasian kingfisher, an attractive river bird with vivid yellow-and-blue plumage.

The highlights for hikers are the Beusnita waterfalls, Sasca Montană (Ochiul Beiului Lake), and Devil's Lake. You can kayak along the Beu to reach the gorges, but the remote Devil's Lake is a lengthy hike, one worth the trek to see the only lake in Romania formed from the collapse of a cave ceiling. The turquoise blue waters of all these lakes are mesmerizing.

AT A GLANCE

Aninei Mountains ▪ 142 square miles (367.7 sq km) ▪ Beusnita waterfalls ▪ Ochiul Beiului Lake ▪ Devil's Lake ▪ Nera River gorge (Cheile Nerei) trail ▪ romaniawanderer.com/cheile-nerei-beusnita-national-park

COZIA

Great hiking, plus rare lichens and old-growth forests

Cozia National Park is located in the Lotrului Mountains along the valley of one of Romania's longest rivers, the Olt. It embraces two old-growth forests in UNESCO's Primeval Beech Forests of the Carpathians site. The park has nine fine hiking trails, many starting at the 18th-century monastery of Turnu, taking you into the mountains via Roman ruins and Orthodox churches. These are challenging hills rather than daunting peaks, which

Spiritual Cozia: Stanisoara Monastery

makes for some of the best hiking in the country.

Wildlife to look for include chamois, deer, wildcat, and vipers. One fish species—*Sabanejewia romanica,* or the Romanian loach—is endemic to this protected area. The park's location on the migratory flyway between central Europe and the Aegean Sea attracts more than 120 bird species to its wetlands and forests of beech, oak, and spruce. Cozia is a mushroom picker's paradise too, with more than 400 known species. The old-growth forests here are cloaked in more than 200 species of gloriously lush moss.

AT A GLANCE

Lotrului Mountains ▪ Hiking trails and rest chalets ▪ 66 square miles (171 sq km) ▪ Old-growth forests ▪ Roman ruins and Orthodox churches ▪ cozia.ro, uncover-romania.com/attractions/nature/cozia-national-park

Danube Delta Biosphere Reserve

The mouth of the Danube and its wildlife is the focal point of this fascinating Romanian biosphere reserve. The end point of one of Europe's great rivers provides a rich preserve for many of the continent's bird and fish species.

A vast colony of Dalmatian pelicans congregate in the delta of the great Danube.

The mighty Danube meanders across Europe for some 1,788 miles (2,877.5 km); it is the continent's second longest river, after the Volga. The great river begins its journey in Germany's Black Forest, then winds its way through a dozen countries, absorbing countless tributaries, before finally emptying into the Black Sea at the Romanian port city of Tulcea, south of the Ukrainian border. Here, nine channels diverge to create a vast sprawling wetland that is home to one of the Earth's great ecosystems. Three of these channels—the Chilia, Sulina, and Sfântu Gheorghe branches—compose the main arteries of the

Danube Delta (Delta Dunării), a constantly evolving wetland of marshes, floating reed islets, and sandbars that sprawls for some 1,616.6 square miles (4,187 sq km).

Romania's Danube Delta National Park, established in 1991, is a small part of this vital wilderness. Under the UNESCO Man and the Biosphere Programme, a part of the Danube Delta shared by both Romania and Ukraine was established as a biosphere reserve in 1998. For more information on visiting these wonderful wetlands, see *romaniatourism.com/danube -delta.html* and *whc.unesco.org/en/ list/588*.

AN AVIAN HAVEN

The park provides sanctuary for more than 300 bird species and some 160 species of fish. The reed marshes, totaling some 603 square miles (1,562 sq km), are among the largest anywhere in the world. In spring, great flocks of rare species convene in the area, and birdwatchers across Europe pack their bags for an annual pilgrimage. This spectacle of squacco herons, colorful rollers, bee-eaters, hoopoes, and red-backed shrikes descending in the hundreds of thousands is like a winged Woodstock for bird lovers. Dalmatian pelicans, great divers, pygmy cormorants, glossy ibis, and swans add to the raucous gathering. April marks the beginning of the migration season, when birds arrive to nest among reeds and inlets until September's cooler winds trigger a mass exodus, and they head south to destinations in North Africa and beyond. In May, when the rains are gone from the delta and the air is warmer, many travelers visit the park and its seaside towns fill up.

SULINA & SFÂNTU GHEORGHE

To protect the birds, much of the Danube Delta is closed to vehicle traffic, so the best route for bird-watchers is taking the ferry from Tulcea to remoter inland destinations such as Sulina or Sfântu Gheorghe that are closer to the Black Sea.

The coastal town of Sulina was once home to the European Commission of the Danube. The Farul Comisiei Europene a Dunarii de Jos, an 1870 lighthouse built by the commission, is now a museum detailing the town's history. The lighthouse offers a fine view of the delta. Wander through the nearby cemetery, Cimitirul Maritim, to get a sense of the multinational character of maritime Sulina. You'll find French, English, German, Italian, Russian, and Romanian names on its headstones. An Anglican section records the names of those lost souls who drowned in ships off the delta's coasts.

The tiny hamlet of Sfântu Gheorghe lies at the end of the southernmost channel and abuts a pristine beach. This is a prime location to view one of the stars of the Danube Delta show, the Egyptian white pelican. The great white pelican is an enormous bird, with a huge pink and yellow bill. Its wingspan can measure more than 11 feet (more than 3 m), the largest for flying animals apart from the great albatross. The park has a vast

Visitors to the Letea Forest may see centuries-old trees and wild horses.

network of boating routes, a maze of canals bordered by thatch, willows, and oaks entangled in lianas. Apart from bird-watching, the fishing is excellent hereabouts, and you'll find several hiking trails along shorelines to villages renowned for seafood.

A TASTE OF THE DANUBE

The delta is a haven for wildlife lovers, bird-watchers, and anglers, and it's also a serious treat for food lovers. The beautiful coastal villages of Sulina and Sfântu Gheorghe offer secluded beaches and fresh sea breezes by day, and a feast of fresh-off-the-boat seafood by night. Throughout the Danube Delta, chefs pride themselves on serving the finest seafood dishes in Romania, particularly one of the best fish soups anywhere in Europe. The local, seemingly infinite variety combines both freshwater and saltwater species, including carp, turbot, sturgeon, and *somn*, a giant catfish native to the region. The soup is served with a garlic sauce and a hearty side of Romanian-style grits (cornmeal porridge) called

mămăligă. Wash it down with a *țuică*, a potent brandy to help you find your sea legs.

LETEA FOREST

The delta is also home to the Letea Forest, Romania's oldest natural reservation, located between the Sulina and Chilia channels in the Danube Delta. This wetlands forest is worth boating or walking through (on wooden pathways). The omnipresence of the silkvine creeper (*Periploca graeca*), and various types of liana, including wild vine and ivy, give the forest a tropical feel. The Letea's rich mix of trees include white and black poplars, elms, English oaks, silver limes, narrow-leaved ashes, and common alders. Bird-watchers will spot colorful residents such as the red-footed falcon, with its mauve feathers and orange-red legs, the white-tailed eagle, the vivid turquoise and orange roller, and the crazily crowned hoopoe. The *Vipera ursinii* is a venomous snake to watch out for here. The park also hosts around 2,000 feral Danube Delta horses.

DEFILEUL JIULUI

Modern art and the Jiu River gorge

Defileul Jiului National Park protects the area along the gorge formed by the Jiu River between the Vâlcan and Parâng Mountains. The Jiu River meanders through the entire length of the park's 20.5 miles (33 km), lined with beech and oak trees with scattered hornbeam and ash. The park hosts a wealth of wildlife: Brown bears, Carpathian deer, marten, and badger all forage in the forests; otters ply the river; and wolves, lynx, and wildcats prowl the hillsides. Chamois climb higher

Brâncuşi's "Table of Silence" sculpture

in the mountains, while great predators such as golden eagles, peregrine falcons, and northern goshawks circle overhead. The park is a popular destination for rafting, horse riding, hiking, cycling, and fishing. It also contains one of the masterpieces of the Romanian sculptor, painter, and photographer Constantin Brâncuşi, who grew up nearby. The huge outdoor sculptural ensemble at Târgu Jiu is an homage to the Romanian heroes of the First World War. It comprises three sculptures—"Table of Silence," "Gate of the Kiss," and "Endless Column"—on an axis that runs 4,265 feet (1,300 m) long, oriented west to east.

DOMOGLED-VALEA CERNEI

A karst wonderland of caves, canyons, cascades, and fine mountain hiking

Domogled-Valea Cernei National Park is karst mountain country filled with sinkholes, caves, pit caves, waterfalls, limestone pavements, and valleys. The protected area stretches over the Cerna and Godeanu Mountains in the west, and the Vâlcan and Medinţi Mountains in the east, as it follows the course of the Cerna River Basin. Thanks to the region's mild Mediterranean climate, the park has an intriguing biodiversity, with a mix of Alpine, Carpathian, and Eurasian species not usually found in

Corcoaia gorge's dramatic walls

the same habitat. The park is also a favored destination for rafters and mountain climbers. Among various hiking destinations is the 131-foot-high (40-m) Vanturatoarea waterfall, a cascade that can be viewed from behind the water, making for interesting photo ops. Another trail leads to the 394-foot (120-m) Cociului waterfall, the highest in the country. Or visit one of the park's many caves, including the Steam Grotto, a wonder of speleology with hot steam hissing from its fissures.

MACIN MOUNTAINS

Mountains filled with raptors and other interesting avian wildlife

The Macin Mountains lie between the Danube to the north and west, the Taița River and Culmea Niculițelului to the east, and the Casimcea plateau to the south. These granite mountains are some of the oldest in Romania, and erosion due to altitudinous temperature differences has created sheer, dramatic slopes. The highest peak within Macin Mountains National Park is Tutuiatu (also known as Greci), at 1,532 feet (467 m). Here, you'll see the park's unique steppe landscapes on the lower slopes, followed by forests of oak, flowering ash, hornbeam, and downy oak, and alpine meadows higher up.

These Balkanic and sub-Mediterranean forests and steppe landscapes attract multitudes of migrant birds. The mountain peaks are prime real estate for high-flying raptors such as the long-legged buzzard, one of Europe's largest buzzards, short-toed eagles, booted eagles, Levant sparrow hawks, and saker falcons. In the forests, you'll find European turtle-doves, red-rumped swallows, isabelline wheatears (a species of Old World flycatchers), and ortolan buntings, among many others.

The park has a dry, rocky landscape, and trails are rough but one good way to explore the Macin massif is along the Greci Village–Tutuiatu Mountain trail. The route is about 4.5 miles (7.2 km) but involves a climb of about 1,310 feet (400 m), so set aside four to five hours, and bring plenty of water. The visitors center in Greci has trail details and a farmers market next door for picnic supplies.

AT A GLANCE

Macin Mountain steppe landscapes ▪ 43 square miles (111.3 sq km) ▪ Large raptors ▪ Greci Village–Tutuiatu Mountain trail ▪ parcmacin.ro/en

PIATRA CRAIULUI

A park of rocky peaks rises amid a rustic backwater of lakes and forests.

The Piatra Craiului mountain range is a series of thin, jagged-edged ridges that can catch early-morning or late-evening light in a spectacular way. Piatra Craiului National Park protects these peaks, Romania's longest and highest limestone ridge at more than 15 miles (24.1 km) long and 6,560 feet (2,000 m) high. Bordered by glacial lakes, the ridge is one of the most cherished destinations in the Carpathians, and a two-day north-south ridge

Rolling limestone hills

trail across it is a rewarding challenge worth taking—if you are reasonably fit. Hikers start at either Plaiul Foii in the northwest or Curmătura in the northeast, then ascend the ridge along the range's narrow spine. The descent at the southern end leads into a karst terrain of deep gorges and pitted slopes, where limestone rock has been carved into a series of caves well worth exploring.

From the villages of Măgura, Peștera, Ciocanu, and Sirnea, several trails lead onto the eastern slopes and are themselves worth visiting to witness the traditional Romanian way of life.

AT A GLANCE

Piatra Craiului ridge ▪ Karst mountain landscapes ▪ 57 square miles (147.7 sq km) ▪ Traditional villages ▪ romaniatourism.com/park-national-piatra-craiului.html

RETEZAT

A Carpathian gem of glacial lakes and soaring alpine peaks

Retezat's soaring mountains and crystalline glacial lakes are the landscapes of ancient legend.

The word *retezat* means "cut off," and legend has it that an angry giant did just that to the summit of the mountain that gives its name to this section of the Carpathians and to one of Romania's most attractive national parks, Retezat.

Gorgeous glacial lakes gleam high in these hills above pristine mixed forests. Crystal clear rivers and streams dance their way down these mountains, carving out gorges and caves. Otters make their home along the fluvial highways, and brown bears, wolves, lynx, and chamois all inhabit this wilderness too. Some 120 bird species ply the skies, including song thrushes, ring ouzels, chiff-chaffs, and golden eagles.

Bucura is Romania's largest glacial lake, and a popular camping ground for hikers. The park's landscapes are strewn with boulders, and the drama of the scenery has given rise to a rich local folklore involving dragons that breathe fire across the plains, not to mention giants chopping mountains down with the edge of their hand.

The park has many trails. A good introduction to its highlights is the Cabana Pietrele to Peleaga loop, a 13.6-mile (22-km) hike up to Bucura Lake and the peak of Peleaga, the park's highest at an altitude of 8,232 feet (2,509 m). The view from the top is a chance to view many of the 80 or so glistening glacial lakes in these mountains, which locals know as "God's eyes." If you camp at Bucura Lake, a 6.2-mile (10-km) trail loops to the Retezat peak with its blunted top.

AT A GLANCE

Carpathian wilderness ▪ Bucura Lake ▪ 146.9 square miles (380.4 sq km) ▪ Cabana Pietrele to Peleaga trail ▪ retezat.ro/index.php/english.html

RODNA MOUNTAINS

A hiking and skiing wonderland with compelling mountain wildlife

The rugged Rodna Mountains offer hikers a panoply of challenging mountain terrain with lush forests, cirques, moraines, high pasturelands, karst caves, and crevasses.

The Rodnas contain one of the longest continuous ridges in Romania, stretching for over 31 miles (50 km) from west to east. The two highest peaks in the park are Pietrosul Rodnei peak at an elevation of 7,556 feet (2,303 m) and Ineu peak, which stands at 7,477 feet (2,279 m). Rodna Mountains National Park protects the whole of the Rodna massif, and the multitude of wildlife that thrives in these mountains, including brown bears, lynx, gray wolves, black capercaillie, and eagles.

The mountains attract many Romanian hikers during summer as well as skiers for a long winter: The ridge is well known for receiving late snowfalls well into the summer months, making it possible to enjoy a day on the pistes in June, and sometimes even into July. Ambitious hikers wishing to take on the whole massif should be well prepared: These are challenging hills and although trails are marked, a trained local guide is recommended, and a good map plus a compass are essential. Be aware that water is hard to come by, although some alpine lakes exist, the largest being Lake Lala. Trails also lead to Izvorul Tăuşoarelor, the deepest cave in Romania, descending some 1,571 feet (479 m) underground, and Jgheabul lui Zalion, which is 794 feet (242 m) deep.

AT A GLANCE Continuous ridge karst landscape ▪ 179.9 square miles (465.9 sq km) ▪ Izvorul Tăuşoarelor and Jgheabul lui Zalion caves ▪ panacomp.net/rodna-mountains

SEMENIC-CHEILE CARAŞULUI

Adventurous hiking and canyon kayaking above a karst underworld

Semenic-Cheile Caraşului National Park protects a mountainous karst region of canyons, pit caves, sinkholes, ridges, valleys, pasturelands, and pristine forests. The Semenic Mountains is a large, sprawling wilderness, and the park has many sites of interest for hikers or kayakers, including Gârlişte Gorge, Caraş Springs, and Nera Springs. The Izvorul Bigăr waterfall is a graceful cascade. A labyrinth of interesting underground destinations here include the caves of Buhui, Comarnic, Popovăţ, and Răsuflătoarei. The park also contains one of the largest areas of virgin beech forests in Europe, protected within the Izvoarele Nerei Reserve.

This is one of the wildest areas in Romania, with vast tracts untouched by humankind. Some of the peaks worth climbing for views of the park are Cracu Roşu peak at 3,957 feet (1,206 m), Căpăţâna peak at 4,367 feet (1,331 m), Capu Muntelui peak, which rises to 4,505 feet (1,373 m), and Piatra Nedeii peak, which stands at 4,715 feet (1,437 m). If you are adventurous, head for Caraş Gorge, close to the village of Caraşova, where you'll likely spot vipers on the rocks as well as eagles and hawks nesting on the cliffs. Round out your day with a visit to the International Sculpture Park in Gărîna, where you can enjoy a series of wooden sculptures alluringly spread out along the meadow.

AT A GLANCE Semenic Mountains landscapes ▪ Comarnic Cave ▪ 137.7 square miles (356.6 sq km) ▪ Virgin beech forests ▪ International sculpture park ▪ pnscc.ro

MOLDOVA

Moldova is the forgotten country of eastern Europe, a small, landlocked country squeezed between Romania on the west and Ukraine in the east, with its access to the Black Sea cut off by the latter. Yet it's a country that has much to offer travelers: Wander through this land of rolling hillsides and green pasturelands and you'll also see vast fields of lavender being harvested by laborers with small hand blades. In Mileștii Mici, you'll find the world's largest wine collection, an amazing 125 miles (200 km) of underground cellars. You'll also discover ornate Orthodox cathedrals and churches near relics from the Cold War era, such as Soviet statuary. Dig a little deeper, and you'll discover caves carved out by 13th-century monks at Orheiul Vechi Monastery in Moldova's sole national park of Orhei.

Opposite: Curchi Monastery is one of the most spectacular sites in Bessarabia; Orhei National Park also encompasses Old Orhei (Orheiul Vechi) Cave Monastery, a UNESCO World Heritage site.

ORHEI

A national park of rare cultural heritage in the heart of Moldova

The Orhei zone has been reborn since the introduction of sustainable farming and ecotourism.

Orhei National Park is a gem of cultural value and natural beauty located just 31 miles (50 km) from Moldova's capital city of Chişinău. The terrain of this large expanse of protected land is characterized by typically Moldovan features of rolling hills, stretches of rivers lined by woods and meadows, and historic villages.

The Orhei zone, the site of Moldova's first—and so far only—national park, was for decades a forgotten hinterland in a poor and neglected countryside. Many significant architectural monuments were abandoned and degraded, and over the last three decades, forests once filled with berries and mushrooms were exploited without much thought for a sustainable future.

In the early 2000s, Moldova's Ministry of Environment started the process of establishing Orhei National Park; in 2013, the national parliament ratified the decision, and Orhei was given a new lease on life. The park authorities have since worked to preserve biodiversity, arrest degradation of the forestry ecosystems, and restore sustainable management of Moldova's valuable forests and pastures. At the same time, the local population has been trained in the importance of conserving biodiversity, and environmentally friendly farming has been promoted. Efforts have also been made to promote sustainable ecotourism, with the result being several walking and biking trails along the park's rivers and through recovering forests.

CULTURAL TREASURES

Orhei embraces a rich rural heritage, and many aspects of national culture are preserved within the park. Local folklore and centuries-old traditions are now being recorded and restored to prominence. Under the protection of Orhei National Park are a wealth of sites worth visiting: the Trebujeni and Țigănești landscape reserves; the Curchi forest; a wide array of archaeological sites; a city from the time of the Golden Horde; and an enhanced medieval Moldovan city, five monasteries, and several boyar aristocratic manors. The park has also become a meditative retreat for followers of transcendental practices, continuing the spiritual heritage of what has long been an isolated rural area of hermitage and retreat.

The Old Orhei open-air museum and Orheiul Vechi Cave Monastery is a complex of historical and architectural monuments located on the banks of the narrow River Râut. The site includes remnants of various ancient monuments and buildings, as well as the famous cave monastery dug into the cliffs by monks in the 13th century. The monastery is currently inhabited by a handful of monks, who hold regular religious services throughout the day.

ARCHAEOLOGICAL TREASURES

Travelers of an archaeological disposition should visit the Orheiul Vechi Archaeological Landscape, which lies along the gorge of the lower course of the Râut River, 8.6 miles (14 km) upstream from its confluence with the Dniester River. This was historically an extremely strategic position, long a key trade route between the northeast Carpathians and the Black Sea Basin, where the remains of many settlements have been found.

If you are a "people person" there is an ethnographic museum worth visiting in Butuceni village, and the Gustar Ethnographical Musical Festival each August in Orheiul Vechi. The park also offers bike tours of Old Orhei and the famous Branesti Cellars, which houses the world's largest collection of wines.

Such has been the success of the region's rehabilitation under the auspices of the national park, that "Old Orhei" is currently a candidate for UNESCO's World Heritage List.

The archaeological and ecclesiastical complex at Old Orhei is known for its Cave Monastery.

AT A GLANCE

Curchi forest ▪ Orheiul Vechi Cave Monastery ▪ 130.5 square miles (338 sq km) ▪ Orheiul Vechi Archaeological Landscape ▪ visit.md/en/tour/stary-j-orhej

UKRAINE

It's not surprising that the huge country of Ukraine boasts so many national parks (called national nature parks), or that these are augmented by a range of smaller nature parks that protect every kind of green space and cultural site, from harbors to meadows to holy mountains. The national nature parks reflect all the tradition and history of a land settled millennia ago by Eastern Slavs, yet they also protect the seminomadic Hutsul culture of the Carpathians, preserved within Ukraine's largest national nature park. These central mountains are also home to European bison, brown bears, wolves, and lynx. At Ukraine's edges too, nature finds refuge: In the Danube Delta Biosphere Reserve, shared with Romania, flocks of cormorants, red-breasted geese, and 70 percent of the world's white pelicans find an eastern refuge.

Karpatskyi National Nature Park is the homeland of the Hutsul people.

Additional National Nature Parks in Ukraine

Biloberezhzhya Svyatoslav National Nature Park

Bug Guard National Nature Park

Charming Harbor (Magic Harbor) National Nature Park

Cheremoskyy National Nature Park

Derman-Ostrog National Nature Park

Dniester Canyon National Nature Park

Dzharylhach National Nature Park

Great Meadow National Nature Park

Halych National Nature Park

Hetman National Nature Park

Holy Mountain National Nature Park

Homilshanski Lisy National Nature Park

Ichnyansky National Nature Park

Kivertsy National Nature Park (Tsumanska Pushcha)

Mezynskyy National Nature Park

Northern Skirts National Nature Park

Nyzhnodnistrovskyy National Nature Park

Nyzhnosulskyy National Nature Park

Oleshkivski Sands National Nature Park

Pripyat-Stokhid National Nature Park

Pyryatynsky National Nature Park

Slobozhansky National Nature Park

Verhovinsky National Nature Park

Zacharovany Krai National Nature Park

Desna-Starogutskiy National Nature Park

RUSSIA

Holosyiyivskyy National Nature Park

Kiev

Kharkiv

Dvurechansky National Nature Park

Desna

Seym

Dnieper

Donets

Kremenchuk Reservoir

UKRAINE

Dnipro

Karmelyukove Podillya N.N.P.

Kakhovka Reservoir

Meotida National Nature Park

Pivdennyy Buh

Azov National Nature Park

Melitopol'

SEA OF AZOV

Dnieper

Dniester

Odesa

Azov-Syvash National Nature Park

Tuzlovski Estuaries National Nature Park

CRIMEA

BLACK SEA

N

0   100 kilometers

0   100 miles

AZOV

A delta parkland with coastal diversity, mineral waters, and medicinal muds

Pryazovskyi is a coastal strip on the northwest of the Azov Sea, about 20 miles (32 km) south of the city of Melitopol. Azov National Nature Park is the second largest national park of Ukraine, encompassing the floodplains, coastal plains, and landforms around the saline Molochnyi River estuary. The estuary forms a wide plain at a point where the "milky" river meets the ocean on the northwest coast of the Sea of Azov. This is a richly diverse area, and the park protects both steppe and aquatic habitats, as well as transition zones in between. These wetlands support large populations of nesting and migratory waterfowl.

The area's estuaries are known in Ukrainian as *limans*, which are enlarged estuaries more in the form of lagoons. These consist of about 80 percent land and 20 percent water. The habitats of these limans encompass a wide diversity: steppe, coastal plain, floodplain swamps, estuaries with variable salinity, spits, peninsulas, sandy-shell islands, sand dunes, and various saline lakes.

Azov has two key wetlands: the Molochnyi Liman (Milky River Delta), and the Berda Liman. The Molochnyi River is the largest of several rivers that course through the park. The park is connected by the thin Fedotova Spit to Biryuchyi Island in Azov-Syvash National Nature Park. There are two main towns, Kyrylivka and Berdiansk, and the area has many beaches and spas as it is known for its mineral waters and medicinal muds.

AZOV-SYVASH

A wilderness of waterways and a dead sea with healing qualities

Azov-Syvash National Nature Park is located in the Ukrainian province of Kherson Oblast, just north of Crimea. The flora of the park is dominated by feather grass and wheatgrass on the steppes. More than 80 percent of this protected area consists of waterways, encompassing the Azov Sea, Utlyutskyy Estuary, and Lake Syvash. Syvash attracts travelers for the healing qualities of its waters and mud, though the lake is, in fact, a "dead sea": Because of the high salinity of Syvash, the water cannot sustain many living

Byriuchyi Island and the Sea of Azov

organisms. Fish do live in the eastern part, and many birds, including pelicans and cormorants, thrive here, as bacteria, algae, and invertebrates are present in these shallow pools. Among the other birds that inhabit the park are bustards, steppe and gray cranes, northern harriers, golden eagle, white-tailed eagles, greater spotted eagles, sakers, peregrine falcons, and steppe kestrels. The park's mammals include ring-necked pheasants, red deer, fallow deer, mouflons (wild sheep), kulans (wild asses), and raccoon dogs.

Opposite: The sun rises in the east over Russia, casting dawn across the Azov Sea to Ukraine.

CARPATHIAN

Classic mountain terrain and old-growth forests combine with Hutsul culture

This is the Ukraine of the Hutsul people, whose traditions and language have endured for centuries in these subalpine western mountains. Although the country has seen turmoil and upheaval for the last three decades, struggling to find its feet in the post-Soviet Europe of the 1990s and beyond, the Hutsuls' homeland in the Carpathian Mountains has endured as a green refuge. Carpathian National Nature Park now works to preserve the forests of pine, beech, and spruce that coat these hills, but also the culture and tradition of the indigenous Hutsuls.

Hiking in these mountains brings you through green valleys along rivers lined with dense forests climbing up hillsides to the alpine meadows. Here the Hutsul drive flocks of sheep in spring to live high on hilltops all summer, producing a thick, rich cheese they sell in the villages below. You can observe the process at one of the many shepherd huts scattered through the meadows.

CARPATHIAN FORESTS

Many of Ukraine's forests were cut in the 18th and 19th centuries, but the sheer remoteness of the Carpathians saved the trees here. The park provides a wealth of habitat for bears, boars, deer, and spotted salamanders. Look in the forests for the Carpathian squirrel, a red squirrel whose coat changes to a winter white and whose ears are distinctively

Snow-cloaked spruces aglow with winter sunlight

spiked. Storks and herons can be spotted in the waters of the park, and high in the peaks you might spot the ominous circling of a golden eagle. Otters ply the park's waterways, and trout fishing here is excellent.

These are vast, somewhat mysterious forests, easily reimagined

as the setting for folkloric tales of witches, giants, ghosts, and all kinds of supernatural goings-on. You can get a flavor of the endless Carpathian stories that swirl around here on the Dovbush Trail, an easy 2.5-mile (4-km) hike from Yaremche (the park's main town) up into the mountainous forest surrounds. The subject of the route is one Oleksa Dovbush, also known as "the Robin Hood of the Carpathians."

Almost all Ukrainian hikers at some point summit Hora Hoverla (Mount Hoverla), a sandstone monument that translates as "the snow fortress" and the country's highest peak. Hoverla stands at 6,762 feet (2,061 m) above sea level. Capped with snow, it is often shrouded in early morning mists that give it a mystical atmosphere.

The Hutsuls

Hutsuls largely regard themselves as a part of a broader Rusyn ethnicity, rather than Ukrainians. Hutsul traditions have endured in the Carpathians, regardless of the politics or ideologies of those in power in faraway Kiev. Or Moscow. These hearty mountain nomads are best described as Transcarpathians, as their range stretches into the Romanian outposts of these vast mountains. Their name is thought to derive from ancient words for "outlaw" or "wanderer." Traditional Hutsul culture is seen in colorful clothing (often beaded), sculpture, wooden architecture, metalworking (especially brassware), rug weaving, pottery, and egg decorating. You can experience these traditions and learn about Hutsul history at the Pysanka Museum and the Museum of Hutsulshchyna and Pokuttya Folk Art, both in Kolomyia.

AT A GLANCE

Carpathian Mountain landscapes ▪ 199 square miles (515 sq km) ▪ Primeval beech forest ▪ The Dovbush Trail ▪ cnnp.if.ua/en

DESNA-STAROGUTSKIY

Wetland, bog, and riparian floodplain along the Desna River

Desna-Starogutskiy National Nature Park protects a middle section of the Desna River in northeastern Ukraine, encompassing a variety of wetland and mixed forest landscapes. The park has two sections, one on the floodplains of the Desna, the other in the southern region of the Bryansk forest on the Russian border.

This national park is also part of the Desniaksyi Biosphere Reserve, a Ukrainian-Russian initiative that incorporates both the Old Rus' and the Bryansk forests. The first habitat nurtures the Pridesniansk plant group. This is named for the Desna River floodplains, around which this vegetation grows. The name Prysdesnyanska can be translated as "near Desna," a zone characterized by riparian floodplain vegetation fed by the Desna River and its many tributaries. The area includes wide meadows with tall grasses, alder swamps, and forest stands of ash, oak, and aspen.

The second vegetation group appears in the Starogutskaya zone. This comprises marshlands and bog areas, and embraces relatively old pine forests with large quantities of sphagnum moss—the condensed moss used to form peat. The Starogutskaya section has mostly pine forests, and hosts mammals such as elk (moose), roe deer, wild swines, squirrels, and wolves. The vulnerable sterlet, a small sturgeon, and the Eurasian otter are among the aquatic creatures here. The park also hosts approximately 700 different varieties of vascular plants.

AT A GLANCE

Old Rus' and Bryansk Forests ▪ Marshlands and bogs ▪ 63 square miles (162 sq km) ▪ ukraine.com/ attractions/national-parks/desnyano-starogutskyi-national-park

DVURECHANSKY

A small park borders the steppe in the southeast of Ukraine.

Dvurechansky National Nature Park lies in a district of the same name in the Kharkiv region, near the villages of Kamyanka, Petro-Ivanivka, Krasne, and Mytrofanivka. The park is set on the edge of the steppe and forest steppe along the banks of the River Oskil. The territory has a dissected topography, with many hills and valleys, and includes areas of chalk steppe, where the chalk rock that underlies the area collapses. In this landscape, you might see such plants as Chinese mugwort, hyssop, and linseed. Stroll near Kamyanka and you may hear the piercing whistle of the marmot. The woods and groves teem with nesting birds, from predators to partridges.

Dvurechansky spans a range of steppe landscapes.

AT A GLANCE

Steppe landscapes ▪ River Oskil ▪ 12 square miles (31.3 sq km) ▪ Marmot colonies ▪ pzf.menr.gov.ua

HOLOSYIYIVSKYY

A park of surprising biodiversity set in the hills around Kiev

Two roads diverge in a Holosiivskyi wood, a green sanctuary for the people of Kiev.

With a tranquil setting in the Kiev hills, Holosyiyivskyy National Nature Park is an ideal escape for stressed-out citizens of the capital. This small park's landscapes embrace a significant range of biodiversity throughout its forests, lakes, and wetlands. The area it protects includes lowlands in the Dniester-Dnieper forest steppe province, and steppe zones in the Holosiivskyi district.

Several ecological trails lead past some wonderful views of the city below with its many onion-domed churches, including the golden-topped Kiev Monastery of the Caves. The southwestern parts of the park are now within the Feofaniya neighborhood, which was known as a settlement of the St. Michael's Kiev monastery. The park's main attractions are the Holy Protection Monastery, with its golden domes, and the Holy Trinity Monastery, its exterior a more subtle green and white. The parklands include several islands of forests located around the southern part of Kiev. A few include age-old oaks worth seeking out, such as the oak of Petro Mohyla.

Some 118 species of moss, 650 species of vascular plants, and more than 60 species of fungi thrive within the nature park, while the fauna includes 181 species of vertebrates and 190 species of insects. Among the surprising species that inhabit this semi-urban environment are reptiles, including European green lizards and smooth snakes; birds such as short-toed snake eagles, greater spotted eagles, and white-backed woodpeckers; numerous bats, including Leisler's bats and Daubenton's bats; as well as stoats, European polecats, and otters.

Among the park's numerous invertebrates are the forest caterpillar hunter; several beetles such as the stag beetle, musk beetle, and hermit beetle; a variety of butterflies including swallowtails, southern festoons, clouded Apollos, and Dukes of Burgundy; as well as carpenter bees and mammoth wasps.

AT A GLANCE

Dniester-Dnieper forest steppe ▪ 17.47 square miles (45.25 sq km) ▪ Holy Trinity Monastery ▪ Rare butterfly species ▪ pzf.menr.gov.ua

HUZULSCHYNA

A Carpathian Mountain wilderness park in the heart of Hutsul land

Huzulschyna National Nature Park, in western Ukraine's Carpathian Mountains, was established in 2002 to protect wildlife, landscapes, and ecosystems unique to these Ukrainian Carpathian Mountains in the Pokutia region.

Part of the park is located in the lower Hutsul Beskyd, known as the Pokutia-Bukovynian Carpathians. Divided into two sections, the park here features both mountainous landscapes reaching altitudes of 4,823 feet (1,470 m) and low foothills,

The Orthodox church in Kryvorivnia

1,148 to 1,640 feet (350 to 500 m) in elevation, with gentle slopes. In this part of the Carpathians, the climate is moderate, supporting a diversity

of local flora and fauna. The more mountainous part of the park is home to forests of spruce, fir, and beech, while the foothills are bearded with beech and beech-hornbeam forests and the lowlands with oak groves.

Hiking, fishing, and horseback riding are popular within the park, and beauty spots include scenic waterfalls and waterways. Huzulschyna means "Hutsul land," as the region is the homeland of this Rusyn ethnic from western Ukraine and Romania.

AT A GLANCE

Western Ukraine Carpathian Mountains ▪ Old oak forests and trails ▪ 124.6 square miles (322.7 sq km) ▪ Ethnic Hutsul lands ▪ pzf.menr.gov.ua

KARMELYUKOVE PODILLYA

An oasis of forests and woodland plants

The national park of Karmelyukove Podillya, located within Ukraine's Vinnytsia region, provides visitors with a forested green oasis in a region known for its rich raw mineral deposits and its recent history of mining and development. Vinnytsia has some 1,159 deposits and manifestations of various mineral resources, as well as multiple peat deposits; significant deposits of granite and kaolin, garnet, and fluorite have also been exploited here.

In such a region, the protected woodlands of the Karmelyukove Podillya are an invitation back to a time before the Earth was altered in the name of industry. These lovely forests consist mainly of English oak and European or common hornbeam, which thrives in mixed stands with oak. Other species are European ash, sycamore, and the wild service tree (aka the chequers or checkers tree).

Flowers found in the park include the martagon lily (or

Turk's cap lily), wild garlic (otherwise known as broad-leaved garlic, wood garlic, bear leek, or bear's garlic), violet helleborine (a lovely orchid), and the lesser butterfly-orchid. The many animals roaming these woodlands and meadows include the European badger and the stoat (aka the short-tailed weasel). And don't forget to look up: The skies are plied by the booted eagle and that fabulously aerodynamic rider of thermal updrafts, the black kite.

AT A GLANCE

Vinnytsia forests ▪ 78.4 square miles (203 sq km) ▪ English oak and European hornbeam ▪ pzf.menr.gov.ua

KHOTYN

Witness to the slings and arrows of Ukraine's national fortunes

This small national nature park celebrates and protects the historic castle complex of Khotyn in western Ukraine. Much of the park's area is covered in the riparian forests along banks of the Dniester River, which runs first through Ukraine and then Moldova before finally discharging back into the Black Sea. The castle has for centuries stood at this crossroads of cultures, marking where great armies fought over this territory of the historical northern Bessarabia region, a land divided in

The castle complex

1940 between Ukraine and Moldova.

The original Khotyn Fortress was built in the 10th century by Prince Vladimir Sviatoslavich as one of the border fortifications of southwestern Kievan Rus'. The fort was located on vital trade routes connecting Scandinavia and Kiev with the Ponyzia (lowlands) and Podillia, as well as Genoese and Greek colonies on the Black Sea, through Moldavia and Wallachia. Construction on the current Khotyn Fortress dates to 1325, with improvements made in the 1380s and 1460s. Through the centuries, the fort has been under Moldovan, Polish, Russian, Austrian-Hungarian, Romanian, German, and Ottoman control.

AT A GLANCE

Medieval fortress ▪ 36.2 square miles (94 sq km) ▪ Over 1,000 years of Ukrainian history ▪ Dniester River ▪ Riparian forests ▪ pzf.menr.gov.ua

KREMENETS MOUNTAINS

A small park with a wealth of protected sites and animals

Kremenets Mountains National Nature Park protects a cluster of mountains and ridges in the Hologoro-Kremenetskiy range in west-central Ukraine. The Hologoro-Kremenetskiy ridge creates a spine of some 106 miles (170 km) across western Ukraine. The massif consists of highly eroded hills of chalk, clay, and limestone, and views of the park are filled with low ridges and plateaus cut by ravines and river valleys. On the northern slopes, the mountains drop at a steep incline down to the valley of the Little Polisia plains, where rocky outcrops form a series of terraces and ledges. The park protects the Dovzhotsky and Veselovsky Botanical Reserves, as well as old-growth oak-hornbeam-ash forests; the Belokrynitsky Zoological Reserve; the Volynsky Zoological Reserve, which shelters the European badger; the Slavic Rock natural monument, a group of large limestone pillars; Mount Stitch, a 1,171-foot (357-m) conical mountain of chalk, marl, sand, and limestone; and Danilova Mountain, with its 12th-century Holy Trinity Church.

Kremenets Mountains also protects the critically endangered species of birch tree, the Klokov birch *(Betula klokovii)*; this species only grows on two mountains, Strakhova and Maslyatyn, both in Kremenets Mountains National Nature Park. These trees thrive on sandy hills in steppe grasses and dry chalkstone or in open woodlands.

AT A GLANCE

Hologoro-Kremenetskiy Mountains ▪ 63 square miles (162 sq km) ▪ Chalk, clay, and limestone landscapes ▪ Danilova Mountain and the Holy Trinity Church ▪ pzf.menr.gov.ua

LOWER POLISSYA

A beautiful park teeming with wildlife in Ukraine's northwest

Water and woodlands are a welcome combination for migrating birds.

Lower Polissya National Nature Park is a beautiful protected area located in the Khmelnytsky region of Ukraine. The park was established in 2013, to protect the wide array of wildlife and flora found in this area. The national nature park consists of a large expanse of the Polissya area and encompasses several lakes and wetland areas, as well as parts of the valleys of the Horyn, Furca, and Gnylyi Rih Rivers. This is a park where forlorn fishermen realize the wisdom of the Wellington boot, and the daylong misery of the wet sock.

BIRD HAVEN

With so much water and woodlands, Lower Polissya is naturally a haven for birds as well as a heaven for bird-watchers. Ukrainian enthusiasts flock here in spring and autumn to follow the migrations of the feathered masses, arriving from and returning to southern and western Europe, and farther afield. The park protects some 186 avian species, including several that are unique to the area. Mammals in the park number approximately 33 species, among them four species that are known to be endangered. These include the magnificent white-tailed eagle (otherwise known as the sea eagle), and the black kite.

A colony of grey herons also passes through the park's wetlands: You'll spot this lovely bird easily, standing at about four feet (1.2 m), and sporting mainly slate-gray plumage with blackish forehead and a bare red crown with a white streak extending from behind the eyes and lores to the upper back. The gray crane is an entertainer: Listen for its loud trumpeting call, given in flight and in times of display. This sound can be piercing and can carry over a considerable distance across the waters of Lower Polissya's lakes. The crane also enacts quite a dancing display, leaping about with its wings uplifted.

Badgers and otters also inhabit the fine forests and fast-running rivers of this impressive park.

ANGLERS' HEAVEN

The park's waters are filled with fish, and anglers will not be disappointed with the 18 species in Lower Polissya's rivers and lakes. One species that is endangered, however, and that should be thrown back if caught, is the Crucian carp, a medium-size carp. This has been described as having a body of "golden-green shining color," although others have described it as more of a bronze and dark green hue with red-flecked fins. If you've caught other carp, you'll know it when you catch it.

Another endangered inhabitant of these lakes is the tiny *Alburnoides bipunctatus,* commonly known as the schneider, spirlin, bleak, or riffle minnow, among several other anglers' monikers.

AT A GLANCE

Khmelnytsky region lake and forest landscapes ▪ 33.83 square miles (87.6 sq km) ▪ Grey crane and Crucian carp ▪ Fine fishing rivers ▪ malepolisja.in.ua

MEOTIDA

In the war-torn Donbas region, where birds still seek sanctuary

Meotida National Nature Park protects coastline and estuaries on the northern edge of the Sea of Azov. The park is close to Mariupol, a city that sits at the mouth of the Kalmius River that is traditionally Russophone, opting to speak Russian after the breakup of the Soviet Union although ethnically the population is evenly split between Russians and Ukrainians. Meotida has thus found itself caught in the crossfire of centuries-old human conflict.

Running the nature park has been disrupted by the latest separatist hostilities in the area. Previously, the protected regions of the park supported vital populations of migratory waterfowl and more than 100 species of nesting birds. As of 2019, the status of wildlife was dependent on the level of military activity. The park's habitats are widely diverse: steppe, coastal plain, floodplain swamps, estuaries with variable salinity, spits, peninsulas, sandy-shell islands, dunes, and saline lakes are all part of the Meotida mix.

The two main coastal sections for birds are the Bilosarayska Spit in the west, and the Kryva Bay and Kryva Spit in the east. The park protected one of the most famous seagull colonies in the ornithological world up to 2014.

In 2018, some *good* news at last came out of the park: "This year the only pair of Dalmatian pelicans—a very rare species of bird—produced young. Isn't this what happiness is?" said Meotida's acting director, Nadia Dolhova.

> **AT A GLANCE**
>
> Diverse Sea of Azov bird habitats ▪ 800 square miles (2,071.9 sq km) ▪ Bilosarayska Spit ▪ Kryva Bay and Kryva Spit ▪ pzf.menr.gov.ua

PODOLSKI TOVTRY

A huge regional park aims for a collective vision for a sustainable future.

The massive Podolski Tovtry National Nature Park extends across the southwest of Ukraine. It is the largest nature conservation area in the country. The park protects the landscape and wildlife of the Podillia region, which nurtures some 1,700 types of flora and 217 species of fauna. The park is a regional enterprise, encompassing many types of industry, housing,

Opposite: The sun blesses the troubled coastline of Meotida.

The gleaming Dniester River

tourist resorts, as well as rural areas of dense forestry, and collective and individual farming. Its aim is to manage and balance many competing interests in the best interests of nature and a sustainable environment. The Zbruch River runs along the park's western border, and the Dniester River runs south toward the mouth of the Ushytsia River. The Lower Smotrych River is a particularly rich wetland, and the park also protects a botanical garden and numerous archaeological sites. Also worth visiting is Kamianets-Podilskyi Castle, a Ruthenian-Lithuanian castle dating from the early 14th century.

> **AT A GLANCE**
>
> Regional national parkland ▪ Lower Smotrych River wetlands ▪ 1,009 square miles (2,613.1 sq km) ▪ Kamianets-Podilskyi Castle ▪ pzf.menr.gov.ua, tovtry.com/en/index.html

SHATSKYI

A silent haven for wildlife and humans alike

The emerald-green Shatskyi lakes glisten with crystalline waters and are surrounded by primeval pine forests, cloaked in a mossy silence. Shatskyi National Nature Park preserves this treasured landscape of more than 30 lakes in the northwest Volyn Polissya region, with Lake Svitiaz as the jewel in its crown. The park's still waters run deep, dropping to depths of 190 feet (58 m), and sometimes referred to as the Ukrainian Baikal. This lake is lined with sandy

Dawn on Lake Svitiaz

beaches and saturated with artesian springs producing its translucent and well-warmed waters. Visitors can row out to the legendary Island

of Love and walk among the lindens and maples, or rent a boat and cast off into waters teeming with bass, pike, bream, roach, catfish, and eel. You can take a basket and gather mushrooms and berries in the Volyn forests. Horseback riding is also popular. In addition, the park runs several environmental trails, such as the 3.7-mile (6-km) Forest Song Trail leading through pine forests between Peremut and Pesochnoye lakes: Watch for elk (moose), wild boar, and roe deer on the way.

AT A GLANCE

Shatskyi lakes ▪ Lake Svitiaz (the Ukrainian Baikal) ▪ 190 square miles (490 sq km) ▪ The Forest Song Trail ▪ ukraine.com/attractions/national-parks

SKOLE BESKYDY

Old-growth beech and spruce-fir forests, rimmed by mineral water spa towns

Skole Beskydy National Nature Park follows the sweep of the Striy and Opir River Valleys. Its territory is located within the areas of the Sanocko-Turczańskie Mountains and Skole Beskids, in the western part of the Ukrainian Carpathians. The park is located near the popular resorts of Skhidnytsia, Skole, and Slavske.

Hiking the beautiful Carpathian trails is popular, as is boating, and skiing facilities are gaining ground. A popular hiking desti-

Traversing the Carpathians

nation is Kamyanetskiy Falls, a spectacular 20-foot (6-m) curtain of water that tumbles from the River Kamyanka, not far from

the village of Dubyna. Watch for rarities such as Miller's water shrews, Bechstein's bats, capercaillie, Aesculapian snakes, and Carpathian newts.

The village of Skhidnytsia, next to the park, offers the chance to rest weary limbs in one of the town's 30 mineral water spas. The park also has more than 30 mineral springs. Healing mineral springs can also be found in the valley of Maydanske Rybnik, around New Kropyvnyk village.

AT A GLANCE

Sanocko-Turczańskie Mountains and Skole Beskids ▪ 137.7 square miles (356.8 sq km) ▪ Kamyanetskiy Falls ▪ Mineral water spa towns ▪ skole.org.ua

SYNEVYR

A peaceful national park in a rustic backwater of lakes and forests

A sleigh ride through the snow-dusted woodlands of northeastern Europe is one of the great experiences of a national park visit in this part of the world. The almost mystical silence of the frozen forests, fog-thick breath of the horses, and exhilarating sensation of gliding as you pick up speed—this is a thrill worth traveling a long way for, and certainly as far as the winter wilderness of Synevyr National Nature Park. Nature may be frozen deep, but your heart races and you'll come alive.

Synevyr welcomes you at its attractive wooden ecological visitors center on the lakeshore, where the vital preservation and environmental work being conducted in the park is presented and explained. A series of other museums in the park invite you to learn the history of the area. At the Alloy Forest Museum, you can learn of the region's wood and its uses. The open-air Skansen Museum, located on the Kolochava riverbank, presents the architectural and household culture of the Hutsul Transcarpathians. Well worth visiting is the Brown Bear Rehabilitation Center, where injured and orphaned bears are nursed toward a return to the wild. This is about as close as you'll ever be—or want to be—to 900 pounds (408 kg) of muscular brown bear.

Synevyr Lake, with its wooded shoreline walkways, is a delight, especially when washed with a pale winter light as steam rises from its waters. Local legend has it that this lake was formed from the tears of a count's daughter named Syn, because her love, the Verkhovynian cowboy Vir, was killed on the orders of her ruthless father. A 43-foot (13-m) sculpture called "Syn i Vir" adorns the lakeside.

A midwinter sleigh ride through the wilds of Synevir is an unforgettable adventure.

AT A GLANCE

Synevyr Lake ▪ Alloy Forest Museum ▪ 156 square miles (404 sq km) ▪ Brown Bear Rehabilitation Center ▪ pzf.menr.gov.ua

TUZLOVSKI ESTUARIES

A group of marine lagoons protected for bird wildlife

During his tenure as fourth president of Ukraine, Viktor Yanukovych ordered several swaths of land protected under national nature park status. One such area is the Tuzlovski Estuaries National Nature Park, located on the coast of the Sea of Azov in southern Bessarabia.

The park is comprised of the Tuzly group of lagoons: These, in turn, consist of parts of the larger lagoons of Shahany, Alibey, and Burnas, as well as the small lagoons called Solone Ozero, Khadzhyder, Karachaus, Buduri, Martaza, Magala, Malyi Sasyk, and Dzhantsheys'ke. The name Tuzly originates from the Turkish *tuzlu,* which means "salty." The salinity of some of these lagoons (or *limans* in Ukrainian, meaning "enlarged estuary") is about 30 percent.

The lagoons are separated from the Black Sea by an 18-mile (29-km) sandbar, which ranges from about 200 to 1,310 feet (60 to 400 m) wide and 3 to 10 feet (1 to 3 m) high.

Walkways bridge some lagoons.

AT A GLANCE

Tuzly Lagoons shore landscapes ▪ 107.6 square miles (278.6 sq km) ▪ Bird-watching and hiking ▪ pzf.menr.gov.ua

UZHANSKY

A UNESCO World Heritage forest on the border with Slovakia and Poland

The remote and mountainous expanses of Uzhansky National Nature Park are located in the far west of the country at the Ukrainian border with Poland and Slovakia. The park is part of the East Carpathian Biosphere Reserve, created to protect the pristine beech forest of the Carpathians.

Uzhansky stretches across the valleys of the Uzh River and its tributaries in the western slopes of the Carpathian Mountains. The park's highest peak, Kinchyk Bukovskyi Mountain, rises to 4,104 feet (1,251 m) and is a fine hike. Hiking Uzhansky's 17 trails takes you through four altitude

The forested peaks of Uzhanian

zones, including beech forest, alder forest, and—above 3,610 feet (1,100 m)—the alpine meadows. In these lovely grasslands, look for some of the park's 23 species of protected orchids. Elsewhere, watch out for signs of the red deer, roe deer, wild boar, red fox, and badgers that inhabit these mountains. Culturally curious visitors should also seek out any of the six wooden churches built here by the indigenous Lemkos ethnic group in the 17th and 18th centuries.

AT A GLANCE

Carpathian Mountains landscapes ▪ 151.1 square miles (391.3 sq km) ▪ Kinchyk Bukovskyi Mountain ▪ Lemkos churches ▪ pzf.menr.gov.ua

VIZHNITSKY

A wealth of wildlife cradled in the woods of the Carpathian lowlands

Vizhnitsky National Nature Park is located in the Carpathian lowlands of southwestern Ukraine. The park protects the landscapes of Bukovina Carpathian with its many historical churches and cultural sites. The town of Vizhnitsky in particular is worth visiting: First mentioned in the Moldova Chronicles of 1501, it was famous for its fairground tradition.

This is a gently rolling landscape, as the park follows the basins of the Cheremosh and Siret Rivers. The eastern part of the park consists of broad valleys of the Siret's many tributaries. The western area follows the Cheremosh River and features more dramatic landscapes, with rocky outcrops, scenic cliffs, waterfalls, and sheer gorges.

Rich forests cover more than 95 percent of the park, mainly consisting of fir-beech mix. Among the endangered species are a number of rare orchid species. The wildlife in the park is particularly rich, due largely to the mild climate within these Western Carpathians. Along the wetlands you'll spot white stork, fire salamander, yellow-bellied toad, and European tree frog; in the forests, you may see hazel dormice, hunted by wildcat, as well as capercaillie and Ural owls; the lesser spotted eagle might swoop down from the park's peaks to hunt. Other mountain birds include rock pipits and grey wagtails, while the Aesculapian snake is seen on some rocks. Brown bear and lynx are among the larger mammals inhabiting Vizhnitsky.

AT A GLANCE

Carpathian lowlands landscapes ▪ 30.6 square miles (79.2 sq km) ▪ Vizhnitsky's fairground heritage ▪ pzf.menr.gov.ua

YAVORIVSKYI

A preserve tucked within a rustic backwater of lakes and forests

The Roztocze is a narrow range of hills that runs for 47 miles (75 km) before rising sharply to the north of the Lesser Polissya and extending into Polish territory. The southeastern part of the Roztocze forms the main European watershed, where many rivers run to basins of the two great seas of the region, the Black Sea and the Baltic. Located within the Ukrainian Roztocze, Yavorivskyi National Nature Park consists of steppe landscapes and large wetlands. Here, floating fields of water lilies are particularly picturesque; look, too, for amphibians in the park, particularly the black and yellow fire salamander.

The nature park enjoys dense forest cover, mainly a mix of hornbeam, oak, and pine stands. Some pristine pine forests exist here too, and in depressions, you'll find alder. Beech grow near the hilly eastern border of the range. In the northeastern part of the park, an interesting relict stand of hundred-year-old spruce, fir, and maple still survives in this remote wilderness.

Due to pastures and settlements within the parklands in centuries past, areas of herbaceous vegetation occupy a much smaller area than in other Ukrainian wildernesses. But visitors hiking through this lush park will find natural meadows as well as wild growths along rivers and channels. The park has several attractive trails and is a popular backwater for river and lake fishing.

AT A GLANCE

Ukrainian Roztocze terrains ▪ Steppes and wetlands ▪ 27 square miles (71 sq km) ▪ Fire salamander ▪ pzf.menr.gov.ua

More National Nature Parks

Ukraine's national nature parks are territories where wildlife and flora, as well as cultural and historic sites, are well protected under the state's Nature Preservation Fund. This includes numerous parks, and the total area under protection is an impressive 4,292 square miles (11,116 sq km).

Dniester Canyon National Nature Park with its forest steppe landscape

The Nature Preservation Fund has gained most ground since the fall of the Soviet Union, with many new parks opened in the 1990s and 2000s. As the map on pages 472–73 shows, most of Ukraine's main parks are in Western Ukraine. For more information on the parks, *pzf.menr .gov.ua* and *en.discovermykolaiv .com.ua* provide English-language website pages.

The **Biloberezhzhya Svyatoslav National Nature Park** is a protected peninsula located between the Dnieper-Buh estuary and the Black Sea. This is million-plus bird migration territory. **Bug Guard National Nature Park** preserves an area that runs alongside the Southern Buh River in south-central Ukraine.

A coastal stretch of the Tarkhankutskyy Peninsula (part of the Crimean Peninsula) is covered by **Charming Harbor (Magic Harbor) National Nature Park,** a treasured Black Sea park. Here the steppe landscape, the Atlesh coast's cliffs and rock formations, and the Bolshoy ruins are also protected.

Set in the northeastern part of the Carpathian Mountains, in the historical region of Bukovina, **Cheremoskyy National Nature Park** protects the deep spruce forests of the area. Ukraine's smallest national nature park, scattered in sections along the Zbytynka River Valley, is the **Derman-Ostrog National Nature Park.** This protects pine-oak forest, marshy river lowlands, and many botanical treasures. **Dniester Canyon National Nature Park** follows Dniester Canyon along the middle course of the Dniester River in western Ukraine. This park encompasses Ukrainian forest steppe landscape and varied geological formations, including two of the world's longest caves.

Dzharylhach National Nature Park protects the island of Dzharylhach, and Dzharylhach Bay, near Crimea; the island has salty lakes and turtle beaches. **Great Meadow** is a beautiful national nature park located on the banks of the River Conca, incorporating the floodplain terrace of the Dnieper River. The fertile marshlands of the Great Meadow host some of Europe's richest vegetation. **Halych National Nature Park,** located along the Dniester River and the lower reaches of its tributaries, protects oak, hornbeam, and beech forests, and wetlands, meadow steppes, and geological formations. The Vorskla River Valley is the focus of **Hetman National Nature Park,** which embraces much of the river's floodplain and its elevated terraces, as well as the vital habitats provided by the river and its pine-forested banks.

Holy Mountain National Nature Park preserves the 17th-century temples of St. Nicholas Church, dramatically set into chalk cliffs. The floodplain woods and mountain terrain here host rare wildlife such as ermine and osprey. The small park of **Homilshanski Lisy** in the northeast of the country has landscapes of lakes and marshes and welcomes 137 species of birds. Located in the Chernihiv region, **Ichnyansky National Nature Park** covers an attractive area of oak and pine forests, forest steppe, wetlands, and lake landscapes along the River Uday. Bird-watching, kayaking, and hiking are all major attractions of **Kivertsy National Nature Park** in western Ukraine, which protects the great forests of Kiversty between Kiev and the Polish border.

Centered around the village of Mezyn, **Mezynskyy National Nature Park** contains ancient archaeological sites, fine oak forests, crystal clear lakes, and brooding moors. An archaeological museum and outdoor wood sculptures add to this area known as "Mezyn Switzerland." Located in Northern Podillya,

Northern Skirts National Nature Park protects area history, culture, archaeology, architecture, and nature. The Olesky and Pidhirtsi castles, monasteries, churches, and beech-hornbeam forests are all part of this park's appeal.

Black Sea lowland is protected by **Nyzhnodnistrovskyy National Nature Park** in southern Ukraine, which is fed by the Dnieper River. **Nyzhnosulskyy National Nature Park,** located in Ukraine's Poltava region, includes wetlands and forests along the Sula River, an area known for its many bat species, among other rich wildlife. The **Oleshkivski Sands National Nature Park** protects the Oleshky Desert, the largest expanse of sand in Ukraine, which is situated inland from the coast of the Black Sea and consists of *kuchuhury* or sand dunes. **Pripyat-Stokhid National Nature Park,** located in Northern Ukraine along the border with Belarus, shelters valuable swamplands, forests, and grasslands.

Pyryatynsky National Nature Park protects vital flora and fauna in the Poltava region of Central Ukraine. It hosts extensive wetlands and reed beds that are home to many bird, fish, and insect species. Set in the Kharkiv region of northeastern Ukraine, **Slobozhansky National Nature Park** protects wildlife and architectural treasures around the valley of the Merlo River (within the Dnieper River Basin). **Verhovinsky National Nature Park** preserves a swath of land in the southwest of Ukraine near the border with Romania.

In Ukraine's southwest, **Zacharovany Krai National Nature Park** protects a small stretch of the Eastern Carpathians. This mountainous area sustains a rich array of fauna, including chamois, brown bear, wild boar, European badger, lynx, wild boar, and wildcat. But the undoubted star of these parts is the magnificent Carpathian red deer, a subspecies valued as a food source for the indigenous Hutsul people. Its distinctive red coat turns grayish brown in winter.

The red deer is found in national parks across much of Europe.

TURKEY

Abundance, profusion, lavish riches. These are the bywords of Turkey, and the lasting impressions visitors have when they step into an ancient bazaar or stand over-
whelmed at the majesty of yet another medieval-era mosque in Istanbul. Wandering
through a Byzantine basilica or simply experiencing the epic drama of a Turkish meal
and its attendant hospitality—all this gives you a sense of sharing in heaven-sent
riches, a feeling that extends to this beautiful country's national parks. Most of these
riches fall in the Asian part of Turkey, among them the otherworldly rock formations
of Cappadocia, the stunning Sümela Monastery in Altındere Valley National Park, and
the avian wildlife of Bird Paradise National Park. Yet, the four European parks are a
fine foretaste for those far-flung pleasures: Gala Lake hosts pelican colonies, Gallipoli
has its heart-wrenching history, Gökçeada gives us underwater Turkey, and İğneada
Longoz is one of Europe's great forest parks.

National Parks in Asiatic Turkey

Aladağlar National Park	Kovada Lake National Park
Altınbeşik Cave National Park	Küre Mountains National Park
Altındere Valley National Park	Marmaris National Park
Başkomutan Historical National Park	Mount Ararat National Park
Beydağları Coastal National Park	Mount Güllük–Termessos National Park
Beyşehir Lake National Park	Mount Honaz National Park
Bird Paradise National Park	Munzur Valley National Park
Boğazköy–Alacahöyük National Park	Nene Hatun Historical National Park
Dilek Peninsula-Büyük Menderes Delta National Park	Saklıkent National Park
Göreme Historical National Park and the Rock Sites of Cappadocia	Sarıkamış Allahuekber Mountains National Park
Hatila Valley National Park	Soğuksu National Park
Ilgaz Mountain National Park	Spil Mountain National Park
Kaçkar Mountains National Park	Sultan Sazlığı National Park
Karagöl–Sahara National Park	Troya Historical National Park
Karatepe–Aslantaş National Park	Uludağ National Park
Kazdağı National Park	Yedigöller National Park
Kızıldağ National Park	Yozgat Çamlığı National Park
Köprülü Canyon National Park	

*Opposite: Flamingos flock to Lake Küçük
Gala in Gala Lake National Park.*

GALA LAKE

A legendary lake park on the crossroads of continental bird migration

The park's vast lakes and forests provide vital habitat for migrating birds.

Gala Lake National Park spans two of western Turkey's great lakes, Pamuklu and Küçük Gala. Here, visitors can stand on a spring or fall day, embraced by nature's silence, stillness, and serenity. Then, a million birds descend.

The park's national protected status is a testament to the activism of biologists who protested against pollution by agricultural pesticides and fertilizer, and demanded a halt to uncontrolled fishing and poaching that was devastating bird numbers. The lakes and forests now provide a safe haven for some 163 species of birds, of which 46 are resident. Bird-watchers flock here to observe huge avian migrations on their way north and south.

The park provides these winged visitors a variety of vital habitat in its wetlands area, lakes, and forest ecosystems. Both Pamuklu and Küçük Gala are known for their large colonies of Dalmatian pelicans, severely endangered birds worldwide. These creatures are mesmerizing to watch in large groups. Other birds that gather here in large numbers are swans, spoonbills, Eurasian coots, great white herons, plovers, spoonbills, avocets, and cormorants in the thousands.

The park has paths through the wetlands, where you may spot glossy ibis, marsh harrier, ruddy shelduck, and little cormorant. Watch in the western part of Gala Lake for large populations of green head ducks. The larger birds of prey are never far away from feasts of fish and feathered foes: The white-tailed eagle, red falcon, and lesser kestrel all keep predatory eyes on the events of these waters.

The flora in the park is a rich mix of lakeside forests and aquatic plants, including water lilies, water hyacinth, reed mats, bamboo, and green algae. Like the birds, anglers find rich pickings here, and among the species you'll catch on Pamuklu and Küçük Gala are European eel, pike perch, carp, and northern pike.

AT A GLANCE

Lake Pamuklu and Lake Küçük Gala ▪ Mountain forests ▪ 23.5 square miles (60.8 sq km) ▪ Bird-watching and angling ▪ nationalparksofturkey.org/lake-gala-national-park-en

GALLIPOLI PENINSULA

A haunting memorial to a turning point in Turkish, Australian, and New Zealand history

The ancient pagan peoples believed in the existence of places in this world that overlap with the hereafter. Walk around certain battle sites, where thousands died violently, and it's chillingly obvious that you have entered into one of these psychic netherworlds. Gettysburg is one such "thin space." Gallipoli Peninsula Historical National Park is another.

THE BATTLE FOR GALLIPOLI

The park was established to honor the soldiers who lost their lives on Gelibolu, aka Gallipoli, in the fierce campaign of World War I when British and colonial forces sought to link up with their Russian allies to the east by attacking the Gallipoli Peninsula and trying to seize Istanbul (formerly Constantinople). The Ottomans dug in and eventually repulsed the attackers in what would become one of the bloodiest slaughters in modern warfare. The first Australian troops landed at Anzac Cove on the morning of April 25, 1915, and only after eight long months of bloodshed were the survivors withdrawn. More than 130,000 men died in the struggle for Gallipoli.

In Turkey, the battle is now seen as a defining moment in history, a last stand of the motherland as the Ottoman Empire crumbled. The battle formed the basis for the Turkish War of Independence and the founding of the Republic of Turkey eight years later under Mustafa Kemal Atatürk, who was a commander at Gallipoli. In Australia and New Zealand, it is solemnly commemorated as the birth of both countries' national consciousness. The story was retold in a fine 1981 movie by Australian filmmaker Peter Weir, simply titled *Gallipoli*.

The park encompasses several memorials, monuments, and cemeteries, and is set amid the natural

The Turkish 57th Infantry Regiment Memorial at Gallipoli

beauty of surrounding forests, Ari Burnu cliffs, and Tuz Gölü (Salt Lake). The green hills, sandy beaches, and blue waters provide a peaceful repose for those who fought and died here at the confluences of three great cultures, Europe (the Balkans), the Aegean Sea, and Anatolia.

The parklands, bays, and beaches are scattered with sunken ships, trenches, castles, towers, and other remnants of the war. As you walk past graves of tens of thousands of young men, the line between life and death is all around you. When you're ready to return to the land of the living, take a ferry from Çanakkale or Kabatepe and head to the largest of the Turkish islands, Gökçeada, to wander around its pristine bays, hills lined with pine and olive trees, and countryside dotted with sacred springs and monasteries.

AT A GLANCE

WWI Memorial Park ▪ Çanakkale Sehitleri Aniti memorial ▪ 127.4 square miles (330 sq km)
▪ nationalparksofturkey.com/gelibolu-gallipoli-peninsula-historical-park

GÖKÇEADA

A marine park teems under Aegean waters around Turkey's largest island.

Off Turkey's westernmost point, beyond the shores of the island to the west of the Gallipoli Peninsula, you'll find Gökçeada Underwater Marine Park. The floor in this watery Aegean world supports vast meadows of *Posidonia* sea grasses interspersed with hard rock and corals. Around the coastal areas of this national park, you'll discover a zone rich with green, brown, and red algae, as well as these sea grasses. These provide rich habitat for a wide range of marine life, including crustaceans and high numbers of pelagic and benthic fish groups. Among the rock caves, you'll find groupers, morays, and octopuses.

Gökçeada is popular with divers, and its onshore activities include hiking, swimming, and fishing in the plentiful Aegean waters. Boating is often rewarded with a sighting of friendly-faced dolphins, or seals sunning themselves on rocks.

To protect wildlife, the park forbids fishing, swimming, and other activities within its own boundaries, so make sure you know where the boundaries lie. The park currently embraces a 1.5-mile (2.4-km) coastal zone from Yıldız Bay to Çiftlik Bay, and extends out into the sea for 660 feet (200 m). Visitors are not totally excluded from these highly sensitive ecosystems, and authorities have set up an underwater trail to educate divers under the tutelage of a park ranger. The visitors center has details of these excursions.

The good news is that preservation measures are having an effect. Research scientists working here have reported a significant increase in the numbers of various fish and lobster species in recent years. More dolphins and endangered Mediterranean monk seals have also started to visit the shores around this fascinating underwater national park.

Be sure to explore the rest of Gökçeada, too, with its pinewoods, dense olive groves, sacred springs, and monasteries.

The Aegean waters off the shores of Gökçeada are a diver's delight.

AT A GLANCE

Gökçeada Island shoreline and Aegean Sea ▪ Yıldız Bay ▪ Çiftlik Bay ▪ .18 square mile (.46 sq km) ▪ Underwater nature trail ▪ gokceadasualtiparki.org

İĞNEADA LONGOZ FOREST

A dark green Eden near the Bulgarian border

Situated at the northernmost tip of the Marmara region, on the last Turkish shore to be washed by the waters of the Black Sea, İğneada Longoz Forest National Park is a secret Eden less than 100 miles (160 km) from Istanbul. These gorgeous dark-green woodlands of the İğneada floodplain cast their spell just outside of İğneada town, which sits on the Bulgarian border.

This small forest park protects an area of floodplains that formed from rivers depositing alluvium on the Black Sea shore, the clay, silt, sand, and gravel that runs down from sources high in the Strandzha Mountains. This rich soil deposit has nurtured a forest of spectacular beauty, which floods each spring as the mountains shed torrents of spring melt and the parklands become a kayakers' playground.

The park's forest floodplains are inundated each springtime

AQUATIC & WOOD HABITATS

The national park protects several rare ecosystems, in addition to the forests. The marshlands, swamps, lakes, and coastal sand dunes here all provide habitat for a host of wildlife. Serving to incubate many species of aquatic plant life, the park's five lakes are Lake Erikli, a lagoon that becomes separated from the sea in the dry summer months; Lake Mert, formed by the Çavuş Dere creek; Lake Saka, a small lake in the south of the park between the floodplain and the dunes; and Lake Hamam and Lake Pedina, which complete the quintet. The dunes are situated on either side of İğneada town, with the northerly dunes stretching from the town to just east of Lake Erikli. The southern sands run from Lake Mert's shoreline to Lake Saka's south coast, reaching a width of 165 to 195 feet (50 to 60 m) at some points.

These dunes extend some 6.2 miles (10 km), protecting several plant species unique to the Black Sea region. The national park also protects the mixed-wood forests of the swamp and marshlands, where many vine species entwine trees that include European ash, oak, alder, beech, and maple. The dense layer of vegetation the vines provide adds to the untamed appeal of this beautiful wilderness.

FISHING, BIRDING & WILDLIFE-WATCHING

Anglers in the park cast for trout, smelt, and grey mullet, among other fish species that thrive in these waterways. The trails are filled with birdsong, and many of Turkey's big hitters fly here, such as white-tailed eagles, European green woodpeckers, grey herons, European cuckoos, kingfishers, black storks, and that Mohawk-headed joker in the park, the hoopoe.

The forests thrum with wildlife, and animals to watch for as you walk the trails include wildcats, wild boar, hares, pine martens, badgers, fox, and weasel. Otters ply the park's watery labyrinth, and big-eared bats use their GPS-like instincts of echolocation to navigate the dense forests. Gray wolves stalk deer, and yellow-necked mice are prey to bigger birds.

AT A GLANCE

İğneada floodplain ▪ Inundated forests ▪ 12.1 square miles (31.5 sq km) ▪ Fishing and kayaking ▪ nationalparksofturkey.com/igneada-longoz-forests-national-park

GEORGIA

A beautiful and mysterious land situated at the crossroads between continents, Georgia now looks toward a European future, yet retains much of the charm and traditions of its Asiatic past. Sitting astride the Caucasus, Georgia is a land of snowcapped mountains where eagles prey, mink sashay, bears prowl, and wolves howl. This is also a land of deep faith, scattered with churches, many of them centuries old. The regions of Svaneti, Khevsureti, and Tusheti are without equal for their rugged beauty and warm hospitality. Few hosts are more affable and welcoming than Georgians, especially in the countryside, where strangers are welcomed with a feast of food and wine and toasts and maybe some polyphonic group singing followed by more wine and more toasts . . . and on into the livelong night the Georgian festivities go.

National Parks in Asiatic Georgia

Algeti
Borjomi-Kharagauli
Javakheti
Kolkheti
Machakhela
Mtirala
Tbilisi
Vashlovani

Above: Georgian mountain goats
Opposite: A low moon rises over the main ridge of the Kavkasioni peaks, Kazbegi National Park.

KAZBEGI

The heights of Georgian mountain landscapes, history, and wildlife

The 14th-century Gergeti Trinity Church, beneath Mount Kazbek in the High Caucasus

Kazbegi National Park is remotely located around the basin of the Tergi River in northeastern Georgia. This is high Caucasus Mountain landscape, close to the Russian border, with alpine pastures, moraines, snow-covered peaks, and low mountain forests. The woods include Litvinov's birch, Sosnovski's pine, junipers, and remarkably at this altitude, sea buckthorn. The park's lowest point is at an altitude of 4,595 feet (1,400 m). These mountains are home to much wildlife, including the goatlike East Caucasian turs, chamois, brown bears, and lynx. Golden eagles, griffon vultures, and bearded vultures swoop down on their prey from the peaks.

The park is set in a region where Christian and pagan beliefs have long been blended into local lore. The area's many historical monuments include the 14th-century Sameba temple, the 10th-century Garbani Church, the Sioni basilica, the Akhaltsikhe basilica, and the 17th-century Sno Castle, the ruins of which rise on a rock next to the Snostskali River. The hospitable local people are called Mokheves ("gorge dwellers"). For centuries, these determined mountain folk defended the main way to Georgia—the deep, narrow gorge of Darialis. Despite the relative poverty of the region and lack of infrastructure, the park attracts Georgians and foreigners who come to relish its rugged, remote mountain wildernesses. A hiking trail starting at the dramatic Darial Gorge takes you to the Devdoraki Glacier; the gorge is also close to the Gveleti waterfall, named for local snakes.

AT A GLANCE

High Caucasus Mountains ▪ Alpine wildlife ▪ 35 square miles (90.3 sq km) ▪ Sioni basilica ▪ Mokheves hospitality ▪ Devdoraki Glacier ▪ georgia.travel/en_US/mtskheta-mtianeti/kazbegi

PSHAV-KHEVSURETI

A Georgian national park established with the future of wildlife in mind

In 2014, the Georgian government looked to the future and, with the help of the World Wide Fund established a protected area in the Mtskheta Mtianeti region for many of the country's species. Pshav-Khevsureti National Park was planned to preserve vital habitat for the East Caucasian tur in particular, extending the turs' range from Tusheti and other areas of Khevsureti. The park will also help protect the mountain leopard in the Caucasus, as well as brown bear, European lynx, Caucasian red deer, and chamois. Another local treasure, the bezoar goat, will benefit from the preserved habitat of Pshav-Khevsureti in future years. This bezoar ibex *(Capra aegagrus aegagrus),* also known as the Anatolian bezoar ibex, Persian ibex, or (by Anatolian locals) *dağ keçisi,* is a wild goat subspecies native to montane forests across much of this region. The bezoar ibex is a popular trophy for hunters, due to its spectacular horns: Bezoars average about 132 pounds (60 kg), and the males' horns can grow as long as 59 inches (1.5 m). The park offers a safe habitat for its population to expand.

The landscape is also remarkably rich in historical and cultural sites: Fortress villages dot the region, including Lebasikari, Shatili, and Mutso, stark ancient settlements marked by iconic crosses. Wherever you travel in this mountainous region, you will see signs of fortress towers, churches, and sanctuaries from afar. As you approach, you'll experience the same sense of anticipation as travelers must have felt many centuries ago when they neared these medieval fortresses.

The old abandoned fortress village of Shatili in the Arghuni gorge

AT A GLANCE

Caucasus Mountains ▪ East Caucasian tur ▪ 293 square miles (758.4 sq km) ▪ Medieval fortress villages ▪ apa.gov.ge/en/protected-areas/national-park, experiencecaucasus.com/en/pshav-khevsurety-national-park-and-its-zones

TUSHETI

Traditional Georgia at its most dramatic

It looks like the village at the end of the world. Like a mythic place travelers might end up at after some kind of epic quest. Perhaps a mission to find the most remote, most impossibly romantic mountain park in Europe.

Welcome to Omalo, stranger, the principal village in the historical region of Tusheti and within Tusheti National Park. You won't be a stranger for long.

The only drivable road to this isolated village is the Abano Pass, at 9,680 feet (2,950 m), the highest mountain road in the Caucasus and a real heart-stopper. Peer over the precipice here and you understand better the roles of faith and destiny in traditional Georgian life. The pass, one of the highest roads in Europe, closes from mid-October until mid-April (depending on snows and road conditions). Many of the roads in these mountains are rough-and-ready and fit only for 4WD vehicles. Or a good mule, if you have the time.

To calm the nerves, there's a spa/bathhouse along the route, known locally as a "giver of life." The indoor swimming pool uses natural thermal waters.

Omalo is located on a natural plateau, connecting four main gorges—Chanchakhovani gorge,

The sun sets on Omalo, at the end of the Abano Pass.

Chaghma gorge, Pirikiti gorge, and Gometsari gorge—all with their own lovely strings of villages.

The highest building you notice as you approach the town is the fortress of Keselo, with its medieval-looking landmark towers. Historically, this served as a refuge for families when the village was attacked. In Omalo today, you'll find shelter in a range of guesthouses and the newly opened 47-room Hotel Samzeo, which overlooks the valley. At the nearby visitors center, you can get maps and information for hiking in the national park.

PEOPLE OF TUSHETI

The people who welcome you to Omalo are mainly ethnic Georgians called Tushs or Tushetians. Many of the families in the region have long practiced a seminomadic way of life, spending summers with their flocks of sheep high up in the mountains between April and October, and wintering in the lower-lying pastures of Alvan at the western end of Kakheti.

The region is known for its high-quality wool and Tushetian Gouda cheese. Try the *khinkali*, Georgian meat-filled dumplings too, washed down by a *chacha* (Georgian pomace brandy) or three. Head to the village of Dartlo for further immersion in traditional Tusheti. Perched on the Caucasus's alpine slopes at

6,070 feet (1,850 m), the village has well-preserved towers, stone houses offering homestays, a café serving mountain cheese, grounds for camping, and fine views of the nearby waterfall. There are petroglyphs to explore, as well as sacred pagan and Christian religious buildings. A visit to the abandoned village of Kvavlo overlooking Dartlo is a must; Chontio is another deserted village where wandering through traditional buildings, long abandoned, gives its visitors a haunting hint of Tusheti's past.

One of the most unspoiled regions anywhere in the Caucasus, Tusheti is now a popular destination for mountain hikers. If you're heading for the hills, however, don't pack any pork products, as this is taboo among Tushetians.

In the forests of Tusheti, you'll walk through preserved pine and birch groves, and among the mountain habitats of Anatolian leopards, bears, chamois, lynx, mountain goats, and wolves, with falcons, golden eagles, and lammergeiers soaring above. Once out on the trails of Tusheti National Park, you'll feel like the last hiker on Earth, gazing over Caucasus Mountains stretching ever eastward. This is the ultimate outpost of European wilderness, and beyond here all paths lead travelers into Asia.

AT A GLANCE

Caucasus Mountains ▪ The Abano Pass ▪ 322.2 square miles (834.5 sq km) ▪ Abandoned villages ▪ georgia4you.ge/where-to-go-in-georgia/tusheti

NOVAYA
ZEMLYA
(see inset)

**National Parks
in Asiatic Russia**

Alkhanay
Anyuysky
Beringia
Bikin
Chikoy
Land of the Leopard
Pribaikalsky
Pripyshminskiye Bory
Saylyugemsky
Shantar Islands
Shorsky
Shushensky Bor
Sochi
Tunkinsky
Udegeyskaya Legenda
Zabaikalsky
Zov Tigra

NORWAY

BARENTS
SEA

Murmansk

ARCTIC CIRCLE

Pechora

Paanajärvi
N.P.

Onezhskoye Pomorye
National Park

Yugyd Va
National Park

U R A L

FINLAND

Kalevalsky
National Park

WHITE SEA

Vodlozersky
National Park

Northern Dvina

Syktyvkar

M O U N T A I N S

Kenozersky
National Park

Sukhona

Kama

ASIA
EUROPE

Lake
Onega

Lake
Ladoga

Russky Sever
National Park

R U S S I A

St. Petersburg

Rybinsk
Reservoir

Kama

ESTONIA

Nechkinsky
N.P.

Taganay
N.P.

LATVIA

Valdaysky
National Park

Pleshcheyevo
Lake N.P.

Mariy Chodra
N.P.

Nizhnyaya Kama
N.P.

Zyuratkul
N.P.

Volga

Ufa

Sebezhsky
N.P.

Losiny Ostrov
N.P.

Moscow

Meschyora
N.P.

Chavash Varmane
N.P.

Bashkiriya
N.P.

Smolenskoye
Poozerye N.P.

Meschyorsky
N.P.

Smolny N.P.

Ugra
N.P.

Sengiley Mts. N.P.

Samarskaya Luka
National Park

Buzuluksky Bor N.P.

BELARUS

Samara

Orlovskoye Polesye
N.P.

Khvalynsky N.P.

Don

KAZAKHSTAN

ARCTIC OCEAN

FRANZ
JOSEF
LAND

UKRAINE

Volga

Caspian Depression

Russian Arctic

National Park

BALTIC SEA

LITHUANIA

Curonian
Spit N.P.

Curonian
Lagoon

BARENTS
SEA

NOVAYA ZEMLYA

Kaliningrad

RUSSIA

Don

KARA
SEA

POLAND

N

0   50 kilometers
0   50 miles

SEA OF
AZOV

CASPIAN SEA

0   200 kilometers
0   200 miles

EUROPE
ASIA

Prielbrusye
National Park

Nal'chik

N

Sochi

Alaniya N.P.

N

0   200 kilometers
0   200 miles

BLACK SEA

GEORGIA

AZERBAIJAN

RUSSIA

The story of Russia is one of extremes. The extreme wealth of the tsars was followed by the October Revolution and a period of harsh austerity during decades of Soviet rule. Then came collapse and calamity and a new era of rampant capitalism; the teahouses, opera halls, and palaces of Moscow and St. Petersburg filled with a newly gilded generation of oligarchs, a new aristocracy to test the extremities of wealth and consumption.

Russia's extremes are spiritual too, as the country has gone from restrictions on religious beliefs to a newfound celebration of the church, and a period of restoration for many Orthodox churches and cathedrals.

And, of course, Mother Russia is a matriarch of geographic extremities, throwing her arms wide to embrace a cross-continental swath of landscapes and peoples from the Baltic to the Bering Sea. Russia runs from the steppes in the west to the Caucasus Mountains, where her Asian east begins; Russia also tracks from the Black Sea to the Caspian Sea. Flying squirrels are seen from her Nordic borders all the way to the shores of the Pacific, and Russian dialects range from Germanic Kaliningrad to the Asiatic accents of the Kamchatka Peninsula. The country's waters include the salty Curonian Spit, shared with Lithuania, and the great Baikal in southern Siberia, the world's largest freshwater lake. The national parks of Russia span this diversity, and the country recently added a new, northerly frontier to its mighty parks system—Russian Arctic National Park—proof that Mother Russia will go to every extreme to expand her embrace of Mother Nature.

Walruses on Hooker Island in Franz Josef Land; the Russian Arctic National Park is the country's latest frontier in conservation.

ALANIYA

A haven for flora, fauna, and mountaineers seeking heady heights

Situated in a glaciated, mountainous region of the Central Caucasus Mountains, Alaniya National Park follows the Urukh River Basin in Russia's North Ossetia region. Urukh is created by the confluence of the Haresidon and Karaugomdon Rivers, and about 70 rivers course through the park. Much of the terrain here is low-growing alpine tundra and coniferous forests.

Many of the park's protected plants are known for their medicinal properties; look for Satan's mushroom with

Sun and shadow on the Caucasus

its compact cap of up to 12 inches (30.5 cm). Martens, wolves, jackals, wildcats, ermine, boar, and chamois all inhabit the park. The rare bearded

vulture, Caucasian grouse, and West Caucasian tur, an indigenous goat-antelope, are also protected here.

The park attracts mountain climbers to its peaks, the two highest being Gora Uilpata at 15,253 feet (4,649 m) and Gora Laboda at 14,153 feet (4,313.7 m). Gora Skalistaya (Rocky) ridge has caves that were inhabited in the Stone Age, and the villages of Kumbulte and Donifarse host Alan (Caucasian tribe) catacombs. Everywhere you'll see medieval towers built by villagers for protection against invaders.

AT A GLANCE

Central Caucasus Mountains ▪ Rare Caucasian wildlife ▪ 212 square miles (549 sq km) ▪ Stone Age caves ▪ Ancient catacombs ▪ rusnature.info/zap/063.htm

BASHKIRIYA

Green space and underground adventure in an industrial region

This large contiguous forest in the southern Ural Mountains provides vital green space between the industrialized flatlands to the west, and the mountainous nature reserves to the east and north. Much of the Bashkiriya National Park is forested, and the old-growth woods at the center are practically impenetrable. The park also boasts striking limestone formations: outcrops, caves, grottoes, and underground rivers. The rocky banks of the

Nugush and Belaya Rivers here reach 492 feet (150 m) in height. The Kuperlya Natural Bridge, a karst formation, spans 66 feet (20

Limestone ridges loom tall.

m) above the ground and 33 feet (10 m) across. Bear, elk (moose), wolf, lynx, beaver, white-tailed eagle, and the vulnerable Siberian salmon all inhabit Bashkiriya, where caving, trail hiking, river rafting, and horseback riding are popular human pursuits. Among the park's 30 caves is Sumgan Cave, the largest in the Urals. The Nugush reservoir is another destination for locals from the industrial town of Meleuz, 20 miles (32 km) to the west.

AT A GLANCE

Ural Mountain karst landscapes ▪ 355 square miles (920 sq km) ▪ Karst caves ▪ Kuperlya Natural Bridge ▪ Nugush reservoir ▪ en.russia.edu.ru/russia/cities/ufa/1166

BUZULUKSKY BOR

A well-protected park with a history of ecological disaster

The Buzuluk Pine Forest, the world's largest grove of isolated high pine trees, is protected by Buzuluksky Bor National Park, an area surrounded by steppes on the East European Plain east of the Volga River and bounded on the south by the Samara River. The Borovka River flows through the forest, cutting a valley of about 330 feet (100 m) into the terrain. Animals making their home here range from squirrels, wolves, foxes, pine martens, mink, and ermines, as well as owls and hawks,

The park's majestic pines

up to large ungulates such as elk (moose), and wild boar. Badgers are particularly welcome, as they eat large numbers of larvae that are pests to the pine trees. Buzuluksky Bor has faced challenges: drought that hastens pine infestations, a 2010 windstorm that felled many pines, and a 2013 forest fire. These setbacks, combined with the park's history of oil leaks—it was drilled up until the 1970s—has led to access restrictions. Hunting and fishing are prohibited, but good hiking trails and a museum welcome visitors.

> **AT A GLANCE**
>
> Steppe and forest landscapes ▪ High pine groves ▪ 409 square miles (1,060 sq km) ▪ Borovka River Valley ▪ buzulukskiybor.ru

---

CHAVASH VARMANE

Reaping rich forestry and wildlife rewards

Chavash Varmane National Park is a large contiguous woodland along the middle course of the Volga River. The park protects both the region's rich biodiversity and the cultural heritage of the Chuvash people, a Turkic ethnic group. The park preserves three types of forest: southern taiga (consisting of conifers), Volga Upland oak forest, and mixed broad-leaved and coniferous forest. Most of the landscape here is woodland—mainly pine, with some birch and aspen—and some marshes, grasslands, and pastures mixed in.

The forests line a labyrinth of valleys cut by the Abamza River from the north and the Bezdna River from the west; these meet in the center of the park and flow south, absorbing numerous tributaries and meandering through flat floodplains. The valleys and forests provide habitat for a wide range of animal life, from hares, squirrels, polecats, and mink to pond frogs, beavers, and badgers. Hunting was prohibited when the park opened in 1993, and brown bears and wolves have since thrived within its boundaries. Rare pallid harriers and greater spotted eagles ply the skies.

Nine species of fish swim the park's rivers and lakes: chub, dace, striped bystranka, common roach, gudgeon, tench, ide, loach, and trout. In recent years, crayfish have returned to the rivers, a sign of improving water purity

> **AT A GLANCE**
>
> Chuvash forest and valley landscapes ▪ 100 square miles (258.9 sq km) ▪ Chuvash culture ▪ Pallid harriers and greater spotted eagles ▪ rusnature.info/zap/046.htm

CURONIAN SPIT

A UNESCO World Heritage site sandbar shared by two countries

The sands of the Curonian Spit shift between Russia and Lithuania.

The Curonian Spit is a massive sandbar that stretches across 60.8 miles (98 km), separating the saltwater Baltic Sea to the west from the freshwater Curonian Lagoon to the east. The spit is protected by national parks in both Russia and Lithuania (see page 366). Russia's Curonian Spit National Park encompasses its southern 25.4 miles (41 km), following the dunes from the Sambian Peninsula in the south to the border with Lithuania, about 25 miles (40 km) north.

The foundations of the spit are unusual; the dunes here formed atop the glacial moraine as the receding glaciers left the Baltic Sea behind about 17,000 years ago. Today, the sand dunes reach an average of 115 feet (35 m) along the spit. The landscapes are diverse, as beaches, dune ridges, various wetlands, meadows, and forests all line these Baltic shores.

The Curonian Spit, situated along Europe's major migratory routes, provides vital habitat for many species. The park's vast wetlands host huge numbers of birds and waterfowl, with an estimated 10 to 20 million birds passing through in spring and fall. The sight of populous flocks of herons and cormorants descending into the park's wetlands draws large number of bird-watchers. A total of 262 species of birds have been recorded here.

The park is also home to 46 species of mammals, including elk (moose), wild boar, fox, marten, raccoon dog, badger, red squirrel, and beaver. The plant life is equally impressive: Some 889 species, hybrids, varieties, and forms of wild vascular plants thrive on this long strip of sand, salt marshes, and forests. As these are among the quickly shifting sands in Europe, the continuing efforts of both national parks to stabilize the sands and reforest the landscapes are vital preservation projects.

AT A GLANCE

Curonian Spit sandbars, marshlands, and forests ▪ 26 square miles (66 sq km) ▪ Wildlife- and bird-watching ▪ whc.unesco.org/en/list/994

KALEVALSKY

Vast forests and small lakes where Russia meets Finland

The Republic of Karelia straddles the border between Russia and Finland. *The Kalevala*, a 19th-century epic poem of Finnish and Karelian oral folklore, sprang from this region and led to an upsurge in interest in Finnish language and stories and, ultimately, to Finland's independence from Russia in 1917. Today, the Russian Karelia is protected by Kalevalsky National Park, which includes one of the last old-growth boreal pine forests in Europe. The park is situated midway along the border with Finland, homeland of both the ethnic Sami and the Karelian peoples, the latter a Baltic-Finnic ethnic group.

The national park lies on the Baltic Shield, which contains the oldest rocks in Europe, including three-billion-year-old Precambrian crystalline granites and gneisses. These are covered by a layer of glacial deposits 65 to 100 feet (20 to 30 m) thick, in a landscape shaped by the last continental ice sheets that scoured the region. The western portion of the park is mostly flat and inundated forest, while the east is hillier. Most of the park is covered in forest, primarily pine, with some spruce, and small stands of birch and aspen planted by farmers. The park also encompasses some marshlands and peat bogs reaching depths of 20 feet (6 m). Here too are many streams, and more than 400 small lakes. Bears, golden eagles, and fish hawks frequent the lakes, while flocks of geese descend on the bogs in spring.

> **AT A GLANCE**
>
> Flooded old-growth pine and spruce forests ▪ 287 square miles (744 sq km) ▪ Republic of Karelia ▪ Europe's oldest rocks ▪ ticrk.ru/en/tourist-sights/nature-objects

KENOZERSKY

A UNESCO biosphere reserve in a deserted northern hinterland

The remote north Russian region of Kenozero was reinvigorated by the opening of Kenozersky in 1991 on the border with the Republic of Karelia. Prior to this, the area suffered a period of chronic depopulation under the Soviet Union, which saw all the villages between Lake Lyokshmozero and Lake Kenozero slowly become ghost towns from the 1950s to the 1980s.

Lake Kenozero is the focal point of the northern part of

Church of St. Nicholas in Vershinino

the park, and you'll find a visitors center in the village of Vershinino, on the lake's northern shore. The rivers Kena and Pocha irrigate the area, along with the Undosha River, which feeds into Lake Pochozero.

The park offers several different hiking trails, one leading to Porzhensky Pogost, the site of St. George's church and its bell tower, surrounded by a wooden wall with gates and towers, all dating from the 18th century. The roads here are rudimentary, but that's all part of the charm of this remote national park.

> **AT A GLANCE**
>
> Lake Kenozero landscapes ▪ 539.2 square miles (1,396.6 sq km) ▪ Porzhensky Pogost hiking trail ▪ Lake Kenozero and the village of Vershinino ▪ kenozero.ru/en

KHVALYNSKY

A raised chalk plateau hosts habitats for rare wildlife and plant life.

The saker falcon is a persistent and relentless hunter

Khvalynsky National Park embraces the Volga Uplands along the west bank of the Volga River. This Khvalanskyaya ridge, known as the Right Bank, is covered in mixed oak, linden, and pine forests. Here the bedrock consists mainly of chalk and marl, so the landscapes reflect extensive erosion out from the center of the ridge, with undulating and hilly terrain and a labyrinth of interconnected ravines and gullies.

This is a park made up of peaks and favored by great birds of prey. The park's highest mountain is Belenkaya, which is almost entirely chalk and rises to 1,211 feet (369 m) in altitude; five other mountains stand at more than 820 feet (250 m). The mountains are mostly covered with upland forest trees, but higher up are outcrops of exposed bedrock, with underground water frequently surfacing in springs.

The park's varied habitats and microclimates support many small mammals, including beavers, foxes, and wolves. Reptiles are common—watch out for the European adder when you're walking. Predatory birds include white-tailed eagles, ospreys, and endangered saker falcons (see sidebar).

Khvalynsky has fine environmental trails, such as the Puteshestvie po Dnu Drevnego Morya (Journey Along the Ancient Sea Bed), which highlights the area's geology. Another trail leads to the Peshchera Monakha (Monk's Cave). You can also visit a museum of peasant life, Derevenskoe Podvorye (Village Farmstead), a chapel, a zoo, and sacred springs. In addition, the park offers a Khvalinskoe safari. Khvalynsky is a sister park to Fossil Butte National Monument, in Wyoming, United States.

The Saker Falcon

The chalk hills of the Volga provide vital habitat for one of nature's most powerful predators, the saker falcon. Khvalynsky protects this bird. Since the collapse of the Soviet Union, the United Arab Emirates has been the main destination for falcons caught and sold illegally on the black market. These beautiful birds breed from central Europe eastward across Asia to Manchuria. Sakers are migratory birds that head north in spring after wintering in many lands, from Ethiopia to the Arabian Peninsula, and from northern Pakistan to western China. These skilled hunters are revered in Arab cultures; the word *saker* means "falcon" in Arabic. Sakers are large hierofalcons, standing at 18 to 22 inches (45 to 57 cm), with a huge wingspan of 38 to 50 inches (97 to 126 cm). Listen in Khvalynsky for their distinctive call—a sharp *kiy-ee* or a repeated *kyak-kyak-kyak*.

AT A GLANCE

Chalk ridge landscapes ▪ Khvalinskoe safaris ▪ 99 square miles (255 sq km) ▪ Journey Along the Ancient Sea Bed Trail ▪ rusnature.info/zap/053.htm

LOSINY OSTROV

Russia's first national park continues to delight visitors in Moscow.

Muscovites tired of the city and the ways of humankind go to Losiny Ostrov (Elk Island) National Park to restore their weary spirits. Here, people may well spot elk (or moose, if you're North American) as they wander the trails through the large forest, the third largest for cities of comparable size (after Table Mountain National Park in Cape Town, South Africa, and Pedra Branca State Park in Río de Janeiro, Brazil). Visitors may also see many other animals in this suburban wilderness: The park

Elk Island in the Moscow suburbs

hosts some 44 species of mammals, plus 170 bird types, nine amphibian species, five species of reptiles, and 19 types of fish. The park protects

habitats including forests, waters, and a small area of swamplands, much of it within Moscow city limits. The landscapes here are mainly the gently undulating forestlands covering the Meschera Lowlands and Klin-Dmitrov chine, which is the watershed of the Moskva River and Klyazma River. Losiny Ostrov National Park was opened in 1983, on land that has long served as hunting grounds of Russian grand princes and tsars. These lands have been preserved since 1799.

AT A GLANCE

Moscow parklands ▪ Meschera Lowlands and Klin-Dmitrov chine ▪ 45 square miles (116 sq km) ▪ Elk (moose) ▪ Ancient royal hunting grounds ▪ elkisland.ru, rusnature.info/zap/037.htm

MARIY CHODRA

Fine forest trails leading into rich habitats of wildlife and birdlife

Mariy Chodra National Park is located in the Mari El Republic, on the northern bank of the Volga River. The park protects more than 115 rare plant species in its meadows and subtaiga forests. Here, you'll walk in oak forests with a mix of maple, linden, pine, elm, and spruce; you'll also find floodplains with oak forests and some small herb fens. As you traverse the woods watch for chipmunks, hares, weasels, ermines, European pole-

cats, and marten; along the rivers you might also spot beavers and otters. The park's birdlife embraces black grouse, capercaillie, and hazel grouse, as well as raptors such as buzzards, goshawks, black kites, and golden eagles. In spring, the floodplain lakes teem with mallard and European teal.

Mariy Chodra has 14 ecological trails. The Yalchik, Glukhoye, and Kichiyer Lakes attract many anglers and swimmers, and raft-

ing on the Ilet and Yushut Rivers is also popular. Maple Mountain is a favored destination for hikers in the park. Travelers should also try to see Pugachev's Oak. Amazingly, this is estimated to date to about A.D. 1500, and measures 47 inches (1.2 m) in diameter, and a towering 85 feet (26 m) in height. Local legend has it that after the Battle of Kazan, Pugachev watched the burning of the town from this oak, under which his troops were sheltering.

AT A GLANCE

Subtaiga forest and lakes landscapes ▪ Rich birdlife ▪ 141 square miles (366 sq km) ▪ Pugachev's Oak ▪ rusnature.info/zap/038.htm

MESCHYORA

A wetland park with teeming lakes, fertile forests, and lush marshes

The medieval Meshchera tribe once inhabited the Meschera Lowlands on the East European Plain.

Meschyora National Park now protects these extensive wetlands east of Moscow, consisting of swamps, peat bogs, rivers, lakes, and meadows. The park is located within the Oka River watershed, and parts of the area are farmed by local communities. Most of the park's territory is wetland, some of which is peatland.

This land is particularly vulnerable to wildfires. Pine trees are found

Pines populate higher, drier grounds.

on drier, sandy hills and ridges. A few small areas of broad-leaved forest (mostly oak) are found in the southeast corner. The remainder of the

forested areas are birch, maple, and alder. The main rivers—the Buzha and the Pol—flow into the Oka in slow, meandering floodplains. The flora reflects this habitat and the park hosts 872 vascular plants, with 61 mosses, 166 lichens, and 24 species of mushrooms. Meschyora's 60 lakes teem with northern pike, perch, common roach, and carp, and beavers are seen busily building dams. In addition, some 208 species of (mainly aquatic) birds inhabit this marshy park.

AT A GLANCE

Meschera Lowlands on the East European Plain ▪ 459 square miles (1,189 sq km) ▪ Extensive wetlands and forests ▪ Peat bogs ▪ en.park-meshera.ru

MESCHYORSKY

Protecting ancient wetlands south of Meschyora

Extending the protected wetlands area of Meschyora to the north, Meschyorsky National Park covers a section of the Pra River, Lake Beloye (White Lake), and surrounding wetlands and forests. Even more of this park is used for agriculture. The landscapes are similar to those of Meschyora, and the forested areas here are dominated by pine where soils are sandy. Elsewhere, the trees are mostly birch, aspen, alder, with some spruce stands. As marshland

is reclaimed for agriculture, manmade meadows are developing with high sedge and secondary forest. The park hosts some 866 species of vascular plants.

At the southern edge of the taiga, large mammals such as elk (moose), wild boar, and brown bear roam the forests. Beavers are multiplying, as are muskrats, in the lakes and canals. Spring brings the migratory masses of birds, especially geese, ducks, and waders in the marshes.

A European green lizard (Lacerta viridis)

AT A GLANCE

Meschera Lowlands on the East European Plain ▪ 26 square miles (66 sq km) ▪ Extensive wetlands and forests ▪ Peat bogs ▪ sovka.narod.ru/7.html

NECHKINSKY

An amazing range of wildlife and forestry in the western Urals

On the western side of the Ural Mountains, that great divide between European and Asiatic Russia, Nechkinsky National Park preserves the valuable biosphere of Udmurtia (the Udmurt Republic). The park's epicenter is in the middle valley of the Kama River, its tributary Siva River, and the Votkinskoye reservoir, near the city of Izhevsk. The terrain here is mostly forest and river floodplains, with the tree-filled valley of the Siva River watershed being prime among the wood-

lands protected. These are typical of the region's Sarmatic mixed forest ecoregion, a strip of low forests, lakes, and wetlands, running from the Baltic Sea east to the Urals.

These forests are a mixture of taiga, mixed woodlands, and steppe forests, with valuable bogs on the lower levels. Siberian spruce dominates, along with oak, birch, and aspen. On both banks of the Siva River are pine forests, with some stands of silver fir and Siberian larch. The park's range of liv-

ing creatures is impressive: Some 50 species of mammals, 191 bird types, five reptile species, 8 types of amphibians, and 37 varieties of fish. The park also hosts 33 species of mollusks, 120 insect types, and 600-odd sorts of spiders. Butterflies and dragonflies thrive here too. The vulnerable Russian desman, a semiaquatic mole, is protected due to historical trapping for its fur. The Dear Ancestors trail is a 15.5-mile (25-km) hike through the human story of the area.

AT A GLANCE

Udmurtia region biosphere ▪ Western Ural Mountains ▪ 80 square miles (208 sq km) ▪ Russian desman ▪ Dear Ancestors hiking trail ▪ rusnature.info/zap/076.htm

NIZHNYAYA KAMA

A wildlife wilderness of rich biodiversity in central Russia

In Tatarstan, in the center of Russia, Nizhnyaya Kama National Park protects the coniferous forests along the banks of the Kama River, which mostly consist of pine trees. This green space consists of three isolated clusters of woodlands: On the right bank of the Kama, Malyy Bor and Tanayavskaya Dacha are located close to the city of Yelabuga, while Bolshoy Bor grows on the peninsula on the left bank of the Kama, outside

The biodiverse banks of the Kama River

the city of Naberezhnye Chelny. The areas around Nizhnekamsk Reservoir are also rich in forests.

The most common trees are pine, birch, and aspen.

Tatarstan is an expansive land and a generous host to large mammals, making a hike through this vast wilderness an adventure into the habitat of elk (moose), roe deer, boar, lynx, badgers, Eurasian beavers, and raccoon dogs. The caves of the park also shelter several species of bats, some of them rare. And don't forget to look up—more than 190 species of birds ply the skies here.

AT A GLANCE

Tatarstan landscapes ▪ Extensive pine forests ▪ 102.6 square miles (265.8 sq km) ▪ Raccoon dogs ▪ rusnature.info/zap/054.htm

ONEZHSKOYE POMORYE

A remote and access-limited park of coastline and pristine forests

Located in Russia's remote northern reaches, Onezhskoye Pomorye National Park is largely inaccessible to the public but well worth a visit if you have the time and the resources to plan a foray into one of Europe's most intriguing environmental outposts. The park also covers an area of the White Sea, but there are no means of transportation from the mainland. Potential visitors must apply to the regional authorities for a permit well in advance (bureaucracy remains a

A dogsled ride is a winter thrill.

Russian speciality that has survived from Soviet times), and the maximum duration for any stay is 10 days.

As expected, most of the area is covered by lush forest, a habitat welcoming for the park's wild inhabitants including elk (moose), brown bears, wolves, and red foxes. There is also a good chance of spotting the beluga whale as they migrate here in the White Sea in spring. In winter, however, the ocean freezes over and ocean life is less easy to see. In May, bears emerge from their long winter hibernation to roam the tide line like ursine beachcombers digging and foraging in seaweed.

AT A GLANCE

Onega Peninsula ▪ Pristine taiga forest and coastlines ▪ 778.6 square miles (2,016.6 sq km) ▪ Beluga whales ▪ onpomor.ru

ORLOVSKOYE POLESYE

A Central Russian Upland park protecting a rare herd of European bison

Orlovskoye Polesye National Park protects parts of the Central Russian Upland. This is a highland area of the East European Plain that mainly takes the form of an undulating plateau, with an average elevation of approximately 790 feet (240 m). This upland stretches across regions in Ukraine as well as the European portion of the Russian Federation. The lands within this national park are a remote area of taiga landscape, with extensive stretches of thick forests, lakes, and elevated grasslands that come ablaze with wildflowers in the spring.

The park is a popular destination for fishing, camping, and hiking on its many trails. Orlovskoye Polesye is perhaps best known as the home range of more than 500 European bison, which have been protected by a special breeding program in these parklands since 1996. In winter, the park runs excellent bison tours for groups of visitors, offering a rare chance to observe these huge creatures as they feed and frolic.

Other animals that may be seen within the park include elk (moose), roe deer, wild boar, otters, alpine hares, European hares, and beavers. The park also hosts a total of 130 nesting bird species, including wood grouse and hazel grouse; many types of owls such as Tengmalm's, little owls, grey owls, long-eared owls; and predatory birds, including the serpent eagle.

AT A GLANCE

Central Russian Upland ▪ Taiga landscapes ▪ 300 square miles (777.4 sq km) ▪ European bison ▪ orlpolesie.ru

PAANAJÄRVI

Pristine forests and lakes with a Finnish cross-border counterpart

Paanajärvi National Park is located in the Loukhsky District of northwestern Republic of Karelia, in northwestern Russia, along the Finnish-Russian border. The park protects vast swaths of pristine taiga forest habitats, lakes, and rivers. The Oulanka National Park in Finland (see page 233) runs adjacent along the border to the west, offering contiguous protection of this Karelian taiga habitat. Paanajärvi also preserves the highland ridges of the Maanselkja rock

Lake Paanajärvi at dawn, lined with alluring woodlands

formation. The park's name derives from Lake Paanajärvi, one of Karelia's deepest lakes. The lake and the watershed of the Olanga River are the park's main features, along with virgin spruce and birch forests.

PLESHCHEYEVO LAKE

Protecting historic hunting grounds around a long-popular lake

Located on the central part of the East European Plain, about 80.7 miles (130 km) northeast of Moscow, Pleshcheyevo Lake National Park protects its namesake's watery ecological habitat and the forested areas. The lake, currently a popular vacation destination for Russians, was a country retreat for tsars in centuries past. The resort town of Pereslavl-Zalessky, located on the southeast shore, is a focal point of the park.

Pleshcheyevo, once a royal retreat

The lake measures about 5.6 miles (9 km) in diameter, and has a 17.3-mile (28-km) shoreline. The surrounding region consists of moraine-type landscape with long ridges, extensive wetlands, and meandering rivers, dotted with sporadic isolated hills. The higher ground above the lake features terraced river valleys, while the middle region is mainly wetlands, including peat bogs and the Berendeyevskoye swamp. Anglers will find 19 species of fish in the lake here, among them the white endemic fish, Ryapushka. Scots pine, spruce, and aspen forest areas frame the lake.

PRIELBRUSYE

Europe's highest mountain, with a wealth of biodiversity

A triumphant mountaineer greets the Russian landscape from atop Mount Elbrus.

The great Mount Elbrus reaches toward the Russian sky at 18,477.6 feet (5,632 m). This is Europe's highest mountain, and the focal point of Prielbrusye National Park. The landscapes of the park are varied, including mountain peaks, side ridges, glaciers, lava flows, lake basins, and low forested river valleys. The headwaters of the Malka River form the glaciers of Elbrus.

The Caucasus eco-region is one of the most biologically diverse eco-regions in the world, due to the confluence of ecological zones and variations in altitude. At the lowest river valleys are dense coniferous forests of mostly pine, with some juniper, barberry, and wild rose mixed in.

The forests are stalked by steppe wolves, European jackals, Caucasian lynx, and Syrian brown bears. Birds here include Caucasian snowcocks, saker falcons, golden eagles, peregrine falcons, and bearded vultures. Watch out too for the endemic Caucasian viper.

Prielbrusye attracts skiers, hikers, and climbers, and the park offers ecotours. Attractions include the Mir station WWII museum, located at 11,483 feet (3,500 m) and accessible by cable car. At the station, you get a 360-degree panorama of Elbrus and Devichy Kosy (Maiden's Braids) waterfall. A drive through the Adyl-Su Valley leads to Narzan springs, where a sulfuric odor rises from these carbonated mineral waters, rich in healing salts.

AT A GLANCE

Mount Elbrus ▪ Caucasus glacier landscapes ▪ 3,900 square miles (10,101 sq km) ▪ Narzan springs ▪ Mir station WWII museum ▪ wild-russia.org/bioregion5/5-PrielbruskyNP/5_priel.htm

RUSSIAN ARCTIC

A new frontier in the icy Arctic waters of the Kara Sea

Originally established in 2009, the Russian Arctic National Park was expanded in 2016 to encompass a remote area of the Arctic Ocean, the northern part of Novaya Zemlya (Severny Island), and all 192 islands of the Franz Josef Land archipelago. The park is located on the Kara Sea.

This magnificent icy wilderness is the habitat of the vulnerable polar bear as well as the beluga whale and gray whale. It also protects one of the largest bird colonies in the Northern Hemisphere, in addition to walrus and seal rookeries.

The range of wildlife in this national park is astonishing: The park hosts a number of endemic species, such as bowhead whales of the Svalbard (Spitsbergen) population. This species, having recently faced extinction, is now making a comeback around the waters of Franz Josef Land. An expedition to the park might also result in a sighting of the "unicorn of the sea," the narwhal, with its strange horned head. Bird-watchers will thrill at the masses of ivory gulls, guillemots, and kittiwakes that nest on the shorelines. The park also offers Arctic travelers a rare chance to see not only polar bears and whales, but also walruses, ringed seals, harp seals, arctic foxes, and even reindeer in their natural habitats.

On planning the park, the Russian government's wish was that the Novaya Zemlya and Franz Josef Land archipelagos would be transformed from a "giant rubbish tip" into a destination for ecotourists. In 2012, Russia initiated a three-year cleanup project to remove more than 110,230 tons (100,000 metric tons) of waste that had accumulated during the Soviet era. As a result, the parklands are being restored to pristine landscapes of glaciers and icy rocky shores where vast

The park also celebrates the rich history of Arctic exploration. Icebreaker ship tours lead you through the discovery and development of the western sector of the Arctic from the 16th century to the present day. Visitors can see traces of the Dutch expedition led by navigator and cartographer Willem Barents (the remains of a winter cabin and a wooden boat) on Novaya Zemlya in Ice Harbor.

A polar bear surveys his shrinking kingdom in Franz Josef Land.

bird colonies can nest. Otherworldly Arctic features are also on view, such as hardened lava flows, petrified trees, and the mysterious sandstone balls on Champ Island; geologists can observe the famous Rubini Rock and the Tegetkhof Cape basaltic dikes at close quarters.

The tours also incorporate the remnants of the Arctic's golden age of discovery in the latter half of the 19th and early 20th centuries. The Franz Josef Land archipelago, base camp for many polar expeditions, was discovered during an expedition to the North Pole in 1873.

AT A GLANCE

Arctic wilderness landscapes ▪ Franz Josef Land archipelago ▪ 5,506 square miles (14,260.4 sq km) ▪ Arctic wildlife ▪ Rubini Rock ▪ Legacy of Arctic exploration ▪ rgo.ru/en/article/russian-arctic-national-park

RUSSKY SEVER

Protecting spiritual and architectural heritage of the Russian Orthodox church

Russky Sever (Russian North) National Park protects the Kirillo-Belozersky Monastery and the Ferapontov Monastery, two hermitages of great historical significance. The monasteries are also priceless architectural monuments: The Kirillo-Belozersky Monastery is now a museum-preserve, while the Ferapontov Monastery is home to the Museum of Dionysius's Frescoes. The park also embraces the Goritsky Monastery and the Nilo-Sorsky Monastery. In 1397, St. Cyril on the White

Frescoes of Ferapontov Monastery

Lake founded the Kirillo-Belozersky Monastery on the shores of Lake Siverskoye. In 1398, St. Therapont of White Lake moved to this location, land that became the Ferapontov Monastery, now a UNESCO World Heritage site. The national park also includes stretches of the Northern Dvina Canal and the Volga-Baltic Waterway. Woods occupy most of Russky Sever, including pristine spruce and pine forests, and visitors can walk ecological trails, shorelines, and hiking routes in the park.

AT A GLANCE

Kirillo-Belozersky Monastery ▪ Ferapontov Monastery ▪ 642 square miles (1,664 sq km) ▪ UNESCO World Heritage site ▪ parkrusever.ru, russia-ic.com/travel/travelling/5158#.XMmdgC-ZP64

SAMARSKAYA LUKA

A UNESCO World Heritage site celebrating cherished waterways

Samarskaya Luka (Samara Bend) National Park protects most of the peninsula formed by the 180-degree bend in the Volga River as it circumvents the Zhiguli Mountains near Samara and Zhigulyovsk. This land has been inhabited since ancient times, and continues to host a rich biodiversity of plant life and wildlife. The Samara Bend is the meeting point of the Volga Upland and the Lower Volga Lowlands, a tectonic trough of clay and sand remain-

The Volga near the city of Samara

ing from the ancient Caspian Sea.

This detour of the Volga around the Zhiguli Mountains runs for almost 125 miles (200 km). The

Zhiguli massif, and most of the bedrock in the park, is a karst (limestone) formation, averaging about 985 feet (300 m) in height. The park extends into the mountainous Zhiguli to the north, and into the floodplains to the south; the remainder consists of forest and forest steppe. The forests are deciduous, with linden, oak, and birch dominating. Watch for the Ural owl, especially on the Witch Lake Trail, a fun 1.2-mile (2-km) hike for children.

AT A GLANCE

Samara Bend in Volga River ▪ 517 square miles (1,339 sq km) ▪ Zhiguli Mountains karst landscapes ▪ Witch Lake Trail ▪ npsamluka.ru/en

SEBEZHSKY

A forested park within the lake district of Russia's northwest

Sebezhsky National Park protects the hilly glacial landscapes of the lake district in the southwest of the Sebezhsky District. This is a wooded area with pine, spruce, and alder forests near Russia's borders with Latvia and Belarus. The town of Sebezh is the gateway to Sebezhsky. Most of the park is located in the river basin of the Velikaya, with some areas in the Daugava Basin. The largest lakes are Lake Necheritsa, Lake Sebezhskoye, and Lake Orono.

This land has been long disputed: Since the 15th century, the region has been controlled by the Grand Duchy of Moscow and subsequently the Grand Duchy of Lithuania, finally becoming part of Russia in 1772. In the 19th century, logging reduced the forests, and commercial fishing on the lakes was common. In the 1950s, swamps were drained and converted into agricultural lands, and by the 1990s, the land was depleted by overfarming. The national park now protects the area's historical and natural landscapes.

The park hosts 291 species of vertebrates, including two species of lamprey, 30 species of fish, eight types of amphibians, five species of reptiles, and 202 bird types. The park's mammals include brown bears, lynx, wolves, wild boar, elk (moose), and roe deer.

Hunting and fishing are permitted here, and a number of huts are maintained for hikers. A permit from the Federal Security Service department is needed to visit the Latvian border security zone.

AT A GLANCE

Glacial woodlands ▪ Velikaya and Daugava River Basins ▪ 193.1 square miles (500.2 sq km) ▪ Lampreys ▪ Lake angling ▪ russia-ic.com/travel/places/3035#.XMmnLS-ZPm0, rusnature.info/zap/020.htm

SENGILEY MOUNTAINS

A park of diverse ecosystems

The small yet vital Sengiley Mountains National Park serves the purpose of protecting valuable forests of birch, pine, and oak in Russia's Ulyanovsk region. It is one of the country's youngest parks, having been established in 2016 to protect vital habitat and ecosystems along the Middle Volga Basin. Aside from its value as a recreational resource offering visitors excellent hiking, fishing, and ecotours, the park also conducts scientific research and

Fall colors in the Sengiley hills

monitoring with a view to long-term ecological education. Russia is increasing its efforts at preservation in recent years: The year 2017 was proclaimed the Year of Protected Areas. In 2016, four other newly protected areas were initiated along with the Sengiley Mountains park: the Ladoga Skerries Nature Park in Karelia, the Solovetsky Archipelago Reserve, Vasyugansky Nature Reserve, and a federal reserve on the New Siberian Islands.

AT A GLANCE

Sengiley Mountains woodlands ▪ 1.9 square miles (5 sq km) ▪ Middle Volga River Basin ▪ Ecological education ▪ revolvy.com/page/Sengiley-Mountains

SMOLENSKOYE POOZERYE

A flat landscape of glacial lakes and wetlands across the Daugava River Basin

In the northwest of Smolenskaya Oblast, near the Belarus border, Smolenskoye Poozerye National Park protects a forest-wetland ecosystem of 35 lakes within the basin of the Daugava River about 40 miles (64 km) north of the city of Smolensk. This is a flatland region encompassing a wide labyrinth of low-lying rivers and lakes and featuring gravel moraines, ridges, and flat floodplains. Two main rivers course through the park, the Yelsha and the Polovya, and its largest lake, the glacial Lake Sapsho, hosts the popular resort town of Przhevalskoye on its banks.

About 75 percent of the national park's terrain is cloaked in forests, with many bogs providing rich animal and plant habitats in these wetland wildernesses. Additional vital habitats include pine, spruce, and broad-leaved forests, and sedge meadows along riverbanks and lakeshores, as well as dry meadows on areas of elevation. Other tree species you'll encounter here are birch, aspen, and black alder. The park hosts 54 mammal species, 232 bird types, and 37 species of fish.

The park protects 17 Neolithic sites, and about 25 Bronze Age memorials. The ancient settlement of Verzhavska is worth visiting. The park offers hikes, including one for children on the Fairy Tales of a Russian Forest Trail, as well as guided bird-watching, ecological, and historical tours.

AT A GLANCE

Wetlands of Smolensk ▪ Daugava River Basin ▪ 565 square miles (1,462 sq km) ▪ Fairy Tales of a Russian Forest Trail ▪ poozerie.ru, becamper.com

SMOLNY

A flat wetland park stretching out on Russia's East European Plain

Smolny National Park protects the deciduous forest and wetlands of the Russian Republic of Mordovia. The predominant landscape here is a lowland river environment with lakes and swamps concentrated largely around the floodplain of the Alatyr River. This is also prime avian habitat, and forests dominate most of the territory. In the park's southern and central areas, the coniferous forests are mainly pine and spruce; also present are bogs and wetlands fed by many springs. To the south, the forests are mostly pine on the terraces above the floodplain, while broad-leaved oak, linden, maple, and ash dominate in the north. Throughout, meadow areas nurture Kentucky bluegrass, fescue, and foxtail. The park also provides rich habitat for mushrooms, mosses, and about 750 species of vascular plants.

The rivers of the park teem with common pike, dace, chub, gudgeon, loach, eel, perch, and silver carp; however, angling is forbidden in these protected waters. Hunting is also banned. The forest steppe landscapes are stalked by elk (moose), wild boar, fox, marten, weasels, and voles. A total of 206 bird species inhabit Smolny National Park, with nesting bird species including the curlew, oystercatcher, owl, imperial eagle, and pallid harrier.

In the village of Smolny, the gateway to the park, you'll find a museum of Mordovian natural history.

Red fox (Vulpes vulpes) *pups venture out into the park.*

AT A GLANCE

Mordovian wetlands ▪ Swamps and bogs ▪ 141 square miles (365 sq km) ▪ Bird-watching ▪ Mordovian natural history museum ▪ eng.russia.travel/objects/285655

TAGANAY

Ural Mountains forested ridges with a spectacularly sited city hub

The Taganay range is a group of mountain ridges in the Southern Urals with the highest peak, Kruglitsa Mountain, reaching 3,865 feet (1,178 m) above sea level. Taganay National Park was established here in 1991 to protect the ecosystems of this mountainous region. At the park's center, the city of Zlatoust enjoys the dramatic backdrop of a lake-filled valley. The city serves as a gateway to the park, which is now a popular wilderness destination for hiking, mountain biking, and rafting in the Ural Mountains.

Taganay National Park also con-

tains Russia's great continental divide: The geographical border between Europe and Asia lies within its boundaries. The park protects both the Southern Urals and the plateaus and flat forest steppes of this mountainous area. Most of the forests here are pine, and the park's fast-running rivers lead to many dramatic waterfalls.

A network of great hiking trails runs through the Taganay's mountains and valleys. These are lined with shelter huts, where hikers can leave backpacks to make their final assault on the peaks unburdened.

Kruglitsa is the most popular challenge for climbers, and the Taganay shelter is nearby. The ascent to this twin-headed peak begins from the base of Belyy Klyuch. The park's most frequented trail follows the eastern slope of the Great Taganay Range.

Loggers from the last century left a series of forestry roads through the park, but these are open only in winter or in the dry season. The landscapes of the park also overlap parts of Zlatoust's highly industrialized mining district, and reforestation of the mountainsides are among the aims of the park administrators.

Frost grips the South Ural Mountains on a winter evening.

AT A GLANCE

Taganay Mountains range ▪ Russia's continental divide ▪ 219.3 square miles (568 sq km) ▪ Extensive hiking trails ▪ Climbing Kruglitsa ▪ eng.russia.travel/objects/305633

UGRA

Conserving a range of wildlife habitats plus historical and cultural sites

The Ugra River Valley in central Russia was designated a UNESCO biosphere reserve in 2002. This is the location of Ugra National Park, which protects several key habitats, including rivers attractive to many avid kayakers.

The northern part of the park comprises the valley of the Ugra from the border with Smolenskaya Oblast downstream to the village of Kurovskoye. Its southern area embraces the valley of the Zhizdra River down to its mouth, and the small Vorotynsk sec-

Ugra resonates with unique history.

tion surrounds an old Soviet village. Park mammals include elk (moose), wild boar, roe deer, Eurasian beaver, and muskrats. The endangered Rus-

sian desman, a small, semiaquatic mammal, also makes its home along the lakes within the park. Look for its distinctive flexible snout and long, flattened tail that it uses as a paddle.

The park also has several historical and cultural attractions, including Optina monastery and the Ugra River site of a 1480 battle between the armies of the Grand Duchy of Moscow and the Golden Horde. The visitors center in Kaluga has information on the history and attractions of the area.

AT A GLANCE

Ugra River Valley landscapes ▪ Several key biospheres ▪ 380,791 square miles (986,245 sq km) ▪ Optina monastery ▪ rusnature.info/zap/045.htm

---

VALDAYSKY

Lovely landscapes of lakes and forests lure travelers north.

Valdaysky National Park is another UNESCO biosphere reserve nestled in the north of Russia.

The park encompasses the town of Valday, Lake Valdayskoye, and the northern part of Lake Seliger, and is one of the most popular destinations for travelers in central Russia.

The park is located in the northern, highest part of the Valdai Hills, where the landscapes are typically glacial, with

a long necklace of some 76 lakes stretched across the hills. The main lakes here are Seliger, Valdayskoye, Velyo, Uzhin, and Borovno, and the Pola, Msta, and Volga Rivers course through the park. These waters host about 40 species of fish. The majority of the park is covered with forests, and several swamplands seep between the lakes. The tree species here are mainly birch, alder, spruce, and pine, although the northern part of the park has

old oak forests. These woods are filled with the birdsong of some 180 species. Valdaysky National Park is inhabited by 50 species of mammals, including elk (moose), wild boar, brown bear, and grey wolf.

The park's attractions include the town of Valday, a number of 19th-century estates, and the Valday Iversky Monastery, built in 1653, which became a focal cultural center of central Russia in the centuries that followed.

AT A GLANCE

Valdai Hills glacial landscapes ▪ Lake Valdayskoye ▪ 612 square miles (1,585 sq km) ▪ Valday Iversky Monastery ▪ valdaypark.ru

VODLOZERSKY

A Karelian park set amid a vast wilderness of lakes and forests

The Church of St. Elijah the Prophet on the banks of Lake Vodlozero is a popular park destination.

In the Republic of Karelia, Vodlozersky National Park protects the taiga (coniferous forests) of northern Russia within what is both one of the largest national parks in Europe and a Russian UNESCO biosphere reserve. This vast wilderness embraces Lake Vodlozero, the basin of the Ileksa River (which is the main inflow of the lake), and the upper course of the Vodla River (the lake's main outflow).

The two parts of the park—the southern portion, around Lake Vodlozero, and the northern section, in the river valley of the Ileksa—enjoy different climates. The northern part has the climate typical for northern taiga, with long, cold winters; the minimum temperature recorded in the park is minus 49°F (-45 °C). The climate in the south is milder. In addition, Vetreny Poyas Ridge (Windy Belt) is a hilly region in the north of the park; the south is almost flat.

The majority of the landscapes are covered by woods. Much of these are spruce and pine forests, with a few scattered birch and aspen stands. Swamps also cover a significant part of the park. In addition to Lake Vodlozero, many lakes feature in the Ileksa River Basin, including Lake Monastyrskoye, Lake Nelmozero, and Lake Luzskoye. Anglers can enjoy pike, bream, whitefish, burbot, and perch in these waters.

The park also protects many monuments of wooden architecture from the 18th and 19th centuries. The best known is Ilyinsky Pogost, a wooden church on an island on Lake Vodlozero. At the start of the 20th century, about 40 villages lined this lake, but most are now deserted. The village of Kuganavolok has a visitors center where a visitor's permit can be bought.

AT A GLANCE

Northern taiga forests ▪ Lake Vodlozero ▪ 1,653 square miles (4,280 sq km) ▪ Ilyinsky Pogost island church ▪ rusnature.info/zap/015.htm

YUGYD VA

An enormous wilderness in the Komi Republic

The environmental pride of the Komi Republic is Yugyd Va National Park. This is mainland Europe's largest national park, and it was Russia's largest national park until the creation of Beringia National Park in the Asiatic region of this vast country. Yugyd Va protects the vast expanses of taiga forests that stretch across the northern Ural Mountains. In 1995, the forested areas of Yugyd Va and the nearby Pechora-Ilych Nature Reserve were collectively recognized as a UNESCO

The park spans the Northern Urals.

World Heritage site under the name Virgin Komi Forests.

Much of the park is taiga boreal forest; the rest is mostly higher-level tundra. Meadows can be found at alpine elevations as well as lower in the river valleys. Some 180 bird species inhabit these lands, and 20 types of fish species ply the park's rivers and lakes. Among the many mammals that can be seen in this huge wilderness are flying squirrels, reindeer, ermines, otters, elk (moose), wolves, foxes, wolverines, bears, pine martens, weasels, and arctic foxes. Rafting, boating, and hiking are popular here in summer, and Nordic skiing in winter.

AT A GLANCE

Europe's largest protected wilderness ▪ Northern Ural taiga forests ▪ 7,303 square miles (18,917 sq km) ▪ Virgin Komi Forests UNESCO World Heritage site ▪ grida.no/resources/4754

ZYURATKUL

One of Russia's finest mountain ranges beckons world-weary hikers.

Retreat into remote Russia at the gorgeous Zyuratkul National Park, where you can simply lose yourself in a natural wilderness that is a wonderland for outdoor enthusiasts. Here, in the heart of Mother Russia, you can hike the hills, go climbing in the Zyuratkul Mountains, or try fishing or swimming in one of Zyuratkul's lovely lakes. Lake Zyuratkul (Heart Lake) is an apropos hub of this most peaceful wilderness, where you can stay for

several days in a log house far from civilization and take a daily *banya* (Russian steam bath), just like Russians have done for centuries.

A kurum (field of loose rocks)

The lake is a rare mountainous body of water for the Urals, sitting 2,474 feet (754 m) above sea level. The waters are slightly mineralized and reputed to be therapeutic.

From here, you can take an easy hike along a boardwalk to several trails in the Zyuratkuls, which are well marked and easy to navigate. But be careful when you reach the *kurum* (field of loose rocks) at the top as these can be wet and easily dislodged.

AT A GLANCE

Zyuratkul Mountains landscapes ▪ Lake Zyuratkul (Heart Lake) ▪ 340.7 square miles (882.4 sq km) ▪ Well-marked mountain trails ▪ welcome-ural.ru/tours

The sun sets on Zyuratkul National Park, one of Europe's last wilderness outposts.

ACKNOWLEDGMENTS

National Geographic Complete National Parks of Europe would not have been possible without the hard work and talents of many people. Special thanks are due to project editor extraordinaire Mary Norris, designer and photo editor Kay Hankins, director of cartography Debbie Gibbons, senior editorial project manager Allyson Johnson, art director Elisa Gibson, photo editor Matt Propert, director of photography Susan Blair, creative director Melissa Farris, and senior production editor Judith Klein. Thanks also to all the authors and editors of the National Geographic Traveler guidebooks, who I've had the pleasure of working with and whose observations I've used in this book—especially to Christopher Somerville, Rudolf Abraham, Fiona Dunlop, and Rosemary Baily. Thanks to all the staff at *National Geographic* magazine's many European offices, and to all the government officials who offered information and assistance, none more so than George Zurabashvili from Georgia. Thanks to photographer Jeff Mauritzen for great company on the road, and to Helen, David, and Al O'Brien for their neverending hospitality through the writing of this book. And finally, my eternal gratitude to Maggie Roberts for her patience, to Baxter Roberts for so many memorable walks in nature, and to Mrs. Ennis for instilling an early love of both poetry and prose.

ABOUT THE AUTHOR

Justin Kavanagh grew up in County Wicklow, the "Garden of Ireland," where youthful weekends were spent hiking on the Wicklow Way or cycling to the ancient monastic site of Glendalough with Conor Williams and other nature-loving friends. Visits to the Williamses' home of Lackafinna, near Cong, County Mayo—where fish caught on Lough Corrib would be cooked for supper—led to a lifelong love of the west of Ireland. Kavanagh now lives in Connemara in the heart of the Galway Gaeltacht (Irish-speaking area) with his wife, Maggie.

Kavanagh studied English literature and philosophy at University College Dublin, before leaving his homeland to work in London, Tokyo, Philadelphia, New York City, and Washington, D.C. He began his career in journalism at the *Irish Press* in Dublin, and he has gone on to write widely on travel, culture, current affairs, and sports for *National Geographic Traveler* (Washington, D.C.), *The Globalist* online magazine (Washington, D.C.), *The Independent* (London), *90:00* (San Diego), *The Title* (Dublin), and *In Dublin* magazine.

Kavanagh has worked as an editor for National Geographic International Editions, which publishes magazines, books, and other media in more than 35 languages; he has also worked as senior editor for National Geographic Books, where he wrote and edited guidebooks on Ireland, New York City, and a host of other destinations worldwide. He currently works for National Geographic Expeditions, where he leads the Ireland: Tales and Treasures of the Emerald Isle tour.

ILLUSTRATIONS CREDITS

INDEX

Boldface page numbers indicate illustrations.

A

Abisko, Sweden 192, **193**
Abruzzo, Lazio & Molise, Italy **284,** 284–
285, **285**
Aggtelek, Hungary 392, **392**
Aigüestortes i Estany de Sant Maurici,
Spain **264,** 264–265, **265**
Aínos, Greece 322, **322**
Alaniya, Russia 504, **504**
Albania 432–445
Bredhi i Drenovë 434
Bredhi i Hotovës-Dangelli 434, **434**
Butrinti 435, **435**
Dajti 435
Divjaka-Karavasta 436, **436**
Karaburun-Sazan 437
Llogara 437, **437**
Lurë-Mount Dejës 438, **438**
map 433
Prespa 439, **439**
Qafë-Shtama 440, **440**
Shebenik-Jabllanicë 441, **441**
Thethi 442, **443**
Tomorri Mountain 444, **444**
Valbona Valley **432,** 445, **445**
Alde Feanen, Netherlands **66,** 66–67, **67**
Alónnissos & Northern Sporades, Greece
323, **323**
Alta Murgia, Italy **257,** 286, **286**
Ånderdalen, Norway 150, **150**
Ängsö, Sweden 194, **194**
Appennino Lucano–Val d'Agri–
Lagonegrese, Italy 287, **287**
Appennino Tosco-Emiliano, Italy 288, **288**
Archipelago, Finland **218,** 218–219, **219**
Archipiélago de Cabrera, Spain 266, **266**
Arcipelago di La Maddalena, Italy 289, **289**
Arcipelago Toscano, Italy **290,** 290–291
Asinara, Italy 292, **292**
Åsnen, Sweden 195, **195**
Aspromonte, Italy 293, **293**
Aukštaitija, Lithuania 364, **365**
Austria 114–123
Donau-auen 116, **116**
Gesäuse 117, **117**
Hohe Tauern **118,** 118–119, **119**
Kalkalpen 120, **120**
map 115
Neusiedler See-Seewinkel 121, **121**
Thayatal 85, 122, **123**
Azov, Ukraine 474
Azov-Syvash, Ukraine 474, **474**

B

Babia Góra, Poland 348
Balaton Uplands, Hungary 393
Bashkiriya, Russia 504, **504**
Bavarian Forest, Germany **90,** 90–91, **91**

Belarus 378–381
Belovezhskaya Pushcha 380, **380**
Braslav Lakes **378,** 380
map 379
Narochansky 381
Pripyatsky 381, **381**
Belgium 60–63
Grenspark De Zoom-Kalmthoutse
Heide 63
Hoge Kempen **60, 62,** 62–63
map 61
Belovezhskaya Pushcha, Belarus 380, **380**
Berchtesgaden, Germany 92, **93**
Białowieża, Poland 348
Biebrza, Poland 349
Biesbosch, Netherlands **64, 68,** 68–69, **69**
Bieszczady, Poland 349, **349**
Biogradska Gora, Montenegro 424, **424**
Bjeshkët e Nemuna, Kosovo 430, **430**
Björnlandet, Sweden 195
Blå Jungfrun, Sweden 196, **196**
Black Forest, Germany **88,** 94, **94**
Blåfjella-Skjækerfjella, Norway 151, **151**
Børgefjell, Norway 152, **152**
Bory Tucholskie, Poland 350
Bosnia & Herzegovina 414–417
Kozara 416, **416**
map 415
Sutjeska **414,** 416
Una 417, **417**
Bothnian Bay, Finland 252, **252**
Bothnian Sea, Finland 220, **220**
Braslav Lakes, Belarus **378,** 380
Brecon Beacons, U.K. **8–9,** 14, **14**
Bredhi i Drenovë, Albania 434
Bredhi i Hotovës-Dangelli, Albania 434,
434
Breheimen, Norway 153, **153**
Brijuni, Croatia 406, **406**
Broads, U.K. 15, **15**
Buila-Vânturarița, Romania 458, **458**
Bükk, Hungary 393
Bulgaria 450–455
Central Balkan 452
map 451
nature parks 452
Pirin 453, **453**
Rila **450, 454,** 454–455, **455**
Burren, Ireland **36,** 36–37, **37**
Butrinti, Albania 435, **435**
Buzuluksky Bor, Russia 505, **505**

C

Cabañeros, Spain 266
Cairngorms, U.K. **16,** 16–17, **17**
Calanques, France **48,** 50, **50**
Caldera de Taburiente, Spain 267, **267**
Călimani, Romania 459
Canary Islands
Caldera de Taburiente 267, **267**
Garajonay **254–255,** 269, **269**

map 263
Timanfaya 281, **281**
Carpathian, Ukraine **336–337,** 476, **476**
Ceahlău, Romania 459
Central Balkan, Bulgaria 452
České Švýcarsko, Czechia 342
Cévennes, France 51, **51**
Cheile Bicazului-Hașmaș, Romania **456,**
460, **460**
Cheile Nerei-Beusnita, Romania 461, **461**
Chuvash Varmane, Russia 505
Cilento, Vallo di Diano & Alburni, Italy **294,**
294–295, **295**
Cinque Terre, Italy 296, **297**
Circeo, Italy **298,** 298–299
Connemara, Ireland 38, **38**
Cozia, Romania 461, **461**
Croatia 404–413
Brijuni 406, **406**
Kornati **339, 404,** 407, **407**
Krka 408, **408**
map 405
Mljet 408
Paklenica 409, **409**
Plitvice Lakes **410,** 410–411, **411**
Risnjak 412, **412**
Sjeverni Velebit 413, **413**
Curonian Spit, Lithuania 85, 366
Curonian Spit, Russia 85, 506, **506**
Czechia 340–345
České Švýcarsko 342
Krkonoše 342
map 341
Podyjí 85, **340,** 343, **343**
Šumava 91, **344,** 345

D

Dajti, Albania 435
Dalby Söderskog, Sweden 197
Danube Delta Biosphere Reserve, Romania
462, 462–463, **463**
Dartmoor, U.K. 18, **18**
Defileul Jiului, Romania 464, **464**
Denmark 140–147
map 141
Mols Bjerge 142, **142**
Skjoldungernes Land 143, **143**
Thy **140, 144,** 144–145, **145**
Vadehavet (Wadden Sea) 146, **147**
Desna-Starogutskiy, Ukraine 477
Divjaka-Karavasta, Albania 436, **436**
Djerdap, Serbia 420, **420**
Djurö, Sweden 197
Dolomiti Bellunesi, Italy 300, **300**
Domogled-Valea Cernei, Romania 464,
464
Doñana, Spain 268, **268, 270–271**
Donau-auen, Austria 116, **116**
Dovre, Norway **154,** 155
Dovrefjell-Sunndalsfjella, Norway 156
Drawa, Poland 350

Drents-Friese Wold, Netherlands 70, **71**
Drentsche Aa, Netherlands 72
Duinen Van Texel, Netherlands 72, **72**
Duna-Dráva, Hungary 394, **395**
Duna-Ipoly, Hungary 396
Durmitor, Montenegro 424
Dvurechansky, Ukraine 477, **477**
Dwingelderveld, Netherlands 72, **72**
Dzūkija, Lithuania 366, **366**

E

Écrins, France **11, 52,** 52–53, **53**
Eifel, Germany 95
Ekenäs Archipelago, Finland 221, **221**
Estonia 372–377
    Karula 374, **374**
    Lahemaa 375, **375**
    map 373
    Matsalu 376, **376**
    Soomaa 377
    Vilsandi **372,** 377
Etna Park, 301, **301**
Exmoor, U.K. 19, **19**

F

Færder, Norway 156, **156**
Färnebofjärden, Sweden 198
Femundsmarka, Norway 157, **157**
Fertő-Hanság, Hungary 396
Finland 216–253
    Archipelago **218,** 218–219, **219**
    Bothnian Bay 252, **252**
    Bothnian Sea 220, **220**
    Ekenäs Archipelago 221, **221**
    Gulf of Finland 222
    Helvetinjärvi 222, **222**
    Hiidenportti 223
    Hossa 223, **223**
    Isojärvi 224, **224**
    Kauhaneva-Pohjankangas 225, **225**
    Koli 226, **226**
    Kolovesi 227, **227**
    Kurjenrahka 228, **228**
    Lauhanvuori 229, **229**
    Leivonmäki 230
    Lemmenjoki 252
    Liesjärvi 230, **230**
    Linnansaari 231, **231**
    map 216
    Nuuksio 232, **232**
    Oulanka **4,** 233, **233, 234–235**
    Päijänne 236, **236**
    Pallas-Yllästunturi 253
    Patvinsuo 237
    Petkeljärvi 237
    Puurijärvi-Isosuo 238, **238**
    Pyhä-Häkki 239, **239**
    Pyhä-Luosto 253
    Repovesi 240, **240**
    Riisitunturi **217,** 253
    Rokua 241, **241**
    Salamajärvi 242, **242**
    Seitsemisharju 243, **243**
    Sipoonkorpi 244
    Southern Konnevesi 244, **245**
    Syöte **246,** 246–247
    Teijo 248, **248**
    Tiilikkajärvi 249, **249**
    Torronsuo 250, **250**

    Urho Kekkonen 253
    Valkmusa 251, **251**
Folgefonna, Norway 158, **159**
Foreste Casentinesi, Monte Falterona &
    Campigna, Italy **302,** 303
Forlandet, Norway 188
Forollhogna, Norway 160, **160**
France 48–59
    Calanques **48,** 50, **50**
    Cévennes 51, **51**
    Écrins **11, 52,** 52–53, **53**
    map 49
    Mercantour 54, **54**
    Port-Cros 55, **55**
    Pyrénées **56,** 56–57
    Vanoise **58,** 58–59, **59**
Fruška Gora, Serbia 420
Fulufjället, Sweden 198, **199**
Fulufjellet, Norway 160

G

Gala Lake, Turkey **490,** 492, **492**
Galičica, North Macedonia 448
Gallipoli Peninsula, Turkey 493, **493**
Garajonay, Spain **254–255,** 269, **269**
Gargano, Italy 304, **304**
Garphyttan, Sweden 200
Gauja, Latvia 370, **370**
Georgia 496–501
    Kazbegi **496,** 498, **498**
    map 497
    Pshav-Khevsureti 499, **499**
    Tusheti **500,** 501
Germany 88–107
    Bavarian Forest **90,** 90–91, **91**
    Berchtesgaden 92, **93**
    Black Forest **88,** 94, **94**
    Eifel 95
    Hainich 95, **95**
    Hamburg Wadden Sea 96, **96**
    Harz 97, **97**
    Hunsrück-Hochwald 98, **98**
    Jasmund 99, **99**
    Kellerwald-Edersee 100
    Lower Oder Valley 100
    Lower Saxony Wadden Sea 101, **101**
    map 89
    Müritz **102,** 103
    Saxon Switzerland **104,** 104–105, **105**
    Schleswig-Holstein Wadden Sea 106,
        106
    Vorpommersche Boddenlandschaft
        107, **107**
Gesäuse, Austria 117, **117**
Glenveagh, Ireland 39, **39**
Gökçeada, Turkey 494, **494**
Gorce, Poland 351, **351**
Gotska Sandön, Sweden 200, **200**
Gran Paradiso, Italy 305, **305**
Gran Sasso & Monti della Laga, Italy 306,
    306
Greece 320–335
    Aínos 322, **322**
    Alónnissos & Northern Sporades 323,
        323
    map 321
    Oeta 324, **324**
    Olympus 325, **325**
    Parnassós **326,** 327
    Párnitha 328

    Pindus 328, **328**
    Prespes 329, **329**
    Samariá 330, **330**
    Sounio 331, **331**
    Víkos-Aóös 332, **333**
    Zákynthos **320, 334,** 334–335, **335**
Greenland 136–139
    map 137
    Northeast Greenland **126, 136, 138,**
        138–139
Grenspark De Zoom-Kalmthoutse Heide,
    Belgium 63
Groote Peel, Netherlands 73
Gulf of Finland, Finland 222
Gulf of Orosei & Gennargentu, Italy 307,
    307
Gutulia, Norway 161

H

Hainich, Germany 95, **95**
Hallingskarvet, Norway 161, **161**
Hamburg Wadden Sea, Germany 96, **96**
Hamra, Sweden 201, **201**
Haparanda Skärgård, Sweden 201
Hardangervidda, Norway **162,** 162–163, **163,**
    164–165
Harz, Germany 97, **97**
Helvetinjärvi, Finland 222, **222**
Hiidenportti, Finland 223
Hoge Kempen, Belgium **60, 62,** 62–63
Hoge Veluwe, Netherlands 75
Hohe Tauern, Austria **118,** 118–119, **119**
Holosyiivskyy, Ukraine 478, **478**
Hortobágy, Hungary 397, **397**
Hossa, Finland 223, **223**
Hungary 390–399
    Aggtelek 392, **392**
    Balaton Uplands 393
    Bükk 393
    Duna-Dráva 394, **395**
    Duna-Ipoly 396
    Fertő-Hanság 396
    Hortobágy 397, **397**
    Kiskunság **390,** 398, **398**
    Körös-Maros 399
    map 391
    Orség 399
Hunsrück-Hochwald, Germany 98, **98**
Huzulshchyna, Ukraine 479, **479**

I

Iceland 128–135
    map 129
    Snæfellsjökull **2–3, 132,** 132–133, **133**
    Þingvellir **124–125, 128, 129, 130,**
        130–131, **131**
    Vatnajökull **134,** 135
İğneada Longoz Forest, Turkey 495, **495**
Indre Wijdefjorden, Norway 188
Ireland 34–47
    Burren **36,** 36–37, **37**
    Connemara 38, **38**
    Glenveagh 39, **39**
    Killarney **34, 40,** 40–41, **41**
    map 35
    Wicklow Mountains **42,** 43, **44–45**
    Wild Nephin Ballycroy 46, **47**
Islas Atlánticas de Galicia Maritime-
    Terrestrial, Spain 272, **272**

Isojärvi, Finland 224, **224**
Isola di Pantelleria, Italy 308
Italy 282–315
    Abruzzo, Lazio & Molise **284,** 284–285,
        285
    Alta Murgia **257,** 286, **286**
    Appennino Lucano–Val d'Agri–
        Lagonegrese 287, **287**
    Appennino Tosco-Emiliano 288, **288**
    Arcipelago di La Maddalena 289, **289**
    Arcipelago Toscano **290,** 290–291
    Asinara 292, **292**
    Aspromonte 293, **293**
    Cilento, Vallo di Diano & Alburni **294,**
        294–295, **295**
    Cinque Terre 296, **297**
    Circeo **298,** 298–299
    Dolomiti Bellunesi 300, **300**
    Etna Park, 301, **301**
    Foreste Casentinesi, Monte Falterona &
        Campigna **302,** 303
    Gargano 304, **304**
    Gran Paradiso 305, **305**
    Gran Sasso & Monti della Laga 306, **306**
    Gulf of Orosei & Gennargentu 307, **307**
    Isola di Pantelleria 308
    Majella 308, **308**
    map 282
    Monti Sibillini 309, **309**
    Pollino **310,** 310–311
    Sila 312, **312**
    Stelvio 313, **313**
    Ta' Qali **316, 318,** 318–319
    Tuscan Archipelago **283**
    Val Grande 314, **314**
    Vesuvio 315, **315**

J
Jasmund, Germany 99, **99**
Jomfruland, Norway 166, **166**
Jostedalsbreen, Norway 167, **167**
Jotunheimen, Norway **149, 168,** 168–169,
    169
Junkerdal, Norway 170, **170**

K
Kalevalsky, Russia 507
Kalkalpen, Austria 120, **120**
Kampinos, Poland 352, **352**
Karaburun-Sazan, Albania 437
Karkonosze, Poland 352
Karmelyukove Podillya, Ukraine 479
Karpatskyi, Ukraine **472**
Karula, Estonia 374, **374**
Kauhaneva-Pohjankangas, Finland 225, **225**
Kazbegi, Georgia **496,** 498, **498**
Kellerwald-Edersee, Germany 100
Ķemeru, Latvia **368,** 370
Kenozersky, Russia 507, **507**
Khotyn, Ukraine 480, **480**
Khvalynsky, Russia 508, **508**
Killarney, Ireland **34, 40,** 40–41, **41**
King's Trail, Sweden 192
Kiskunság, Hungary **390,** 398, **398**
Koli, Finland 226, **226**
Kolovesi, Finland 227, **227**
Kopaonik, Serbia 385
Kornati, Croatia **339, 404,** 407, **407**
Körös-Maros, Hungary 399

Kosovo 428–431
    Bjeshkët e Nemuna 430, **430**
    map 429
    Sharri **428, 429,** 431, **431**
Kosterhavet, Sweden **191,** 202, **202**
Kozara, Bosnia & Herzegovina 416, **416**
Kremenets Mountains, Ukraine 480
Krka, Croatia 408, **408**
Krkonoše, Czechia 342
Kurjenrahka, Finland 228, **228**

L
Lahemaa, Estonia 375, **375**
Láhko, Norway 170, **170**
Lake District, U.K. **20,** 20–21, **21**
Lake Skadar, Montenegro 425, **425**
Langsua, Norway 171
Latvia 368–371
    Gauja 370, **370**
    Ķemeru **368,** 370
    map 369
    Rāznas 371
    Slitere 371, **371**
Lauhanvuori, Finland 229, **229**
Lauwersmeer, Netherlands 76, **76**
Leivonmäki, Finland 230
Lemmenjoki, Finland 252
Lierne, Norway 171
Liesjärvi, Finland 230, **230**
Linnansaari, Finland 231, **231**
Lithuania 362–367
    Aukštaitija 364, **365**
    Curonian Spit 85, 366
    Dzūkija 366, **366**
    map 363
    Trakai **362,** 367, **367**
    Zemaitija 367
Llogara, Albania 437, **437**
Loch Lomond & the Trossachs, U.K. 22, **23**
Lofotodden, Norway 172
Lomsdal-Visten, Norway 172, **172**
Loonse en Drunense Duinen, Netherlands
    77, **77**
Losiny Ostrov, Russia 509, **509**
Lovćen, Montenegro 426, **426**
Lower Oder Valley, Germany 100
Lower Polissya, Ukraine 481, **481**
Lower Saxony Wadden Sea, Germany 101, **101**
Lurë-Mount Dejës, Albania 438, **438**

M
Maasduinen, Netherlands 78
Macin Mountains, Romania 465
Magura, Poland 353, **353**
Majella, Italy 308, **308**
Majjistral Nature and History Park, Malta 319
Malá Fatra, Slovakia 384, **384**
Malta 316–319
    Majjistral Nature and History Park 319
    map 317
    Salini 319
Mariy Chodra, Russia 509
Matsalu, Estonia 376, **376**
Mavrovo, North Macedonia 448, **448**
Meinweg, Netherlands 78
Meotida, Ukraine **482,** 483
Mercantour, France 54, **54**
Meschyora, Russia 510, **510**
Meschyorsky, Russia 510, **510**

Mljet, Croatia 408
Moldova 468–471
    map 469
    Orhei **468, 470,** 470–471, **471**
Mols Bjerge, Denmark 142, **142**
Monfragüe, Spain 273, **273**
Montenegro 422–427
    Biogradska Gora 424, **424**
    Durmitor 424
    Lake Skadar 425, **425**
    Lovćen 426, **426**
    map 423
    Prokletije **422,** 427, **427**
Monti Sibillini, Italy 309, **309**
Mount Etna, Italy 301, **301**
Møysalen, Norway 173, **173**
Muddus, Sweden 203
Muránska Planina, Slovakia 385, **385**
Müritz, Germany **102,** 103

N
Narew, Poland 354
Narochansky, Belarus 381
Nechkinsky, Russia 511
Netherlands 64–87
    Alde Feanen **66,** 66–67, **67**
    Biesbosch **64, 68,** 68–69, **69**
    Drents-Friese Wold 70, **71**
    Drentsche Aa 72
    Duinen Van Texel 72, **72**
    Dwingelderveld 72, **72**
    Groote Peel 73
    Hoge Veluwe 75
    Lauwersmeer 76, **76**
    Loonse en Drunense Duinen 77, **77**
    Maasduinen 78
    map 65
    Meinweg 78
    Oosterschelde 79, **79**
    Sallandse Heuvelrug 80
    Schiermonnikoog 80
    Utrechtse Heuvelrug 81, **81**
    Veluwezoom 82, **82**
    Weerribben-Wieden 83, **83**
    Zoom-Kalmthoutse Heide 63, **84,** 84–85,
        85
    Zuid-Kennemerland 86, **87**
Neusiedler See-Seewinkel, Austria 121, **121**
New Forest, U.K. 24, **24**
Nizhnyaya Kama, Russia 511, **511**
Nízke Tatry, Slovakia 385
Nordenskiöld Land, Norway 189
Nordre Isfjorden, Norway 189
Nordvest-Spitsbergen, Norway 189
Norra Kvill, Sweden 203
North Macedonia 446–449
    Galičica 448
    map 447
    Mavrovo 448, **448**
    Pelister **446,** 449, **449**
North York Moors, U.K. **6, 26,** 26–27, **27**
Northeast Greenland, Greenland **126, 136,**
    138, 138–139
Northumberland, U.K. 25, **25**
Norway 148–189
    Ånderdalen 150, **150**
    Blåfjella-Skjækerfjella 151, **151**
    Børgefjell 152, **152**
    Breheimen 153, **153**
    Dovre **154,** 155

Dovrefjell-Sunndalsfjella 156
Færder 156, **156**
Femundsmarka 157, **157**
Folgefonna 158, **159**
Forlandet 188
Forollhogna 160, **160**
Fulufjellet 160
Gutulia 161
Hallingskarvet 161, **161**
Hardangervidda **162,** 162–163, **163, 164–165**
Indre Wijdefjorden 188
Jomfruland 166, **166**
Jostedalsbreen 167, **167**
Jotunheimen **149, 168,** 168–169, **169**
Junkerdal 170, **170**
Láhko 170, **170**
Langsua 171
Lierne 171
Lofotodden 172
Lomsdal-Visten 172, **172**
map 148–149
Møysalen 173, **173**
Nordenskiöld Land 189
Nordre Isfjorden 189
Nordvest-Spitsbergen 189
Øvre Anárjohka 174, **174**
Øvre Dividal 175, **175**
Øvre Pasvik 176, **176**
Pilgrim's Route 155
Raet 177, **177**
Rago 178
Reinheimen 178
Reisa 179, **179**
Rohkunborri 180, **180**
Rondane 181, **181**
Saltfjellet-Svartisen **182,** 182–183
Sassen-Bünsow Land 189
Seiland 184
Sjunkhatten 184, **184**
Skarvan & Roltdalen 185, **185**
Sør-Spitsbergen 189
Stabbursdalen 186, **186**
Svalbard parks **188,** 188–189, **189**
Varangerhalvøya 186
Ytre Hvaler 187, **187**
Nuuksio, Finland 232, **232**

O
Oeta, Greece 324, **324**
Ojców, Poland 354, **354**
Olympus, Greece 325, **325**
Onezhskoye Pomorye, Russia 512, **512**
Oosterschelde, Netherlands 79, **79**
Ordesa & Monte Perdido, Spain **262, 274,** 275
Orhei, Moldova **468, 470,** 470–471, **471**
Orlovskoye Polesye, Russia 512
Orség, Hungary 399
Oulanka, Finland **4,** 233, **233,** 234–235
Øvre Anárjohka, Norway 174, **174**
Øvre Dividal, Norway 175, **175**
Øvre Pasvik, Norway 176, **176**

P
Paanajärvi, Russia 513, **513**
Padjelanta, Sweden 204
Päijänne, Finland 236, **236**
Paklenica, Croatia 409, **409**
Pallas-Yllästunturi, Finland 253

Parnassós, Greece **326,** 327
Párnitha, Greece 328
Patvinsuo, Finland 237
Peak District, U.K. 28, **28**
Pelister, North Macedonia **446,** 449, **449**
Pembrokeshire Coast, U.K. 29, **29**
Peneda-Gerês, Portugal **258, 260,** 260–261
Petkeljärvi, Finland 237
Piatra Craiului, Romania 465, **465**
Picos de Europa, Spain **276,** 276–277, **277**
Pieljekaise, Sweden 204, **204**
Pieniny, Poland 355
Pieniny, Slovakia 386, **386**
Pilgrim's Route, Norway 155
Pindus, Greece 328, **328**
Pirin, Bulgaria 453, **453**
Pleshcheyevo Lake, Russia 513, **513**
Plitvice Lakes, Croatia **410,** 410–411, **411**
Podolski Tovtry, Ukraine 483, **483**
Podyjí, Czechia 85, **340,** 343, **343**
Poland 85, 346–361
    Babia Góra 348
    Białowieża 348
    Biebrza 349
    Bieszczady 349, **349**
    Bory Tucholskie 350
    Drawa 350
    Gorce 351, **351**
    Kampinos 352, **352**
    Karkonosze 352
    Magura 353, **353**
    map 347
    Narew 354
    Ojców 354, **354**
    Pieniny 355
    Polesie 355, **355**
    Roztocze 356
    Słowiński 356
    Stołowe Mountains 357, **357**
    Świętokrzyskie 357
    Tatra 85, **346, 358,** 358–359, **359**
    Warta Mouth 360
    Wielkopolski 360, **360**
    Wigry 361, **361**
    Wolin 361
Polesie, Poland 355, **355**
Pollino, Italy **310,** 310–311
Poloniny, Slovakia 386
Port-Cros, France 55, **55**
Portugal 258–261
    map 259
    Peneda-Gerês **258, 260,** 260–261
Prespa, Albania 439, **439**
Prespes, Greece 329, **329**
Prielbrusye, Russia 514, **514**
Pripyatsky, Belarus 381, **381**
Prokletije, Montenegro **422,** 427, **427**
Pshav-Khevsureti, Georgia 499, **499**
Puurijärvi-Isosuo, Finland 238, **238**
Pyhä-Häkki, Finland 239, **239**
Pyhä-Luosto, Finland 253
Pyrénées, France **56,** 56–57

Q
Qafë-Shtama, Albania 440, **440**

R
Raet, Norway 177, **177**
Rago, Norway 178

Rāznas, Latvia 371
Reinheimen, Norway 178
Reisa, Norway 179, **179**
Repovesi, Finland 240, **240**
Retezat, Romania 466, **466**
Riisitunturi, Finland **217,** 253
Rila, Bulgaria **450, 454,** 454–455, **455**
Risnjak, Croatia 412, **412**
Rodna Mountains, Romania 467
Rohkunborri, Norway 180, **180**
Rokua, Finland 241, **241**
Romania 456–467
    Buila-Vânturarița 458, **458**
    Călimani 459
    Ceahlău 459
    Cheile Bicazului-Hașmaș **456,** 460, **460**
    Cheile Nerei-Beusnita 461, **461**
    Cozia 461, **461**
    Danube Delta Biosphere Reserve **462,** 462–463, **463**
    Defileul Jiului 464, **464**
    Domogled-Valea Cernei 464, **464**
    Macin Mountains 465
    map 457
    Piatra Craiului 465, **465**
    Retezat 466, **466**
    Rodna Mountains 467
    Semenic-Cheile Carașului 467
Rondane, Norway 181, **181**
Roztocze, Poland 356
Russia 502–525
    Alaniya 504, **504**
    Bashkiriya 504, **504**
    Buzuluksky Bor 505, **505**
    Chuvash Varmane 505
    Curonian Spit 85, 506, **506**
    Kalevalsky 507
    Kenozersky 507, **507**
    Khvalynsky 508, **508**
    Losiny Ostrov 509, **509**
    map 502
    Mariy Chodra 509
    Meschyora 510, **510**
    Meschyorsky 510, **510**
    Nechkinsky 511
    Nizhnyaya Kama 511, **511**
    Onezhskoye Pomorye 512, **512**
    Orlovskoye Polesye 512
    Paanajärvi 513, **513**
    Pleshcheyevo Lake 513, **513**
    Prielbrusye 514, **514**
    Russian Arctic **503,** 515, **515**
    Russky Sever 516, **516**
    Samarskaya Luka 516, **516**
    Sebezhsky 517
    Sengiley Mountains 517, **517**
    Smolenskoye Poozerye 518
    Smolny 518, **519**
    Taganay 520, **520**
    Ugra 521, **521**
    Valdaysky 521
    Vodlozersky 522, **522**
    Yugyd Va 523, **523**
    Zyuratkul 523, **523,** 524–525
Russian Arctic, Russia **503,** 515, **515**
Russky Sever, Russia 516, **516**

S
Salamajärvi, Finland 242, **242**
Salini, Malta 319

Sallandse Heuvelrug, Netherlands 80
Saltfjellet-Svartisen, Norway **182,** 182–183
Samariá, Greece 330, **330**
Samarskaya Luka, Russia 516, **516**
Sarek, Sweden 205, **205**
Sassen-Bünsow Land, Norway 189
Saxon Switzerland, Germany **104,** 104–105, **105**
Schiermonnikoog, Netherlands 80
Schleswig-Holstein Wadden Sea, Germany 106, **106**
Sebezhsky, Russia 517
Seiland, Norway 184
Seitsemisharju, Finland 243, **243**
Semenic-Cheile Carașului, Romania 467
Sengiley Mountains, Russia 517, **517**
Serbia 418–421
    Djerdap 420, **420**
    Fruška Gora 420
    Kopaonik 421
    map 419
    Tara **418,** 421, **421**
Sharri, Kosovo **428, 429,** 431, **431**
Shatskyi, Ukraine 484, **484**
Shebenik-Jabllanicë, Albania 441, **441**
Sierra de Guadarrama, Spain 278, **278**
Sierra Nevada, Spain 279, **279**
Sila, Italy 312, **312**
Sipoonkorpi, Finland 244
Sjeverni Velebit, Croatia 413, **413**
Sjunkhatten, Norway 184, **184**
Skarvan & Roltdalen, Norway 185, **185**
Skjoldungernes Land, Denmark 143, **143**
Skole Beskydy, Ukraine 484, **484**
Skuleskogen, Sweden **206,** 206–207, **207**
Slitere, Latvia 371, **371**
Slovakia 382–389
    Malá Fatra 384, **384**
    map 383
    Muránska Planina 385, **385**
    Nízke Tatry 385
    Pieniny 386, **386**
    Poloniny 386
    Slovenský Kras 387, **387**
    Slovenský Raj 388, **388**
    Tatranský 85, **382,** 389, **389**
    Veľká Fatra 389
Slovenia 400–403
    map 401
    Triglav **400, 401, 402,** 402–403, **403**
Slovenský Kras, Slovakia 387, **387**
Slovenský Raj, Slovakia 388, **388**
Słowiński, Poland 356
Smolenskoye Poozerye, Russia 518
Smolny, Russia 518, **519**
Snæfellsjökull, Iceland **2–3, 132,** 132–133, **133**
Snowdonia, U.K. **30,** 31
Söderåsen, Sweden 208, **208**
Sonfjället, Sweden 209, **209**
Soomaa, Estonia 377
Sør-Spitsbergen, Norway 189
Sounio, Greece 331, **331**
South Downs, U.K. 32, **32**
Southern Konnevesi, Finland 244, **245**
Spain **254–255,** 262–281
    Aigüestortes i Estany de Sant Maurici **264,** 264–265, **265**
    Archipiélago de Cabrera 266, **266**
    Cabañeros 266

    Caldera de Taburiente 267, **267**
    Doñana 268, **268, 270–271**
    Garajonay **254–255,** 269, **269**
    Islas Atlánticas de Galicia Maritime-Terrestrial 272, **272**
    map 263
    Monfragüe 273, **273**
    Ordesa & Monte Perdido **262, 274,** 275
    Picos de Europa **276,** 276–277, **277**
    Sierra de Guadarrama 278, **278**
    Sierra Nevada 279, **279**
    Tablas de Daimiel 280, **280**
    Teide 281
    Timanfaya 281, **281**
Stabbursdalen, Norway 186, **186**
Stelvio, Italy 313, **313**
Stenshuvud, Sweden 210, **210**
Stołowe Mountains, Poland 357, **357**
Stora Sjöfallet, Sweden 211
Store Mosse, Sweden 211
Šumava, Czechia 91, **344,** 345
Sutjeska, Bosnia & Herzegovina **414,** 416
Svalbard parks, Norway **188,** 188–189, **189**
Sweden 190–215
    Abisko 192, **193**
    Ängsö 194, **194**
    Åsnen 195, **195**
    Björnlandet 195
    Blå Jungfrun 196, **196**
    Dalby Söderskog 197
    Djurö 197
    Färnebofjärden 198
    Fulufjället 198, **199**
    Garphyttan 200
    Gotska Sandön 200, **200**
    Hamra 201, **201**
    Haparanda Skärgård 201
    King's Trail 192
    Kosterhavet **191,** 202, **202**
    map 190
    Muddus 203
    Norra Kvill 203
    Padjelanta 204
    Pieljekaise 204, **204**
    Sarek 205, **205**
    Skuleskogen **206,** 206–207, **207**
    Söderåsen 208, **208**
    Sonfjället 209, **209**
    Stenshuvud 210, **210**
    Stora Sjöfallet 211
    Store Mosse 211
    Tiveden 212, **212**
    Töfsingdalen 213
    Tresticklan 213
    Tyresta 214, **214**
    Vadvetjåkka 215, **215**
Świętokrzyskie, Poland 357
Swiss National Park, Switzerland **110,** 110–111, **111, 112–113**
Switzerland 108–113
    map 109
    Swiss National Park **110,** 110–111, **111, 112–113**
Synevyr, Ukraine 485, **485**
Syöte, Finland **246,** 246–247

T
Ta' Qali, Italy **316, 318,** 318–319
Tablas de Daimiel, Spain 280, **280**
Taganay, Russia 520, **520**

Tara, Serbia **418,** 421, **421**
Tatra, Poland 85, **346, 358,** 358–359, **359**
Tatranský, Slovakia 85, **382,** 389, **389**
Teide, Spain 281
Teijo, Finland 248, **248**
Thayatal, Austria 85, 122, **123**
Thethi, Albania 442, **443**
Þingvellir, Iceland **124–125, 128, 129, 130,** 130–131, **131**
Thy, Denmark **140, 144,** 144–145, **145**
Tiilikkajärvi, Finland 249, **249**
Timanfaya, Spain 281, **281**
Tiveden, Sweden 212, **212**
Töfsingdalen, Sweden 213
Tomorri Mountain, Albania 444, **444**
Torronsuo, Finland 250, **250**
Trakai, Lithuania **362,** 367, **367**
Tresticklan, Sweden 213
Triglav, Slovenia **400, 401, 402,** 402–403, **403**
Turkey 490–495
    Asiatic Turkey national parks 491
    Gala Lake **490,** 492, **492**
    Gallipoli Peninsula 493, **493**
    Gökçeada 494, **494**
    İğneada Longoz Forest 495, **495**
    map 491
Tuscan Archipelago, Italy **283**
Tusheti, Georgia **500,** 501
Tuzlovski Estuaries, Ukraine 486, **486**
Tyresta, Sweden 214, **214**

U
Ugra, Russia 521, **521**
Ukraine 472–489
    Azov 474
    Azov-Syvash 474, **474**
    Carpathian **336–337,** 476, **476**
    Desna-Starogutskiy 477
    Dvurechansky 477, **477**
    Holosyiyivskyy 478, **478**
    Huzulshchyna 479, **479**
    Karmelyukove Podillya 479
    Karpatskyi **472**
    Khotyn 480, **480**
    Kremenets Mountains 480
    Lower Polissya 481, **481**
    map 472–473
    Meotida **482,** 483
    national nature parks 473, **488,** 488–489
    Podolski Tovtry 483, **483**
    Shatskyi 484, **484**
    Skole Beskydy 484, **484**
    Synevyr 485, **485**
    Tuzlovski Estuaries 486, **486**
    Uzhansky 486, **486**
    Vizhnitsky 487
    Yavorivskyi 487
Una, Bosnia & Herzegovina 417, **417**
United Kingdom 12–33
    Brecon Beacons **8–9,** 14, **14**
    Broads 15, **15**
    Cairngorms **16,** 16–17, **17**
    Dartmoor 18, **18**
    Exmoor 19, **19**
    Lake District **20,** 20–21, **21**
    Loch Lomond & the Trossachs 22, **23**
    map 13
    New Forest 24, **24**
    North York Moors **6, 26,** 26–27, **27**

Northumberland 25, **25**
Peak District 28, **28**
Pembrokeshire Coast 29, **29**
Snowdonia **30,** 31
South Downs 32, **32**
Yorkshire Dales **12,** 33, **33**
Urho Kekkonen, Finland 253
Utrechtse Heuvelrug, Netherlands 81, **81**
Uzhansky, Ukraine 486, **486**

V

Vadehavet, Denmark 146, **147**
Vadvetjåkka, Sweden 215, **215**
Val Grande, Italy 314, **314**
Valbona Valley, Albania **432,** 445, **445**
Valdaysky, Russia 521
Valkmusa, Finland 251, **251**
Vanoise, France **58,** 58–59, **59**
Varangerhalvøya, Norway 186
Vatnajökull, Iceland **134,** 135
Vel'ká Fatra, Slovakia 389
Veluwezoom, Netherlands 82, **82**
Vesuvio, Italy 315, **315**
Víkos-Aóös, Greece 332, **333**
Vilsandi, Estonia **372,** 377
Vizhnitsky, Ukraine 487
Vodlozersky, Russia 522, **522**
Vorpommersche Boddenlandschaft,
    Germany 107, **107**

W

Wadden Sea, Denmark 146, **147**
Wadden Sea, Germany 96, **96,** 101, **101,**
    106, **106**
Warta Mouth, Poland 360
Weerribben-Wieden, Netherlands 83, **83**
Wicklow Mountains, Ireland **42,** 43, **44–45**
Wielkopolski, Poland 360, **360**
Wigry, Poland 361, **361**
Wild Nephin Ballycroy, Ireland 46, **47**
Wolin, Poland 361

Y

Yavorivskyi, Ukraine 487
Yorkshire Dales, U.K. **12,** 33, **33**
Ytre Hvaler, Norway 187, **187**
Yugyd Va, Russia 523, **523**

Z

Zákynthos, Greece **320, 334,** 334–335, **335**
Zemaitija, Lithuania 367
Zoom-Kalmthoutse Heide, Netherlands 63,
    84, 84–85, **85**
Zuid-Kennemerland, Netherlands 86, **87**
Zyuratkul, Russia 523, **523, 524–525**

Since 1888, the National Geographic Society has funded more than 13,000 research, exploration, and preservation projects around the world. National Geographic Partners distributes a portion of the funds it receives from your purchase to National Geographic Society to support programs including the conservation of animals and their habitats.

National Geographic Partners
1145 17th Street NW
Washington, DC 20036-4688 USA

Get closer to National Geographic explorers and photographers, and connect with our global community. Join us today at nationalgeographic.com/join

For information about special discounts for bulk purchases, please contact National Geographic Books Special Sales: specialsales@natgeo.com

For rights or permissions inquiries, please contact National Geographic Books Subsidiary Rights: bookrights@natgeo.com

Additional cartographic assistance provided by Mapping Specialists Ltd.

ISBN 978-1-4262-2096-8

Library of Congress Control Number:2019946218

Printed in China

19/RRDH/1

The information in this book has been carefully checked and to the best of our knowledge is accurate. However, details are subject to change, and the publisher cannot be responsible for such changes, or for errors or omissions. Assessments of sites, hotels, and restaurants are based on the author's subjective opinions, which do not necessarily reflect the publisher's opinion.